Helping Skills

Helping Skills

The Empirical Foundation

Edited by

Clara E. Hill

American Psychological Association

Washington, DC

Published by
American Psychological Association
750 First Street, NE
Washington, DC 20002
www.apa.org

To order
APA Order Department
P.O. Box 92984
Washington, DC 20090-2984

Tel: (800) 374-2721, Direct: (202) 336-5510
Fax: (202) 336-5502, TDD/TTY: (202) 336-6123
Online: www.apa.org/books/
Email: order@apa.org

In the U.K., Europe, Africa, and the Middle East, copies may be ordered from
American Psychological Association
3 Henrietta Street
Covent Garden, London
WC2E 8LU England

Typeset in Times Roman by EPS Group Inc., Easton, MD
Printer: Goodway Graphics of Virginia, Inc., Springfield, VA
Dust jacket designer: Minker Design, Bethesda, MD
Technical/Production Editor: Amy J. Clarke

The opinions and statements published are the responsibility of the authors, and such opinions and statements do not necessarily represent the policies of the American Psychological Association.

On the cover: *Breton Girls Dancing, Pont-Aven* (1888, oil on canvas) by Paul Gauguin, from the Collection of Mr. and Mrs. Paul Mellon, © 2001 Board of Trustees, National Gallery of Art, Washington, DC. Reprinted with permission.

Library of Congress Cataloging-in-Publication Data
Helping skills : the empirical foundation / edited by Clara E. Hill.
    p. cm.
  Includes bibliographical references.
  ISBN 1-55798-817-X (pb : acid-free paper)
  1. Counseling.   2. Helping behavior.   I. Hill, Clara E.   II. American Psychological
Association.
  BF637.C6 H46 2001
  158'.3—dc21
                                                    .2001022591

British Library Cataloguing-in-Publication Data
A CIP record is available from the British Library.

Printed in the United States of America
First Edition

CONTENTS

CONTRIBUTORS

Edgar O. Angelone
Hassan F. A. Azim
Victoria Balenger
R. Gayle Benefield
Nancy E. Betz
Donald B. Boulet
Wilfried Busse
Charles D. Claiborn
Mary C. Cogar
Andrew Cooper
Maureen M. Corbett
Paul Crits-Christoph
Daniel W. Denman III
E. Thomas Dowd
Robert Elliott
David R. Fairweather
Dana R. Falk
Jenny Firth-Cozens
M. S. Forgatch
Bruce R. Fretz
Myrna L. Friedlander
Robin Gagnon
Maria Gomez
James Gormally
Barbara R. Gronsky
Richard F. Haase
William E. Hanson
Gillian E. Hardy
Janet E. Helms
Colin B. Herring
Shirley A. Hess
Clara E. Hill
Mary Hill
Anthony S. Joyce
Bettina Kanitz
Barbara Kerr

Dennis M. Kivlighan, Jr.
Sarah Knox
Richard Lightsey
Susan P. Llewelyn
Lester Luborsky
Karen Blackwell Mahoney
Alvin R. Mahrer
Frank R. Margison
Mary McCallum
Patricia R. McCarthy
William R. Miller
Thomas Mullin
Kevin E. O'Grady
Douglas H. Olson
G. R. Patterson
Elgin S. Perry
David A. Petersen
William E. Piper
Peggy Rios
Kenneth Roach
Michael J. Scheel
Scott Seaman
David A. Shapiro
Larry Siegelman
Joseph C. Speisman
Sharon B. Spiegel
Alicia Stephany
William B. Stiles
Frank Sturniolo
Rick Taffe
Donald T. Tepper, Jr.
Barbara J. Thompson
Victoria Tichenor
J. Scott Tonigan
Teresa L. Wonnell

INTRODUCTION

Clara E. Hill

Students in classes on helping skills ought to be thinking deeply not only about how to acquire the skills to help others but also about how to evaluate and conduct research on helping skills. One way to examine the effects of helping skills is through personal experience as a therapist and as a client. However, personal experience can be limited by individual bias. Examining the effects of helping skills through scientific investigation helps limit the effects of bias.

In this book, we have gathered studies that form the empirical foundation for the Hill and O'Brien (1999) helping skills model. By putting major studies in one book, we hope to show the intellectual basis for the model, educate people about what has been done in the area of helping skills, and stimulate more and better research on helping skills. This book can be used to accompany the Hill and O'Brien (1999) helping skills text.

This book can also be used by students in undergraduate and graduate classes in research methodology. By studying a coherent body of literature, students can learn more about the current methods used to study psychotherapy process. Many methods have been used to study helping skills, so it is instructive to examine the variety of results that can be obtained with different methods.

Researchers will also find this book to be a valuable reference. Having many of the major studies of helping skills in one source can be enormously helpful for assessing what has been done and identifying the exciting areas for future research.

Please note that for this Introduction, we use the terms *client* (rather than patient) and *therapist* (rather than helper) to refer to the participants in the therapy endeavor because these are the terms that have been used most often in the research literature on therapy process. In addition, we use the term *helping skills* because it is more generic, although therapist interventions have also been called *verbal response modes* or *techniques* in most of the research literature.

Methodological Issues in Studying Helping Skills

Much has been written about methodological issues in conducting psychotherapy research (see Heppner, Kivlighan, & Wampold, 1999; Hill & Lambert, in press; and Kazdin, 1994). Our focus here is on two major concerns for helping skills research: the measures and the methods.

Measures

Beginning with several researchers in the 1940s (e.g., Porter, 1943; Robinson, 1950; Synder, 1945), more than 30 systems have been developed to assess helping skills. Most researchers develop their own system, use it for one or two studies, and then abandon the whole area. Similarly, many studies included in this collection use different definitions of skills and different ways of identifying them within sessions, making it difficult to aggregate results across studies. When comparing across studies, readers need to be aware of the definitions and measures used because they influence the results obtained.

We suggest that established definitions of the various helping skills, such as those developed by Hill and O'Brien (1999), be used in future research so that more consistency across studies can be attained. Furthermore, we suggest that researchers be very careful about procedures used to identify helping skills, so that readers can have some assurance that skills were coded accurately.

Methods

Several methods have been used for studying helping skills. Each method has advantages and disadvantages, and readers need to be aware of these in evaluating the studies because the methods influence the results obtained. Gelso (1979) coined the term *bubble hypothesis,* which refers to the phenomenon that occurs when someone tries to get rid of an air bubble trapped under a sticker on a car window: Typically, the bubble is just moved around to another spot but does not disappear. Similarly in research, when researchers try to solve one methodological problem, they often create others. Because researchers studying helping skills are at such a primitive level in terms of our research methods, all of the methods have "bubbles," as the brief descriptions below show.

Descriptive Approaches

In descriptive approaches, researchers simply describe what naturally occurs in therapy, often in terms of frequencies or proportions of events. For example, in 1987, Elliott et al. (see chapter 1) described the helping skills used by therapists of differing theoretical orientations. In accord with the theories, the behavioral therapist used more information and advisement, whereas the client-centered therapist used more reflection of feelings. Elliott et al., however, did not investigate the effectiveness of any of the helping skills.

The descriptive approach is valuable because it provides an idea of how often different skills occur in therapy and thus can show important differences among types of therapists, therapies, clients, and so forth. This type of descriptive information is important because it can provide guidelines for trainees in examining how their own skills compare with others. The disadvantage is that the descriptive approach does not provide an evaluation of the effectiveness of these skills. Hence, other methods are clearly needed to evaluate the skills.

Experimental Approach

In the experimental method, researchers manipulate a helping skill and observe the effects on some outcome variable. For example, in 1978, Tepper and Haase (see chapter 12) developed videotapes in which therapists assumed different verbal and nonverbal stances. They then asked therapists and clients to watch these videotapes and evaluate the therapist's level of empathy, respect, and genuineness. Differences among the videotapes were assumed to be due to differences in verbal and nonverbal behaviors because other variables were controlled.

The advantage of the experimental method is that skills can be carefully defined and implemented and extraneous variables can be controlled, so researchers can be confident that the manipulated variable caused the results (i.e., high internal validity). The disadvantage is that the setting is artificial, so results often cannot be generalized to naturally occurring therapy (i.e., low external validity).

Correlational Approaches

Many process researchers have used a correlational strategy, in which they relate the frequency or proportion of occurrence of a process variable to another process variable or to an outcome. For example, in 1966, Fretz (see chapter 10) correlated the frequency of naturally occurring client and therapist nonverbal behaviors (e.g., head movements, hand movements, smiling, leaning forward) with client and therapist perceptions of therapist facilitative conditions (i.e., regard, unconditionality of regard, empathy, congruence), satisfaction, and charisma. He found that vertical hand movements were the best indicator of satisfaction for both clients and therapists, whereas hand clasping was the best indicator of unconditionality of regard (i.e., feeling respect) for both clients and therapists.

An advantage of the correlational approach is that it allows researchers to study naturally occurring events. Furthermore, it is relatively simple to count behaviors and correlate them with another variable. However, correlational designs have been criticized because they do not take into account the timing, appropriateness, quality, or context of the process variable (Gottman & Markman, 1978; Hill, 1982; Hill, Helms, Tichenor, et al., 1988, see chapter 4; Russell & Trull, 1986; Stiles, 1988; Stiles & Shapiro, 1994). This criticism argues that one moderately deep interpretation given to an introspective client who is pondering why she or he behaves in a particular way may be more helpful than 10 poorly timed interpretations (see Spiegel & Hill, 1989). Furthermore, Stiles noted that correlational designs fail to account for client needs. For example, disturbed clients may need more of some interventions (e.g., interpretations) but still may end up with a poor outcome, not because the interventions were ineffective but because clients could not effectively use the interventions and needed more guidance to fully understand them.

Sequential Analyses

Rather than testing process in relation to an outcome at the end of treatment as in the traditional correlational approach, several writers have recommended using sequential analyses to study the temporal contiguity (or immediate effects) of one process variable on another (Bakeman, 1978; Bakeman & Gottman, 1986; Russell & Trull, 1986). For example, in 1988, Hill, Helms, Tichenor, et al. (see chapter 4) studied the link between therapist helping skills and the subsequent client experiencing level. They found the highest levels of client experiencing following therapist self-disclosure and the lowest level following direct guidance and confrontation.

The advantage of sequential analyses is that researchers can determine immediate effects, which are often of great interest to therapists, because that is what they observe in therapy sessions. On the negative side, sequential analyses are limited because only stable, immediate effects can be determined, whereas the effects of many therapist interventions are delayed and may even change over time. For example, clients who immediately reject a therapist confrontation might then go home and think about it and recognize its validity but may or may not bring that realization back to discuss in therapy. Furthermore, sequential analyses do not allow one to link the helping skills to longer term outcomes (i.e., how all the skills operate together to help the client change).

Analyses of Patterns

An extension of sequential analysis is to consider longer sequences of events. This type of analysis is more sophisticated because it typically does not only involve units that occur next to each other temporally but can also involve units of different sizes. Hence, the first step in analyzing patterns is often segmenting the process into units (or stages) that can be coded. Methods for analyzing prolonged sequences are relatively new and have been much discussed and advocated (e.g., comprehensive process analysis, Elliott, 1989; task analysis, Greenberg, 1984, 1986, 1991). An example is Elliott et al.'s (1994, and see chapter 19) description of the five stages involved in helping clients attain insight. They found that the most common therapist skill leading to client insight was interpretation. The interpretation was delivered after a therapeutic alliance was established, the therapist had an adequate amount of information about the client, and the client expressed puzzlement over their reactions. The interpretation was followed by the client thinking over the interpretation, coming to an insight, and then exploring and elaborating on the insight. Hence, the process clearly was not just a simple sequence of therapist interpretation leading to client insight but entailed a more prolonged series of events that enabled the therapist interpretation to lead to client insight.

An advantage of analyzing patterns is that it provides data that mirror the clinical phenomenon. Methodological issues that need to be addressed in future research include how to identify units (stages), how to identify transitions between stages, how to assess the process within stages, and how to study the relationship between resolution of events and longer term outcome.

Qualitative Research

With qualitative methods, researchers use open-ended, data-gathering techniques (e.g., interviews) and then develop categories from the data. They use words rather than numbers to summarize data. For example, in 1997, Knox, Hess, Petersen, and Hill (see chapter 22) qualitatively analyzed interviews with clients about their experiences of helpful therapist self-disclosures. They found that clients thought that their therapists had given disclosures (which were typically about personal historical information) to normalize their feelings and reassure them. Furthermore, clients indicated that the therapist disclosures led to new insight or perspective, made therapists seem more real and human, improved the therapeutic relationship, and resulted in clients feeling more "normal" or reassured.

An advantage of qualitative methods is that researchers can investigate clinically rich or infrequently occurring phenomena that are often difficult to investigate through quantitative methods, especially when minimal research exists in the area. Disadvantages involve difficulties in determining the validity and reliability of the data, the possible biases of the judges who evaluate the data, and difficulty aggregating results across studies.

Summary

Several methods have been used to assess the effects of helping skills. None are perfect; each has its advantages and disadvantages. We encourage researchers to use all the methods but to be aware of the potential limitations of each when interpreting their results. Replication of results across different methods is the best evidence of the "true" effects. Furthermore, we encourage researchers to develop new methods that have fewer limitations.

Critiquing the Studies

Because no study is perfect, we need to evaluate the results of each within the context of its limitations. When evaluating the studies in this book, readers need to think carefully about the methods used to determine the limits of what can be concluded from each study. Excellent references for further reading on the methodological issues for studying helping skills are Heppner et al. (1999) and Hill and Lambert (in press). The questions in Exhibit I.1 will be helpful to keep in mind while evaluating each study.

Overview of This Book

This book is a collection of studies that investigate the skills discussed in the Hill and O'Brien (1999) helping skills model (e.g., although challenge, interpretation, and self-disclosure are included, paradoxical interventions are not because they are not included in Hill & O'Brien). We also note that not all of the studies in this collection used the same definitions and ways of assessing the skills as Hill and O'Brien did. Furthermore, only studies about the effectiveness of skills in helping situations are included; hence, studies about the effects of training or the effects of skills in other situations (e.g., medical settings) are not included. We include studies that involve a variety of methodologies because we can learn something about helping skills from each of the methods, although we must take the limitations of the method into account when interpreting the results. Finally, we include only studies that were published in either the *Journal of Counseling Psychology* or the *Journal of Consulting and Clinical Psychology* because as the premier journals in counseling and clinical psychology, these represent most of the best studies available on helping skills.

Exhibit I.1—*Questions to Ask When Evaluating Sections of*
Empirical Studies on Helping Skills

I. Introduction
   A. Have the researchers convinced you of the need for the study?
   B. Are the purposes or hypotheses clearly stated?
II. Method
   A. Design
      1. Was the design appropriate for answering the questions posed in the study?
      2. Internal validity: Were variables clearly defined and implemented? Were extraneous variables (i.e., those not of interest in the study) controlled?
      3. External validity: Can the results be generalized to naturally occurring therapy?
   B. Participants
      1. Were clients and therapists adequately sampled from the population?
      2. Were therapists trained to deliver the skills competently?
      3. Were clients motivated for receiving help?
      4. Were clients and therapists in a therapeutic relationship?
   C. Measures
      1. Did the measures have adequate validity (i.e., assess what they were supposed to assess) and reliability (assess the construct consistently)?
      2. Were the measures from several perspectives (client, therapist, external judges) and types (self-report, observations) to reduce perspective bias?
   D. Procedures
      1. Could one replicate this study given the description of the procedures?
      2. Did the researchers conduct the study ethically?
      3. Was the helping interaction realistic in terms of naturally occurring therapy?
      4. If appropriate, were manipulation checks conducted to determine whether procedures were delivered as promised?
III. Results
   A. Was the number of analyses appropriate given the number of participants and variables?
   B. Were appropriate analyses used to test the data?
   C. Could you understand what was done in the analyses?
IV. Discussion
   A. Did the authors interpret beyond their results?
   B. Did the authors discuss the limitations of their results?
   C. Did the authors provide feasible ideas for future research directions?
V. Overall was the writing understandable and the logic clear?
VI. What ideas come to mind for future research in this area?

The book is divided into seven parts, each of which corresponds to a section of the Hill and O'Brien (1999) text. In Part I, we focus on the overall process of helping (therapist intentions, therapist helping skills or response modes, client reactions, and client behaviors). In Parts II and III, we focus on the exploration stage, with Part II involving studies about nonverbal communication (attending and listening) and Part III highlighting a study that compares the effects of restatement, probe, reflection of feelings, and nonverbal behaviors. In Parts IV to VI, the insight stage is the focus, with Part IV including studies on challenge, Part V focusing on studies on interpretation, and Part VI containing studies on self-disclosure. Part VII encompasses studies on the action stage. Prior to each of the seven parts, we include Part

Introductions, in which we review what is known about the topic and what still remains to be investigated.

Conclusion

This collection of studies is offered to stimulate critical thinking about helping skills. One exciting aspect about the field of helping skills is that there are so many things yet to be discovered and so many challenges in terms of conducting the research. For example, some skills (e.g., restatement, open question, reflection of feelings, immediacy, information, process advisement) have largely been ignored and need more empirical attention. Another issue confronting researchers is the need to use consistent definitions so that the results can be aggregated across studies. We need to do further research about the complexity of the helping skills, including the accompanying nonverbal behaviors, the quality of the intervention, the manner or style of the intervention, and the timing of the intervention. We need to study the effects of different types of helpers using the various helping skills with different types of clients during different moments of the helping process. We need to study the immediate and delayed effects of interventions, how clients continue the work of therapy outside therapy sessions, the cumulative effects of interventions, the relationship between the therapeutic alliance and the helping skills, and how all of the process variables operate together to yield ultimate outcome.

We also need to understand more about how to teach helping skills to novice helpers. The exploration skills seem to be relatively easy to teach, but the insight and action skills (and integrating the skills) are more difficult to teach. Research in teaching helping skills was vibrant and active in the 1960s and 1970s and needs to be revived again, with better methodologies for assessing how students best learn them.

It is hoped that much more research will be conducted on helping skills in the future. We hope that future researchers will rise to the challenge of finding new and better methods for studying helping skills that are more suited to the clinical experience of therapy. It is also hoped that these researchers will fill in some of the holes in the knowledge about how to define helping skills, when to use helping skills in therapy, with whom to use the different skills, how to sequence the use of the various skills, how helping skills interact with the therapeutic relationship, and the effects of the various helping skills in terms of immediate and long-term outcome. Conducting helping skills research is challenging, but if science has discovered how to send people into space, how to clone animals, and how to cure cancer, then certainly we can discover more about the complexity of how helping skills work in therapy.

References

Bakeman, R. (1978). Untangling streams of behavior: Sequential analysis of observation data. In G. P. Sackett (Ed.), *Observing behavior. Vol. 2: Data collection and analysis methods* (pp. 63–78). Baltimore, MD: University Park Press.

Bakeman, R., & Gottman, J. M. (1986). *Observing interaction: An introduction to sequential analysis.* New York: Cambridge University Press.

Elliott, R. (1989). Comprehensive process analysis: Understanding the change process in significant therapeutic events. In M. J. Packer & R. B. Addison (Eds.), *Entering the circle: Hermaneutic investigation in psychology* (pp. 165–184). Albany, NY: State University of New York Press.

Elliott, R., Shapiro, D. A., Firth-Cozens, J., Stiles, W. B., Hardy, G. E., Llewelyn, S. P., & Margison, F. R. (1994). Comprehensive process analysis of insight events in cognitive–behavioral and psychodynamic–interpersonal psychotherapies. *Journal of Counseling Psychology, 41,* 449–463.

Gelso, C. J. (1979). Research in counseling: Methodological and professional issues. *The Counseling Psychologist, 8,* 7–35.

Gottman, J. M., & Markham, H. J. (1978). Experimental designs in psychotherapy research. In S. L. Garfield & A. E. Bergin (Eds.), *Handbook of psychotherapy and behavior change* (2nd ed., pp. 23–62). New York: Wiley.

Greenberg, L. S. (1984). Task analysis: The general approach. In L. N. Rice & L. S. Greenberg (Eds.), *Patterns of change: Intensive analysis of psychotherapeutic process* (pp. 124–148). New York: Guilford Press.

Greenberg, L. S. (1986). Change process research. *Journal of Consulting and Clinical Psychology, 54,* 4–9.

Greenberg, L. S. (1991). Research on the process of change. *Psychotherapy Research, 1,* 3–16.

Heppner, P. P., Kivlighan, D. M., Jr., & Wampold, B. E. (1999). *Research design in counseling* (2nd ed.). Pacific Grove, CA: Brooks/Cole.

Hill, C. E. (1982). Counseling process research: Philosophical and methodological dilemmas. *The Counseling Psychologist, 10*(4), 7–19.

Hill, C. E., & Lambert, M. J. (in press). Methodological issues in assessing psychotherapy processes and outcomes. In M. J. Lambert (Ed.), *Handbook of psychotherapy and behavior change.* New York: Wiley.

Hill, C. E., & O'Brien, K. M. (1999). *Helping skills: Facilitating exploration, insight, and action.* Washington, DC: American Psychological Association.

Kazdin, A. E. (1994). Methodology, design, and evaluation in psychotherapy research. In A. E. Bergin & S. L. Garfield (Eds.), *Handbook of psychotherapy and behavior change* (4th ed., pp. 19–71). New York: Wiley.

Porter, E. H., Jr. (1943). The development and evaluation of a measure of counseling interview procedures. *Educational and Psychological Measurement, 3,* 105–126.

Robinson, F. R. (1950). *Principles and procedures in student counseling.* New York: Harper.

Russell, R. L., & Trull, T. J. (1986). Sequential analysis of language variables in psychotherapy process research. *Journal of Consulting and Clinical Psychology, 54,* 16–21.

Snyder, W. U. (1945). An investigation of the nature of nondirective psychotherapy. *Journal of General Psychology, 33,* 193–223.

Spiegel, S. B., & Hill, C. E. (1989). Guidelines for research on therapist interpretation: Toward greater methodological rigor and relevance to practice. *Journal of Counseling Psychology, 36,* 121–129.

Stiles, W. B. (1988). Psychotherapy process–outcome correlations may be misleading. *Psychotherapy, 25,* 27–35.

Stiles, W. B., & Shapiro, D. A. (1994). Drugs, recipes, babies, bathwater, and psychotherapy process–outcome relations. *Journal of Consulting and Clinical Psychology, 56,* 955–959.

Part I

The Process of Helping

INTRODUCTION

Hill and O'Brien (1999) posited a description of what goes on between therapists and clients in the moment-by-moment process of therapy sessions. First, therapists have intentions for what they want to accomplish (e.g., encourage the client to talk about feelings) and choose specific skills to implement these intentions (e.g., reflection of feelings). The client has an immediate reaction to the therapist intervention (e.g., feeling misunderstood or worse) and then makes a decision about how to respond to the therapist (e.g., resisting). The therapist observes the client's behaviors and revises his or her subsequent intentions to be as helpful as possible to the emerging client need (e.g., the therapist might change intentions to provide more support given that the client appeared distressed). The articles reprinted here are about the parts of this process model and about the links between the parts of the model.

Therapist Intentions

Several studies have been conducted on therapist intentions. The development and use of the Intentions List was presented in 1985 by Hill and O'Grady (see chapter 5) using both a case study of brief therapy with a volunteer client and middle sessions of long-term therapy. Hill and O'Grady showed that therapists of different theoretical orientations used different intentions and that intentions varied across sessions and across therapy.

In 1991, Kivlighan and Angelone (see chapter 9) found that novice therapists used different proportions of intentions with introverted versus nonintroverted volunteer clients. Specifically, novice therapists used more intentions aimed at identifying cognitions and challenging clients' beliefs and fewer intentions aimed at supporting the client, working on the therapeutic relationship, and dealing with their own needs when they were paired with introverted as compared to nonintroverted volunteer clients. This study is important because it used a slightly different methodology for assessing intentions than did Hill and O'Grady. Specifically, because Martin, Martin, and Slemon (1987) found that therapists often coded similar statements of intention into different categories on the Intentions List, Kivlighan trained novice therapists about how to use the Intentions List reliably before allowing them to use the list in the research.

In 1993, Hill, Thompson, Cogar, and Denman (see chapter 8) studied middle sessions of long-term therapy and found that a match between therapist intentions and client perceptions of therapist intentions was not related to session outcome. These results replicated four other studies that found that client awareness of therapist intentions either was not related to or was negatively related to episode or session outcome (Fuller & Hill, 1985; Horvath, Marx, & Kamann, 1990; Martin, Martin, Meyer, & Slemon, 1986; Martin et al., 1987), suggesting that clients do not need to be aware of therapists' intentions.

Hill, O'Grady, et al. (1994, see chapter 6) did an evaluation of the psychometric properties (validity and reliability) of therapist intentions. They found that therapist intentions were consistent over time. Intentions reported during videotape review sessions conducted immediately after sessions were similar to those reported during therapy sessions. Furthermore, therapist intentions reported during a videotape review two weeks after the therapy session were similar to those reported both during the session and the videotape review that occurred right after the session.

Therapist intentions is a rich area for future research. We need to know more about how to measure intentions unobtrusively, how therapists develop their intentions, and how aware therapists are of their intentions (see also Stiles, 1987).

Therapist Skills (Also Known as Response Modes or Techniques)

In this section, studies are presented that involve testing all the skills simultaneously (note that studies testing the effects of individual skills are presented in parts III–VII of the book). In 1987, Elliott et al. (see chapter 1) compared six of the most frequently used systems for categorizing helping skills and found considerable overlap for six specific skills (question, information, advisement, reflection, interpretation, and self-disclosure), indicating that the systems are fairly interchangeable at least for these skills. Elliott et al. also found that therapists from different theoretical orientations had different profiles of using the various skills, and these profiles were consistent with the therapists' stated orientations.

In 1988, Hill, Helms, Tichenor, et al. (see chapter 4) investigated three methods for assessing the links between skills and outcome. First, they examined the correlational method of relating the proportion of skills to session and treatment outcome. Because of problems with correlational studies (see p. xii of the Introduction), however, they did not think that these results were valid, especially as the results were discrepant from previous findings and from findings using other methods in the same study. Then, they did a sequential analysis linking skills with immediate outcome and found that the most helpful therapist skills from the client perspective were interpretation and self-disclosure. Finally, they added other variables to the process model and found that client state and therapist intentions needed to be considered in addition to therapist skills. Specifically, when clients were at a low level of experiencing (i.e., were not expressing their feelings), the most helpful interventions were ones in which therapists helped clients explore feelings and behaviors through using the skills of paraphrase, interpretation, and confrontation. However, when clients were at a moderate level of experiencing (i.e., expressing their feelings but not aware of why they were having these feelings), all therapist interventions were perceived as equally helpful. In other words, the type of therapist intervention made a difference when clients were not very involved in therapy but did not matter as much when clients were involved in the tasks of therapy.

In summary, a great deal of research activity has gone into measuring therapist skills, describing how the skills are used by different types of therapists in different types of situations, and figuring out how to test the effects of the skills. However, it is important to note that there is more to a therapist intervention than just the skill used. There is the intention behind the skill (e.g., to intensify feelings, to provide support), the nonverbal behaviors that accompany it, the manner or style with which the helping skill is offered (e.g., empathetically, judgmentally), and the quality or competence with which the skill is delivered. In addition, there is the content of what is being talked about in the therapy session (e.g., interpersonal concerns, careers concerns), the working alliance between the therapist and client, the time in the session (beginning, middle, end), and the stage of therapy (beginning, middle, termination). The challenge for future researchers is to create innovative methods for considering more of the complexity of skills in determining their effectiveness.

Client Reactions

In 1988, Hill, Helms, Spiegel, and Tichenor (see chapter 3) described the development of a system of client reactions. Hill et al. found that about 60% of the client reactions were positive (e.g., client felt understood, learned new ways to behave), whereas about 40% were negative (e.g., client felt worse, stuck, or had no reaction). Furthermore, clients who were more initially disturbed reported having more negative reactions during sessions. They also found that therapist intentions were associated with client reactions in predictable ways (e.g., when the therapist intended to support and instill hope, the client typically reported feeling supported), indicating that therapists were able to communicate their intentions and clients were able to perceive the intentions.

In 1990, Hill and Stephany (see chapter 7) investigated whether client reactions were systematically linked with their nonverbal behaviors. They found that when clients had therapeutic work reactions and felt supported, they used more horizontal head movements. Interestingly, there were no specific nonverbal behaviors associated with negative client reactions, which indicates that therapists cannot readily gauge negative client reactions from nonverbal behaviors.

The Hill, Thompson, et al. (1993, see chapter 8) study, which was discussed with the studies on therapist intentions, also included a study on client reactions to therapist interventions. Hill et al. found that clients in long-term therapy were more likely to hide negative than supported reactions (7% vs. 1% respectively), that 65% of clients left at least one thing unsaid during session and that these things were usually negative, and that 46% of clients had secrets that they had not told their therapists. Overwhelming emotions, desire for avoidance, shame, and embarrassment were major reasons for not revealing things left unsaid and secrets. Therapists were more accurate at guessing positive than negative client reactions, replicating earlier studies by Hill, Thompson, and Corbett (1992) and Thompson and Hill (1991).

Hill, O'Grady, et al. (1994, see chapter 6) also did an evaluation of the psychometric properties (validity and reliability) of the client reactions system. They found that client reactions reported were consistent over time during videotape review sessions conducted immediately after sessions were similar to those reported during therapy sessions. Furthermore, client reactions reported during a the videotape review two weeks after the therapy session were similar to those reported both during the session and videotape review that occurred right after the session.

In summary, client reactions is a vital area to study because it reveals information about the process of therapy about which therapists are not always aware. It is particularly important to study hidden negative client reactions because of their potential impact on therapy. It appears that clients give few nonverbal clues to their negative reactions, and it also appears that therapists are not very good at guessing when clients have negative reactions. Perhaps it is more effective for therapists to ask clients about their reactions rather than to guess at them in the hope that they perceive them accurately, but this needs to be tested empirically.

Client Behaviors

Hill, Corbett, et al. (1991, see chapter 2) described the development of the client behavior system. Similar to the manner in which therapist skills are measured above, client behaviors are assessed as discrete behaviors (e.g., insight, resistance) that can be measured in each client sentence. Hill et al. found that the most frequent client behaviors were recounting and cognitive–behavioral exploration. Clients were at highest levels of experiencing when they were engaged in affective exploration, insight, and cognitive–behavioral exploration. They were at the lowest levels of experiencing when they were engaged in agreement, requests, and resistance.

Although space does not permit us to reprint a number of other excellent measures of client involvement, it is useful to note them here: the client Experiencing Scale (Klein, Mathieu-Coughlan, & Kiesler, 1986), the client Vocal Quality Measure (Rice & Kerr, 1986), the Rutgers Psychotherapy Progress Scale (Holland, Roberts, & Messer, 1998), the Assimilation Scale (Stiles et al., 1990), and the Client Resistance Scale (Mahalik, 1994). These measures typically involve a progression from limited involvement to deep involvement in the therapy process.

References

Fuller, F., & Hill, C. E. (1985). Counselor and helpee perceptions of counselor intentions in relationship to outcome in a single counseling session. *Journal of Counseling Psychology, 32,* 329–338.

Hill, C. E., & O'Brien, K. M. (1999). *Helping skills: Facilitating exploration, insight, and action.* Washington, DC: American Psychological Association.

Hill, C. E., Thompson, B. J., & Corbett, M. M. (1992). The impact of therapist ability to perceive displayed and hidden client reactions on immediate outcome in first sessions of brief therapy. *Psychotherapy Research, 2,* 143–155.

Holland, S. J., Roberts, N. E., & Messer, S. B. (1998). Reliability and validity of the Rutgers Psychotherapy Progress Scale. *Psychotherapy Research, 8,* 104–110.

Horvath, A. O., Marx, R. W., & Kamann, A. M. (1990). Thinking about thinking in therapy: An examination of clients' understanding of their therapists' intentions. *Journal of Consulting and Clinical Psychology, 58,* 614–621.

Klein, M. H., Mathieu-Coughlan, P., & Kiesler, D. J. (1986). The Experiencing Scales. In L. S. Greenberg & W. M. Pinsof (Eds.), *The psychotherapeutic process: A research handbook* (pp. 21–72). New York: Guilford Press.

Mahalik, J. R. (1994). Development of the Client Resistance Scale. *Journal of Counseling Psychology, 41,* 58–68.

Martin, J., Martin, W., Meyer, M., & Slemon, A. (1986). An empirical test of the cognitive mediational paradigm for research on counseling. *Journal of Counseling Psychology, 33,* 115–123.

Martin, J., Martin, W., & Slemon, A. (1987). Cognitive mediation in person-centered and rational–emotive therapy. *Journal of Counseling Psychology, 34,* 251–260.

Rice, L. N., & Kerr, G. P. (1986). Measures of client and therapist vocal quality. In L. S. Greenberg & W. M. Pinsof (Eds.), *The psychotherapeutic process: A research handbook* (pp. 73–106). New York: Guilford Press.

Stiles, W. B. (1987). Some intentions are observable. *Journal of Counseling Psychology, 34,* 236–239.

Stiles, W. B., Elliott, R., Llewelyn, S. P., Firth-Cozens, J. A., Margison, F. R., Shapiro, D. A., & Hardy, G. (1990). Assimilation of problematic experiences by clients in psychotherapy. *Psychotherapy, 27,* 411–420.

Thompson, B., & Hill, C. E. (1991). Therapist perceptions of client reactions. *Journal of Counseling and Development, 69,* 261–265.

Chapter 1
PRIMARY THERAPIST RESPONSE MODES:
Comparison of Six Rating Systems

Robert Elliott, Clara E. Hill, William B. Stiles, Myrna L. Friedlander,
Alvin R. Mahrer, and Frank R. Margison

The psychotherapy or counseling process can be divided into four aspects: content (what is said), action (what is done), style (how it is said or done), and quality (how well it is carried out; Elliott, 1984; Russell & Stiles, 1979). Categories or dimensions of verbal action are referred to by linguists and philosophers as speech acts (Searle, 1969) and by process researchers as response modes (Goodman & Dooley, 1976).

Measures of therapist response modes have gradually accumulated, resulting in some 20 or 30 systems to date (Elliott et al., 1982; Goodman & Dooley, 1976; Hill, 1982; Russell & Stiles, 1979). Some of these systems have been incorporated into skills training packages for beginning counselors (e.g., Ivey & Gluckstern, 1974), whereas others have been used to discriminate between treatments or to predict therapy outcome (e.g., Sloane, Staples, Cristol, Yorkston, & Whipple, 1975).

The multiplicity of rating systems makes it difficult to compare studies or to tell whether differences between studies are due to rating systems or to the interviews rated. Furthermore, to our knowledge, no published studies have compared different response-mode rating systems.

Barriers to the comparison of response-mode systems include (a) the use of different labels for similar categories; (b) the failure to report reliabilities for specific response modes, making it difficult to evaluate specific categories within and across systems; (c) different measurement assumptions and rating procedures (e.g., differences in scoring units); and (d) theoretical biases, resulting in overemphasis on certain verbal behaviors and restricted applicability to therapist behaviors of a particular orientation. Thus, a need exists for comparing response-mode systems on a single sample of therapy sessions.

In this study, six developers of rating systems collaborated to rate a common set of actual therapy sessions. The sessions represented a range of theoretical orientations, a range of client types, and a mixture of initial and later sessions, providing a variety of therapist verbal behaviors.

Our goals were (a) to compare interrater reliabilities, (b) to seek a common set of primary modes, and (c) to assess the discriminant validity of the primary modes by contrasting response use by different therapists.

Reprinted from *Journal of Consulting and Clinical Psychology, 55,* 218–223 (1987). Copyright © 1987 by the American Psychological Association. Used with permission of the first author.

An earlier version of this article was presented at the annual meeting of the Society for Psychotherapy Research, Lake Louise, Alberta, Canada, June 1984. The authors thank the six teams of raters, as well as Henya Rachmiel and Mee-Ok Cho, for their assistance in data entry and analysis. This article was written while the first and third authors were Visiting Researchers at the Social and Applied Psychology Unit at the University of Sheffield, Sheffield, United Kingdom.

Method

Sample

Seven therapy sessions were rated: (a) *John Paul Brady: Behavioral Treatment of Stuttering* (Brady, 1983), an initial session demonstrating deconditioning of stuttering with a young woman; (b) *Albert Ellis: John Jones* (Ellis, 1983), the 15th session of rational–emotive therapy with a young male homosexual; (c) Clara Hill, the 5th session of a 12-session, time-limited, relationship-insight-oriented treatment with a female college student (Hill, Carter, & O'Farrell, 1983); (d) Robert Hobson (1982), an initial session of conversational therapy (a relationship–dynamic treatment conducted by its originator, a British psychiatrist) with a young woman with interpersonal problems; (e) *Ira Progoff: Gregg* (Progoff, 1983), Jungian dream analysis with a male client (the session appears to be one of the last from a long-term therapy); (f) *Carl Rogers: Miss Munn* (Rogers, 1983), the 17th session of a client-centered treatment with a young woman; (g) Faith Tanney, an intake session with a male client with procrastination problems that was conducted by a counseling center therapist with a gestalt–dynamic orientation (Hill, 1978).

Response Mode Systems

The six response mode systems used in the study are summarized below and in Table 1.

1. Hill's Counselor Verbal Response Mode Category System (Hill, 1978) consists of 14 mutually exclusive categories. Response modes are judged for each response unit, which is defined as a grammatical sentence that has been unitized separately (brief phrases such as "mm-hmm" and "yes" are also treated as separate units). Unitized transcripts were rated independently by three trained undergraduates. Final ratings were based on agreement by two of the three judges; three-way disagreements were resolved by discussion.
2. Friedlander's (1982) refinement of Hill's (1978) rating system includes nine mutually exclusive categories, combining several of Hill's categories (e.g., "open question" and "closed question" are combined as "information seeking"). The scoring unit is generally the same as Hill's, except that each unit must minimally contain a verb phrase (i.e., "uh-huh" is not rated and compound predicates are scored separately). Ratings were done from unitized transcripts. Three raters were used. Procedures for final ratings and resolution of disagreements were identical to those of Hill (1978).
3. Stiles' Verbal Response Mode System (Stiles, 1978, 1979) consists of eight mutually exclusive categories. Verbal form (literal meaning) and speaker intention (meaning intended in the situation) are rated separately, and the unit is defined as the independent clause or nonrestrictive dependent clause. Three trained undergraduate students unitized and rated transcripts. A two-out-of-three convention was used for resolving disagreements; three-way disagreements were defined as unclassifiable.

4. Elliott's Response Mode Rating System (Elliott, 1985) consists of 10 non-mutually exclusive dimensions that are rated using 0–3 confidence ratings. The unit is flexible, but in this study Hill's (1978) verbal sentence units were used. Ratings were made from unitized transcripts and tapes. Final ratings were achieved by rescaling confidence ratings to 0–1 scales, then averaging ratings across the four raters (three undergraduates and coauthor Friedlander).

5. The Conversational Therapy Rating System (Goldberg et al., 1984; referred to here as the Margison system) was developed to rate the therapist behaviors described in Hobson's Conversational Model of Therapy (Hobson, 1985). The system includes 11 mutually exclusive function categories, rigidly defined by formal cues, with particular emphasis on types of questions and advisement. The final ratings represent a combination of ratings by two judges (a psychology research assistant and coauthor Margison).

6. Mahrer's Taxonomy of Procedures and Operations in Psychotherapy (Mahrer, 1983) contains 35 mutually exclusive categories. The unit is defined as the therapist's speaking turn. Disagreements (less than 50% agreement) are resolved by rerating responses or by labeling responses as unclassifiable. Between eight and 12 raters (graduate students and coauthor Mahrer) were used on each session. Ratings were made from tapes and transcripts.

Results

Reliability Analyses

To compare systems, the *phi* statistic, a simplification of the product-moment correlation (for pairs of dichotomous variables) was used. The response-mode systems using nominal scale measurement (all except Elliott's) were treated as sets of dichotomous dimensions, each corresponding to separate response-mode categories. Correlations were then calculated between each pair of raters for each category or dimension in each system. The means of these correlations, provided in Table 1, can be interpreted as the reliability of the average rater for each category or dimension within each rating system. The median values (across categories) for five of the seven systems were quite similar (Hill = .61, Friedlander = .59, Elliott = .56, Stiles-Intent = .55, and Mahrer = .52, or .57 if the 12 categories with zero or near zero baserates are excluded). These small differences probably reflect differences in the training and sophistication of the raters. The median reliability for Stiles-Form ratings was .73, presumably because response form is easier to rate than speaker intent. (The other response-mode systems are primarily intent based.) The typical values for the Margison system were higher yet (*Mdn* = .88), probably because these categories have been rigidly defined and require highly experienced raters. When median reliability values were grouped by mode, question categories were rated most reliably (.71), followed by advisement (.66), information (.64), self-disclosure (.61), reassurance (.58), interpretation (.56), reflection (.53), confrontation (.48), and other (.37).

Alpha reliability coefficients were also calculated in order to obtain a measure of actual reliability. These were substantially higher than the average rater figures

Table 1—*Reliability Estimates of Response Mode Systems Organized by Primary Mode*

Primary mode	Hill	Friedlander	Stiles (form/intent)	Elliott	Margison	Mahrer
Question	Closed question (.78), open question (.73)	Information seeking (.82)	Question (.86/.76)	Closed question (.76), open question (.64)	Closed question (.87), open question (.71), understanding question (.67)	Inquiry about ongoing self (.71), information about distantiated self (.71), descriptive clarification of patient in situation (.43), go on, tell me (.66), simple clarification (.59), agree or disagree (.56)
Information	Information (.73)	Providing information (.53)	Edification (.78/.56)	Information (.64)	Information–explanation (.88)	General structuring (.64), defining external behavior (.55), explanation of external world (.61)
Advisement	Direct guidance (.61)	Direct guidance–advice (.67)	Advisement (.73/.66)	Process advisement (.60), general advisement (.52)	Topic area defined (.82), process defined (.79), general instruction (.89), advice (.37)[c]	Identification of concerns (.59), behavior change consideration (.20)[a] Advised extra-therapy behavior (.52), carrying out behavior as patient (.69)
Reflection	Restatement (.59), reflection (.48), nonverbal reference (.52)	Reflection–restatement (.59)	Reflection (.53/.46)	Reflection (.59)	Restatement (.91)	Reflection (.49), repetition–restatement (.53), summary conclusion (.32)

Interpretation	Interpretation (.62)	Interpretation (.44)	Interpretation (.50/.43)	Interpretation (.56)	Understanding hypothesis (.93)	Explanation of patient (.64)
Self-disclosure	Self-disclosure (.56)	Self-disclosure (.71)	Disclosure (.80/.55)	Self-disclosure (.55)	Therapist-owned (.90)	Self-disclosure (.61)
Reassurance	Approval–reassurance (.58)	Encouragement–approval–reassurance (.60)		Reassurance (.56)		Approval–reassurance (.57)
Confrontation	Confrontation (.55)	Confrontation (.49)		Disagreement (.38)[b]		Observed discrepancy (.29), challenge to defend (.48)
Acknowledgment	Minimal encourager (.94)		Acknowledgment (.88/.75)			Simple answer (.56), simple acknowledgment (.89)
Other	Other (.62)	Unclassifiable (.32)[a]	Confirmation (.71/.30)[a] Unclassifiable/other (.20/.25)[a]	Other (.37)	Miscellaneous (.92)	Ridiculous description of patient (.22)[c]
No. Units	2,079	1,573	2,909	2,041	796 (4 sessions only)	1,169
No. Raters	32 undergraduates	Friedlander and 2 graduate students	3 undergraduates	3 undergraduates, 1 graduate student	Margison and graduate-level research assistant	Mahrer and 7 graduate students

Note. Reliability values in parentheses are mean intercorrelations among raters. Not included in table are 10 zero base-rate Mahrer categories.
[a] Alpha was less than .60. [b] Alpha was between .60 and .70. [c] Low base-rate and unreliable category; not analyzed.

because they were averages of 2–12 ratings. Only 19 of the 97 different categories or dimensions had alpha reliabilities less than .70. All of these involved either zero or very low base-rate categories (13 instances, most in the Mahrer system); other or unclassifiable categories (3 instances); or had alphas between .60 and .70, indicating that the data were still usable (3 instances).

Comparison of Rating Systems on Primary-Response Modes

The final ratings were assembled into a master file, first using Hill's response units and then subdividing to accommodate the smaller units used by Stiles and (occasionally) by Friedlander. If Stiles' raters divided a Hill unit into smaller parts, then the other systems' ratings were duplicated over the same parts of the response. The exception occurred when Stiles or Hill created a unit for something not rated in other systems (e.g., initial "yes," "well," "you know"); in this case, a missing value was entered for the system in which the unit was not rateable. Finally, because there was disagreement among systems as to whether acknowledgments or minimal encouragers (e.g., "uh-huh") and silence should be considered units, these were dropped from the analyses.

In the initial comparisons among systems, the original categories were used. It became clear, however, that differences in "fine-grainedness" of categories were distorting the results. For example, Friedlander's reflection–restatement category is superordinate to Hill's reflection, restatement, and nonverbal referent categories. To compare categories across systems, similar categories were identified by careful checking of category definitions and examples and by initial correlational analyses. We found six primary response modes (question, information, advisement, interpretation, reflection, and self-disclosure) that were measured by all the systems and two modes (reassurance and confrontation) that were common to four of the systems.

In all, 138 tests of convergence (correlations between same primary modes across different systems) were performed on 50 measures of primary-response modes.[1] The very large sample size ($N = 1,947$) and the nonindependence of observations (units within sessions) rendered the usual statistical significance criteria meaningless. However, 117 of these tests (85%) had correlations of at least .20 and 98 (71%) of the correlations exceeded .30. An estimate of discriminant validity was given by comparing these with the 930 correlations of different modes in different systems; only 10 exceeded .20 (1.1%), and none exceeded .30.

Mean intercorrelations showed that convergence across systems for comparable modes was highest for question and reassurance (.61 and .52, respectively), and was moderate for information (.40), reflection (.38), advisement (.35), self-disclosure (.33), confrontation (.31), and interpretation (.28). These convergence figures, interestingly, average only about .20 lower than the reliability estimates for categories within systems.

To provide an index of each response-mode system's convergent validity, each was compared with an index consisting of all other measures of the same mode. These corrected item–total correlations are presented in Table 2 for the six primary modes. (The comparable values for reassurance are Hill, .68; Friedlander, .62; Elliott,

---

[1]These data are available from the first author.

Table 2—*Proportions and Item-Total Correlations for Primary Response Modes*

Rating system	Question	Information	Advisement	Reflection	Interpretation	Self-disclosure
			Proportions			
Hill	.14	.24	.02	.12	.27	.01
Friedlander	.11	.37	.05	.17	.15	.01
Stiles-form	.13	.32	.04	.16	.07	.16
Stiles-intent	.15	.15	.06	.18	.22	.07
Elliott	.17	.16	.10	.20	.31	.05
Margison	.13	.27	.07	.19	.19	.29
Mahrer	.18	.18	.07	.08	.38	.02
			Item–total correlations			
Hill	.82	.58	.50	.58	.62	.32
Friedlander	.76	.51	.73	.61	.49	.34
Stiles-form	.73	.32	.58	.49	.17	.59
Stiles-intent	.84	.62	.73	.70	.45	.57
Elliott	.84	.68	.67	.66	.67	.48
Margison	.73	.37	.46	.35	.26	.52
Mahrer	.49	.51	.33	.47	.52	.39

Note. Categories are treated as separate dimensions within each system. The item–total correlation is the correlation between a category in a system and the proportion for the category for all the remaining systems.

.73; and Mahrer, .52. For confrontation, comparable values are Hill, .47; Friedlander, .51; Elliott, .45; and Mahrer, .29.) Hill's system showed particularly good convergence relative to other systems for its measures of question, interpretation, and confrontation, whereas its measure of self-disclosure appeared to differ from that of the other systems. Friedlander's version of the Hill system showed good convergence on measures of advisement and confrontation but not on measures of self-disclosure. Elliott's system converged relatively strongly in its measures of question, information, reflection, and interpretation. Stiles-Intent converged well for question, information, advisement, reflection, and self-disclosure. Stiles-Form converged well only for self-disclosure and diverged somewhat for information and interpretation. The Mahrer and Margison systems appeared to be most divergent from the other systems, generally showing lower item–total correlations.

Discrimination of Therapists by Response-Mode Use

As a further test of the discriminant validity of the primary response modes, we compared the proportions of response modes used by the seven therapists. We developed a composite response-mode index, calculated by finding the proportion of systems scoring the given mode as present for a given unit. These composite indices were then averaged across the 1,947 units (see Table 3). Finally, dummy variable correlations were used for each mode to compare each therapist with all other therapists. Effect sizes ($rs > .10, .20, .30$) are also given in Table 3 because conventional significance levels were not useful (for $r = .10$, $p < .001$).

Each therapist was characterized by a unique profile of response-mode use: Brady (a behavior therapist) used more information and advisement but was low on reflection, interpretation, and confrontation. In comparison, Progoff also used more information but less advisement and confrontation. Tanney (a gestalt/dynamic therapist) frequently used information, self-disclosure, and question and avoided use of reflection and interpretation. Consistent with his treatment model, Rogers used more reflection than did any other therapist for that mode or, in fact, for any one mode. Hill's relatively high use of interpretation and reflection modes is consistent with her bridging of the relationship and dynamic therapy traditions. Ellis was unique in his high use of both reassurance and confrontation and gave fewer information and self-disclosure responses. Hobson was not characterized by relatively greater use of any response mode, although he did use less information.

Discussion

The present results suggest that a set of fundamental response-mode categories or dimensions underlies a variety of systems with different origins and purposes. We have reported evidence for the convergent and discriminant validity of six primary response modes (question, advisement, information, reflection, interpretation, and self-disclosure) rated in all the systems studied.

Convergence was obtained despite a variety of methodological differences between rating systems, including levels of rater training experience (a few weeks to several years), rater sophistication (advanced undergraduates to seasoned therapy

Table 3—*Mean Composite Ratings by Therapist for Response Modes*

Response mode	Total	Brady	Ellis	Hill	Hobson	Progoff	Rogers	Tanney
Question	.15	.20	.17	.06[a]	.14	.11	.10	.21[a]
Information	.24	.38[a]	.14[a]	.17[a]	.13[a]	.31[a]	.02[a]	.33[a]
Advisement	.06	.20[c]	.03	.03	.09	.01[a]	.00	.06
Reflection	.16	.05[a]	.14	.22[a]	.18	.13	.71[c]	.10[a]
Interpretation	.23	.03[b]	.28	.38[b]	.28	.26	.14	.13[b]
Self-disclosure	.09	.07	.01[a]	.10	.11	.07	.04	.13[a]
Reassurance	.05	.03	.09[a]	.02	.03	.07	.02	.04
Confrontation	.05	.00[a]	.16[a]	.06	.02	.01[a]	.00	.05
Other	.03	.03	.04	.01	.03	.03	.00	.03
N	1,947	216	269	357	239	364	65	437

Note. Values in the table are mean composite response ratings (proportion of systems scoring a unit as a given mode, averaged across all units). Dummy variable correlations were used to compare each therapist with all others for each mode (correlating composite response mode ratings with a set of variables coded 1 for each therapist vs. 0 for all other therapists). Effect sizes are given because conventional significance levels were not useful (for $r = .10$, $p < .001$).
[a] $r > .10$. [b] $r > .20$. [c] $r > .30$.

researchers), rating units (clauses to complete responses), thoroughness of definitions and examples (brief descriptions to complete expositions), and measurement structure (nominal scale vs. set of rating dimensions).

The factors that did seem to affect interrater reliability or convergent validity were (a) the category itself, with question being the easiest category to rate reliably; (b) the form versus intention distinction introduced by Goodman and Dooley (1976) and incorporated by Stiles (1978, 1979); and (c) whether or not the system was designed to measure a particular approach to therapy.

At the same time, the results make it clear that the response-mode measures do not converge entirely. The intersystem validity coefficients are still about .20 lower than the typical interrater correlations within systems (i.e., .30–.40 vs. .55–.60). Although the systems measure the same primary modes, they are still defined somewhat differently.

We conclude that there generally is not a best response-mode rating system. Reliability values were comparable and convergent validity varied by category, with no one system clearly proving best on all modes. However, to promote comparability across studies, researchers measuring therapist speech acts should examine the six primary modes and may also want to consider measuring reassurance, confrontation, or acknowledgment. Researchers should select or adjust response-mode systems according to their needs in relation to the features and strengths of particular systems.

At present, the therapist response modes are probably the most widely studied therapist process variables. Response modes are conceptually clear and can be thoroughly specified; they also discriminate between different approaches to therapy. On the other hand, therapist response modes predict outcome or therapist effectiveness only weakly or moderately (Elliott et al., 1982). The response modes measure only one aspect of therapist responses: action. A more complete description of therapist responses requires additional ratings of content, style, quality, or effectiveness (Elliott, 1984; Russell & Stiles, 1979). Finally, therapist response modes also take their meaning and impact from context, in particular, from background characteristics of the client, from the current status of the relationship, from the current important helping tasks, and from the client's immediately prior statement (Elliott, 1984).

References

Brady, J. P. (1983). *Behavioral treatment of stuttering* (AAP Tape Library Catalogue, Tape No. 38). Salt Lake City, UT: American Academy of Psychotherapists.

Elliott, R. (1984). A discovery-oriented approach to significant events in psychotherapy: Interpersonal process recall and comprehensive process analysis. In L. Rice & L. Greenberg (Eds.), *Patterns of change* (pp. 249–286). New York: Guilford Press.

Elliott, R. (1985). Helpful and nonhelpful events in brief counseling interviews: An empirical taxonomy. *Journal of Counseling Psychology, 32,* 307–322.

Elliott, R., Stiles, W. B., Shiffman, S., Barker, C. B., Burstein, B., & Goodman, G. (1982). The empirical analysis of helping communication: Conceptual framework and recent research. In T. A. Wills (Ed.), *Basic processes in helping relationships* (pp. 333–356). New York: Academic Press.

Ellis, A. (1983). *John Jones* (AAP Tape Library Catalogue, Tape No. 11). Salt Lake City, UT: American Academy of Psychotherapists.

Friedlander, M. L. (1982). Counseling discourse as a speech event: Revision and extension of the Hill Counselor Verbal Response Category System. *Journal of Counseling Psychology, 29,* 425–429.

Goldberg, D. P., Hobson, R. F., Maguire, G. P., Margison, F. R., O'Dowd, T., Osborn, M., & Moss, S. (1984). The clarification and assessment of a method of psychotherapy. *British Journal of Psychiatry, 144,* 567–580.

Goodman, G., & Dooley, D. (1976). A framework for help-intended communication. *Psychotherapy: Theory, Research and Practice, 13,* 106–117.

Hill, C. E. (1978). The development of a system for classifying counselor responses. *Journal of Counseling Psychology, 25,* 461–468.

Hill, C. E. (1982). Counseling process research: Philosophical and methodological dilemmas. *Counseling Psychologist, 10,* 7–19.

Hill, C. E., Carter, J. A., & O'Farrell, M. K. (1983). A case study of the process and outcome of time-limited counseling. *Journal of Counseling Psychology, 30,* 3–18.

Hobson, R. (1982). *Louise R.* Unpublished tape, Central Manchester Health Authority, Manchester, England.

Hobson, R. F. (1985). *Forms of feeling.* London: Tavistock.

Ivey, A. E., & Gluckstern, N. B. (1974). *Basic attending skills: Participant manual.* North Amherst, MA: Microtraining Associates.

Mahrer, A. R. (1983). *Taxonomy of procedures and operations in psychotherapy.* Unpublished manuscript, University of Ottawa, Canada.

Progoff, I. (1983). *Gregg.* (AAP Tape Library Catalogue, Tape No. 12). Salt Lake City, UT: American Academy of Psychotherapists.

Rogers, C. R. (1983). *Miss Munn* (AAP Tape Library Catalogue, Tape No. 5). Salt Lake City, UT: American Academy of Psychotherapists.

Russell, R. L., & Stiles, W. B. (1979). Categories for classifying language in psychotherapy. *Psychological Bulletin, 86,* 404–419.

Searle, J. R. (1969). *Speech acts: An essay in the philosophy of language.* Cambridge, England: Cambridge University Press.

Sloane, R. B., Staples, F. R., Cristol, A. H., Yorkston, N. J., & Whipple, K. (1975). *Psychotherapy versus behavior therapy.* Cambridge, MA: Harvard University Press.

Stiles, W. B. (1978). Verbal response modes and dimensions of interpersonal roles: A method of discourse analysis. *Journal of Personality and Social Psychology, 36,* 693–703.

Stiles, W. B. (1979). Verbal response modes and psychotherapeutic technique. *Psychiatry, 42,* 49–62.

Chapter 2
CLIENT BEHAVIOR IN COUNSELING AND THERAPY SESSIONS:
Development of a Pantheoretical Measure

Clara E. Hill, Maureen M. Corbett, Bettina Kanitz, Peggy Rios,
Richard Lightsey, and Maria Gomez

To understand the interaction between counselors and clients, researchers need measures of client behavior. A measure of client behavior can aid in describing and evaluating client behavior, ascertaining the ways in which clients respond to counselor interventions, and assessing the ways in which clients change over the course of treatment.

In considering the importance of client behavior in counseling and therapy, it is puzzling that a single measure or even a single type of measure has not emerged as the standard in the field. In measuring counselor behavior, in contrast, response modes have been widely accepted as a standard type of measure, with several different versions created by different researchers (cf. Elliott et al., 1987). In contrast, several different types of measures of client behavior, most of which were developed from single theoretical perspectives (e.g., client experiencing: Klein, Mathieu-Coughlan, & Kiesler, 1986; client vocal quality: Rice & Kerr, 1986; client perceptual processing: Toukmanian, 1986; interactional patterns: Benjamin, 1979; and response modes: Snyder, 1945; Stiles, 1986; Hill et al., 1981). Although these measures are useful for specific research purposes, pantheoretical measures are needed so that client behavior can be studied across theoretical approaches to determine the effects of different therapeutic interventions.

Hill and O'Grady (1985) developed a generic model for describing the counseling process. Briefly, this model specifies that counselor intentions lead counselors to select particular response modes to use in their interventions, which in turn create specific reactions in clients, who then select their behaviors accordingly. Measures have been developed for each of these dimensions (Hill, 1992), including the Client Verbal Response Category System (Hill, 1986; Hill et al., 1981).

Hill et al.'s (1981) system includes nine nominal, mutually exclusive categories: simple responses, requests, description, experiencing, insight, discussion of plans, discussion of client–counselor relationship, silence, and other. Although Hill et al. obtained high interjudge agreement using this system (mean kappa = .92) and found predicted relationships with counselor interventions, there are several problems with

Reprinted from *Journal of Counseling Psychology, 39*, 539–549 (1992). Copyright © 1992 by the American Psychological Association. Used with permission of the first author.

This study was supported in part by a National Institute of Mental Health Research Grant (MH 37837). The Computer Science Center of the University of Maryland, College Park, provided computer support.

A version of this article was presented in June 1991 at the annual meeting of the Society for Psychotherapy Research, Lyon, France.

We wish to express our appreciation to Daniel Denman for statistical consultation and to Barbara Thompson for her helpful comments on an earlier draft of this article.

the system. First, most of the responses fell into the description (54%) and simple responses (25%) categories, which resulted in a restricted characterization of the therapy process. Particularly problematic, the system seems to focus most on behaviors valued in client-centered or psychodynamic therapies, such as experiencing or insight, and to disregard behaviors valued more in cognitive or behavioral therapies, such as cognitive or behavioral exploration.

Second, there are no categories for describing client resistance. Given that clients sometimes have difficulty engaging in therapeutic tasks, either because of their own issues or because of ineffective counselor interventions, inclusion of resistant behaviors in a measure of client behavior is important. Chamberlain, Patterson, Reid, Kavanagh, and Forgatch (1984) developed the Therapy Process Code to measure resistant behavior in families. They found that families who dropped out of treatment had more instances of resistance than families who completed treatment and that agency-referred families had more resistance than self-referred families. Patterson and Forgatch (1985) found that client resistance was higher when therapists were teaching and confronting and lower when therapists were supporting or facilitating. Furthermore, resistance was highest in the middle phase of treatment relative to early and late phases of treatment (Chamberlain et al., 1984; Chamberlain & Ray, 1988). Chamberlain and Ray (1988) also found that resistance by mothers was negatively correlated with therapist liking of mothers, indicating that therapists disliked resistant mothers. Also, children of more resistant mothers had poorer treatment outcomes. Thus, the research on client resistance in family treatment suggests that resistance is an important behavior that needs to be included in a comprehensive measure of client verbal behavior.

Third, the Hill et al. (1981) system includes categories that are at different conceptual levels. Simple responses and silence categories do not seem to be conceptually similar to the overt verbal categories. Simple responses (e.g., "Mmhmm") are often conversation-maintaining devices, rather than overt verbal communication. Silence, which can have many different functions in therapy, is clearly not a form of verbal communication. Although both simple responses and silence can be very important client behaviors in counseling, they do not convey what the client is doing in the same manner that overt behaviors such as insight or requests do. Furthermore, the category of discussion of the client–counselor relationship seems to be more global than do the other categories. For example, when talking about the relationship, the client could be involved in description, experiencing, or insight. From a methodological standpoint, measures should assess behaviors at the same level of abstraction (Greenberg & Pinsof, 1986).

Fourth, the Hill et al. (1981) system uses transcripts to code client behaviors, thus ignoring nonverbal and paralinguistic cues that would be available from use of videotapes. Because nonverbal and paralinguistic behaviors are important in communication (cf. Harper, Wiens, & Matarazzo, 1978), the lack of attention to nonverbal cues is a serious limitation of the Hill et al. system.

Finally, the Hill et al. (1981) system relies on unit (sentence) judgments of client behaviors, which present a molecular analysis of what the client is saying. However, counselors probably respond to the most predominant or central aspect of what the client communicates in an entire speaking turn. Moreover, the use of multiple behaviors within speaking turns results in a lack of independence of data in statistical analyses. Hill, Carter, and O'Farrell (1983) tried to address this issue by examining the first two units (sentences) of the speaking turn, but that approach still missed the essential or predominant message. O'Farrell, Hill, and Patton (1986) used predominant judgments rather than unit judgments but did not report interjudge agreement levels for these predominant judgments.

Our overall purpose was to revise the Hill et al. (1981) measure by correcting several of its deficiencies (adding cognitive–behavioral exploration and resistance; eliminating simple responses, discussion of counselor–client relationship, and silence; adding categories of nonverbal and paralinguistic cues and requiring the use of videotapes for the judgment process; and adding predominant judgments). We first revised the system, creating the new client behavior system (CBS) and then conducted two studies to examine the interjudge agreement and validity of the CBS.

Revision of the Client Behavior System

In revising the Hill et al. (1981) system, we followed several guidelines: (a) categories should be nominal and mutually exclusive, (b) categories should represent the range of possible client behaviors in therapy, (c) categories should cover the range of client behaviors that would be expected from different theoretical perspectives, and (d) categories should all be at the same level of abstraction. We revised the Hill et al. categories on the basis of our examination of other systems (Chamberlain & Ray, 1988; Klein et al., 1986; Mahrer, Nadler, Sterner, & White, 1989; McCullough, 1990; Rice & Kerr, 1986; Snyder, 1945; Stiles, 1986).

The preliminary categories were revised several times as judges applied them to videotapes of counseling sessions (other than those used in Study 1). After several iterations of refining our categories and applying them to new sessions, the present eight-category system was developed (see the Appendix).

We asked 16 (9 female, 7 male) post-PhD counseling and clinical psychologists to examine the final version of the CBS. Psychologists who examined the CBS thought that it was clear, complete, and adequate for measuring what we set out to measure. They suggested minor wording changes for the categories, which we incorporated. Thus, the psychologists provided us with evidence of face and content validity for the CBS.

To gain an overall sense of the valence of the categories, we also asked the 16 psychologists to rate how involved and productive clients generally are when engaged in each of the eight CBS behaviors, using a 9-point scale ranging from *totally uninvolved in therapy and not working productively* (1) to *totally involved in therapy and working productively* (9). Means and standard deviations of ratings for each of the CBS categories are presented in Table 1. A repeated measures multivariate analysis of variance used to test differences between categories was significant with Pillai's trace $F(7, 9) = 16.29$, $p < .001$, indicating overall differences between categories. Because of the limited sample size, all post hoc comparisons could not be computed. Instead, we compared ratings on the first four categories (resistance, agreement, request, recounting) with ratings on the final four categories (cognitive–behavioral exploration, affective exploration, insight, changes) because we had hypothesized differences between these clusters on the basis of past research (Hill, Helms, Tichenor, et al., 1988). A post hoc orthogonal contrast was significant,

Table 1—*Ratings by Psychologists of Client Involvement and Productivity for the Client Behavior System Categories*

Category	M	SD
Resistance	3.31	2.09
Agreement	4.41	1.16
Request	5.25	1.40
Recounting	3.66	1.48
Cog–beh exploration	7.16	1.40
Affective exploration	8.06	0.79
Insight	7.91	0.93
Changes	7.16	1.34

Note. Cog–beh = Cognitive–behavioral. Ratings of client involvement and productivity were made by 16 post-PhD psychologists on a 9-point scale, ranging from *totally uninvolved and not working productively* (1) to *totally involved and working productively* (9).

$F(1, 15) = 119.24$, $p < .001$, indicating that psychologists viewed the final 4 categories as reflecting more productive behaviors than the first 4 categories.

Study 1

The first purpose of Study 1 was to examine the interjudge reliability for each of the categories, and the overlap between categories. Reliability was determined for both response units (grammatical sentences) and predominant (speaking turn) judgments. We used predominant judgments in our data analyses because (a) they presented a more global picture of what the counselor responds to in client behavior in a speaking turn than did unit judgments and (b) use of predominant judgments addresses the problem of lack of independence of unit data for statistical analyses. Thus, obtaining adequate reliability for predominant judgments was critical. The second purpose was to describe client behavior in actual therapy sessions to provide some initial normative data.

The third purpose was to establish convergent validity by comparing categorizations on the CBS with ratings on the Client Experiencing Scale (Klein, Mathieu, Gendlin, & Kiesler, 1970), both measures of judge-rated client behavior. We expected that higher levels of experiencing would be related to the more productive CBS categories (cognitive–behavioral exploration, affective exploration, insight, therapeutic changes). The fourth purpose was to establish construct validity by comparing CBS categorizations to client ratings of the helpfulness of the preceding counselor interventions (using archival data). We expected that when clients rated counselor interventions as more helpful, they would engage in more productive CBS behaviors.

Using the CBS, four trained judges coded one middle session from each of eight cases from an archival data set (Hill, 1989). Middle sessions were used because we thought that they would contain a wide range of client behaviors.

Method

Data Set

The data set for this study consisted of eight cases of brief therapy reported on elsewhere (Hill, 1989; Hill, Helms, Spiegel, & Tichenor, 1988; Hill, Helms, Tichenor, et al., 1988). The 8 (4 female, 4 male; 6 White, 2 Black) therapists averaged 46.38 ($SD = 13.47$) years of age, had an average of 18.50 ($SD = 10.85$) years of postdoctoral experience, and rated themselves, using 5-point Likert scales ranging from *low* (1) to *high* (5), on average as 3.75 ($SD = 0.46$) on psychoanalytic orientation, 2.62 ($SD = 0.74$) on humanistic orientation, and 2.50 ($SD = 1.07$) on behavioral theoretical orientation. The 8 female (6 White, 1 Arabic American, 1 Asian American) clients averaged 42.38 ($SD = 9.41$) years of age. All had elevated scores on the Depression and Psychasthenia subscales of the Minnesota Multiphasic Personality Inventory. Clients and therapists were unaware of the specific purposes of the study but were fully informed about all research procedures and signed consent forms before and after treatment.

This data set was chosen because it included ratings of client experiencing, as well as client ratings of the helpfulness of therapist interventions, both of which we used to validate the CBS. The Client Experiencing Scale (Klein et al., 1970; Klein, Mathieu-Coughlan, & Kiesler, 1986) is a 7-point scale used to describe a client's level of involvement in the therapy. In the Hill, Helms, Tichenor, et al. (1988) data set, six raters obtained an intraclass correlation (alpha) of 0.99 on two randomly selected sessions. The Helpfulness Scale (Elliott, 1985) is a 9-point Likert scale, ranging from *extremely unhelpful* (1) to *extremely helpful* (9), used by clients during a videotape review to rate therapist interventions.

Judges

Four women (3 White, 1 Hispanic; 3 master's-level students; 1 professor), all authors of the study, served as judges.

Measures

The CBS described above was used for this study. The CBS includes eight nominal, mutually exclusive categories: resistance, agreement, appropriate request, recounting, cognitive–behavioral exploration, affective exploration, insight, and therapeutic changes.

Procedure

Data preparation.   Transcripts for the eight sessions were available from the previous studies. Client verbal behavior was unitized (divided into grammatical sentences) by two trained judges using rules in Hill et al. (1981). These two judges had a 92% agreement rate for unitizing. Unitizing discrepancies were discussed until agreement was reached on consensus units.

CBS judgment process. Judgments were made in a two-step process of first judging response units (grammatical sentences) and then judging predominant behaviors (in speaking turns). Using videotapes and transcripts of a session, the judges independently assigned each response unit (grammatical sentence) to one category of the CBS. Interjudge agreement was calculated on these independent judgments. After completing all judgments for a session, judges met to resolve discrepancies. Any units in which fewer than three of the four judges agreed on the categorization were discussed until a consensus judgment was achieved. Once consensus judgments were reached for all units within a speaking turn (everything a client said between two counselor speeches), judges independently coded the predominant (major, primary) behavior for that speaking turn. In the occasional event that a behavioral shift resulted in two categories predominating in a turn, the behavior that came early in the turn (in response to the counselor's speaking turn) was weighed as most important in making the predominant judgment. When fewer than three judges agreed on the predominant categorization, judges discussed their judgments until they reached a consensus.

We should note that the rules used to define predominant judgments could differ on the basis of the research question. We used the rule of attending more to the initial part of the speaking turn in the occasional instances in which a shift in client behavior resulted in more than one predominant category. We weighed the initial portion more heavily because we conceptualized client responses as occurring in response to counselor interventions. If future researchers were more interested in examining client behavior as a stimulus for counselor interventions, they could weigh the latter portion of the speaking turn more heavily.

Results

Reliability

Response units. We expected interjudge agreement to be somewhat low because of the difficulty in discriminating client behaviors, so we used four rather than the more typical two or three judges. Use of more judges should allow for a more reliable estimate of the "true" judgment. The kappa statistic, generally regarded as the most appropriate index of agreement between judges because it corrects for chance (Tinsley & Weiss, 1975), is used with pairs of judges and therefore does not reflect the advantage of using additional judges. Because of this problem with kappa values, we present both the average number of judges who agreed on their independent judgments and kappa values.

Table 2 shows that an average of 3.26 judges agreed on categorizations, indicating high agreement levels. The average kappa value between pairs of judges was .54 ($SD = 0.02$), which according to Fleiss (1981) is fair to good agreement.

More than three judges usually agreed on categorizations for agreement, requests, recounting, and cognitive–behavioral exploration, whereas fewer than three judges usually agreed on categorizations for resistance, affective exploration, insight, and changes. Thus, these latter categories appeared to be more difficult to judge.

To determine areas of difficulty in judging among categories, we constructed a confusion matrix by plotting the categorizations for each judge against the categorization of every other judge (e.g., one judge coded Category 1, whereas another

Table 2—*Average Number of Judges Agreeing on Categories of the Client Behavior System for Response Unit and Predominant (Speaking Turn) Judgments for Study 1 and Study 2*

| | Study 1 | | | | Study 2 | | | |
| | Unit | | Predominant | | Unit | | Predominant | |
Category	M	SD	M	SD	M	SD	M	SD
Resistance	2.37	0.92	3.91	0.34	2.61	0.94	3.50	0.75
Agreement	3.13	0.92	3.92	0.36	—	—	—	—
Request	3.27	0.80	3.94	0.25	3.69	0.63	—	—
Recounting	3.52	0.73	3.94	0.27	3.36	0.80	3.68	0.65
Cog–beh exploration	3.22	0.74	3.83	0.46	3.12	0.75	3.59	0.64
Affective exploration	2.78	1.03	3.62	0.78	2.96	1.01	3.56	0.63
Insight	2.51	0.94	3.85	0.46	2.32	0.99	3.33	0.58
Changes	2.61	1.16	3.57	0.76	1.78	0.90	3.40	0.55
Total	3.26	0.85	3.86	0.43	3.21	0.84	3.61	0.65

Note. Cog–beh = cognitive–behavioral. Four judges categorized each unit or speaking turn (predominant judgment). In Study 2, dashes indicate that no categorizations were made in the agreement category for response units or in the agreement or requests categories for the predominant judgments.

judge coded Category 4). Thus, we could examine which categories were most likely to be confused with other categories (i.e., the area of most disagreement among judges). Because the matrix was an overlay of categorizations of each response unit for six pairs of judges, this matrix was simply examined for patterns of overlap between categories. Our criterion for examining the table was to note whether judgments of the other seven categories occurred about as often as judgments of the same category. Cognitive–behavioral exploration overlapped with resistance, recounting, affective exploration, and insight; resistance overlapped with recounting.

Predominant categorizations. Table 2 reveals that overall an average of 3.84 judges agreed on the predominant categorizations, again indicating high agreement levels. The average kappa between pairs of judges was 0.92 ($SD = 0.01$), which according to Fleiss (1981) indicates strong agreement. In addition, more than three judges agreed on the categorizations for each category. Examination of the confusion matrix indicated no major overlap among categories.

Proportions of Client Behavior System Categories

Table 3 presents the means and standard deviations for the proportions of the eight CBS categories for categorizations on both response units and predominant judgments. The most frequently occurring category for response units was recounting (49%), whereas the most frequently occurring category for predominant judgments was cognitive–behavioral exploration (39%). In the remaining analyses, we use the predominant judgments.

Table 3—*Proportions of Client Behavior System Categories
for Eight Clients in Study 1*

	Unit		Predominant	
Categories	M	SD	M	SD
Resistance	.08	.05	.11	.07
Agreement	.03	.01	.06	.04
Request	.01	.01	.03	.01
Recounting	.49	.15	.30	.12
Cog–beh exploration	.33	.11	.39	.08
Affective exploration	.03	.02	.06	.02
Insight	.03	.02	.05	.05
Changes	.02	.01	.11	.07

Note. Cog–beh = cognitive–behavioral.

Client Behavior System Categories and Experiencing Ratings

Table 4 shows the means and standard deviations of the experiencing ratings for each CBS category. We conducted an analysis of variance (ANOVA), with the main effects of case and predominant judgments on the eight CBS categories, using experiencing ratings as the dependent variable. Case was included as a main effect to control for the effects of eight different cases but was not interpreted. Thus, we

Table 4—*Average Client Experiencing and Helpfulness
Ratings for Each Predominant Categorization on the
Client Behavior System in Study 1*

	Experiencing Scale		Helpfulness Scale	
Category	M	SD	M	SD
Resistance	2.10	0.31_b	6.79	1.22_a
Agreement	2.00	0.00_b	6.55	1.47_{ab}
Request	2.06	0.25_b	6.26	1.05_{ab}
Recounting	2.19	0.48_b	6.12	1.35_b
Cog–beh exploration	2.26	0.53_b	6.69	1.23_a
Affective exploration	2.88	0.40_a	6.69	1.28_a
Insight	2.59	0.91_a	6.31	1.95_{ab}
Changes	2.47	0.62_{ab}	6.76	1.56_{ab}

Note. Cog–beh = cognitive–behavioral. The Experiencing Scale is a 7-point scale ranging from *low experiencing* (1) to *high experiencing* (7); the Helpfulness Scale is a 9-point scale ranging from *extremely unhelpful* (1) to *extremely helpful* (9). In each column, categories with the same subscripts are not significantly different from each other (e.g., a and b are significantly different, whereas a and ab are not significantly different).

determined the effects of CBS categories on experiencing independent of case differences. Controlling for case, a significant effect was found for the predominant CBS categories, $F(7, 609) = 14.25$, $p < .001$. Post hoc comparisons between all pairs of CBS categories, with Tukey's Studentized range test, which controlled for the Type I experimentwise error rate, indicated that affective exploration and insight were associated with higher experiencing levels than resistance, requests, agreement, recounting, and cognitive–behavioral exploration (changes fell in between).

Client Behavior System Categories and Client Helpfulness Ratings

Table 4 also shows the means and standard deviations for client ratings of the helpfulness of therapist interventions that preceded each CBS category of client behavior. We conducted an ANOVA, with the main effects of case (included to control for the effects of the eight different cases) and the predominant judgments on the eight CBS categories, using client helpfulness ratings as the dependent variable. Controlling for case, a significant effect was found for the predominant CBS categories, $F(7, 639) = 6.21$, $p = .0001$. Post hoc comparisons between all pairs of CBS categories with Tukey's Studentized range test (to control for the Type I experimentwise error rate) indicated that interventions preceding resistance and cognitive–behavioral exploration were rated as more helpful than interventions preceding recounting (agreement, requests, affective exploration, insight, and changes fell in between).

Discussion

The psychometric properties of the CBS appear to be adequate. We were able to establish reliability (in terms of interjudge agreement levels), convergent validity with client experiencing ratings, and construct validity with client ratings of the helpfulness of preceding counselor interventions.

We contend that it is most appropriate to examine the predominant client behavior during a speaking turn, which most likely is what counselors respond to in sessions. Agreement levels were higher for predominant judgments than for unit judgments, which was probably partially due to the procedure of making predominant judgments after discussing unit judgments. After judges independently judged all units within a speaking turn, they discussed their judgments until a consensus was reached and then independently judged the predominant client behavior. Use of linked judgments is somewhat problematic in terms of the independence of judgments, but other methods of obtaining predominant judgments, such as using separate teams of judges, are even more problematic in that judges might not agree on the behavior in the initial units.

Examination of the predominant behaviors in our sample (Table 3) indicates that we were able to describe a more complete range of client behavior than the earlier Hill et al. (1981) system. Whereas the majority of the comparable responses obtained with the earlier Hill et al. system were in the description category (Hill et al., 1983; O'Farrell et al., 1986), four categories accounted for the majority of the responses obtained with the CBS: cognitive–behavioral exploration (39%), recounting (30%), resistance (11%), and changes (11%). Thus, it appears that we were able to separate the large category of description into the important therapeutic behaviors of resistance, recounting, and cognitive–behavioral exploration. Separating the behaviors yielded a lower interjudge agreement level than Hill et al. had achieved but provides a better description of client behavior.

We were particularly pleased to see that resistance accounted for 11% of the total client behavior, given the significance of resistance in counseling (Chamberlain et al., 1984; Chamberlain & Ray, 1988; Patterson & Forgatch, 1985). Interjudge agreement on resistance was lower than for the other categories, however, indicating that judges found it difficult to code resistance. What seems to be defensive behavior to one judge may not appear to be defensive behavior to another judge. The key to distinguishing between resistance and other categories is often in the nonverbal and paralinguistic cues, which suggests that watching the videotape of the therapy session is essential. Problems remain, however, in differentiating resistance from other categories.

Although Chamberlain et al. (1984) specified several subtypes of resistant behaviors, we could not distinguish among these subtypes reliably in our preliminary development of the CBS. Because resistant behaviors occurred relatively infrequently, we decided that it was most important simply to know that a resistant behavior occurred rather than to know the specific subtype. Therefore, we combined all of the resistant behaviors (e.g., sidetracking, complaining) into one category. Further research could clarify differences among subtypes of resistance.

To establish convergent validity, we compared the CBS categories with the Experiencing Scale (Klein et al., 1986), which has been used extensively in psychotherapy research. When clients exhibited affective exploration and insight, as compared with other CBS behaviors, they were rated by trained judges as having higher levels of experiencing. Given that the Experiencing Scale emphasizes affect and insight, these findings make sense. Interestingly, cognitive–behavioral exploration was not associated with higher levels of experiencing than recounting, perhaps because the Experiencing Scale does not discriminate among different types of nonaffective responding. We should note that scores on the Experiencing Scale were low and that the range was restricted ($M = 2.31$, $SD = 0.15$ on a 7-point scale), which may have precluded finding more relationships with the CBS categories.

To establish construct validity, we compared the CBS categorizations with client ratings of the helpfulness of the previous counselor intervention. Interventions preceding client resistance and cognitive–behavioral exploration were rated as more helpful than other interventions. Thus, when clients viewed counselor interventions as very helpful, their responses were likely to be resistant or exploratory. The results for cognitive–behavioral exploration are logical in that helpful interventions would be expected to lead to productive client work. We are somewhat surprised with the results for resistance, but we speculate that clients might resist a helpful intervention if that intervention seemed especially challenging or threatening.

Study 2

The purpose of Study 2 was to provide evidence of construct validity for the CBS with another data set. We hypothesized that interviewees would exhibit different CBS behaviors in response to different interviewer queries. We designed nine queries to elicit different CBS categories from the interviewees. The nine queries and the CBS categories that we hypothesized would be elicited are shown in Table 5.

Table 5—*Queries Used for Study 2, Hypothesized Client Behavior in Response to Each Query, and Actual Client Behavior in Response to Each Query*

Query	Hypothesized CBS Category	Actual CBS Category
Understand: Tell me something you understand about yourself	Insight	Cognitive–behavioral exploration
Bad: Tell me something bad someone did to you	Resistance	Recounting
Decision: Tell me something you have made a decision about	Changes	Recounting
Trivial: Tell me something trivial that has happened to you recently	Recounting	Recounting
Feelings: Tell me something you have strong feelings or emotions about	Affective exploration	Cognitive–behavioral exploration
Worried: Tell me something you are worried about	Affective exploration	Affective exploration
Don't Understand: Tell me something you do but don't understand why you do it	Cognitive–behavioral exploration	Cognitive–behavioral exploration
Don't Like: Tell me something you do not like about yourself	Cognitive–behavioral exploration	Cognitive–behavioral exploration
Not Fault: Tell me something that someone blamed you for that you don't think is your fault	Resistance	Recounting

Note. CBS = Client behavior system.

Method

Interviewees

Thirty-nine undergraduate students (17 female, 22 male; 26 White, 5 Black, 5 Asian American, 2 Arabic American, 1 Hispanic American), ages 18–42 ($M = 19.87$, $SD = 2.51$) years, participated. The students were enrolled in psychology courses and received course credit for their participation.

Interviewers

The interviewers were the four judges from Study 1.

Judges

Two new judges (both graduate students) and two of the judges from Study 1 (a graduate student and a post-PhD professor) served as judges. The two additional judges are also authors of the study. The new judges obtained training by practicing on three transcripts from Study 1 and comparing their judgments to consensus judgments.

Measures

The CBS, described in Study 1, was used.

Procedure

Interview. Interviewees were informed that they would be asked to talk for 3–5 min about each of several topics, that the interviewer would respond only minimally, and that sessions would be videotaped. Prior to participating, each interviewee signed a consent form. Interviewees were randomly assigned to one of the four interviewers. Interviewers were trained to respond only minimally after presenting each query so that responses would reflect the interviewee rather than the interviewer. Thus, interviewers were instructed to appear interested and to use minimal encouragers, such as "Mmhmm" but not to probe further or respond to the interviewee. If the interviewee asked about how to respond, the interviewer repeated the query and reassured the interviewee that whatever she or he wanted to say was fine. Interviewees were not held to any time restriction in their responses. The nine queries (shown in Table 5) were arranged in a different random-order sequence for each interviewee. After the interview, subjects were debriefed about the purpose of the study, allowed to ask any questions, and given referral information about the university counseling center.

Data preparation. The interviewee responses to each of the nine queries were excerpted from the videotapes of each interview. Interviewer queries were not excerpted so that judges would be unaware of the stimuli preceding the interviewee response. When interviewers responded to interviewees with more than minimal encouragers, the interviewer response and subsequent interviewee response was not excerpted, in keeping with the intent that only the interviewee response to the standard stimuli be recorded. Thus, if an interviewer reflected feelings or asked a further probing question during the interviewee's response, the response to this second intervention was not excerpted. Each excerpted session was then transcribed verbatim (excluding the interviewer queries). Because high interrater reliability had been established in Study 1, only one judge unitized (divided into grammatical sentences) the client speech in all the transcripts.

Client behavior system judgment process. The judgment process occurred several months after the interviews were done, so that even though two of the judges had also been interviewers, there was minimal chance that they would recall the specific interviewer queries preceding client responses (especially as these queries were not excerpted). Units (sentences) within sessions were categorized independently by each of the four judges into one of the CBS categories while the judges watched the videotape and read the transcript. Following independent judgments of each entire session, the judges met to discuss and resolve discrepancies. Any units in which fewer than three of the four judges agreed on the categorization were discussed until a consensus judgment was achieved. Once consensus judgments were reached for all units within a speaking turn, judges independently determined a predominant categorization for the speaking turn. When fewer than three judges agreed on the predominant categorization, judges discussed their judgments until they reached a consensus.

Results

Reliability

As in Study 1, interjudge agreement was determined by calculating both the average number of judges agreeing before discussion and the kappa value. For response units, an average of 3.21 (SD = 0.84) of 4 judges agreed across all categorizations, indicating high agreement. Average kappa values between pairs of judges was .48, indicating fair to good agreement (Fleiss, 1981). Table 2 shows that more than three judges agreed on the categorizations for requests, recounting, and cognitive–behavioral exploration, whereas fewer than three agreed on resistance, affective exploration, insight, and changes.

For predominant judgments, an average of 3.61 (SD = 0.65) judges agreed across all categorizations, and the average kappa value between pairs of judges was .59, again indicating fair to good agreement. Table 2 shows that more than three judges agreed on the categorization for all eight categories.

Predominant Client Behavior in Response to Different Queries

The frequency of predominant responses by CBS category and query is shown in Table 6. Each query was analyzed with a separate chi-square analysis because each interviewee received all nine queries and chi-square analyses require independent data within cells. The assumption underlying the chi-square analyses was that each client behavior was equally likely to occur in response to the interviewer query. Because agreement and appropriate requests never occurred in the predominant judg-

Table 6—*Frequency of Predominant Judgments in Each of Six Client Behavior System (CBS) Categories in Response to Nine Interview Queries in Study 2*

CBS Category	Interviewer Query								
	1	2	3	4	5	6	7	8	9
Resistance	2	7	0	6	1	1	2	1	8
Recounting	12	23	26	31	8	4	8	5	19
Cog–beh exploration	22	8	8	2	21	8	27	28	9
Affective exploration	0	1	1	0	9	25	0	5	0
Insight	1	0	0	0	0	0	2	0	0
Changes	1	0	4	0	0	0	0	0	0
N	38	39	39	39	39	38	39	39	36

Note. Cog–beh = Cognitive–behavioral; Interviewer Query 1 = Understand, 2 = Bad, 3 = Decision, 4 = Trivial, 5 = Feelings, 6 = Worried, 7 = Don't Understand, 8 = Don't Like, 9 = Not Fault. The CBS categories of agreement and requests were never coded as predominant.

ments, only six categories were examined for these analyses. The sample size is slightly different for some of the analyses because interviewers occasionally forgot to ask a question.

The overall chi-square values for all nine queries were significant at the .05 level: for Category 1, $\chi^2(5, N = 38) = 62.44$; for Category 2, $\chi^2(5, N = 39) = 59.92$; for Category 3, $\chi^2(5, N = 39) = 77.46$; for Category 4, $\chi^2(5, N = 39) = 115.35$; for Category 5, $\chi^2(5, N = 39) = 38.31$; for Category 6, $\chi^2(5, N = 38) = 73.87$; for Category 7, $\chi^2(5, N = 39) = 86.15$; for Category 8, $\chi^2(5, N = 39) = 89.47$; and for Category 9, $\chi^2(5, N = 36) = 48.34$. Because of the lack of independence between queries, results of the chi-square analyses across the queries could not be compared.

Cell chi-square tests were conducted to determine which behaviors occurred more or less often than chance for each query. Because six separate cell chi-square tests were conducted for each query, a Bonferroni-adjusted alpha of .001 was used (critical value = 10.8). Cell chi-square tests indicated that interviewees responded with the following behaviors more often than chance: recounting to the queries labeled bad, decision, trivial, and not fault; cognitive–behavioral exploration to queries labeled understand, feelings, don't understand, and don't like; and affective exploration to the query labeled worried (see Table 5).

Discussion

Different standard interviewer queries resulted in different client behavior. Evidence for construct validity is provided by the findings that different client behaviors were elicited by different interviewer queries.

As predicted, interviewees most often responded with recounting when interviewers asked them to talk about something trivial that had happened to them. Interviewees did tend to tell a story about some recent event, although interestingly a certain number indicated that nothing trivial ever happened to them. Contrary to our predictions, interviewees also responded with recounting when interviewers asked them to talk about something bad that had happened to them, something someone blamed them for that was not their fault, or a decision they had made. We had predicted that interviewees would respond to the first two queries with resistance and to the third with changes. Perhaps in a brief, structured interview, interviewees are more likely to respond cautiously and superficially (with recounting) than they would in a more emotionally provocative situation.

Additionally, as predicted, interviewees responded with cognitive–behavioral exploration when interviewers asked them to talk about something they did not understand about themselves and something they did not like about themselves. Contrary to expectation, when the interviewer asked the interviewee to talk about something about which they had strong feelings or emotions, interviewees responded with cognitive–behavioral exploration rather than affective exploration. Rather than exploring some feeling or emotion, interviewees typically talked about some issue on which they had definite opinions, such as abortion or feelings about gay men and lesbians. Also contrary to our expectations, interviewees responded with cognitive–behavioral exploration rather than insight when interviewers asked them to talk about something they understood about themselves. Perhaps without the stimulus of the interviewer helping them achieve insight, it was difficult for these people to gain insights about themselves.

Furthermore, as predicted, interviewees responded with affective exploration to the query of what they were worried about. Interestingly, affective exploration occurred much more often in response to the request to discuss something that worried participants than it did in ongoing therapy (see Study 1). Our sense is that counselors typically reflect feelings but seldom ask a direct question about a specific feeling in counseling. These results are reminiscent of the findings of Hill and Gormally (1977) that probes for feelings elicited more client affect than did reflections of feelings or restatements.

We were not able to elicit resistance, insight, or therapeutic changes at a level greater than chance to any of the questions. These are all behaviors that may be less likely to occur in brief structured interviews than in ongoing counseling, in which there is more interaction between the counselor and client.

Interjudge agreement was lower in Study 2 than in Study 1, particularly for the predominant judgments. One explanation for the low agreement level was that it was more difficult to judge behavior in these brief structured interviews than in therapy. In the interviews, interviewees engaged in long speaking turns, which make it more difficult to determine a predominant behavior. Furthermore, interviewees did not engage in the CBS categories of minimal resistance, agreement, or insight. When they did engage in cognitive–behavioral or affective exploration, it was seldom as deep as occurred in actual therapy, making it more difficult for judges to distinguish these categories from recounting.

General Conclusions

The CBS, the revised version of the earlier Hill et al. (1981) Client Verbal Response Category System, appears to have adequate validity and reliability. Several of the problems with the earlier version have been corrected: (a) Categories of cognitive–behavioral exploration and resistance have been included to make the CBS more comprehensive and pantheoretical; (b) the CBS incorporates nonverbal and paralinguistic cues in the definitions of the categories and requires observation of the videotapes of sessions; (c) predominant judgments are used instead of unit (sentence) judgments; and (d) categories at different levels of abstraction (minimal encourager, silence, and discussion of the client–counselor relationship) were dropped.

Determining the superiority of the revised system over the previous system is difficult. The interjudge agreement levels are lower, seemingly because of the addition of more clinically meaningful but difficult to differentiate categories. The categories from the new system operate as we expected them to operate for the most part, providing evidence for construct validity. Thus, we assert that the new version is superior from a validity perspective.

Although the interjudge agreement levels fall within the fair-to-good range, they are not as high as we would like them to be. We attribute this to the difficulty in categorizing client behavior. In contrast to judgment of counselor behavior for which there are identifiable discrete techniques, clients are not as likely to engage in discrete, differentiated tasks. For example, resistance, recounting, and cognitive–behavioral exploration seem to be qualitatively rather than structurally distinct. Although difficulties in distinguishing client behavior may be part of the reason why client behavior measures are not as well developed as therapist behavior measures, we need to keep struggling to define client behaviors so that we can study client change in counseling.

The CBS can be used in several ways in future research. First, the measure could be used as an index of the context in which counselor interventions are delivered. Second, the measure could be used as an index of the immediate outcome of counselor interventions, providing an assessment of the ways in which clients respond to different interventions. Third, the CBS could be used to describe client behavior as well as client change both within and across the course of sessions. If counselor interventions have an effect on clients, then there ought to be a change in client behavior over the course of therapy. For example, as a result of therapy, clients might engage in more exploration and insight, behaviors that counselors often consider desirable.

As is true for all counseling process measures, several methodological procedures need to be examined for the CBS: the necessary level of experience of judges (Moras & Hill, 1991), the potential for bias due to judges' personality characteristics or perceived similarity with clients (Mahalik, Hill, O'Grady, & Thompson, 1993), and the most appropriate methods for training judges (cf. Hill, 1991; Lambert & Hill, 1994). Furthermore, interjudge agreement levels need to be tested with other sets of judges.

In sum, the CBS provides a promising alternative to other measures of client in-session behavior. Additionally, this measure completes the battery of instruments needed to test a process model of counseling and psychotherapy, which includes counselor intentions, counselor response modes, client reactions, and client behaviors (Hill, 1992; Hill & O'Grady, 1985). We hope that this model can now be tested more completely to determine how faithfully it describes the therapy process.

References

Benjamin, L. S. (1979). Use of structural analysis of social behavior (SASB) and Markov chains to study dyadic interactions. *Journal of Abnormal Psychology, 88*, 303–319.

Chamberlain, P., Patterson, G. R., Reid, J. B., Kavanagh, K., & Forgatch, M. S. (1984). Observation of client resistance. *Behavior Therapy, 15*, 144–155.

Chamberlain, P., & Ray, J. (1988). The Therapy Process Code: A multidimensional system for observing therapist and client interactions in family treatment. In R. J. Prinz (Ed.), *Advances in behavioral assessment of children and families*, (Vol. 4, pp. 189–217). Greenwich, CT: JAI Press.

Elliott, R. (1985). Helpful and nonhelpful events in brief counseling interviews: An empirical taxonomy. *Journal of Counseling Psychology, 32*, 307–322.

Elliott, R., Hill, C. E., Stiles, W. B., Friedlander, M. L., Mahrer, A. R., & Margison, F. R. (1987). Primary therapist response modes: Comparison of six rating systems. *Journal of Consulting and Clinical Psychology, 55*, 218–223.

Fleiss, J. L. (1981). *Statistical methods for rates and proportions*. New York: Wiley.

Greenberg, L., & Pinsof, W. (Eds.). (1986). *The psychotherapeutic process: A research handbook*. New York: Guilford Press.

Harper, R. G., Wiens, A. N., & Matarazzo, J. D. (1978). *Nonverbal communication: The state of the art*. New York: Wiley.

Hill, C. E. (1986). An overview of the Hill Counselor and Client Verbal Response Modes Category Systems. In L. S. Greenberg & W. M. Pinsof (Eds.), *The psychotherapeutic process: A research handbook* (pp. 131–160). New York: Guilford Press.

Hill, C. E. (1989). *Therapist techniques and client outcomes: Eight cases of brief psycho-therapy.* Newbury Park, CA: Sage.

Hill, C. E. (1991). Almost everything you ever wanted to know about how to do process research on counseling and psychotherapy but didn't know who to ask. In C. E. Watkins & L. J. Schneider (Eds.), *Research in counseling* (pp. 85–118). Hillsdale, NJ: Erlbaum.

Hill, C. E. (1992). An overview of four measures developed to test the Hill process model: Therapist intentions, therapist response modes, client reactions, and client behaviors. *Journal of Counseling and Development, 70,* 728–739.

Hill, C. E., Carter, J. A., & O'Farrell, M. K. (1983). A case study of the process and outcome of time-limited counseling. *Journal of Counseling Psychology, 30,* 3–18.

Hill, C. E., & Gormally, J. (1977). Effects of reflection, restatement, probe, and nonverbal behavior on client affect. *Journal of Counseling Psychology, 24,* 92–97.

Hill, C. E., Greenwald, C., Reed, K. G., Charles, D., O'Farrell, M., & Carter, J. (1981). *Manual for Counselor and Client Verbal Response Modes Category Systems.* Columbus, OH: Marathon Consulting and Press.

Hill, C. E., Helms, J. E., Spiegel, S. B., & Tichenor, V. (1988). Development of a system for categorizing client reactions to therapist interventions. *Journal of Counseling Psychology, 35,* 27–36.

Hill, C. E., Helms, J. E. Tichenor, V., Spiegel, S. B., O'Grady, K. E., & Perry, E. S. (1988). Effects of therapist response modes in brief psychotherapy. *Journal of Counseling Psychology, 35,* 222–233.

Hill, C. E., & O'Grady, K. E. (1985). List of therapist intentions illustrated in a case study and with therapists of varying theoretical orientations. *Journal of Counseling Psychology, 32,* 3–22.

Klein, M. H., Mathieu, P. L., Gendlin, E. T., & Kiesler, D. J. (1970). *The Experiencing Scale: A research and training manual* (Vols. 1 & 2). Madison, WI: Wisconsin Psychiatric Institute, Bureau of Audio Visual Instruction.

Klein, M. H., Mathieu-Coughlan, P., & Kiesler, D. J. (1986). The Experiencing Scales. In L. Greenberg and W. Pinsof (Eds.), *The psychotherapeutic process: A research handbook* (pp. 21–72). New York: Guilford Press.

Mahalik, J. R., Hill, C. E., O'Grady, K. E., & Thompson, B. J. (1993). Rater characteristics influencing the Checklist of Psychotherapy Transactions—Revised. *Psychotherapy Research, 3*(1), 47–56.

Mahrer, A. R., Nadler, W. P., Sterner, I., & White, M. V. (1989). Patterns of organization and sequencing of "good moments" in psychotherapy sessions. *Journal of Integrative and Eclectic Psychotherapy, 8,* 125–139.

McCullough, L. (1990). *Psychotherapy Interaction Coding System Manual.* Beth Israel Hospital, New York.

Moras, K., & Hill, C. E. (1991). Rater selection in psychotherapy process research: Observations on the state-of-the-art. *Psychotherapy Research, 1,* 114–124.

O'Farrell, M. K., Hill, C. E., & Patton, S. (1986). Comparison of two cases of counseling with the same counselor. *Journal of Counseling and Development, 65,* 141–145.

Patterson, G. R., & Forgatch, M. S. (1985). Therapist behavior as a determinant for client noncompliance: A paradox for the behavior modifier. *Journal of Consulting and Clinical Psychology, 53,* 19.

Rice, L. N., & Kerr, G. P. (1986). Measures of client and therapist vocal quality. In L. Greenberg and W. Pinsof (Eds.), *The psychotherapeutic process: A research handbook* (pp. 73–105). New York: Guilford Press.

Snyder, W. U. (1945). An investigation of the nature of nondirective psychotherapy. *Journal of General Psychology, 33,* 193–223.

Stiles, W. B. (1986). Development of a taxonomy of verbal response modes. In L. S. Greenberg & W. M. Pinsof (Eds.), *The psychotherapeutic process: A research handbook* (pp. 131–160). New York: Guilford Press.

Tinsley, H. E. A., & Weiss, D. J. (1975). Interrater reliability and agreement of subjective judgments. *Journal of Counseling Psychology, 22*, 358–376.

Toukmanian, S. G. (1986). A measure of client perceptual processing. In L. S. Greenberg & W. M. Pinsof (Eds.), *The psychotherapeutic process: A research handbook* (pp. 107–139). New York: Guilford Press.

Appendix
The Client Behavior System

Instructions

Client behavior should be judged by trained judges using both videotapes and transcripts. Minimal verbalizations (such as "Mmhmm" or "yeah") and silence are not coded within this system. Events such as role-playing, problem-solving, dream reports, or guided fantasies should be judged for the client behaviors exhibited during each response unit and speaking turn within the event. Each client response unit (grammatical sentence) and speaking turn (called a predominant judgment) should be assigned to *one* category. With predominant judgments, judges should decide in advance (depending on the research question) to either weight the initial or latter portion of the speaking turn most heavily when there is a shift of emphasis or topic.

Categories

Resistance

Includes complaining or blaming others inappropriately, defenses (e.g., projection, denial, intellectualization, avoidance, dissociation, etc.), sidetracking (changing the topic), and inappropriate requests (reflecting excessive helplessness or dependency). Resistant behavior tends to block progress in therapy and is often used to suggest that the client cannot change. These statements may be used by clients to protect themselves from an abusive or hostile therapist. The client's tone of voice is often defensive, whiny, defeated, abusive, or hostile.

Agreement

Indicates understanding or approval of what the therapist has said without adding substantially to the therapist's statement. Must be more than a simple response (e.g., "Mmhmm" or "yeah") that serves to maintain conversation.

Appropriate Request

An attempt to obtain clarification, understanding, information, or advice from the therapist. If client acts helpless or overly dependent, code as resistance.

Recounting

Small talk or statements that answer questions or give factual information about past events. Client reports in a storytelling style (e.g., "I said ..., he said ..., then I said") rather than actively and presently exploring feelings and thoughts or interacting and working with the therapist. Tone of voice tends to be monotonic or conversational with minimal involvement in the immediate moment.

Cognitive–Behavioral Exploration

Statements that indicate the client is currently involved and exploring therapeutically significant thoughts or behaviors. Clients exhibit a quality of actively thinking about their issues, which typically indicates that they do not have all the answers and are exploring to understand more. Disagreeing with or challenging the therapist would be coded here if clients are actively exploring their own thoughts or behaviors. In general, this category is not coded when a client is talking about another person *unless* understanding that person's behavior has a significant implication for the client. Voice tone tends to have a lot of energy and to be irregular with pauses and thoughtfulness.

Affective Exploration

Statements that indicate that the client is currently involved and exploring feelings about therapeutically significant material. Specific feeling words must be stated (e.g., happy, sad, anxious), or clearly visible nonverbal behavior (e.g., audible sighs, clenched fists, lowering of the head, crying or shifting body position) must accompany affective material. The client's voice must sound as if feelings are being experienced in the present moment. Discussion of past feelings would be coded as recounting unless the client is reexperiencing the feelings in the present moment. Disagreeing with or challenging the therapist would be coded here if clients are actively exploring their feelings.

Insight

Client expresses an understanding of something about himself or herself and can articulate patterns or reasons for behaviors, thoughts, or feelings. Insight usually involves an "aha" experience, in which the client perceives himself/herself or his/her world in a new way. The client takes appropriate responsibility rather than blaming others, using "shoulds" imposed from the outside world, or rationalizing (Note: these behaviors would be coded as resistance).

Therapeutic Changes

Client expresses changes in his or her own behaviors, thoughts, and/or feelings in therapeutically significant areas. Changes can be increases in positive target areas, decreases in negative areas, or indications of action-oriented plans or decisions. If client reports changes, but no change is apparent to judges, code as resistance.

Chapter 3
DEVELOPMENT OF A SYSTEM FOR CATEGORIZING
CLIENT REACTIONS TO THERAPIST INTERVENTIONS

Clara E. Hill, Janet E. Helms, Sharon B. Spiegel, and Victoria Tichenor

Covert feelings undoubtedly influence a client's behavior in therapy. Rice and Greenberg (1984) noted that "people in therapy are goal-setting beings who actively construe the task and situation and act in terms of their goals and construals. Clients will respond differentially to the same interventions depending on how they perceive the situation and in terms of their own goals and intentions" (p. 13).

Client reactions to therapist interventions have just begun to receive attention in the literature. Elliott (1985) developed a taxonomy of therapeutic impacts that assesses the client's subjective experience of the helpful and hindering events within sessions. Because his taxonomy was developed from brief sessions with volunteer students as clients, Elliott cautioned that actual counseling sessions need to be studied to determine generalizability.

In reviewing Elliott's (1985) recall methodology, we found that we needed to modify it for our purposes. To use Elliott's (1985) system, we would first have had the client go through the tape and rate the helpfulness of every therapist intervention, then have had an interrogator go through the videotape with the client, using Interpersonal Process Recall (Kagan, 1975) to elicit statements about the impact of the interventions, and then have had raters code the open-ended statements into Elliott's (1985) categories. This procedure is not only time-consuming and impractical for reviewing whole sessions (Elliott, 1985, reviewed only selected segments), but the raters' codings into categories may not reflect the clients' experiences. We wanted to use a structured procedure whereby clients would use a list of possible reactions and directly indicate which reactions fit their experience. We felt that such a structured procedure would shorten the amount of time involved and would reduce error in having raters interpret what the clients meant by their open-ended statements. Elliott and Shapiro (1988) recently developed a structured system, but because it was developed only on the most and least helpful events in sessions, we felt that it did not fit our need to be descriptive of all moments in sessions.

Further, Elliott's (1985) taxonomy does not include several categories needed for a complete description of therapy according to our process model (Hill & O'Grady, 1985). This process model essentially postulates that therapist intentions lead to therapist response modes that in turn lead to client reactions and then to overt behavior. Whereas measures of therapist intentions (Hill & O'Grady, 1985), therapist

Reprinted from *Journal of Counseling Psychology, 35,* 27–36 (1988). Copyright © 1988 by the American Psychological Association. Used with permission of the first author.

A version of this article was presented to the meeting of the Society for Psychotherapy Research, Evanston, Illinois, on June 21, 1985.

This study was sponsored by National Institute of Mental Health Research Grant MH-37837 to Clara E. Hill. The Computer Science Center of the University of Maryland provided computer funds.

Special thanks are due Robert Elliott for sharing his impact system with us prior to publication and for consulting with us about how to develop a structured recall procedure.

response modes (Hill, 1978, 1985), and client overt behavior (Klein, Mathieu, Gendlin, & Kiesler, 1970) have been developed that fit the model, no appropriate measure of client reactions is available.

Development of the Reactions System

To generate categories for the reactions system, we (a) used Elliott's (1985) taxonomy, and (b) brainstormed possible positive and negative client reactions to the Intentions List (Hill & O'Grady, 1985). This lengthy and redundant list was then organized into rationally distinct categories, which were reviewed and revised until they seemed clear and understandable, yielding 18 positive and 18 negative categories.

Four Pilot Cases

The 36-category system was used with four cases of brief psychotherapy (12–20 sessions) with experienced therapists and anxious, depressed female clients. Clients were given a copy of the Reactions System and asked to familiarize themselves with it. Following each session, clients viewed the videotape and wrote down the numbers of all reactions that best described their experience of each therapist speaking turn (defined as everything the therapist said between two client speeches).

The clients reported that occasionally none of the categories reflected their reactions. In these instances, we asked them to write down their specific reactions. We used these remarks to create one new negative and three neutral categories.

Purpose of This Study

Our main purpose in this study was to use the revised 40-category Reactions System on a new sample of clients. Our first goal was to reduce the number of categories because pilot clients had complained that it was difficult to remember and use so many categories. Further, having a large number of infrequently used categories (as was true for the pilot data) makes data analyses more difficult. Thus, as an initial reduction strategy, we used multidimensional scaling to determine underlying clusters. Our second reduction strategy was to determine if we could drop or combine some categories. Those categories that were (a) used infrequently, (b) never used alone or used frequently with other reactions, and (c) given similar helpfulness ratings were combined.

The second goal was to obtain preliminary data for the revised measure by studying possible correlates of reactions. We hypothesized that (a) clients with different levels of pretreatment symptomatology (defined as the number of scores above 70 on the 10 clinical scales of the Minnesota Multiphasic Personality Inventory [MMPI] taken prior to treatment) would react differently to therapist interventions, (b) therapist intentions would be related to client reactions more for the successful than for the unsuccessful cases, (c) proportions of reactions would be related to client-rated session and treatment outcome, and (d) reactions would change across the course of treatment for successful versus unsuccessful cases.

The data for this study came from reactions obtained during structured reviews of 65 videotaped sessions in five cases of brief (maximum of 20 sessions) psychotherapy cases with experienced therapists and anxious/depressed, adult, female clients. These selection criteria were used to obtain a group of relatively homogeneous clients who typically respond well to brief psychotherapy (see review by Highlen & Hill, 1984).

Method

Therapists

The two male and two female therapists ranged in age from 34 to 78 years ($M = 50.00$ years; $SD = 19.25$) with 5 to 42 years of postdoctoral experience ($M = 19.75$ years, $SD = 15.73$). On 5-point scales (1 = *low*, 5 = *high*), the therapists rated themselves as more psychoanalytic ($M = 3.75$, $SD = .50$) than either humanistic ($M = 2.75$, $SD = .96$) or behavioral ($M = 1.50$, $SD = .58$). One of the therapists treated two of the clients in this sample.

Clients

Clients were recruited through newspaper advertisements that announced the availability of free individual psychotherapy for women who had problems with self-esteem and relationship issues, were over 25 years of age, available for three hours during the day, planned to remain in the area for at least one year, had no previous psychotherapy, did not use psychotropic drugs, and had no alcohol or drug dependency. Persons not selected for this study were given appropriate referrals.

Five women ranging in age from 32 to 46 ($M = 38.80$, $SD = 5.54$) who met all the stated criteria were selected. Further testing revealed that all five clients had valid profiles and elevated scores on the MMPI Depression ($M = 75.00$, $SD = 7.65$), Psychasthenia ($M = 69.80$, $SD = 9.58$), and Social Introversion Scales ($M = 72.20$, $SD = 6.38$) and were judged by clinical interviewers to be appropriate and motivated for brief individual psychotherapy. Three of the clients were given primary diagnoses of dysthymic (mildly depressed), and one was cyclothymic (mildly manic–depressive).

Clients were fully informed about all selection and treatment procedures and gave informed consent at the initial testing and following treatment. Clients were not paid for their participation. One client dropped out after four sessions and was replaced with another client. Both were included in this study to provide a broader range of reactions.

Measures

The preliminary *Client Reactions System* contained 40 non-mutually exclusive categories of possible ways a client might experience a therapist's interventions. The 40 reactions were rationally divided into three groups: *positive* (Supported, Understood, Hopeful, Relief, Clear, Feelings, Negative Thoughts or Behavior, Responsibility, Challenged, Overcame Block, Feel Better about Therapist, Attracted to Therapist, Better Self-Understanding, New Perspective, Educated, New Ways to Behave, Resolutions, and Progress); *negative* (Misunderstood, Attacked, Angry at Therapist, Disregard for Therapist, Pressured, Lack Direction, Confused, Distracted, Pitied, Worse, Less Hopeful, Felt Like Avoiding, Scared, Feared Disapproval, Stuck, Impatient or Bored, Envious of Therapist, Felt Like Giving Up, Doubtful or Disagreed with Therapist); and *neutral* (Just Information, Social Conversation, No Particular Reaction). Clients used the measure during a review of the taped session by selecting up to five reactions per therapist speaking turn that were most descriptive of their subjective experience at the time. The total number of reactions listed for each category was divided by the total number of reactions listed by each client. As Marsden, Kalter, and Ericson (1974) have discussed, such proportion scores are preferable to frequency counts because they correct for amount of therapist activity as well as for client endorsement of different numbers of reactions.

The *Therapist Intentions List* (Hill & O'Grady, 1985) includes 19 pantheoretical, nominal, non-mutually exclusive intentions (Set Limits, Get Information, Give Information, Support, Focus, Clarify, Hope, Cathart, Cognitions, Behaviors, Self-Control, Feelings, Insight, Change, Reinforce Change, Resistance, Challenge, Relationship, and Therapist Needs). During a review of a taped session, therapists listed up to five intentions that were most descriptive of their subjective goals or aims at the time.

The *Helpfulness Rating Scale* (Elliott, 1985; Elliott, Barker, Caskey, & Pistrang, 1982) is a 9-point bipolar adjective-anchored rating scale, in which 1 = *extremely hindering*, 5 = *neutral*, and 9 = *extremely helpful*. The rating unit is the therapist speaking turn. Informants rated how helpful they perceived the response to be at the time it was delivered. Elliott (1986) reviewed evidence supporting the reliability and validity of the scale.

The *Session Evaluation Questionnaire*, Form 4 (SEQ; Stiles & Snow, 1984) scales of depth and smoothness were used to measure global session impact. Depth measures perceptions of the value of the session, whereas smoothness measures perceptions of comfort, relaxation, and pleasantness. Each scale consists of six bipolar adjectives arranged in 7-point semantic differential formats. Stiles and Snow reported that factor analyses indicated that depth and smoothness were orthogonal factors for clients and counselors.

Outcome Measures

To measure outcome from the perspective of the client, 8 indexes were used. Waskow and Parloff (1975) recommended several of these measures for inclusion in outcome batteries, and all have sufficient reliability and validity data. The Depression, Psychasthenia, and Social Introversion scales of the MMPI and the Global Severity Scale of the Hopkins Symptom Checklist–90 (SCL-90; Derogatis, Rickels, & Rock, 1976) measured symptomatology. The total scale of the Tennessee Self Concept Scale (TSCS; Fitts, 1965) measured positive functioning. Fear of Negative Evaluation and the Social Avoidance and Distress (Watson & Friend, 1969) scales measured the client's affective state. The Target Complaints (TC; Battle et al., 1965) measured individualized change in problem areas that the client selected as a focus for treatment.

Scores on each of the eight outcome measures were standardized ($M = 50$, $SD = 10$). An average change score was computed for each client, ranging from 4.88 to 15.62 ($M = 10.28$, $SD = 4.94$).

Procedures

Pretreatment

Prior to treatment, clients completed the battery of outcome measures and had a clinical interview that included the Target Complaints. Clients were randomly assigned to therapists on the basis of time availability. Prior to treatment, therapists were allowed to examine the client's MMPI profile, a history questionnaire, and the client's Target Complaints (without the severity ratings). Following the first session, the therapists rated their perceptions of the client's severity on the Target Complaints. Neither client nor therapist was aware of specific hypotheses being studied, nor were they allowed to see any evaluation measures completed by the other participant.

Treatment

Therapists were instructed to use their clinical judgment to determine what interventions to use within sessions. All sessions were approximately 50 min and were videotaped and monitored by a researcher from an adjacent room. Number of sessions for each of the five cases was: 4, 12, 12, 17, and 20 ($M = 13.00$, $SD = 6.08$).

Postsession Evaluation

After each session, participants completed postsession measures and then reviewed the videotape. Prior to the first videotape review, a researcher met with each client to review the Reactions System. For the review, a partition was placed between the participants so that they could see the videotape, but not each other. The researcher's role was to monitor the process by determining when to stop the videotape (therapist speaking turns were divided if they contained more than one "thought" unit), saying the number of the speaking turn to be rated so that accurate data would be generated and recording the key words for later identification.

Participants were instructed to review the videotape and try to recall what they were feeling at that moment during the session. Clients rated the helpfulness and listed the numbers of up to five reactions that best described their feelings about the therapist intervention. Therapists rated the helpfulness and listed the numbers of up to five intentions that were most descriptive of their goals for that intervention. All ratings were done privately, and communication was discouraged.

Posttreatment

One to two weeks after treatment, clients returned and completed the outcome measures that were listed earlier.

Results

Revision of System

A total of 12,223 reactions were listed in the five cases. Because clients were allowed to list up to 5 reactions to each therapist intervention, we could examine the overlap between reactions. The 5,705 reactions that were listed with other reactions were listed in a co-occurrence table. Multidimensional scaling on the co-occurrence of the 40 categories suggested only that positive and negative (which included neutral) reactions were on opposite dimensions. Separate multidimensional scaling solutions for the positive and negative reactions resulted in too many underlying dimensions to interpret, so this was not a productive method for revising the system.

We identified 19 reactions that either occurred only rarely (each occurred less than 1% of the time) or always occurred with other reactions. By combining these reactions with other reactions with which they co-occurred and that received similar helpfulness ratings, we created a 21-category system. Because of this reduction of overlap between categories, the resulting 21 categories were relatively independent.

To determine if the 21 categories could be subdivided into a smaller number of clusters on a statistical basis, McQuinty's (1957) elementary linkage analysis, in which reactions were assigned to clusters on the basis of common occurrence, was used. Two positive clusters were identified if we eliminated Understanding and Challenged, which clustered with many reactions; four negative clusters were identified.

A discriminant analysis provided only partial support for the clustering, indicating a positive cluster (excluding Challenged) and a negative cluster (excluding No Reaction). Thus, across all analyses, there was consistent support for a positive and a negative cluster, although none of the categories within clusters replicated exactly.

Because the clustering procedures did not replicate completely, the next strategy was to examine client helpfulness ratings. In instances of conflicting evidence among analyses, reactions were assigned to clusters on the basis of their helpfulness ratings. Thus, Challenged was placed with the positive cluster and No Reaction with the negative cluster. Positive reactions accounted for 58% of the total number of client reactions and received an average client helpfulness rating of 7.19 ($SD = 1.24$). The negative reactions cluster accounted for 42% of the total, with an average helpfulness rating of 5.67 ($SD = 1.57$). With analyses of variance (ANOVAS), we found highly significant differences between the two clusters, $F(1, 12221) = 3,575.57$, $p < .0001$. However, because collapsing the 21 reactions into two clusters would have obscured the potential individual differences among reactions within the clusters, all analyses were done with the 21 reactions.

Definitions of the 21 reactions and their cluster assignments are shown in the Appendix. The order of categories was determined by placing categories that co-occurred together and that clustered together close to each other. Table 1 shows the proportion of occurrence of each reaction, as well as the average client helpfulness ratings for each reaction.

Reactions and Pretreatment Symptomatology

Table 2 shows the correlations between proportions of reactions and client pretreatment symptomatology (number of scores > 70 on the 10 scales of the MMPI), with

Table 1—*Proportions and Helpfulness of Reactions*

Reaction	Proportion		Helpfulness	
	M	SD	M	SD
Positive	.59	.17	7.19	1.24
Understood	.12	.05	6.62	1.43$_g$
Supported	.08	.03	7.41	1.32$_{cde}$
Hopeful	.03	.02	7.22	1.21$_e$
Relief	.02	.01	7.29	1.40$_e$
Thoughts	.04	.02	7.28	1.41$_e$
Self-Understanding	.04	.02	7.77	1.05$_{ab}$
Clear	.03	.03	7.29	1.14$_e$
Feelings	.04	.02	6.92	1.40$_f$
Responsibility	.02	.02	7.48	1.12$_{cd}$
Unstuck	.01	.01	7.95	0.88$_a$
Perspective	.04	.02	7.23	1.26$_e$
Educated	.03	.04	7.07	1.14$_e$
New Ways	.01	.01	7.63	1.14$_{bc}$
Challenged	.05	.04	7.30	1.20$_{de}$
Negative	.40	.17	5.67	1.57
Scared	.10	.06	5.99	1.82$_{hi}$
Worse	.05	.03	5.89	1.81$_{hij}$
Stuck	.02	.01	5.68	1.91$_{jk}$
Lack Direction	.01	.01	6.21	1.66$_h$
Confused	.05	.03	5.50	1.48$_k$
Misunderstood	.02	.02	5.22	1.43$_l$
No reaction	.15	.08	5.32	0.88$_l$

Note. Reactions with the same subscript are not significantly different; a = highest rating.

an alpha of .10 because there were only five cases. High pretreatment symptomatology was positively related to four negative reactions (Scared, Worse, Stuck, Lack Direction) and negatively related to three positive reactions (Clear, New Perspectives, Educated).

Therapist Intentions and Client Reactions

Co-occurrence tables were examined for intentions and reactions that were listed together in the same speaking turn. Because dyads had different activity levels, cases were analyzed separately (the four-session case was omitted because of insufficient data). Chi-squares between all 19 intentions and 21 reactions were highly significant for all four cases: Case 1, χ^2 (360, N = 11,521) = 2,174.39; Case 2, χ^2 (360, N = 4,193) = 1,531.01; Case 3, χ^2 (360, N = 2,527) = 890.75; and Case 5, χ^2 (360, N = 3,574) = 826.01 (all ps < .0001). These results indicated that the two systems were related.

Individual chi-squares for each intention–reaction pair were also computed. A Bonferroni adjustment to correct for the large number of tests resulted in an alpha

Table 2—*Correlations Between Mean Proportions of Reactions and Pretreatment Symptomatology, Mean Depth and Smoothness, and Outcome*

Reaction	Presymp	Depth	Smoothness	Outcome
Understood	−.39	.73	−.27	.65
Supported	−.39	.58	−.07	.17
Hopeful	.11	.10	.20	−.53
Relief	.18	.67	−.55	.42
Thoughts	.74	−.40	−.77	.51
Self-Understanding	−.07	.08	−.22	.22
Clear	−.88*	.22	.70	−.39
Feelings	−.24	.82	−.53	.81
Responsibility	.33	−.27	.30	−.72
Unstuck	.00	.17	−.27	.20
Perspective	−.83*	.61	.66	−.45
Educated	−.83*	−.07	.86*	−.54
New Ways	−.19	−.36	.70	−.88*
Challenged	.49	−.46	−.42	.18
Scared	.93**	−.56	−.64	.32
Worse	.85*	−.70	−.36	.03
Stuck	.97***	−.57	−.49	.04
Lack Direction	.85*	−.74	−.36	−.10
Confused	.17	.49	−.39	.43
Misunderstood	.47	−.22	.12	−.45
No Reaction	−.32	−.11	.58	−.41

Note. $N = 5$. Presymp = pretreatment symptomatology defined as the number of the 10 scales >70 on the Minnesota Multiphasic Personality Inventory; Outcome = average change score pre–post on 8 outcome measures.

*$p < .10$.   **$p < .05$.   ***$p < .01$.

of .00013 and a critical value of 14.71. Eight intention–reaction pairs were significantly associated in at least two cases. The intention Get Information was associated more often than by chance with No Reaction, but less often than by chance with Understood and Supported. Support and Hope were both associated more often than by chance with the reaction of Supported. Clarify was associated more often than by chance with No Reaction. Feelings and Insight were associated less often than by chance with No Reaction.

The two cases with the highest average change score on outcome measures had more significant connections (15 and 21) than did the two cases with the smallest average change score (8 and 6), indicating more congruence between therapist intentions and client reactions for the more successful cases.

Reactions and Mean Session and Treatment Outcome

Table 2 shows the correlations between mean proportions of reactions and mean depth and mean smoothness for cases; that is, all scores were averaged across sessions within cases, using an alpha of $p < .10$. Use of mean scores provides the most stable estimate of the overall levels on all the variables. Mean depth was marginally positively related to Feelings. Mean smoothness was positively related to Educated. The number of significant correlations was not greater than would be expected by chance.

Proportions of reactions were also correlated with the mean change score on client-rated treatment outcome. Outcome was negatively related to New Ways and marginally positively related to Feelings, although again the number of correlations was not greater than would be expected by chance.

Reactions With Session Outcome Within Cases

Although correlations between mean levels, as in the previous analysis, present the overall association between two sets of variables, they do not show individual variability across sessions. Table 3 presents the correlations between proportions of reactions and client-rated depth within each of the five cases. Misunderstood was negatively related to depth in all five cases, indicating that sessions in which clients felt misunderstood were perceived as less valuable or deep. Confused and Lack Direction were each negatively related in two cases, and Better Self-Understanding was positively related in two cases. Thus, some clients additionally valued sessions in which they gained better self-understanding and felt less confused and unfocused.

Table 3—*Correlations Between Proportions of Reactions and Depth Within Cases*

Reaction	Case 1	Case 2	Case 3	Case 4	Case 5
Understood	.08	−.09	.31	.42	.05
Supported	.45	.25	−.03	.36	−.52
Hopeful	.10	.19	.00	.65*	−.35
Relief	.36	.30	.13	.00	.10
Thoughts	.26	−.28	−.98*	−.15	.36
Self-Understanding	.23	.21	.92	.26	.69*
Clear	.18	.26	.29	−.41	.30
Feelings	.30	.20	−.12	.10	.44
Responsibility	.38	.08	.91	−.39	.09
Unstuck	.26	.30	.58	.14	−.10
Perspective	.00	.30	.50	.29	.80**
Educated	−.16	.42	.89	.02	.19
New Ways	.28	.02	.80	.41	.24
Challenged	.15	.36	−.90	.40	−.21
Scared	−.20	−.12	−.99*	.08	−.47
Worse	−.28	−.28	−.96*	−.22	−.44
Stuck	−.39	−.10	−.67	−.60*	−.06
Lack Direction	−.20	.17	−.96*	−.51	−.41
Confused	−.44	−.25	−.96*	.05	.08
Misunderstood	−.46	−.38	−.96*	−.56	−.71**
No Reaction	−.47	−.04	−.65	.11	−.45

Note. Correlations are based on the number of sessions within cases: Case 1 = 17 sessions; Case 2 = 20 sessions; Case 3 = 4 sessions; Case 4 = 12 sessions; Case 5 = 12 sessions.

*p < .05.   **p < .01.

Table 4 presents the correlations between proportions of reactions and client-rated smoothness for all five cases. Negative Thoughts and Behaviors, Scared, Worse, and Lack Direction were each negatively related to smoothness in two cases. Thus, for some clients, sessions in which they had negative thoughts and behaviors, felt scared, worse, or lacked direction or had some combination of these reactions were perceived as rough and unpleasant.

Change in Reactions Across Treatment

The four cases with at least 12 sessions were divided into three stages: first 4 sessions, middle 4 sessions, and final 4 sessions. One-way ANOVAs for linear and curvilinear trends were calculated. Twelve of the 21 reactions showed significant linear or curvilinear trends across the three stages for at least one client. None of the reactions changed in the same manner for all four clients. For three clients, Scared decreased linearly from the first to the third stage (although only significantly so for two of the clients), whereas there was a significant curvilinear function for one client, such that Scared increased in the middle stage. For two clients, Clear increased across stages, but there was no change for the other two clients. New Ways to Behave increased for three clients, though only significantly for two.

Table 4—*Correlations Between Proportions of Reactions and Smoothness Within Cases*

Reaction	Case 1	Case 2	Case 3	Case 4	Case 5
Understood	−.20	.30	.23	.64*	.26
Supported	.19	.09	.17	.36	.51
Hopeful	−.01	−.10	.06	.42	.07
Relief	−.08	.27	.39	−.01	−.38
Thoughts	−.05	.10	−.97*	.05	−.52
Self-Understanding	−.13	.20	.99*	.45	−.34
Clear	.06	−.03	.04	−.27	−.48
Feelings	−.23	.04	−.37	−.04	−.69*
Responsibility	.50*	.27	.86	−.03	−.41
Unstuck	−.11	−.14	.70	.49	−.12
Perspective	.03	.31	.66	−.18	−.51
Educated	.41	−.04	.78	.31	−.14
New Ways	.43	.02	.62	.37	.16
Challenged	.31	−.24	−.76	.06	.06
Scared	−.18	−.48*	−.96*	−.30	.24
Worse	−.22	−.39	−.98*	−.37	.29
Stuck	−.10	−.47*	−.45	−.46	−.11
Lack Direction	−.07	−.22	−.98*	−.54	.38
Confused	.10	−.01	−.98*	.07	.00
Misunderstood	.30	−.30	−.98*	−.33	.48
No Reaction	.11	.25	−.47	.38	.72**

Note. Correlations are based on numbers of sessions within cases: Case 1 = 17 sessions; Case 2 = 20 sessions; Case 3 = 4 sessions; Case 4 = 12 sessions; Case 5 = 12 sessions.
*$p < .05$. **$p < .01$.

Changes in reactions across stages were not related to pretreatment symptomatology or to session or treatment outcome.

Because there were too few sessions for us to divide the four-session case into stages, correlations were computed between the proportions of reactions and session number, using an alpha of $p < .10$. Over time, the client felt more Clear ($r = .97$, $p = .02$) and Educated ($r = .82$, $p = .09$), but less Supported ($r = -.83$, $p = .09$), Challenged ($r = -.82$, $p = .09$), and Stuck ($r = -.93$, $p = .04$).

Discussion

A 21-category Client Reactions System, with 14 positive reactions and 7 negative reactions, was developed. Results indicated that therapist intentions were related to client reactions more for successful cases than unsuccessful cases, pretreatment symptomatology was highly predictive of which reactions the clients reported, some reactions changed across time in treatment in consistent ways, and within-case correlations of reactions with client-rated session depth and smoothness indicated some similarities across cases. Each of these findings is explored in greater detail.

Relation to Therapist Intentions

When therapists intended to Support and Instill Hope, the clients indeed reported reactions of Support. Apparently, therapists were quite able to communicate support to clients. In contrast, when therapists intended to promote Feelings and Insight, clients were apparently aroused (i.e., they felt less No Reaction), although not in the specific direction that the therapists intended (e.g., Feelings, Better Self-Understanding, New Perspectives). Of course, the intentions Feelings and Insight are more demanding of the client than is Support and may engender resistance.

When therapists intended to Get Information and Clarify, clients reported No Reaction, which indicated that they felt nothing in particular. However, clients generally gave low helpfulness ratings to No Reaction. Additionally, when therapists intended to Get Information, clients also reported fewer amounts of Understood and Supported, again suggesting that these were negative feelings. Thus, when the therapists did a lot of data gathering, the clients got impatient and felt it was not helpful. These data clearly confirm hypotheses from skills training programs about the undesirability from the client perspective of gathering information (e.g., Carkhuff, 1969).

The two cases with better outcome had more significant associations than did the two cases with less improvement. Success appeared to be related to convergence between the therapist's intentions and the client's reactions. However, it should be recalled that only eight of the intention–reaction pairs occurred together at levels greater than by chance for more than one case. Apparently, therapist intentions do not often match client reactions, even when the therapists are experienced.

According to the Hill and O'Grady (1985) process model, several events must transpire before the therapist intentions lead to specific reactions in the client. First, the therapist must accurately perceive the client's reaction. In our data, a comparison of postsession interviews of therapists with the reactions data indicated that therapists often did not perceive reactions accurately. After the therapist perceives the client's reactions, he or she must develop intentions and then communicate these intentions through appropriate interventions.

The client reacts to the therapist's input, filtering it through his or her needs and perceptions. Classic examples can be found of clients' "absorbing" something other than what the therapist intended. For example, the therapist may intend to promote insight, but the client may be focused on something that happened 5 min ago and may not hear what the therapist has said. Or the client may absorb what he or she expects from therapy on the basis of personality dynamics. Finally, the client must exhibit reactions overtly so that the therapist can decode the client reactions and plan the next intervention accordingly. Perhaps in the good outcome cases, the consistency was due both to the therapist intentions and client reactions being obvious as well as to the therapist's ability to decode the reaction and plan the next intention and intervention accordingly. Further examination of the links between therapist and client overt and covert processes is needed.

Pretreatment Symptomatology

Clients who were initially more disturbed felt more frightened (Scared, Worse) and stuck (Stuck, Lack Direction) during treatment and had more difficulty gaining new ways of looking at their problems (Clear, New Perspectives, Educated), all of which seem to describe defensiveness or resistance. Interestingly, pretreatment symptomatology was not related to feeling Understood, Supported, Hope, and Relief.

Perhaps therapists could use pretreatment testing to provide clues about which clients will potentially feel distressed in treatment. If therapists were aware of high pretreatment disturbance, they could establish a more receptive environment than normal to offset clients' tendency to be frightened and stuck and to facilitate clients' thinking about new ways to look at their problems. Alternatively, these findings may suggest that therapists should be attentive to signs of negative reactions in treatment to offset possible negative effects in treatment.

Relation to Session and Treatment Outcome

No more significant correlations were found between proportions of reactions and mean session and treatment outcome than would have been expected by chance. Perhaps the low variability between cases on all outcome measures (ANOVAS indicated no significant differences between cases) prevented us from obtaining significance. Further research with a greater variety of cases is needed to determine the relation of client reactions to outcome.

In the within-case correlations between proportions of reactions and client-rated depth and smoothness, we found more significant and meaningful results than in the correlations between means. For all clients, sessions in which they felt Misunderstood were perceived as less valuable. Further, for at least some clients, sessions in which they gained more Self-Understanding and felt less confused and unfocused were rated as more valuable. Thus, clients placed a high premium on those sessions in which they did not experience negative reactions to what the therapist did.

In the within-session correlations, smoothness was related to reactions in a different manner than was depth, supporting Stiles and Snow's (1984) findings that they were separate dimensions. Sessions in which some clients felt more Negative Thoughts or Behaviors, Scared, Worse, and Lack Direction were rated as less smooth. It makes sense that these reactions would make clients anxious. Therapists had not intended for the clients to have these reactions. Further, these reactions were generally the same as those related to pretreatment symptomatology.

One factor that can be noticed clearly in an examination of Tables 3 and 4 is the individual nature of the correlations between reactions and client-rated outcome. For example, Client 5 valued those sessions in which she felt more Self-Understanding and New Perspective, whereas Client 4 valued those sessions in which she felt more Hopeful. Thus, except for Misunderstood, which is negatively related to depth for all clients, there is a great deal of individual variability in what clients value in sessions.

One possible problem with all of these correlational analyses is the use of a correlational design to study such phenomena. Gottman and Markman (1978) have noted that correlational designs cannot detect sequential patterns. One would not necessarily expect that proportions of reactions would be related to outcome. A single reaction of one type may be more powerful than dozens of other types. For example, one instance of Better Self-Understanding may be enough to cause a deep session. Thus, moment-by-moment helpfulness ratings may be a better index of the impact of the intervention than are the more distant session and treatment outcome indexes.

Time in Treatment

Across the course of therapy, some clients felt less Scared, and some clients became more Clear and Learned New Ways to Behave, indicating some general changes across treatment. These changes in reactions make sense in that therapists' goals are generally to set clients at ease and help them clarify and learn new ways to deal with their problems. However, none of the other reactions changed in predictable manners for more than one client. Nor was treatment outcome a good moderating variable of change in reactions across treatment. Further visual examination of the data revealed no alternative stage structures, either for all clients or for individual clients. Generally, these data indicate that little can be generalized from client to client, but that clients are very individual in how they react and how they progress in the therapy situation. The absence of meaningful stages in this study is similar to Hill, Carter, and O'Farrell's (1983) and O'Farrell, Hill, and Patton's (1986) findings of no consistent stages across two cases of brief psychotherapy, in which they used a variety of process measures.

Theories of brief therapy (e.g., Mann, 1973) would lead one to believe that stages should be demonstrable, but no consistent stages for client reactions could be found in this study. Of course, although our therapists were experienced in doing brief therapy, none of them consistently followed any of the models that have been advanced for brief therapy. For example, one therapist focused on time in treatment by reminding the client of the number of sessions remaining, as Mann suggests, but other principles such as developing a primary focus (e.g., Strupp & Binder, 1984) or intensively discussing termination (Mann, 1973) were not used by these therapists. Perhaps therapists need to follow the prescriptions of techniques from these brief therapies for hypothesized stages to be demonstrable.

Descriptions of Reactions

The original system of 40 reactions was reduced to 21 reactions, which were grouped into a positive and a negative cluster. All reactions within the positive cluster had higher client helpfulness ratings than any of the reactions within the negative cluster.

Although we originally postulated that reactions could be divided into positive, neutral, and negative categories, the data did not support a grouping of neutral reactions. In fact, No Reaction received some of the lowest helpfulness ratings.

We should note that none of the reactions were consistently perceived as negative, but some were perceived as less helpful. The entire range of the 9-point scale was used, but most of the ratings were above 5.

Positive Reactions

The positive reactions that received the highest helpfulness ratings were Unstuck, Better Self-Understanding, Learned New Ways to Behave, and Took Responsibility. On the other hand, the positive reactions that got the lowest helpfulness ratings were Feelings and Understood. Thus, clients rated as most helpful those therapist interventions in which they indicated that they had learned something new about themselves, their problems, or the world. Those interventions that got the clients in touch with their feelings or that made them feel understood were perceived as less helpful.

The positive reaction that received the highest average helpfulness rating was Unstuck. According to the definition of Unstuck, the client had to have felt blocked previously and the therapist's intervention had to have helped him or her feel freed up and more involved in the therapy. This definition is reminiscent of Bordin's (1983) concept of the importance of the "tear and repair" process in the working alliance. He noted that it was not just maintaining a working alliance that was important, but also working through errors or "tears" in the alliance that increased the strength of the relationship between the therapist and client.

Better Self-Understanding, which is defined as gaining new insight, received the second highest helpfulness rating, which lends support to the notion that clients like to have insight into their problems, a primary goal of psychoanalytic therapies. Interestingly, Learned New Ways to Behave, a primary goal of behavioral therapy, received similar helpfulness ratings. A common goal in psychoanalytic, humanistic, and behavioral therapies alike is to help clients accept Responsibility for their role in events while blaming others less, which also received high helpfulness ratings. Thus, major goals for all theories received equivalent ratings of helpfulness from clients.

These data on higher helpfulness ratings for task reactions fits with Parloff, Waskow, and Wolfe's (1978) review of the literature, which indicated that therapist facilitative conditions are necessary but not sufficient for therapeutic change. However, it still remains to be demonstrated how relationship (i.e., Understood, Supported) and task (i.e., Self-Understanding, New Ways to Behave) reactions interact.

For example, how much of and which of the relationship reactions do clients need to experience before they can hear specific task interventions? Further research is needed to uncover these complex interactions between reactions for individual clients.

Negative Reactions

The negative reactions of Sacred and Worse were particularly interesting to us because they received higher helpfulness ratings than most of the other negative reactions. Further, these reactions were endorsed often by clients with high pretreatment symptomatology and tended to decline across the course of treatment. Our speculation is that such painful reactions are necessary in successful therapy. The common sense notion is that clients often have to feel worse before they can feel better. In fact, if one considers the feelings of being confronted and coming up with new insights, it is not surprising that clients feel worse and want to run away and avoid the pain. There is probably a balance needed between a certain level of painful feelings and feeling Understood, so that the client can tolerate the pain.

Additionally, it is helpful to be reminded that clients are often very frightened about therapy. Perhaps a certain level of being scared motivates clients, but it may be that for some clients the feeling of being scared and feeling worse is too intense and needs to be dissipated before they can experience the positive benefits of treatment.

The reactions of Stuck, Confused, and Misunderstood received relatively low helpfulness ratings and may have been indicative of client perceptions of therapist errors as discussed by Elliott (1985) and Kepecs (1979). Alternatively, endorsement could be reflective of client pathology, given the correlation with high pretreatment symptomatology. The client could want more direction either because the therapist was inadequate or because of dependency needs.

Although the No Reaction category was added to measure neutral reactions, we were surprised to find that clients actually gave it one of the lowest helpfulness ratings. Apparently, clients do not respond well to neutral interventions. Although they would probably never be labeled as *hindering* events, as in Elliott's methodology, it is clear that clients do not perceive such reactions as helping them to change.

Methodological Issues

Critics may claim that the results of the cases presented in this study cannot be generalized to real therapy because the structured review of the videotape may have changed the nature of the therapy process. Our observations and posttherapy interviews with therapists and clients, however, indicated that these sessions were similar to those in naturally occurring therapy. The participants told us that they were generally not aware of the research being conducted during the sessions, but several noted the beneficial nature of the videotape review. Whereas the videotaping and the review may indeed have had some effect on the process, we would assert that this cost is trivial compared with the rich source of information about the therapy process uncovered by this procedure.

No indices of reliability were presented here, because reliability is difficult to demonstrate with this type of data. Given that reactions refer to fleeting experiences known only to the subject, traditional measures of inter- and intrarater reliability are not appropriate. As Hill and O'Grady (1985) argued in the development of the measure of therapist intentions, test–retest reliability may be more a measure of memory loss or guessing than an accurate assessment of the phenomena. One can certainly argue that test–retest stability is not an accurate index of reliability, but that it merely reflects the fact that one's perceptions alter with intervening experiences. An experience that may have felt extremely painful at one moment may be experienced later as having been necessary. For example, Elliott, Cline, and Reid (1982) demonstrated that a client's perceptions of impacts changed when measured immediately after a session and again after treatment.

Further, we should note that we studied only immediate reactions. One would expect the most direct impact of therapist interventions to be measurable in the immediate moment, but it may be that a reaction does not occur until a delayed point. The client may not always absorb the impact immediately but may go home and think about what the therapist has said. Clearly, future research should attempt to measure these more delayed reactions.

Implications for the Practice of Psychotherapy

The Reactions System may be applicable to the work of practitioners. Therapists could use the measure to review sessions with their clients, as an easy, relatively nonthreatening structured procedure for uncovering reactions during sessions. Through the use of this methodology, therapists could learn a great deal about a client's reactions to his or her interventions that may not have been apparent in the session. In our experience, clients were generally willing to disclose their reactions to the researchers when asked specifically to do so. However, as Rennie (1985) found and as was our experience in observing the cases, clients did not reveal many of their reactions to their therapists. We were often surprised to discover that our impressions from observations of the therapy sessions as well as the therapists' impressions as reported in postsession interviews were often not verified by the clients' reports of their reactions. Rennie reported that most client secrets involve negative or angry feelings toward the therapist. Thus, if therapists automatically assume that they know how the client is reacting without verifying their perceptions, they may be operating on faulty assumptions. Obviously, therapists who are quite skilled at processing client reactions discover these secrets in sessions. For example, the therapist in the first pilot case routinely asked the client about her feelings, and we noticed that there were few secrets in that case.

A further potential application of the Reactions System is in training therapists. Feedback from the client can be a potent tool in correcting misperceptions. Given the lack of association we noted between therapist intentions and client reactions, it might be useful to train therapists to be more attentive to cues connected with client reactions. If therapists could perceive the client's reactions accurately, they might be able to develop more appropriate intentions and interventions.

We have used the intentions and reactions measures for training of undergraduate and graduate counselors and have received good evaluations of their utility. However, more refined research is needed to demonstrate whether this method of self-instruction helps trainees learn anything different or to learn faster than in other forms of feedback such as supervisor feedback.

Future Research

Now that measures have been developed to test the complete process outlined by Hill and O'Grady (1985), the next step is to test the full model, that is, to answer the question of whether specific therapist intentions lead to specific therapist response modes and then to identifiable client reactions and responses. Additionally, their model can be refined to determine if linkages between therapist intentions, response modes, and reactions vary systematically on the basis of stage of treatment or events engaged in at the specific moment in treatment.

In addition to the verification of the process model, it seems important to discover what other types of variables can be clarified through their relations with client reactions. Possible avenues for further exploration include the correspondence between client reactions and overt behavior, the predictability of reactions by observers other than the client (e.g., therapist, outside observer), and redefinition of core therapy constructs such as empathy from the perspective of the client. In the long run, the development of techniques that permit one to value the client's contribution to the therapy process should enhance psychotherapy research and practice.

References

Battle, C. G., Imber, S. D., Hoehn-Saric, R., Stone, A. R., Nash, E. R., & Frank, J. D. (1965). Target complaints as criteria of improvement. *American Journal of Psychotherapy, 20,* 184–192.

Bordin, E. S. (1983, February). *Myths, realities, and alternatives to clinical trials.* Paper presented at the International Conference on Psychotherapy, Bogotá, Colombia.

Carkhuff, R. R. (1969). *Human and helping relations* (Vols. 1 & 2). New York: Holt, Rinehart & Winston.

Derogatis, L. R., Rickels, K., & Rock, A. F. (1976). The SCL-90 and the MMPI: A step in the validation of a new self-report scale. *British Journal of Psychiatry, 128,* 280–289.

Elliott, R. (1985). Helpful and nonhelpful events in brief counseling interviews: An empirical taxonomy. *Journal of Counseling Psychology, 32,* 307–322.

Elliott, R. (1986). Interpersonal process recall (IPR) as a process research method. In L. S. Greenberg & W. M. Pinsof (Eds.), *The psychotherapeutic process: A research handbook* (pp. 503–528). New York: Guilford.

Elliott, R., Barker, C. B., Caskey, N., & Pistrang, N. (1982). Differential helpfulness of counselor verbal response modes. *Journal of Counseling Psychology, 29,* 354–361.

Elliott, R., Cline, J., & Reid, S. (1982, June). *Tape-assisted retrospective review: A method for assessing the changing effects of therapist interventions in psychotherapy.* Paper presented at the meeting of the Society for Psychotherapy Research, Smuggler's Notch, VT.

Elliott, R., & Shapiro, D. A. (1988). Brief structured recall: A more efficient method for studying significant therapy events. *British Journal of Medical Psychology, 61*(2), 141–153.

Fitts, W. H. (1965). *Manual for the Tennessee Self Concept Scale.* Nashville, TN: Counselor Recordings and Tests.

Gottman, J. M., & Markman, H. J. (1978). Experimental designs in psychotherapy research. In S. L. Garfield & A. E. Bergin (Eds.), *Handbook of psychotherapy and behavior change* (2nd ed., pp. 23–62). New York: Wiley.

Highlen, P. S., & Hill, C. E. (1984). Factors affecting client change in counseling: Current status and theoretical speculations. In S. D. Brown & R. W. Lent (Eds.), *Handbook of counseling psychology* (pp. 334–396). New York: Wiley.

Hill, C. E. (1978). Development of a counselor verbal category system. *Journal of Counseling Psychology, 25,* 461–468.

Hill, C. E. (1985). *Manual for Counselor Verbal Response Category System* (rev. ed.). Unpublished manuscript, University of Maryland, College Park.

Hill, C. E., Carter, J. A., & O'Farrell, M. K. (1983). A case study of the process and outcome of time-limited counseling. *Journal of Counseling Psychology, 30,* 3–18.

Hill, C. E., & O'Grady, K. E. (1985). A list of therapist intentions illustrated in a case study and with therapists of varying theoretical orientations. *Journal of Counseling Psychology, 32,* 3–22.

Kagan, N. (1975). *Interpersonal process recall: A method of influencing human interaction.* (Available from N. Kagan, Department of Education, University of Houston, Houston, TX 77004)

Kepecs, J. G. (1979). Tracking errors in psychotherapy. *American Journal of Psychotherapy, 23,* 365–377.

Klein, M. H., Mathieu, P. L., Gendlin, E. T., & Kiesler, D. J. (1970). *The Experiencing Scale: A research and training manual.* Madison: Wisconsin Psychiatric Institute, Bureau of Audio Visual Instruction.

Mann, J. (1973). *Time-limited psychotherapy.* Cambridge, MA: Harvard University Press.

Marsden, G., Kalter, N., & Ericson, W. A. (1974). Response productivity: A methodological problem in content analysis studies in psychotherapy. *Journal of Consulting and Clinical Psychology, 42,* 224–230.

McQuinty, C. C. (1957). Elementary linkage analysis for isolating orthogonal and oblique types and typal relevancies. *Educational and Psychological Measurement, 17,* 207–229.

O'Farrell, M. K., Hill, C. E., & Patton, S. (1986). Comparison of two cases of time-limited counseling with the same counselor. *Journal of Counseling and Development, 65,* 141–145.

Parloff, M. B., Waskow, I., & Wolfe, B. E. (1978). Research on therapist variables in relation to process and outcome. In S. L. Garfield & A. E. Bergin (Eds.), *Handbook of psychotherapy and behavior change* (2nd ed., pp. 233–282). New York: Wiley.

Rennie, D. (1985, June). *The inner experience of psychotherapy.* Paper presented at the meeting of the Society for Psychotherapy Research, Chicago, IL.

Rice, L. N., & Greenberg, L. S. (1984). The new research paradigm. In L. N. Rice & L. S. Greenberg (Eds.), *Patterns of change: Intensive analysis of psychotherapy process* (pp. 7–25). New York: Guilford.

Stiles, W. B., & Snow, J. S. (1984). Counseling session impact as viewed by novice counselors and their clients. *Journal of Counseling Psychology, 31,* 119–130.

Strupp, H. H., & Binder, J. L. (1984). *Psychotherapy in a new key: A guide to time-limited dynamic psychotherapy.* New York: Basic.

Waskow, I. E., & Parloff, M. B. (1975). *Psychotherapy change measures.* Washington, DC: Department of Health, Education, and Welfare.

Watson, D., & Friend, R. (1969). Measurement of social-evaluative anxiety. *Journal of Consulting and Clinical Psychology, 33,* 448–457.

Appendix
Client Reactions System

Instructions

Review the tape immediately after the session. Try to remember what you were experiencing during the session. Stop the tape after each therapist intervention and list the numbers of the reactions that you felt when you first heard what the therapist said. Choose those reactions that best describe your experience, even if every part of the definition does not apply or the phrasing is not exactly accurate.

Positive Reactions

1. *Understood:* I felt that my therapist really understood me and knew what I was saying or what was going on with me.
2. *Supported:* I felt accepted, reassured, liked, cared for, or safe. I felt like my therapist was on my side or I came to trust, like, respect, or admire my therapist more. This may have involved a change in my relationship with my therapist, such that we resolved a problem between us.
3. *Hopeful:* I felt confident, encouraged, optimistic, strong, pleased, or happy, and felt like I could change.
4. *Relief:* I felt less depressed, anxious, guilty, angry, or had fewer uncomfortable or painful feelings.
5. *Negative thoughts or behaviors:* I became aware of specific negative thoughts or behaviors which cause problems for me or others.
6. *Better self-understanding:* I gained new insight about myself, saw new connections, or began to understand *why* I behaved or felt a certain way. This new understanding helped me accept and like myself.
7. *Clear:* I got more focused about what I was really trying to say, what areas I need to change in my life, what my goals are, or what I want to work on in therapy.
8. *Feelings:* I felt a greater awareness or deepening of feelings or could express my emotions better.
9. *Responsibility:* I accepted my role in events and blamed others less.
10. *Unstuck:* I overcame a block and felt freed up and more involved in what I have to do in therapy.
11. *New perspective:* I gained a new understanding of another person, situation, or the world. I understand *why* people or things are as they are.
12. *Educated:* I gained greater knowledge or information. I learned something I had not known.
13. *New ways to behave:* I learned specific ideas about what I can do differently to cope with particular situations or problems. I solved a problem, made a choice or decision, or decided to take a risk.
14. *Challenged:* I felt shook up, forced to question myself, or to look at issues I had been avoiding.

Negative Reactions

15. *Scared:* I felt overwhelmed, afraid, or wanted to avoid or not admit to having some feeling or problem. I may have felt that my therapist was too pushy or would disapprove of me or would not like me.

16. *Worse:* I felt less hopeful, sicker, out of control, dumb, incompetent, ashamed, or like giving up. Perhaps my therapist ignored me, criticized me, hurt me, pitied me, or treated me as weak and helpless. I may have felt jealous of or competitive with my therapist.

17. *Stuck:* I felt blocked, impatient, or bored. I did not know what to do next or how to get out of the situation. I felt dissatisfied with the progress of therapy or having to go over the same things again.

18. *Lack of direction:* I felt angry or upset that my therapist didn't give me enough guidance or direction.

19. *Confused:* I did not know how I was feeling or felt distracted from what I wanted to say. I was puzzled or could not understand what my therapist was trying to say. I was not sure I agreed with my therapist.

20. *Misunderstood:* I felt that my therapist did not really hear what I was trying to say, misjudged me, or made assumptions about me that were incorrect.

21. *No reaction:* I had no particular reaction. My therapist may have been making social conversation, gathering information, or was unclear.

Chapter 4
EFFECTS OF THERAPIST RESPONSE MODES
IN BRIEF PSYCHOTHERAPY

Clara E. Hill, Janet E. Helms, Victoria Tichenor, Sharon B. Spiegel,
Kevin E. O'Grady, and Elgin S. Perry

Therapist techniques are generally regarded as an important component of effective counseling and psychotherapy. The most common method of operationalizing therapist techniques has been through response modes (e.g., Hill, 1978; Porter, 1943; Robinson, 1950; Snyder, 1945; Stiles, 1979; Strupp, 1955), which refer to the grammatical structure of the therapist's verbal response, independent of the topic or content of the speech (Hill, 1982).

Research on the differential effects of response modes on outcome is not particularly illuminating. When response modes have been used to predict the outcome of sessions or treatment, conflicting and often insignificant results have been found. Several methodological problems have obscured the potential impact of response modes: (a) the methodological paradigm and outcome measures that were used, (b) the lack of inclusion of other process variables in conjunction with response modes, and (c) the lack of attention to individual differences in clients' reactions to response modes.

Methodological Paradigm and Type of Outcome Measure

Russell and Trull (1986) noted that the most typical means for studying the effects of response modes has been to correlate the frequency or proportion of occurrence of response modes with outcome. Such correlational designs have been criticized (Gottman & Markman, 1978; Russell & Trull, 1986) because whereas correlational designs can show that overall occurrences of classes of behavior are related to one another, they cannot indicate whether certain therapist response modes lead systematically to client behaviors.

A further problem with the use of correlational designs to study response modes is that they measure only the frequency of occurrence of the response modes in relation to outcome. There is no reason to believe, however, that the quantity of a type of response mode is related to perceived quality or impact of the response mode. For instance, one helpful interpretation could have more impact than several mediocre interpretations.

Relatedly, the impact of response modes may be obscured if they are examined

Reprinted from *Journal of Counseling Psychology, 35*, 222–233 (1988). Copyright © 1988 by the American Psychological Association. Used with permission of the first author.

This study was sponsored by National Institute of Mental Health Research Grant MH-37837 to Clara E. Hill. The Computer Science Center of the University of Maryland provided part of the computer funds.

We express gratitude to all of the therapists, clients, transcribers, and raters and to Pauline Price for her work with the data entry.

in relation to session or treatment outcome rather than to immediate outcome. Because outcome is probably determined by the cumulative effects of response modes in conjunction with other process variables, the contribution of any individual response mode to outcome becomes less apparent when distal outcome is used. Thus, the impact is more likely to be observed in the immediate client response.

Several studies have examined the immediate effects of therapist response modes. Elliott, Barker, Caskey, and Pistrang (1982) found that clients rated interpretation and advisement as the most helpful and question as the least helpful response modes. Elliott (1985) found that general advisement, interpretation, and information were all positively correlated with ratings of client helpfulness. In an examination of client activity in two cases of time-limited counseling, Hill, Carter, and O'Farrell (1983) and O'Farrell, Hill, and Patton (1986) found that counselor interpretation was associated with decreased client description of the problem and increased experiencing and insight in both cases, whereas direct guidance, confrontation, and silence were helpful for one case but not the other. In sum, interpretation was the only response mode that was effective across all studies.

Inclusion of Other Process Variables

Elliott et al. (1982) and Elliott (1985) noted that the differences among response modes on client helpfulness ratings were small, which suggests that other moderating variables accounted for most of the variance. Because we know clinically that response modes occur in conjunction with other process variables, creating a more complex model will help in describing and understanding the psychotherapy process. On the basis of the process model proposed by Hill and O'Grady (1985), we suggest that therapist intentions and client state be studied in conjunction with response modes.

Therapist Intentions

Not only which response mode the therapist uses but why the therapist is using that response mode at a particular moment (i.e., the therapist's intention) is important information. Elliott (1985) and Hill and O'Grady (1985) studied the co-occurrence of therapist intentions with therapist response modes. Hill and O'Grady found that each response mode can be used to implement several different intentions; for example, open questions were used with intentions of get information, cognitions, feelings, catharsis, and relationship. Using their cognitive–mediational paradigm, Martin, Martin, Meyer, and Slemon (1986) found that consistency between counselor intentions and behaviors and client cognitive processes and behaviors were related to counselor-related session outcome.

Client State

The context of the intervention or how the client is behaving when the therapist delivers a response undoubtedly moderates the effect of therapist interventions (Rice

& Greenberg, 1984). We assume that therapist response modes are not delivered at random but because a client is in a particular state, which we operationalize by the Experiencing scale (Klein, Mathieu, Gendlin, & Kiesler, 1970). No research has been conducted on the effectiveness of response modes or intentions for clients at differing states or experiencing levels.

Individual Differences

Several studies have shown that clients vary in their reactions to different response modes (Garduk & Haggard, 1972; O'Farrell, Hill, & Patton, 1986; Snyder, 1963). Certainly in clinical settings therapists often talk about developing different interventions based on client problems. In the Hill, Helms, Spiegel, and Tichenor (1988) study, clients' reactions to therapist interventions were related to client symptomatology. Therefore we wondered if client pretreatment symptomatology would influence therapist response-mode usage and immediate outcome.

Purpose of the Present Study

The first purpose of the present study was to examine the effects of response modes in treatment. Because most previous research has studied the effects of response modes without consideration of other interrelated process variables, we wanted to establish a baseline for comparison with previous research. Thus, we studied response modes in relation to pretreatment symptomatology, immediate outcome (therapist and client helpfulness ratings, client experiencing, client reactions), session outcome (therapist- and client-rated depth and smoothness), and treatment outcome (changes in anxiety, depression, and self-concept).

The second purpose of the study was to test the effects of therapist response modes on immediate outcome when they are measured in conjunction with the related process variables of therapist intentions and previous client experiencing.

Method

Therapists

Fifty therapists in agencies, private practice, and academic departments who responded to our inquiry each nominated the 10 best therapists in the area. Of the 16 highest rated nominees who were invited, 8 (4 men and 4 women) agreed to participate in the study for a nominal fee. The therapists ranged from 34 to 78 years of age ($M = 46.38$, $SD = 13.47$) and had from 5 to 42 years of postdoctoral experience ($M = 18.50$, $SD = 10.85$). Using 5-point scales ($1 = low$ to $5 = high$), the therapists rated themselves as more psychoanalytic ($M = 3.75$, $SD = .46$) than either humanistic ($M = 2.62$, $SD = .74$) or behavioral ($M = 2.50$, $SD = 1.07$). Therapists were fully informed about all research procedures and signed consent forms before and after treatment.

Clients

Newspaper advertisements announced the availability of free individual psychotherapy for women over 25 years of age with self-esteem and relationship problems. Volunteers were required to be available during the day for 3 hours, plan to remain in the area for at least 1 year, have no previous psychotherapy, and have no history of alcohol or drug dependency. Of 94 who made appropriate telephone inquiries, 53 women completed a battery of psychological tests. Of those tested, 15 women who approximated our desired Minnesota Multiphasic Personality Inventory (MMPI) profile (*T* scores >70 on Scales 2 and 7 and <60 on Scales 4, 6, and 8) were interviewed to determine whether they were appropriate and motivated for brief therapy.

The 8 women who were finally selected as clients all had valid profiles on the MMPI and elevated scores on the scales of Depression ($M = 76.12$, $SD = 5.64$) and Psychasthenia ($M = 70.12$, $SD = 6.44$). The clients ranged in age from 32 to 60 years ($M = 42.38$, $SD = 9.41$). Primary diagnoses, as judged by the researchers according to the *Diagnostic and Statistical Manual of Mental Disorders* (American Psychiatric Association, 1981; *DSM–III*), were dysthymic ($n = 5$), generalized-anxiety disorders ($n = 2$), and cyclothymic ($n = 1$). Clients were fully informed about all selection and treatment procedures and gave informed consent at the initial testing and following treatment; they were not paid for their participation. The women not selected for this study were given referrals.

Process Measures

The revised Hill Counselor Verbal Response Modes Category System (Hill, 1985, 1986) includes nine pantheoretical, nominal, mutually exclusive therapist verbal response modes: approval, information, direct guidance, closed question, open question, paraphrase (which includes restatement, reflection, summary, and nonverbal referent), interpretation, confrontation, and self-disclosure. Three additional categories (minimal encourager, silence, and other) were coded but not used for this study. The judges coded the response modes on the basis of transcripts of the sessions. To correct for different amounts of talking, proportions of response modes were used rather than frequencies in all analyses. Elliott et al. (1987) found concurrent validity for these categories with those of other response-modes systems.

The *Therapist Intentions List* (Hill & O'Grady, 1985) includes 19 pantheoretical, nominal, nonmutually exclusive intentions: set limits, get information, give information, support, focus, clarify, hope, cathart, cognitions, behaviors, self-control, feelings, insight, change, reinforce change, resistance, challenge, relationship, and therapist needs. The therapists used this measure during a videotape review following sessions. Hill and O'Grady demonstrated that therapists from divergent theoretical orientations used the intentions differentially and in the predicted manner and that intentions changed in a consistent manner both within and across sessions.

The Client Experiencing scale (Klein et al., 1970; Klein, Mathieu-Coughlan, & Kiesler, 1986) is a 7-point scale used by the judges to describe a client's level of involvement. At a low level, disclosure is markedly impersonal or superficial; at higher levels, feelings are explored and experiencing serves as the basic referent for problem resolution and self-understanding. Klein et al. (1986) reported high interrater reliability for 15 previous studies and indicated that experiencing had been found to be related to self-exploration, insight, working through, absence of resistances, and high-quality free association. For this study the peak or highest level of experiencing within each client speaking turn was used. Ratings of client's experiencing were used in two ways, (a) as an index of the client's state in the turn prior to the therapist response mode (referred to as previous client experiencing) and (b) as a measure of immediate outcome (referred to as client experiencing).

Immediate Outcome Measures

Therapists and clients rated the helpfulness of each therapist speaking turn by using the Helpfulness scale (Elliott, 1985; Elliott et al., 1982), a 9-point scale (1 = *extremely hindering* to 9 = *extremely helpful*). Elliott (1986) reported adequate reliability and validity for this measure.

During a videotape review following the sessions, the clients also indicated their specific reactions to each therapist speaking turn by using the Client Reactions System (Hill et al., 1988), which consists of 21 nominal, non-mutually-exclusive reactions grouped into five clusters, (a) supported (which consists of understood, supported, hopeful, and relief), (b) therapeutic work (negative thoughts and behaviors, better self-understanding, clear, feelings, responsibility, unstuck, new perspective, educated, new ways to behave), (c) challenged, (d) negative reactions (scared, worse, stuck, lack direction, confused, misunderstood), and (e) no reaction. Hill et al. (1988) demonstrated that therapist intentions and pretreatment symptomatology were related to client reactions.

Client behavior from an observer perspective was measured through judges' ratings of the level of the client's experiencing (described previously) following each therapist speaking turn.

Session Outcome Measures

Clients and therapists completed the Session Evaluation Questionnaire (SEQ; Stiles & Snow, 1984). Depth and Smoothness scales, which factor analyses have shown to be distinct orthogonal factors. Each scale has six bipolar adjectives arranged in 7-point semantic-differential formats.

Treatment Outcome Measures

The Anxiety and Depression scales of the Symptom Checklist-90—Revised (SCL-90-R; Derogatis, Rickels, & Rock, 1976) and the Tennessee Self Concept Scale (TSCS; Fitts, 1965) were all completed by the clients before and after therapy. Adequate reliability and validity have been reported for each measure. Change was determined by using squared-difference scores (Beutler & Crago, 1983) retaining the signs between pre- and postadministrations.

Procedure

Prior to treatment, clients completed the MMPI, SCL-90-R, and TSCS. We randomly assigned clients to therapists on the basis of mutual time availability. Neither clients nor therapists were aware of the specific purpose of the study.

All the therapists conducted 12 to 20 sessions of 50-min with their assigned clients. The therapists used their clinical judgment to select interventions. All sessions were videotaped and monitored by a researcher from an adjacent room.

After each session the client and therapist each completed the SEQ. Immediately following completion of the postsession measures, the therapists and clients reviewed the videotape. Before the first review a researcher met with each client to explain the Client Reactions System. For the videotape review a partition was placed between the therapist and client so that they could see the videotape and the researcher but not each other. The researcher monitored the videotape review, stopping the videotape after each speaking turn of the therapist. If a therapist's speaking turn consisted of more than one distinct section (e.g., a summary followed by a change of topic), the researcher divided it. Clients and therapists were instructed to review the videotape and to try to recall what they felt during the session rather than what they felt at the time of the review. Clients rated the helpfulness and wrote down the numbers of up to five reactions that described their feelings about the therapist intervention. Therapists rated the helpfulness and wrote down the numbers of up to five intentions that described their goals for that intervention. During the review all ratings were done in writing, and talking was discouraged. Neither participant was allowed to see the postsession measures completed by the other participant.

The client returned and completed the outcome measures 1 to 2 weeks after treatment.

Verbatim transcripts were obtained for each of the sessions ($N = 127$). One person typed a rough draft, and then another person corrected it by listening to the tape. The transcripts were then unitized by trained judged into the response units (grammatical sentences) on the basis of the guidelines in Hill (1985).

Undergraduates (6 women and 3 men) were selected to judge the therapists' response modes. Training, which consisted of reading the manual (Hill, 1985), participating in discussions, and practicing with transcripts from previous studies, continued for 20 hr until high agreement was reached. After their training, rotating teams of three judges read each transcript and independently categorized all therapists' response units into response modes. Judges listened to the audio- or videotape of the first session of each case to become familiar with the therapist's style. Data analyses used master judgments (the category selected by at least two judges or the category agreed upon after discussion for three-way disagreements).

For the Experiencing scale, 4 female and 2 male graduate students were trained using the transcripts and audiotapes in the manual (Klein et al., 1970). Following training, rotating sets of two judges used the transcript and audiotape of the session to rate each client speaking turn for the peak experiencing level.

Results

Given that this was an exploratory study with a small number of cases ($N = 8$) and a Type II error would potentially have more serious consequences than would a Type

I error, a significance level of .10 was used for the correlational analyses of the entire sample.

Preliminary Analyses

Reliability

For response modes the average kappa (agreement corrected for chance) between raters for the independent (prior to discussion) judgments was .67. For the Experiencing scale an intraclass correlation on two randomly selected sessions rated by all six raters indicated an interrater reliability of .99.

Response Mode Profile

Overall, the therapists used information in the highest proportion ($M = .33$, $SD = .12$), followed in descending order by paraphrase ($M = .20$, $SD, = .09$), closed question ($M = .14$, $SD = .07$), open question ($M = .10$, $SD = .05$), interpretation ($M = .08$, $SD = .06$), approval ($M = .05$, $SD = .04$), direct guidance ($M = .04$, $SD = .04$), confrontation ($M = .04$, $SD = .04$), and self-disclosure ($M = .01$, $SD = .02$). One-way analyses of variance (ANOVA) indicated significant differences ($ps < .001$) in the therapists' usage of all response modes.

Response Modes in Relation to Measures of Immediate Outcome

Correlations between immediate outcome measures based on all turns for all subjects combined were all significant: For client and therapist helpfulness ratings, $r(10, 560) = .18$, $p < .001$; for client helpfulness and experiencing, $r(10, 560) = .14$, $p < .001$; and for therapist's helpfulness and client's experiencing $r(10, 560) = .03$, $p < .001$. Because the magnitudes of the correlations were small (none accounted for more than 3% of the variance), these measures were not combined in subsequent analyses.

The data presented numerous problems for choosing the appropriate analyses. Response modes are nominal, whereas the dependent variables are interval, which ruled out loglinear analyses unless the data were transformed. Further, response modes do not occur independently either within or across therapist's speaking turns or sessions, which thus violates some of the assumptions of the ANOVA. After careful consideration we chose to use ANOVAs, recognizing that they were not completely appropriate. We were less concerned about the violation of assumptions given the large sample and the lower alpha ($p < .01$). An additional issue was that therapist's speaking turns consisted of up to 34 response modes, many of which were redundant. Duplicates of response modes were thus eliminated, so that any response mode type was counted only once per turn.

A multivariate analysis of variance (MANOVA) with one main effect (response modes) using Pillai's F approximation indicated that response modes were significantly related to the three immediate outcome measures, $F(24, 48780) = 23.46$, $p < .0001$.

Post hoc ANOVAs indicated that both main effects (response modes and subjects) were significant for all three measures. The unique variance for each effect (sr^2) was obtained by dividing the sum of squares. For therapist helpfulness rating ($R^2 = .45$), response modes, $F(8, 16275) = 32.73$, $p < .0001$, $sr^2 = .01$, and subject, $F(7, 16275) = 1,823.57$, $p < .0001$, $sr^2 = .43$. For client helpfulness rating ($R^2 = .38$), response modes, $F(8, 16275) = 27.96$, $p < .0001$, $sr^2 = .01$, and subject, $F(7, 16265) = 1,354.10$, $p < .0001$, $sr^2 = .36$. For client experiencing rating ($R^2 = .06$), response modes, $F(8, 16275) = 17.35$, $p < .0001$, $sr^2 = .01$, and subject, $F(7, 16275) = 111.32$, $p < .0001$, $sr^2 = .05$. Means and standard deviations are shown in Table 1.

Differences between response modes on each measure, found by using Student-Newman-Keuls tests, are indicated in Table 1 by letters following the means and standard deviations. Response modes that share the same subscript letter are not significantly different. Therapists gave the highest helpfulness ratings for interpretation. Clients gave the highest helpfulness ratings and had the highest experiencing levels for self-disclosure.

One-way ANOVAs comparing therapist and client helpfulness ratings indicated that clients gave higher ratings for approval, $F(1, 1038) = 53.02$, $p < .001$, information, $F(1, 3926) = 29.87$, $p < .001$, closed question, $F(1, 3024) = 11.16$, $p < .001$, paraphrase, $F(1, 3312) = 55.09$, $p < .001$, interpretation, $F(1, 1190) = 10.25$, $p < .01$, and self-disclosure, $F(1, 122) = 86.18$, $p < .001$, but lower ratings for direct guidance, $F(1, 766) = 3.80$, $p = .05$, and open question, $F(1, 2156) = 4.86$, $p < .05$.

After eliminating the duplicate response modes that occurred in the same turn, we formed a co-occurrence table for all subjects by pairing each therapist response mode with every client reaction listed for each turn. Therapist self-disclosures were dropped because of their infrequent occurrence. A chi-square analysis, which is analogous to a sequential analysis, indicated that therapist response mode and the clusters of client reactions covaried systematically, $\chi^2(28, N = 19789) = 1,488.88$, $p < .0001$. Cell chi-squares were tested for each response mode and reaction pair using a Bonferroni adjustment to control the error rate involved in the use of multiple comparisons ($\alpha = .001$; critical value $= 10.41$). Those client reactions occurring with each response mode more or less often than expected by chance are found in Table 1.

Response Modes in Relation to Session Outcome

Table 2 reports the correlations between mean proportions of response modes and mean depth and smoothness. For therapists confrontation was significantly negatively related to both depth and smoothness, whereas information and direct guidance were significantly positively related to smoothness. The pattern of correlations was similar for depth and smoothness, reflecting the high correlation between the mean scores on the two scales for therapists, $r(6) = .88$, $p < .01$.

For clients information was significantly negatively related whereas interpretation was significantly positively related to depth. Open question was significantly negatively related to smoothness. Thus, different response modes were correlated with depth and smoothness, reflecting the nonsignificant relationship between the two session-outcome measures for clients, $r(6) = .03$.

We computed the differences between the independent correlations between therapists and clients on the correlations between proportions of response modes and session-outcome measures. For depth there were significant differences for infor-

Table 1—*Therapist Helpfulness Ratings, Client Helpfulness Ratings, Client Experiencing, and Client Reactions for Therapist Response Modes*

Response modes	N	%	Therapist helpfulness		Client helpfulness		Client experiencing		Client reactions	
			M	SD	M	SD	M	SD	Most likely	Least likely
Approval	1,041	.06	6.25	1.20$_d$	6.67	1.42$_b$	2.36	.65$_b$	Supported	Challenged Negative No reaction
Information	3,929	.24	6.29	1.30$_{cd}$	6.46	1.45$_c$	2.26	.58$_{cd}$	Supported	Challenged
Direct guidance	769	.05	6.42	1.26$_b$	6.28	1.54$_d$	2.24	.54$_d$		
Closed question	3,029	.19	6.13	1.14$_e$	6.24	1.41$_d$	2.26	.55$_{cd}$	No reaction	Supported
Open question	2,160	.13	6.42	1.16$_b$	6.33	1.50$_d$	2.40	.65$_b$	Challenged Negative No reaction	Supported
Paraphrase	3,316	.20	6.46	1.23$_b$	6.71	1.50$_b$	2.34	.63$_{bc}$	Supported	Negative No reaction
Interpretation	1,192	.08	6.57	1.21$_a$	6.77	1.65$_b$	2.34	.67$_{bc}$	Therapeutic work	No reaction
Confrontation	759	.05	6.38	1.18$_{bc}$	6.49	1.54$_c$	2.19	.49$_d$	Negative	No reaction
Self-disclosure	124	.01	5.73	.97$_f$	7.13	1.36$_a$	2.49	.73$_a$	—	—
Total	16,319		6.34	1.20	6.49	1.47	2.31	.59		

Note. Duplicate response modes in the same turn were eliminated. Helpfulness was rated on 9-point scales (1 = *extremely hindering* to 9 = *extremely helpful*); experiencing was rated on a 7-point scale (7 = *high*). Within each dependent measure (client or therapist helpfulness ratings or client experiencing), response modes that share the same subscript letter (a–f) were not significantly different; a = highest ratings; f = lowest ratings.

Table 2—Correlations Between Proportions of Response Modes and Client Pretreatment Symptomatology, Session Outcome, and Treatment Outcome

Measure	Response mode								
	App	Inf	DrG	CIQ	OpQ	Par	Int	Con	Dis
Pretreatment									
Anxiety	.19	.11	.18	.48	-.35	-.63*	.07	.28	.41
Depression	.08	-.28	-.30	.81***	.12	-.54	.09	.73**	-.02
TSCS	.58	.12	-.30	.19	-.49	.18	-.32	-.42	.49
Session outcome									
Therapist depth	.12	.42	.59	-.16	-.18	.11	-.57	-.64*	-.31
Therapist smoothness	.28	.62*	.62*	-.36	-.51	.08	-.49	-.79**	.02
Client depth	-.02	-.71**	-.54	.39	.16	.26	.68*	.05	-.14
Client smoothness	.28	.41	.21	.13	-.66*	-.58	.14	.10	.49
Treatment outcome									
Anxiety	-.44	-.38	-.49	-.54	.65*	.64*	.17	.18	-.16
Depression	.04	-.48	-.54	.29	.15	.04	.38	.31	.31
TSCS	-.66*	-.52	-.26	-.63*	.54	.83***	.55	-.20	-.17

Note. $N = 8$ cases. App = approval, Inf = information, DrG = direct guidance, CIQ = closed question, OpQ = open question, Par = paraphrase, Int = interpretation, Con = confrontation, Dis = self-disclosure. Anxiety and Depression are subscales of the Symptom Checklist; TSCS = the total score from the Tennessee Self Concept Scale. Session outcome was determined by the Session Evaluation Questionnaire; treatment outcome was determined by squared difference scores between pre- and posttesting.

*$p < .10$. **$p < .05$. ***$p < .01$.

mation, $z = 2.13$, $p < .05$, direct guidance, $z = 2.03$, $p < .05$, and interpretation, $z = 2.34$, $p < .05$, reflecting the significant negative correlation between mean therapist- and client-rated depth, $r(6) = -.62$, $p < .10$. For smoothness, no significant differences were found, reflecting the nonsignificant correlation between mean therapist- and client-rated smoothness, $r(6) = .04$.

Response Modes in Relation to Measures of Treatment Outcome

Table 2 also reports the correlations between mean proportions of response modes and the three treatment outcome measures. Open question and paraphrase were significantly positively related to greater positive change on the Anxiety subscale of the SCL-90-R. Approval was significantly negatively related whereas paraphrase was significantly positively related to positive change on the TSCS.

Individual Differences

Finally, Table 2 includes the correlations between proportions of response modes and client scores on the pretests of the Anxiety and Depression subscales of the SCL-90-R. Therapists used more closed question and confrontation with more depressed clients, and less paraphrase when clients were anxious.

Additionally, mean therapist helpfulness was significantly negatively related to pretest Anxiety scores, $r(6) = -.68$, $p < .10$, such that therapists rated their interventions as less helpful with anxious clients. Mean client helpfulness ratings were significantly positively related to pretest TSCS scores, $r(6) = .78$, $p < .05$, as were mean client experiencing ratings, $r(6) = .65$, $p < .05$. Thus, clients who began treatment with higher self-concept gave higher helpfulness ratings and had higher experiencing.

Response Modes With Interventions and Previous Client Experiencing

After eliminating duplicates or response modes within turns, we computed a multifactor MANOVA with four main effects (intentions, response modes, previous client experiencing, selected interactions, and subject) using Pillai's F approximation (see Table 3). Significant effects were found for intentions, previous client experiencing, Response Modes × Intentions, and Intentions × Previous Experiencing.

Table 3 also shows the results of the post hoc univariate ANOVAS involving the same main effects and interactions for each of the three immediate outcome measures. For therapist helpfulness ratings, intentions, the Intentions × Previous Experiencing interaction, and subject were significant. For client helpfulness ratings, intentions, previous experiencing, Response Modes × Intentions, Intentions × Previous Experiencing, and subject were significant. For client experiencing, all effects were significant. In all of the univariate, ANOVAS, the sum of the unique variance contributed by each factor did not equal the total R^2 because the factors were correlated.

A comparison of the first set of analyses (with response modes and subjects) with the second set of analyses (adding therapist intentions and previous client ex-

Table 3—*Multivariate and Univariate Effects for Therapist Response Modes, Therapist Intentions, Client Experiencing in the Previous Turn, and Subjects*

Source	Multivariate analysis of variance		Univariate analysis of variance						
				Therapist helpfulness		Client helpfulness		Client experiencing	
	df	F	df	F	sr^2	F	sr^2	F	sr^2
Response modes (A)	24, 47451	1.43	8, 16101	1.20	.00	1.35	.00	1.94	.00
Intentions (B)	54, 47451	2.25**	18, 16101	1.96*	.00	1.84	.00	2.98**	.00
Previous client experiencing (C)	15, 47451	9.39**	5, 16101	.53	.00	8.29**	.00	20.50**	.01
A × B	420, 47451	1.31**	140, 16101	1.16	.01	1.46**	.01	1.35*	.01
A × C	108, 47451	1.06	36, 16101	.41	.00	.60	.01	2.20**	.04
B × C	210, 47451	2.64**	70, 16101	2.19**	.01	2.51**	.01	3.27**	.01
Subjects	21, 47451	859.47**	7, 16101	1,844.48**	.41	1,275.25**	.33	63.43**	.02
R^2					.49		.42		.13

*$p < .01.$ **$p < .001.$

periencing) indicated that the additional variables increased the R^2 only about .05. The sr^2s for response modes consistently decreased from .01 to .00. Thus, these analyses indicated that response modes need to be considered in conjunction with other process variables.

To examine the interaction of response modes with intentions and previous experiencing (which yielded 1,197 categories, many of which occurred infrequently), we had to simplify the data. We examined post hoc tests for experiencing ratings and the co-occurrence table of intentions and response modes to determine whether we could collapse or eliminate categories.

Previous Experiencing Levels

Post hoc analyses (Student-Newman-Keuls) revealed significant differences between levels of previous client experiencing when client helpfulness ratings and subsequent experiencing were the dependent variables. In effect clients rated therapist responses as more helpful and attained higher experiencing levels when they had been at higher previous experiencing levels. Therapist helpfulness ratings did not vary by previous client experiencing, reflecting the nonsignificant F value found in the univariate ANOVA. The experiencing data were collapsed into two levels, low (scale Points 1 and 2, which measure superficial client disclosure) and high (scale Points 3 to 7, in which the client begins to explore problems with feelings and insight). About 75% of the ratings were in the low level.

Therapist Intentions and Response Models

A co-occurrence table was formed by pairing every therapist intention with every therapist response mode within that same speaking turn for all subjects combined. The chi-square, $\chi^2(144, N = 27474) = 6,986.53$, $p < .0001$, indicated that intentions and response modes covaried systematically. The cell chi-squares between each therapist intention and response mode were tested (Bonferroni adjusted $\alpha = .0003$; critical value = 13.12). Thirty-three intention/response-mode pairs occurred significantly more often whereas 41 pairs occurred significantly less often than chance. Pairing the intentions with the response modes probably provides a more pure form of the intervention because pairs that occurred together by chance were eliminated. The 33 intention/response-mode pairs that occurred together more often than expected by chance were retained for further analyses.

Therapist Intention/Response-Mode Pairs Delivered at Low Versus High Experiencing

The frequency of occurrence of the 33 intention/response-mode pairs is shown in Table 4 for low previous experiencing and in Table 5 for high previous experiencing. An overall chi-square test indicated that the 33 intention/response modes covaried systematically across the two experiencing levels, $\chi^2(32, N = 12058) = 281.43$, $p < .001$. Cell chi-square tests (Bonferroni adjusted $\alpha = .0008$, critical value = 11.34) indicated which pairs occurred more and less often than expected by chance. At low

Table 4—Frequency, Therapist and Client Helpfulness Ratings, Client Experiencing, and Client Reactions to Therapist Intention/Response Modes Delivered at Low Client Experiencing

Intentions/response modes	N	Therapist helpfulness		Client helpfulness		Client experiencing		Client reactions most likely
		M	SD	M	SD	M	SD	
Set limits/information	300	6.21	1.36$_{efghi}$	5.99	1.40$_h$	2.10	.37$_c$	No reaction
Set limits/direct guidance	80	6.40	1.29$_{bcdefgh}$	6.19	1.49$_{fgh}$	2.12	.43$_{bc}$	
Get information/closed question	851	5.88	1.10$_{hi}$	5.99	1.25$_h$	2.22	.48$_{abc}$	No reaction
Get information/open question	424	6.21	1.21$_{efghi}$	6.29	1.31$_{efgh}$	2.35	.60$_{abc}$	No reaction
Give information/information	703+	6.44	1.56$_{bcdefgh}$	6.22	1.45$_{fgh}$	2.15	.44$_{bc}$	
Give information/direct guidance	143	6.76	1.28$_{abcde}$	6.51	1.48$_{defgh}$	2.10	.31$_c$	
Give information/self-disclosure	29	5.69	1.11$_i$	7.31	1.44$_{abc}$	2.24	.44$_{abc}$	
Support/approval	321	6.33	1.31$_{cdefgh}$	6.72	1.33$_{cdefgh}$	2.31	.58$_{abc}$	Supported
Support/information	666	6.37	1.40$_{cdefgh}$	6.67	1.30$_{cdefgh}$	2.24	.52$_{abc}$	Supported
Support/paraphrase	466	6.35	1.25$_{cdefgh}$	6.73	1.37$_{cdefg}$	2.28	.54$_{abc}$	Supported
Focus/direct guidance	77	6.05	1.13$_{fghi}$	6.09	1.43$_{fgh}$	2.34	.62$_{abc}$	
Focus/open question	151	6.24	1.37$_{defgh}$	6.16	1.48$_{fgh}$	2.42	.69$_{ab}$	Challenged
Clarify/closed question	813	6.29	1.12$_{cdefgh}$	6.05	1.35$_{gh}$	2.18	.47$_{bc}$	No reaction
Clarify/open question	627	6.46	1.06$_{bcdefgh}$	6.10	1.42$_{fgh}$	2.26	.54$_{abc}$	Challenged Negative No reaction
Hope/approval	35	6.66	1.08$_{abcdef}$	7.23	1.26$_{abcd}$	2.34	.59$_{abc}$	
Hope/information	133	6.61	1.32$_{abcdef}$	6.99	1.31$_{abcd}$	2.23	.61$_{abc}$	
Cognitions/confrontation	79	6.30	1.11$_{cdefgh}$	6.42	1.20$_{defgh}$	2.14	.47$_{bc}$	
Behavior/paraphrase	219	7.02	1.17$_{ab}$	7.41	1.24$_{ab}$	2.27	.62$_{abc}$	
Behavior/interpretation	103	7.11	1.29$_a$	7.50	1.45$_a$	2.29	.64$_{abc}$	
Behavior/confrontation	63	7.11	1.02$_a$	7.35	1.47$_{abc}$	2.14	.43$_{bc}$	

	N							
Feelings/open question	375	6.88	1.18_{abcd}	6.52	1.51_{defgh}	2.48	$.63_a$	Challenged Negative
Feelings/paraphrase	625–	6.89	1.19_{abc}	6.96	1.46_{abcde}	2.32	$.58_{abc}$	
Feelings/interpretation	234	7.11	1.12_a	7.20	1.62_{abc}	2.37	$.64_{abc}$	
Insight/interpretation	446	6.63	1.20_{abcdef}	6.44	1.67_{defgh}	2.30	$.67_{abc}$	
Insight/confrontation	178	6.54	$1.18_{abcdefg}$	6.31	1.63_{defgh}	2.10	$.41_c$	
Change/information	223	6.22	1.27_{efghi}	7.01	1.04_{abcd}	2.24	$.51_{abc}$	Therapeutic work
Change/direct guidance	73	5.93	1.28_{ghi}	6.92	1.10_{abcde}	2.18	$.48_{bc}$	
Reinforce change/approval	73	6.64	1.21_{abcdef}	6.81	1.43_{bcdef}	2.32	$.62_{abc}$	Supported
Resistance/confrontation	44	6.48	$1.32_{bcdefgh}$	6.50	1.41_{defgh}	2.09	$.36_c$	Negative
Challenge/confrontation	166	6.56	$1.14_{abcdefg}$	6.20	1.56_{fgh}	2.13	$.44_{bc}$	Negative
Relationship/information	140	6.66	1.23_{abcdef}	6.94	1.41_{abcde}	2.26	$.58_{abc}$	
Therapist needs/information	69	5.16	$.78_j$	6.23	1.10_{fgh}	2.20	$.47_{abc}$	No reaction
Therapist needs/self-disclosure	11	5.00	1.00_j	6.18	1.40_{fgh}	2.09	$.30_c$	

Note. Within each measure, response modes that share the same subscript letter (a–j) were not significantly different; a = highest ratings; j = lowest ratings. In the N column, a plus indicates that this pair occurred more often than expected by chance for this experiencing level; a minus indicates less-than-chance occurrence.

Table 5—*Frequency, Therapist and Client Helpfulness Ratings, Client Experiencing, and Client Reactions for Therapist Intention/Response Modes Delivered at High Client Experiencing*

Intentions/response modes	N	Therapist helpfulness		Client helpfulness		Client experiencing		Client reactions most likely
		M	SD	M	SD	M	SD	
Set limits/information	62	6.32	1.52_{ab}	6.61	1.50_{abc}	2.34	$.63_{ab}$	
Set limits/direct guidance	16	6.50	1.83_{a}	7.31	1.40_{abc}	2.44	$.63_{ab}$	
Get information/closed question	273	5.90	1.08_{ab}	6.34	1.35_{bc}	2.40	$.59_{ab}$	No reaction
Get information/open question	157	6.26	1.23_{ab}	6.49	1.36_{bc}	2.53	$.69_{ab}$	
Give information/information	126−	6.65	1.62_{a}	6.83	1.55_{abc}	2.28	$.59_{ab}$	
Give information/direct guidance	26	7.00	1.96_{a}	7.00	1.67_{abc}	2.27	$.53_{ab}$	
Give information/self-disclosure	10	6.30	1.16_{ab}	8.40	$.97_{a}$	2.90	$.99_{ab}$	
Support/approval	160	6.42	1.20_{ab}	7.16	1.27_{abc}	2.53	$.68_{ab}$	Supported
Support/information	218	6.33	1.28_{ab}	7.15	1.37_{abc}	2.48	$.72_{ab}$	Supported
Support/paraphrase	238+	6.32	1.11_{ab}	7.13	1.39_{abc}	2.54	$.73_{ab}$	Supported
Focus/direct guidance	30	6.63	1.43_{a}	7.03	1.75_{abc}	2.53	$.86_{ab}$	
Focus/open question	54	6.54	1.19_{a}	6.72	1.52_{abc}	2.76	$.97_{ab}$	No reaction
Clarify/closed question	229	6.28	1.18_{ab}	6.51	1.29_{bc}	2.44	$.62_{ab}$	Challenged
Clarify/open question	198	6.57	1.09_{a}	6.63	1.42_{abc}	2.57	$.76_{ab}$	
Hope/approval	16	6.38	1.26_{ab}	8.00	$.97_{ab}$	2.56	$.73_{ab}$	
Hope/information	34	6.47	1.24_{ab}	7.41	1.37_{abc}	2.38	$.60_{ab}$	
Cognitions/confrontation	23	6.61	1.12_{a}	6.96	1.19_{abc}	2.39	$.66_{ab}$	
Behavior/paraphrase	66	6.76	1.15_{a}	7.52	1.39_{abc}	2.39	$.76_{ab}$	
Behavior/interpretation	30	7.10	1.09_{a}	7.43	1.65_{abc}	2.37	$.76_{ab}$	
Behavior/confrontation	24	6.67	1.17_{a}	7.42	1.35_{abc}	2.33	$.56_{ab}$	Challenged
Feelings/open question	192+	6.84	1.10_{a}	6.58	1.54_{bc}	2.61	$.65_{ab}$	Negative

Response mode	N						No reaction
Feelings/paraphrase	372+	6.83	1.16_a	7.11	1.47_{abc}	2.55	$.75_{ab}$
Feelings/interpretation	128+	6.99	1.08_a	7.44	1.65_{abc}	2.56	$.81_{ab}$
Insight/interpretation	155	6.61	1.20_a	7.26	1.64_{abc}	2.56	$.84_{ab}$
Insight/confrontation	48	6.69	1.31_a	6.85	1.57_{abc}	2.33	$.63_{ab}$
Change/information	59	6.27	1.16_{ab}	7.12	1.22_{abc}	2.54	$.70_{ab}$
Change/direct guidance	16	6.12	1.09_{ab}	7.31	$.95_{abc}$	2.19	$.54_{ab}$
Reinforce change/approval	56+	6.39	$.82_{ab}$	7.55	1.16_{abc}	2.71	$.78_{ab}$
Resistance/confrontation	8	5.88	2.03_{ab}	7.12	$.35_{abc}$	2.00	$.00_b$
Challenge/confrontation	39	6.62	1.27_a	6.64	1.55_{abc}	2.28	$.46_{ab}$
Relationship/information	40	6.20	1.14_{ab}	7.80	1.22_{abc}	2.65	1.05_{ab}
Therapist needs/information	14	5.07	1.21_b	6.07	1.38_c	2.21	$.43_{ab}$

Note. Within each measure, response modes that share the same subscript letter (a–d) were not significantly different; a = highest ratings; d = lowest ratings. In the N column, a plus indicates that this pair occurred more often than expected by chance for this experiencing level; a minus indicates less-than-chance occurrence. Therapist needs/self-disclosure was dropped because it occurred only once.

experiencing, information/information occurred more often whereas feelings/paraphrase occurred less often than expected by chance. At high experiencing, reinforce change/approval, feelings/approval, support/paraphrase, feelings/paraphrase, feelings/interpretation all occurred more often whereas information/information occurred less often than expected by chance.

The results of separate post hoc tests (Student-Newman-Keuls) for the helpfulness and experiencing ratings within each experiencing level across all 33 intention/response-mode pairs are also shown in Tables 4 and 5. In general, fewer post hoc differences were found for high than for low previous experiencing.

The overall relationship of the 33 intention/response-mode pairs to the five reactions was tested by a chi-square for each experiencing level. For low experiencing, $\chi^2(128, N = 10900) = 1,901.38$, $p < .001$; for high experiencing, $\chi^2(128) = 835.54$, $p < .001$. The cell chi-square tests (Bonferroni adjusted $\alpha = .0003$, critical value = 13.05) indicated which reactions occurred more and less often than chance to the 33 interventions.

Discussion

We first discuss the results of the analyses based solely on response modes in relation to outcome. Then we discuss the results of the analyses of response modes in conjunction with therapist intentions and levels of previous client experiencing.

Response Modes in Relation to Measures of Immediate Outcome

Response modes were significantly related to all immediate outcome measures (therapist and client helpfulness ratings, client experiencing, and client reactions), although the amount of unique variance accounted for was small (about 1%), which is consistent with previous research (Elliott, 1985; Elliott et al., 1982). Considering that response modes were not used independently (i.e., frequently more than one type of response mode was used per therapist speaking turn) and that other process variables that interact with response modes (e.g., intentions, client state, nonverbal behaviors, etc.) were not considered, the amount of variance accounted for is substantial. The response modes are discussed in the order of their overall effectiveness.

Interpretation

Therapists and clients concurred that interpretation was quite helpful. Additionally, interpretation led to moderate experiencing levels and to clients reporting reactions of therapeutic work, which indicates growth and change within treatment. Clients seldom reported no reaction, indicating that they were rarely bored or indifferent when presented with an interpretation. Perhaps interpretation was effective because of the level of motivation and suitability of these clients for brief therapy. The effectiveness of interpretation is consistent with a great deal of theory (Frances & Perry, 1983; Greenson, 1967; Levy, 1963) and past research (Elliott, 1985; Elliott et al., 1982; Hill et al., 1983; O'Farrell et al., 1986).

Self-Disclosure

Self-disclosure received the highest client helpfulness ratings of all response modes and led to the highest client experiencing levels. Clients may have valued therapist disclosures for a variety of reasons, such as providing a glimpse that therapists are also human and have problems or shifting the power balance in the relationship so that clients feel less vulnerable. Further, the infrequent use of self-disclosure (one therapist never disclosed, five disclosed 1% or less, and two used disclosures 2%) may have made clients value them even more.

In contrast to the high client ratings, therapists were quite divided in their evaluation of self-disclosures. Three therapists rated it as the most helpful response mode, whereas the others rated it as one of the least helpful. Therapists may have felt more vulnerable when disclosing their own reactions or may have felt uncomfortable with the shift in the power dynamics. This variability in reaction to disclosures is reflected in the theoretical literature. Psychoanalytic writers (e.g., Curtis, 1981) have underscored the potential deleterious effects of self-disclosure on the transference process, whereas humanistic therapists, for example, Meador and Rogers (1984) and Carkhuff (1969), have emphasized its usefulness in demonstrating therapist genuineness and building the therapeutic relationship.

Paraphrase

Paraphrase was rated as moderately helpful by clients and therapists and led to moderate experiencing. Clients reported feeling supported and seldom felt negative reactions or no reaction. This finding is consistent with skills training programs (Carkhuff, 1969; Egan, 1984) that suggest that paraphrase requires the counselor to listen to what the client is saying and demonstrate a sense of understanding the client. Thus the responsibility is shared by the therapist and the client to work to understand the client's experience.

Approval

Approval was similar to paraphrase in terms of its moderate client helpfulness ratings, moderate experiencing levels, and types of reactions, but it was rated as less helpful by therapists. Perhaps therapists felt that they were too supportive or "gratifying," which is contrary to the neutral stance advocated by psychoanalytic therapists (e.g., Greenson, 1967).

Open Question

Therapists rated open question as moderately helpful, reflecting the value therapists place on the self-exploration process (Carkhuff, 1969). Clients, on the other hand, gave low helpfulness ratings to open question. Perhaps the low ratings by clients are explained by the findings that open question led to high client experiencing and to reactions of challenged, negative reactions (particularly scared) and no reaction, but not to feeling supported.

Evidently open question was a very powerful intervention that made clients feel uncomfortable. It did lead to exploration and experiencing (e.g., Carkhuff, 1969; Egan, 1984), which may be why clients felt challenged. An analogy to convergent and divergent thinking may help explain these findings. In convergent thinking there is one right answer, whereas in divergent thinking there can be many right answers. Similarly, with closed question the therapist wants a specific answer, but with an open question there is not a right answer. Thus the client is called on to explore and may not be sure that he or she is saying what the therapist wants to hear. For example, the open question, "How would your life be different if you got divorced?" could feel quite threatening, albeit impactful and useful, to a client. The feelings of threat could have resulted in lower client helpfulness ratings for open question.

Confrontation

Confrontation received moderate helpfulness ratings from therapists but was rated low by clients and led to low experiencing levels and to negative reactions. Clients seldom reported no reaction, indicating that they were aroused by confrontation. Confrontation often interrupts the client's thinking by presenting discrepancies and another point of view. Because challenging may increase anxiety, it is not surprising that confrontation does not feel good to clients. Although confrontation feels negative at the time, such disruption may be a necessary foundation for change.

Information

Information was moderately low on all criteria, leading to client reactions of feeling supported but not challenged. This response usually is educative and appears not to arouse much feeling.

Direct Guidance

Direct guidance led to the lowest experiencing levels and the lowest client helpfulness ratings, in contrast to the high helpfulness ratings found by Elliott et al. (1982) and Elliott (1985). This group of highly motivated clients clearly did not like being given advice but instead preferred the more insight-oriented interventions of interpretation, paraphrase, and disclosure. Therapists gave moderately high helpfulness ratings for direct guidance. In fact, this was the only response mode that therapists rated higher than did clients. Perhaps the therapists felt a need to be active and give the clients some specific advice in the brief therapy format because they did not have a long period of time to help the clients change.

Closed Question

Closed question was consistently rated as least helpful and led to no reaction, which indicated a sense of neutrality. One client stated that she found these questions to be boring; she knew the information already but had to repeat it for the therapist. These results are similar to data reported by Elliott et al. (1982) and Elliott (1985) and fits with skills training (Carkhuff, 1969). Of course, closed question was not typically rated as hindering but rather as less helpful. Therapists may feel a need to obtain specific information from clients but should be aware that too many closed questions may be negative.

Response Modes in Relation to Measures of Session Outcome

Cases that were characterized by more interpretation and less information were associated with higher client ratings of depth. These findings are consistent with higher client helpfulness and experiencing ratings for interpretation and lower ratings for information. Cases in which therapists used more open question were viewed by clients as rougher, which confirms that clients generally viewed open questions as threatening.

From the therapist perspective cases in which they offered more information and direct guidance and less confrontation were associated with higher ratings of depth and smoothness. These data confirm the results of the immediate outcome measures only for direct guidance, which was rated positively by therapists.

Response Modes in Relation to Measures of Treatment Outcome

Cases in which the therapist used more open question and paraphrase had more decreases in anxiety. Thus, although open question was viewed negatively by clients when they were given, the increase in experiencing and awareness of feelings may have enabled them to deal with the anxiety and begin to conquer it. Cases with more paraphrase but less approval and closed question had more increases in self-concept. Thus, whereas approval may have felt good to the client on an immediate level, frequent therapist approval may have prevented the dyad from going beyond a superficial level. Similarly, use of many closed questions may have structured the situation but left the client unchanged. Paraphrase and open question, on the other hand, may have offered the client the opportunity to explore.

Individual Differences

There were large individual differences between clients, accounting for most of the explained variance in the relationship between response modes and outcome. Participants apparently had different anchor points in using the scales, that is, for one client the helpfulness rating mean was 7.78 ($SD = 1.11$), whereas for another it was 5.12 ($SD = 5.12$). Interestingly, the rank order for the helpfulness ratings of response modes was similar across clients. The amount of variance accounted for by subjects in the Experiencing scale was much lower than that of the client Helpfulness scale (5% vs. 36%), undoubtedly because it was rated by outside judges. Observers saw some differences between clients, but the clients' diverse manners of using the scale accounted for a lot of variance in the helpfulness ratings.

Furthermore, clients with higher initial self-concept gave higher helpfulness ratings and had higher experiencing, which supports the notion that clients who are initially functioning at a higher level engage in more productive client behavior and are more positive about the therapeutic interaction.

Therapists used more closed question and confrontation with depressed clients. The more depressed clients in this study were quieter and less self-revealing, which may have forced the therapists to be more structured. With clients who were more anxious, therapists used less paraphrase. Perhaps paraphrases are too unstructured for anxious clients.

Summary of Response Modes Analyses

A comparison of the results of the immediate versus session and treatment outcome measures indicates that response modes fare differently depending on when outcome is measured. However, we must recall that measures of immediate outcome rely on aggregate ratings of each intervention. Evaluations of response modes based on correlations with session and treatment outcome on the other hand rely on frequency of usage of the various response mode. In effect a comparison of these two methodologies is like comparing apples and oranges. This is best illustrated with therapist self-disclosure, in that it was not amount but type and quality that made these interventions effective. Another example is that a well-timed interpretation might be very effective, but that does not necessarily mean a high number of interpretations would be effective. In fact, we may argue that interpretations and confrontations should be used sparingly and judiciously.

In agreement with Gottman and Markman (1978), we recommend that future studies abandon the design of correlating response modes with distal outcome. Use of immediate outcome measures such as helpfulness ratings, experiencing, and reactions seem to be better indicators of the effects of response modes. New methodologies need to be developed to study the links between the ratings on individual interventions and what makes good sessions. A few critical interventions may be a better predictor of session outcome than a simple summary of all transactions.

Response Modes With Intentions and Previous Client Experiencing

When response modes are the only process variable to be analyzed, they had a small but significant effect on outcome. However, when other related process variables are added, the unique contribution of response modes dropped to nothing. Examination of the data revealed that therapist intentions accounted for more of the unique variance than did response modes. A variety of response modes within the same cluster could be used to accomplish the same purpose. For example, the therapist could help the client explore behaviors and feelings equally well through an open question, paraphrase, interpretation, or confrontation. Similarly, the therapist could assess equally well through closed or open questions or direct guidance. In effect, the differences among response modes were due to the underlying intentions rather than to the response mode.

Previous client experiencing also accounted for more variance, both as a main effect and in interaction with intentions, than did response modes. Thus, the context or client state when the therapist delivered the intervention was important in determining the outcome of the intervention.

At low previous experiencing levels, which includes most of the client behavior (75%), the client is generally at a superficial level of discourse, telling stories or describing details of situations. When the client is experiencing at a low level, therapists offered more information but fewer interpretations aimed at feelings. Therapists and clients concurred that the most helpful interventions were those in which the therapist helped the client explore feelings and behaviors through paraphrase, interpretation, and confrontation. Both participants gave moderate ratings to interventions intended to support, instill hope, and reinforce change through approval, information, or paraphrase as well as to interventions with intentions of cognitions, insight, challenge, and resistance implemented through interpretation and confrontation. Both participants gave low helpfulness ratings to interventions with intentions of set limits, information, and therapist needs implemented through information and direct guidance and the intentions of get information, focus, and clarify implemented through closed and open question and direct guidance. The only disagreements were that therapists rated feelings/open question and information/direct guidance as very helpful whereas clients rated it as not very helpful. Clients, on the other hand, rated information/self-disclosure, and change through information or direct guidance as very helpful whereas therapists rated it as not very helpful. In sum, when the client was at a low level of experiencing, therapist interventions aimed at exploration, restructuring, and support were most helpful.

When previous client experiencing was high, subsequent client helpfulness ratings and experiencing ratings were uniformly higher than when the client was at a low experiencing level. Thus, clients have better immediate outcome when they begin at higher levels of experiencing. Therapists used more interventions aimed at support and exploring feelings and fewer interventions designed to give information at the higher experiencing levels. Interestingly, few post hoc differences in effectiveness were found between therapist interventions. Apparently, when the client is functioning at a high level, then almost anything the therapist does is perceived as helpful by the client.

Previous client experiencing did not account for much of the variance in therapist helpfulness ratings. Presumably, therapists use those response modes that they anticipate will be most helpful at a given moment, which may explain the lower amounts of variance due to anything besides intentions for therapists.

Conclusions

Several conclusions can be drawn from this study. First, immediate outcome measures such as therapist and client helpfulness ratings, client experiencing, and client reactions, are more sensitive measures of the effects of therapist interventions than are measures of session and treatment outcome.

Second, response modes account for an insignificant amount of variance in immediate outcome ratings when other process variables are considered. Future researchers should consider using therapist intentions, either alone or in conjunction with response modes, as a more adequate descriptor of therapist interventions.

Third, the results indicate that there is some overlap among Hill and O'Grady's (1985) intentions, suggesting that there are only seven unique intentions that occur frequently enough to be used for future research, (a) set limits, (b) assessment (includes get information, focus, and clarify), (c) support (includes support, hope, and reinforce change), (d) educate (includes give information), (e) explore (includes cognitions, behaviors, and feelings), (f) restructure (includes insight, challenge, and resistance), and (g) change.

Fourth, the effectiveness of therapist interventions depends on the previous client experiencing level. At low levels of experiencing, both therapists and clients rate as most helpful those interventions that are aimed at exploration of feelings and behaviors. However, clients gave high ratings to interventions that are aimed at change or in which the therapist discloses in order to educate, whereas therapists gave high ratings to feelings through open question and information through direct guidance. At high levels of previous client experiencing, most therapist interventions were rated as helpful. These results provide evidence that context and timing are important variables in the psychotherapy process.

Fifth, individual differences both in the frequency of usage and evaluation of therapist interventions for different clients remind one that different interventions work for different clients. Preliminary evidence was presented relating these individual differences to pretreatment symptomatology.

Finally, therapists and clients diverge in what they perceive as helpful. Of course, the finding that therapists and clients view the process differently is certainly not new within the psychotherapy literature (e.g., Fuller & Hill, 1985). We would caution though that we cannot choose between the two perspectives because they offer different ways of looking at the process.

We recommend that further research on the effects of therapist interventions take into account context, timing, and individual differences between clients. Further attention is also needed for measuring delayed effects of interventions. Whereas the effects of some interventions are only immediate (e.g., questions used to get information), the effects of others may be more delayed. For instance, a client may reject a confrontation when it is first offered but go home and think it over, returning later to tell about how it helped them to reanalyze the situation.

References

American Psychiatric Association. (1981). *Diagnostic and statistical manual of mental disorders* (3rd ed.). Washington, DC: Author.

Beutler, L. E., & Crago, M. (1983). Self-report measures of psychotherapy outcome. In M. L. Lambert, E. R. Christensen, & S. S. DeJulio (Eds.), *The assessment of psychotherapy outcome* (pp. 453–497). New York: Wiley.

Carkhuff, R. R. (1969). *Human and helping relations* (Vols. 1 and 2). New York: Holt, Rinehart, & Winston.

Curtis, J. M. (1981). Indications and contraindications in the use of therapist's self-disclosure. *Psychological Reports, 49*, 499–507.

Derogatis, L. R., Rickels, K., & Rock, A. F. (1976). The SCL-90 and the MMPI: A step in the validation of a new self-report scale. *British Journal of Psychiatry, 128*, 280–289.

Egan, G. (1984). *The skilled helper* (4th ed.). Monterey, CA: Brooks/Cole.

Elliott, R. (1985). Helpful and nonhelpful events in brief counseling interviews: An empirical taxonomy. *Journal of Counseling Psychology, 32*, 307–322.

Elliott, R. (1986). Interpersonal process recall as a research tool. In L. Greenberg & W. Pinsof (Eds.), *The psychotherapeutic process: A research handbook* (pp. 503–528). New York: Guilford.

Elliott, R., Barker, C. B., Caskey, N., & Pistrang, N. (1982). Differential helpfulness of counselor verbal response modes. *Journal of Counseling Psychology, 29,* 354–361.

Elliott, R., Hill, C. E., Stiles, W. B., Friedlander, M. L., Mahrer, A. R., & Margison, F. R. (1987). Primary therapist response modes: Comparison of six rating systems. *Journal of Consulting and Clinical Psychology, 55,* 218–223.

Fitts, W. H. (1965). *Manual for the Tennessee Self Concept Scale.* Nashville, TN: Counselor Recordings and Tests.

Frances, A., & Perry, S. (1983). Transference interpretations in focal therapy. *American Journal of Psychiatry, 140,* 405–409.

Fuller, F., & Hill, C. E. (1985). Counselor and helpee perceptions of counselor intentions in relation to outcome in a single counseling session. *Journal of Counseling Psychology, 32,* 329–338.

Garduk, E. L., & Haggard, E. A. (1972). Immediate effects on patients of psychoanalytic interpretations. *Psychological Issues, 7*(28), 3–82.

Gottman, J. M., & Markman, H. J. (1978). Experimental designs in psychotherapy research. In S. L. Garfield & A. E. Bergin (Eds.), *Handbook of psychotherapy and behavior change* (2nd ed., pp. 23–62). New York: Wiley.

Greenson, R. R. (1967). *The technique and practice of psychoanalysis* (Vol. 1). New York: International Universities Press.

Hill, C. E. (1978). Development of a counselor verbal category system. *Journal of Counseling Psychology, 25,* 461–468.

Hill, C. E. (1982). Counseling process research: Methodological and philosophical issues. *Counseling Psychologist, 10*(4), 7–19.

Hill, C. E. (1985). *Manual for the Hill Counselor Verbal Response Modes Category System* (rev. ed.). Unpublished manuscript, University of Maryland.

Hill, C. E. (1986). An overview of the Hill Counselor and Client Verbal Response Modes Category Systems. In L. Greenberg & W. Pinsof (Eds.), *The psychotherapeutic process: A research handbook* (pp. 131–160). New York: Guilford.

Hill, C. E., Carter, J. A., & O'Farrell, M. K. (1983). A case study of the process and outcome of time-limited counseling. *Journal of Counseling Psychology, 30,* 3–18.

Hill, C. E., Helms, J. E., Spiegel, S. B., & Tichenor, V. (1988). Development of a system for categorizing client reactions to therapist interventions. *Journal of Counseling Psychology, 35,* 27–36.

Hill, C. E., & O'Grady, K. E. (1985). A list of therapist intentions: Illustrated in a single case and with therapists of varying theoretical orientations. *Journal of Counseling Psychology, 32,* 3–22.

Klein, M. H., Mathieu, P. L., Gendlin, E. T., & Kiesler, D. J. (1970). *The Experiencing scale: A research and training manual* (2 vols.). Madison, WI: Bureau of Audio Visual Instruction.

Klein, M. H., Mathieu-Coughlan, P., & Kiesler, D. J. (1986). The Experiencing scales. In L. Greenberg & W. Pinsof (Eds.), *The psychotherapeutic process: A research handbook* (pp. 21–72). New York: Guilford.

Levy, L. H. (1963). *Psychological interpretation.* New York: Holt, Rinehart & Winston.

Martin, J., Martin, W., Meyer, M., & Slemon, A. (1986). Empirical investigation of the cognitive mediational paradigm for research on counseling. *Journal of Counseling Psychology, 33,* 115–123.

Meador, B. D., & Rogers, C. R. (1984). Person-centered therapy. In R. Corsini (Ed.), *Current psychotherapies* (3rd ed.). Itasca, IL: Peacock.

O'Farrell, M., Hill, C. E., & Patton, S. (1986). A comparison of two cases of counseling. *Journal of Counseling and Development, 65,* 141–145.

Porter, E. H., Jr. (1943). The development and evaluation of a measure of counseling interview procedures. *Educational and Psychological Measurement, 3,* 105–126.

Rice, L. N., & Greenberg, L. S. (1984). *Patterns of change.* New York: Guilford.

Robinson, F. P. (1950). *Principles and procedures in student counseling.* New York: Harper.

Russell, R. L., & Trull, T. J. (1986). Sequential analyses of language variables in psychotherapy process research. *Journal of Consulting and Clinical Psychology, 54,* 16–21.

Snyder, W. U. (1945). An investigation of the nature of nondirective psychotherapy. *Journal of General Psychology, 33,* 193–223.

Snyder, W. U. (1963). *Dependency in psychotherapy: A casebook.* New York: MacMillan.

Stiles, W. B. (1979). Verbal response modes and psychotherapeutic technique. *Psychiatry, 42,* 49–62.

Stiles, W. B., & Snow, J. S. (1984). Counseling session impact as viewed by novice counselors and their clients. *Journal of Counseling Psychology, 31,* 3–12.

Strupp, H. H. (1955). An objective comparison of Rogerian and psychoanalytic techniques. *Journal of Consulting Psychology, 19,* 1–7.

Chapter 5
LIST OF THERAPIST INTENTIONS ILLUSTRATED IN A CASE STUDY AND WITH THERAPISTS OF VARYING THEORETICAL ORIENTATIONS

Clara E. Hill and Kevin E. O'Grady

Intentions can be defined as a therapist's rationale for selecting a specific behavior, response mode, technique, or intervention to use with a client at any given moment within the session. Intentions represent what the therapist wants to accomplish through his or her behavior within the session. An intention is the cognitive component that mediates the choice of intervention. Intentions refer to *why*, whereas interventions or techniques refer to *what* the therapist does. Intentions seem to be a step closer to describing how therapists think about their subjective experience in sessions than are such variables as response modes (e.g., questions, restatements) or nonverbal behaviors (e.g., head nods, arm movements), all of which have received considerable attention in the research literature (Hill, 1978; Stiles, 1979; Strupp, 1955).

Exploration of intentions can be of enormous benefit for teaching or supervision because such a process enables one to clarify and think through what one is doing in sessions. For research, the explication of intentions can be beneficial by providing more in-depth representation of therapist behavior. Further, knowledge of intentions may provide explanations for why similar techniques result in divergent outcomes. For example, two therapists may use a lot of closed questions: One may use them to get information, whereas the other may use them in a very different way to stimulate insight. Thus, intentions may be a moderating variable for understanding verbal or nonverbal therapist behavior.

Research

Recently, cognitive psychologists have explored the role of cognitions in mediating behavior (Mahoney & Arnkoff, 1978). The role of the therapist's cognitions in mediating choice of interventions within therapy sessions has concomitantly been of growing interest. Theoreticians have discussed links between intentions and interventions; for example, Goodman and Dooley (1976) assumed that advisements carry the intention of guiding the client's behavior. Until recently, however, minimal re-

Reprinted from *Journal of Counseling Psychology, 32*, 3–22 (1985). Copyright © 1985 by the American Psychological Association. Used with permission of the first author.

We would like to acknowledge Lynda Birckhead, Jean A. Carter, Daniel McKitrick, Mary K. O'Farrell, Terri B. Thames, and Douglas Varvil-Weld for their extensive involvement in the preliminary stages of the development of this measure and also the many counselors and therapists who generously contributed their time to participate in this study. The final stages of this research were partially supported by National Institute of Mental Health Grant No. MH-37837.

A version of this study was presented at the Society for Psychotherapy Research, Sheffield, England, June 1983.

search attempts have been made to verify whether intentions do systematically vary with choice of interventions.

Elliott and Feinstein (1978) developed a list originally containing 6 and now 10 intentions ("gather information," "give information," "communicate my understanding," "explain," "advise," "guide," "reassure," "disagree," "share myself," and "other"). Elliott (1986) reported finding small but significant correlations between client, counselor, and observer ratings of the same counselor intention variables (values in the .20s) and found little overlap among the 10 therapist intention variables. Further, client and therapist perceptions of gathering information and explaining were associated with increased client exploration. Elliott also reported that response modes (determined by external trained judges) were correlated with intentions (as determined by the counselor), such that both open and closed questions were related to the intention "gather information," process advisement was related to "guide," general advisement was related to "advise," reflection was related to "communicate my understanding," interpretation was related to "explain," reassurance was related to "reassure," disagreement was related to "disagree," self-disclosure was related to "share myself," information was related to "give information," and the response mode of other was related to "other."

Elliott and Feinstein's system, although useful, seems incomplete and nonrepresentative of some important intentions from particular theoretical perspectives, for example, set limits, identify cognitive behaviors, intensify feelings, promote self-control, cause change, challenge, or deal with relationship issues. Also, there seems to be a lack of differentiation between intentions and response modes in Elliott and Feinstein's list, such that it is not clear that they are actually measuring separate variables. For example, the intention of general advisement and the response mode of advise sound so similar that rather than being two separate concepts they may just be the same variable judged from two perspectives.

Thus, although there appears to be some preliminary interest in the area of intentions, further measure development seems warranted. In this article we first outline our theoretical model for how intentions fit into the psychotherapy process. Then we discuss some general methodological issues related to measure development. Next, we describe the development of the present 19-item Intentions List. Finally, we detail the use of the Intentions List in two studies.

Theoretical Model

Our theory about how intentions operate in the counseling/psychotherapy process is that therapists compute an enormous amount of data from global input variables (e.g., presenting problem, diagnosis, setting, attractiveness) as well as immediate stimulus variables (e.g., the behavioral observations, clinical hypotheses, personal reactions, overall treatment plan, and specific task engaged in at that point in treatment) in an incredibly quick and sophisticated manner. Based on their experience and training, therapists develop these data into intentions or goals for what they want to accomplish next in the session. These intentions guide the choice of interventions. An intention can be implemented by a range of interventions, both nonverbal and verbal. For example, if the intention is to intensify feelings, the therapist might choose from a range of behaviors to implement that intervention: leaning forward, touching, reflection of feelings, silence, confrontation, self-disclosure, or an empty chair technique. The therapist's choice undoubtedly depends on many factors, such as familiarity and comfort with specific techniques, the client's behavior and dynamics, and the desired consequences.

After each counselor intervention or turn, the client responds. The client goes through a similar process of integrating the immediate stimulus variables, trying to figure out what the therapist meant; experiencing positive or negative emotional reactions, all influenced by his or her readiness for hearing the therapist's statement; deciding or filtering what to say next; and choosing how to respond.

Based on the client's response, the therapist reacts and adjusts the subsequent intention and response accordingly. Obviously, as the process continues, more and more data enter into the stimulus variables, so that the therapist probably develops rather stable notions about client dynamics and response patterns. Similarly, the client develops stable expectations for the therapist's interventions and reactions. It may even be that after a certain point the therapist and client develop rather fixed notions about the other person that are relatively difficult to change even with new information. This process, although seemingly similar to a computer, is actually much more sophisticated because the therapist can take human factors (e.g., feelings and interpersonal reactions) into account.

Relationship of Intentions to Theoretical Orientation

A great deal of controversy exists over whether the various forms of psychotherapy actually differ. Several major reviews of the literature (Bergin & Lambert, 1978; Luborsky, Singer, & Luborsky, 1975; Smith, Glass, & Miller, 1980) have found all forms of psychotherapy to be equally effective for most client problems, with the exception that the behavioral therapies are superior for treating phobias. Despite such findings, many psychologists still believe that the various forms of treatment do differ in process and outcome. Perhaps our current outcome measures are not sensitive enough to pick up the different effects. Alternatively, it may be that various treatments have different means or methods of achieving relatively similar results. Process measures would seem to present a possible means for demonstrating such differences.

A related field of research that has received considerable attention is that of nonspecific or common factors across therapies (Frank, 1973; Goldfried, 1980). Such theories suggest that the curative elements are those that exist in or are common to all forms of treatment rather than those that are unique to each form of treatment. However, such common factors are usually described in very ambiguous and global terms rather than in an operational fashion. A system such as the Intentions List, which is designed to measure cognitions specifically related to most forms of treatment but which uses neutral language acceptable to all orientations, offers a promising means to investigate the common versus the specific factors across treatments. For example, it may be that although therapists of various orientations do differ on the use of some of the intentions, they may all use other intentions equally. If these intentions were found to be the important ones leading to client change, this would bolster evidence that the important factors are those common to all therapies.

Methodological Issues

Since intentions are covert, they cannot be measured directly by observations of overt behavior. Further, thoughts cannot be measured directly during an actual session because such intrusion would destroy the nature of the therapeutic interaction. The most promising means to measure intentions seems to be through the therapist's retrospective recall of videotaped or audiotaped sessions, using methods of interpersonal process recall developed by Kagan (1975) and refined for research by Elliott (1986). The tape is stopped after each therapist statement, and the therapist recollects the rationale for each statement by indicating which intentions were being used.

An additional issue raised in devising our list of intentions was the use of generic labels devoid of a specific theoretical orientation. Generic labels and definitions were seen as more appropriate for capturing processes that underlie all theoretical orientations. These intentions should apply to counselors and therapists in all forms of counseling and therapy, all theoretical orientations, and all modalities (individual, group, family, and consultation). (Since there is no empirical evidence that different behaviors occur between *counselors* and *psychotherapists*, we will use the terms interchangeably.)

Further, by design, the intentions do not focus on change in specific content areas such as sexuality, assertiveness, or interpersonal relationships. Rather, the intentions are phrased as generally related to thoughts, feelings, behaviors, and attitudes.

The focus of this system was restricted to immediate intentions, that is, the intentions therapists have for the immediate effect of their verbal response on the client. This decision was made to help differentiate intentions from broader conceptualizations, such as strategies (Goldfried, 1980), which cover larger portions of sessions.

Finally, while the underlying rationale for all interventions is to lead ultimately to change, that concept is too general and elusive to denote the type of change. Thus, we conceptualized intentions as smaller and more specific categories that serve as the building blocks toward change. Some of these intentions, however, are still more general and may occur throughout larger portions of treatment (e.g., to support and build rapport), whereas others may be more specific and contained (e.g., to focus).

At any given time, more than one intention may be operating. For instance, a therapist may intend to identify maladaptive behaviors while also trying to support. Thus, intentions are not mutually exclusive and more than one may be used simultaneously.

Development of the Intentions List

The original system was rationally derived; that is, intentions were suggested that might be used by counselors or therapists from a variety of styles, orientations, and approaches. The major theoretical orientations were reviewed for what they postulated as major aims or goals for treatment. Meador and Rogers (1984) proposed that clients ideally would come to experience feelings with immediacy and richness of detail and to accept ownership of these feelings. Psychoanalytic theorists (Fine, 1973; Malan, 1979) have suggested that clients should gain understanding and insight into their thoughts and feelings, overcome resistance, and resolve transferences. For Haley (1976) and Minuchin (1974), a reframing is crucial to change. For Ellis (1962), changes in thoughts or cognitions from irrational to rational would be the desired client behavior change. For Lazarus (1981), changes in behavior, affect, sensation, imagery, cognition, interpersonal relationships, and drug/biological areas are necessary. Frank (1973) suggested that major change needs to occur in the restoration of hope. These examples illustrate the diversity of theoretical goals that therapists have for client behavior.

Several sources were also reviewed for discussions of general aims and goals common to all forms of treatments. For example, Goldfried (1980) noted that therapists from all orientations give feedback about behavior; Orlinsky and Howard (1975) measured client reactions of self-control, hope, and cathart (in addition to those mentioned above for specific theories) on their Therapy Session Report. Sloane, Staples, Cristol, Yorkston, and Whipple (1975) listed several specific aims that differentiated psychoanalytic and behavior therapies.

The rationally derived Intentions List was revised through several stages. First, five experienced counseling psychologists reviewed an audiotape of a counseling session and told a researcher what their intentions were for each response. These open-ended statements were used by a team of researchers to modify the list. In the next stage, seven experienced counselors each reviewed an audiotape and used the list to indicate their intentions. Further, the therapist statements in these tapes were judged according to response modes (Hill et al., 1981) by two trained judges. These data were analyzed to determine whether intentions were associated with specific response modes. The list was again revised based on feedback.

At this point, we wanted to know when the hypothetical links occurred between intentions and response modes, and we wanted feedback from a larger number of therapists about the list. Twelve experienced counselors and 12 graduate students were provided the two lists and asked which response modes they would use to implement each of the intentions. Their feedback and the results of the analysis were used to revise the list. The study was then replicated using the revised list with a new sample of 40 experienced counselors and therapists. The two studies yielded fairly consistent results, indicating that therapists do systematically link two or three response modes with each intention. Further, there was an encouraging amount of convergence in the results of the two studies.

The list was again revised for a case study (Hill, Carter, & O'Farrell, 1983) to include intentions representative of the counselor's cognitive processes. The counselor and two judges independently categorized the intentions based on reading transcripts several months after the sessions occurred. These categorizations were then discussed until a consensus view was reached.

Based on the results of the case study, the list was again revised. The new list was given to 15 therapists who were asked to estimate on a 1–5 scale how much they would use each intention in the next session with two different clients. A correlational analysis was then used to determine categories that could be combined to reduce overlap.

The final list contains 19 categories with minimal overlap between categories. Throughout the stages of development, the list was used by practitioners from a wide variety of orientations and was seen to have face validity, to be inclusive of the range of intentions, and to have a neutral language with terms acceptable to all orientations. The final list is shown in Table 1.

Study 1

A case study approach was used to capture the variety of responses that occur across the stages of treatment. A 20-session, time-limited therapy case between an experienced female counseling psychologist and a young, neurotic female client was used for this study. Details of the case (measures and outcome data) are reported elsewhere (O'Farrell, Hill, & Patton, 1984). The following questions were studied: (a) Do intentions vary across 20 sessions of treatment? (b) Are intentions linked systematically with therapist response modes? and (c) Are intentions linked systematically with client response modes?

Method

Measures

The 19-item Intentions List was used to measure therapist intentions.

The Counselor Verbal Response Category System (Hill, 1978; Hill et al., 1981) includes 14 nominal, mutually exclusive categories: minimal encourager, silence, approval–reassurance, information, direct guidance, closed question, open question, restatement, reflection, interpretation, confrontation, self-disclosure, nonverbal referent, and other. Client reactions were measured via the Client Verbal Response Category System (Hill et al., 1981), which includes nine nominal, mutually exclusive categories: simple responses, requests, description, experiencing, exploration of relationship, insight, discussion of plans, silence, and other. Both of these systems have adequate face and content validity as well as high agreement levels, as established in previous research (Hill, 1986).

Procedure

Since highly accurate transcripts were desired to answer our three questions, judgments of intentions for a given session were done approximately 1–2 months after that session had been completed, when transcripts were available. To facilitate memory and simulate the actual experiential quality of the sessions, the therapist reviewed case notes, discussed the case with her co-researchers, and reviewed several sessions at the same time. For each session, the therapist read the transcript and after each of her speaking turns marked as many intentions as applied. If a turn contained distinct segments, the therapist marked intentions separately, indicating where each segment began.

Counselor and client response modes were judged by separate teams of three trained judges for each session. These judges had no knowledge of the Intentions List. To do the ratings, judges independently rated all response units on a transcript

Table 1—*List of Intentions*

Instructions

To judge intentions, the therapist should review the tape within 24 hours so that the session is as fresh and vivid in memory as possible. The therapist should stop the tape after each therapist turn (everything the therapist says between two client speech acts, excluding minimal phrases) and indicate as many intentions as applied for that turn. You should strive to remember exactly what was going through your mind right at the time of the intervention *and* be as honest as possible in reporting what you were actually thinking. Remember that there are no right or wrong answers; the purpose is simply to uncover what you planned to do at that moment. Also remember that you should indicate your intentions only for that immediate intervention, rather than report global strategies for the entire session. Note that not every phrase in the definition for each intention needs to fit to judge that the intention applies. In general, the therapist should choose those intentions that best apply, even if all the phrasing is not exactly applicable to the current situation or does not fit the way he or she would say it.

Intentions

1. **Set limits:** To structure, make arrangements, establish goals and objectives of treatment, outline methods to attain goals, correct expectations about treatment, or establish rules or parameters of relationship (e.g., time, fees, cancellation policies, homework).
2. **Get information:** To find out specific facts about history, client functioning, future plans, and so on.
3. **Give information:** To educate, give facts, correct misperceptions or misinformation, give reasons for therapist's behavior or procedures.
4. **Support:** To provide a warm, supportive, empathic environment; increase trust and rapport and build relationship; help client feel accepted, understood, comfortable, reassured, and less anxious; help establish a person-to-person relationship.
5. **Focus:** To help client get back on the track, change subject, channel or structure the discussion if he or she is unable to begin or has been diffuse or rambling.
6. **Clarify:** To provide or solicit more elaboration, emphasis, or specification when client or therapist has been vague, incomplete, confusing, contradictory, or inaudible.
7. **Hope:** To convey the expectation that change is possible and likely to occur, convey that the therapist will be able to help the client, restore morale, build up the client's confidence to make changes.
8. **Cathart:** To promote relief from tension or unhappy feelings, allow the client a chance to let go or talk through feelings and problems.
9. **Cognitions:** To identify maladaptive, illogical, or irrational thoughts or attitudes (e.g., "I must be perfect").
10. **Behaviors:** To identify and give feedback about the client's inappropriate or maladaptive behaviors and/or their consequences, do a behavioral analysis, point out games.
11. **Self-control:** To encourage client to own or gain a sense of mastery or control over his or her own thoughts, feelings, behaviors, or impulses; help client become more appropriately internal rather than inappropriately external in taking responsibility for his or her role.
12. **Feelings:** To identify, intensity, and/or enable acceptance of feelings; encourage or provoke the client to become aware of or deepen underlying or hidden feelings or affect or experience feelings at a deeper level.

Table continues

Table 1—*Continued*

13. **Insight:** To encourage understanding of the underlying reasons, dynamics, assumptions, or unconscious motivations for cognitions, behaviors, attitudes, or feelings. May include an understanding of client's reactions to others' behaviors.
14. **Change:** To build and develop new and more adaptive skills, behaviors, or cognitions in dealing with self and others. May be to instill new, more adaptive assumptive models, frameworks, explanations, or conceptualizations. May be to give an assessment or option about client functioning that will help client see self in new way.
15. **Reinforce change:** To give positive reinforcement or feedback about behavioral, cognitive, or affective attempts at change to enhance the probability that the change will be continued or maintained; encourage risk taking and new ways of behaving.
16. **Resistance:** To overcome obstacles to change or progress. May discuss failure to adhere to therapeutic procedures, either in past or to prevent possibility of such failure in future.
17. **Challenge:** To jolt the client out of a present state; shake up current beliefs or feelings; test validity, adequacy, reality, or appropriateness of beliefs, thoughts, feelings, or behaviors; help client question the necessity of maintaining old patterns.
18. **Relationship:** To resolve problems as they arise in the relationship in order to build or maintain a smooth working alliance; heal ruptures in the alliance; deal with dependency issues appropriate to stage in treatment; uncover and resolve distortions in client's thinking about the relationship that are based on past experiences rather than current reality.
19. **Therapist needs:** To protect, relieve, or defend the therapist; alleviate anxiety. May try unduly to persuade, argue, or feel good or superior at the expense of the client.

and then met and resolved discrepancies. Average interjudge agreement levels (Kappas) were .71 for the counselor system and .71 for the client system.

Results

To determine whether intentions varied across treatment, two-tailed correlations were done between session number and proportion of each category of intention used per session. (Graphs also were drawn to check whether relationships were linear.) Results indicated that "set limits" decreased across sessions ($r = -.44$, $p < .05$), "get information" decreased ($r = -.55$, $p < .01$), "support" decreased ($r = -.53$, $p < .05$), "clarify" decreased ($r = -.62$, $p < .01$), "hope" decreased ($r = -.64$, $p < .01$), "cathart" decreased ($r = -.61$, $p < .01$), "insight" increased ($r = .53$, $p < .05$), "change" increased ($r = .68$, $p < .001$), and "reinforce change" increased ($r = .15$, $p < .05$).

An analysis for within-session trends compared the first third to the final two thirds of all 20 sessions, using t tests for related measures. Results showed decreases in "get information," $t(19) = 2.31$, $p < .05$; decreases in "clarify," $t(19) = 2.77$, $p < .05$; and decreases in "cathart," $t(19) = 2.27$, $p < .05$.

A sequential analysis was done to determine whether intentions predictably led to certain therapist response modes. A sequential analysis essentially examines the proportion of the occurrence of a given response mode in relationship to the occurrence of all response modes that occur after that intention and then compares that number to the total occurrence of the given response mode to all other response modes. A sequential analysis was seen as an appropriate statistic because of our theoretical assumption that intentions precede and guide behaviors. Sequential analyses also were used in a previous case study (Hill et al., 1983). The results are presented in Table 2.

Another sequential analysis was done to determine whether intentions predictably led to certain client response modes. The results are presented in Table 3. It was disappointing that no associations were found between any of the intentions and the client response mode of insight, although the low frequency of occurrence of insight may have affected results.

Table 4 presents the average usage of each of the 19 intentions for the entire case study.

Discussion

Results from the analysis of the case indicated that the most frequently used intentions for this particular therapist were "insight," "behaviors," "feelings," "change," "challenge," and "self-control," supporting her self-description as relationship/insight-oriented and active-directive. Thus, a profile of intentions usage can provide a process measure of orientation based on actual cognitive behavior.

Intentions varied systematically across treatment, with decreases in "set limits," "get information," "support," "clarify," "hope," and "cathart," as compared to increases in "insight," "change," and "reinforce change." These findings suggest that in the beginning of treatment the therapist focused on assessment and support, followed by greater efforts to instill insight and promote change. These changes across treatment provide tentative support for a stage model (Carkhuff, 1969; Cashdan, 1973). It is interesting that somewhat similar patterns were found for changes within sessions, such that "get information," "clarify," and "cathart" decreased. This suggests that the pattern of therapist behavior within sessions is similar to the overall pattern across treatment.

Evidence was found for linkages between therapist intentions and therapist response modes. Several of the sequences between intentions and therapist response modes had been found in the preliminary stages of measure development, providing greater support for these associations. Those sequences that have been replicated in at least two of the four sequential analyses (three pilot studies and Study 1) using similar items are shown in Table 5. Also shown in Table 5 are results for nine of the intentions in the present list ("set limits," "clarify," "hope," "cathart," "behaviors," "self-control," "reinforce change," "resistance," and "relationship") that had no clear precursor items in previous versions; these sequences need to be viewed with more caution because they may be idiosyncratic to the therapist in Study 1.

These data provide a preliminary empirical pattern of associations between therapist intentions and response modes that should be quite useful for training. Indeed, training models have made such connections before (e.g., Carkhuff, 1969; Goodman & Dooley, 1976), but they were not empirically derived. These findings also support the notion that there are various verbal channels to implement intentions, rather than a fixed one-to-one correspondence between an intention and a specific response

Table 2—A Sequential Analysis of Therapist Response Modes Most Likely to Follow Therapist Intentions

Intention	Therapist response mode									
	Approval reassurance	Information	Direct guidance	Closed question	Open question	Restatement	Reflection	Interpretation	Confrontation	Self-disclosure
1. Set limits	.05$^+$	.65^{+++}	.17^{+++}	.04^{++}	.02	.01^{---}	.01$^-$	.04^{---}	.02^{--}	.00$^-$
2. Get information	.01	.14	.01	.39^{+++}	.36^{+++}	.07	.00	.01^{---}	.01^{---}	.00
3. Give information	.06^{++}	.50^{+++}	.04	.01	.00^{--}	.02^{--}	.02	.22^{---}	.11^{---}	.01
4. Support	.15^{+++}	.08^{--}	.01$^-$	.01	.02	.18^{+++}	.06^{+++}	.35	.11$^-$	.03
5. Focus	.07	.29^{++}	.00	.02	.13^{+++}	.07	.02	.29	.11^{--}	.00
6. Clarify	.02	.07^{--}	.00^{--}	.07^{+++}	.03	.29^{+++}	.04^{++}	.37	.09^{--}	.01
7. Hope	.15^{+++}	.31^{+++}	.04	.00	.02	.04	.04	.28$^-$	.12^{--}	.01
8. Cathart	.02	.06	.00	.05	.17^{+++}	.13$^+$	.20^{+++}	.24$^-$	.07^{--}	.05
9. Cognitions	.01^{--}	.04^{---}	.02$^-$	.01	.07^{+++}	.06	.01$^-$	.38	.39^{+++}	.01^{--}
10. Behaviors	.02$^-$	.10^{---}	.03	.01	.02$^-$	.06	.01$^-$	.36	.36^{+++}	.03$^+$
11. Self-control	.02$^-$	.06^{---}	.03	.01$^-$	.03	.07	.01$^-$	.40	.37^{+++}	.00^{--}
12. Feelings	.03	.06^{--}	.02	.02	.05^{+++}	.08	.08^{+++}	.39$^+$	.26	.01$^-$
13. Insight	.02^{--}	.08^{---}	.02^{--}	.01^{---}	.02^{---}	.05^{--}	.01$^-$	.59^{+++}	.21$^-$	.01$^-$
14. Change	.05^{+++}	.15$^+$	.09^{+++}	.01	.02	.05^{--}	.01$^-$	.37	.23$^-$	.01$^-$
15. Reinforce change	.18^{+++}	.05^{---}	.01	.01	.01$^-$	.07	.04$^+$	.46^{+++}	.15^{--}	.00
16. Resistance	.02	.16	.09^{+++}	.02	.04	.03^{--}	.00^{--}	.34	.23	.06^{+++}
17. Challenge	.01^{---}	.06^{---}	.01^{---}	.00	.01^{---}	.08	.01$^-$	.25$^+$	.57^{+++}	.01^{--}
18. Relationship	.01^{---}	.17^{++}	.02	.02	.07^{+++}	.08	.01	.42$^+$	.13$^-$	.06^{+++}
19. Therapist needs	.05	.38^{+++}	.03	.01	.03	.01^{---}	.00	.22^{--}	.15^{--}	.12^{+++}

Note. Table figures refer to the proportion of therapist response modes that occurred in response to each therapist intention with the case study in Study 1. Higher numbers indicate more frequent occurrence. Pluses indicate that this sequence occurred more than would be expected by chance ($+ = p < .05$; $++ = p < .01$; $+++ = p < .001$). Minuses indicate less-than-chance occurrence ($- = p < .05$; $-- = p < .01$; $--- = p < .001$).

Table 3—*Sequential Analysis of Client Response Modes Most Likely
to Follow Therapist Intentions*

	Client response mode				
Intention	Requests	Description	Experiencing	Relationship	Insight
1. Set limits	$.18^{+++}$	.57	$.22^-$	.00	.03
2. Get information	.02	$.75^{+++}$	$.23^{--}$	.00	.00
3. Give information	$.13^{+++}$	.63	.24	.00	.00
4. Support	.02	.62	.35	.02	.00
5. Focus	.04	.75	.17	.04	.00
6. Clarify	$.01^-$	.61	.33	.05	.01
7. Hope	.08	.50	.35	.02	.05
8. Cathart	.00	.66	.25	$.09^{++}$	.00
9. Cognitions	.03	.58	.34	.02	.03
10. Behaviors	.05	$.64^+$	$.28^-$	.03	.01
11. Self-control	.02	.58	.34	.02	.02
12. Feelings	.02	$.50^{--}$	$.44^{+++}$	.02	.01
13. Insight	.04	.55	.38	$.01^{--}$	.03
14. Change	.04	.52	.41	.01	.01
15. Reinforce change	.01	.52	.43	.01	.03
16. Resistance	.05	.51	.36	$.07^{++}$	.01
17. Challenge	.02	$.63^+$	.32	.01	.02
18. Relationship	.03	$.49^-$	.33	$.12^{+++}$	.02
19. Therapist needs	.05	.58	.27	$.08^+$	.02

Note. Table figures refer to the proportion of client response modes that occurred in response to each therapist intention with the case study in Study 1. Higher numbers indicate more frequent occurrence. Pluses indicate that this sequence occurred more than would be expected by chance ($+ = p < .05$; $++ = p < .01$; $+++ = p < .001$). Minuses indicate less-than-chance occurrence ($- = p < .05$; $-- = p < .01$; $--- = p < .001$).

mode. For example, therapists choose to set limits via information, direct guidance, or closed question, all of which probably have different impacts. This analysis also shows the danger in assuming that any single therapist response mode always has a uniform intention. Self-disclosure, for example, is done to deal with resistance, resolve issues in the relationship, or handle therapist needs. All of these seem quite different and probably result in different client reactions.

The linkage of intentions with client response modes also indicated some clear connections: Clients make more requests after "set limits" and "give information"; do more description after "get information" and less after "feelings"; do more experiencing after "feelings" and less after "get information"; and discuss the relationship more after "cathart," "resistance," and "relationship" and less after "insight." These linkages make clinical sense in that the client did respond as the therapist intended in some cases. However, we were particularly disappointed in the results from the client measure because it did not seem parallel to the therapist intentions measure and was therefore unable to pick up the richness of the client's response. For instance, there was no way of knowing if the client focused more, understood irrational cognitions, or felt challenged. Further, if we believe that sub-

Table 4—*Proportions of Intentions From Study 1 and Study 2*

	Study 1		Study 2	
Intentions	M	SD	M	SD
1. Set limits	.03	.03	.04	.04
2. Get information	.02	.02	.08	.08
3. Give information	.03	.04	.04	.04
4. Support	.03	.04	.07	.07
5. Focus	.01	.01	.06	.05
6. Clarify	.04	.03	.15	.13
7. Hope	.02	.03	.02	.02
8. Cathart	.01	.01	.03	.04
9. Cognitions	.06	.04	.03	.04
10. Behaviors	.10	.05	.03	.04
11. Self-control	.09	.05	.03	.03
12. Feelings	.10	.04	.10	.08
13. Insight	.15	.06	.13	.10
14. Change	.10	.08	.08	.12
15. Reinforce change	.04	.04	.04	.05
16. Resistance	.03	.04	.02	.02
17. Challenge	.10	.05	.04	.04
18. Relationship	.05	.06	.02	.04
19. Therapist needs	.02	.03	.00	.01

Note. Study 1 was a case study with 20 sessions; Study 2 had 42 therapists each doing a middle session with a neurotic client.

jective reports are crucial, a measure that studies the client's subjective reactions in addition to objective judges' ratings would be helpful. We are in the process of developing such a measure.

An additional problem with the linkage of intentions with client response modes was that we examined only the immediate client response. Some intentions may have an immediate effect whereas others may have delayed effects. Further work with more delayed sequential patterns might be useful to uncover these more complicated relationships.

Study 2

A demonstration of the applicability of the Intentions List across theoretical orientations was needed to show that the list was truly pantheoretical and inclusive of the range of possible intentions. Further, some construct validity could be shown if the Intentions List could differentiate therapeutic orientations.

Research has demonstrated that theoretical orientations differ in therapist's verbal response modes as judged by external judges (Brunink & Schroeder, 1979; Hill, Thames, & Rardin, 1979; Snyder, 1945; Stiles, 1979; Strupp, 1955). Extension of these findings to intentions would indicate that orientations differ in more than simple technical aspects.

Table 5—*Relationship Between Therapist Intentions and Response Modes*

Intentions	Therapist response modes	
	Most likely	Least likely
Get information[a]	Closed question	Interpretation
	Open question	Confrontation
Give information[a]	Information	Open question
		Restatement
Support[a]	Approval	Confrontation
Focus[a]	Closed question	
	Restatement	
Cognitions[a]	Open question	Information
Feelings[a]	Open question	Information
	Reflection	
Insight[a]	Interpretation	Approval
Change[a]	Direct guidance	Restatement
Challenge[a]	Confrontation	Approval
Therapist needs[a]	Approval	
	Self-disclosure	
Set limits[b]	Information	Restatement
	Direct guidance	Interpretation
	Closed question	Confrontation
Clarify[b]	Closed question	Information
	Restatement	Direct question
	Reflection	Confrontation
Hope[b]	Approval	Confrontation
	Information	
Cathart[b]	Open question	Confrontation
	Reflection	
Behaviors[b]	Confrontation	Approval
		Information
Self-control[b]	Interpretation	Information
		Closed question
		Confrontation
Reinforce change[b]	Approval	Information
	Interpretation	Confrontation
Resistance[b]	Direct guidance	Restatement
	Self-disclosure	Reflection
Relationship[b]	Information	Approval
	Open question	Confrontation
	Self-disclosure	

Note. These sequences were all significant at the *p* < .01 level.
[a]Sequences replicated in at least two of the four studies in this article (Pilot 2, 3, or 4 or Study 1).   [b]Sequences tested only in Study 1.

A problem immediately encountered in pursuing this question was in clearly delineating theoretical orientations. Several surveys (e.g., Garfield & Kurtz, 1974; Norcross & Prochaska, 1983) have indicated the growing number of practitioners who select eclectic as their primary preference rather than a specific orientation. In a recent survey of a random sample of 200 registrants of the National Register of Health Service Providers in Psychology, Wellner (1983) reported that 34% selected eclectic as their primary preference, whereas 20% indicated psychoanalytic, 14% indicated interpersonal relationship, and 10% indicated behavioral orientation as their preference. Further, Wellner (personal communication, July 2, 1984) reported that of 729 new members of the register, 38% selected eclectic, 19% were psychoanalytic, 10% were rational emotive, 9% were systems, 7% were interpersonal relationship, and 7% were behavioral. One problem with many of these surveys about orientation is that they require participants to choose a single orientation, which leads those who combine orientations to use the eclectic label. A preferable and yet simple way to measure orientation would be to have participants rate how much they believe in and adhere to each of the three major orientations (psychoanalytic, humanistic, and behavioral). This would perhaps give a better overall picture of orientation.

Several issues guided us in the design of this study. First, as demonstrated in Study 1, intentions differed based on stage of treatment, and therefore stage of treatment needed to be controlled. Since the major work of all treatments seems to occur in the middle of treatment, it seemed that middle sessions would have the greatest probability of revealing differences between orientations. Second, because in Study 1 and also in our past research (Hill, 1978; Hill et al., 1979; Hill et al., 1983) we have found differences within thirds of sessions, it seemed important to examine within-session changes. Third, because results of the pilot studies indicated that therapists probably have different intentions for different clients, client type needed to be controlled. For this study, only neurotic adult clients were studied. Fourth, clients from a variety of settings (counseling centers, private practice, community agencies) were desired to enhance the generalizability of results. Finally, it seemed desirable to study only experienced therapists, who were more likely to have developed their own styles and to have thought through what they hope to accomplish with clients.

Thus, the purpose of this study was to compare experienced therapists of psychoanalytic, humanistic, and behavioral orientations for their usage of intentions in middle sessions of an ongoing treatment with a neurotic individual or family. The following questions were studied: (a) Can persons holding different theoretical orientations be distinguished? (b) Is there a relationship between orientation and usage of the intentions? (c) Does usage of intentions vary across thirds of sessions? (d) Is usage of intentions related to experience, sex of therapist or client, or therapist-rated quality of the session? and (e) Can dimensions or clusters of intentions be identified?

Method

Participants

Forty-two (28 male, 14 female) practicing, experienced (i.e., postinternship) PhD therapists known to the authors from graduate school, present employment, professional societies, or referral by other therapists participated. Participants were from both the United States and Europe and represented a wide range of settings and orientations. The sample was highly experienced: The reported number of years' experience doing therapy averaged 10.24 ($SD = 6.27$). Of the 42 sessions, 38 involved individual (at least one hypnosis and one vocational) and 4 involved family therapy.

Measures

The 19-item Intentions List was used to measure therapist intentions.

For a measure of therapeutic orientation, therapists were asked to rate on a 5-point Likert scale (1 = *low,* 5 = *high*) how much they believed in and adhered to the techniques in psychoanalytic, humanistic, and behavioral orientations and to provide a short phrase describing their therapeutic orientation.

Therapists also were asked to rate overall quality of the session on a 1–5 scale where 1 = *very poor* and 5 = *very good.*

Procedure

Therapists were sent a cover letter containing an invitation to participate, a brief theoretical explanation of intentions (similar to the introduction of this article), the Intentions List, and instructions to audiotape a middle (i.e., not introductory or termination) session with a neurotic client. Within 24 hours of the session, therapists were to listen to the audiotape and record as many intentions as applied for each therapist turn (everything between two client speeches). To protect confidentiality, therapists were asked to return only their intentions recording sheet and not the tape of the session.

Each of the sessions was divided into thirds based on the number of speaking turns. (Because the tape was not available, exact division based on time was not possible. The present division, although not precise because therapists talk different amounts during different portions of sessions, was the best possible within constraints of the data.) The total number of intentions used in each category was calculated; this frequency was divided by the total number of intentions used during that period to give a proportion of the total. Proportion of the total was used rather than frequency to control for number of speaking turns (activity level) and the possible use of multiple intentions per turn.

Results

The average number of speaking turns per session was 61.50 ($SD = 34.29$). The average number of intentions was 100.24 ($SD = 62.97$). The average number of intentions used per turn was 1.47 ($SD = .53$). The average of rated overall quality of the session was 3.27 ($SD = .58$).

The right half of Table 4 presents the average usage of each of the 19 intentions for the entire sample. The most commonly used intentions by these experienced therapists in middle sessions with neurotic clients were "clarify," "insight," "feelings," "get information," "change," "support," and "focus," in total accounting for 67% of the intentions. It should be noted that the standard deviations for each intention were approximately the same as the mean, indicating a large variability.

Orientation

Regarding ratings (using 1–5 scales) on orientations, the average for the entire sample on psychoanalytic orientation was 2.98 ($SD = 1.05$), on humanistic orientation it was 3.33 ($SD = .69$), and on behavioral orientation it was 2.79 ($SD = 1.05$). The correlation between ratings on psychoanalytic and behavioral orientations was $-.45$ ($p < .01$), whereas none of the other correlations was significant. Years' experience, sex of therapist, therapist-rated quality of sessions, number of speaking turns per session, number of intentions, and number of intentions per turn were not significantly correlated with ratings of the three orientations, except in one instance: Number of intentions was related to humanistic ratings ($r = .31$, $p < .05$).

Of the 42 therapists in the sample, only 4 (10%) identified themselves solely with only one of the three orientations (i.e., rated the preferred orientation with a 4 or 5 while rating the other two orientations with a 1 or 2; two of these therapists were psychoanalytic, one was humanistic, and one was behavioral. It was much more typical ($N = 22$, 52%) for therapists to rate two of the three orientations at approximately equal high levels, such that psychoanalytic and humanistic orientations were rated 3 or 4 while behavioral was rated 1 or 2 ($N = 13$, 31%), or humanistic and behavioral orientations were rated 3 or 4 while psychoanalytic was rated 1 or 2 ($N = 9$, 21%). Also, a relatively high proportion ($N = 16$, 38%) rated all three at approximately equally high levels or did not have a clear pattern. Further, the short phrase describing their orientations proved to be vague and unhelpful in categorizing therapists. These results suggested that each therapist's ratings on all three orientations needed to be considered in combination rather than categorizing each therapist into a single orientation.

Effects of Orientation and Thirds of Sessions

To examine the relationship between therapist orientations and intentions across thirds of sessions, a multivariate multiple regression profile analysis was performed. Sessions were divided into thirds to determine whether the relative use of the 19 intentions varied across a session.

Three contrasts among these 57 dependent variables (relative proportion of use of the 19 intentions *within* thirds of a session) were employed to test three separate hypotheses. The first contrast was a test for each of the 19 intentions across the session. The independent variables, or predictors, were the ratings given by the therapists on the three orientations. Thus, this first analysis can be considered to correspond to a "main effect" of orientations, adjusted for the session "factor." The second contrast involved a comparison of the relative proportion of use of the 19 intentions during the first third of the session with the relative proportion of use during the second third of the session and, simultaneously, a comparison of the relative proportion of use of the 19 intentions during the second third of the session with the relative proportion of use during the final third of the session. The predictor variable in this case was simply the constant term, or grand mean effect. This test corresponds, then, to a test of the "main effect" of sessions—it answers the question of whether there is a change in the relative proportion of use of the 19 intentions across the sessions of the 42 therapists. Finally, the third analysis employs the same contrasts described above, with the predictor variables in this case being the therapist's three orientation ratings. This analysis, then, can be seen as a test of the "interaction" of therapists and sessions and an assessment of the question of whether therapists with differing orientations use the 19 intentions differentially across a session.

Each of the three effects was tested for significance at the .1 level. This more liberal alpha was chosen because the small sample size relative to the number of variables in an analysis such as this one uniformly produces low power to reject the null hypothesis. All tests of hypotheses were based on Pillai's F approximation to Pillai's V. All post hoc tests were determined by simultaneous test procedures, as described in Harris (1975).

Results of the test for the "main effect" of therapist orientations revealed a significant effect, $F(57, 66) = 1.39$, $p < .1$, canonical $R = .89$. A significant weighted contrast resulting from the post hoc multiple comparison procedure involved seven intentions: "give information," "clarify," "self-control," "feelings," "insight," "change," and "therapist needs." This weighted contrast model with the seven intentions resulted in an R of .796, a decrease in fit of only 3.22% over the model including all 19 intentions.

In an attempt to construct a prediction equation that might prove useful in interpreting these results, and to provide some utility for individuals who might make use of the intention measure in future research, an even more simplified prediction equation was constructed that weighted the predictors—that is, the three orientations ratings—as well as the seven criteria. Based on an examination of the regression coefficient and the unstandardized discriminant function coefficients, the following prediction equation was derived:

$$2P + H - B = 6GI + 2Cl + 5SC + 3F + 3I + 3Ch + 18N + 1.8,$$

where P = psychoanalytic, H = humanistic, B = behavioral, GI = give information, Cl = clarify, SC = self-control, F = feeling, I = insight, Ch = change, and N = therapist needs. This even more simplified prediction equation results in an R of .789, a loss of only 4.70% of the explained variation found in the equation involving all 19 intentions. The mean square error of this equation is 1.0. Thus, for example, a "pure" psychoanalytic therapist, who would provide ratings of 5, 1, and 1 on the respective orientation scales, would have a score of 10 (i.e., $2 \times 5 + 1 - 1$) on the orientations side of the equation and would be expected to have a sum of approximately 10 when adding the 7 weighted predictor intentions together. A "pure" behaviorist, on the other hand, who provided orientation ratings of 1, 1, and 5, would be expected to score -2 on the linear combination of the 7 weighted intentions. A therapist deviating more than approximately ± 2 points would be beyond the 95%

confidence level; this prediction equation could be used by future researchers as a rough guideline to compare similarity to this sample of therapists.

This analysis took the pattern of rating on all three orientations into account in the prediction equation because, as described earlier, therapists do not ascribe to a single orientation. It reveals that intentions are predictable based on the relative importance given to these orientations. But this analysis does not provide information about how individual intentions relate to each orientation. Keeping the cautionary note in mind that orientation patterns are more appropriate than single orientation ratings, we did univariate correlations of the intentions with the orientations. These indicated significant relationships for 7 of the 19 intentions: "Set limits" was positively related to behavioral ratings ($r = .43$, $p < .01$); "focus" was negatively related to psychoanalytic ratings ($r = -.32$, $p < .05$); "feelings" was positively related to psychoanalytic ratings ($r = .33$, $p < .05$) and negatively related to behavioral ratings ($r = -.39$, $p < .01$); "insight" was positively related to psychoanalytic ratings ($r = .51$, $p < .001$); "change" was negatively related to psychoanalytic ratings ($r = -.34$, $p < .05$) and positively related to the behavioral ratings ($r = .50$, $p < .001$); "reinforce change" was positively related to behavioral ratings ($r = .33$, $p < .05$); and "therapist needs" was positively related to humanistic ratings ($r = .31$, $p < .05$).

Results of the test for the "main effect" for sessions also revealed a significant effect, $F(38, 1) = 95.67$, $p < .1$, canonical $R = .99$. Post hoc simultaneous test procedures showed that the use of the 19 intentions, considered simultaneously, differed between the first third of the session and the second third of the session, and likewise between the second and final thirds. Multiple comparison procedures on the respective change in the relative use of each of the 19 intentions considered individually, for these two contrasts, showed the pattern of changes found in Table 6.

The interaction term was nonsignificant ($p > .1$), indicating that there was not an interaction between orientation and time in the session. Thus, these changes across the session were patterns that held true for all orientations.

Relationship to Other Variables

Use of intentions was not related to sex of therapist or client. The therapist's years of experience was negatively related to use of only one intention, "support" ($r = -.33$, $p < .05$), which could be due to chance.

Ratings of overall quality of the session were correlated with the usage of the following intentions: "get information" ($r = -.29$, $p = .06$), "support" ($r = -.33$, $p = .03$), "focus" ($r = .34$, $p = .03$), and "feelings" ($r = .36$, $p = .02$). Ratings of quality were not related to ratings on the three orientations. Thus, across the whole sample, the sessions the therapists considered best were ones in which they intended more to focus on and deal with feelings than to get information and support.

Multidimensional Scaling of Intentions

Because the instructions allowed for therapists to list multiple intentions, a co-occurrence table was constructed to determine which intentions were used alone and

Table 6—*Mean Change in Relative Use of the 19 Intentions Across the Session*

Intentions	Rank order 1st third	Rank order 2nd third	Rank order 3rd third	1st third vs. 2nd third	2nd third vs. 3rd third
1. Set limits	9	16	17	.02	.04*
2. Get information	2	2	14	.07*	.16*
3. Give information	7	10	6	.03*	−.05*
4. Support	5	7	13	.05*	.07*
5. Focus	3	9	3	.17*	−.12*
6. Clarify	1	1	5	.23*	.07*
7. Hope	8	13	10	.02	−.03*
8. Cathart	13	11	1	−.03*	−.26*
9. Cognitions	16	17	15	−.04*	.01
10. Behaviors	15	18	11	−.01	−.05*
11. Self control	10	14	12	.01	−.02
12. Feelings	19	3	7	−.24*	.03
13. Insight	18	12	2	−.11*	−.16*
14. Change	17	5	4	−.16*	−.02
15. Reinforce change	4	6	9	.04*	.04
16. Resistance	12	19	18	.02	.03*
17. Challenge	11	4	8	−.12*	.04*
18. Relationship	6	8	19	.04*	.17*
19. Therapist needs	14	15	16	−.01*	.04*

Note. An asterisk indicates a significant change. A positive value indicates an intention used proportionally more often during the earlier third than the later third of the session.

which were used in combination with others. A lower triangular table was made of all possible combinations of intentions, regardless of the order in which they were listed. A nonmetric multidimensional scaling analysis (ALSCAL; Young & Lewyckyj, 1979) was then done on these data to examine potential structure among the 19 intentions. A two-dimensional solution provided the optimal fit for these data, accounting for approximately 83% of the variance. The first dimension seemed to reflect support–assessment versus change, whereas the second dimension seemed to be of relationship problems versus therapeutic work. Five clusters could be identified: (a) "get information," "focus," "clarify"; (b) "feelings," "insight," "cognitions," "behaviors," "self-control"; (c) "challenge," "hope," "relationship," "support," and "cathart"; (d) "resistance," "therapist needs," "give information," and "set limits"; and (e) "change" and "reinforce change." Figure 1 presents graphically how these clusters are arranged along the two dimensions.

Discussion

Only 7 ("give information," "clarify," "self-control," "feelings," "insight," "change," and "therapist needs") of the 19 intentions were needed to differentiate the three therapeutic orientations in the multivariate multiple regression profile anal-

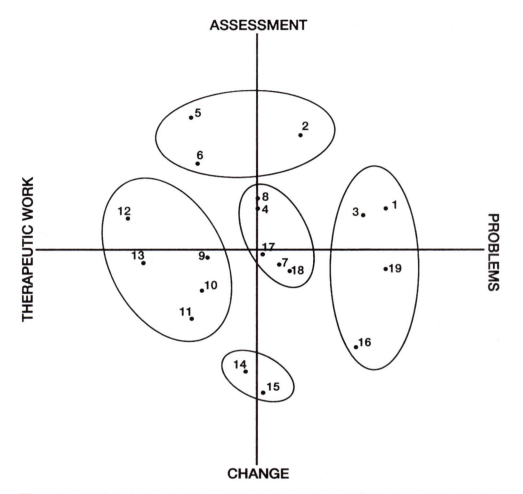

Figure 1. Multidimensional scaling solution to the structure of 19 intentions. (1 = set limits, 2 = get information, 3 = give information, 4 = support, 5 = focus, 6 = clarify, 7 = hope, 8 = cathart, 9 = cognitions, 10 = behaviors, 11 = self-control, 12 = feelings, 13 = insight, 14 = change, 15 = reinforce change, 16 = resistance, 17 = challenge, 18 = relationship, 19 = therapist needs.)

ysis. Further, in univariate correlations, "feelings" and "insight" were more frequently associated with the psychoanalytic orientation; "change," "set limits," and "reinforce change" were highly associated with the behavioral orientation; and "therapist needs" was associated with the humanistic orientation. These intentions seem to represent the central differences between orientation and, for the most part, fit with the theoretical formulations. Psychoanalytic theorists (e.g., Fine, 1973; Greenson, 1975) do discuss insight as a primary goal in treatment. It was surprising that "feelings" was associated more with the psychoanalytic orientation than with the humanistic orientation with its emphasis on experiencing. Examination of the multidimensional scaling solution indicated that "insight" and "feelings" were often used together, suggesting that this definition may have tapped primarily an emotional insight. It is interesting that "resistance," "relationship," and "therapist needs" were not seen as associated primarily with psychoanalytic theory, as one might expect from the literature. Perhaps because these were written in a neutral language, practitioners from all orientations could identify these intentions as ones they used. Evidently the need for these particular intentions arises only occasionally, because the incidence also is low.

Intentions associated with the behavioral orientation fit behaviorists' purposes of providing a great deal of structure and dealing with specific observable changes (e.g., Goldfried & Davison, 1976; Rimm & Masters, 1974). It is interesting that the intentions of "cognitions" and "behaviors" were not used more by behaviorists, again perhaps suggesting that when written in a neutral language, these are intentions used by all orientations.

Ability to admit to having personal needs fits with the humanistic valuing of openness (Meador & Rogers, 1984; Polster & Polster, 1974). But it was surprising that none of the more substantive intentions was related to the humanistic orientation. A perusal of the data, however, suggested very few "pure" humanistic types and rather found that humanistic values and techniques have been integrated into other orientations.

The other 10 intentions were used with equal frequency by therapists from varying orientations. This lends support to Goldfried's (1980) notions of commonalities among treatment. Perhaps these intentions depend more on client and situational variables. Thus, while the hallmark of a psychodynamic therapist might be to stimulate insight, perhaps he or she will focus on the relationship only if it seems particularly appropriate during that session. And in fact, if the relationship is interfering with progress in therapy, a behavioral therapist might be just as likely to discuss it as a psychodynamic therapist. These findings suggest that further research could seek those factors that stimulate therapists to use specific intentions at a given time.

What seemed more related to usage of intentions than orientation was the breakdown into thirds of sessions. Apparently, therapists across all orientations move through their middle sessions in a fairly similar manner, such that the beginning of a session is characterized by intentions to "clarify" and "get information," whereas the emphasis toward the end of a session shifts to intentions of "cathart,' "insight," and "change." The decreases in "clarify" and "get information" were also found in Study 1, indicating a strong tendency for sessions to progress along a consistent pattern. Thus, in the beginning of a session, therapists seem to wait to hear what the client brings up. They try to get information and clarify the problem. As the problem becomes clearer, they proceed to try to promote relief, to stimulate insight, and to help the client figure out how to change, all of which require more active therapeutic work. Further research could identify whether these patterns differ between good versus bad sessions. Another important question worth study is how therapists know to shift from assessment to therapeutic work.

Therapists' ratings of quality for the sessions were positively related to "focus" and "feelings" and negatively related to "get information" and "support," suggesting that all therapists have consistent notions about what makes a good session. This further suggests that if therapists get stuck in the preliminary assessment/supportive activities in a session, they are dissatisfied. They need to move on to other activities before they feel good about a session. Further work is needed in examining perceived effectiveness of each of the intentions.

Multidimensional Scaling

The multidimensional scaling solution, along with the results of change both within and across sessions, provided evidence of several clusters of intentions. The first cluster can be labeled *assessment*. These intentions generally seem to be used at the beginning of treatment and of each session. They represent the goals of finding out more about the presenting problems. These seem to be very basic skills used by all orientations to determine what the course of treatment will be. The second cluster, *therapeutic work*, is used when the therapist helps the client to reach a deeper or new cognitive or emotional understanding and to internalize responsibility. This cluster seems to be most associated with psychoanalytic orientation ratings. In the third cluster, *change*, the therapist actively tries to help the client learn and maintain new behaviors, feelings, or attitudes. These intentions are used more by behavioral therapists. The fourth cluster, *problems*, involves activities that generally block or prevent therapeutic working. Generally these problems must be overcome before therapeutic work can be done. The fifth cluster, *nonspecific factors*, involves intentions used during all points in treatment by all orientations. These intentions are connected to intentions in each of the other clusters. The first three clusters are similar to the stages of exploration, understanding, and action described by Carkhuff (1969) and Egan (1982). However, the term *stages* does not seem appropriate because they recur within sessions. Cluster seems to be a more appropriate concept, with the notion that with each new problem area or session, the therapist begins the assessment procedure anew. The final two clusters add substantially to Carkhuff's and Egan's models by providing intentions for working with clients during problem and relationship-maintaining periods, which certainly seem to occur with most clients.

General Discussion

Throughout the course of several stages, we have developed a promising measure of therapist intentions. Therapists from a wide variety of theoretical orientations have both helped to validate the measure and used it to track their intentions within sessions. Comments by these therapists indicated that reviewing their sessions with the aid of the intentions measure was quite useful in helping them clarify often unverbalized reactions, suggesting that this measure might be a useful supervision tool. Therapists also indicated that the measure made clinical sense, covering most of the range of their thinking about their within-session behaviors.

Across both studies, the most frequently used intentions were "insight," "clarify," "feelings," and "change." Apparently these intentions are applicable across a wide variety of situations. Other intentions, such as "resistance," "hope," "relationship," or "therapist needs," seemed to occur less frequently and may be appropriate only for very specific circumstances. A comparison of the two studies indicated that the case study therapist in Study 1 used less "focus" but more "behaviors," "self-control," "challenge," and "therapist needs." One explanation for these differences is that in Study 1 all sessions were analyzed, whereas in Study 2 therapists were allowed to choose which session to analyze. Given that the mean quality rating was

3.27 out of a possible 5, it seems reasonable to assume that therapists chose good sessions that contained more focus and less anxiety with little need to challenge.

Conceptual Issues

Reliability of the intentions raises a particularly difficult issue, because we are essentially measuring the therapist's memory of what he or she was thinking at the moment. Clearly, memory fades over time, and the longer one waits to measure memory the less sure one can be as to what phenomenon one is measuring. Elliott (1986) emphasized the importance of having the review within 24 hours of the session to facilitate the actual memory of the intention. Thus, one can question whether it is actually possible to get an index of intrarater reliability. It seems that rather than test reliability, one would actually test memory loss. A similar problem exists with measuring interrater reliability. If intentions are a subjective phenomenon, only the therapist can be an accurate judge of what he or she was thinking, rendering the concept of interrater reliability meaningless. One would imagine that an outside judge may determine a therapist's intentions based on grammatical cues or on what he or she personally might have intended, rather than by actually being able to read the other person's mind. Further studies on this problem are certainly necessary to determine how to measure cognitions most accurately.

Another issue is whether therapists are actually intentional in their work. Because some therapists (e.g., Haley, 1976; Minuchin, 1974) carefully plan their strategies prior to sessions it is easy to see their work as intentional. Others, for example within a humanistic framework (e.g., Meador & Rogers, 1984; Napier & Whitaker, 1978; Polster & Polster, 1974), do not plan ahead but react to what the client brings up within the session. While these therapists might not determine their intentions in a structured manner, it seems they are still acting on an intentional basis; that is, they want the client to react in a certain manner, such as greater experiencing.

We have also discussed whether *intentions* is the best label or whether better terms would be *strategies, tactics, retrospections, aims, goals*, or *plans*. While the term *intentions* seems to capture the type of therapist activity being examined, questions can be raised regarding whether it is ever possible to capture with any degree of certainty the therapist's thought processes. There is a problem with remembering exactly what one was thinking at any retrospective point. Further, unknown demand characteristics might subtly bias the therapist's report. For example, a therapist's report. For example, a therapist might be reluctant to report that he or she was trying to relieve personal anxiety and might rather claim a more socially desirable response. Another problem is that at any given time a therapist can report only those intentions that were at a conscious level of awareness. If, for example, a therapist responds based on countertransference issues of which he or she is unaware, these issues cannot be reported.

An important issue is whether intentions add a great deal beyond simply measuring response modes (Hill, 1978). At minimum, intentions provide a measure of the therapist's perspective as opposed to objective judges' perceptions required for response modes. Beyond this, however, intentions seem to provide a measure that is more complex and clinically relevant in that it seems to capture more of what happens than does a simple grammatical measure such as response modes. Stiles (1979) has argued that many measures of response modes confuse intent and grammatical structure and has recommended that these are constructs that should be determined separately by objective judges. However, because intentions are by definition a subjective cognitive process, it does not seem feasible to have judges determine a therapist's intentions. Rather, it makes more sense to ask therapists directly what their intentions were. This illustration again points up the difference between response modes and intentions because therapists rarely will say what the grammatical structure was, but will say what they hoped to accomplish. Thus, response modes generally refer to a grammatical structure that can be observed behaviorally, whereas intentions refer to the internal processes of a therapist that might be quite undetectable to an outsider. These internal processes can be inferred by other persons but accuracy would always be in question. Indeed, it would be interesting to study whether other persons can judge a therapist's intentions. We would recommend that both response modes and intentions be measured as different aspects of the therapeutic process.

Work also needs to be done on the relationship between intentions (which are defined as occurring during speech turns) and more general strategies (which cover large portions of sessions). For example, Goldfried's (1980) strategy of giving feedback seems to be a constellation of specific intentions (e.g., behaviors, challenge, relationship), response modes (e.g., interpretation, self-disclosure, information), and nonverbal behaviors (e.g., eye contact). Measuring both general strategies and intentions seems desirable to study different levels of the process. For example, a therapist might be building toward a big shift by getting the client in touch with feelings and then challenging him or her. Looking only at the intentions for the immediate response would lose that long-term goal. It seems likely that more general strategies have to be measured via other methodologies, such as open-ended questions of the therapist.

Another conceptual challenge is further development of the sequential model presented at the beginning of this article. For example, how are the global input variables and immediate stimulus variables integrated in forming intentions? Are particular variables, such as problem severity or behavioral observations, more salient than other variables? One possibility is that intentions are affected by situation or context variables. Some recent theorists (Elliott, 1983; Rice & Greenberg, 1984) have pointed out the importance of examining the context in which process events occur. Thus, it is not as important to summarize frequency of intentions across a whole session as it is to examine what elicits a given intention. For example, it may be that certain conditions (e.g., a certain level of client experiencing) must be present before the therapist attempts to promote insight or behavior change. Conversely, the therapist undoubtedly has different intentions when presented with an angry client versus a friendly one or a client who is in a storytelling mood versus one at a crisis point. Similarly, different client types may evoke entirely different treatment strategies; for example, a therapist's intentions for dealing with a depressed client probably differ from those for dealing with a psychopathic client.

Another part of the model that needs to be tested is how therapists use feedback from clients to modify their intentions. Let's say that following the therapist's intention of challenge, the client becomes quiet and defensive. How does the therapist process that information and come up with a new intention? Clinicians (e.g., Greenson, 1975) have emphasized the importance of following up on an interpretation.

But we have little empirical data about when and how therapists think about their intervention, either when to shift or when to stick to the same strategy. In addition, we need much further specification of the range of behaviors that therapists use to implement their intentions. Nonverbal behaviors could certainly be examined in conjunction with verbal behaviors. From the other side of the equation, the client's reactions and responses need to be studied more thoroughly.

An obvious extension of these findings is to training and supervision. Many supervisors have told us that they typically review the supervisee's rationales or intentions to enable the supervisee to become more aware of what he or she is trying to accomplish. Reviewing intentions enables trainees to examine their motivations more carefully. After questioning and understanding their own intentions, trainees can more systematically examine their interventions and subsequent client reactions. We hope the development of the Intentions List can enhance this supervision process. Further research can determine how to best utilize these intentions in the training process.

References

Bergin, A. E., & Lambert, M. J. (1978). The evaluation of therapeutic outcomes. In S. L. Garfield & A. E. Bergin (Eds.), *Handbook of psychotherapy and behavior change* (2nd ed., pp. 139–190). New York: Wiley.

Brunink, S. A., & Schroeder, H. E. (1979). Verbal therapeutic behavior of expert psychoanalytically oriented, gestalt, and behavior therapists. *Journal of Consulting and Clinical Psychology, 47,* 567–574.

Carkhuff, R. R. (1969). *Human and helping relations* (Vols. 1 & 2). New York: Holt, Rinehart & Winston.

Cashdan, S. (1973). *Interactional psychotherapy: Stages and strategies in behavioral change.* New York: Grune & Stratton.

Egan, G. (1982). *The skilled helper.* Monterey, CA: Brooks/Cole.

Elliott, R. (1983). Fitting process research to the practicing psychotherapist. *Psychotherapy: Theory, Research and Practice, 20,* 49–55.

Elliott, R. (1986). Interpersonal process recall as a psychotherapy process research method. In L. S. Greenberg & W. M. Pinsof (Eds.), *The psychotherapeutic process: A research handbook* (pp. 503–528). New York: Guilford Press.

Elliott, R., & Feinstein, L. (1978). *Helping intention rating procedures: Overview and uses.* Unpublished manuscript, University of Toledo, Toledo, OH.

Ellis, A. (1962). *Reason and emotion in psychotherapy.* New York: Lyle Stuart & Citadel Press.

Fine, R. (1973). Psychoanalysis. In R. Corsini (Ed.), *Current psychotherapies* (pp. 1–33). Itasca, IL: Peacock.

Frank, J. D. (1973). *Persuasion and healing: A comparative study of psychotherapy* (rev. ed.). Baltimore, MD: Johns Hopkins University Press.

Garfield, S. L., & Kurtz, R. (1974). A survey of clinical psychologists: Characteristics, activities, and orientations. *The Clinical Psychologist, 28,* 7–10.

Goldfried, M. R. (1980). Toward the delineation of therapeutic change principles. *American Psychologist, 33,* 991–999.

Goldfried, M. R., & Davison, G. C. (1976). *Clinical behavior therapy.* New York: Holt, Rinehart & Winston.

Goodman, G., & Dooley, D. (1976). A framework for helping-intended communication. *Psychotherapy: Theory, Research and Practice, 13*, 106–117.

Greenson, R. R. (1975). *The technique and practice of psychoanalysis* (Vol. 1). New York: International Universities Press.

Haley, J. (1976). *Problem-solving therapy.* New York: Harper.

Harris, R. J. (1975). *A primer of multivariate statistics.* New York: Academic Press.

Hill, C. E. (1978). Development of a counselor verbal category system. *Journal of Counseling Psychology, 25*, 461–468.

Hill, C. E. (1986). An overview of the Hill counselor and client verbal response modes category systems. In L. S. Greenberg & W. M. Pinsof (Eds.), *The psychotherapeutic process: A research handbook* (pp. 131–160). New York: Guilford Press.

Hill, C. E., Carter, J. A., & O'Farrell, M. K. (1983). A case study of the process and outcome of time-limited counseling. *Journal of Counseling Psychology, 30*, 3–18.

Hill, C. E., Greenwald, C., Reed, K. G., Charles, D., O'Farrell, M. K., & Carter, J. A. (1981). *Manual for Counselor and Client Verbal Response Category Systems.* Columbus, OH: Marathon Consulting and Press.

Hill, C. E., Thames, T. B., & Rardin, D. K. (1979). Comparison of Rogers, Perls, and Ellis on the Hill Counselor Verbal Response Category System. *Journal of Counseling Psychology, 29*, 198–203.

Kagan, N. (1975). *Interpersonal process recall: A method of influencing human interaction.* Unpublished manuscript. (Available from N. Kagan, 434 Erickson Hall, College of Education, Michigan State University, East Lansing, MI 48824)

Lazarus, A. A. (1981). *The practice of multimodal therapy.* New York: McGraw-Hill.

Luborsky, L., Singer, B., & Luborsky, L. (1975). Comparative studies of psychotherapies. *Archives of General Psychiatry, 32*, 995–1008.

Mahoney, M. J., & Arnkoff, D. (1978). Cognitive and self-control therapies. In S. L. Garfield & A. E. Bergin (Eds.), *Handbook of psychotherapy and behavior change* (2nd ed., pp. 689–722). New York: Wiley.

Malan, D. H. (1979). *Individual psychotherapy and the science of psychodynamics.* London: Butterworths.

Meador, B. D., & Rogers, C. R. (1984). Person-centered therapy. In R. J. Corsini (Ed.), *Current psychotherapies* (3rd ed., pp. 142–195). Itasca, IL: Peacock.

Minuchin, S. (1974). *Families and family therapy.* Cambridge, MA: Harvard University Press.

Napier, A. Y., & Whitaker, C. A. (1978). *The family crucible.* New York: Bantam.

Norcross, J. C., & Prochaska, J. O. (1983). Psychotherapists in independent practice: Some findings and issues. *Professional Psychology: Research and Practice, 14*, 869–881.

O'Farrell, M. K., Hill, C. E., & Patton, S. (1984). *A comparison of two cases treated by the same therapist.* Unpublished manuscript, University of Maryland, College Park.

Orlinsky, D. E., & Howard, K. I. (1975). *Varieties of psychotherapeutic experience.* New York: Teachers College Press.

Polster, E., & Polster, M. (1974). *Gestalt therapy integrated.* New York: Random House.

Rice, L. N., & Greenberg, L. S. (1984). The new research paradigm. In L. Rice & L. Greenberg (Eds.), *Patterns of change: Intensive analysis of psychotherapy process* (pp. 7–25). New York: Guilford.

Rimm, D. C., & Masters, J. C. (1974). *Behavior therapy: Techniques and empirical findings.* New York: Academic Press.

Sloane, R. B., Staples, F. R., Cristol, A. H., Yorkston, N. J., & Whipple, K. (1975). *Psychotherapy vs. behavior change.* Cambridge, MA: Harvard University Press.

Smith, M. L., Glass, G. V., & Miller, M. I. (1980). *The benefits of psychotherapy.* Baltimore, MD: Johns Hopkins University Press.

Snyder, W. A. (1945). An investigation of the nature of nondirective psychotherapy. *Journal of General Psychology, 33*, 193–223.

Stiles, W. B. (1979). Verbal response modes and psychotherapeutic techniques. *Psychiatry, 42*, 49–62.

Strupp, H. H. (1955). An objective comparison of Rogerian and psychoanalytic techniques. *Journal of Psychology, 19*, 1–7.

Wellner, A. M. (Ed.) (1983). Characteristics of services—preliminary overview. *Register Report, 18*, 3–4.

Young, F. W., & Lewyckyj, R. (1979). *ALSCAL–4: User's guide.* Chapel Hill, NC: Author.

Chapter 6
METHODOLOGICAL EXAMINATION OF VIDEOTAPE-ASSISTED REVIEWS IN BRIEF THERAPY:
Helpfulness Ratings, Therapist Intentions, Client Reactions, Mood, and Session Evaluation

Clara E. Hill, Kevin E. O'Grady, Victoria Balenger, Wilfried Busse, Dana R. Falk, Mary Hill, Peggy Rios, and Rick Taffe

One of the continuing issues in process research has concerned the impact that the methods and measures used have on the data collected and the conclusions drawn (see Hill, 1991, and Lambert & Hill, 1994, for reviews). For example, an ongoing concern has been that data collection may be unduly intrusive and may alter the quality or nature of the therapeutic interaction. Other concerns have been expressed about the reliability and validity of process measures and the effects of situational variables on data. Because the results of any study are only as good as the quality of the data generated, researchers need to have evidence that supports the efficacy of their methods and measures.

In this study, we focused on several issues that may influence the results of process studies: (a) the validity of videotape-assisted reviews as a means of studying process, in terms of whether ratings made during videotape-assisted reviews reflect experiences during sessions and whether videotape-assisted reviews influence mood and evaluations of session quality; (b) the stability and validity of helpfulness ratings; (c) the stability of therapist intentions and client reactions; and (d) the effects of client and therapist mood on postsession judgments.

Validity of Videotape-Assisted Reviews

An increasing number of studies involve videotape-assisted reviews to collect data from therapists and clients about their experiences during therapy sessions (e.g., Elliott, 1985, 1986; Hill, 1989; Hill, Thompson, & Corbett, 1992; Kivlighan, 1990; Martin, Martin, Meyer, & Slemon, 1986; Thompson & Hill, 1991). The use of videotape-assisted reviews to collect process data has been viewed as a major methodological breakthrough because participants can provide subjective information about what was happening during sessions without an intrusion into the therapy process (Elliott, 1986; Elliott & Shapiro, 1988). Only one study was found, however, that examined the issue of the similarity of reviews to sessions. In that analogue

Reprinted from *Journal of Counseling Psychology, 41*, 236–247 (1994). Copyright © 1994 by the American Psychological Association. Used with permission of the first author.

An earlier version of this article was presented at the annual meeting of the Society for Psychotherapy Research, Pittsburgh, Pennsylvania, in June 1993.

We thank Joan Jeranek and Cindy Schaffer for coding the data and Robert Elliott for his comments as a discussant on the article. We also acknowledge that the suggestion to study the effects of mood on process judgments came from Changming Duan, University of Missouri—Columbia.

study, Katz and Resnikoff (1977) found moderate correlations between live ratings of comfort or discomfort and ratings recalled during videotape stimulation.

Hence, questions remain about whether responses obtained during videotape reviews are accurate representations of experiences during actual sessions (Friedlander, 1992). Establishing the accuracy of such data is crucial for the support of claims that videotape-assisted review data are valid.

Elliott (1986) has suggested that videotape-assisted reviews be done within 48 hr of the session to increase the likelihood that participants will be able to return to the experiential framework of the session. Anecdotal information from clients and therapists in our research indicated that they could reexperience the events of sessions when reviews were conducted immediately after the session. Such subjective impressions are hardly reliable evidence, however, in the determination of whether participants can actually reexperience what they were feeling and thinking during sessions. In reality, placing oneself back into the experience of the session may be difficult or impossible. During therapy sessions, participants are involved and actively participating, whereas during reviews of sessions, participants take on observer or evaluative roles. These different perspectives (experiential vs. evaluative) may result in different feelings and judgments about what happens in sessions.

Furthermore, the evaluation of a session event during a review may be influenced by events that occurred subsequent to a particular event during the session. For example, therapist confrontations may strike clients as very unhelpful in the immediate moment, and they may rate them negatively if given an opportunity at that particular moment. But if therapists handle the events well, clients may come to trust and respect their therapists more, thus leading them to rate the confrontations more positively in a subsequent review. In effect, resolving events within sessions may lead clients to assimilate new learnings, which might lead to changes in their perceptions of events (see Barkham, 1988). Similarly, therapist perspectives might change after they view the effects of their interventions. For example, when clients initially react defensively but then go on to explore productively, therapists might evaluate the initial response more favorably because they recall what came later. Related research on anchoring of clinical judgment has found that data presented in earlier parts of an interview influence judgments of later parts of the same interview (Ellis, Robbins, Schult, Ladany, & Banker, 1990; Pain & Sharpley, 1988, 1989).

Thus, the first purpose of this study was to examine the effects of videotape-assisted reviews. We wanted to determine whether data (helpfulness ratings, therapist intentions, and client reactions) reported during therapy sessions were similar to data reported during videotape-assisted reviews. To accomplish this goal, we had participants judge the same events during sessions and reviews.

In designing the study, however, we were concerned that interrupting the session might result in a sensitization or rehearsal effect, so that the ratings made during the session might be imprinted on the participants' minds. Thus, participants might have an accurate recall because they remembered these events or their ratings rather than because they rated recall and in-session events similarly. Thus, our second purpose was to use two methods to test whether a rehearsal effect was operating. First, we had participants judge several additional events during videotape-assisted reviews that had not been judged during the sessions. We then compared the mean helpfulness ratings of the repeated judgments with those of the review-only judgments. Second, we compared the correlations between the in-session ratings and the review-only ratings with ratings after 2 weeks. Larger correlations for in-session ratings with reratings would suggest that these ratings had somehow been imprinted more strongly in the participants' minds.

Our third purpose was to determine whether mood and evaluation of sessions are different after videotape-assisted reviews than after sessions. Checking for the effects of mood and evaluation is another way of examining the effects of reviews on participants. If participants can put themselves back into the experience of sessions, there would be no differences in ratings of mood and session evaluation between sessions and reviews. However, if participants become self-critical or fatigued during videotape-assisted reviews, their ratings of mood and session evaluation might be lower. If ratings after reviews differ from those given after sessions, issues about when session outcome measures should be administered would be raised.

Related research on the efficacy of videotape self-confrontation suggests mixed results. Sanborn, Pyke, and Sanborn (1975) concluded that videotape self-confrontation is efficacious, helps eliminate distortion, and adds humanness to therapy. Gur and Sackheim (1978) were not as positive in their evaluation of the literature. They concluded that reactions to videotape self-confrontation are a function of personality structure and type of psychopathology. They noted that videotape self-confrontation can be detrimental to client well-being at times. Given these ambiguities in the literature, more research is needed to determine the effects of videotape reviews.

Stability and Validity of Helpfulness Ratings

Clients and therapists have often rated the helpfulness of therapist interventions using a 3-, 5-, or 9-point scale during videotape-assisted reviews of sessions (e.g., Elliott, 1985; Fuller & Hill, 1985; Hill, Helms, Tichenor, et al., 1988; Hill, Thompson, Cogar, & Denman, 1993). Although these scales have become very popular, minimal psychometric data have been reported for them. Elliott, Cline, and Reid (1982) estimated stability levels from .40 to .60 for helpfulness ratings. Elliott (1986) reported a predictive validity of .60 for helpfulness ratings with session outcome.

Thus, the fourth purpose of this study was to determine the stability of helpfulness ratings over a 2–3 week period. We also wanted to determine the predictive validity of helpfulness ratings by relating them to ratings of session quality. Furthermore, we wanted to estimate the consistency between therapist and client helpfulness ratings to provide an estimate of concurrent validity.

Stability of Therapist Intentions and Client Reactions

The Therapist Intentions List and Client Reactions System have been criticized by reviewers for not providing estimates of stability across time. Hill and O'Grady (1985) and Hill, Helms, Spiegel, and Tichenor (1988) have argued that estimates of stability are not relevant because they test participant memory more than the stability of the measures. We conjectured that participants would not be able to reexperience what occurred during past sessions and that reactions to various events might change over time on the basis of events that occur within subsequent sessions or in life experiences outside of therapy. Because of these arguments, stability was never tested. Yet whether the measures are stable remains an empirical question. Perhaps watching the videotape allows participants to reexperience what they felt during sessions, and high stability would be expected. Thus, our fifth purpose was to test the stability of therapist intentions and client reactions over a 2–3 week period.

Effects of Mood on Judgments

In all likelihood, mood prior to sessions influences how participants experience sessions. In the social and cognitive psychology literature, mood has been found to influence learning. People who felt happy, sad, or angry selectively attended to and learned more about stimulus materials that were congruent with their feelings at the time (Bower, 1983; Bower, Gilligan, & Montiero, 1981; Forgas & Bower, 1987). Furthermore, bad mood has sometimes been found to lead to a negative perception of the world. For example, people in a bad mood tend to rate ambiguous stimuli as less pleasant (Forest, Clark, Mills, & Isen, 1979; Isen & Shalker, 1982), express more negative conceptions of others (Gouaux, 1971; Veitch & Griffitt, 1976), and perceive negative affect in others' ambiguous facial expressions (Schiffenbauer, 1974). However, minimal research has been conducted on the effects of mood on perceptions of therapy process and outcome. Therefore, our final purpose was to examine whether mood is related to helpfulness ratings and session evaluations.

Method

Design

Before each of three therapy sessions, clients and therapists completed measures of mood. Each session was interrupted five times for clients and therapists to complete process evaluations. Immediately after each session, clients and therapists completed mood and session evaluation measures. They then reviewed the videotape of the therapy session, completing process evaluations at the same 5 points as during the session and at an additional 5 points. After the review, clients and therapists completed mood and session evaluation measures. Clients and therapists returned 1–2 weeks after the third session and reevaluated the videotape of the second session, completing process evaluations at the same 10 points as they had during the original review of that session.

We made several choices regarding methodology in designing the study. Because previous research has shown that the accuracy of judgments improves when more sensory modalities are used (Weiss, Marmar, & Horowitz, 1988), we used videotapes rather than audiotapes for the reviews in this study. Furthermore, we were aware that to obtain an estimate of participant experience during sessions, we had to intrude on sessions to collect data. Such intrusion undoubtedly changes the nature of therapeutic interactions, making it difficult to generalize findings to naturally occurring therapy. We hoped that by preparing participants for the intrusion, we would minimize the effects on the therapy experience and participants' judgments. Finally, because different types of clients might respond differently to videotape-assisted reviews (see

Gur & Sackheim, 1978), we somewhat arbitrarily selected clients who had problems with anxiety. Anxiety is a commonly occurring problem on college campuses, yet it includes a broad range of people. By choosing clients who were anxious, we hoped to ensure that clients were at least minimally distressed and therefore similar to actual clients.

Participants

Therapists

Six therapists (4 women and 2 men; 5 advanced preinternship doctoral students in counseling psychology, all of whom had completed at least three practicums, and 1 professor with 18 years of clinical experience; and 5 White and 1 Hispanic) were chosen on the basis of their expertise and ability to conduct sessions without extensive individual supervision. Each therapist was paired with 4 clients, with an attempt to assign both male and female clients to each therapist.

Clients

Twenty-four (17 women and 7 men; 23 White and 1 non-White) undergraduate students, ranging in age from 19 to 32 years ($M = 21.67$, $SD = 2.44$), were the clients for this study. Before therapy, all of the clients had elevated scores on the Beck Anxiety Inventory (>14; $M = 24.38$, $SD = 7.48$) and the Penn State Worry Questionnaire (>58 for women and >53 for men; $M = 68.79$; $SD = 5.68$). All of the volunteers indicated that they were participating because they were anxious and wanted a therapy experience.

Researcher

A white female graduate student served as the researcher for all cases. She interrupted sessions using an intercom from an adjacent room and monitored the videotape-assisted review.

Selection Measures for Anxiety

The Beck Anxiety Inventory (BAI; Beck, Epstein, Brown, & Steer, 1988) is a 21-item self-report inventory that measures the severity of anxiety. Beck et al. (1988) reported that the BAI has high internal consistency ($\alpha = .92$) and moderate test–retest reliability over 1 week (.75). They also found that the BAI discriminated anxious diagnostic groups (panic disorder, generalized anxiety disorder, etc.) from nonanxious diagnostic groups (major depression, dysthymic disorder, etc.). Furthermore, they found that the BAI was moderately correlated with the revised Hamilton Anxiety Rating Scale (.51) but only mildly correlated with the revised Hamilton Depression Rating Scale (.25), suggesting that it measures anxiety independent of depression. Beck et al. stated that scores of 0–9 are considered in the normal range, scores of 10–18 indicate mild to moderate anxiety, scores of 19–29 indicate moderate to severe anxiety, and scores of 30–63 indicate extremely severe anxiety.

The Penn State Worry Questionnaire (PSWQ; Meyer, Miller, Metzger, & Borkovec, 1990) is a 16-item self-report inventory rated on a 5-point scale (5 = *high*) that measures the trait of worry. Factor analyses have revealed one general factor for the PSWQ. High internal consistency has been found (αs = .91–.95). Test–retest reliability ranged from .74 to .93 across 2–10 weeks. The PSWQ correlated positively with psychological measures related to worry but not with measures more remote from the construct, and it was not related to social desirability; thus concurrent and discriminant validity have been established. The PSWQ discriminated among college samples who met all, some, or none of the *Diagnostic and Statistical Manual of Mental Disorders* (3rd ed., rev.; American Psychiatric Association, 1987) criteria for generalized anxiety disorder and also discriminated among persons diagnosed with generalized anxiety disorder versus those with posttraumatic stress disorder. For 405 college students (228 women and 177 men), Meyer et al. reported a mean of 48.80 (*SD* = 13.8), with female students averaging 51.20 and male students averaging 46.10.

Mood Measure

Our measures of positive and negative mood were taken from the Differential Emotions Scale—IV (DES–IV; Blumberg & Izard, 1985, 1986). The DES–IV includes 36 adjectives, and each are judged on 5-point Likert scales (5 = *high*), with 3 adjectives on each of 12 scales. Each scale represents a fundamental, discrete emotion that is universally discernible in facial expression (Izard, 1977). Several studies have found evidence for construct validity of the DES–IV (e.g., Blumberg & Izard, 1985, 1986; Fridlund, Schwartz, & Fowler, 1984; Schwartz, 1982). Factor analysis (Izard, Libero, Putnam, & Haynes, 1993) found two easily interpretable factors: Positive Emotionality (scales of Interest, Enjoyment, and Surprise all loaded from .73 to .86) and Negative Emotionality (scales of Distress, Anger, Disgust, Contempt, Fear, Shame, Guilt, Shyness, and Hostility Inward all loaded from .66 to .82). For the present study, correlations between Positive Emotionality and Negative Emotionality (averaged across sessions for presession, postsession, and postreview) ranged from .28 to .52 for clients and from .49 to .57 for therapists (all at $p < .05$).

Process Measures

The Helpfulness Scale (Elliott, 1985) is a 9-point, Likert-type scale (9 = *extremely helpful*) used by clients and therapists during a videotape review to rate the helpfulness of therapist interventions. In Elliott et al.'s (1982) comparison of original and retrospective helpfulness ratings, they reported stability levels ranging from .40 to .60. This moderate level of stability may be due to memory fluctuation over time or to change in attitude after completion of therapy. Elliott (1986) reported evidence of predictive validity ($r = .60$) for helpfulness and empathy ratings with session outcome in three studies, although the separate correlations of each measure with outcome were not reported. Hill, Helms, Spiegel, and Tichenor (1988) found that client helpfulness ratings were related to client reactions, so that positive reactions were associated with higher helpfulness ratings than were negative reactions.

The Therapist Intentions List—Revised (Hill, Helms, Tichenor, et al., 1988; Hill & O'Grady, 1985) has 19 pantheoretical, nonmutually exclusive intentions organized in eight clusters: set limits, assess (get information, focus, and clarify), support (support, instill hope, and reinforce change), educate (give information), explore (identify and intensify cognitions, behaviors, and feelings), restructure (insight, resistance, and challenge), change, and miscellaneous (relationship, cathart, self-control, and therapist needs). Intentions are therapist rationales for their selection of particular interventions to use with clients at given moments within sessions. Hill and O'Grady (1985) and Hill, Helms, Tichenor, et al. (1988) reported content and construct validity for the Therapist Intentions List: Psychoanalytic therapists used more feelings and insight intentions, whereas behavioral therapists used more change, set limits, and reinforce change intentions; therapists decreased their use of assessment intentions and increased their use of restructuring both within and across sessions; and specific therapist intentions were connected reliably with specific therapist response modes.

The Client Reactions System (Hill, Helms, Spiegel, & Tichenor, 1988) consists of 21 nominal, nonmutually exclusive reactions organized into five clusters: supported (understood, supported, hopeful, and relief), therapeutic work (negative thoughts and behaviors, better self-understanding, clear, feelings, responsibility, unstuck, new perspective, educated, and new ways to behave), challenged, negative reactions (scared, worse, stuck, lack direction, confused, and misunderstood), and no reaction. The Client Reactions System is used by clients to indicate their reactions to therapist interventions. Hill, Helms, Spiegel, and Tichenor (1988) found that therapist intentions were related to client reactions more for successful cases than for unsuccessful cases, that pretreatment symptomatology was highly predictive of which reactions the clients reported, and that there were some predictable changes in reactions across time in treatment.

The Session Evaluation Questionnaire—Form 4 (SEQ; Stiles & Snow, 1984) is a widely used, 24-item, bi-polar, adjective-anchored self-report measure for evaluating a therapy session from the perspective of therapists and clients. The SEQ has four subscales derived from factor analyses: Depth (quality), Smoothness, Positivity, and Arousal. Higher scores on each scale indicate higher levels of the variable. Stiles and Snow reported internal consistency alphas for therapists and clients, respectively, of .91 and .87 for Depth, .89 and .93 for Smoothness, .86 and .89 for Positivity, and .82 and .78 for Arousal.

Procedure

Therapist Training

Before conducting the sessions, therapists read about the etiology and treatment of anxiety disorders and then met to discuss what could reasonably be accomplished in three sessions of therapy with anxious students. Therapists were instructed to be as helpful as possible during sessions but were not required to follow any specific treatment approach. Therapists were all familiar with the process measures from previous usage. Therapists received group supervision every other week to deal with concerns about cases.

Recruiting

Clients were recruited through announcements in undergraduate psychology classes offering credit for attending three sessions of therapy and an additional 4 hr of watching videotapes of their own sessions. Announcements emphasized that prospective clients had to (a) have problems with anxiety, (b) be willing to be videotaped, (c) be willing to be interrupted during sessions, and (d) be willing to review the videotape of the session. Within time availability constraints, volunteer clients were randomly assigned to therapists, who called them to screen them for eligibility (clients had to be anxious and motivated to talk in therapy) and, if eligible, to set up an appointment for testing ($N = 46$). During the phone call, therapists used a script to describe the requirements of the study, emphasizing the videotaping, the interruptions during the sessions, and the reviews immediately following the sessions.

Screening

Volunteers who attended testing sessions ($N = 42$) signed consent forms and completed the BAI and the PSWQ in a random order. To be eligible for the study, volunteers had to score greater than 14 on the BAI and greater than 58 (for women) or 53 (for men) on the PSWQ. Volunteers who scored below these cutoffs ($N = 17$) were referred to the campus counseling center.

Practice Session

Immediately after pretesting, therapists gave copies of the Helpfulness Scale and the Client Reactions System (with definitions of categories) to eligible clients and reviewed what each category meant. To ensure that clients were able to appropriately use the measures and knew what to do when the session was stopped, therapists then conducted a 15–20 min practice session with each eligible client. Clients were assured that therapists would never have access to their data. To practice how the sessions would proceed, therapists asked for a brief description of what clients planned to discuss in the sessions and then paraphrased what clients said. The researcher interrupted the practice session from an adjacent room by saying "stop" using an intercom. Each time the tape was stopped, clients and therapists evaluated the therapist intervention as they would during the actual sessions. Immediately after this brief practice session, therapists and clients reviewed the videotape, with a researcher stopping the tape after each therapist statement, so that participants could evaluate the therapist intervention. One client who went through the testing and practice session dropped out before therapy, which left 24 clients who completed the study.

Treatment

Therapists and clients completed the DES–IV before each session. Dyads met for three 45-min weekly therapy sessions. Therapists were allowed to use whatever interventions they thought were clinically appropriate for clients.

The researcher in the adjoining room listened to sessions and chose 10 interruption points spaced at least 3 min apart within the first 35 min of each session. The researcher usually interrupted at the end of therapist speaking turns (defined as everything therapists say, excluding minimal responses, between two client statements). In two instances in which clients were visibly upset, the researcher allowed a little more time to elapse before interrupting. Five interruptions were administered during the sessions, and five interruptions were put onto the tapes of the sessions. The order of the immediate and delayed interruptions was randomly determined, with no more than three of either type in a row, in accordance with rules for series specified in Gellerman (1933).

At the five immediate interruptions, the researcher said "stop" using an intercom from the adjoining room (referred to hereinafter as Turns 1–5). As soon as they heard the word *stop*, clients and therapists stopped talking and wrote down their ratings of the helpfulness of the therapist intervention using the Helpfulness Scale. In addition, therapists wrote down the numbers of up to three intentions using the list and definitions provided, and clients wrote down the numbers of up to three reactions for that turn using the list and definitions provided. All of the ratings were done on sheets of paper hidden from the view of the other person. When ratings were completed, therapists often briefly paraphrased what had been occurring before the interruption (e.g., "You were talking about your reaction to tests").

At the five delayed interruptions, which were interspersed among the immediate interruptions, the researcher inserted the word *stop* onto the videotape sound track, which could not be heard by the clients and therapists as they conducted the sessions (referred to hereinafter as Turns 6–10). The voice quality of the two types of stops was equivalent on the final videotape, so that cues differentiating immediate and delayed stops were minimized.

Postsession Review

Immediately after each session, the client and therapist went to an adjoining room equipped with a videomonitor and computer terminals. The client and therapist were seated so that each could see his or her respective videomonitor and a copy of either the Therapist Intentions List or Client Reactions System, but could not see each other's computer terminal. The client and therapist first completed paper-and-pencil versions of the DES–IV and the SEQ in a random order and then began the review of the session. All data collected during the review were entered directly into the computer. Participants were instructed to respond according to how they felt during sessions rather than according to their immediate feelings. At each of the 10 stops (5 actual interruptions and 5 interruptions superimposed by the researcher during the session), the researcher stopped the tape. The tape was stopped as quickly as possible to eliminate cues indicating whether the stop had been heard during the actual session. Both participants rated the helpfulness of the therapist intervention. Clients also entered the numbers of up to three reactions to the intervention using the list and definitions provided; therapists also entered the numbers of up to three intentions using the list and definitions provided. After the reviews of the sessions, therapists and clients again completed the DES–IV and the SEQ in a random order.

Reassessment of the Second Session

Approximately 1 week after the third (and final) session, clients and therapists once again reviewed the videotape of the second session. Participants were instructed to try to remember how they felt during the actual session. At each of the 10 points (Turns 1–10) indicated by the researcher's voice on the videotape sound track, the researcher stopped the tape. Therapists rated the helpfulness of the therapist intervention and indicated up to three intentions for each, whereas clients rated the helpfulness of the intervention and indicated up to three reactions. After the review, clients completed the BAI and the PSWQ in a random order. Therapists debriefed clients about the purpose of the study and provided referrals to the campus counseling center.

Results

Preliminary Analyses

Although not a stated purpose of the study, we first examined client pre- and post-treatment change scores to provide a context within which to evaluate the process results. From pre- to posttreatment, clients changed from 24.38 ($SD = 7.48$) to 17.42 ($SD = 11.61$) on the BAI and from 68.79 ($SD = 5.68$) to 64.83 ($SD = 9.98$) on the PSWQ. A repeated measures multivariate analysis of variance (MANOVA) with main effects for therapists (as the between-subjects variable) and time (as the repeated variable) conducted on the BAI and the PSWQ indicated a significant effect for time, $F(2, 17) = 6.76$, $p < .01$, but no significant effect for therapists. Thus, clients improved over the course of treatment, but no significant differences in treatment outcome were found among the six therapists. Using a Bonferroni adjusted alpha of .025, we found that only the BAI showed significant change, $F(1, 18) = 10.94$, $p < .01$. On average, clients were still mildly to moderately anxious after therapy, even though there was a decrease of 7 points from pre- to posttreatment. This mean difference, approximately two thirds of the error standard deviation, is somewhat less than are changes reported for 12-session therapies for anxiety (e.g., Borkovec & Costello, 1993).

Testing the Validity of the Videotape-Assisted Review

Relationship Between Helpfulness Ratings in Sessions and in Reviews

To determine the consistency of mean ratings, we computed intraclass correlations (ICC(3,2); Shrout & Fleiss, 1979) for clients and therapists between Turns 1–5 when rated during the three sessions and these same turns when rerated during videotape-assisted reviews. The effects of individual therapists, sessions, speaking turns, and time (session vs. review) and all possible interactions between these variables were partialed out in these analyses. The intraclass correlation was .94 for client helpfulness ratings and .76 for therapist helpfulness ratings. Thus, clients and therapists were quite consistent in their helpfulness ratings of the same turns across sessions and reviews.

To determine whether there were therapist effects for helpfulness ratings, therapists were considered to be a random effect, whereas session, turn, and session or review were considered to be fixed effects in the analysis of variance model used above. Appropriate error terms for each effect were then derived. Therapist effects were not significant for client helpfulness ratings, although they were for therapist helpfulness ratings, $F(5, 11) = 7.41$, $p < .01$. Thus, therapists differed in their anchor points when they used the Helpfulness Scale. Means for individual therapists ranged from 5.23 to 6.96, with the most experienced therapist (the professor) in the middle of the range.

Mean client and therapist helpfulness ratings for Turns 1–5 in sessions and reviews after sessions are presented in Table 1. No significant differences were found between the mean helpfulness ratings in the sessions and those in the reviews, indicating that clients and therapists judged events similarly in the reviews as they did in the sessions.

Differences Between Rerated and New Helpfulness Ratings in Reviews

Mean client and therapist helpfulness ratings for Turns 1–5 and 6–10 completed during the postsession reviews are also shown in Table 1. No significant differences were found between the means; thus no evidence was found for a rehearsal effect.

Relationship Between Intentions in Session and Review

We calculated the consistency of reported intentions across the sessions and reviews in three ways: (a) by noting the proportion of hits versus misses for each intention cluster, (b) by estimating kappa (Cohen, 1960) between the sessions and reviews for all categories, and (c) by estimating kappa between the sessions and reviews for the

Table 1—*Means and Standard Deviations for the Client and Therapist Helpfulness Ratings During Sessions and Reviews Immediately After Sessions*

| | Session Turns 1–5 | | Review | | | |
| | | | Turns 1–5 | | Turns 6–10 | |
Rating	M	SD	M	SD	M	SD
Client	7.08	1.41	7.22	1.32	7.29	1.00
Therapist	6.28	1.22	6.15	1.29	6.13	0.74

Note. Helpfulness is rated on a 9-point scale (9 = *high helpfulness*). Turns 1–5 = actual interruptions; Turns 6–10 = interruptions superimposed on videotape.

clusters. We counted duplicate matches if more than one category within a cluster was reported. The proportion of hits (i.e., therapist reported an intention in the same cluster vs. another cluster) was 100% ($n = 1$) for set limits, 71% ($n = 190$) for assess, 68% ($n = 139$) for support, 62% ($n = 8$) for educate, 70% ($n = 156$) for explore, 67% ($n = 140$) for restructure, 59% ($n = 39$) for change, and 43% ($n = 96$) for miscellaneous. For categories (including a category for no intention listed), kappa was .43 ($z = 42.60$, $p < .0001$), whereas for clusters (including a cluster for no intention listed), kappa was .64 ($z = 47.05$, $p < .0001$). Thus, therapists were consistent in their reports of intentions across sessions and reviews, with relatively high proportions of hits for all except the miscellaneous cluster.

Relationship Between Reactions in Session and Review

We used the same methods for assessing consistency of reactions as we used for intentions. The proportion of hits was 69% ($n = 325$) for supported, 70% ($n = 338$) for therapeutic work, 29% ($n = 48$) for challenged, 47% ($n = 57$) for negative reactions, and 45% ($n = 20$) for no reaction. For categories (including a category for no reaction listed), kappa was .25 ($z = 25.20$, $p < .0001$), whereas for clusters (including a cluster for no reactions listed), kappa was .54 ($z = 14.76$, $p < .0001$). Thus, clients reported similar reactions across sessions and reviews.

Changes on the DES–IV and the SEQ

Table 2 contains the scores for the client- and therapist-rated DES–IV averaged across the three sessions for before the session (presession), after the session (postsession), and after the review (review). Table 2 also contains the scores for the client-

Table 2—*Means and Standard Deviations for Client- and Therapist-Rated Differential Emotions Scale—IV (DES–IV) Positive Emotionality and Negative Emotionality Scales Across All Three Sessions*

Measure	Presession		Postsession		Review	
	M	*SD*	*M*	*SD*	*M*	*SD*
Client DES–IV						
Positive	2.39	0.57	2.65	0.76	2.49	0.75
Negative	2.08	0.68	1.85	0.56	1.77	0.57
Therapist DES–IV						
Positive	2.40	0.89	2.77	0.75	2.54	0.72
Negative	1.33	0.25	1.34	0.31	1.29	0.25
Client SEQ Depth	—	—	5.31	0.69	5.24	0.68
Therapist SEQ Depth	—	—	4.84	0.64	4.75	0.57

Note. The DES–IV Positive Emotionality and Negative Emotionality scales use a 5-point Likert scale ($5 = high$); the Session Evaluation Questionnaire (SEQ) Depth scale uses a 7-point Likert scale ($7 = high$). Dashes indicate that measures were not administered at this point.

and therapist-rated SEQ averaged across the three treatment sessions for (a) after the session (postsession) and (b) after the review (review).

Separate repeated measures MANOVAs were conducted on the client- and therapist-rated DES–IV, with effects for therapists (as the between-subjects factor) and time (presession, postsession, and review), session, scales (Positive Emotionality and Negative Emotionality), and all possible interactions. Another set of repeated measures MANOVAs was conducted on the client- and therapist-rated SEQ with effects for therapists (as the between-subjects actor), time (postsession and review), session, scales (Depth, Smoothness, Positivity, and Arousal), and all possible interactions. Only the results for time and scales and the interaction of Time × Scales (balanced for the other effects) were interpreted, because these were the only effects of interest in this study.

On the client-rated DES–IV, there were significant main effects for time, $F(2, 17) = 12.93$, $p < .001$, and scales, $F(1, 18) = 29.65$, $p < .001$, and a significant Time × Scales interaction, $F(2, 17) = 6.57$, $p < .01$ (see Figure 1). Post hoc univariate tests for each scale were conducted with a Bonferroni adjusted alpha of .0125 (.05 divided by 4 tests). Positive emotionality increased between pre- and postsession, $F(1, 18) = 8.91$, $p < .01$, and decreased between postsession and review, $F(1, 18) = 14.19$, $p < .01$. Negative emotionality decreased between pre- and postsession, $F(1, 18) = 10.79$, $p < .004$, but showed no change between postsession and review. Thus, clients felt more positive and less negative after sessions; they still felt less negative after reviews but no longer felt as positive.

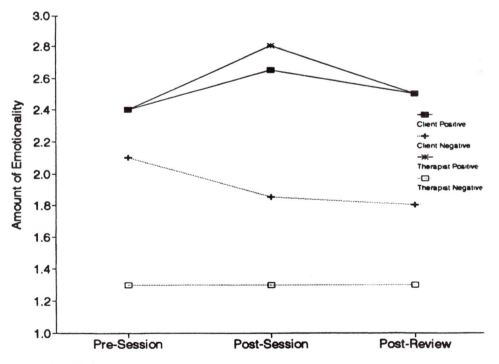

Figure 1. Changes in client and therapist positive and negative emotionality across the course of sessions and videotape-assisted reviews.

On the therapist-rated DES–IV, there was a significant Time × Scales interaction, $F(2, 17) = 8.55$, $p < .01$, and significant main effects for time, $F(2, 17) = 28.05$, $p < .001$, and scales, $F(1, 18) = 234.50$, $p < .001$ (see Figure 1). Post hoc univariate tests for each scale, with a Bonferroni-corrected alpha of .01, indicated that positive emotionality increased between pre- and postsession, $F(1, 18) = 22.05$, $p < .001$, and decreased between postsession and review, $F(1, 18) = 22.26$, $p < .001$. Negative emotionality did not change significantly between time periods. Thus, therapists became more positive after sessions but less positive after reviews.

On the client-rated SEQ, there was only a significant main effect for scales, $F(3, 16) = 21.42$, $p < .01$, which was not of interest to this study. On the therapist-rated SEQ, there was a significant main effect for time, $F(1, 18) = 7.55$, $p < .05$, but none were found for scales, indicating that the mean of all four scales decreased over the two testings. Thus, therapist evaluations of the quality of sessions decreased after the reviews.

Validity and Stability of Helpfulness Ratings

Predictive Validity

Average helpfulness ratings during sessions (Turns 1–5) were significantly related to postsession depth for both clients, $r(20) = .64$, $p < .001$, and therapists, $r(22) = .42$, $p < .05$. Likewise, average helpfulness ratings during reviews (Turns 1–5) were significantly related to postsession depth for clients, $r(21) = .73$, $p < .001$, but not for therapists, $r(21) = .33$. (Note that Turns 1–5 were examined to keep a comparable statistic across sessions and reviews; also postsession depth rather than review depth was used because depth is typically assessed immediately after sessions.)

Consistency Between Therapists and Clients

The intraclass correlations, ICC(3,2), between therapist and client helpfulness ratings, with the effects of therapists, sessions, turns, and their interactions partialed out, was .79 for Turns 1–5 during sessions and .77 for Turns 1–5 during reviews, indicating concurrent validity for therapist and client helpfulness ratings. Helpfulness ratings were significantly higher for clients than for therapists both during sessions, $F(1, 5) = 10.69$, $p < .05$, and during reviews, $F(1, 5) = 16.65$, $p < .01$ (see Table 1). No therapist effects were found in these analyses.

Stability

Means and standard deviations for helpfulness ratings given during the videotape-assisted reviews immediately after Session 2 and 2–3 weeks later are shown in Table 3. Intraclass correlations, ICC(3,2), with the effects of therapists, turns, and their interaction partialed out, were computed between the helpfulness ratings completed during the videotape-assisted review of Session 2 and the reratings of these same stimuli completed 2–3 weeks later. The intraclass correlations for all 10 helpfulness ratings were .90 and .89 for clients and therapists, respectively, thus indicating sta-

Table 3—*Means and Standard Deviations for the Client and*
Therapist Helpfulness Ratings for Videotape-Assisted Review of Session 2
Done Immediately After Session and 2–3 Weeks Later

Ratings	Session 2		Rerated Session 2	
	M	*SD*	*M*	*SD*
Client				
Turns 1–5	7.18	1.33	6.98	1.35
Turns 6–10	7.33	1.12	6.98	1.42
Turns 1–10	7.25	1.23	6.98	1.38
Therapist				
Turns 1–5	6.17	1.23	6.16	1.13
Turns 6–10	6.18	1.21	6.31	1.17
Turns 1–10	6.18	1.22	6.23	1.15

Note. Helpfulness is rated on a 9-point scale (9 = *high helpfulness*).
Turns 1–5 = actual interruptions; Turns 6–10 = interruptions superimposed
on video.

bility across 2 weeks when participants viewed the same material. For Turns 1–5,
the intraclass correlations were .76 and .78 for clients and therapists, respectively,
and for Turns 6–10 the intraclass correlations were .86 and .87, respectively, suggesting that there was not a rehearsal effect (i.e., the intraclass correlation for Turns
1–5 was not larger than that for Turns 6–10).

When therapist effects were tested for the 10 turns with therapists considered as
a random effect and all other effects considered as fixed effects, no effect was found
for client helpfulness ratings, but significant effects were found for therapist helpfulness ratings, $F(5, 16) = 5.32$, $p < .01$. No mean shifts were found across time
(see Table 3).

Stability of Intentions and Reactions Across 2 Weeks

Allowing for more than one match per cluster if more than one category was reported
in a given cluster, kappa for Session 2 with the same session rerated 2 weeks later
(including a cluster for nothing reported) was .57 ($z = 59.99$, $p < .0001$) for intentions
clusters and .47 ($z = 38.20$, $p < .0001$) for reactions clusters. Thus, therapists and
clients were significantly better than chance at reporting the same clusters of responses during the initial and delayed reviews.

Effects of Mood on Judgments

We report only on Turns 1–5 for the effects of mood on judgments, so that results
will be comparable across correlations for sessions and reviews. Table 4 contains the
correlations between positive and negative emotionality and ratings of helpfulness
and session depth for both clients and therapists. Client presession positive emotionality generally was marginally or significantly related to client helpfulness ratings
and client-reported depth in sessions and reviews. Similarly, client preview positive

Table 4—*Correlations Between Average Mood and*
Helpfulness Ratings and Session Depth

Rating	Positive	Negative
Client		
Presession		
In-session helpfulness	.37	.10
Session depth	.40	.04
Review helpfulness	.44*	.18
Review depth	.50*	.14
Prereview		
Review helpfulness	.56*	.05
Review depth	.63**	−.01
Therapist		
Presession		
In-session helpfulness	−.01	−.44*
Session depth	.02	−.53*
Review helpfulness	−.04	−.31
Review depth	.12	−.33
Prereview		
Review helpfulness	.16	−.33
Review depth	.32	−.21

Note. For all correlations, $df = 22$.
*$p < .05$.   **$p < .001$.

emotionality was significantly related to client ratings of helpfulness and depth in reviews. Client negative emotionality was not significantly related to any of their evaluations. Thus, the more positively clients felt before sessions and reviews, the more positively they evaluated therapist helpfulness and session quality in reviews.

In contrast, therapist presession negative emotionality was significantly related to therapist helpfulness ratings and therapist-reported depth in sessions. Thus, therapist negative mood before sessions influenced their ratings of their own helpfulness and of session depth, so that the more negative their mood the lower they rated the helpfulness of their interventions and the quality of the sessions. However, the effects of presession negative mood did not carry over to the correlations with review ratings, nor was prereview negative emotionality related to review ratings. Therapist positive emotionality was not related to any of their evaluations.

Discussion

The results of this study should be considered within the context of the brevity of the therapy (three sessions), the use of anxious and worried clients, and the use of mostly graduate student therapists. The clients did become less anxious over the three sessions, although in the absence of a control group we cannot assume that these changes were due to the treatment.

Validity of Videotape-Assisted Reviews

We found that client and therapist helpfulness ratings, therapist intentions, and client reactions were highly consistent between sessions and reviews. These findings support the validity of videotape-assisted reviews as a means of assessing in-session experiences, and confirm previous research (Katz & Resnikoff, 1977). In addition, these findings did not seem to be the result of participants simply remembering their in-session evaluations during reviews, which would have suggested a rehearsal effect. Apparently, the stimulus of the videotape was enough to enable participants to reexperience sessions. Kagan (1975) has noted that viewing a videotape has the effect of creating a flashback, which enables viewers to relive the experience as if they were there again. However, we hesitate to generalize these findings to audiotape- or transcript-assisted reviews because participants may be less able to reexperience their feelings when fewer sensory channels are used.

Although participants made similar process judgments during sessions and videotape-assisted reviews, their mood did vary after sessions compared with their mood after reviews. Both therapists and clients experienced an increase in positive emotionality after sessions, which dissipated after reviews. Thus, the sessions created an immediate positive feeling that was dampened by the experience of going through the review. For clients, the increase in positive mood was accompanied by a decrease in negative mood after the sessions, and this decrease was maintained after the reviews. Therapists reported no change in their negative mood, but they rarely expressed any negative mood. These changes in mood are in keeping with participant reports of feeling bored and less engaged during reviews and support the literature that not all videotape self-confrontation is efficacious (Gur & Sackheim, 1978). Given these mood shifts, researchers might be careful not to do too many reviews after sessions. For example, rather than reviewing every session in a 12-session therapy, they might only review 2–4 sessions to get a representative sampling of the therapy, thereby avoiding participant fatigue and ill will.

In addition, therapists evaluated sessions more negatively after they watched the sessions on videotape than they did immediately after the sessions. This finding suggests that watching the tape had a chilling effect on therapist evaluation, perhaps because they became self-critical and anxious watching themselves on videotape. Similarly, Walz and Johnston (1963) found that therapist assessment of their own performance tended to decrease after self-observation. Clients did not evaluate sessions more negatively after watching the videotape, perhaps because they were not the focus of evaluation.

Psychometric Properties of the Helpfulness Scale

We found mostly positive evidence for the predictive validity of the Helpfulness Scale. Client helpfulness ratings during sessions and reviews were related to their after-session evaluations of depth. Therapist helpfulness ratings during sessions were related to their after-session evaluations of depth, but helpfulness ratings during reviews were not related to after-session ratings of depth.

We found evidence of the concurrent validity of helpfulness ratings in that therapist and client ratings were highly related. As has been commonly reported, client ratings were significantly higher than were therapist ratings (Stiles & Snow, 1984). Helpfulness ratings were also quite stable across a 2-week period, when clients and therapists viewed the same videotape for a second time.

Compared with Elliott's (1986) findings, our findings allow us to be more sanguine about the psychometric properties of the Helpfulness Scale. Since Elliott's methodology was not clear, we cannot completely explain the discrepancy. We guess, however, that we found higher reliabilities because we used a homogeneous client sample in a very brief therapy and accounted for much of the error variance (due to therapists, sessions, speaking turns, and time) in our statistics.

Stability of Intentions and Reactions Across Time

Contrary to earlier arguments that intentions and reactions would not be stable over time because of fading memories, we found evidence for the stability of intentions and reactions. One explanation for this, as discussed above, is that videotape cues allowed participants to reexperience sessions. A comparison of participants' stability levels with observers' stability levels would be an interesting area for future research.

Effects of Mood on Judgments

The effects of mood on process judgments were quite different for clients and therapists. Client positive mood was related to client ratings of therapist helpfulness and session depth, whereas therapist negative mood was related to therapist ratings of their own helpfulness and session depth. When clients felt positively before the session, they generalized this positive feeling to other evaluations. When therapists felt negatively before the session, they likewise generalized this negative feeling to other evaluations. The differential effects of positive versus negative emotions may be attributable to the fact that the therapists, rather than the clients, were being evaluated. Therapists tend to be self-critical and anxious, which may have been exacerbated by any negative feelings they had before going into the sessions. The generally low level of negative emotions for therapists may reflect therapists' belief that their own feelings should not enter into the therapy process.

Limitations

To determine whether videotape-assisted reviews are representative of actual sessions, we interrupted sessions to obtain data from clients and therapists about their immediate experiences. Obviously, because such interruptions do not generally occur in therapy, this procedure introduced a change that reduces the generalizability of the findings. Note that the interruptions did not appear to be as detrimental to the process as we had feared. Clients had been thoroughly informed that the interruptions would occur and had agreed to participate under these conditions. It is interesting that participants often picked up the discussion after the interruption with almost no discernible loss of train of thought. Occasionally the pauses even seemed beneficial, in that they provided an opportunity for participants to think about what they wanted to say.

Although we provided some evidence that reratings were not substantially different from new ratings made during the videotape reviews, it is still possible that the entire process of doing in-session evaluations resulted in a sensitizing effect. Participants may have been more reflective during the recall because they had stopped throughout the session and evaluated how they were responding.

In addition, because of the clients' volunteer status, we cannot infer that they were similar to clients who seek help at agencies. We were careful, however, to select clients who had real concerns and who had elevated scores on anxiety and worry measures to ensure that they were similar to actual anxious clients who might seek and profit from brief therapy.

Of course, clients who are not anxious might respond quite differently to videotape-assisted reviews. As Gur and Sackheim (1978) recommended, further research needs to examine the interaction of diagnosis with reactions to videotape-assisted reviews.

Another potential limitation is that we did not require therapists to use any specific treatment nor did we check to determine what treatment components were used. Thus, we do not know whether certain therapist treatment modalities or interventions would lead to more or less accurate recall.

Finally, given that we used a structured videotape-assisted review with minimal contact between participants and researchers, we cannot generalize these results to unstructured recall techniques (cf. Elliott, 1986). Rhodes and Johnson (1993), in their qualitative analysis of client experiences of open-ended recalls, found that although clients reported gaining a great deal from such recalls, some also felt a sense of shame in having another person see their private thoughts. Research needs to examine differences between the structured and open-ended recall methods.

Implications

The major implication of this study is that researchers can feel somewhat reassured that judgments made during videotape-assisted reviews are representative of judgments made during therapy sessions if these reviews are done within 2 weeks. In addition, researchers can be more confident about the psychometric properties of the Helpfulness Scale, the Therapist Intentions List, and the Client Reactions System. Researchers should be aware, however, that videotape-reviews appear to have some dampening effects on client and therapist mood and on therapist evaluations of session quality. Finally, presession mood does appear to affect process ratings.

Because of the change in mood and evaluation after reviews, researchers should probably be careful to administer session evaluation measures directly after sessions rather than after reviews. Also, researchers should consider including presession mood as a variable in the examination of process evaluations.

Further investigation of the long-term effects of videotape-assisted review is indicated. Researchers have often assumed that the potential self-assessment in the videotape-assisted reviews was beneficial, as Kagan (1975) and Sanborn et al. (1975) suggested. But our findings about lowered positive mood, along with Gur and Sackheim's (1978) conclusion about detrimental effects of videotape self-confrontation, raise concerns about the impact of reviews.

Additional research on the effects of mood on process judgments would also be interesting. One possibility would be to study therapist mood throughout the course of several consecutive clients in the same day to determine whether mood after particularly good or difficult sessions impinges on therapist mood and behavior with subsequent clients.

Finally, we encourage more investigation of the methodologies and measures used in process research. Issues such as bias in judgment (e.g., Hill, O'Grady, & Price, 1988; Mahalik, Hill, O'Grady, & Thompson, 1993), individual differences among therapists and clients, and the validity and reliability of process measures need to be explored.

References

American Psychiatric Association. (1987). *Diagnostic and statistical manual of mental disorders* (3rd ed. rev.). Washington, DC: Author.

Barkham, M. (1988). Empathy in counseling and psychotherapy: Present status and future directions. *Counselling Psychology Quarterly, 1*, 407–428.

Beck, A. T., Epstein, N., Brown, G., & Steer, R. A. (1988). An inventory for measuring clinical anxiety: Psychometric properties. *Journal of Consulting and Clinical Psychology, 56*, 893–897.

Blumberg, S. H., & Izard, C. E. (1985). Affective and cognitive characteristics of depression in 10- and 11-year-old children. *Journal of Personality and Social Psychology, 49*, 194–202.

Blumberg, S. H., & Izard, C. E. (1986). Discriminating patterns of emotions in 10- and 11-year-old children. *Journal of Personality and Social Psychology, 51*, 852–857.

Borkovec, T. D., & Costello, E. (1993). Efficacy of applied relaxation and cognitive–behavioral therapy in the treatment of generalized anxiety disorder. *Journal of Consulting and Clinical Psychology, 61*, 611–619.

Bower, G. H. (1983). Affect and cognition. *Philosophical Transactions of the Royal Society of London: B. Biological Sciences, 302*, 387–402.

Bower, G. H., Gilligan, S. G., & Montiero, D. P. (1981). Selectivity of learning caused by affective states. *Journal of Experimental Psychology: General, 110*, 451–473.

Cohen, J. (1960). A coefficient of agreement for nominal scales. *Educational and Psychological Measurement, 20*, 37–46.

Elliott, R. (1985). Helpful and nonhelpful events in brief counseling interviews: An empirical taxonomy. *Journal of Counseling Psychology, 32*, 307–322.

Elliott, R. (1986). Interpersonal Process Recall (IPR) as a psychotherapy process research method. In L. S. Greenberg & W. M. Pinsof (Eds.), *The psychotherapeutic process: A research handbook* (pp. 503–528). New York: Guilford Press.

Elliott, R., Cline, J., & Reid, S. (1982, June). *Tape-assisted retrospective review: A method for assessing the changing effects of therapist interventions in psychotherapy.* Paper presented at the annual meeting of the Society for Psychotherapy Research, Jeffersonville, VT.

Elliott, R., & Shapiro, D. (1988). Brief structured recall: A more efficient method for identifying and describing significant therapy events. *British Journal of Medical Society, 61*, 141–153.

Ellis, M. V., Robbins, E. S., Schult, D., Ladany, N., & Banker, J. (1990). Anchoring errors in clinical judgments: Type I error, adjustment, or mitigation? *Journal of Counseling Psychology, 37*, 343–351.

Forest, D., Clark, M. S., Mills, J., & Isen, A. M. (1979). Helping as a function of feeling state and nature of the helping behavior. *Motivation and Emotion, 3*, 161–169.

Forgas, J. P., & Bower, G. H. (1987). Mood effects on person–perception judgments. *Journal of Personality and Social Psychology, 53*, 53–60.

Fridlund, A. J., Schwartz, G. E., & Fowler, S. C. (1984). Pattern recognition of self-reported emotional state from multiple-site facial EMG activity during affective imagery. *Psychophysiology, 21*, 622–637.

Friedlander, M. L. (1992). Psychotherapeutic process: About the art, about the science. *Journal of Counseling and Development, 70*, 740–741.

Fuller, F., & Hill, C. E. (1985). Counselor and helpee perceptions of counselor intentions in relation to outcome in a single counseling session. *Journal of Counseling Psychology, 32*, 329–338.

Gellerman, L. W. (1933). Chance orders of alternating stimuli in visual discrimination experiments. *Journal of Genetic Psychology, 42*, 206–208.

Gouaux, C. (1971). Induced affective states and interpersonal attraction. *Journal of Personality and Social Psychology, 20*, 37–43.

Gur, R. C., & Sackheim, H. A. (1978). Self-confrontation and psychotherapy: A reply to Sanborn, Pyke, and Sanborn. *Psychotherapy: Theory, Research, and Practice, 15*, 258–265.

Hill, C. E. (1989). *Therapist techniques and client outcomes: Eight cases of brief psychotherapy.* Newbury Park, CA: Sage.

Hill, C. E. (1991). Almost everything you ever wanted to know about how to do process research on counseling and psychotherapy but didn't know who to ask. In C. E. Watkins & L. J. Schneider (Eds.), *Research in counseling* (pp. 85–118). Hillsdale, NJ: Erlbaum.

Hill, C. E., Helms, J. E., Spiegel, S. B., & Tichenor, V. (1988). Development of a system for categorizing client reactions to therapist interventions. *Journal of Counseling Psychology, 35*, 27–36.

Hill, C. E., Helms, J. E., Tichenor, V., Spiegel, S. B., O'Grady, K. E., & Perry, E. (1988). Effects of therapist response modes in brief psychotherapy. *Journal of Counseling Psychology, 35*, 222–233.

Hill, C. E., & O'Grady, K. E. (1985). List of therapist intentions illustrated in a case study and with therapists of varying theoretical orientations. *Journal of Counseling Psychology, 32*, 3–22.

Hill, C. E., O'Grady, K. E., & Price, P. (1988). A method for investigating sources of rater bias. *Journal of Counseling Psychology, 35*, 346–350.

Hill, C. E., Thompson, B. J., Cogar, M. C., & Denman, D. W., III (1993). Beneath the surface of long-term therapy: Therapist and client report of their own and each other's covert processes. *Journal of Counseling Psychology, 40*, 278–287.

Hill, C. E., Thompson, B. J., & Corbett, M. M. (1992). The impact of therapist ability to perceive displayed and hidden client reactions on immediate outcome in first sessions of brief therapy. *Psychotherapy Research, 2*, 143–155.

Isen, A. M., & Shalker, T. E. (1982). The influence of mood state on evaluation of positive, neutral, and negative stimuli: When you "accentuate the positive", do you "eliminate the negative"? *Social Psychology Quarterly, 45*, 58–63.

Izard, C. E. (1977). *Human emotions.* New York: Plenum.

Izard, C. E., Libero, D. Z., Putnam, P., & Haynes, O. M. (1993). Stability of emotion experiences and their relations to traits of personality. *Journal of Personality and Social Psychology, 64*, 847–860.

Kagan, N. (1975). *Interpersonal process recall: A method of influencing human interaction.* (Available from N. Kagan, Educational Psychology Department, University of Houston, University Park, Houston, Texas 77004.)

Katz, D., & Resnikoff, A. (1977). Televised self-confrontation and recalled affect: A new look at videotape recall. *Journal of Counseling Psychology, 24*, 150–152.

Kivlighan, D. M. (1990). Relation between counselors' use of intentions and clients' perception of working alliance. *Journal of Counseling Psychology, 37*, 27–32.

Lambert, M. J., & Hill, C. E. (1994). Assessing psychotherapy process and outcome. In A. E. Bergin & S. L. Garfield (Eds.), *Handbook of psychotherapy and behavior change* (4th ed., pp. 72–113). New York: Wiley.

Mahalik, J., Hill, C. E., O'Grady, K. E., & Thompson, B. (1993). Rater bias in the Checklist of Psychotherapy Transactions—Revised. *Psychotherapy Research, 3,* 47–56.

Martin, J., Martin, W., Meyer, M., & Slemon, A. (1986). An empirical test of the cognitive mediational paradigm for research on counseling. *Journal of Counseling Psychology, 33,* 115–123.

Meyer, T. J., Miller, M. L., Metzger, R. L., & Borkovec, T. D. (1990). Development and validation of the Penn State Worry Questionnaire. *Behavior Research and Therapy, 28,* 487–495.

Pain, M. D., & Sharpley, C. F. (1988). Case type, anchoring errors, and counselor education. *Counselor Education and Supervision, 28,* 53–58.

Pain, M. D., & Sharpley, C. F. (1989). Varying the order in which positive and negative information is presented: Effects on counselors' judgments of clients' mental health. *Journal of Counseling Psychology, 36,* 3–7.

Rhodes, R., & Johnson, B. (1993, June). *The impact of videotape-assisted interpersonal process recall on clients in long-term therapy: Balancing validity and impact when choosing process measures.* Paper presented at the annual meeting of the Society for Psychotherapy Research, Pittsburgh, PA.

Sanborn, D. E., Pyke, H. F., & Sanborn, C. J. (1975). Videotape playback and psychotherapy: A review. *Psychotherapy: Theory, Research, and Practice, 12,* 179–186.

Schiffenbauer, A. (1974). Effect of observer's emotional state on judgments of the emotional state of others. *Journal of Personality and Social Psychology, 30,* 31–35.

Schwartz, G. E. (1982). Psychophysiological patterning and emotion revisited: A systems perspective. In C. E. Izard (Ed.), *Measuring emotions in infants and children* (Vol. 1, pp. 67–93). Cambridge, England: Cambridge University Press.

Shrout, P. E., & Fleiss, J. L. (1979). Intraclass correlations: Uses in assessing rater reliability. *Psychological Bulletin, 86,* 420–428.

Stiles, W. B., & Snow, J. S. (1984). Counseling session impact as viewed by novice counselors and their clients. *Journal of Counseling Psychology, 31,* 3–12.

Thompson, B. J., & Hill, C. E. (1991). Therapist perceptions of client reactions. *Journal of Counseling and Development, 69,* 261–265.

Veitch, R., & Griffitt, W. (1976). Good news–bad news: Affective and interpersonal affects. *Journal of Applied Social Psychology, 6,* 69–75.

Walz, G. R., & Johnston, J. A. (1963). Counselors look at themselves on video tape. *Journal of Counseling Psychology, 19,* 232–236.

Weiss, D. S., Marmar, C. R., & Horowitz, M. J. (1988). Do the ways in which psychotherapy process ratings are made make a difference? The effects of mode of presentation, segment, and rating format on interrater reliability. *Psychotherapy, 25,* 44–50.

Chapter 7
RELATION OF NONVERBAL BEHAVIOR
TO CLIENT REACTIONS

Clara E. Hill and Alicia Stephany

One of a therapist's tasks is to observe and understand the client's experience in therapy (Hill & O'Grady, 1985). Unfortunately, Rennie (1985) found that clients often hide their negative reactions to therapists. Furthermore, Thompson and Hill (1988) found that therapists are not as accurate in detecting negative client reactions, for example, if the client felt worse or felt misunderstood, as they are in detecting positive client reactions, for example, if the client felt supported or gained better self-understanding, to therapist interventions. These findings bode poorly for therapy if, as Hill and O'Grady suggested, therapists need to be aware of client reactions to plan effective interventions.

We wondered whether clients emit clues that therapists could use to predict client reactions. Nonverbal behaviors seemed like a good source of clues for reactions because previous research has found them to be particularly important in the communication of emotion (Ekman, 1964; Harper, Wiens, & Matarazzo, 1978; Mehrabian, 1972; Siegman & Feldstein, 1987). Harman (1971) noted that

> there appears to be adequate research to support the idea that specific nonverbal acts have specific psychological meaning. The ability to interpret such acts will add to the counselor's repertoire of skills. Understanding non-verbal behavior is another way of "hearing" the feelings the client is expressing. (p. 191)

Highlen and Hill (1984) suggested that nonverbal behavior served the following functions: (a) to express or communicate emotion, (b) to show sensitivity to changes in the relationship, (c) to regulate the interaction by rules for such things as turn-taking, (d) to provide clues to a person's attempt to conceal emotion, (e) to convey a person's attitude toward self, and (f) to repeat, contradict, complement, accent, or regulate the meanings of verbal behavior. They suggested that by observing their clients, counselors could avoid misreading and mislabeling client communications.

Of particular interest is the function of nonverbal behavior in concealing emotion. Research has indicated that nonverbal behaviors can reveal when persons are involved in deception (Zuckerman, DePaulo, & Rosenthal, 1981). Although clients may not consciously be trying to deceive when they hide their negative reactions, they may in some cases be altering their behaviors so that therapists cannot read their reactions. In such cases Ekman and Friesen's (1969a, 1969b) theory of a leakage

Reprinted from *Journal of Counseling Psychology, 37*, 22–26 (1990). Copyright © 1990 by the American Psychological Association. Used with permission of the first author.

This study was conducted as an undergraduate honor's thesis by Alicia Stephany under the direction of Clara E. Hill and was supported in part by National Institutes of Mental Health Research Grant MH37837 to Clara E. Hill. The Computer Science Center of the University of Maryland provided computer support.

We express our appreciation to Kevin E. O'Grady for statistical consultation and to Bruce Fretz and Barbara J. Thompson for reviewing the article.

hierarchy may apply. Ekman and Friesen noted that all nonverbal and verbal channels can be arranged on a continuum of controllability. Verbal content and the face seem to be more controllable, whereas the body and tone of voice are less controllable. Thus one expects that negative reactions may be evinced more in arm and leg movements than in facial movements.

In noting the problems with research in the nonverbal area, Highlen and Hill (1984) suggested that the traditional strategy of relating the frequency of nonverbal behaviors to outcome measures was not appropriate because the amount of a behavior may not be as important as the timing and appropriateness of the behavior. They suggested that researchers instead must look at critical moments within sessions to see which nonverbal behaviors occur. Negative client reactions constitute such critical moments.

Our study used the data set developed by Thompson and Hill (1988). During a videotape review the clients reported up to three reactions to each therapist intervention and the therapists reported up to three reactions that they judged clients to be experiencing to their interventions. For this study every 5 s of client behavior was judged for the presence or absence of nine nonverbal behaviors, although only those units that occurred at the time of the therapist intervention were included in the analyses. These nine nonverbal behaviors were chosen to represent a range of presumably controllable (smiles, speech hesitancies, and vertical and horizontal head movements) and uncontrollable (arm movements, leg movements, postural shifts, adaptors, and illustrators) behaviors.

The first purpose of the study was to determine how client nonverbal behaviors corresponded to client-reported reactions. We realized, however, that simply looking at client-reported reactions would not provide any clues to therapist misperceptions of client reactions. In Thompson and Hill's (1988) study, they found that client-reported and therapist-perceived reactions did not always converge, which indicated that therapists might be responding to different nonverbal behaviors in their determination of client reactions. Therefore, the second purpose was to determine how client nonverbal behavior corresponded to therapist-perceived reactions.

Method

Stimulus Materials

In the Thompson and Hill (1988) study, 16 therapists each saw 2 different clients for single 50-min sessions. For this study only one session from each therapist ($N = 16$) was used because of the need to eliminate some sessions in which judges knew the clients.

Therapists

Sixteen therapists, ranging in age from 24 to 46 years ($M = 33.29$, $SD = 6.24$), participated. Eight (4 women and 4 men) were advanced graduate students with 3–11 years of predoctoral counseling experience ($M = 4.81$, $SD = 2.73$), and 8 (4 women and 4 men) were experienced therapists with 2–20 years of postdoctoral experience ($M = 10.13$, $SD = 5.57$). Using three 5-point ($5 = high$) Likert scales to rate how much they believed in and adhered to major theoretical orientations, the therapists rated themselves at moderate levels on humanistic ($M = 3.56$, $SD = .80$), psychoanalytic ($M = 2.75$, $SD = 1.32$), and behavioral ($M = 2.69$, $SD = 1.00$) orientations.

Volunteer Clients

Eight female and 8 male volunteer clients were recruited from upper level psychology classes. Selection criteria included motivation to discuss a specific personal problem with a therapist and a lack of severe pathology, that is, no T scores greater than 70 on the Hopkins Symptom Checklist (Derogatis, Rickels, & Rock, 1976). All volunteer clients signed consent forms.

Judges

To judge the presence of nonverbal behaviors, 13 judges (8 women and 5 men) were recruited from upper level undergraduate psychology courses and given course credit for participation in this study. Selection criteria included good reasons for wanting to participate (i.e., research experience rather than just course credit) and a grade point average of at least 3.0 on a 4-point scale. Judges signed statements to affirm that they did not know any of the volunteer clients and to promise to keep all material confidential. Judges were unaware of the hypotheses of the study.

Measures

Client Reactions System (Hill, Helms, Spiegel, & Tichenor, 1988)

The Client Reactions System consists of 21 nominal, nonmutually exclusive reactions grouped into five clusters: (a) supported (understood, supported, hopeful, and relief), (b) therapeutic work (negative thoughts and behaviors, better self-understanding, clear, feelings, responsibility, unstuck, new perspectives, educated, and new ways to behave), (c) challenged (challenged), (d) negative (scared, worse, stuck, lack direction, confused, and misunderstood), and (f) no reaction (no reaction). Hill et al. (1988) demonstrated that therapist intentions and pretreatment symptomatology were related to client reactions.

Nonverbal Behaviors

On the basis of the literature (Ekman & Friesen, 1969b; Fretz, 1966; Haase & Tepper, 1973; Hill, Siegelman, Gronsky, Sturniolo, & Fretz, 1981; Smith-Hanen, 1977), definitions were developed for nine nonmutually exclusive nonverbal behaviors: (a) *Speech hesitancies* were silences of at least 3 s of duration; (b) *vertical head movements* were any up-and-down movements of the head, including any forward–backward motion of the head such as bobbing, not directly associated with a horizontal movement; (c) *horizontal head movements* were any horizontal movements of the head not directly associated with a vertical movement, including any side-to-side nodding; (d) *arm movements* were any vertical or horizontal movements of the arm; (e) *leg movements* were any vertical or horizontal movements of the leg; (f) *postural shifts* were changes in trunk lean or body orientation; (g) *adaptors* were behaviors such as biting, licking the lips, playing with hair, picking with fingers, scratching, holding oneself, tapping hand movement, rubbing, or massaging; (h) *illustrators* were any arm or hand movements directly tied to speech; and (i) *smiles* were any upward turning of the lips.

Procedure

Four judges were trained on each nonverbal behavior (except speech hesitancy for which only 2 judges were trained). Each judge was trained on two different nonverbal behaviors. The judges first discussed the definition and criteria for their assigned nonverbal behavior and then practiced rating these behaviors on tapes other than those used for this study. They were trained until they reached 80% agreement for each category of behavior on 100 segments that each lasted 5 s.

The judges rated the entire session for nonverbal behaviors. A grid that segmented each min into twelve 5-s intervals was used to record each category of behavior. Segments were announced by a tape-recorded voice. Judges marked a check in the unit if they observed their category of behavior in the 5-s period. The judges who recorded head movements distinguished between vertical and horizontal head movements. Similarly, judges recording adaptors and illustrators distinguished between them. Because the nonverbal categories are not mutually exclusive and were judged by different judges, all nine behaviors could potentially have been judged to occur during any given 5-s unit.

To protect the confidentiality of the volunteer clients, who along with the judges were undergraduate students, only 1 judge listened to the audio portion of the session. This judge was responsible for recording therapist and client speaking turns and speech hesitancies. The rest of the judges watched the session with the audio portion turned off.

The judges worked in pairs assigned for each therapy session. One judge did ratings for 5 min and then switched with the other judge, so that only 1 judge was rating at a time. Reliability was measured in half of the sessions by having each pair of judges record their behavior together for a randomly determined 5 min interval.

In choosing which units of nonverbal behavior to analyze, we chose the last two 5-s units of a therapist speaking turn and the first two 5-s units of a client speaking turn. It seemed most likely from the research on turn-taking (Harper et al., 1978) that clients would display their reactions to therapist interventions through their nonverbal behavior at the time that they were required to respond to the therapist.

More than one client-reported reaction or therapist-perceived reaction was typically reported for any given speaking turn, so each reaction was related to all nonverbal behaviors observed for that speaking turn. The data is presented in the form of the proportion of times each nonverbal behavior actually occurred out of the total number of 5-s units in which a given reaction was reported. Proportions were used to correct for unequal numbers of reactions.

Results

Interrater Reliability

Both the percentage of agreement and kappa were computed for all nonverbal be-haviors except speech hesitancies: horizontal head movements, 99%, $\kappa = .75$; vertical head movements, 94%, $\kappa = .68$; arm movements, 94%, $\kappa = .88$; leg movements, 97%, $\kappa = .90$; postural shifts, 95%, $\kappa = .58$; adaptors, 89%, $\kappa = .68$; illustrators, 91%, $\kappa = .82$; and smiles, 94%, $\kappa = .70$. For this particular data the percentage of agreement is probably a more accurate estimate of interrater reliability than kappa because there was not an even distribution among the cells, which is required for the kappa statistic. No reliability was computed for speech hesitancies because it was operationally defined clearly and because only 1 judge listened to the session to preserve confidentiality among the students.

Correspondence Between Reactions and Nonverbal Behavior

Before the analyses, arc sine transformations were used to correct for possible skew-ing of the data due to the small proportions. Separate analyses were done for each nonverbal behavior because there was no a priori reason to believe that the nonverbal behaviors were related. We tested whether proportions of each nonverbal behavior differed across the five reactions with profile analysis, a multivariate analogue of repeated measures analysis of variance. Profile analysis was used because it does not have the restrictive assumptions (e.g., circularity) of repeated measures analyses of variance (Harris, 1985).

Because of the large number of tests, an alpha level of .01 was used for all analyses to provide the best balance between power and the limited sample size.

Client-Reported Reactions and Nonverbal Behavior

Table 1 shows the means and standard deviations of the proportions of each of the nonverbal behaviors for each client-reported reaction. A significant main effect for reactions was found for horizontal head movements, $F(4, 12) = 15.88, p < .001$. Post hoc analyses, in which we used simple mean comparisons (univariate tests) with a Bonferroni adjusted alpha of .001, indicated that there were more horizontal head movements when clients reported feeling supported than negative reactions, $F(1, 15) = 57.31, p < .001$, or no reaction, $F(1, 15) = 16.40, p = .001$. More horizontal head movements were also found when clients reported therapeutic work than negative reactions, $F(1, 15) = 17.76, p = .001$. A significant main effect for reactions was also found for vertical head movements, $F(4, 12) = 7.96, p = .002$. More post hoc analyses indicated that clients had more vertical head movements for supported than for chal-lenged, $F(1, 15) = 31.62, p < .001$.

Therapist-Perceived Reactions and Nonverbal Behavior

Table 2 shows the means and standard deviations of the proportions of each of the nonverbal behaviors for each therapist-perceived reaction. A significant main effect

Table 1—Proportions of Client Nonverbal Behaviors Occurring During 5-S Time Units
That Corresponded to Client Reports of Each of Five Reactions

	Reactions									
	Supported		Therapeutic work		Challenged		Negative		No reaction	
Nonverbal behavior	M	SD	M	SD	M	SD	M	SD	M	SD
Speech hesitancy	.02	.03	.03	.04	.03	.06	.02	.04	.02	.03
Negative head movements[a]	.07	.07	.06	.07	.05	.18	.03	.07	.05	.09
Positive head movements[a]	.01	.02	.02	.03	.00	.01	.01	.02	.01	.03
Arm movements	.18	.12	.18	.12	.18	.24	.13	.15	.20	.22
Leg movements	.14	.18	.11	.16	.10	.24	.08	.14	.14	.24
Postural shifts	.03	.03	.02	.04	.01	.04	.02	.05	.03	.12
Adaptors	.09	.10	.10	.11	.08	.15	.08	.13	.12	.20
Illustrators	.13	.09	.12	.08	.13	.21	.10	.13	.14	.14
Smiles	.05	.06	.04	.05	.04	.08	.04	.10	.03	.04

Note. The data in this table are raw proportions; arc sine transformations were computed on the raw data prior to data analysis.
[a]Significant results were found between the reactions for this nonverbal behavior.

Table 2—Proportions of Client Nonverbal Behaviors Occurring During 5-S Time Units That Corresponded to Therapist Reports of Each of Five Perceived Client Reactions

| | Reactions | | | | | | | | | |
| | Supported | | Therapeutic work | | Challenged | | Negative | | No reaction | |
Nonverbal behavior	M	SD	M	SD	M	SD	M	SD	M	SD
Speech hesitancy[a]	.03	.04	.05	.05	.09	.17	.08	.10	.02	.03
Negative head movements[a]	.16	.13	.12	.11	.09	.13	.04	.07	.08	.14
Positive head movements	.03	.04	.01	.02	.04	.08	.03	.06	.02	.03
Arm movements	.36	.12	.36	.15	.29	.28	.35	.25	.29	.20
Leg movements	.28	.29	.26	.30	.20	.33	.20	.30	.26	.31
Postural shifts	.04	.05	.04	.06	.03	.08	.05	.07	.02	.03
Adaptors	.17	.14	.20	.14	.13	.16	.12	.13	.15	.17
Illustrators	.28	.12	.25	.13	.19	.17	.17	.16	.21	.17
Smiles	.10	.08	.08	.09	.09	.14	.05	.09	.09	.11

Note. The data in this table are raw proportions; arc sine transformations were computed on the raw data prior to data analysis.
[a]Significant results were found between the reactions for this nonverbal behavior.

for reactions was found for speech hesitancies, $F(4, 12) = 6.98$, $p < .01$. The post hoc analyses indicated that clients had more speech hesitancies when therapists perceived therapeutic work than when they perceived supported, $F(1, 15) = 18.20$, $p = .001$. A significant main effect for reactions was also found for horizontal head movements, $F(4, 12) = 5.30$, $p = .01$. The post hoc analyses indicated that clients had more horizontal head movements when therapists perceived therapeutic work than when they perceived negative reactions, $F(1, 15) = 16.64$, $p = .001$.

Discussion

Client reactions were associated with three client nonverbal behaviors: horizontal head movements, vertical head movements, and speech hesitancies. The results differed somewhat, however, depending on whether the reactions were reported by clients or perceived by therapists.

Clients and therapists agreed that horizontal head movements were associated with the client reactions of therapeutic work, and the clients also associated horizontal movements with feeling supported. These findings indicate that horizontal head movements may serve as signals of client involvement in the therapy process.

Vertical head movements were also associated with clients' reporting reactions of supported. Thus, clients showed signs of agreement when they felt good about what was happening in the session. It was somewhat surprising that the therapists did not recognize that the vertical head movements were associated with positive reactions.

An additional finding was that for therapists clients' speech hesitancies were associated with therapeutic work. Therapists apparently thought that clients were deep in thought and working inwardly when they paused in their speech. From the clients' reports, however, they were not necessarily reacting in any particular manner. Apparently, therapists mistakenly attributed speech hesitancies to therapeutic work.

Although we had hoped to discover specific nonverbal behaviors that were associated with negative reactions, we instead found that clients were generally less active, particularly with their head movements, when they had negative reactions. Perhaps when clients are less active, therapists ought to be curious about possible negative reactions.

No associations were found between the other nonverbal behaviors that we measured (arm movements, leg movements, postural shifts, and smiles) and client reactions. Given Ekman and Friesen's (1969a) theory of a leakage hierarchy, these results make sense for head movements and smiles because they are more controllable behaviors. However, the results are not consistent with Ekman and Friesen's theory for arm and leg movements and postural shifts, which are less controllable and thus ought to be more indicative of emotions. A possible explanation is that these body movements occur infrequently in therapy and are not good predictors of reactions in such a confined setting. An alternate explanation is that clients may use these nonverbal behaviors in idiosyncratic ways to express reactions. One client may smile, whereas another client may fidget when feeling negative reactions.

Dittmann (1987) concluded that body language is a limited method of communication because few nonverbal behaviors have universal meanings. He suggested that people tend to focus primarily on the verbal communication because it is of higher information density and greater intensity than nonverbal behavior. Future studies may investigate whether therapists focus differentially on verbal or nonverbal cues in decoding negative client reactions.

In conclusion, this study makes a step toward examining nonverbal behavior during critical events in therapy rather than examining all nonverbal behaviors that occur within a therapy session, as was suggested by Highlen and Hill (1984). However, we must caution that we did not study individual differences between clients or cultural factors in using nonverbal behaviors. Persons undoubtedly express their reactions through different nonverbal behaviors. Future studies on nonverbal behavior need to consider individual differences between clients in their use of nonverbal behavior, so that therapists can learn more about how different clients express their reactions to therapist interventions.

References

Derogatis, L. R., Rickels, K., & Rock, A. F. (1976). The SCL-90 and the MMPI: A step in the validation of a new self-report scale. *British Journal of Psychiatry, 128*, 280–289.

Dittmann, A. T. (1987). The role of body movement in communication. In A. W. Siegman & S. Feldstein (Eds.), *Nonverbal behavior and communication* (2nd ed., pp. 37–64). Hillsdale, NJ: Erlbaum.

Ekman, P. (1964). Body position, facial expression, and verbal behavior during interviews. *Journal of Abnormal and Social Psychology, 63*, 295–301.

Ekman, P., & Friesen, W. V. (1969a). Nonverbal leakage and clues to deception. *Psychiatry, 32*, 88–106.

Ekman, P., & Friesen, W. V. (1969b). The repertoire of nonverbal behavior: Categories, origins, usage, and coding. *Semiotica, 1*, 49–98.

Fretz, B. R. (1966). Postural movements in a counseling dyad. *Journal of Counseling Psychology, 13*, 335–343.

Haase, R. F., & Tepper, D. T. (1973). Nonverbal components of empathic communication. *Journal of Counseling Psychology, 19*, 417–424.

Harman, R. L. (1971). Nonverbal behavior in counseling. *School Counselor, 18*, 189–192.

Harper, R. G., Wiens, A. N., & Matarazzo, J. D. (1978). *Nonverbal communication: The state of the art.* New York: Wiley.

Harris, R. J. (1985). *A primer of multivariate statistics* (2nd ed.). New York: Academic.

Highlen, P. S., & Hill, C. E. (1984). Factors affecting client change in counseling. In S. D. Brown & R. Lent (Eds.), *Handbook of counseling psychology* (pp. 334–396). New York: Wiley.

Hill, C. E., Helms, J. E., Spiegel, S. B., & Tichenor, V. (1988). Development of a system for categorizing client reactions to therapist interventions. *Journal of Counseling Psychology, 35*, 27–36.

Hill, C. E., & O'Grady, K. E. (1985). List of therapist intentions illustrated in a case study and with therapists of varying theoretical orientations. *Journal of Counseling Psychology, 32*, 3–22.

Hill, C. E., Siegelman, L., Gronsky, B., Sturniolo, F., & Fretz, B. R. (1981). Nonverbal communication and counseling outcome. *Journal of Counseling Psychology, 28*, 203–212.

Mehrabian, A. (1972). *Nonverbal communication.* Chicago: Aldine-Atherton.

Rennie, D. (1985, June). *The inner experience of psychotherapy.* Paper presented at the Society for Psychotherapy Research, Evanston, IL.

Siegman, A. W., & Feldstein, S. (Eds.). (1987). *Nonverbal behavior and communication* (2nd ed.). Hillsdale, NJ: Erlbaum.

Smith-Hanen, S. S. (1977). Effects of nonverbal behaviors on judged levels of counselor warmth and empathy. *Journal of Counseling Psychology, 24,* 87–91.

Thompson, B. J., & Hill, C. E. (1988, June). *Therapist perceptions of client reactions.* Paper presented at the Society for Psychotherapy Research, Evanston, IL.

Zuckerman, M., DePaulo, B. M., & Rosenthal, R. (1981). Verbal and nonverbal communication of deception. In L. Berkowitz (Ed.), *Advances in experimental social psychology* (Vol. 14, pp. 2–59). New York: Academic Press.

Chapter 8
BENEATH THE SURFACE OF LONG-TERM THERAPY:
Therapist and Client Report of Their Own and Each Other's Covert Processes

Clara E. Hill, Barbara J. Thompson, Mary C. Cogar,
and Daniel W. Denman III

Hill and O'Grady (1985) and Martin (1984) provided cognitive–mediational models that describe the influence of covert processes (such as therapist intentions and client reactions) on the therapy process. Consider, for example, an overt exchange in which the therapist recommends that the client do a homework exercise and the client agrees. If we were to examine the underlying thoughts and feelings, we might find that the therapist really meant to encourage the client but that the client felt misunderstood. If this were the case, the client probably would not do the homework, and the therapy relationship would suffer. However, if the therapist were aware that the client had a negative reaction to the homework directive, he or she could address the negative reaction and perhaps repair the misunderstanding event. If the client were aware that the therapist meant to encourage rather than to direct, she or he might be more receptive to the therapist and feel encouraged.

The underlying assumption in these models is that attention to covert processes on the part of both clients and therapists is helpful in therapy. The more open and revealing clients are about their thoughts and feelings, the more therapists ought to be able to help them (see also Stiles, 1987). The more transparent therapists are about their intentions, the greater the sense of collaboration about the therapeutic process clients ought to feel.

Client Covert Processes

We consider research relevant to three types of client covert processes: reactions, things left unsaid, and secrets. *Reactions*, which can be displayed or hidden, refer to thoughts and feelings clients have in response to specific therapist interventions. *Things left unsaid* refer to thoughts or feelings clients have during sessions that they do not share with their therapists. *Secrets* are major life experiences, facts, or feelings that clients do not tell their therapists. In effect, hidden reactions, things left unsaid, and secrets all refer to hidden thoughts and feelings but differ in terms of the time

Reprinted from *Journal of Counseling Psychology, 40*, 278–288 (1993). Copyright © 1993 by the American Psychological Association. Used with permission of the first author.

A version of this article was presented in June 1992 at the annual meeting of the Society for Psychotherapy Research, Berkeley, California.

This research was supported by National Institute of Mental Health Research Grant MH37837 to Clara E. Hill, Principal Investigator.

We express our appreciation to the therapists and the clients who gave so generously of their time, to Joan Jeranek for coding the data, and to Maureen M. Corbett and Elizabeth Nutt for commenting on a draft of this article.

frame, with reactions being directed toward a specific therapist intervention, things left unsaid being felt within a session, and secrets occurring over a longer time frame and not necessarily arising from events within the therapy.

Client Reactions

Using a qualitative methodology, Rennie (1985, 1992) found that clients often reported hiding negative reactions from their therapists. While overtly cooperative and pleasant, clients sometimes were secretly questioning and even resentful toward their therapists. Clients admitted being reluctant to reveal these negative reactions. Some clients felt that it was not their place to challenge the experts. Other clients felt that it was childish to express criticisms and that they should overlook minor faults if they generally valued the therapy. Still other clients were afraid that criticism might jeopardize their relationship with their therapists.

Hill, Thompson, and Corbett (1992) and Thompson and Hill (1991) used a quantitative methodology to examine hidden reactions. During a videotape-assisted review of the session, clients reported their reactions and therapists reported what they perceived the client's reactions to have been for each therapist intervention. These two studies found that clients hid negative reactions more often than they hid positive reactions; that therapists were more accurate at recognizing positive than negative client reactions; and that when therapists were aware of negative client reactions, their next interventions were actually perceived as less helpful than when therapists were not aware of negative client reactions. Because these studies were of single sessions or of very brief therapy, questions remain as to whether similar results would be found in longer term therapy in which clients might feel more comfortable revealing negative feelings and therapists might be more adept at interpreting these reactions.

Client Things Left Unsaid

Regan and Hill (1992) asked clients to indicate in writing what thoughts or feelings they had during the session that they did not share with their therapists. They also asked therapists to indicate what thoughts or feelings they thought clients had but did not share. Regan and Hill found that most of the things clients left unsaid were negative. Therapists were able to match (indicate the same thing left unsaid) on only 17% of the total number of things clients left unsaid during sessions. Therapists rated the sessions as rougher, and clients indicated lower satisfaction with treatment when therapists matched (versus did not match) what clients indicated they left unsaid.

Client Secrets

On the basis of what encounter group participants anonymously wrote that they kept secret, Yalom (1970) found three predominant themes: (a) a deep conviction of basic inadequacy, (b) a deep sense of interpersonal alienation, and (c) some variety of sexual secret. In a study of what undergraduates were most disinclined to share in their encounter groups, Norton, Feldman, and Tafoya (1974) found that the highest proportion of secrets were sex related (27%) or about failure (16%). To our knowledge, secrets have not been studied in individual therapy.

Purposes of the Present Study

In sum, the overall purpose of the part of the present study dealing with client covert processes was to study three different types of such processes (reactions, things left unsaid, and secrets) and to investigate their impact on long-term therapy. The first purpose was to investigate client reactions by using a tape-assisted review of sessions in an effort to replicate the findings of brief therapy by Thompson and Hill (1991) and Hill et al. (1992) in long-term therapy. We examined whether (a) therapists would be able to match overall client reactions at a level greater than chance, (b) therapists would be as able to match negative reactions as other reactions, (c) clients would hide more negative reactions than other reactions, and (d) therapist awareness of negative reactions would be perceived as helpful by clients and therapists.

The second purpose was to examine things left unsaid in an effort to replicate the findings for brief therapy by Regan and Hill (1992) in long-term therapy. We examined whether (a) clients leave things unsaid during sessions, (b) the things left unsaid are positive or negative, (c) therapists are aware of things clients left unsaid, and (d) therapist awareness of things clients left unsaid is related to outcome. Furthermore, we explored why clients leave things unsaid in therapy sessions.

The third purpose was to investigate secrets within long-term therapy. We examined whether (a) clients keep secrets from their therapists, (b) client secrets can be categorized into particular content areas, and (c) clients who have secrets are less satisfied with their treatment. Finally, we explored client reasons for keeping secrets from their therapists.

Therapist Covert Processes

Several studies have been based on the hypothesis that therapists should be transparent about their intentions to enhance client collaboration and hence improve outcome. Three of four studies (Fuller & Hill, 1985; Horvath, Marx, & Kamann, 1990; Martin, Martin, Meyer, & Slemon, 1986; Martin, Martin, & Slemon, 1987) found that client awareness of therapists intentions either was not related to or was negatively related to episode or session outcome. These authors (Fuller & Hill, 1985; Martin et al., 1986, 1987) suggested that when clients are focusing on what therapists are doing, they are not involved in their own tasks in therapy.

The four studies on client awareness of therapist intentions had several limitations. They all used a correlational strategy of linking frequency of events with outcome. Correlational designs are problematic because of lack of attention to timing, appropriateness, quality, and context of the behavior (Gottman & Markman, 1978; Lambert & Hill, 1994; Russell & Trull, 1986; Stiles, 1988). Thus, studying immediate outcome may be more appropriate than investigating episode or session outcome because of the temporal proximity of immediate outcome to the process variable. Furthermore, client awareness of different types of intentions has not been examined separately, which might obscure differences. Finally, all previous studies have involved single sessions or brief therapy, and findings need to be replicated within longer term therapy.

Thus, the overall purpose of the therapist covert processes part of the present study was to investigate client ability to detect therapist intentions in long-term therapy. We examined whether (a) clients would be able to match therapist intentions at a level greater than chance, (b) clients would be better able to match on some intentions than others, (c) client match on therapist intentions would be positively related to session outcome and client satisfaction with treatment, and (d) client match on specific therapist intentions would lead to higher client and therapist helpfulness ratings.

Method

Design

Therapy cases from a wide variety of theoretical orientations were included in the study because we were interested in the general construct of covert processes that occur across all forms of therapy (Hill & O'Grady, 1985; Martin, 1984). Furthermore, we excluded beginning and termination sessions because stage theorists (e.g., Egan, 1986; Mann, 1973) have suggested that different events occur in the beginning, middle, and termination stages of therapy.

Participants in long-term therapy were asked to audiotape or videotape a middle session of therapy in which termination was not being discussed or planned immediately. There were two parts of the research: (a) the videotape- or audiotape-assisted review, in which client and therapist indicated the helpfulness of each intervention and then indicated their own covert processes and their perceptions of the other's covert processes, and (b) the written evaluation, in which participants evaluated the session, reported what was left unsaid, and indicated any secrets. Nineteen dyads completed both the review and written evaluation parts of the study, and an additional 7 dyads completed the written evaluation only. Examination of demographic data showed no differences between the two groups, so the data were combined for the written evaluation portion of the study (things left unsaid and secrets).

Participants

Twenty-three therapists (14 female and 9 male; 22 White and 1 Black; 19 psychologists, 3 counselors, and 1 psychiatrist) practicing in the United States, Canada, England, Germany, and the Philippines participated in this study. Therapists averaged 41.50 ($SD = 9.36$) years of age and had an average of 10.42 ($SD = 8.86$) years of postgraduate experience conducting therapy. Using 5-point scales to indicate how much they believed in and adhered to the techniques of different orientations, therapists rated themselves as 3.81 ($SD = 0.98$) on humanistic approaches, 3.38 ($SD = 1.27$) on psychoanalytic approaches, and 2.35 ($SD = 1.26$) on behavioral approaches.

Clients were 18 women and 8 men (24 White, 1 Black, and 1 Asian), averaging 32.62 ($SD = 7.71$) years of age. Diagnoses and presenting problems were mixed, although therapists reported that clients were predominantly depressed or anxious.

All sessions were from the middle of therapy (defined as the period of therapy excluding the first few and the final few sessions). Therapists indicated that they had met with their clients for an average of 86.23 ($SD = 85.87$, range = 8–375) sessions prior to doing the research and estimated that they would conduct an average of 68.84 ($SD = 98.89$, range = 10–500) additional sessions.

In all but one case, therapists initiated the research project. One therapist participated with 2 clients in the complete version of the study (review plus written evaluation), and 2 therapists participated with 2 clients each in the short version (just the written evaluation). One person participated once as a therapist and once as a client in separate dyads in the complete version.

Measures

The helpfulness of therapist interventions was rated with the Helpfulness Scale (Elliott, 1985), which has a 9-point Likert scale ranging from *extremely unhelpful* (1) to *extremely helpful* (9). Elliott (1986) reported evidence of predictive validity ($r = .60$), with session outcome and temporal stability ranging from .40 to .60 between original and retrospective (after-therapy) helpfulness ratings.

The Client Reactions System (Hill, Helms, Spiegel, & Tichenor, 1988) consists of 21 nominal, nonmutually exclusive reactions organized into five clusters: supported (understood, supported, hopeful, relief), therapeutic work (negative thoughts and behaviors, better self-understanding, clear, feelings, responsibility, unstuck, new perspective, educated, new ways to behave), challenged (challenged), negative reactions (scared, worse, stuck, lack direction, confused, misunderstood), and no reaction (no reaction). Participants used all 21 reactions in completing the tasks, but these were collapsed into the five reaction clusters for the analyses. Hill, Helms, Spiegel, and Tichenor (1988) demonstrated validity for the Client Reactions System, showing that therapist intentions and pretreatment symptomatology were related to client reactions and that the supported, therapeutic work, and challenged reaction clusters received higher client helpfulness ratings than did negative and no reaction clusters.

The Therapist Intentions List (Hill & O'Grady, 1985; Hill, Helms, Tichenor, et al., 1988) has 19 pantheoretical, nonmutually exclusive intentions organized into eight clusters: set limits; assess (get information, focus, and clarify); support (support, instill hope, and reinforce change); educate (give information); explore (identify and intensify cognitions, behaviors, and feelings); restructure (insight, resistance, and challenge); change; and miscellaneous (relationship, cathart, self-control, and therapist needs). Intentions are a therapist's rationale for selecting a particular intervention to use with a client at any given moment within a session and are identified by therapists during an audiotape- or videotape-assisted review conducted immediately after the session. In the present study, therapists used all 19 intentions in completing the task, but these were collapsed into the eight clusters for the analyses. Hill and O'Grady (1985) reported content and construct validity for the measure. They also reported that psychoanalytic therapists used more feelings and insight intentions, whereas behavioral therapists used more change, set limits, and reinforce change intentions. Furthermore, there were decreases in assessment intentions and increases in restructuring intentions both within and across sessions. Therapist intentions were predictably connected with therapist response modes (Hill, Helms, Tichenor, et al., 1988).

The things left unsaid inventory (adapted from Regan & Hill, 1992) is a pencil-and-paper measure that uses an open-ended format to elicit information about what was experienced but not stated overtly during a session. Clients were asked, "What, if any, thoughts or feelings did you have during the session that you did not share with your therapist?" (e.g., "I was angry when the therapist asked about my mother but did not tell him"), and "Why didn't you tell your therapist?" Therapists were asked, "What, if any, thoughts or feelings do you think the client had but did not share with you?"

The things left unsaid valence rating (Regan & Hill, 1992) of the affective tone of the statement was made on a 5-point Likert-type scale assigned by independent judges ranging from *very negative* (1), for example, "One thing I did not tell her was that I felt the sessions were worthless and leading to nowhere," to *very positive* (5), for example, "I felt very supported and accepted throughout the session." Regan and Hill obtained an intraclass correlation of .96 among four judges for valence.

Match between therapists and clients on client things left unsaid was determined by judges through comparison of lists of client things left unsaid with therapist perceptions of things left unsaid, as was done in Regan and Hill (1992). For each client unsaid item, judges indicated whether any of the therapist's perceptions definitely matched, might have matched, or definitely did not match. Regan and Hill reported that at least three of four judges agreed on the categorization (same, maybe, different) for 93% of the items, and all four agreed on 80% of the items. We counted agreement (including both matches on things left unsaid and agreement that nothing was left unsaid) divided by the number of cases. (Note that Regan and Hill did not include agreement that nothing was left unsaid; they just divided the number of matches on things left unsaid by the number of things clients left unsaid.)

The secrets question is a pencil-and-paper measure that uses an open-ended format to elicit information about what secrets clients possess but have not told their therapists. Clients were asked, "What secrets do you have that you have not told your therapist?" (e.g., homosexuality, drug use, childhood sexual abuse, affairs, fears that therapy won't help), and "Why have you not told your therapist?"

The 17-category list developed by Norton et al. (1974) for types of secrets was used by judges to assign the secrets to categories. The categories were the following: sex, violence or destruction, mental health, masking, failure, stealing, loneliness, defective relationships, cheating, alcohol, drugs, phobia, physical health, ego vanity, goals and plans, habits, and no secrets. Norton et al. reported an average percentage agreement rate of 88% among four judges for this category system.

The Session Evaluation Questionnaire—Depth scale (SEQ–Depth; Stiles & Snow, 1984) is a bipolar, adjective-anchored scale developed to measure client and therapist estimates of session impact or quality. Stiles and Snow found minimal correlation, $r(15) = -.18$, *ns*, between counselor and client ratings of depth, indicating minimal overlap between perspectives. Stiles and Snow reported internal consistency of .91 for counselors and .87 for clients.

The 8-item Client Satisfaction Questionnaire (CSQ; Larsen, Attkisson, Hargreaves, & Nguyen, 1979) is a self-report measure assessing consumer satisfaction with mental health services. The CSQ evaluates various dimensions of consumer satisfaction: physical surroundings, type of treatment, treatment staff, quality of service, amount of service, outcome of service, general satisfaction, and procedures. For each item, scores range from 0 to 4, with higher scores reflecting greater satisfaction. In a sample of 3,120 respondents, the mean was 27.09 ($SD = 4.01$). Internal consistency of the CSQ has ranged from .84 to .93. When factor analyzed, the CSQ has repeatedly yielded only one factor (e.g., Nguyen, Attkisson, & Stegner, 1983). In terms of validity, the CSQ was related to clients' ratings of global improvement and symptomatology and therapists' ratings of clients' progress and likability; less satisfied clients had higher dropout rates. For the present study, the words *services* and *program* were replaced with *therapy* in each item.

Procedure

Dyad Recruitment

Letters of invitation were sent to approximately 300 therapists whom we knew through professional organizations and thought might have been currently involved in providing long-term therapy. The 29 therapists who indicated that they were interested in participating were sent the materials for the study. Therapists were asked to recruit clients with whom they were in the middle phase (i.e., the period excluding the first few and the final few sessions) of long-term therapy (i.e., therapy in which no termination was currently planned) and whom they thought would be willing to participate. Therapists were asked to stress to clients that all data would be kept confidential and that neither the client nor the therapist would see the other's responses.

Session

Prior to the research session, clients and therapists signed consent forms and reviewed the Therapist Intentions List and the Client Reactions System. The session was then audiotaped or videotaped but otherwise proceeded as usual.

Postsession Evaluation

For the 19 dyads who completed the review portion of the study, clients and therapists reviewed the videotape or audiotape together within 24 hr of the session (usually immediately after the session). They were instructed to review the tape and to recall what they felt during the session rather than what they were feeling at the time of the review. They were also instructed to record the data in writing, with no talking during the review. Therapists stopped the tape after the first sentence of the client response to each therapist speaking turn (defined as everything between two client speeches) and said the number of the speaking turn (to ensure that they were at the same spot on the review sheet). Each time the tape was stopped, clients rated the helpfulness of the therapist intervention, wrote down the numbers of up to 3 reactions (out of 21) to the therapist intervention (circling any hidden reactions), and wrote down the numbers of up to 3 intentions they thought the therapist might have had for the intervention. At the same time, therapists rated the helpfulness of their intervention, wrote down the numbers of up to 3 intentions they had for the intervention, and wrote down the numbers of up to 3 reactions (out of 21) they thought clients were experiencing (circling any reactions that they thought the client was hiding). The reactions that were uncircled were considered displayed, and the reactions that were circled were considered hidden.

All clients responded in writing to the things left unsaid inventory, the secrets question, the brief demographic questionnaire, the SEQ–Depth scale, and the CSQ; all therapists responded in writing to the things left unsaid inventory, the brief demographic form, and the SEQ–Depth scale.

When participants finished all tasks, each put his or her forms into an envelope, which was sealed immediately to ensure confidentiality. The forms were returned to us by mail, although the videotape or audiotape of the session was not sent.

Data Preparation

All responses to the things left unsaid inventory were typed and coded to preserve anonymity. The responses were coded into thought units (separate coherent thoughts) by the three judges. Two of the three judges agreed on 95% of the units, and all three agreed on 84% of the units. Discrepancies between judges were resolved through discussion.

Coding Things Left Unsaid

Three judges (Clara E. Hill, Barbara J. Thompson, and Mary C. Cogar) were trained to rate valence using material from a previous study. After training, each judge independently rated each item left unsaid for its valence. The intraclass correlation (alpha) for the three judges on the actual data was .76. After completing the valence ratings, the same judges independently compared lists of client things left unsaid and therapist guesses of things left unsaid for each session. For each item that the client left unsaid during a given session, judges determined whether any of the therapist guesses definitely did, might have, or definitely did not match. Two of the three judges agreed on 100% of the matches, and all three agreed on 85% of the matches. Discrepancies between judges were resolved through discussion. A match was counted if the therapist definitely or maybe matched the client, including instances in which both agreed that the client left nothing unsaid as matches.

Coding Reasons for Things Being Left Unsaid

On the basis of a rational appraisal of the responses, the three judges developed a preliminary list of reasons for leaving things unsaid: (a) therapist wouldn't understand, (b) emotions were overwhelming, (c) client wanted to avoid dealing with disclosure, (d) therapist didn't ask or didn't seem interested, (e) client was unsure about feelings, (f) client trusted therapist to ask important things, and (g) no reason was listed even though something was left unsaid. The judges reviewed the responses again and independently categorized each reason into one of the categories on the list. Two of the three judges agreed on 100% of the categorizations of the reasons, and all three agreed on 90% of the categorizations.

Coding Secrets

At a different point in time from the other judgments, the three judges independently coded each of the secrets into 1 of the 17 categories in Norton et al.'s (1974) list. Two of the three judges agreed on 100% of the matches, and all three agreed on 86% of the matches.

Coding Reasons for Nondisclosure of Secrets

On the basis of client responses, the three judges developed a preliminary list of reasons for not disclosing secrets: (a) felt ashamed or embarrassed, (b) therapist couldn't handle the disclosure, (c) client couldn't handle the disclosure, and (d) no reason provided. Then the judges went through the responses again and independently categorized each reason into one of the categories on the list. All three judges agreed on 100% of the categorizations.

Results

Average therapist-rated SEQ–Depth was 4.79 ($SD = 1.20$) and client-rated SEQ–Depth was 5.50 ($SD = 1.09$), both of which are within one standard deviation of scores reported by Stiles and Snow (1984). The average score on the CSQ was 28.31 ($SD = 2.71$), which is within one standard deviation of the scores reported by Larsen et al. (1979). Thus, the clients in this study were comparable to other client samples on these measures. The client-rated SEQ–Depth score was significantly related to the CSQ, $r(24) = .47$, $p < .01$.

Match on Reactions

The average proportion of displayed and hidden client reactions in each of the five clusters is shown in Table 1. The proportions within each cluster are within one standard deviation of those reported by Hill et al. (1992).

Calculating Match

A match was counted if therapists identified the same reaction cluster as their clients did for a given speaking turn. Therapists did not have to match on the exact reaction within the cluster but simply had to indicate a reaction within the cluster. More than one match could occur per cluster if clients listed more than one reaction within a cluster. The average number of observed matches across clusters as well as within clusters is shown in Table 2.

Average therapist match ratio (defined as the number of matches divided by the

Table 1—*Mean Proportion of Each of Five Reaction Clusters Reported by Clients as Displayed Versus Hidden*

Reaction cluster	Displayed		Hidden		Total	
	M	SD	M	SD	M	SD
Supported	.28	.14	.01	.04	.29	.13
Therapeutic work	.32	.20	.05	.13	.37	.19
Challenged	.06	.08	.01	.03	.08	.07
Negative reactions	.11	.14	.07	.07	.18	.17
No reaction	.08	.08	.00	.00	.08	.08
Total	.87	.26	.13	.29	—	—

Note. Proportions were computed for each case and then averaged across cases. Dashes indicate not applicable.

number of client-reported reactions) across all reactions was .45 ($SD = .12$), which is comparable to ratios of past studies (e.g., Thompson & Hill, 1991). Therapist match ratio was significantly correlated with client age, $r(17) = .49$, $p < .05$, but not with therapist age, years of experience, theoretical orientation ratings, or number of transpired or expected sessions.

Calculating Chance

The overall expected number of matches was determined by calculating the number of matches expected assuming random guessing, given the number of reactions indicated by the client for each turn as well as the number indicated by the therapist for each turn, taking into account that there were five clusters with different numbers of reactions within clusters and summing this across the session. The calculation for separate clusters accounted for the number of reactions reported by the client and therapist as well as the number of reactions within that given cluster. Table 2 shows the average number of expected matches across and within the five reaction clusters.

Calculating the Difference Between Match and Chance

The difference scores between the observed and expected number of matches were summed across turns for each case. The total difference score was weighted by the inverse of the variance for each case (calculated from the chance probability model). This weighting controlled for the different numbers of reactions within turns and gave more weight to those cases having less variability under the null hypothesis (chance model). Thus, if a client reported fewer reactions, we had more confidence that matching was not by chance. To determine whether the number of matches was greater than chance across all reactions, we conducted a one-sample *t* test to compare the average weighted difference score to zero (the expected difference score if chance were operating). Results indicated that therapists matched client reactions at a level greater than chance (see Table 2).

Additionally, analyses were done for the five reaction clusters compared to

Table 2—*Observed and Expected Number of Matches and Weighted Difference Scores for the Five Reaction Clusters*

Reaction cluster	n	Observed matches		Expected matches		Weighted difference		t
		M	SD	M	SD	M	SE	
Support	19	14.47	14.11	2.52	1.66	4.13	2.02	2.04
Therapeutic work	19	18.74	16.42	12.50	8.32	3.39	0.72	4.69*
Challenged	18	1.83	2.26	0.09	0.15	0.72	1.70	0.43
Negative	17	6.65	8.43	3.09	2.38	1.73	0.76	2.28
No reaction	18	2.94	3.99	0.03	0.03	1.28	4.49	0.29
Overall	19	43.68	20.11	38.17	16.90	5.37	0.48	11.14**

Note. *SE* = standard error of the mean.
*Significant at the alpha ($p < .006$) set for the five reaction clusters. **Significant at the alpha ($p < .001$) set for the overall analysis.

chance. One-sample t tests compared the weighted difference score (the actual number of matches minus the expected number of matches) to zero. Multiple t tests, with
a Bonferroni adjusted alpha of .01 (.05/5), were used because different results were
expected for the different reactions. Table 2 indicates that therapists were better than
chance at matching on therapeutic work.

Differences Between Clusters on Hidden Reactions

An additional question was whether more reactions were hidden in the negative
cluster than in other clusters. A repeated measures analysis of variance conducted on
the number of hidden reactions within each of the five clusters was significant, $F(4,
15) = 5.36$, $p < .01$. Post hoc univariate analyses, with a Bonferroni corrected alpha
of .01 (.05/4), contrasted the negative reaction cluster with each of the other clusters.
As predicted, clients hid more negative reactions than supported reactions, $F(1, 18)
= 8.45$, $p < .01$, challenged reactions, $F(1, 18) = 9.17$, $p < .01$, or no reaction, $F(1,
18) = 15.57$, $p < .001$, but not more than therapeutic work reactions. Thus, clients
hid more negative reactions than supported reactions, challenged reactions, or no
reaction, but they hid as many therapeutic work reactions as negative reactions.

Therapist Match on Reactions in Relation to Immediate Outcome

Our goal was to determine whether therapist match on reactions was related to the
helpfulness ratings of subsequent therapist interventions. Separate analyses of variance were conducted for each reaction cluster because we predicted that the results
would vary on the basis of the reaction cluster. The main effects for each analysis
were case (19 cases) and match status (match vs. no match), and the dependent
variable was either client or therapist helpfulness ratings. Separate analyses were
conducted for client and therapist helpfulness ratings because of the low correlation
generally found between these variables (see Hill, Helms, Tichenor, et al., 1988).
The case main effect was not interpreted because we were interested only in the
effect for the match variables, with the case effect controlled. None of the interaction
effects were significant. A significant difference was found on therapeutic work, $F(1,
18) = 10.59$, $p < .001$, such that therapists gave higher helpfulness ratings when they
matched on therapeutic work than when they did not match.

Things Left Unsaid

Seventeen of the 26 clients (65%) left at least one thing unsaid during sessions, with
an average of 0.81 ($SD = 0.69$) things left unsaid per client and an average valence
of 2.52 ($SD = 1.43$) on the 5-point scale ranging from negative (1) to positive (5).
Similarly, 17 (65%) of 26 therapists indicated that clients left something unsaid
during sessions. However, in only 7 (27%) of the 26 cases were therapists accurate
about their perceptions (including agreement that nothing was left unsaid).
    In terms of reasons for not revealing the 21 things left unsaid by the 17 clients,
clients indicated overwhelming emotions ($n = 7$), wanting to avoid dealing with
disclosure ($n = 4$), fear that therapists wouldn't understand ($n = 3$), that therapists

didn't seem interested ($n = 1$), that they were unsure about their feelings ($n = 1$), that they trusted that their therapist would ask if it were important ($n = 1$), and no reason provided ($n = 5$).

The number of things clients left unsaid and whether there was a match between therapists and clients on things left unsaid were not significantly related to therapist-rated SEQ–Depth, client-rated SEQ–Depth, or client-rated CSQ.

Secrets

Twelve (46%) of the 26 clients indicated that they had secrets, with 9 indicating one secret and 3 indicating two secrets. The number of secrets was not related to the length of time in therapy, therapist-rated SEQ–Depth, or client-rated CSQ, although they were in the predicted direction (more secrets related to poorer outcome) and approached significance for client SEQ–Depth, $r(24) = -.36$, $p = .07$, and CSQ, $r(24) = -.37$, $p = .06$.

Table 3 shows the comparison of secrets in each of the categories along with Norton et al.'s (1974) data for encounter groups. The long-term clients had more mental health secrets, the same amount of sex secrets, but fewer of all other kinds of secrets than did the clients in Norton et al.'s encounter groups.

Of the 15 secrets withheld, the 16 listed reasons (1 client indicated two reasons) for lack of revelation were the following: felt ashamed or embarrassed ($n = 8$), client couldn't handle the disclosure ($n = 3$), client thought therapist couldn't handle the disclosure ($n = 2$), and no reason ($n = 3$).

Match on Intentions

Therapists reported an average proportion of .34 ($SD = .11$) intentions in the assessment cluster, .19 ($SD = .09$) in the support cluster, .18 ($SD = .12$) in the exploration cluster, .16 ($SD = .07$) in the restructure cluster, .05 ($SD = .06$) in the education

Table 3—*Percentage of Secrets in Each Category for Long-Term Clients as Compared With Norton, Feldman, and Tafoya's (1974) Data for Encounter Group Clients*

Category	Long-term clients (%)	Encounter group (%)
Sex	27	27
Failure	7	16
Mental health	7	2
Other	9	43
No secrets	50	12

Note. Other is a miscellaneous category that includes all of Norton et al.'s (1974) categories of violence or destruction, masking, stealing, loneliness, defective relationships, cheating, alcohol, drugs, phobia, physical health, ego vanity, goals and plans, and habits.

cluster, .04 (SD = .04) in the miscellaneous cluster, .02 (SD = .02) in the change cluster, and .02 (SD = .05) in the set limits cluster. These proportions are similar (within one standard deviation) to data of experienced therapists in the Hill and O'Grady (1985) and Fuller and Hill (1985) samples, except that the current therapists reported fewer change intentions than either of the other two samples (.02 in the present sample vs. .08 in each of the other two samples).

The average number of observed and expected matches and the weighted difference scores were calculated in exactly the same manner as they were for client reactions. The average number of observed and expected matches across clusters as well as within the eight clusters is shown in Table 4.

Average client match ratio (defined as the number of matches divided by the number of therapist-reported intentions) across all intentions was .50 (SD = .12). Using Pearson product–moment correlations, we found that client match ratio was not related to client age, therapist age, therapist years of experience, therapist ratings on theoretical orientations, or number of transpired or expected sessions.

To determine whether the number of matches was greater than chance across all intentions, a one-sample t test compared the average weighted difference score to zero (the expected difference score if chance were operating). Overall, clients matched therapist intentions at a level greater than chance (see Table 4).

Additionally, analyses were done for the eight intention clusters compared to chance. One-sample t tests compared the weighted difference score to zero. Multiple t tests, with a Bonferroni adjusted alpha of .006 (.05/8), were done because different results were expected for the different intentions. Table 4 indicates that clients were better than chance at matching on assessment, support, and restructure.

Client Match on Intentions in Relation to Session Outcome and Satisfaction

Client match ratio was not significantly related to client-rated SEQ-Depth, therapist-rated SEQ-Depth, or client-rated CSQ.

Client Match on Intentions in Relation to Immediate Outcome

To determine whether client match on each of the intention clusters was related to the helpfulness ratings, we conducted analyses of variance. Separate analyses were conducted for each cluster because we predicted that the results would vary by cluster. The main effects for each analysis were case (19 cases) and match status (match vs. no match), and the dependent variable was either client or therapist helpfulness ratings. The case main effect was not interpreted because we were interested only in the effect for the match variables, with the case effect controlled.

No significant interaction effects were found. A significant main effect for match status was found on the assessment cluster for both client helpfulness ratings, $F(1, 18) = 13.71$, $p < .001$, and therapist helpfulness ratings, $F(1, 18) = 44.27$, $p < .001$, such that both clients and therapists gave lower helpfulness ratings when clients matched on assessment intentions than when they did not match. Significant main effects for match status were also found on the explore cluster for therapist helpfulness ratings, $F(1, 18) = 4.55$, $p < .05$, and on the restructure cluster for therapist helpfulness ratings, $F(1, 18) = 33.71$, $p < .001$, such that therapists gave higher

Table 4—*Observed and Expected Number of Matches and Weighted Difference Scores for the Eight Intention Clusters*

Intention cluster	n	Observed matches		Expected matches		Weighted difference		
		M	SD	M	SD	M	SE	t
Set limits	5	2.20	3.90	0.10	0.14	0.56	6.10	0.09
Assessment	19	16.58	6.19	2.22	1.14	13.26	0.92	14.42*
Support	19	10.37	9.53	1.72	1.41	5.93	1.66	3.57*
Educate	16	1.31	2.52	0.07	0.08	0.84	1.86	0.45
Explore	19	9.16	9.74	2.99	2.64	2.27	0.95	2.39
Restructure	19	7.95	5.28	1.58	1.06	3.77	0.90	4.17*
Change	14	0.64	1.39	0.04	0.04	0.16	1.62	0.10
Other	16	0.75	1.00	0.74	0.96	0.16	0.40	0.39
Overall	19	46.84	17.90	25.53	12.49	20.12	0.56	35.73**

Note. SE = standard error of the mean.
*Significant at the alpha ($p < .006$) set for the five reaction clusters.   **Significant at the alpha ($p < .001$) set for the overall analysis.

helpfulness ratings when clients matched on explore and restructure intentions than when they did not match. Thus, both clients and therapists gave higher helpfulness ratings for assessment interventions when clients did not match these therapist intentions. In contrast, therapists gave higher helpfulness ratings to exploration and restructuring intentions when clients matched these therapist intentions.

Discussion

Our purpose in this study was to investigate client and therapist covert processes as well as each person's awareness of the other person's covert processes in long-term therapy. We found that clients did hide negative reactions, thoughts, and feelings during sessions. We also found that therapists were seldom aware of how clients were reacting or what clients were not saying. Furthermore, many clients had secrets they did not share with their therapists. Client match on therapist intentions was either neutrally or negatively related to either immediate or session-level outcome. The results for client and therapist covert processes are discussed separately.

Client Covert Processes

Clients in this study of long-term therapy hid negative reactions more often than they hid positive reactions, as did clients in brief therapy (Hill et al., 1992; Thompson & Hill, 1991). Thus, the finding that clients hide negative reactions is very robust, having been shown across single sessions, brief therapy, and long-term therapy. Apparently, when clients feel scared, worse, stuck, lacking in direction, confused, or misunderstood, they do not want their therapists to know.

In contrast to findings in past studies, these clients also hid reactions in the therapeutic work cluster (e.g., better self-understanding, unstuck, educated, and new ways to behave). This finding was somewhat surprising and needs to be replicated to determine whether it is typical for clients in long-term therapy to hide therapeutic work reactions. Given that hiding such reactions seems counterproductive, determining why clients hide therapeutic work reactions would be useful.

Experienced long-term therapists had a match ratio of .45 in their ability to perceive client reactions, which is comparable to ratios reported for inexperienced graduate student therapists in first sessions of brief therapy (Hill et al., 1992) and therapists with a range of experience in single sessions (Thompson & Hill, 1991). The long-term therapists in this study were as adept at perceiving negative as positive reactions, whereas the less experienced therapists in brief therapy were less adept at perceiving negative than positive reactions. Recognizing negative reactions may be an important component of long-term therapy.

Furthermore, the findings suggest that therapist awareness of negative client reactions was not detrimental to the therapy process, as had been found in the earlier studies of brief therapy (Hill et al., 1992; Thompson & Hill, 1991). Undoubtedly, the experience level of therapists, the long-term nature of the treatment, and the selectivity of the cases all contributed to the differences in findings between the studies. Experienced therapists in long-term therapy are probably less anxious when they perceive negative reactions because they have skills to deal with negative reactions and because the therapeutic relationship has had an opportunity to develop. In fact, in long-term therapy, therapists might even welcome the emergence of negative reactions because of the entree provided to deal with interpersonal relationship or transference issues. Furthermore, therapists probably selected clients for this study who could tolerate self-examination and with whom they had good relationships.

Additionally, in concert with Thompson and Hill (1991), therapist awareness of therapeutic work reactions (e.g., better self-understanding) resulted in higher therapist helpfulness ratings in subsequent turns. These results suggest that experienced therapists in long-term therapy are more adept at recognizing and managing therapeutic work and negative reactions than are inexperienced therapists (as in Hill et al., 1992).

Things Left Unsaid

The majority (65%) of clients left something unsaid during sessions, and most of the things left unsaid were slightly negative in valence. The number of things left unsaid for clients was similar to Regan and Hill's (1992) findings. Examples of things clients left unsaid are the following: "When we spoke about my husband, she made me feel like I was wrong and bad to him"; "I felt unsupported in talking about possible hospitalization"; "I felt stuck and needed prompting"; "I felt afraid of hurting her feelings"; "Frustration and anger that he was trying to change the feelings I have inside about death"; and "Her responses were ahead of where I wanted to be." Many of these unvoiced opinions reflect client discomfort with therapist behavior and may represent therapist errors.

Only 27% of therapists were accurate in their guesses about client nondisclosures, which is similar to the level found by Regan and Hill (1992). These data suggest that clients are pretty good at hiding what they do not want to tell therapists, that therapists are not very good at guessing what clients withhold, or both.

Clients indicated that they did not reveal things to their therapists because the emotions felt too overwhelming, they wanted to avoid dealing with the disclosures, or they were afraid their therapists would not understand or were not interested. These findings serve as a reminder that even in long-term therapy, clients get anxious about dealing with difficult emotions.

Secrets

About half of the clients in long-term therapy reported having secrets that they had not shared with their therapists. However, the proportion of clients who reported having secrets was much lower in long-term therapy than it was in encounter groups (Norton et al., 1974).

The content of several secrets was sexual, for example, "I am more sexually attracted to my therapist than I have let on"; "unorthodox sexual persuasions"; "I have been sexually abused to some degree"; "that I, being gay, fancy him"; and "childhood sexual abuse." Examples of secrets about the therapy process were the following: "I fear that therapy will end and I'll be left to fend for myself" and "I do fear that the therapy at times isn't helping."

Why do clients not reveal their secrets to their therapists? Shame and insecurity seemed to be the primary reasons. The client's reason for not revealing childhood sexual abuse was "embarrassment." The client's reason for not revealing sexual attraction to therapist was "I wish it wasn't so." The gay client said, "I don't want to worry him and cause anxiety." The client who felt therapy was not helping indicated, "I am scared of being rejected" as the reason for not revealing this.

Thus, although secrets were only present in about half of the cases, the secrets were major issues for clients and occasionally for the therapy process. Therapists might attend to methods to enable clients to feel more comfortable and less embarrassed about revealing secrets. Therapists sometimes become inoculated after hearing so much in therapy and forget how painful it is for clients to reveal what they perceive as shameful and embarrassing.

We should note that therapists might reinforce this shame and insecurity about sexual issues as a result of their own discomfort in discussing sexual issues. Therapists set a tone that lets clients know what is permissible to discuss in therapy. Courtois (1988), for example, suggested that therapists need to ask clients directly about sexual abuse to give permission and encouragement to admit abuse openly.

Therapist Covert Processes

Clients had a match ratio of .50 for therapist intentions, with more matches than expected for chance on assessment, support, and restructure intention clusters. The findings for assessment and support replicate those of Fuller and Hill (1985), who suggested that clients are able to recognize these intentions because they occur frequently in daily life and have grammatical and nonverbal cues that make them easy to perceive. The additional finding that clients were aware of therapists' restructuring intentions may be a result of the long-term nature of the therapy. Over time, clients may become clearer as to when therapists are trying to accomplish restructuring.

We found no relationship between overall match rate and session outcome, which replicates the findings of three other studies of neutral or negative relationships (Fuller & Hill, 1985; Martin et al., 1986, 1987). Thus, there seems to be fairly substantial evidence that overall client match is not related to session outcome.

However, overall match rate has the potential of obscuring discrepant findings for client awareness of different intentions. Indeed, in our analyses, we found evidence of differential results for different intentions clusters. Both clients and therapists gave higher helpfulness ratings in subsequent interventions when clients did not match on therapist intentions of assessment. Corbett and Hill (1991) also found that supervisees and supervisors gave higher helpfulness ratings when supervisees did not match supervisor intentions of assessment. Thus, across similar relationships, awareness of assessment was not perceived as being helpful or beneficial. Perhaps, as Corbett and Hill suggested, assessment feels less tangibly useful in comparison with other intentions. Alternatively, in longer term therapy, clients might believe that therapists should already have factual information and might feel upset if therapists do not know them as well as they thought the therapists did.

Furthermore, we found that therapists gave higher helpfulness ratings to exploration and restructuring intentions when clients matched on these therapist intentions. Perhaps when clients are aware of these intentions, therapists are more likely to feel that there is a good working relationship. We must emphasize, however, that client views of helpfulness were not influenced by their awareness of therapist exploration and restructuring intentions.

Thus, using both overall match and specific intention match, match between therapist intention and client perceptions seems to be either neutrally or negatively related to either immediate or session-level outcome, as assessed by the client perspective. Apparently, unless therapists are doing too much assessment in therapy, clients do not focus on therapist intentions. In fact, if therapists are being facilitative, clients may not notice so much what their therapists are doing as what they themselves are experiencing or thinking.

Limitations and Conclusions

A limitation of the present study is the small sample size, which reduces the generalizability of the findings. As was true for Vachon, Susman, and Wynne (1991), many therapists we contacted chose not to participate because of the time commitment, fears that the audiotaping or videotaping and review would interfere with therapy, and feelings that their clients could not tolerate the research. The cases in the current study probably represent a sample of therapists who were open to scrutiny and felt comfortable in a research setting. Furthermore, these therapists probably chose clients who had high ego strength and with whom they had good relationships. The comparability of the data for this study with normative data on the SEQ–Depth scale and the CSQ, as well as the comparability of findings for both reactions and things left unsaid with earlier studies (Hill et al., 1992; Regan & Hill, 1992; Thompson & Hill, 1991), provides some reassurance about the validity of the findings; however, this sample should not be considered representative of clients in long-term therapy.

Other limitations include the heterogeneity of the sample in terms of both therapist orientation, client diagnosis, and point in therapy. Additionally, use of data from a single session is problematic in that participants may have behaved differently in this research session than in typical sessions. Given the difficulties in obtaining even one session to study, however, it is difficult to imagine gaining access to more than one session using the present methodology.

A final limitation of this study is that we do not know whether participants gave accurate responses to our questions about hidden reactions, things left unsaid, and secrets. They may have had trouble remembering whether reactions were hidden or whether things were left unsaid. Furthermore, if they were not honest with their therapists, clients may not have been honest with researchers about their covert experiences. Rhodes and Geller (1992) suggested that clients may feel less vulnerable to researchers than to therapists because the relationship is less intimate; thus, clients may be better able to "confess" negative feelings. However, clients may also feel bad if they betray their therapists by revealing negative feelings about the relationship. Further research needs to be done on the accuracy and the experience of respondents in this type of research.

We encourage further research of covert events in therapy. In future studies researchers might examine what therapists do to encourage clients to reveal hidden reactions, experiences, and secrets. More knowledge is also needed about specific methods for dealing with the feelings of avoidance and shame that keep clients from disclosing their feelings. Because of the sensitive nature of these disclosures, however, therapists need to have respect for client boundaries both in therapy and in research.

Another interesting avenue of research would be to determine whether match on covert process is consistent with match on recall of significant therapeutic events (Cummings, Hallberg, Martin, & Slemon, 1992; Cummings, Martin, Hallberg, & Slemon, 1992; Martin & Stelmaczonek, 1988). Both match on covert processes and match on recall of important events may be indicative of therapist empathy or a strong working alliance.

References

Corbett, M. M., & Hill, C. E. (1991, August). *Intentions and reactions in supervision.* Paper presented at the 99th Annual Convention of the American Psychological Association, San Francisco.

Courtois, C. A. (1988). *Healing the incest wound.* New York: Norton.

Cummings, A. L., Hallberg, E., Martin, J., & Slemon, A. (1992). Participants' memories for therapeutic events and ratings of session effectiveness. *Psychotherapy: An International Quarterly, 6,* 113–124.

Cummings, A. L., Martin, J., Hallberg, E., & Slemon, A. (1992). Memory for therapeutic events, session effectiveness, and working alliance in short-term counseling. *Journal of Counseling Psychology, 39,* 306–312.

Egan, G. (1986). *The skilled helper* (3rd ed.). Monterey, CA: Brooks/Cole.

Elliott, R. (1985). Helpful and nonhelpful events in brief counseling interviews: An empirical taxonomy. *Journal of Counseling Psychology, 32,* 307–322.

Elliott, R. (1986). Interpersonal Process Recall (IPR) as a psychotherapy process research method. In L. S. Greenberg & W. M. Pinsof (Eds.), *The psychotherapeutic process: A research handbook* (pp. 503–528). New York: Guilford Press.

Fuller, F., & Hill, C. E. (1985). Counselor and helpee perceptions of counselor intentions in relation to outcome in a single counseling session. *Journal of Counseling Psychology, 32,* 329–338.

Gottman, J. M., & Markman, H. J. (1978). Experimental designs in psychotherapy research. In S. L. Garfield & A. E. Bergin (Eds.), *Handbook of psychotherapy and behavior change* (2nd ed., pp. 23–62). New York: Wiley.

Hill, C. E., Helms, J. E., Spiegel, S. B., & Tichenor, V. (1988). Development of a system for categorizing client reactions to therapist interventions. *Journal of Counseling Psychology, 35,* 27–36.

Hill, C. E., Helms, J. E., Tichenor, V., Spiegel, S. B., O'Grady, K. E., & Perry, E. S. (1988). Effects of therapist response modes in brief psychotherapy. *Journal of Counseling Psychology, 35,* 222–233.

Hill, C. E., & O'Grady, K. E. (1985). List of therapist intentions illustrated in a case study and with therapists of varying theoretical orientations. *Journal of Counseling Psychology, 32,* 3–22.

Hill, C. E., Thompson, B. J., & Corbett, M. M. (1992). The impact of therapist ability to perceive displayed and hidden client reactions on immediate outcome in first sessions of brief therapy. *Psychotherapy Research, 2,* 148–160.

Horvath, A. O., Marx, R. W., & Kamann, A. M. (1990). Thinking about thinking in therapy: An examination of clients' understanding of their therapists' intentions. *Journal of Consulting and Clinical Psychology, 58,* 614–621.

Lambert, M. J., & Hill, C. E. (1994). Assessing psychotherapy outcomes and processes. In A. E. Bergin & S. L. Garfield (Eds.), *Handbook of psychotherapy and behavior change* (4th ed., pp. 72–113). New York: Wiley.

Larsen, D. L., Attkisson, C. C., Hargreaves, W. A., & Nguyen, T. D. (1979). Assessment of client/patient satisfaction: Development of a general scale. *Evaluation and Program Planning, 2*, 197–207.

Mann, J. (1973). *Time-limited psychotherapy.* Cambridge, MA: Harvard University Press.

Martin, J. (1984). The cognitive mediational paradigm for research on counseling. *Journal of Counseling Psychology, 31*, 558–571.

Martin, J., Martin, W., Meyer, M., & Slemon, A. (1986). Empirical investigation of the cognitive mediational paradigm for research on counseling. *Journal of Counseling Psychology, 33*, 115–123.

Martin, J., Martin, W., & Slemon, A. (1987). Cognitive mediation in person-centered and rational–emotive therapy. *Journal of Counseling Psychology, 34*, 251–260.

Martin, J., & Stelmaczonek, K. (1988). Participants' identification and recall of important events in counseling. *Journal of Counseling Psychology, 35*, 385–390.

Nguyen, T. D., Attkisson, C. C., & Stegner, B. L. (1983). Assessment of patient satisfaction: Development and refinement of a service evaluation questionnaire. *Evaluation and Program Planning, 6*, 299–314.

Norton, R., Feldman, C., & Tafoya, D. (1974). Risk parameters across types of secrets. *Journal of Counseling Psychology, 21*, 450–454.

Regan, A. M., & Hill, C. E. (1992). Investigation of what clients and therapists do not say in brief therapy. *Journal of Counseling Psychology, 39*, 168–174.

Rennie, D. L. (1985, June). *Client deference in the psychotherapy relationship.* Paper presented at the annual meeting of the Society for Psychotherapy Research, Evanston, IL.

Rennie, D. L. (1992). Qualitative analysis of the client's experience of psychotherapy: The unfolding of reflexivity. In S. G. Toukmanian and D. L. Rennie (Eds.), *Psychotherapy process research: Paradigmatic and narrative approaches* (pp. 211–233). Newbury Park, CA: Sage.

Rhodes, R., & Geller, J. (1992, June). *Clinical issues in research on what clients don't tell their therapists.* Paper presented at the annual meeting of the Society for Psychotherapy Research, Berkeley, CA.

Russell, R. L., & Trull, T. J. (1986). Sequential analysis of language variables in psychotherapy process research. *Journal of Consulting and Clinical Psychology, 54*, 16–21.

Stiles, W. B. (1987). "I have to talk to somebody": A fever model of self-disclosure. In V. J. Derlega & J. H. Berg (Eds.), *Self-disclosure* (pp. 257–282). New York: Plenum Press.

Stiles, W. B. (1988). Psychotherapy process–outcome correlations may be misleading. *Psychotherapy, 25*, 27–35.

Stiles, W. B., & Snow, J. S. (1984). Counseling session impact as viewed by novice counselors and their clients. *Journal of Counseling Psychology, 31*, 3–12.

Thompson, B. J., & Hill, C. E. (1991). Therapist perceptions of client reactions. *Journal of Counseling and Development, 69*, 261–265.

Vachon, D. O., Susman, M., & Wynne, M. E. (1991, November). *Therapists' refusal to participate in psychotherapy process research: A survey.* Paper presented at the North American Society for Psychotherapy Research, Panama City, FL.

Yalom, I. (1970). *The theory and practice of group psychotherapy.* New York: Basic Books.

Chapter 9
HELPEE INTROVERSION, NOVICE COUNSELOR INTENTION USE, AND HELPEE-RATED SESSION IMPACT

Dennis M. Kivlighan, Jr., and Edgar O. Angelone

Few of the studies examining counseling process have taken into account Kiesler's (1966) client uniformity myth by deliberately including client variables in the design. Recent exceptions include Hill, Helms, Spiegel, and Tichenor's (1988) examination of client's reaction as a function of the client's pretreatment symptomatology and Cummings's (1989) study in which she looked at differences in counselor response mode use as a function of client problem type. In addition, Nocita and Stiles (1986) examined client session evaluation as a function of client's level of introversion. Nocita and Stiles's study is significant because introversion "is a venerable and pervasive constituent of personality theories and theoretically based personality tests" (Nocita & Stiles; 1986, p. 235). The research by Nocita and Stiles indicated that less-introverted clients, as compared with more-introverted clients, rated their sessions as relatively smoother and their postsession mood as relatively more positive. There was, however, no difference in session depth as a function of client introversion. This finding is important because recent research has shown that session smoothness, and not depth, was positively correlated with counseling outcome as measured by changes in client Minnesota Multiphasic Personality Inventory (MMPI) scores and by client and therapist target complaints (Stiles, Shapiro, & Firth-Cozens, 1990). Two explanations for these findings are the following: (a) More-introverted clients may experience the sessions differently than less-introverted clients, and (b) counselors behave differently with introverted and nonintroverted clients.

The effect of the client's behavior on the counselor's approach has been discussed on theoretical grounds (Kiesler, 1988; Leary, 1957) and documented empirically. In theoretical terms, "interpersonal acts are designed to invite, pull, elicit, draw, entice, or evoke restricted classes of reactions from those with whom we interact" (Kiesler, 1988, p. 10). This process seems to occur at an unconscious level. Therefore, counselors are likely to respond in a different manner to a socially withdrawn, anxious, and uncomfortable introverted client than to an impulsive, spontaneous, and socially at ease extraverted one (Nocita & Stiles, 1986). In other words, more more-introverted clients would be expected to elicit different behaviors from their counselors than would less-introverted clients. This variation in counselor approach may account for the differences in reports of session smoothness found between more- and less-introverted clients.

A number of researchers have argued that counselors should alter their approach

Reprinted from *Journal of Counseling Psychology, 38*, 25–29 (1991). Copyright © 1991 by the American Psychological Association. Used with permission of the first author.

We gratefully acknowledge the assistance of Michael Patton and two anonymous reviewers for their comments and suggestions on this article.

on the basis of client individual differences (e.g., DiLoreto, 1971; Kiesler, 1966). For example, DiLoreto (1971) suggested that introverts derive greater benefit from directive approaches to treatment, whereas extraverts obtain greater benefit from nondirective approaches. If, as this research suggests, introverted and extraverted clients require different treatment approaches and counselors recognize and respond to these client differences, then one would expect to see a relationship between the client's level of introversion and counselor intention use.

Hill and O'Grady (1985) suggested that counselor approach or activity includes two parts: the "how" part and the "why" part. The how part of counselor activity consists of different ways of intervening and can be operationalized as response modes (Elliot et al., 1987). The why part of counselor activity involves different reasons for intervening and can be operationalized as therapist intentions (Hill & O'Grady, 1985). Recent research suggests that counselor intentions are related to the working alliance and to the client's perception of sessions (Fuller & Hill, 1985; Hill & O'Grady, 1985; Kivlighan, 1990). Also, Hill et al. (1988) indicated that counselor intentions are better descriptors of counselor interventions than are counselor response modes. Therefore, we hypothesized that there would be a relationship between the helpee's level of introversion and the novice counselor's use of intentions.

The purpose of this study was twofold: (a) to attempt to replicate Nocita and Stiles's (1986) findings regarding the relationship between client introversion and session impact, and (b) to examine possible relations between helpee introversion and novice counselor intention use.

Method

Participants

Novice counselors were 36 counseling students in a Masters of Education degree program who were enrolled in a prepracticum counseling skills course at a large state-supported midwestern university. There were 25 female and 11 male novice counselors. Their ages ranged from 21 to 36 years ($M = 26.14$, $SD = 2.12$). The course in which they were enrolled consisted of a combination of lecture/didactic and laboratory/skills-building components. In the lecture portion of the course, the students used a text by Strupp and Binder (1984), *Psychotherapy in a New Key*. The laboratory portion of the course consisted of modeling and practicing counseling skills, group interactions, videotaped interviews with recruited helpees, and tape review and supervision by peers and instructors. Strupp and Binder view their text as a treatment manual for conducting interpersonal/dynamic psychotherapy. They stress the importance of the counselor–client relationship as the medium for diagnosing and mediating client interpersonal difficulties. This treatment manual was used to define learning objectives for the course. Novice counselors were taught to examine the helpee's immediate experience and to reflect and interpret aspects of the helpee–counselor relationship.

The helpee sample consisted of 36 undergraduate students enrolled in undergraduate child or adolescent development courses who were recruited because they acknowledged a variety of personal concerns and showed willingness to talk to a novice counselor about their problems. The participants received extra credit toward their course grade for taking part in the study. Their mean age was 20.76 years (*SD* = 1.32), with a range of 19 to 27 years. Of the helpees, 75% were women and 25% were men; 85% were White and 15% were Black. The helpees saw their novice counselor for four sessions over the course of one academic semester. Typical helpee concerns included the following: conflicts with roommates or parents, loneliness, difficulties with assertiveness, and depressed mood.

Instruments

Session Evaluation Questionnaire

The impact of the counseling sessions was measured with the Session Evaluation Questionnaire (SEQ; Stiles & Snow, 1984), which consists of 11 bipolar-item scales presented in 7-point semantic differential format. Two session impact dimensions were identified from factor analysis, the depth/value and the smoothness/ease dimensions. Stiles and Snow reported good test–retest reliability (.80 or greater). In addition, the SEQ has been used in a number of studies as a session outcome measure (e.g., Kivlighan, 1989; Nocita & Stiles, 1986).

Intentions List

The Intentions List (Hill & O'Grady, 1985) is a 19-item, non-mutually exclusive, nominal, pantheoretical measure of therapists' cognitive behavior. The 19 intention categories are the following: set limits, get information, give information, support, focus, clarify, hope, cathart, cognitions, behaviors, self-control, feelings, insight, change, reinforce change, resistance, challenge, relationship, and therapist needs. The Intentions List was rationally derived by examining various theoreticians' descriptions of treatment goals. Researchers submitted the list to several trials with expert counselors, used the list in postsession reviews, and then revised the list on the basis of counselors' feedback. The Intentions List has been used extensively to analyze the therapeutic process (Hill et al., 1988; Hill & O'Grady, 1985; Kivlighan, 1989, 1990).

Reliability data for the Intentions List is not available. Hill and O'Grady (1985) argued that interrater reliability and test–retest reliability are not appropriate for intentions in cases in which the intentions are supplied by the counselor. Construct validity and concurrent validity have been established by examining the relationship among therapist intention use, client and therapist session evaluation (Fuller & Hill, 1985), and therapist response mode use (Hill & O'Grady, 1985).

Martin, Martin, and Slemon (1989), however, found that counselors often coded similar statements of intention into different categories of the Intentions List. Accordingly, Martin et al. modified Hill and O'Grady's (1985) method of collecting counselor intentions. Their procedure involved a stimulated-recall interview in which the counselor reviewed videotaped segments containing selected statements and then responded to probes about his or her intention. Counselor statements concerning intention were transcribed, and judges rated the transcripts for the presence of the intentions described by Hill and O'Grady.

Because the novice counselors were conducting their first sessions with clients, we wanted to be sure that they were familiar with the intention construct. Prior to the initial interview, all novice counselors were given specific detailed instructions concerning the meaning of the intention items. Then the novice counselors were given written statements in which counselors had explained their intentions; the novices were asked to say which of the 19 categories from the Hill and O'Grady (1985) list they would choose if this had been their intention. These written statements, along with their intention classification, were obtained from a previous study (Kivlighan, 1990). Written statements were presented to the novice counselors in groups of 50 statements. The trainees individually categorized each statement and then compared their categorization with that derived in the Kivlighan (1990) study. Training proceeded in this manner until all novice counselors achieved 90% agreement with the criterion categorizations (Cohen's kappa = .87 for the final set of 50 statements). Five groups of 50 statements each were presented before this agreement level was reached by all of the novice counselors. Only after this training did the novice counselors begin interviews, which involved use of the Intentions List.

To assess rater drift, 50 additional written statements were presented to the novice counselors after they completed their four counseling sessions. The average agreement across the 36 trainees, with the criterion categorization, was .90 (Cohen's kappa). This result suggests that the novice counselors were using the Intentions List in a consistent manner.

Minnesota Multiphasic Personality Inventory—Social Introversion Scale

Client introversion was measured by the Social Introversion (Si) scale of the MMPI (Hathaway & McKinley, 1983). The Si scale is a 70-item scale developed to assess subjects' inclination to withdraw from social contacts and responsibilities (Graham, 1987). The correlation of actual amount of overlap between the Si scale and the basic clinical scales ranged from $r = .00$ to $r = -.15$ (Wheeler, Little, & Lehner, 1951). Several studies have used the Si scale alone to measure social introversion (e.g., Cope, Kunce, & Newton, 1989; Klein, 1984; J. T. Kunce, personal communication, April 11, 1990; Terry & Berg, 1984). Other studies have shown high correlations between Si and other introversion measures (e.g., Si scale and the Personality Style Inventory Introversion Scale, $r = .72$; Kunce & Newton, 1989). The Si scale was selected in order to replicate the Nocita and Stiles (1986) study.

Procedure

The potential helpees initially attended a group orientation session, in which a graduate teaching assistant explained the nature of the project and obtained informed consent from those students interested in participating in the research. During the orientation, the volunteers were also informed verbally and in writing about other counseling services available through the university. The participating helpees completed the Si scale prior to the first session and the SEQ at the end of each of the four counseling sessions.

Helpees were randomly assigned to novice counselors within mutual time availability. Helpees were asked to discuss a real personal concern or problem during each of the 50-min interviews. Each counseling session was videotaped and the videotapes were reviewed immediately after each session by the novice counselors and during the following week by a supervisor. During the tape review, the novice counselors stopped the tape after each of his or her turns (periods during which the counselor spoke) and categorized his or her intentions for that turn with the Intentions List. To control for speaking activity levels, the proportion of the total intentions, rather than the frequency of intention use, was used in analysis (Hill et al., 1988).

Finally, videotapes of the four counseling sessions were reviewed by the graduate teaching assistant to make sure that no additional counseling was needed. Upon completion of the project, participants were again reminded of available counseling services.

Results

Preliminary Analyses

The 19 intentions used by the novice counselors were not normally distributed; accordingly, we used arc sine transformations (Cohen & Cohen, 1983). We based all subsequent analyses on the transformed scores of these 19 intentions. With a preliminary correlational analysis, we explored whether novice counselor or helpee demographic variables were related to use of intentions or session depth and smoothness. Neither novice counselor sex or age variables nor helpee sex or age variables were significantly correlated with intention use, depth, or smoothness rating (Pearson product–moment correlations ranged from $-.07$ to $.09$, all ns). Data were collapsed across age and sex categories in subsequent analyses.

To establish the comparability of our sample of counselors having limited experience with another sample of more experienced counselors, the frequency of intention use from the novice counselors in our sample was compared with the frequencies in the Hill and O'Grady (1985) sample. A multivariate t test yielded nonsignificant results, indicating that there was no difference in intention use for the novice counselors in this study and the sample of more experienced therapists.

Helpee Introversion and Session Impact

We used a Pearson product–moment correlational analysis to examine the relationship between helpee introversion and session impact evaluation. Scores for depth, smoothness, and proportions of intention use were obtained by averaging the respective scores across the four sessions. The means and standard deviations for helpee introversion/extraversion, helpee-rated depth and smoothness, and novice counselor intention use are presented in Table 1. The correlations between these measures are presented in Table 2.

Helpee introversion was significantly related to session smoothness ($r = -.50$, $p < .01$) but not to session depth ($r = -.05$, $p > .01$). This result is similar to that reported by Nocita and Stiles (1986).

The cognitive ($r = .38$) and challenge ($r = .40$) intentions were positively related to helpee social introversion; the support ($r = -.39$), relationship ($r = -.43$), and therapist needs ($r = -.38$) intentions were negatively related to helpee social intro-

Table 1—*Means and Standard Deviations for the Proportion*
of Novice Counselor Intention Use, Helpee Minnesota
Multiphasic Personality Inventory Social Introversion (Si)
Scale Scores, and Helpee-Rated Session Depth
and Smoothness

Measure	M	SD
Counselor intention		
Set limits	.01	.01
Get information	.12	.07
Support	.03	.03
Give information	.12	.08
Focus	.05	.03
Clarify	.11	.06
Hope	.01	.01
Cathart	.02	.02
Cognitions	.03	.02
Behaviors	.03	.03
Self-control	.02	.07
Feelings	.16	.06
Insight	.11	.05
Change	.04	.02
Reinforce change	.02	.01
Resistance	.01	.02
Challenge	.07	.06
Relationship	.03	.03
Therapist needs	.01	.01
Si *T* scores	50.08	10.55
SEQ smoothness	5.04	1.00
SEQ depth	5.90	0.62

Note. $N = 36$. SEQ = Session Evaluation Questionnaire.
For the smoothness and depth dimensions of the SEQ, responses were measured on a scale ranging from *shallow/rough*
(1) to *deep/smooth* (7).

version. The novice counselors used more challenge and cognitive intentions and
fewer support, relationship, and therapist needs intentions with the more-introverted
helpees than with the less-introverted helpees.

Discussion

Before discussing the results of this study, we point out several important limitations.
First, the helpees studied were recruited undergraduates rather than clients voluntarily
seeking clinical services. These helpees entered counseling with the expectations
associated with having only four sessions. Clients who enter counseling with other
expectations may behave and react differently. There was, however, a similar relationship between helpee introversion and session impact in this study and in the
study by Nocita and Stiles (1986).

Table 2—*Correlations Among Helpee-Rated Depth and Smoothness,*
Helpee Introversion, and Novice Counselor Intention Use

Counselor intention	SEQ Evaluation		MMPI–Si
	Depth	Smoothness	
Set limits	−.19	−.20	.30
Get information	.13	.12	.04
Support	−.02	.40*	−.39*
Give information	−.11	.14	−.15
Focus	−.05	.02	.05
Clarify	−.13	−.11	−.22
Hope	.00	−.09	.03
Cathart	.24	.08	.15
Cognitions	.16	−.04	.38*
Behaviors	.01	.00	.22
Self-control	−0.3	.10	.07
Feelings	.08	−.15	−.09
Insight	.27	.05	.28
Change	.02	−.01	.16
Reinforce change	−.17	−.04	−.06
Resistance	−.28	−.26	.08
Challenge	.02	−.45*	.40*
Relationship	−.18	−.15	−.43*
Therapist needs	−.06	−.19	−.38*

Note. N = 36. MMPI–Si = Minnesota Multiphasic Personality Inventory Social Introversion scale (higher scores indicate more social introversion).
*p < .05.

Second, the novice counselors in this study were students in a counseling class.
How similar the use of intentions by novice counselors are to the use of intentions
by more experienced therapists is open to question. This limitation is of fundamental
importance because more experienced counselors may be either more or less responsive to client behavior (Tracey & Hays, 1989). We did compare the relative use
of intentions by the novice counselors with the relative use of intentions by experienced counselors (Hill & O'Grady, 1985) and found no significant differences. This
finding, however, indicates only that the two groups of counselors were similar on
this one dimension.

Third, the therapeutic encounters were relatively brief (four sessions) in this
study. We cannot be certain of the impact that this limited period of counseling had
on the counseling interactions. Perhaps, more counseling sessions could reduce or
eliminate the relationship between introversion, helpee-rated session evaluations, and
novice counselors' use of intentions.

Fourth, correlational studies merely demonstrate relationships between sets of
variables. Thus, more powerful statistical tools and research designs are necessary
to address cause–effect questions among these variables. Finally, the training procedure used to ensure consistency in the use of the Intentions List may have biased
the way in which the novice counselors rated their intentions. In other words, the
novice counselors might have learned to associate a question, for example, with a

get-information intention rather than examining the intention of the question in each specific case.

In spite of these limitations, the findings in this study both replicate and extend those of Nocita and Stiles (1986). Helpee introversion was negatively related to session smoothness and was unrelated to ratings of session depth. In addition, the magnitude of the relationships was similar to that found by Nocita and Stiles. More-introverted clients, whether recruited or actual, rated their sessions as rougher in comparison with their less-introverted counterparts.

Nocita and Stiles (1986) suggested that introverts' evaluations of sessions as less smooth could result from differences in counselor approach or from different internal evaluations for objectively similar counselor approaches. The results of this study offer support for the proposition that novice counselors respond differently on the basis of the helpee's level of introversion. The use of the support, cognition, challenge, and therapist needs intentions was significantly related to helpee introversion level. The novice counselors in this study approached their introverted helpees in a more cognitive and challenging manner. In addition, the novice counselors were less likely to confront difficulties in the helpee–counselor relationship, attend to their own needs, or provide support with the more-introverted helpees than with less-introverted helpees. Additional research is necessary to discern whether this difference is purposeful or reactive.

Why would the novice counselors use more of the intentions that are related to rougher sessions with more-introverted helpees? Kiesler (1988) would assert that the novice counselors were being "pulled," at an unconscious level, to respond to their clients in a complementary manner. He labels this phenomenon, "being hooked." For example, the Si scale measures social withdrawal, anxiety, and discomfort. Perhaps the novice counselors were frustrated with introverted helpees, who were uncomfortable and anxious in the social situation of the counseling interview. A possible indication and result of this type of frustration is the reduced level of support and increased level of challenge intended that were evident with more-introverted helpees. This challenging style could lead to further anxiety and withdrawal for the introverted helpee, with an eventual impact of this cycle being decreased perceptions of session smoothness. It is also important to remember that the novice counselors were less likely to address problems in their relationship with introverted helpees, so there was a reduced chance of interrupting this negative cycle. It would be interesting to see if different results would be obtained with more experienced counselors.

The results of this study a number of avenues for future research. First, replication of these analyses with clients seeking clinical services and with more experienced counselors would be essential in order to determine the generalizability of the findings. Such conditions might be especially important to examine if, as suggested by Tracey and Hays (1989), more experienced therapists are less responsive to the introverted clients' style. Second, other aspects of counselor behavior, such as response modes (Elliot et al., 1987), could be explored to see if other counselor response differences are evidenced as a function of client introversion. Third, structural equation modeling could be used to further examine the relationships among client introversion, counselor approach (intention use), and session evaluation. Fourth, counselor social introversion could be examined to see if other main or interaction effects occur.

References

Cohen, J., & Cohen, P. (1983). *Applied multiple regression/correlation analysis for the behavioral sciences.* Hillsdale, NJ: Erlbaum.

Cope, C. S., Kunce, J. T., & Newton, R. M. (1989, August). *Counseling alcoholics: Normal and psychopathological personality characteristics and treatment considerations.* Paper presented at the 94th Annual Convention of the American Psychological Association, New Orleans, LA.

Cummings, A. L. (1989). Relationship of client problem type to novice counselor response modes. *Journal of Counseling Psychology, 36,* 331–335.

DiLoreto, A. O. (1971). *Comparative psychotherapy: An experimental analysis.* Chicago: Aldine–Atherton.

Elliot, R., Hill, C. E., Stiles, W. B., Friedlander, M. L., Mahrer, A. R., & Margison, F. R. (1987). Primary therapist response modes: Comparison of six rating systems. *Journal of Consulting and Clinical Psychology, 55,* 218–223.

Fuller, F., & Hill, C. E. (1985). Counselor and helpee perception of counselor intentions in relation to outcome in a single counseling session. *Journal of Counseling Psychology, 32,* 329–338.

Graham, J. R. (1987). *The MMPI: A practical guide.* New York: Oxford University Press.

Hathaway, S. R., & McKinley, J. C. (1983). *The Minnesota Multiphasic Personality Inventory Manual.* New York: Psychological Consultation.

Hill, C. E., Helms, J. E., Spiegel, S. B., & Tichenor, V. (1988). Development of a system for categorizing client reactions to therapist interventions. *Journal of Counseling Psychology, 35,* 27–36.

Hill, C. E., & O'Grady, K. E. (1985). List of therapist intentions illustrated with a case study and with therapists of varying theoretical orientations. *Journal of Counseling Psychology, 32,* 3–22.

Kiesler, D. J. (1966). Some myths of psychotherapy research and the search for a paradigm. *Psychological Bulletin, 65,* 110–136.

Kiesler, D. J. (1988). *Therapeutic metacommunication.* Palo Alto, CA: Consulting Psychologists Press.

Kivlighan, D. M. (1989). Changes in counselor intentions and response modes and in client reactions and session evaluation after training. *Journal of Counseling Psychology, 36,* 471–476.

Kivlighan, D. M. (1990). Relation between counselors' use of intentions and clients' perception of working alliance. *Journal of Counseling Psychology, 37,* 27–32.

Klein, S. (1984). Birth order and introversion–extraversion. *Journal of Research in Personality, 18,* 110–113.

Kunce, J. T., & Newton, R. M. (1989). Normal and psychopathology personality characteristics of individuals in alcohol rehabilitation. *Journal of Counseling Psychology, 36,* 308–315.

Leary, T. (1957). *Interpersonal diagnosis of personality.* New York: Ronald.

Martin, J., Martin, W., & Slemon, A. G. (1989). Cognitive–mediational models of action–act sequences in counseling. *Journal of Counseling Psychology, 36,* 8–16.

Nocita, A., & Stiles, W. B. (1986). Client introversion and counseling session impact. *Journal of Counseling Psychology, 33,* 235–241.

Stiles, W. B., Shapiro, D. A., & Firth-Cozens, J. A. (1990). Correlations of session evaluations with treatment outcome. *British Journal of Clinical Psychology, 29,* 13–21.

Stiles, W. B., & Snow, J. S. (1984). Counseling session impact as viewed by novice counselors and their clients. *Journal of Counseling Psychology, 31,* 3–12.

Strupp, H. H., & Binder, J. L. (1984). *Psychotherapy in a new key.* New York: Basic Books.

Terry, R. L., & Berg, A. J. (1984). The relationship between WAIS Pa and MMPI Si is mediated by MMPI Pd. *Journal of Clinical Psychology, 40,* 970–971.

Tracey, T. J., & Hays, K. (1989). Therapist complementarity as a function of experience and
    client stimuli. *Psychotherapy, 26,* 462–468.
Wheeler, W. M., Little, K. B., & Lehner, G. F. J. (1951). The internal structure of the MMPI.
    Journal of Consulting Psychology, 15, 134–141.

Part II

Attending and Listening— Nonverbal Behaviors

INTRODUCTION

Several studies have examined client and therapist nonverbal behaviors in therapy. These studies are included here because nonverbal behaviors are assumed to be the mechanism through which attending and listening are communicated. Attending and listening are important to give clients an opportunity to tell their stories and to feel heard and valued. Attending and listening are important skills for therapists to use throughout therapy but are especially important for therapists to use in the exploration stage when they are establishing a therapeutic relationship with clients.

In 1966, Fretz (see chapter 10) conducted one of the first studies in which client and therapist nonverbal behaviors in therapy were coded. His work was influential in helping establish the existence of different categories of nonverbal behavior. He found that therapists used significantly more positive nods, whereas clients used more negative nods or points, vertical hand movements, and hand clasping. Furthermore, clients perceived the therapeutic relationship as being good when they engaged in high levels of leaning forward and backward. Therapists perceived the therapeutic relationship as being good when they engaged in vertical and horizontal hand movements, smiling, talk-stopping (hands to lap or chin on hand), and hand clasping.

Tepper and Haase's 1978 study (see chapter 12) is included to represent several analogue (i.e., nontherapy) studies on the influence of nonverbal behaviors (see Gladstein, 1974). In these studies, participants rated their perceptions of therapist-offered facilitative conditions based on their observations of brief videotaped vignettes in which therapists assumed different verbal and nonverbal stances. Tepper and Haase found that nonverbal behaviors (trunk leaning, eye contact, vocal intonation, and facial expression) accounted for more of the variance in judged facilitative conditions than did the verbal message. Although these results tell us something about how people respond to brief exposures of verbal and nonverbal behaviors, the study is limited because it did not assess how clients react to therapists in actual therapeutic situations.

In 1981, Hill, Siegleman, Gronsky, Sturniolo, and Fretz (see chapter 11) found minimal relationships among client and therapist nonverbal behaviors and client and therapist perceptions of therapist facilitative conditions and session outcome (which is in contrast to Fretz's findings). Hill et al. also found no relationship between therapist decoding ability (detecting emotions through nonverbal behaviors) and encoding ability (sending emotions through nonverbal behaviors) and perceptions of therapist facilitative conditions and session outcome. They did, however, find relationships among therapist congruence (consistency in feelings expressed through verbal and nonverbal behaviors) and therapist-rated facilitative conditions.

Unfortunately, few studies of therapist nonverbal behaviors have been conducted in recent years, perhaps because the method of correlating the frequency of various nonverbal behaviors with outcome has had minimal payoff. It is hoped that more researchers will take up the challenge of investigating this area in the future so that we can begin to understand the influence of therapist nonverbal behaviors on the therapeutic process. Perhaps researchers could examine therapist nonverbal behaviors during critical moments of therapy rather than correlating the frequency of all nonverbal behaviors with outcome. In addition, researchers might use replays of tapes of therapy sessions to investigate qualitatively how clients react to various nonverbal behaviors.

Reference

Gladstein, G. A. (1974). Nonverbal communication and counseling/psychotherapy. *The Counseling Psychologist, 4,* 35–57.

Chapter 10
POSTURAL MOVEMENTS IN A COUNSELING DYAD[1]

Bruce R. Fretz

Although research on body movements has been in progress for nearly 40 years, neither past nor present research provides data which can be easily and reliably utilized by counselors as they participate in the counseling process. Presently, body movement research generally takes the form of (1) complex, minute analysis of the elements of movements and their meanings (Birdwhistell, 1953, 1963) or (2) the more traditional movement–meaning type of research in which selected movements are directly correlated with selected meanings (Allport & Vernon, 1933; Nielsen, 1962; Thompson & Meltzner, 1964). A variation of the traditional movement–meaning type of research is found in investigations of movements occurring in various situational conditions such as stress (Russell & Snyder, 1963; Sainsbury, 1955), anger and depression (Dittman, 1962).

While all of the cited research has produced useful information about movements, the difficulties in understanding movements have not been greatly reduced. Researchers have not pursued the question of what are the most useful and meaningful movements to study. Can a few select movements, molar or molecular, represent the functions and meanings of entire groups of movements?

It was the purpose of the present research to demonstrate that the movements of the client and counselor in a counseling dyad can be reduced and codified into a small, yet inclusive, number of units; that observers can simultaneously observe and categorize these movements into meaningful units, with meaningfulness determined not by observer inferences, but by empirical patterns and relationships revealed in the present research; and that these units can provide a basis for formulating experimental paradigms for the study of movements.

Method

Subjects

The counselors in this study were 12 graduate students, 4 males and 8 females, who were enrolled in an introductory counseling psychology practicum. All the counselors had completed a graduate level introductory course on the principles of counseling and most of them had completed or were enrolled in a counseling diagnostic course and laboratory.

The clients, 10 males and 7 females, were undergraduate students enrolled in an educational skills program. This course attracts, primarily, students with academic

Reprinted from *Journal of Counseling Psychology, 13*, 335–343 (1966). Copyright © 1966 by the American Psychological Association. Used with permission of the author.

[1]This article is based on the author's doctoral dissertation completed at the Ohio State University under the supervision of Lyle Schmidt and Frank Fletcher.

difficulties who wish to improve their study skills. The clients, 12 freshmen, 4 sophomores, and 1 junior, were all single, ranged in age from 18 to 23 and had a median percentile of 27 on the university entrance examinations (Ohio State Psychological and American College Test). The range of percentiles was 1 to 86.

The observers used in the study included 6 males and 7 females selected from volunteers in an upper level undergraduate introductory course in counseling psychology.

Procedures

In an orientation session the observers were shown their places in the observation room, how they could see their subjects through the two-way mirror, and how to record their observations on audio tapes. The only instructions given were to (1) describe all movements in physiognomic terms, that is, actual movements such as "squints" or "smiles" instead of "looks puzzled" or "amused," and (2) to maintain a continuous description of ongoing activity.

The first, third, and sixth interviews of the counseling relationship were chosen for observation. In the practicum (one academic quarter) most relationships terminate with the seventh interview; the sixth interview was chosen to avoid "halo" contamination of the criterion measures during a final seventh interview. The first interview was chosen as a base line against which to observe change and the third interview was chosen as the mid-point of the relationship.

After the third and sixth interviews, counselors and clients completed the Barrett-Lennard Relationship Inventory and a satisfaction and "charisma" questionnaire (see description below).

Criterion Measures

The Barrett-Lennard Relationship Inventory (1962) provided scores on (1) level of regard, (2) unconditionality of regard, (3) empathy, (4) congruence and (5) the total relationship. Table 1 presents the obtained intercorrelations of the parts of this inventory as well as its correlations with the satisfaction and charisma variables described below. For clients, the subscales significantly correlate with the total score, but, generally, not with each other. For counselors, on the other hand, the subscales are highly intercorrelated.

The satisfaction and charisma (charisma defined in the traditional sense of "mystical healing") questionnaire provided two separate scores. This questionnaire utilized (1) 14 questions from a satisfaction questionnaire developed by Cundick (1962) at the Ohio State University Counseling Center, and (2) 10 questions designed by the writer to assess the clients' and counselors' perceptions of 4 dimensions of persuasive healing suggested by Frank (1961): (1) healers must be believed, e.g., "Do you think your counselor will be able to help you with all other problems you might bring up in future counseling sessions?" (2) confession must be elicited, e.g., "Are you able to tell your counselor about things you've never told anyone else?" (3) the situation must be emotionally charged, e.g., "At times during counseling do you feel as if you will lose some control of your emotions?" (4) the therapeutic value of the process must be well known and validated in the common culture, e.g., "To what extent do you feel counselors have made worthwhile contributions to the self-improvement of their clients?"

As can be seen in Table 1, satisfaction is somewhat significantly correlated with the various scales of the Barrett-Lennard Relationship Inventory, but only on the first administration. Charisma, on the other hand, is significantly correlated with no variable except satisfaction during the second administration. Internal reliability coefficients on these measures ranged from .58 to .76 during the first administration and from .68 to .94 during the second administration.

Movement Measures

Observers' reports of movements provided the data for both the definition of "a movement" and for a factor analysis of movements. The observers' implicit definition of "a movement" was as economical as possible. "A movement" was as large as the grossest applicable concept, for example, "slides back in chair." At other times, the grossest applicable concept was "little finger moves up." "A movement" lasted as long as (1) it was the only perceptible movement phenomenon away from a conceived homeostatic condition, e.g., "hand out and back to lap" equals one movement, whereas "hand out, leans forward, hand back to lap" equals three movements; or (2) repeated itself without perceptible intervening pauses, e.g., finger tapping was

Table 1—*Significant Intercorrelations of Client and Counselor Inventory Scores*[a]

Counselors	Regard I	Regard II	Empathy I	Empathy II	Unconditionality I	Unconditionality II	Congruence I	Congruence II	Total I	Total II	Satisfaction I	Satisfaction II	Charisma I	Charisma II
Regard I[b]		.57								.76				
Regard II[c]	.61			.54				.67		.78		.64		
Empathy I									.57					
Empathy II		.58	.63					.74		.83	.55	.64		
Unconditionality I	.50		.51			.51			.71					
Unconditionality II	.51		.66		.74					.62				
Congruence I		.54	.60	.44	.59	.71			.68					
Congruence II		.46	.47	.64		.45	.43			.85	.57	.76		
Total I	.66	.48	.72		.88	.85	.79				.46	.75		
Total II	.51	.76	.67	.78		.77	.70	.78	.71					
Satisfaction I	.56	.56	.43	.45				.46	.49	.55		.44		
Satisfaction II		.54												.58
Charisma I												.42		.71
Charisma II														

[a]$p < .10$, $n = 17$; intercorrelations for counselors below the diagonal.
[b]I Indicates first administration (third interview).
[c]II Indicates second administration (sixth interview).

considered only one movement as long as it continued uninterruptedly. If it stopped and started again, it was considered as separate movements.

The observers' descriptive reports included 131 separate movements, only 60 of which were used by three or more subjects. A score sheet was then constructed on which the frequencies of each of the 60 movements could be recorded for the first five 5-minute segments of the three observed interviews.

In order to minimize the extreme variance present in the original frequency scores of the movements, e.g., scores on positive nod ranged from zero to 41, all segment cells were rescored either "1" (movement observed at least once or more during five-minute segment) or "0" (movement not observed). The data for factor analysis included, then, 60 rows (60 movements), each with 255 cells (3 interviews × 5 segments each × 17 subjects). The clients' movement data yielded 19 unrotated factors, the counselors' 22 unrotated factors.[2] Only 10 of these 41 factors appeared to be common factors; the remaining 31 factors were assumed to contain mostly specific and error variance. A normalized varimax rotation yielded further clues to the principal components of the factors; however, the unrotated factors remained the better source of identifying clusters of different movements each with eigenvalues greater than one. Since it was the aim of this study to provide as simplified categories as possible, rather than a strict factor analysis of movements, the movements given for each factor for Table 2 include *only* those that could be meaningfully related. The median percentage of inclusiveness of movements with eigenvalues greater than one, on each factor, was 67 per cent.

Factor 8 was labeled "talk-stop" since hand movements to lap and chin convey a cessation of other hand movements that were probably in progress while the subject was speaking. Factor 9 was labeled "thinking," simply on the basis that "eyebrows raised" and "look up" seemed to imply reflection upon what had been said.

Since the majority of the factors applied to both counselors and clients, and since the total number of factors was small, all ten factors were utilized for both clients and counselors in all subsequent analysis. Also, horizontal and vertical hand movements were made logically inclusive; that is, any hand movement in a horizontal plane was scored as one horizontal hand movement, and similarly for vertical hand movements.

The final step prerequisite to criterion data analysis was the scoring of all the observer tapes for the ten movement factors. Interjudge ($N = 2$) reliability of the scoring of the videotapes was .98.

Results

Table 3 presents the intercorrelations of the 10 movement factors for counselors and for clients. The number of significant intercorrelations among counselor movements is twice that of the client movements.

Table 4 indicates significant differences in the movement repertoires of clients and counselors. Counselors used significantly more positive nods and total number of movements than did clients. Clients used more negative nods/points, vertical hand

---

[2] The writer wishes to thank the Ohio State University Numerical Computation Laboratory for the use of the IBM 7094 in performing the factor analyses.

Table 2—*The Movement Factors*

Factors	Loading	Clients	Loading	Counselors
1) Horizontal Hand Movements	.54	Both Hands Out	.39	Both Hands Out
	.57	Both Hands Circle		
	.34	Right Hand Out	.48	Right Hand Out
	.42	Right Hand to Knee	.39	Right Hand to Knee
	.46	Right Hand Circles		
	.40	Left Hand Out	.50	Left Hand Out
	.32	Left Hand Circles		
2) Vertical Hand Movements			.44	Both Hands Clasp at Chin
	.49	Right Hand to Chin		
	.46	Right Hand Up & Down	.40	Right Hand Up & Down
	.65	Left Hand Up & Down	.51	Left Hand Up & Down
3) Head Movements Other Than Nods	.44	Head Erect	.43	Head Erect
	.39	Head Forward	.65	Head Forward
	.61	Head Back	.31	Head Back
	.67	Head Turn Left	.37	Head Turn Left
	.55	Head Turn Right	.49	Head Turn Right
	.39	Head Tilts		
4) Positive Nod			.62	Positive Nod
5) Negative Nod/ Points	.35	Negative Nod/	.80	Negative Nod
	.45	Points		
6) Smile and Laugh	.58	Smile	.56	Smile
	.38	Laugh	.36	Laugh
7) Lean Forward, Lean Back			.35	Lean Forward
			.39	Lean Back
8) "Talk-Stop"	.36	Right Hand to Lap		
	.47	Left Hand to Lap		
	.31	Chin Leans on Hand		
9) "Thinking"	.30	Looks up	.60	Looks Up
	.45	Eyebrows Raised	.82	Eyebrows Raised
10) Clasping Movements	.46	Both Hands Clasp		
	.54	Both Hands Clasp at Lap		
	.39	Finger Play		
	.34	Plays With Something		

movements, clasping and total number of movements with positive nods subtracted than did counselors. The low frequency and high variance of the "talk-stop" and "thinking" factors suggest that these factors must be interpreted cautiously until further research demonstrates greater use and stability for them.

Table 3—*Significant Intercorrelations of Client and Counselor Movement Factors*[a,b]

Counselors	Positive Nod	Negative Nod/Pts.	Smile and Laugh	Head Movements	Lean Forward	Horizontal Hand	Vertical Hand	"Talk-stop"	Thinking	Clasping	Total
											Clients
Positive Nod		.30	.42						.18		.51
Negative Nod/Pts.						.18					.45
Smile and Laugh	.27										.41
Head Movements			.28						.39		.44
Lean Forward	.20			.30		.33					.21
Horizontal Hand			.22	.24			.22				.52
Vertical Hand	-.20					.53					.33
"Talk-stop"							.30				
"Thinking"		.25					.16				.33
Clasping			.21	.19		.21					.25
Total	.73		.62	.43	.35	.42	.25		.20		

[a] $p < .01$, $n = 255$ (5 segments $\times$ 3 interviews $\times$ 17 subjects).
[b] Intercorrelations of counselor movement factors below the diagonal.

Table 4—*Means, Standard Deviations, and Counselor–Client Differences on Movement Factors*

Movement categories	Client		Counselor		Significance of difference[b]
	Mean[a]	Sigma	Mean[a]	Sigma	
Positive Nod	6.4	5.4	21.8	9.9	$p < .01$
Negative Nod/Pts.	2.8	2.9	.4	.7	$p < .01$
Smile and Laugh	3.0	3.5	3.2	3.4	n.s.
Head Movements	2.7	3.9	1.8	2.2	n.s.
Lean Forward	.9	1.2	.9	1.2	n.s.
Horizontal Hand	6.8	6.1	4.4	3.8	n.s.
Vertical Hand	3.9	2.7	2.1	2.2	$p < .01$
"Talk-Stop"	.6	1.0	.4	.7	n.s.
"Thinking"	.7	1.8	.5	.8	n.s.
Clasping	2.8	2.4	1.5	1.6	$p < .05$
Total	30.7	13.8	37.2	13.6	$p < .01$
Total–Positive Nod	24.3	9.6	15.4	11.7	$p < .10$

[a] For five minute segments.
[b] As determined by *t* ratios.

Table 5 presents the results of a standard analysis of variance of changes in movements during the six interview series. An analysis of variance for "repeated measurements," in which the "individual differences residual" of the denominator of the F ratio is partialled out, probably would have raised the larger F values to more acceptable significance levels.

The significant correlations of the movement scores and the criterion variables

Table 5—*Analysis of Variance of Changes in Frequencies of Movements in a Counseling Series*

Movement Categories	Five Minutes Means		Interview 6	F value
	Interview 1	Interview 3		
Positive Nod				
Client	6.8	5.1	7.8	.90
Counselor	24.7	22.4	17.9	1.54
Negative Nod/Pts.				
Client	3.0	2.6	2.9	.10
Counselor	.3	.4	.4	.23
Smile and Laugh				
Client	3.5	3.0	2.8	.20
Counselor	4.8	2.7	2.4	1.30
Head Movements				
Client	2.7	4.0	1.8	.96
Counselor	1.8	1.7	1.6	.72
Lean Forward				
Client	.9	.8	1.0	.27
Counselor	1.1	.7	.9	.53
Horizontal Hand				
Client	8.7	6.8	4.8	1.22
Counselor	4.2	4.6	4.5	.40
Vertical Hand				
Client	4.5	3.8	3.5	1.02
Counselor	1.6	2.1	2.5	.53
"Talk-stop"				
Client	.5	.5	.6	.60
Counselor	.3	.4	.6	1.72
"Thinking"				
Client	.8	1.1	.3	.88
Counselor	.3	.6	.5	1.93
Clasping				
Client	4.0	2.6	1.7	2.72*
Counselor	1.5	1.6	1.4	.13
Total				
Client	34.2	30.5	27.7	1.75
Counselor	40.4	39.1	32.9	.80
Total–Positive Nod				
Client	29.1	26.4	21.8	2.04
Counselor	16.0	16.0	15.8	.05

*p significant beyond the .10 level.

are given in Table 6. By noting the cells with two significant correlations, the following observations can be made: (1) vertical hand movements were the best indicator of satisfaction for both clients and counselors, and (2) clasping was the best indicator of unconditionality for both groups.

By noting the row frequencies of significant correlations, additional observations include: (1) clients' leaning forward and back was the best indicator of clients' relationship inventory variables, (2) counselors' clasping was the best indicator of the counselors' relationship inventory variables; moreover, all hand movements, as well as smile and laugh, were significantly related to the majority of the Barrett-Lennard Relationship Inventory variables, (3) negative nods/points showed negative correlations for all client relationship inventory variables in contrast to all positive correlations for all counselor relationship inventory variables.

The concentration of the significant correlations in Table 6 among the various scales of the Barrett-Lennard Relationship Inventory, rather than among the satisfaction and charisma columns, is most probably a result of the significant intercorrelations of the subscales of the inventory. A final general observation of note is that head movements have the fewest significant correlations with criterion variables.

Discussion

The factors identified in this study must be considered *only* as a first attempt to reduce the complexity of movement observation. Each of the factors described included only about two-thirds of the movements with significant loadings on that factor. Consequently, the statistical stability of the factors is questionable. Nevertheless, the goal of identifying some logically, and at least somewhat statistically, related movements was attained. From a pragmatic viewpoint, it is the subsequent usefulness of the movement factors, which more appropriately might be called categories, that is of most importance. Indeed, the emphasis in the present study was in identifying relationships of the movement categories with other variables in the counseling relationship.

Considering, then, the relationships of the movement categories, perhaps the most intriguing finding was the counselors' greater use of positive nod in contrast to the clients' greater use of negative nods/points. The negative correlations of negative nods/points with the relationship inventory variables suggest that clients did feel the relationship was less acceptable when they frequently shook their heads "no." The slight, but insignificant, decline in frequency of positive nod for counselors (Table 5) suggests positive nod may be related to an initial accepting listening or to an initial strong need for approval on the part of the beginning counselors used in this study. Rosenfeld's (1965) finding that a greater percentage of positive nods were used by subjects in an approval-seeking condition tends to support the latter hypothesis.

In view of the intercorrelations of the parts of the Barrett-Lennard Relationship Inventory, perhaps the most attention should be given to the relationships of the *total* inventory score and the movement categories; significant correlations of the subscales and the movement categories cannot really be considered independent relationships. For clients, leaning forward and back was the only significant positive indicator of a good relationship as measured by the given inventory. The leaning forward and back may well indicate a more active involvement of the clients; therefore, a better relationship. The counselors, on the other hand, used more hand movements and smiling when they perceived a good relationship; however, these same movement categories are significantly intercorrelated for counselors; therefore, the number of significant correlations may really reflect only one general relationship. It may well be that further research will show that the various hand movement categories for counselors can be collapsed into fewer categories.

The independence of the significant correlations of satisfaction and charisma, with the movement categories (Table 6), from those of the relationship inventory gives some support to the aforementioned independence of satisfaction and charisma. On the other hand, the lesser magnitude of these correlations raises some questions as to the existence of any stable relationships between satisfaction and charisma with the movement categories.

Some general limitations to the study may be construed as impetus for specific extensions of movement research. One of the first such extensions should ascertain the reliability with which the ten movement factors can be observed. Although interscorer reliability for scoring audio tapes of observers' reports was highly acceptable, no measure of reliability of live observation has been established.

A second extension should give attention to four other limitations to the generalization of the results of the present study: (1) counselors were inexperienced, (2) clients were typically low ability and motivated primarily toward improving education skills, (3) observers were homogeneous in age, education, and vocational aim (helping professions), and (4) counselors and clients sat in armchairs not adjacent to an elbow-level desk or table. All of these limitations can be examined by having the limiting variable, for example, counselor experience, serve as the independent variable in an experimental design.

A third type of further research is suggested by Rosenfeld's (1965) previously mentioned findings that subjects in an approval-seeking condition emitted higher percentages of smiles, gesticulations, and positive nods while subjects in approval-avoidance conditions emitted higher percentages of negative nods and postural shifts.

Such correlational studies can, in turn, provide the basis for experimental paradigms to answer the questions: (1) "Under what conditions do selected movements occur?" and (2) "Are the movements a consequence of the condition or are the conditions a consequence of the movements?" The results of the present research, combined with those of Rosenfeld (1965), suggest three hypotheses relevant to the first question:

1. Clients who perceive highly favorable relationships with their counselors, as compared with clients who perceive unfavorable relationships, utilize (a) significantly fewer negative nods/points, and (b) significantly more leaning forward and back.
2. Counselors who perceive highly favorable relationships with their clients, as compared with counselors who perceive unfavorable relationships, utilize (a) significantly more hand movements and (b) significantly more smiles and laughs.
3. Counselors in approval seeking conditions, as compared with counselors in non-approval seeking conditions, utilize (a) significantly more positive nods and (b) significantly more smiles and laughs.

Table 6—*Significant Correlations of Movement Factors and Criterion Variables*

Movement categories	Criterion variables						
	Regard	Empathy	Unconditionality	Congruence	Total	Satisfaction	Charisma
Positive Nod							
Client			−.30*		−.29*		
Counselor							
Negative Nod/Pts.							
Client	−.31*		−.33**		−.34**		
Counselor		.45***	.38***		.40**		
Smile and Laugh							
Client	.43***						
Counselor		.33**	.64***	.45***	.56***		−.29*
Head Movements							
Client							
Counselor							.32**
Lean Forward							
Client	.29*	.50***	.32*	.29*	.45***		
Counselor		−.30*					
Horizontal Hand							
Client		.42**					
Counselor	.29*		.56***	.48***	.50***	.38**	
Vertical Hand							
Client		.45***				.31*	
Counselor		.33**	.51***	.36**	.49***	.39**	

"Talk-stop"							
Client				−.30*			−.31*
Counselor		.57***	.73***	.40**	.64***		
"Thinking"							
Client						.38*	
Counselor	.30*						
Clasping							
Client			.36**				
Counselor	.54***	.51***	.38**	.42**	.55***	.39**	
Total Movements							
Client			.60***	.31*	.46***		
Counselor						.32**	

*Correlations >.29. Significant beyond the .10 level.
**Correlations >.33. Significant beyond the .05 level.
***Correlations >.43. Significant beyond the .01 level.

Confirmation of these and similar hypotheses would make movement data immediately useful as (1) measures of selected counselor or client characteristics and counseling process variables and as (2) a means of improving counselor sensitivity to client characteristics, emotional states, and feelings about the relationship.

Finally, although the present research has shown significant relationships between postural movements and situational variables in the counseling relationship, there remains the important task, for future research, of identifying the causal variable, that is, do given movements occur as a result of situational conditions or are the conditions a consequence of the given movements?

References

Allport, G., & Vernon, P. *Studies in expressive movement*. New York: Macmillan, 1933.

Barrett-Lennard, G. Dimensions of therapist response as causal factors in therapeutic change. *Psychol. Monogr.*, 1962, **76**, No. 43.

Birdwhistell, R. *Introduction to kinesics*. Louisville, Ky.: Univer. of Louisville Press, 1953.

Birdwhistell, R. The kinesics level in the investigation of the emotions. In P. Knapp (Ed.), *Expression of the emotions in man*. New York: International Univer. Press, Inc., 1963.

Cundick, B. The relation of student and counselor expectations to rated counseling satisfaction. Unpublished doctoral dissertation. The Ohio State University, 1962.

Dittman, A. The relationship between body movements and moods in interviews. *J. consult. Psychol.*, 1962, **26**, 480.

Frank, J. *Persuasion and healing*. Baltimore: Johns Hopkins, 1961.

Nielsen, G. *Studies in self-confrontation*. Copenhagen: Munksgaard, 1962.

Rosenfeld, H. Gestural and verbal communication of interpersonal affect. Paper given at Midwestern Psychological Assoc., 1965.

Russell, P., & Snyder, W. Counselor anxiety in relation to amount of clinical experience and quality of affect demonstrated by clients. *J. Consult. Psychol.*, 1963, **27**, 358–363.

Sainsbury, P. Gestural movement during psychiatric interviews. *Psychosom. Med.*, 1955, **17**, 458–469.

Thompson, D., & Meltzner, L. Communication of emotional intent by facial expression. *J. Abnorm. Soc. Psychol.*, 1964, **68**, 129–135.

Chapter 11
NONVERBAL COMMUNICATION AND COUNSELING OUTCOME

Clara E. Hill, Larry Siegelman, Barbara R. Gronsky,
Frank Sturniolo, and Bruce R. Fretz

Nonverbal behavior is an extremely important mode of communication. In the popular media, numerous books purport to teach the reader how to understand body language. In counselor training (e.g., Carkhuff, 1969; Ivey, 1971) time is usually spent teaching attending skills so that counselors can learn to exhibit the "appropriate" nonverbal behaviors to communicate undistracted listening and to detect unverbalized feelings in the client. However, the scientific study of nonverbal communication is fairly recent. At present, the role of nonverbal communication in counseling/psychotherapy has not been empirically established. Reviewers have called for more research, particularly in the study of nonverbal behavior in naturalistic settings (Gladstein, 1974; Harper, Wiens, & Matarazzo, 1978; Hughey, 1974).

From the study of nonverbal communication in general psychology, we identified three major areas that seemed relevant to counseling effectiveness: nonverbal abilities, nonverbal behaviors, and congruence between verbal and nonverbal channels of communication. The first area of abilities to send (encode) and receive (decode) nonverbal messages comes from the study in personality and social psychology of traits and individual differences. If some persons are more skilled than others in interpreting and communicating nonverbal messages, then this has implications for the selection of counselors for training and perhaps for the selection of clients for specified types of counseling.

The second area, nonverbal behaviors, has been studied more often in counseling psychology. Gladstein (1974) reviewed 77 empirical studies but found that only 33 of these had used real helpers/helpees and actual counseling/psychotherapy. The typical study has used an analogue format with short videotaped vignettes or still photographs. The results of these studies need to be replicated in more naturalistic settings to determine if specific nonverbal behaviors are necessary for counseling effectiveness. The findings have implications for counselor training.

The third area is potentially the most exciting in that it begins to tap the complex interplay between verbal and nonverbal communication. Congruence, or the consistency of emotions expressed in verbal and nonverbal channels of communication, has also received more empirical attention from social psychologists. For example, DePaulo (Note 1) found that discrepant messages are harder to decode, and Mehr-

Reprinted from *Journal of Counseling Psychology, 28*, 203–212 (1981). Copyright © 1981 by the American Psychological Association. Used with permission of the first author.

The order of names of the second through the fifth authors was randomly determined. This project was planned and conducted cooperatively by the entire research team. The decoding portion of Experiment 1 was based on a master's thesis by Barbara Gronsky; Experiment 2 was based on an undergraduate honors thesis by Frank Sturniolo; and Experiment 3 was based on a master's thesis by Larry Siegelman.

We thank Judy Hall for her consultation on this project, Jim Gormally and Mary Ann Hoffman for their reviews of an earlier draft, and Jo Shaffer for her many preparations of the manuscript.

abian (1972) hypothesized that when there is a contradiction between verbally and nonverbally expressed attitudes, the nonverbal portion will be taken as the true attitude (e.g., sarcasm). The concept of congruence has also received a lot of theoretical attention from counselors, beginning with Rogers (1957), who labeled it as one of the necessary and sufficient conditions for a therapeutic relationship. However, the measurement of this concept has been problematic, and no behavioral measures have been developed that tap congruence of channels of communication within actual counseling sessions.

Furthermore, past research has examined counselor nonverbal variables to the exclusion of those of clients. The underlying assumption is that counselor skills are the sole determinant of counseling effectiveness. This assumption has been increasingly challenged (cf. Garfield, 1978). Currently the assumption has been that both counselor and client behaviors are important contributors to the counseling process.

The purpose of the present investigation was to comprehensively examine the relationship of both counselor and client nonverbal communication (on nonverbal abilities, nonverbal behaviors, and verbal–nonverbal congruence) with counseling outcome. Based on previous literature, nonverbal measures were selected that were hypothetically related to counseling outcome measures; therefore, one-tailed tests of significance were used. Additionally, because of the large number of significance tests conducted, an alpha level of $p < .01$ was maintained throughout the study. The three areas of nonverbal communication are relatively distinct, so the data will be presented as three separate experiments. The shared methodology will be explicated in Experiment 1.

Experiment 1: Decoding and Encoding

Mehrabian (1972) defined decoding as the inference of another's state, relation, or attitude from subtle cues. The Profile of Nonverbal Sensitivity (PONS; Hall, Rosenthal, Archer, DiMatteo, & Rogers, 1978; Rosenthal, Archer, Koivumaki, DiMatteo, & Rogers, 1974) was developed to measure decoding ability; adequate reliability and validity have been demonstrated for this instrument. Three studies utilizing the PONS have provided preliminary evidence of an association between counselors' decoding ability and clinical skills. Hall et al. (1978) found weak but significant correlations between clinician scores on the PONS and supervisory ratings of clinical skill. In an unpublished study by Burruss (cited in Hall et al., 1978), therapist scores on the PONS predicted change among alcoholic patients better than ratings of therapist skills by the therapists themselves, supervisors, or colleagues. DiMatteo, Friedman, and Taranta (1979) found that scores on the body channel of the PONS were significantly correlated with physicians' interpersonal success with patients in a clinical setting. However, this relationship was not supported in a fourth study by Lee, Halberg, Kocsis, and Haase (1980), in which no relationship was found between counselor PONS scores and client ratings of the counselors. Thus, there is some evidence of a weak relationship between nonverbal abilities and clinical skills, although this has not replicated in a counseling setting.

Encoding can be defined as an ability to transmit or send nonverbal cues of emotion (i.e., the capacity to be emotionally expressive). Only one study has examined the relationship of encoding to clinical effectiveness. Friedman, DiMatteo, and Taranta (1980) found a weak but positive relationship between physician encoding ability and patient satisfaction within a physician–patient relationship. Because the process of encoding is idiosyncratic, no standardized or objective measures have been developed, and researchers have used different methodologies.

The nonverbal abilities (decoding and encoding) have been studied extensively in social psychology but have only recently received attention in the counseling literature. We intuitively believe that counselors vary individually in nonverbal sensitivity. Hence, it seems appropriate to study these variables further. The purpose of the first experiment was to investigate the relationship of decoding and encoding abilities of both counselors and clients to outcome measures of counseling.

Method

Participants

The clients were 20 males and 20 females between 17 and 20 years of age. Students volunteered in response to announcements made in introductory psychology classes. Only those volunteers were selected who indicated on a sign-up sheet that they were very or somewhat willing to talk about a personal problem and had never been in counseling. Subjects received course credit for participation.

Twenty doctoral-level students (10 males, 10 females) in the counseling psychology, clinical psychology, and counselor education programs at a large eastern university served as counselors. All counselors had completed at least 2 years of graduate training, including at least 1 year of practicum experience.

Outcome Measures

Barrett-Lennard Relationship Inventory (BLRI; Barrett-Lennard, 1962).   The BLRI measures perceptions of counselor-offered empathy, regard, congruence, and unconditionality of regard. There are 64 items (16 on each scale), each of which is rated on a 6-point scale (from −3 to +3). Split-half reliability of the scales ranges from .82 to .96. Content validation was established by counselor rating of the valence of the items; only those items were retained for which experienced counselors had full agreement as to the positive or negative valence.

Counseling Evaluation Inventory (CEI; Linden, Stone, & Schertzer, 1965).   The CEI measures counseling climate, satisfaction with counseling, and counseling comfort. The measure consists of 19 randomly ordered items, each rated on a 5-point scale. Discriminative validity has been established for the three scales and the total score, using counselor trainees' practicum grades as a criterion. Total test–retest reliability ranges from .62 to .83.

Counselor Rating Form (CRF; Barak & LaCrosse, 1975).   The CRF measures clients' perceptions of counselors' expertness, attractiveness, and trustworthiness. A total score combines the three scales. The total measure contains 36 randomly ordered 7-point bipolar items, with 12 items on each scale. Split-half reliability for the three dimensions, based on a normative group of undergraduates, ranges from .75 to .92.

Table 1 presents the means and standard deviations for all outcome measures

Table 1—*Means and Standard Deviations for*
Counseling Outcome Measures

Variable	Client		Counselor	
	M	SD	*M*	*SD*
BLRI	98.33	38.73	88.23	41.64
CEI	25.75	9.35		
CRF	214.03	24.84		

Note. BLRI = Barrett-Lennard Relationship Inventory;
CEI = Counseling Evaluation Inventory; CRF = Counselor
Rating Form.

(client BLRI, CEI, and CRF, and counselor BLRI). The three client measures were all at least moderately correlated (for BLRI and CRF, $r = .35$; for BLRI and CEI, $r = .39$; for CRF and CEI, $r = .77$). The client and counselor forms of the BLRI were also moderately correlated ($r = .34$).

Decoding and Encoding Measures

The PONS (Hall et al., 1978; Rosenthal et al., 1974) assesses ability to understand nonverbal communication transmitted through different nonverbal channels. The PONS is a film comprised of 220 2-sec audio and/or video segments. In each segment, a young woman portrays one of 20 randomly ordered situations such as "criticizing someone for being late" or "talking to a lost child." For each scenario, the subject chooses, from a pair of descriptions of cross-culturally relevant situations, the best description of what has just been seen and/or heard. Each scenario is represented in 11 different channels of nonverbal communication involving various combinations of face, full body, and two forms of verbal content-filtering, which make the speech unintelligible. Adequate reliability and validity has been established on over 4,000 subjects varying in cultural background, age, occupational status, and other criteria (Hall et al., 1978).

Encoding task

Since there are no standardized measures of encoding, this measure was modeled after commonly used procedures according to Hall (Note 2).

Each participant was seated in an armchair directly facing the camera for a full body shot and was videotaped while briefly enacting each of eight scenarios, similar to those used on the PONS. The sequence of scenarios for each person was determined randomly (with 10 random sequences).

The 480 scenarios (60 participants, i.e., 40 clients and 20 counselors × 8 scenarios) were divided into two stimulus tapes. Each tape contained four consecutive scenarios from each subject, with the order of subjects randomly determined for each tape. To insure equal duration of all segments, all utterances were truncated to 3 sec. A ROVOCO Model 104 Voice Control Filter with bandpass filters set for optimal frequencies was used to make the words unintelligible while leaving the expressive qualities of the voice more or less intact; this was done to ensure that judges looked for the nonverbal characteristics rather than the verbal content of the message.

Seven undergraduate assistants, selected for high-decoding ability (as measured by the PONS) served as judges. After watching each 3-sec filtered videotaped segment, they attempted to identify which of the eight scenarios the subject was expressing. The total encoding score for each subject was the average number of judges accurately identifying each segment. The seven judges had an average accuracy score of 2.75 out of 8 identifications, which is better than chance (1 of 8). The average agreement level between pairs of judges was low (average $\kappa = .20$).

Procedure

Counselors conducted two 30-minute counseling sessions, one with a male and one with a female client. The two sessions were separated by varying intervals of time (from no separation to 2 weeks). They were informed that the study would focus on the counseling interaction, but they remained blind as to the exact purposes of the study. Counselors were instructed to be as helpful as possible with their clients, making appropriate referral for clients who wished further help for their personal problems. Clients were instructed to come prepared to discuss a personal problem for a half hour. The client and counselor were seated in armchairs directly facing each other at a distance of approximately 55 inches (1.40 m) from the centers of the chairs. Each session was videotaped.

After the session, clients completed the BLRI, the CRF, and the CEI. The counselors also completed the BLRI.

Approximately 2 weeks later, clients and counselors ($N = 60$) completed the encoding and decoding tasks and were debriefed about the study.

Results

On the PONS, clients' mean score was 175.96 ($SD = 19.57$) and the counselors' mean score, 184.68 ($SD = 6.64$). On the encoding measure, the clients' mean score was 2.35 ($SD = .93$) and the counselors' mean score, 2.55 ($SD = .90$). In comparing the PONS scores of the counselor sample to the general norms (Rosenthal et al., 1974), the means were very similar, but the standard deviations were significantly smaller ($p < .01$). The client sample did not differ from the norm group on the PONS scores.

None of the relationships between the nonverbal measures and the four outcome measures was significant. The PONS scores were not related to encoding scores for either counselor or client.

Discussion

Nonverbal abilities had virtually no impact on evaluations of counseling effectiveness. Consequently, neither client nor counselor decoding or encoding skills, as measured in this study, helped to explain what determines a good counseling session.

These findings are similar to a recent study (Lee et al., 1980), which used a similar methodology and found no relationship between counselor PONS scores and client ratings of the counselor. However, these results contradict earlier findings by Hall et al. (1978), Burruss (cited in Hall et al., 1978), and DiMatteo, Friedman, and Taranta (1979), all of which used different methodologies and found weak relationships.

Both measures in this study had methodological problems. Counselors not only scored higher than clients on the PONS ($t = 4.64$, $p < .001$), but their standard deviations were quite low, suggesting the presence of a ceiling effect. The resulting restricted range may have reduced the possibility for significant relationships with outcome measures. On the encoding measure, very low agreement among judges was obtained. Judges found the task to be aversive because the segments were brief (3 sec) and so little information was presented. Although the decoding and encoding measures were the most commonly used, they did not appear to be methodologically adequate. These measures may be more appropriate for social psychology experiments than for counseling settings. They do not seem to tap the nonverbal skills that differentially affect a counseling situation.

Experiment 2: Nonverbal Movements

A number of studies have shown that nonverbal behaviors are not random activity but have communicative value (Ekman, 1964; Mehrabian, 1972). In fact, nonverbal behaviors alone (e.g., voice-tone, facial expression, and body movements) can reliably communicate emotions and relationship characteristics (Allport & Cantrill, 1934; Buck, Miller, & Caul, 1970; Davitz & Davitz, 1959; Dusenbury & Knower, 1939; Fairbanks & Pronovost, 1939; Fretz, 1966; Howell & Jorgensen, 1970; Knower, 1945; Munn, 1940; Pfaff, 1954; Thompson & Meltzer, 1964; Zuckerman, Lipets, Koivumaki, & Rosenthal, 1975).

Given the obvious significance of communication in counseling, nonverbal behaviors have received an increasing amount of attention. Hughey (1974) theorized that nonverbal behavior serves several purposes in the counseling relationship: communication of meaning, leakage of information, deception, regulation of the interaction and attitudes, and indication of change in the therapeutic relationship. Despite the reported importance of nonverbal behavior within the counseling process, few studies have examined actual counseling sessions (Gladstein, 1974). Most social and counseling psychology studies have utilized an analogue methodology, which shows short videotaped vignettes or still photographs as stimuli and has subjects rate the counselor on any of several measures. This procedure seems to measure impression formation rather than the impact of specific behaviors in the counseling process.

The purpose of this study was to examine the relationship between counselor and client nonverbal behaviors and outcome in a more naturalistic setting. Based on the past literature, the frequencies of the following counselor behaviors were hypothesized to be related to counseling outcome: affirmative head nods would be positively correlated (Hackney, 1974; LaCrosse, 1977; Sobelman, 1974); smiles would be positively correlated (Bayes, 1972; Fretz, 1966); a body orientation directly facing the client would be positively related (Haase & Tepper, 1972; LaCrosse, 1977; Sobelman, 1974); a forward trunk lean would be positively related (Genther & Moughan, 1977; Haase & Tepper, 1972; LaCrosse, 1977; Sobelman, 1974; Tepper

& Haase, 1978); a leg position of the ankle of one leg resting on the knee of the other leg would be negatively correlated (Smith-Hanen, 1977); and both vertical and horizontal arm movements would be positively correlated (Fretz, 1966; LaCrosse, 1977; Sobelman, 1974).

Method

The research participants, procedures for conducting the counseling sessions, and outcome measures were reported in Experiment 1.

Definitions of Nonverbal Behaviors

Affirmative head nods were any vertical movements of the head not directly associated with a horizontal movement. Smiles were defined as a turning upward of the lips. Direct facing of the body was defined as squarely facing the other person. Forward trunk lean occurred when the person's shoulders were in front of the bottom of his/her seated body. The leg position was defined as when the ankle of one leg rests on the knee of the other leg. Vertical arm movements were any up and down movements of the arm, whereas horizontal arm movements were any sideways movements.

Procedure

Videotapes of the 40 counseling sessions provided the data for the nonverbal behaviors. The audio portion of each tape was erased, and numbered beeps were dubbed onto the tapes at 5-sec intervals, yielding approximately 360 numbered segments per 30-min session. The 5-sec interval was chosen so that the nonverbal behaviors would be readily observable yet not so gross (e.g., 1-min block) as to exclude potentially important data regarding repetitions of a movement.

To provide judgments of the frequency of the nonverbal behaviors, eight female undergraduates were selected from a pool of approximately 60 volunteers on the basis of high grade point averages and high scores on the PONS, a measure of the individual's ability to decode communication. Pairs of raters were trained to observe two specific behaviors (e.g., smiles and head nods). After definitions and trials, training tapes were rated and raters discussed the criteria they used to make decisions. This procedure was repeated until the two raters consistently agreed on at least 80% of the segments. After training, raters worked independently to complete their ratings on all 40 tapes. Raters indicated whether or not a given behavior occurred in each 5-sec segment. Each behavior was rated by one rater, with 10% of the tapes rated again by a second rater to assess reliability. Final reliabilities ranged from .71 (smiles) to .99 (leg position and direct facing). Average reliability for all seven movements was .91. The proportion of occurrence of nonverbal behaviors was calculated by dividing the number of occurrences within the 5-sec segments by the total number of segments in the session.

Results

Means and standard deviations of client and counselor nonverbal movements are shown in Table 2.

Table 3 presents the correlations between counselor nonverbal movements and counseling outcome measures. A review of this table indicates that only counselor vertical arm movements were significantly correlated ($-.32$) with any client-rated outcome. Counselor smiles and forward trunk lean were significantly correlated with counselor BLRI. However, these three correlations were of weak magnitude and only slightly above the number which could be expected to occur by chance.

Of the 28 correlations between client nonverbal behavior and counseling outcome, only one significant result was found, which could be attributed to chance.

Discussion

Frequency of occurrence of specific nonverbal behaviors appeared to have minimal impact on evaluations of counseling effectiveness. The most likely explanation for the lack of significant results in this study as compared with past research is the use of more naturalistic methods rather than the usual analogue methodology. In an analogue, when subjects are shown a still photograph or a videotape segment of counselor behavior, nonverbal cues probably assume a greater importance simply because of the lack of other information available. In a naturalistic setting, the client or counselor responds to many additional cues (e.g., verbal content and relationship factors).

Further, the use of frequency data did not seem adequate for tapping the complexity of the role of nonverbal behavior in the counseling process. It may not be the frequency of occurrence of nonverbal behavior but an occurrence at a specific moment that is important. Also, the interaction between counselor and client nonverbal behavior as well as the interaction between verbal and nonverbal behaviors cannot be examined through simple frequency counts. The context, content, and

Table 2—*Means and Standard Deviations of Client and Counselor Nonverbal Behaviors*

Movement	Client		Counselor	
	M	*SD*	*M*	*SD*
Head nods	9.5	5.5	49.6	16.5
Smiles	11.0	9.3	6.2	5.3
Direct facing	96.8	9.7	94.4	13.4
Trunk forward	7.1	22.1	18.2	31.2
Legs: Ankle on knee	9.3	23.3	38.0	43.2
Vertical arm	8.8	5.9	11.4	7.4
Horizontal arm	3.0	2.8	7.4	5.3

Note. All entries are percentages of all the 5-sec segments in which this movement occurred.

Table 3—*Correlations Between Counselor Nonverbal*
Behaviors and Counseling Outcome

Movement	Counseling outcome measure			
	Client			Counselor
	BLRI	CEI	CRF	BLRI
Head nods	.01	.14	.07	.06
Smiles	.26	.13	.13	.31*
Direct facing	−.20	−.04	−.04	−.22
Trunk forward	.00	−.13	.09	.36**
Legs: Ankle on knee	−.08	−.11	−.12	−.25
Vertical arm	.00	−.26	−.32*	−.13
Horizontal arm	−.08	−.10	−.11	−.11

Note.   BLRI = Barrett-Lennard Relationship Inventory: CEI = Counseling Evaluation Inventory; CRF = Counselor Rating Form.
   $*p < .01.$ $**p < .001.$

dynamics all probably need to be considered in answering the complicated question
of how nonverbal behavior operated in the counseling process.

Experiment 3: Congruence

A recurring theme throughout the research in nonverbal communication in counsel-
ing/psychotherapy is the degree of consistency between verbal and nonverbal channels of communication. Haase and Tepper (1972) concluded that even highly empathic verbal messages are undermined by inconsistent or contradictory nonverbal
cues and that congruence may be an essential underpinning to all core facilitative
conditions. Graves and Robinson (1976) demonstrated that judged counselor congruence is significantly less when verbal and nonverbal cues are inconsistent. Barrett-
Lennard (1962) stated that level of congruence is conceived to set an upper limit to
the degree to which empathic understanding of another is possible. Consequently, a
certain degree of congruence between verbal and nonverbal messages would appear
to be critical for the successful communication of empathy.

Despite the importance of the concept of congruence, no measure has been
developed to assess the consistency of verbal and nonverbal messages within a counseling session. Previous measures have assessed participants' perceptions of congruence after the session (Barrett-Lennard, 1962) or have used judges to rate congruence
(Carkhuff, 1969). The first purpose of this study was to assess and compare counselor
and client perceptions of their own verbal–nonverbal congruence and validate this
type of congruence with the Congruence subscale of the BLRI. A second purpose of
the study was to determine if congruence was related to outcome measures of counseling.

Method

The research participants, procedures for conducting the counseling sessions, and the outcome measures were reported in Experiment 1.

Congruence Measure

For this measure, congruence was defined as a state in which feelings the counselor is experiencing are available to him or her and available to his or her awareness and he or she is able to live these feelings, be them in the relationship, and is able to communicate them. For purposes of this study, we assumed this definition would hold for clients as well as counselors. We also believed that this definition would best be operationalized by allowing counselors and clients to rate their own experiences of congruence. Affect within the session was ascertained using a recall method, modeled after Kagan's (Note 3) Interpersonal Process Recall. A series of five standardized questions were asked for each 1-minute segment of replayed videotape. A 1-minute time period was used (based on a pilot experiment) so that the segment was long enough to judge congruence yet not so long as to contain several affects. Counselors and clients were asked the following five questions: (a) What was your major feeling during this segment? (b) What feelings were you expressing through your words? (c) What feelings were you expressing through your voice tone? (d) What feelings were you expressing through your movements, facial expression, and/or gestures? (e) What do you believe the other person was feeling in this segment? Each of these five questions was answered by recording 1 of the 13 categories on the following Affect Adjective List.

Affect Adjective List. To facilitate the subjects' identification of feelings, an Affect Adjective Checklist was developed by the authors. First, feeling words ($n = 471$) and affect category labels ($n = 13$) were culled from several lists (Gazda, 1973; McNair, Lorr, & Droppleman, 1971; Zuckerman & Lubin, 1965). Next, 73 undergraduate students were asked to assign each feeling word to one of the 13 categories. Those adjectives that were placed under a given category by more than half the subjects were used for the final list, which contains 225 adjectives in 13 categories: calm–relaxed, happy–joyful, vigorous–active, competent–powerful, concerned–caring, respectful–loving, tense–anxious, sad–depressed, angry–hostile, tired–apathetic, confused–bewildered, criticized–shamed, and inadequate–weak.

Types of congruence. Congruence was then operationalized as a consistency of response between two or more of the five questions; the same affect had to be recorded for congruence to be scored for any given minute. Five types of congruence were identified from the responses to the five questions: (a) *verbal congruence* (consistency between Questions 1 & 2), (b) *paralinguistic congruence* (consistency between Questions 1 & 3), (c) *kinesic congruence* (consistency between Questions 1 & 4), (d) *intracongruence* (consistency between Questions 1, 2, 3, & 4), and (e) *intercongruence* (consistency between Questions 1 & 5). The total possible score for any of the five types was 30 (given the 30 minutes of the session).

Procedure

While the session was conducted (see Experiment 1 for Procedure), beeps at 1-minute intervals were superimposed onto the videotape to be used in the recall.

Postsession process recall. After completion of the counseling session and the counseling outcome measures, both the counselor and client were taken into a room containing a television monitor. The counselor and client were separated by a partition; both had a clear view of the split-screen videotape of their session but were unable to observe or speak to each other. The subjects were given the Affect Adjective Checklist to use in completing the congruence measure. The experimenter stopped the tape after each successive 1-min segment of the video-audio replay. Following each segment, both client and counselor wrote down 1 of the 13 categories from the Affect Adjective Checklist that they felt best described their response to each of the five questions of the congruence measure. This recall procedure required approximately 60–75 minutes to complete.

Results

Means and standard deviations for the five types of congruence are presented in Table 4. The types of congruence that depend only on one's own perceptions (verbal, paralinguistic, kinesic, and intracongruence) were highly intercorrelated; the range of correlations for the client was from .63 to .88 ($p < .001$) and for the counselor, .69 to .90 ($p < .001$). These four types of congruence were not related to intercongruence for either counselor or client.

Correlations between all five types of counselor congruence and counselors' scores on the Congruence subscale of the BLRI were significant ($r = .50, .56, .33, .49,$ and $.29$, respectively, $p < .05$). However, of the correlations between counselor congruence and client's scores on the Congruence subscale of the BLRI, only the intercongruence measure was significantly correlated ($r = .30, p < .05$). These results help to establish the validity of this new measure.

Correlations between client and counselor congruence and the counseling outcome measures are presented in Table 5. Of the client congruence measures, verbal congruence was related to client CRF, and intracongruence was related to both client CEI and CRF. All three correlations involved client perceptions (e.g., client perceptions of his/her congruence and client perceptions of outcome) but did not involve counselor perceptions of client congruence or outcome. Of the counselor congruence

Table 4—*Means and Standard Deviations for Congruence Measures*

Congruence measure	Client		Counselor	
	M	*SD*	*M*	*SD*
Verbal	15.08	6.40	17.25	7.17
Paralinguistic	12.75	6.75	16.55	7.20
Kinesic	10.73	6.56	15.35	7.67
Intracongruence	5.73	6.51	11.18	7.88
Intercongruence	5.00	2.54	10.65	7.91

Table 5—*Correlations Between Congruence Measures
and Counseling Outcome*

| | Counseling outcome measure | | | |
| | Client | | | Counselor |
Congruence measure	BLRI	CEI	CRF	BLRI
Client				
Verbal	.09	.23	.37**	.03
Paralinguistic	.09	.24	.30	−.04
Kinesic	−.02	.21	.26	−.21
Intracongruence	.05	.38**	.41**	−.02
Intercongruence	.09	−.16	−.05	.20
Counselor				
Verbal	.20	.05	.08	.47**
Paralinguistic	.09	−.02	.06	.39**
Kinesic	.06	.10	.00	.19
Intracongruence	.17	.18	.13	.34**
Intercongruence	.38**	.22	.21	.37**

Note. BLRI = Barrett-Lennard Relationship Inventory; CEI = Counseling Evaluation Inventory; CRF = Counselor Rating Form.
$*p < .01.$ $**p < .005.$

measures, four of the five types of congruence (verbal, paralinguistic, intracongruence, and intercongruence) were related to the counselor BLRI. Additionally, congruence between client and counselor perceptions of counselor expression of feeling (counselor intercongruence) was also related to the client BLRI.

Discussion

Counselor congruence was positively related to counselor facilitativeness. If the counselor was congruent, he/she rated himself/herself as more facilitative. If the counselor's feelings were accurately communicated to the client (counselor intercongruence), then the client also perceived the counselor as more facilitative. These findings correspond with past theory and research on other types of congruence measures (Barrett-Lennard, 1962; Graves & Robinson, 1976; Haase & Tepper, 1972). Thus, the importance of consistent portrayal of affect among various channels (verbal, paralinguistic, and kinesic) within an actual counseling session was empirically demonstrated.

The high correlation between counselor ratings on both congruence measures (the one derived for this study and the Congruence subscale of the BLRI) provided concurrent validity for the new measure. The advantage of this new measure over previous ones is that it is more relevant for demonstrating actual congruence within the session. This measure more closely approximates the behaviors involved in the concept of congruence than does the BLRI, which is completed after the session and tests global impressions rather than actual in-session behavior.

That client congruence was related to clients' own evaluations of the counseling suggests that when clients perceived themselves as being consistent in the portrayal of emotions through the various channels, they felt better about the session. In fact, clients appeared to rely more heavily on their perceptions of their own congruence rather than counselor congruence in judging outcome. The same was true for counselors, which suggests that especially in an initial session, each participant is more aware and critical of his/her own behavior. If congruence reflects anxiety, an anxious person not expressing himself/herself well may tend to devalue the session.

The methodology employed in this study seemed particularly useful for future research. In effect, the use of a set of questions for each 1-minute segment of the replay of the videotape standardized the Interpersonal Process Recall (Kagan, Note 3) method. It enabled subjects to go back and recapture what they were experiencing at the time. The counselors particularly reported that this portion of the research was helpful and revealing to them. This same method could be used in further research on nonverbal behavior to pinpoint the moments when the verbal or nonverbal channels were ascendant in importance.

General Discussion

The results of this three-part study suggested that the effects of nonverbal communication cannot be examined in isolation to determine their influence on counseling. When we studied nonverbal abilities and frequency of nonverbal movements alone, we found minimal impact on counseling outcome. When we looked at the congruence between verbal and nonverbal behaviors, we found more promising results. There remains much intuitive and clinical evidence that nonverbal behaviors have a large impact on counseling process and outcome. However, nonverbal communication seems to be a very subtle phenomenon and, based on the present results, one must look at other aspects, such as how nonverbal behavior interacts with other variables (e.g., verbal content, timing in counseling, and the interaction between counselor and client behavior).

Perhaps one outcome of this study is that future researchers in counseling will be encouraged to abandon some of the more traditional methods of doing nonverbal research in counseling. Clearly, new methods need to be developed to look at this complex issue. One possibility might be the use of sequential patterns of nonverbal behaviors as the unit of examination. That is, sequences rather than specific behaviors may be more appropriate for illuminating the importance of nonverbal behaviors for counseling outcome. Another method might involve expanding the Interpersonal Process Recall methodology to include client and counselor specification of the nonverbal behavior they perceived as critical. A critical-incidents analysis could then be conducted. Single case designs in naturalistic settings may be the best generator of more fruitful hypotheses regarding the relationship of nonverbal abilities and behaviors to counseling outcome.

Reference Notes

1. DePaulo, B. M. *Liking, disliking, ambivalence, deception: Who hides it? Who finds it?* Paper presented at the meeting of the American Psychological Association, Toronto, Canada, August–September 1978.

2. Hall, J. Personal communication, September 1978.
3. Kagan, N. *Interpersonal Process Recall: A method of influencing human interaction.* Unpublished manuscript, 1975. (Available from N. Kagan, 434 Erickson Hall, College of Education, Michigan State University, East Lansing, Michigan 48824.)

References

Allport, G. W., & Cantrill, H. Judging personality from voice. *Journal of Social Psychology*, 1934, *5*, 37–54.

Barak, A., & LaCrosse, M. B. Multidimensional perceptions of counselor behavior. *Journal of Counseling Psychology*, 1975, *22*, 471–476.

Barrett-Lennard, G. T. Dimensions of therapist response as causal factors in therapeutic changes. *Psychological Monographs*, 1962, *76*(43, Whole No. 562).

Bayes, M. A. Behavioral cues of interpersonal warmth. *Journal of Consulting and Clinical Psychology*, 1972, *39*, 333–339.

Buck, M. A., Miller, R. E., & Caul, W. F. Sex, personality, and physiological variables in the communication of affect via facial expression. *Journal of Personality and Social Psychology*, 1970, *30*, 587–596.

Carkhuff, R. R. *Helping and human relations: A primer for lay and professional helpers* (Vol. 1). New York: Holt, Rinehart & Winston, 1969.

Davitz, J., & Davitz, L. The communication of feelings by content-free speech. *Journal of Communication*, 1959, *9*, 6–13.

DiMatteo, M. R., Friedman, H. S., & Taranta, A. Sensitivity to bodily nonverbal communication as a factor in practitioner–patient rapport. *Journal of Nonverbal Behavior*, 1979, *4*, 18–26.

Dusenbury, D., & Knower, F. H. Experimental studies of the symbolism of action and voice —II. A study of the specificity of meaning in abstract tonal symbols. *Quarterly Journal of Speech*, 1939, *25*, 67–75.

Ekman, P. Body position, facial expression, and verbal behavior during interviews. *Journal of Abnormal and Social Psychology*, 1964, *63*, 295–301.

Fairbanks, G., & Pronovost, W. An experimental study of the pitch characteristics of the voice during the expression of emotion. *Speech Monographs*, 1939, *6*, 87–104.

Fretz, B. R. Postural movements in a counseling dyad. *Journal of Counseling Psychology*, 1966, *13*, 335–343.

Friedman, H. S., DiMatteo, M. R., & Taranta, A. A study of the relationship between individual differences in nonverbal expressiveness and factors of personality and social interaction. *Journal of Research in Personality*, 1980, *14*, 351–364.

Garfield, S. L. Client variables in psychotherapy. In S. L. Garfield & A. E. Bergin (Eds.), *Handbook of psychotherapy and behavior change.* New York: Wiley, 1978.

Gazda, G. M. *Vocabulary of affective adjectives in human relationship development: A manual for educators.* Boston, Mass.: Allyn & Bacon, 1973.

Genther, R. W., & Moughan, J. Introverts and extraverts' responses to nonverbal attending behavior. *Journal of Counseling Psychology*, 1977, *24*, 244–246.

Gladstein, G. A. Nonverbal communication and counseling/psychotherapy: A review. *Counseling Psychologist*, 1974, *4*(3), 34–57.

Graves, J. R., & Robinson, J. D. Proxemic behavior as a function of inconsistent verbal and nonverbal messages. *Journal of Counseling Psychology*, 1976, *23*, 333–338.

Haase, R. F., & Tepper, D. T. Nonverbal components of emphathic communication. *Journal of Counseling Psychology*, 1972, *19*, 417–424.

Hackney, H. Facial gestures and subject expression of feeling. *Journal of Counseling Psychology*, 1974, *21*, 173–178.

Hall, J. A., Rosenthal, R., Archer, D., DiMatteo, M. R., & Rogers, P. L. Profile of nonverbal sensitivity. In P. McReynolds (Ed.), *Advances in psychological assessment* (Vol. 4). San Francisco: Jossey-Bass, 1978.

Harper, R. G., Wiens, A. N., & Matarazzo, J. D. *Nonverbal communication: The state of the art.* New York: Wiley, 1978.

Howell, R. J., & Jorgensen, E. C. Accuracy of judging unposed emotional behavior in a natural setting: A replication study. *Journal of Social Psychology*, 1970, *81*, 269–270.

Hughey, A. R. Nonverbal behaviors, their use in counseling and implications for counselor education (Doctoral dissertation, University of Pittsburgh, 1973). *Dissertation Abstracts International*, 1974, *35*, 189–90A. (University Microfilms No. 74-14, 962)

Ivey, A. E. *Microcounseling: Innovations in interviewer training.* Springfield, Ill.: Charles C Thomas, 1971.

Knower, F. H. Studies in the symbolism of the voice and action: V. The use of behavioral and tonal symbols as tests of speaking achievement. *Journal of Applied Psychology*, 1945, *29*, 229–235.

LaCrosse, M. B. Comparative perceptions of counselor behavior: A replication and extension. *Journal of Counseling Psychology*, 1977, *24*, 464–471.

Lee, Y. L., Halberg, E. T., Kocsis, M., & Haase, R. F. Decoding skills in nonverbal communication and perceived interviewer effectiveness. *Journal of Counseling Psychology*, 1980, *27*, 89–92.

Linden, J. D., Stone, S. C., & Schertzer, B. Development and evaluation of an inventory for rating counselors. *Personnel and Guidance Journal*, 1965, *43*, 267–276.

McNair, D. M., Lorr, M., & Droppleman, L. F. *Profile of mood manual.* San Diego, Calif.: Educational and Industrial Testing Service, 1971.

Mehrabian, A. *Nonverbal communication.* Chicago: Aldine-Atherton, 1972.

Munn, N. L. The effect of knowledge of the situation upon judgment from facial expressions. *Journal of Abnormal and Social Psychology*, 1940, *35*, 324–338.

Pfaff, P. L. An experimental study of communication of feeling without contextual material. *Speech Monographs*, 1954, *21*, 155–156.

Rogers, C. R. The necessary and sufficient conditions of therapeutic personality change. *Journal of Consulting Psychology*, 1957, *21*, 95–103.

Rosenthal, R., Archer, D., Koivumaki, J. H., DiMatteo, M. R., & Rogers, P. L. Assessing sensitivity to nonverbal communication: The PONS test. *Personality and Social Psychology Bulletin* (APA Division 8), 1974, 1–3.

Smith-Hanen, S. S. Effects of nonverbal behaviors on judged levels of counselor warmth and empathy. *Journal of Counseling Psychology*, 1977, *24*, 87–91.

Sobelman, S. A. The effects of verbal and nonverbal components of the judged level of counselor warmth (Doctoral dissertation, American University, 1973). *Dissertation Abstracts International*, 1974, *35*, 273A. (University Microfilms No. 74-14, 199)

Tepper, D. T., & Haase, R. F. Verbal and nonverbal components of facilitative conditions. *Journal of Counseling Psychology*, 1978, *25*, 35–44.

Thompson, D. F., & Meltzer, L. Communication of emotional intent by facial expression. *Journal of Abnormal and Social Psychology*, 1964, *68*, 129–135.

Zuckerman, M., Lipets, M. S., Koivumaki, J. H., & Rosenthal, R. Encoding and decoding nonverbal cues of emotion. *Journal of Personality and Social Psychology*, 1975, *32*, 1068–1076.

Zuckerman, M., & Lubin, B. *Multiple Affect Adjective Checklist manual.* San Diego, Calif.: Educational and Industrial Testing Service, 1965.

Chapter 12
VERBAL AND NONVERBAL COMMUNICATION
OF FACILITATIVE CONDITIONS

Donald T. Tepper, Jr., and Richard F. Haase

It is becoming increasingly apparent that nonverbal communication in the counseling process is of critical importance in furthering our understanding of the conditions under which counseling is effective. Within the past decade nonverbal communication has gained increasing prominence as an object of study; within the past 5 years the counseling literature has begun to reflect the importance of the *total* communication process to the texture and outcome of the counseling relationship. Defined in a rather broad fashion, nonverbal behaviors which have been demonstrated to have measurable impact on the counseling process include eye contact, trunk lean, distance, body orientation, movement, facial expression, vocal intonation, gestures, and selected features of the spatial environment (Broekman & Moller, 1973; Chaikin, Derlega, & Miller, 1976; Dinges & Oetting, 1972; Ekman & Friesen, 1968; Fretz, 1966; Graves & Robinson, 1976; Haase, 1970; Haase & DiMattia, 1970, 1976; Haase & Tepper, 1972; Hackney, 1974; LaCrosse, 1975; Lee, Zingle, Patterson, Ivey, & Haase, 1976; Smith, 1975; Stone & Morden, 1976; Strahan & Zytowski, 1976; Sweeney & Cottle, 1976. A comprehensive review of much of the evidence relating nonverbal behavior to counseling can be found in Gladstein (1974).

The evidence which relates directly to counseling, as well as the more general literature in nonverbal communication, suggests that there exists a delicate balance between the verbal and nonverbal channels of communication of affect and attitude. Haase and Tepper (1972) found that the ratio of nonverbal to verbal message variance was 2:1 in the judged communication of empathy. Mehrabian (1968) indicates that as much as 55% of the communicational significance of the message is nonverbal; similar ratios have been reported by Birdwhistell (1970) and Argyle, Alkema, and Gilmour (1971). It seems fairly clear that the balance between verbal and nonverbal cues in the communication process is critical for the perceived impact of the overall message. As early as 1965 Argyle and Dean demonstrated that shifting the balance between verbal and nonverbal channels alters the perception and the communicational significance of the message. Inasmuch as the counseling process is so heavily rooted in a complex communicational context, an understanding of the balance and interplay between verbal and nonverbal cues in the relationship becomes important.

Of the many variables which have received attention in the counseling literature, the facilitative conditions proposed by Rogers (1951, 1957) have achieved wide acceptance in counseling practice. These conditions have been noted to be essential to the quality of the relationship; research evidence suggests that helping relationships depend heavily on these conditions in myriad forms (Bergin & Garfield, 1971; Carkhuff, 1971). Haase and Tepper (1972) have shown that the communication of empathy is heavily dependent on the verbal message but not to the exclusion of the

---

Reprinted from *Journal of Counseling Psychology, 25*, 35–44 (1978). Copyright © 1978 by the American Psychological Association. Used with permission of the first author.

211

nonverbal channels of communication. They demonstrated that even high-quality verbal emphathic messages are undermined by contradictory and inconsistent nonverbal cues. Fretz (1966) and Shapiro (1968) demonstrated that the communication of empathy is dependent on nonverbal as well as verbal communications. Graves and Robinson (1976) have shown that judged counselor genuineness is significantly less when verbal and nonverbal cues are inconsistent and that a behavioral outcome variable (proximity to the counselor) was also significantly affected by the inconsistency. With the exception of these studies, little work has been completed which is aimed at disentangling the relative contribution of verbal and nonverbal cues in the communication of the basic facilitative conditions of empathy, respect, and genuineness (congruence).

The purpose of the present study was, therefore, (a) to replicate the earlier findings of Haase and Tepper (1972) with regard to the judged empathy of multichannel communication; (b) to extend multichannel research to the facilitative conditions of respect and genuineness; (c) to operationalize the nonverbal cues of vocal intonation and facial expression which have not received extensive attention in the counseling literature; and (d) to include a sample of actual clients as well as counselors as judges of communicated attitude in the study.

Method

Subjects

The two groups of subjects used in this study consisted of 15 male students in varying stages of counseling at the University of Massachusetts Counseling Center, who ranged from age 18 to 25 and represented a variety of presenting concerns, and 15 experienced male counselors (8 doctoral level and 7 doctoral level counselors in training) who represented several theoretical orientations. Only male subjects were used to avoid the inclusion of a sixth factor in the design and to control for a source of extraneous variance.

Stimulus Materials

A videotape stimulus was especially designed for this study which consisted of 32 role-played interactions between an actor counselor and an actor client. Both the counselor and client were male and relatively unknown to most of the subject-judges. The interactions showed a full view of the counselor as seen across the shoulder of the client. The client's shoulder served as a spatial frame of reference from which the subjects judged the counselor's response to the client's statement.

The 32 stimulus interactions represented all combinations of two levels of trunk lean (forward–backward), two levels of eye contact (direct contact–no contact), two levels of vocal intonation (concerned–indifferent), two levels of facial expression (concerned–indifferent), and two levels of verbal message (high–low).

The operational definitions of trunk lean and eye contact were as follows: in the backward-trunk-lean condition, the counselor leaned backward in a professional swivel chair with his hands on the arms of the chair, while in the forward condition he leaned forward with his arms on his legs. The counselor's body orientation was maintained facing toward the client in all stimulus interactions. In the eye-contact condition, the counselor looked directly at the client's eyes and in the no-eye-contact condition looked downward into his own lap.

To operationally define the three independent variables of vocal intonation, facial expression, and verbal message, three preliminary operations were performed. The first was to select the high- and low-level message. Using as a guide verbatim excerpts extracted from Truax and Carkhuff (1967) and Carkhuff and Berenson (1967), 30 interactions were formed which represented varying degrees of counselor-communicated core conditions of empathy, respect or positive regard, and genuineness. These excerpts, consisting of one client statement and one counselor response, were mimeographed on four sheets of paper and given in random sequence to a group of counselors and counselors in training for judging. Each judge was given a booklet of statements and a criterion sheet which briefly described the dimension of empathy and positive regard and also the scale point identifications for judging the level of each. Each statement was judged according to a 5-point scale taken from Carkhuff (1969) for its level of emphathic understanding and also for its level of positive regard or respect shown for the client. The statements were not judged for genuineness because genuineness is defined as the congruence between at least two simultaneous cues only one of which (the verbal message) was present at this stage. There was at least a 1-day separation between the judging of empathy and the judging of positive regard, so as to reduce criterion contamination.

Two levels of verbal message were used in this study.[1] The statement which was most consistently judged highest for both empathy and positive regard and also one which was judged lowest in empathy and positive regard served as the two levels of the verbal message independent factor.

Determining the operational definitions for the vocal intonation and facial expression variables was somewhat more complicated. For the purpose of this study, an appropriate nonverbal intonational and facial response to a client utterance signifying depression was chosen and defined as that which conveys an understanding of and a concern for perceived client depression. The polar opposite of concern was defined as indifference; these two ends of the continuum defined the two levels of vocal intonation and facial expression.

Determination of the two levels of intonation was accomplished by having the counselor recite both the high- and the low-level message into a tape recorder. He was instructed to vary his intonational pattern (rate, pitch, volume, etc.) while attempting to convey varying levels of concern and indifference. These coded excerpts were rated by a group of adults according to 5-point, Likert type scale along an indifference–concern continuum for level of communicated concern. The judges were instructed to make their ratings on the basis of intonation only. Two statements were selected from the high-verbal-statement group (one with concerned intonation and one with indifferent intonation) and two statements from the low-verbal-statement group (one concerned and one indifferent). The concerned intonation was

---

[1]A Thurstone Equal Appearing Intervals Technique (Edwards, 1957) was used to scale and select all high and low levels of the independent factors.

characterized by soft, low tones and slow rhythm, while the indifferent intonation was harsher, higher pitched, and faster paced. These selected combinations of verbal message and vocal intonation were then retrieved from the coded master tape for later use in preparation of the stimulus videotape.

Facial expression was operationally defined by making 36 photographs of the counselor's face as he attempted to convey feelings from indifference to concern. An effort was made to vary the furrow of the brow, the pitch of the eyebrow, and the position of the cheekbone, since these facial features were believed through experience to convey concern (Darwin, 1872; Ekman, 1973). The photographs were then coded and judged by a group of adults along a 5-point Likert type scale for communicated concern and both a concerned and an indifferent facial expression were selected for duplication in the stimulus videotape. A concerned facial expression was characterized by a furrowed brow and lowered eyebrows, while the indifferent expression was typically bland and without meaningful contortion.

Employing these operational definitions for the two levels of each of the five independent variables, the stimulus tape was produced by seating the counselor in a swivel tilt armchair opposite the client at a distance of 55 in (140 cm). This distance was chosen because Kelly (1972) concluded that "closer distances (36″) communicate positive counselor regard, while middle (55″) and far (72″) interactional distances tend to convey neutral and negative evaluative counselor feelings respectively" (p. 345). In order not to bias the stimulus communications, the neutral distance of 55 in (140 cm) was chosen.

For each of the 32 interaction conditions, a card was made which indicated the combination of independent variables for that particular interaction. The counselor was instructed to position himself according to the designated conditions listed on the reference card. For example, the instructions on one card were for the counselor to lean forward, maintain eye contact, speak a low-level message, and use an indifferent intonation while showing a concerned facial expression. The master audiotape recorder holding the appropriate verbal message–vocal intonation combinations (described earlier) was started simultaneously with the videotape recorder. The counselor timed his lip response to coincide with the audio portion which was dubbed directly onto the videotape. In this way, only the four segments which were previously judged to be concerned or indifferent intonation and high and low statements were recorded onto the stimulus tape. The 32 interactions were recorded onto four tapes of 8 interactions each to provide for random presentation to the judges.

Procedure

Each of the 30 judges was shown the stimulus videotape either alone or with 1 other subject in a small room which was free from distractions. The subjects were seated behind a small desk about 4 ft (122 cm) from the television monitor and provided with pencils, answer sheet, and the appropriate instruction sheet for the dependent measure being judged. The four sets of 8 interactions each were then randomly presented to the subjects who made their ratings directly on a Digitek answer sheet. Each subject rated all 32 interactions on all three dependent measures (empathy, respect, and genuineness) one dependent measure at a time with at least 1 and not more than 7 days between each rating. The order of rating the dependent measures was randomized for each subject.

All subjects were given instructions to make their judgments according to a 5-point scale taken from Carkhuff (1969) on the basis of brief descriptions of empathy, positive regard, and genuineness found in Carkhuff and Berenson (1967). The descriptions were written so that persons without previous knowledge of the technical terms would be able to make judgments easily. They were instructed to make the ratings according to their feeling about the attitude communicated by the counselor.

Design

Each of the three dependent variables of judged empathy, respect, and genuineness were evaluated by a $2 \times 2 \times 2 \times 2 \times 2 \times 2$ analysis of variance design with repeated measures on five factors. This design had one between-subjects factor (group) with two levels (counselors and clients) and five within-subjects factors. The within-subjects factors all had two levels and consisted of trunk lean (forward–backward), eye contact (direct contact–no contact), vocal intonation (concerned–indifferent), facial expression (concerned–indifferent), and verbal message (high–low).

A repeated measures design was chosen in this study for several reasons, chief among which is the efficiency of the design relative to the number of subjects required. Although only 15 subjects in each group were employed, the design actually yields 960 individual observations. To attempt to reproduce this design as a completely randomized analysis of variance is prohibitive. Moreover, a completely randomized design cannot control for intersubject variance which is a major source of error. A repeated measures design, by its very nature, eliminates this source of variation from the error terms involved and therefore increases the power of the F tests involved. It should also be noted that each subject therefore responded to 32 videotaped segments, each of which differed only by the dictates of the levels of each factor described earlier. Hence a certain amount of redundancy and carryover effect must be expected. It was for this reason that the additional precaution of randomizing the presentation of segments of stimulus materials was instituted in this study. Any carryover effect which might occur would at least, in this case, be equally distributed across all conditions and might lower the overall level of the effect measured, but would not differentially affect comparisons between factors within the design (Winer, 1972). In addition to the usual analysis of variance, variance components were calculated following a procedure outlined by Vaughn and Corballis (1969).

Results

The Results section has been divided in separate sections for each of the three facilitative conditions. Main and interaction effects for each analysis are further separated to emphasize the multichannel nature of the communication studied here.

Empathy

Five of the six main effects achieved statistical significance for the dependent variable of empathic communication. The effects of trunk lean, $F(1, 28) = 63.14$, $p < .001$, eye contact, $F(1, 28) = 79.35$, $p < .001$, vocal intonation, $F(1, 28) = 21.13$, $p < .001$, facial expression, $F(1, 28) = 96.55$, $p < .001$, and verbal message, $F(1, 28) = 86.18$, $p < .001$, all proved to be highly potent in accounting for variability in the judged quality of the empathic communication. There were no overall differences between counselors' and clients' judgments of the videotaped interactions, $F(1, 28) = 2.14$. Calculated variance components reveal that the effect sizes of the variables included in this study were sizable. Facial expression accounted for 26.01% of the variability in judged empathy, followed by the verbal message (16.94%), eye contact (6.03%), trunk lean (3.14%), and vocal intonation (1.14%). The calculation of variance components reveals that even a highly statistically significant effect such as vocal intonation can actually account for a relatively minor portion of the variance in the response variate. Considering only the main effects, the nonverbal cues which were included accounted for over two times the variability in judged empathy accounted for by the verbal message alone.

In addition to the significant main effects, 14 of the interactions tested in this factorial arrangement also reached statistical significance. The complexity of the communicational value of empathy is reflected in the fact that all of the main effects are involved in at least 1 of these interactions, which must alter the outright interpretation of the main effects as independent entities.

Five of the 14 significant interactions in the judgment of empathy suggested that counselors and clients perceive the relative contribution of verbal and nonverbal cues differentially. The first-order Group × Eye Contact interaction, $F(1, 28) = 6.84$, $p < .05$, $\theta^2 = .81\%$, reflects a greater judged difference between conditions of eye contact and no-eye contact for the clients than was the case for the counselors. While both groups judged the no-eye-contact condition about equally, the clients gave a higher judgment of empathy in the condition of eye contact than the counselors. The Group × Vocal Intonation interaction showed a similar pattern, but is superseded by a higher order interaction involving groups, vocal intonation, and facial expression, $F(1, 28) = 14.65$, $p < .001$, $\theta^2 = .92\%$. This interaction reveals that the counselors perceived relatively equal differences between concerned and indifferent facial expressions, and these were distributed as generally higher judgments under conditions of concerned intonation than under conditions of indifferent intonation. The meaning of the interaction is within the client group who perceived little difference between concerned and indifferent facial expressions at both levels of intonation, but who judged the concerned face–concerned intonation combination higher than the concerned face–indifferent intonation. This judgment was also higher than the counselors offered at both levels of intonation. The clients were apparently more influenced by the congruent presence of cues in this interaction.

A significant Group × Facial Expression × Verbal Message interaction revealed similar differences between counselors and clients, $F(1, 28) = 5.97$, $p < .05$, $\theta^2 = 1.18\%$. The general pattern of this interaction suggests that the counselors were more influenced by the nature of the verbal message, while the clients seemed to base their judgments more on the basis of the nonverbal cues in the message. The key point of difference is within the high-verbal message wherein the clients assigned a greater discrepancy between conditions of concerned and indifferent facial expression than did the counselors.

Two first-order interactions involving Trunk Lean × Facial Expression, $F(1, 28)$ = 18.78, $p < .001$, $\theta^2 = 1.11\%$, and Vocal Intonation × Facial Expression, $F(1,28)$ = 17.42, $p < .001$, $\theta^2 = .78\%$, reflect a frequent finding in nonverbal communication literature, that is, one which might be called an additive model in which congruent pairs of stimuli produce higher ratings than pairs of cues which are opposed. In both of these interactions, empathy was judged higher when each of the cues was paired in the high or positive direction, followed sequentially by successively lower judgments of empathy.

Respect

For the dependent variable of respect, five main effects and 22 interactions reached at least the .05 level of significance. The main effects and the more salient interactions are reviewed here.

With the exception of the group factor, all other main effects representing the nonverbal and verbal cues in the paradigm showed significant influence on the judgment of respect or positive regard. These significant effects included forward trunk lean, $F(1, 28) = 72.97$, $p < .001$, $\theta^2 = 3.21\%$, maintaining eye contact, $F(1, 28) =$ 107.25, $p < .001$, $\theta^2 = 6.95\%$, concerned vocal intonation, $F(1, 28) = 10.12$, $p < .01$, $\theta^2 = .32\%$, concerned facial expression, $F(1, 28) = 278.91$, $p < .001$, $\theta^2 = 39.62\%$, and a high level of verbal message, $F(1, 28) = 77.68$, $p < .001$, $\theta^2 = 9.62\%$. Clearly the most potent independent cue in the judgment of respect is facial expression, accounting for two fifths of the variance in the judgments and two thirds of the variability accounted for by the main effects. The rank order of the importance of the main effects is identical to that found for the dependent judgment of empathy. Considered independently, maintaining a high-verbal message, direct eye contact, concerned vocal intonation, concerned facial expression, and a forward trunk lean all add to the increased perception of respect or positive regard in two-person encounters.

The main effects and their impact are altered by the numerous interactions among them occurring in this study. Counselor and client groups were involved in two of the interactions, one third-order and a second-order interaction involving groups, facial expression, and verbal message, $F(1, 28) = 5.06$, $p < .05$, $\theta^2 = 1.18\%$. This interaction reveals that counselors' and clients' judgments are almost parallel in every respect except for the High Message × Indifferent Facial Expression interaction in which the clients tend to assign higher judgments of respect than do the counselors. Counselors apparently discount the impact of the verbal message under indifferent facial expression more than do the clients who are giving greater weight in the judgment to the verbal message.

Among the more noteworthy interactions (i.e., $\theta^2 > 1.00\%$), all of the verbal and nonverbal cues are represented; the pattern of the interactions is highly consistent with the additive model, that is, congruence between levels of the cues produces the highest judged levels of respect, while incongruence renders judgments that are perceived as communicating significantly less respect. The interactions of Trunk Lean × Facial Expression, $F(1, 28) = 17.93$, $p < .001$, $\theta^2 = 1.07\%$, Eye Contact × Facial

Expression, $F(1, 28) = 17.72$, $p < .001$, $\theta^2 = 1.50\%$, Vocal Intonation × Facial Expression, $F(1, 28) = 16.69$, $p < .001$, $\theta^2 = 1.25\%$, and Verbal Message × Facial Expression, $F(1, 28) = 9.19$, $p < .01$, $\theta^2 = 1.18\%$, all reflect the additive nature of these combinations of cues. It is notable that the facial expression is involved in each of these interactions, reflecting its power as a cue in the judgment of respect.

Genuineness

The analysis of variance for the dependent variable of genuineness yielded four significant main effects and nine significant interactions. Significant main effects were found for trunk lean, $F(1, 28) = 27.58$, $p < .001$, $\theta^2 = 2.47\%$, eye contact, $F(1, 28) = 90.43$, $p < .001$, $\theta^2 = 11.06\%$, vocal intonation, $F(1, 28) = 18.58$, $p < .001$, $\theta^2 = 1.25\%$, and facial expression, $F(1, 28) = 25.79$, $p < .001$, $\theta^2 = 9.16\%$. The main effect for verbal message was not significant and accounted for none of the judged level of genuineness of the message, $F(1, 28) = .09$, $\theta^2 = .00\%$.

Among the most important and significant interactions accounting for variability in the judgments of genuineness was the Facial Expression × Verbal Message interaction, $F(1, 28) = 16.34$, $p < .001$, $\theta^2 = 6.19\%$. The essence of this interaction lies in the difference between concerned and indifferent facial expressions at the level of high-verbal message. Under this condition the concerned facial expression clearly amplifies the judgment of genuineness and indifferent facial expressions suppress it. At the low-verbal message, the difference between concerned and indifferent facial expressions is less pronounced, while the level of the judgment for both of these conditions is below that of the optimum combination. Even under conditions of low-verbal message a concerned facial expression raises the judgment of genuineness, but not to the degree that is observed under conditions of high-verbal message.

Several statistically and practically significant interactions were found in the judgment of genuineness which involved the group differences between counselors and clients. The Group × Verbal Message interaction, $F(1, 28) = 19.82$, $p < .001$, $\theta^2 = 6.65\%$, is explained by the clients tending to be more discriminating about the level of genuineness communicated by the verbal message than the counselors. The judgment of the counselors was approximately equal for both high- and low-verbal message, while the clients assigned a greater degree of genuineness to the high- than to the low-verbal message. This is paralleled by a Group × Facial Expression × Verbal Message interaction, $F(1, 28) = 7.56$, $p < .05$, $\theta^2 = 1.50\%$, which reveals that the counselors and clients discriminate levels of judged empathy in accord with expectations when concerned and indifferent facial expressions occur simultaneously with high-verbal messages. With the low-verbal message, however, counselors rated the concerned and indifferent facial expression equally, while the clients discriminated in the expected direction for concerned and indifferent facial expressions. The clients apparently were more responsive to the various combinations of cues, especially in the low-message condition, than were the counselors.

A similar pattern is revealed between counselors and clients in the Group × Eye Contact × Vocal Intonation interaction, $F(1, 28) = 6.69$, $p < .05$, $\theta^2 = 1.29\%$. Finally, group differences in the judgment of genuineness were revealed in a third-order Group × Eye Contact × Vocal Intonation × Verbal Message interaction, which is not interpreted here.

Overall, the main effects and interaction effects in this study accounted for 68%, 84%, and 68% of the total variability in the judgments of empathy, respect, and genuineness, respectively. For the dependent variables of empathy and respect the main effects accounted for more variability as a group than did the interactions. However, in the ratings of genuineness, the interactions proved to account for greater variability than the main effects.[2]

Discussion

The results of the analyses presented here clearly substantiate that complex combinations of verbal and nonverbal cues play an important role in the determination of perceived levels of empathy, respect, and genuineness. The major contribution of this study reflects the following: (a) the overwhelming importance of nonverbal cues in the communication process, and especially the factorial complexity of combinations of verbal and nonverbal cues; (b) the extension of nonverbal communication research beyond empathy to include the important facilitative constructs of respect and genuineness; (c) the inclusion of the nonverbal cues of vocal intonation and facial expression which have not received attention in the counseling literature; and (d) the inclusion of both clients and counselors as judges of the facilitative conditions of empathy, respect, and genuineness.

The importance of nonverbal cues to the eventual judged level of empathy, respect, and genuineness cannot be overemphasized. With respect to each of these dependent variables, the results of this study clearly indicate that the nonverbal cues play a dominant role in the determination of message significance. Considering only the main effects, the ratios of nonverbal to verbal variance were 2:1 for empathy, 5:1 for respect, and 23:1 for genuineness. These figures compare favorably to similar ratios reported in the literature (Argyle et al., 1971; Haase & Tepper, 1972; Mehrabian, 1968). In the case of genuineness, the ratio reflects the overwhelming importance of the nonverbal cues.

Of even more importance, however, is that the cues manipulated in this study clearly operate as a *system* and depend heavily on the relative balance between the cues in terms of the message which is ultimately perceived. The sheer number and character of the interactions found in this study support the conceptualization of the communication process as a multichannel process. To continue to perform research which systematically manipulates only one cue within the context of what we now know to be a factorially complex transaction can only serve to cloud our understanding of the communication process in counseling.

The study described here has extended a more factorially complex perspective to the study of respect and genuineness in addition to empathy. With the exception of Graves and Robinson (1976) and Smith-Hanen (1977), few studies have focused on these two important dimensions of counseling relationship effectiveness. The results of the study regarding respect again indicate that the judgments or respect communicated in two-person encounters are dependent upon a delicate balance of the cues in the situation—verbal and nonverbal. All of the main effects studied

---

[2]Copies of the complete analysis of variance tables, means, and standard deviations are available on request from the first author.

entered into an interaction dictating the levels of judged respect. In general, all of these interactions were of the additive nature, that is, an interaction wherein positive combinations of cues resulted in the highest judged levels of respect, negative combinations of cues resulted in the lowest judgments, and the positive–negative combination of cues resulted in midlevel judgments. Such interactions have been found to be common (Graves & Robinson, 1976; Haase & Tepper, 1972; Kelly, 1972; Smith, 1975) and attest to the balancing quality of cues in multichannel communications.

With regard to the judgment of respect, it is notable that the facial expression cue played such a dominant role. Obviously a tremendous amount of the judgment of respect is made by employing the facial expression as a sort of benchmark in the decoding process. The additive model of the interactions for respect also played a key role in the results of judged empathy in this study.

The results of the judgment of genuineness are interesting from a number of perspectives. First, the complete absence of impact due to the verbal message main effect is revealing ($\theta^2 = .00\%$). All the nonverbal cues in the design accounted individually for some portion of the variability in the judgments of genuineness, ranging from 1.25% to 11.06%. That the verbal message as an individual entity accounted for none of this message variance suggests that it is the least powerful of the cues for communicating a condition of genuineness on the part of the counselor. To discount the role of the verbal message altogether is not possible, as this cue entered into several significant interactions with other cues in the paradigm. Nonetheless, the fact that judges were able to make some discrimination in their own minds about genuineness on the basis of the nonverbal cues and were not able to do so with the verbal message is a finding worthy of further more refined research. The Facial Expression × Verbal Message interaction is an apt illustration. In this case it appears that the verbal message serves as somewhat of an anchor point which cues from the second channel altered the decoded message in the expected direction. We chose to call the verbal message the anchor point, because even under conditions of low-verbal message the concerned facial expression is capable of raising the judged level of genuineness above the double negative combination. Furthermore, the Group × Verbal Message × Facial Expression interaction reveals that clients tended to be more responsive to the entire range of cues presented in making their judgments of genuineness than were the counselors. This phenomenon could possibly be due to the level of sophistication of the counselors, both about the constructs under examination and about the role of nonverbal cues in the communication process.

Although no significant main effects were detected in this study between counselors and clients, the presence of several significant interactions involving the group factor was detected—indicating that counselors and clients did indeed differ in response tendency and that these differences are dependent upon the presence or absence of additional conditions, namely, the verbal and nonverbal cues examined in this study. The presence of significant interactions clearly vitiates the meaningfulness of the preceding main effects (whether significant or not). That counselors and clients did differ significantly under certain other conditions in their judgments of empathy, respect, and genuineness raises an important issue. The issue centers around the fact that in any style of counseling which demands these core conditions for effectiveness, the conditions must be perceived by the client to be maximally effective. Previous research has suggested that clients and counselors often do not perceive these conditions in the same way (Caracena & Vicory, 1969; Hansen, Moore, & Carkhuff, 1968). The data presented in this study lead to the same conclusion, but help to clarify some of the other cues in the multichannel communication process which may begin to explain the basis of these differences between counselor and client perception of facilitative conditions.

In a similar vein, Sweeney and Cottle (1976) reported no differences between a group of counselors and noncounselors in terms of their nonverbal acuity, but their noncounselor group employed a group of graduate students in a noncounseling discipline. The results of the study reported here employed clients not confederates.

The differences which were found between counselors and clients in this study were across all three of the dependent variables. In general the interactions involving groups in this study seem to reflect a greater range of usage of all the cues present by the clients than by the counselors. The range of judgments was greater for the clients in the majority of the interactions. These findings are similar to those presented by Lee et al. (1976), who also found client–counselor differences, but with respect to the judgment of counselor effectiveness. It is difficult to attach substantive meaning to the client–counselor differences found in this study beyond recognizing that differences in perception occur with some degree of regularity and that the principal factor to which this difference is attached is the role differentiation between the groups. It is impossible to speak of which set of perceptions is more accurate, since standards of accuracy against some external, and operationally well defined, criterion do not exist. Smith (1975) is one of the few authors who has attempted to grapple with this problem of definition of standards of judgment in the context of multichannel research in the counseling process. Nonetheless, the client–counselor differences found in this study cannot be ignored in future research or the development of training models in nonverbal communication. These differences may ultimately mean the difference between perceived and ignored facilitative conditions.

Finally, the present study has studied two additional nonverbal cues which have not appeared frequently in the counseling literature and which were operationalized in a fashion which has directly interpretable consequences for counseling encounter (Strahan & Zytowski, 1976). The cues of vocal intonation and facial expression proved significant contributors to the results of this study. The facial expression stimulus was especially powerful as a determinant of message variance in the judgment of facilitative conditions. The findings that the independent contribution of the facial expression main effect accounted for 26% and 40% of the message variance in the judgment of empathy and respect indicates the almost unbelievable power of the facial expression in the communication process (see also Hackney, 1974). The role of facial expression should prove a fruitful area of further research in the counseling process and the communication of emotion. New models for the study of facial expression which are being developed (Ekman & Friesen, 1976) have great implications for their application in the study of how individuals interact under the rather specialized social rules of the counseling interview. Other nonverbal cues are similarly important in the study of these specialized communication settings. Aside from the specific results presented here and elsewhere in the counseling literature in the past 5 years, the incontrovertible importance of studying the communication process in a multichannel, factorially complex fashion is paramount. At the present time, there are limits to this activity. However, as our hypotheses become more sophisticated and our research tools expand to meet this sophistication, the pace of our understanding should quicken commensurately.

References

Argyle, M., Alkema, G., & Gilmour, R. The communication of friendly and hostile attitudes by verbal and non-verbal signals. *European Journal of Social Psychology,* 1971, *1,* 385–402.

Argyle, M., & Dean, J. Eye contact, distance and affiliation. *Sociometry,* 1965, *28,* 289–304.

Bergin, A. E., & Garfield, S. L. *Handbook of psychotherapy and behavior change.* New York: Wiley, 1971.

Birdwhistell, R. *Kinetics in context.* Philadelphia: University of Pennsylvania Press, 1970.

Broekman, N. C., & Moller, A. T. Preferred seating position and distance in various situations. *Journal of Counseling Psychology,* 1973, *20,* 504–508.

Caracena, P. F., & Vicory, J. R. Correlates of phenomenological and judged empathy. *Journal of Counseling Psychology,* 1969, *16,* 510–515.

Carkhuff, R. R. *Helping and human relations* (Vol. 2). New York; Holt, Rinehart & Winston, 1969.

Carkhuff, R. R. *The development of human resources.* New York; Holt, Rinehart & Winston, 1971.

Carkhuff, R. R., & Berenson, B. G. *Beyond counseling and therapy.* New York: Holt, Rinehart & Winston, 1967.

Chaikin, A. L., Derlega, V. J., & Miller, S. J. Effects of room environment on self-disclosure in a counseling analogue. *Journal of Counseling Psychology,* 1976, *23,* 479–481.

Darwin, C. *The expression of emotion in man and animals.* London, England: Murray, 1872.

Dinges, N., & Oetting, E. R. Interaction distance anxiety in the counseling dyad. *Journal of Counseling Psychology,* 1972, *19,* 146–149.

Edwards, A. L. *Techniques of attitude scale construction.* New York: Appleton-Century-Crofts, 1957.

Ekman, P. *Darwin and facial expression.* New York: Academic Press, 1973.

Ekman, P., & Friesen, W. V. Nonverbal behavior in psychotherapy research. In J. M. Schlien (Ed.), *Research in psychotherapy* (Vol. 3). Washington, DC: American Psychological Association, 1968.

Ekman, P., & Friesen, W. V. Measuring facial movement. *Environmental Psychology and Nonverbal Behavior,* 1976, *1,* 56–75.

Fretz, B. R. Postural movements in a counseling dyad. *Journal of Counseling Psychology,* 1966, *13,* 335–343.

Gladstein, G. A. Nonverbal communication and counseling/psychotherapy. *Counseling Psychologist,* 1974, *4,* 35–57.

Graves, J. R., & Robinson, J. D. Proxemic behavior as a function of inconsistent verbal and nonverbal messages. *Journal of Counseling Psychology,* 1976, *23,* 333–338.

Haase, R. F. The relationship of sex and instructional set to the regulation of interpersonal distance in a counseling analogue. *Journal of Counseling Psychology,* 1970, *17,* 233–236.

Haase, R. F., & DiMattia, D. J. Proxemic behavior: Counselor administrator and client preferences for seating arrangement in dyadic interaction. *Journal of Counseling Psychology,* 1970, *17,* 319–325.

Haase, R. F., & DiMattia, D. J. Spatial environments and verbal conditioning in a quasi-counseling interview. *Journal of Counseling Psychology,* 1976, *23,* 414–421.

Haase, R. F., & Tepper, D. T. Nonverbal components of empathic communication. *Journal of Counseling Psychology,* 1972, *19,* 417–426.

Hackney, H. Facial gestures and subject expression of feelings. *Journal of Counseling Psychology,* 1974, *21,* 173–178.

Hansen, J. E., Moore, C. D., & Carkhuff, R. R. The differential relationship of objective and client percpetions of counseling. *Journal of Clinical Psychology,* 1968, *24,* 244–246.

Kelly, F. D. Communicational significance of therapist proxemic cues. *Journal of Consulting and Clinical Psychology,* 1972, *39,* 345.

LaCrosse, M. B. Nonverbal behavior and perceived counselor attractiveness. *Journal of Counseling Psychology,* 1975, *22,* 563–566.

Lee, D. Y., Zingle, H., Patterson, J., Ivey, A. E., & Haase, R. F. Development and validation of the Microcounseling Skill Discrimination Scale. *Journal of Counseling Psychology,* 1976, *23,* 468–472.

Mehrabian, A. E. Communication without words. *Psychology Today,* 1968, *2,* 52–56.

Rogers, C. R. *Client-centered therapy.* Cambridge, Mass.: Riverside Press, 1951.

Rogers, C. R. The necessary and sufficient conditions of therapeutic personality change. *Journal of Consulting Psychology,* 1957, *22,* 95–103.

Shapiro, J. Relationships between visual and auditory cues of therapeutic effectiveness. *Journal of Clinical Psychology,* 1968, *24,* 236–239.

Smith, C. W. *Counselor perception of anger: Verbal and nonverbal cues.* Unpublished doctoral dissertation, University of Pennsylvania, 1975.

Smith-Hanen, S. S. Effects of nonverbal behaviors on judged levels of counselor warmth and empathy. *Journal of Counseling Psychology,* 1977, *24,* 87–91.

Stone, G. L., & Morden, C. J. Effect of distance on verbal productivity. *Journal of Counseling Psychology,* 1976, *23,* 486–488.

Strahan, C., & Zytowski, D. G. Impact of visual, vocal and lexical cues on judgments of counselor qualities. *Journal of Counseling Psychology,* 1976, *23,* 387–393.

Sweeney, M. A., & Cottle, W. C. Nonverbal acuity: A comparison of counselors and non-counselors. *Journal of Counseling Psychology,* 1976, *23,* 394–397.

Truax, C. B., & Carkhuff, R. R. *Toward effective counseling and psychotherapy.* Chicago: Aldine, 1967.

Vaughn, G. M., & Corballis, M. C. Beyond tests of significance: Estimating strength of effects in selected ANOVA designs. *Psychological Bulletin,* 1969, *72,* 204–213.

Winer, B. J. *Statistical principles in experimental design.* New York: McGraw-Hill, 1972.

Part III

Exploration Stage

INTRODUCTION

The exploration stage sets the foundation for the helping process. By encouraging clients to talk about their problems, therapists are able to help clients hear their thoughts and feelings in a new way. Hearing clients allows therapists the opportunity to get to know their clients and understand their concerns. This stage is based on a client-centered tradition, which stresses that clients can heal themselves if they are provided with empathy, warmth, and genuineness. When a therapist believes in them, clients come to believe in themselves and figure out what they want and need.

Although the exploration stage is posited by Hill and O'Brien (1999) to be the foundation of helping, only one study was found that could be included in this section. In 1977, Hill and Gormally (see chapter 13) experimentally manipulated skills (restatement, open question about feelings, and reflection of feelings) and nonverbal behavior (presence or absence of nodding and smiling) in face-to-face brief interviews. Clients discussed their feelings more when therapists asked open questions about feelings than when they gave restatements or reflections of feelings, but no differences were found for nonverbal behaviors. This study needs to be replicated in naturally occurring therapy with more refined measures of client behaviors and reactions. Given the large role that exploration skills are accorded in the Hill and O'Brien (1999) model, more studies are needed to determine their differential effects, when to use each one, and whether indeed these skills are necessary for the potentiation of the insight and action skills.

Reference

Hill, C. E., & O'Brien, K. M. (1999). *Helping skills: Facilitating exploration, insight, and action.* Washington, DC: American Psychological Association.

Chapter 13
EFFECTS OF REFLECTION, RESTATEMENT, PROBE, AND NONVERBAL BEHAVIORS ON CLIENT AFFECT

Clara E. Hill and James Gormally

The emphasis in counselor education in recent years has been to train counselors in specific skills that appear to facilitate client exploration of feelings. Several analogue studies have attempted to determine those counselor behaviors that produce greater discussion of feelings. Minimal verbal stimuli, such as "mm hmm," "go on," and "I see," when applied contingently immediately after the client's expression of feeling, have been found to be effective reinforcers of affect (Hoffnung, 1969; Kennedy & Zimmer, 1968; Rogers, 1960; Salzinger & Pizoni, 1960). Although these minimal verbal stimuli do occur during real counseling sessions, they are not representative of all the responses a counselor makes.

Other studies have found conflicting results for the effects of more complex, noncontingent counselor statements, the most common of which are reflections, restatements, and probes. Some studies that measured reflection of feelings found increases in affect (Hoffnung, 1969; Merbaum, 1963; Merbaum & Southwell, 1965), whereas others found no increases (Barnabei, Cormier, & Nye, 1974; Waskow, 1962). Similarly for restatements (paraphrase of content), some studies reported increases in affect (Hoffnung, 1969; Kennedy & Zimmer, 1968), whereas others did not (Auerswald, 1974; Waskow, 1962). The only study that measured probes (defined broadly as any questions) found no superiority of probes to reflections, confrontations, or unspecified responding (Barnabei et al., 1974).

Comparison of the results of these studies is difficult because of the lack of consistent operational definitions, and the variable number of counselor statements made in the session. Most of these studies are flawed by the use of only one counselor with unspecified training, and the lack of manipulation checks to determine if the counselor actually behaved in the appropriate experimental manner. In order to make comparisons between types of responses, various portions of counselor responses were manipulated in the present study. All three verbal modes focused on the content of the subject's discussion but varied according to whether the counselor reflected the subject's feelings (reflection), asked what the subject was feeling (probe), or omitted any mention of feeling (restatement).

Another possible source of confounding in the past studies was the counselor's nonverbal behavior. For example, in certain verbal conditions, counselors may have inadvertently relied on nonverbal behavior to complement verbal behaviors. Research has indicated that nonverbal variables such as head nods, smiles, and eye contact do play a significant role in the counseling interaction (Fretz, 1966; Haase & Tepper,

Reprinted from *Journal of Counseling Psychology, 24,* 92–97 (1977). Copyright © 1977 by the American Psychological Association. Used with permission of the first author.

This research was supported by a General Research Board grant from the University of Maryland. The authors are indebted to Jill Colman, Dona Lenkin, and Carol Rice for their help with this study.

1972; LaCrosse, 1975). In the present study, nonverbal behavior was manipulated such that subjects received either head nods and smiles or no head nods and smiles.

Therefore, the present study attempted to isolate various verbal and nonverbal counselor behaviors and to determine if these factors influence a client's expression of feelings. Specifically, each client received an equal number of reflections, probes, or restatements delivered on a predetermined variable-interval schedule. The design of the study followed a simple ABAB format of baseline (minimal verbal stimuli and no-nonverbal behavior), counseling intervention (manipulation of verbal and nonverbal stimuli), return to baseline, and return to counseling intervention. The use of the ABAB design permits intrasubject replication to ensure reliability, a crucial issue for an analogue interview study. This design also more clearly establishes whether the effects were the result of counselor behaviors rather than warm-up, that is, passage of time in the interview.

Method

Subjects

Twenty-four male and 24 female subjects, who were 18–25 years old and had no previous counseling, were selected from a large pool ($N = 100$) of volunteers from undergraduate psychology classes. Students were asked to volunteer only if they were interested in and felt they could profit from talking with a counselor, a procedure used to obtain subjects at least minimally motivated for counseling. All subjects received research credit for their participation. In addition to the 48 subjects, 3 subjects could not complete the interview because of stress they experienced at the outset of the interview and 2 additional subjects could not be used in the analysis because of inaudible audiotapes.

Two counseling psychologists, one female and one male, served as counselors. Both had 1 year of postdoctoral experience, were in the late 20s, were of average physique and appearance, and held similar counseling orientations. Counselor training lasted 7 hours and included detailed description of the operational definitions of the verbal and nonverbal techniques, drills in responding to hypothetical client statements, and practice trials on each of the six possible interview conditions with pilot subjects.

Experimental Facilities and Apparatus

An interview room and an adjoining monitor room were used. A vertical 2 × 4 inch (5 × 10 cm) panel with four 71/2-W light bulbs (white, red, green, and amber) was located on the wall of the interview room directly behind the subject. The control panel for the lights and a Sony reel-to-reel audiotape recorder were located in the monitor room. A one-way observation window located behind the subject permitted a research assistant to watch the interview, operate the tape recorder, and control the light switches.

Procedure

The research assistant randomly assigned subjects to one of the two nonverbal conditions and to one of the five predetermined variable-interval schedules for counselor statements. Each of the two counselors interviewed two females and two males in each of the six combinations of verbal and nonverbal conditions. Counselors were not aware of the experimental condition to be used until the onset of the counseling period.

Warm-Up

The counselors began each session with the following instructions (adapted from Rogers, 1960): (a) The subject would discuss feelings about a personally relevant problem (brief examples of feelings were given), (b) the subject would be doing most of the talking for the half-hour interview, and (c) the talking would probably be helpful to the subject. Clients were also assured that the tape of the interview would be treated as confidential material. When the client seemed relaxed, the counselor assumed a standard position (both feet flat on the floor, arms on the chair arms, with upright posture, directly facing the subject) and said, "You may begin anywhere you like." This was a cue for the research assistant to begin timing.

Baseline (6 Minutes)

The counselor responded to the subject with minimal verbal stimuli whenever a response was necessary. Minimal verbal stimuli were defined as one- or two-word nonobtrusive vocalizations such as "mm hmm," "I see," or "go ahead." No questions were asked even if silences occurred. Although the counselor did maintain relatively steady eye contact, he or she did not nod, smile, or gesture for any of the clients in the six groups.

Counseling (9 Minutes)

The counselor was cued via a white light that the counseling period had begun. The white light stayed on continuously for the no-nonverbal condition and blinked for the nonverbal condition. For each of the verbal responses, the counselor was cued via a light (red = reflection; green = restatement; amber = probe) on a variable-interval schedule of one response per minute, with a 30-sec mean interval. This meant that the counselor gave nine responses per counseling period. The counselor also used minimal verbal stimuli if necessary.

Return to Baseline (6 Minutes)

When the white light was turned off, the counselor returned to baseline conditions.

Return to Counseling (9 Minutes)

This condition was the same as the first counseling period. When the research assistant signaled the end of the half-hour interview by flashing all lights, the counselor terminated as soon as possible.

Following the interview, the research assistant questioned the subjects about their perceptions of the purpose of the study and informed them of the intended purpose of the study.

Treatment Conditions

Reflection

The verbal condition was adapted from Carkhuff (1972) and consisted of a statement with a subject, verb, feeling word, and subordinate clause beginning with "because." The feeling word reflected the subject's overt feelings, and the subordinate clause restated the content, for example, "You feel angry because your father doesn't support you anymore."

Probe

This verbal condition was adapted from Hackney and Nye (1973) and consisted of a statement that began with "How" or "What" and contained a subject, verb, and a subordinate clause that began with "about." The first part of the sentence asked an open-ended question that required more than a one-word answer, and the subordinate clause restated the content, for example, "How do you feel about your father not supporting you anymore?"

Restatement

This verbal condition consisted of a restatement of the content, in a manner equivalent to the subordinate clause described above. No mention was made of any feelings, even if the subject specifically mentioned feelings, for example, "Your father doesn't support you anymore."

Nonverbal Condition

The counselors used head nods and smiles only during the two counseling periods for those subjects in the nonverbal condition. In the no-nonverbal condition, counselors did not nod or smile during any period. A head nod was defined as any time the chin went downward toward the chest. A smile was any turning up of the lips. The counselors' nods and smiles were used at appropriate times during the subject's discussion, usually at the end of a response unit, and they were not contingent on client expression of feelings. No gestures were used at any time, and the counselors maintained a relatively stable body position.

Dependent Measures

The 48 interviews were audiotaped and converted to verbatim typescripts. Two undergraduate assistants categorized all of the client verbalizations into response units, using techniques described by Auld and White (1956). This system approximates that each response unit lasts 5 sec and counts silences of that length as response units. A silence of 5 sec was defined as a pause. The interrater agreement for unitizing response units was 96.8%. Disagreements were discussed until both raters agreed on the classification. A 3 × 2 (Verbal × Nonverbal Conditions) analysis of variance for number of response units for the entire interview revealed no significant differences across groups.

The response units were then analyzed by the same two assistants for affective self-referents, as described by Salzinger and Pizoni (1960). To be classified as an affective self-referent, a response had to begin with an "I" or "We," followed by a feeling word. The interrater reliability was 91.4%. Disagreements were discussed until a satisfactory classification could be made.

To control for individual differences in response rates, a proportion of affective self-referents to total response units was used. A measure of the subject's loquacity was derived by computing the proportion of pauses to total response units. Because of statistical difficulties with proportion scores, arc sine transformations were performed on the data before the analysis.

Results

Manipulation Checks

To check the counselor's performance of the appropriate verbal conditions, each counselor's statement was classified by a naive, trained psychology graduate student as either a reflection, restatement, or probe. Three sessions contained only 16, as opposed to the prescribed 18, counselor statements. But all sessions met the predetermined criteria of 14 appropriate counselor statements out of the possible 18 statements, and thus no session had to be eliminated from the analysis.

On the basis of the postexperimental inquiry, the research assistant rated each subject on a Likert-type 1–5 scale of awareness of the purpose and procedures in the study. A 3 × 2 (Verbal × Nonverbal Conditions) analysis of variance indicated no significant differences between groups. Some subjects in each group noted changes in counselor's behaviors, but none could specify what the counselor was manipulating.

To determine if counselor characteristics or sex of subject contributed to the results, 2 × 2 (2 Counselors × Sex of Subject) analyses of variance were computed on each of the two dependent variables. Because no significant effects were found, it appears that the two counselors provided similar conditions and that sex of subject did not influence the results.

Effects of Counselor Statements

Means and standard deviations for the proportion of affective self-referents to total response units are presented in Table 1.

A 3 × 2 × 4 (Verbal × Nonverbal × Time Periods) repeated-measures analysis of variance was computed on the arc sine transformations of the proportion of affective self-referent to response units. The Verbal Condition × Time Periods inter-

Table 1—*Means and Standard Deviations for the Proportion of Affective Self-Referents to Response Units*

Condition	Baseline 1		Counseling 1		Baseline 2		Counseling 2	
	M	*SD*	*M*	*SD*	*M*	*SD*	*M*	*SD*
Reflection	.07	.04	.07	.05	.07	.04	.08	.04
Nonverbal	.05	.04	.05	.03	.07	.03	.06	.02
No-nonverbal	.09	.04	.10	.05	.08	.04	.10	.04
Restatement	.07	.05	.06	.04	.08	.05	.07	.04
Nonverbal	.05	.04	.05	.02	.06	.04	.06	.03
No-nonverbal	.10	.06	.08	.04	.10	.04	.08	.05
Probe	.08	.07	.10	.05	.06	.05	.10	.05
Nonverbal	.08	.08	.12	.06	.05	.03	.10	.06
No-nonverbal	.07	.06	.09	.05	.07	.07	.10	.05

Note. $ns = 16$ for reflection, restatement, and probe conditions; half ($n = 8$) of the subjects in each verbal condition received the nonverbal treatment and half ($n = 8$) received the no-nonverbal treatment.

action was significant, $F(6, 126) = 2.35$, $p < .05$. A post hoc trend analysis indicated a significant cubic trend, $F(2, 126) = 6.95$, $p < .001$. An inspection of the means, graphically presented in Figure 1, indicated that the cubic trend was a result of increases in affective self-referents that occurred in the probe condition, whereas reflection and restatement showed no increases.

There was also a significant main effect for the nonverbal condition, $F(1, 42) = 5.65$, $p < .05$, such that the group which received the no-nonverbal condition produced more affective self-referents during all time periods. Because subjects received

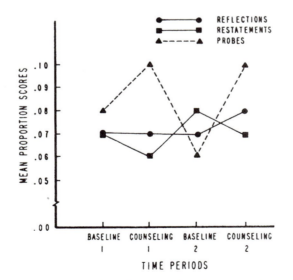

Figure 1. Mean proportion scores for affective self-referents produced by subjects during the four time periods.

equivalent conditions in both baseline periods, random assignment apparently failed to create equivalent groups. Therefore, further analyses were necessary using the baseline production of affective self-referents as the covariate for testing and conditioning effects. The 3 × 2 (Verbal × Nonverbal Conditions) analysis of covariance on the first counseling period using the first baseline as a covariate revealed a significant main effect for the verbal condition, $F(2, 42) = 3.67$, $p < .05$. A similar analysis of covariance on the second counseling period using the second baseline as a covariate revealed a marginally significant main effect for verbal conditions, $F(2, 42) = 2.86$, $.05 < p < .10$. An inspection of the means confirms the results from the previous analysis, such that the probes elicited more affective self-referents than reflections, which elicited more than restatements.

In an experiment such as this, the counselor's statements may merely serve to increase client verbal productivity rather than increasing discussion of feelings. To test for this, a 3 × 2 × 4 (Verbal × Nonverbal × Time Periods) repeated-measures analysis of variance was computed on the proportion of pauses to response units. Means and standard deviations of the pause data are presented in Table 2. A significant main effect resulted for time periods, $F(3, 126) = 8.59$, $p < .001$. Inspection of the means indicated that fewer pauses occurred during the counseling periods than during baselines. There was also a significant Verbal × Nonverbal Conditions interaction, $F(2, 42) = 3.48$, $p < .05$, again suggesting that random assignment did not occur. Therefore, a 3 × 2 (Verbal × Nonverbal Conditions) analysis of covariance was conducted, with the proportion of pauses to response units during the baseline as the covariate. Analyses of both counseling periods using the respective baselines as covariates revealed no significant effects. All subjects talked more during the counseling periods than during baselines, regardless of the counselor's behavior.

Discussion

The three counselor responses were designed to permit comparison between them. That is, each type of response included content but varied with respect to how

Table 2—*Means and Standard Deviations for the Proportion of Pauses to Response Units*

Condition	Baseline 1		Counseling 1		Baseline 2		Counseling 2	
	M	*SD*	*M*	*SD*	*M*	*SD*	*M*	*SD*
Reflection	.05	.05	.03	.04	.07	.09	.07	.10
Nonverbal	.05	.05	.03	.04	.12	.12	.10	.13
No-nonverbal	.05	.06	.03	.04	.03	.02	.05	.05
Restatement	.09	.14	.07	.10	.16	.20	.08	.12
Nonverbal	.16	.16	.11	.13	.26	.25	.13	.16
No-nonverbal	.01	.03	.03	.02	.07	.06	.02	.05
Probe	.04	.06	.03	.05	.07	.10	.04	.07
Nonverbal	.04	.06	.02	.03	.04	.04	.01	.02
No-nonverbal	.03	.06	.04	.06	.10	.13	.07	.09

Note. ns = 16 for reflection, restatement, and probe conditions; half ($n = 8$) of the subjects in each verbal condition received the nonverbal treatment and half ($n = 8$) received the no-nonverbal treatment.

feelings were discussed by the counselor. The probe condition resulted in more discussion of feelings than did either reflections or restatements. From these results, it appeared that the crucial component for eliciting client feelings was the direct questioning of the client concerning feelings. Furthermore, the increase in the probe condition seemed to be a reliable phenomenon because the increase occurred after both baselines, thus eliminating the possible effects of warm-up on discussion of feelings.

Perhaps probes elicited more discussion of feelings simply because questions contain demand characteristics for answering. However, the percentage of feelings discussed was relatively low, even for the probe condition. Apparently, subjects did not typically answer the questions by stating their feelings. An analysis of the typescripts indicated that many of the clients responded to the probes by giving further explanations of content rather than discussing feelings. With reflections or restatements, on the other hand, the clients usually did not even acknowledge the counselor's statement.

Even though probes did result in a greater percentage of affect discussion, it seems inaccurate to say that this happened because of the reinforcing properties of probes. The counselor's statements were not made contingent on the client production of affect, but rather were emitted on a predetermined variable-interval schedule, such that the particular response was given regardless of whether the client had discussed feelings or whether such a response might be considered clinically appropriate. Perhaps the probe provided a discriminative stimulus for the subject in structuring what was an appropriate response during the session. None of these subjects had had previous counseling, so they were probably naive as to what occurs in a counseling session. Perhaps the role of a counselor was to teach the client how to be a client. If so, the probe may be the most effective tool for teaching appropriate behavior, particularly in an initial session.

The procedures in the present study for the warm-up and baseline periods were modeled after Auerswald (1974). Interestingly, the baseline production of affective self-referents is higher in her study (.16 and .21 for her two groups) than in the present research (an average of .07 for the entire sample), even though subjects were selected similarly. The only procedural differences for the baselines between the two studies were the systematic attempts of counselors in the present study to control nonverbal behaviors by not nodding and smiling during the baseline, which may have depressed the production of affective self-referents. Because the later introduction of nodding and smiling did not significantly increase the production of affective self-referents, it may be critical to establish these behaviors in the initial period of the interview. Further research is needed to specify the possible effects of timing on nonverbal behaviors.

The major advantage of this type of analogue research is the control over the independent variable, such that the specific effects of various counselor behaviors can be determined. However, the corresponding limitations are the possible lack of similarity to real counseling clients as well as the imposed artificiality and possible inappropriateness of the counselor statement in response to the client's immediate message. Because of the complexity of determining the effect of the counselor's statements on the client, both analogue and naturalistic research can be valuable in seeking such answers and in cross-validating results. Thus, this question needs to be addressed in other settings and with other methodologies before general conclusions can be drawn.

References

Auerswald, M. Differential reinforcing power of restatement and interpretation on client production of affect. *Journal of Counseling Psychology,* 1974, *21,* 9–14.

Auld, F., & White, A. M. Rule for dividing interviews into sentences. *Journal of Psychology,* 1956, *42,* 273–281.

Barnabei, F., Cormier, W. H., & Nye, L. S. Determining the effects of three counselor verbal responses on client verbal behavior. *Journal of Counseling Psychology,* 1974, *21,* 355–359.

Carkhuff, R. R. *The art of helping.* Amherst, Mass.: Human Resource Development Press, 1972.

Fretz, B. R. Personality correlates of postural movements. *Journal of Counseling Psychology,* 1966, *13,* 344–347.

Haase, R. F., & Tepper, D. T. Nonverbal components of empathic communication. *Journal of Counseling Psychology,* 1972, *19,* 417–424.

Hackney, H., & Nye, L. S. *Counseling strategies and objectives.* Englewood Cliffs, N.J.: Prentice-Hall, 1973.

Hoffnung, R. J. Conditioning and transfer of affective self-references in a role-played counseling interview. *Journal of Consulting and Clinical Psychology,* 1969, *33,* 527–531.

Kennedy, J. J., & Zimmer, J. M. Reinforcing value of five stimulus conditions in a quasi-counseling situation. *Journal of Counseling Psychology,* 1968, *15,* 357–362.

LaCrosse, M. B. Nonverbal behavior and perceived counselor attractiveness and persuasiveness. *Journal of Counseling Psychology,* 1975, *22,* 563–566.

Merbaum, M. The conditioning of affective self-references by three classes of generalized reinforcers. *Journal of Personality,* 1963, *31,* 179–191.

Merbaum, M., & Southwell, E. A. Conditioning of affective self-references as a function of the discriminative characteristics of experimenter intervention. *Journal of Abnormal and Social Psychology,* 1965, *70,* 180–187.

Rogers, J. M. Operant conditioning in a quasi-therapy setting. *Journal of Abnormal and Social Psychology,* 1960, *60,* 247–252.

Salzinger, K., & Pizoni, S. Reinforcement of verbal affect responses of normal subjects during the interview. *Journal of Abnormal and Social Psychology,* 1960, *6,* 127–130.

Waskow, I. E. Reinforcement in a therapy-like situation through selective responding to feelings or content. *Journal of Consulting Psychology,* 1962, *26,* 11–19.

Part IV

Insight Stage—Challenge

INTRODUCTION

Although exploration is sometimes enough for clients to heal themselves, many clients need additional help from therapists in terms of insight and action. Insight is particularly important because we seem to be meaning-making creatures who want to understand why we act as we do. Because of defenses, it is often difficult for clients to come to insight on their own, so therapists need to help clients by challenging, interpreting, self-disclosing, and discussing the immediate relationship. The research on the insight stage is discussed in the next three parts, focusing first on challenge.

In 1990, Olson and Claiborn (see chapter 15) studied the effects of *confrontations,* which they defined as a discrepancy between the client's statement in the interview and their behavior outside the interview (these are called *challenges* in Hill and O'Brien, 1999). In their experimental study, they found that therapist confrontation led to greater client arousal (as shown by galvanic skin response) than did reflection of feelings. Furthermore, clients had lower arousal and greater acceptance of an "interpretation" (which were more like information and direct guidance according to Hill and O'Brien) following a confrontation than a reflection of feeling. Replication of this study in naturally occurring therapy is needed.

In 1985, Patterson and Forgatch (see chapter 16) did two studies relevant to the effects of therapist challenges. The first study involved a sequential analysis of naturally occurring therapy. In this study, Patterson and Forgatch found that clients (mothers of children with management problems) were more noncompliant when therapists taught or confronted than when therapists facilitated or supported. The second study involved an experimental manipulation in which therapists increased "teaching" and "confronting" behaviors during some 12-minute blocks and refrained from using these teaching or confronting behaviors in alternating 12-minute blocks. Once again, client noncompliance was highest when therapists did more teaching and confronting.

In a 1992 comparison of a directive–confrontive style and a client-centered style for clients who were problem drinkers, Miller, Benefield, and Tonigan (see chapter 14) found that the directive–confrontational style yielded significantly more resistance than the client-centered approach. Furthermore, the more therapists confronted during the two-session intervention, the more the clients drank at a 1-year follow-up.

Future research needs to examine the effects of challenges delivered by different types of therapists to different types of clients. Some therapists seem more comfortable with challenging than do others, and some clients seem to respond better to being challenged than do others. Furthermore, it seems likely that the manner in which challenges are delivered (supportively versus hostilely) is particularly important given that therapists are ultimately disagreeing with clients whenever they challenge. Another interesting area to investigate is the relationship among therapist countertransference (i.e., therapist reactions to clients based on their own personal issues), challenges, and effectiveness. Therapists might challenge either too much or too little when their countertransference issues are stimulated, and both might be harmful.

Reference

Hill, C. E., & O'Brien, K. M. (1999). *Helping skills: Facilitating exploration, insight, and action.* Washington, DC: American Psychological Association.

Chapter 14

ENHANCING MOTIVATION FOR CHANGE IN PROBLEM DRINKING:
A Controlled Comparison of Two Therapist Styles

William R. Miller, R. Gayle Benefield, and J. Scott Tonigan

A commonly acknowledged problem within health psychology in general, and in the area of addictive behaviors in particular, is lack of motivation for change. Lack of compliance with advice, failure to seek or persist in treatment, and unsuccessful outcomes are all commonly attributed to poor patient motivation. Such inadequate motivation is in turn often ascribed to client traits, defense mechanisms, or intentionality that are relatively resistant to change.

There is reason to believe, however, that motivation for change in problem drinking can be affected by relatively brief interventions. Two dozen randomized trials have indicated that problem drinkers receiving brief motivational interventions showed outcomes significantly better than those of untreated controls or comparable to those from more extensive treatment (Bien, Miller, & Tonigan, 1993; Institute of Medicine, 1989).

What strategies are optimal for overcoming resistance and motivating change in problem drinkers? For several decades, U.S. alcoholism treatment emphasized a hard-hitting, directive, exhortational style intended to overwhelm robust defense mechanisms (DiCicco, Unterberger, & Mack, 1978; Moore & Murphy, 1961). More recently, the emphasis has shifted:

> Aggressive, confrontational counseling was [once] regarded as the only way to get an alcoholic to listen. A good counselor needed a loud voice and an arsenal of four-letter words. . . . It's true that we once used confrontation. But we found a better way, and we went with it. (Hazelden Foundation, 1985, p. 2)

The core of this "better way" is described as a more reasoned, respectful, and individualized approach.

This transition in therapeutic style is consonant with what the outcome literature reveals about therapist effects. Groups of substance abusers assigned at random to different therapists show dramatically different outcomes (Luborsky, McLellan, Woody, O'Brien, & Auerbach, 1985; Miller, Taylor, & West, 1980). In every study in which therapist characteristics have been systematically evaluated and effects were found, more favorable outcomes have been associated with a therapeutic style approximating what Rogers termed *accurate empathy* (Rogers, 1959; Truax & Carkhuff, 1967). Ends and Page (1957) found that a client-centered group approach to alcoholism treatment yielded the highest rate of improvement when compared with

Reprinted from *Journal of Consulting and Clinical Psychology, 61*, 455–461 (1993). Copyright © 1993 by the American Psychological Association. Used with permission of the first author.

This study was supported in part by a grant from the Research Allocation Committee of the University of New Mexico. Data analyses were supported in part by Grants T32-AA07460 and K05-AA00133 from the National Institute on Alcohol Abuse and Alcoholism.

three other styles. Valle (1981) reported that relapses among alcoholics could be predicted for up to 2 years from the counselors' levels of interpersonal skills, including empathy. Miller et al. (1980) similarly obtained a correlation of .82 between therapist empathy and 6-month outcomes among problem drinkers. Even 1 year (r = .71) and 2 years (r = .51) after treatment, therapist empathy remained a potent predictor of outcomes (Miller & Baca, 1983). Brief interventions with positive outcomes have also commonly emphasized an empathic counseling style as a key component (e.g., Chafetz, 1961; Edwards et al., 1977). Even hostile versus supportive vocal tone has been found to be predictive of therapist effectiveness with alcoholics (Milmoe, Rosenthal, Blane, Chafetz, & Wolf, 1967).

Can such effects be controlled experimentally? In a study of family therapy, Patterson and Forgatch (1985) used an ABAB design by having therapists switch back and forth between a directive–confrontive and a supportive–reflective style during 12-min blocks within sessions. Client resistance reliably covaried with therapist behavior, increasing during confrontational blocks and diminishing during supportive–reflective periods. In this study, we sought to apply this approach in a randomized between-groups design with problem drinkers.

Method

Subjects

Through the news media of the Albuquerque metropolitan area, we announced the availability of a free Drinker's Check-Up (DCU; Miller, Sovereign, & Krege, 1988). It was emphasized that the DCU was intended not for alcoholics but for drinkers who wanted to find out whether alcohol was harming them in any way. We further stressed that the DCU was completely confidential and not part of any treatment program and that it would be up to the individual to decide what, if anything, to do with the objective feedback provided.

The desired sample of 42 individuals was readily recruited from a single advertisement. Only 2 applicants were excluded from the study. One of these failed to keep numerous appointments for the DCU; the other was inadvertently given incorrect feedback because of scoring errors. When the error was detected, this subject was given corrected feedback but was excluded from analyses.

Group Assignment and Pretesting

Following initial screening and informed consent procedures, subjects completed preintervention questionnaires including the Alcohol Use Inventory (Horn, Wanberg, & Foster, 1987) and the Self-Evaluation of Drinking (Appel & Miller, 1984). All assessment was completed before either the subject or the interviewer knew the subject's group assignment. Subjects were then assigned at random to receive an immediate or a delayed (waiting-list control) DCU. Two thirds of subjects were immediately scheduled for a DCU (within 1 week), and the remaining one third were told that they would receive the DCU after a 6-week wait. After completing the DCU, all subjects were further randomly assigned to receive one of two styles of feedback: directive or client centered. Randomization was constrained to yield 14 subjects in each group.

Interventions

The DCU has been described in detail elsewhere (Miller et al., 1988). In this study it consisted of a 2-h evaluation based on measures sensitive to early alcohol-related risk and impairment. The DCU interview included a breath test to ensure sobriety at the time of testing, the Brief Drinker Profile (Miller & Marlatt, 1987), and a 1-h neuropsychological test battery. Subjects were then referred to a local laboratory for the drawing of a serum sample to be assayed for biomedical indexes of alcohol impairment.

Approximately 1 week after the DCU session, subjects returned for a feedback visit. Each subject received a personal feedback sheet reporting individual scores on 34 measures, accompanied by information permitting comparison with normal ranges. Feedback encompassed four measures of alcohol consumption, three serum tests (serum glutamic oxalcetic transaminase [SGOT], gamma glutamyl transpeptidase [GGTP], and high-density lipoprotein cholesterol [HDL]), eight neuropsychological measures (Trails A and B, Digit Symbol, Block Design, finger-tapping speed for dominant and nondominant hands, and Tactual Performance Test total time and location score), and 19 other scores derived from the Alcohol Use Inventory and the Brief Drinker Profile.

With each subject's written permission, we also attempted to interview two significant others following the DCU session in order to corroborate client self-reports. To obtain quantitative information, a structured interview protocol was used, paralleling the subject's self-report format (Miller, Crawford, & Taylor, 1979; Miller & Marlatt, 1987). These collateral data were used for research purposes but were not divulged to the subject.

The directive and client-centered groups differed only in the style with which feedback was presented and discussed during the second session. Assessment and feedback sessions were conducted by the same interviewer, with assessment completed before the client's assignment to feedback condition was revealed to the interviewer. Thus, both preintervention assessment and the DCU assessment were conducted double-blind.

In both conditions, the interviewer reviewed the objective feedback, helping the subject to interpret results in relation to normative standards. The therapeutic styles differed primarily in how the interviewer reacted to client responses.

In the directive feedback condition, interviewers were instructed to confront client resistance by emphasizing the evidence of alcohol problems, giving direct advice, and disagreeing with client minimization of problems. Using a broad definition of alcoholism as drinking in a way that causes problems (World Health Organization, 1952), subjects in the directive condition were told (as appropriate) that their drinking problems could be considered alcoholism. When a subject disputed any feedback, the interviewer argued from facts and findings that the subject did indeed have an alcohol problem and needed to do something about it.

In the client-centered feedback condition, interviewers were instructed to respond to subject statements in an empathic fashion, using the clinical skill of reflective listening (Truax & Carkhuff, 1967). No direct attempt was made to prove points to the subject or to force him or her to "face up to reality." The label *alcoholism* was not applied to the subject, and if asked about it, the interviewer deemphasized labeling in favor of considering what negative effects alcohol might be having and what (if anything) the client might need to do about it. The style of feedback in this group adhered closely to what has been described elsewhere as motivational interviewing (Miller, 1983; Miller & Rollnick, 1991).

Ensuring Intervention Integrity

To ensure that the two feedback conditions were in fact different, we audiotaped all sessions and submitted them to coding via a structured behavior checklist. Each tape was coded for therapist and client behaviors by two independent raters. The behavior classification system used was a modification of Patterson's code for quantifying client resistance and related therapist behavior (Chamberlain, Patterson, Reid, Kavanagh, & Forgatch, 1984; Patterson & Forgatch, 1985). The code was adapted to an alcoholic population and to the particular purposes of the DCU feedback session, resulting in a catalog of 38 therapist behaviors and 30 client responses. The raters received approximately 20 h of training including detailed coding of practice sessions, with discussions to resolve questions and disagreements about behavior classifications, and were aware that all tapes would be coded independently by a second rater.

The interviewers were one graduate and seven undergraduate psychology trainees who received specific training and supervision in assessment and feedback procedures. The separate feedback styles were explained, demonstrated, and practiced in weekly training meetings. Each interviewer then practiced both intervention styles, with direct observation and feedback from the senior author, until criterion performance was reached and practice sessions were appropriately discriminable on therapist behavior codes. Interviewers and feedback styles were completely crossed. Subjects were assigned at random to interviewers, and all interviewers completed at least one case within each feedback style. Total prestudy training for interviewers approximated 30 hr. We attempted to provide equally positive expectancies for success with each approach, both of which were novel for the interviewers. Our observations suggested that about half of the trainees had more difficulty with the directive style, whereas the remainder found the client-centered approach more challenging. Unfortunately, we collected no data on the interviewers' perceptions of the two styles.

Following the feedback session, the interviewer reminded the subject that follow-up interviews would be conducted in 6 weeks and again at the 1-year anniversary of the check-up. Subjects in the waiting-list condition were scheduled for a DCU at times paralleling the 6-week follow-up for subjects in the other two groups (Week 7). We chose the 6-week span because our prior research on brief interventions indicated that behavior change is observed within this period (e.g., Miller & Taylor, 1980; Miller et al., 1980).

Dependent Measures

Interventions were designed to affect alcohol consumption, which was measured both at intake and follow-up by the Drinker Profile structured interview (Miller & Marlatt,

1984, 1987). Average weekly consumption was expressed in standard ethanol content (SEC) units equivalent to 0.5 oz (15 ml) absolute alcohol (Miller, Heather, & Hall, 1991). Because mean volume of consumption does not fully capture the degree of intoxication, we also estimated number of weekly drinking days and subjects' weekly peak blood alcohol concentration (BAC) by computer projection (Markham, 1990) on the basis of drinking patterns reported on the Drinker Profile. This approach to quantifying consumption has been found to yield estimates comparable to those from a timeline follow-back approach (Cervantes, Miller, & Tonigan, 1990). Collateral reports obtained by a parallel interview have been found, at long-term follow-up, to be significantly correlated with client self-reports of weekly SECs ($r = .76$, $p < .001$) and peak BAC ($r = .39$, $p < .001$; Miller, Leckman, Delaney, & Tinkcom, 1992).

Follow-Up

Six weeks after the feedback session, subjects were scheduled for a brief follow-up visit. The second author, who at this point was still unaware of group assignment, administered the Follow-Up Drinker Profile (Miller & Marlatt, 1987). All 42 subjects completed this follow-up. The same procedure was repeated in follow-up interviews 12 months after the DCU, which was conducted by a new team of interviewers who were unaware of group assignment and of the purposes of this study. Collaterals were also interviewed at this time.

As an incentive for participation, subjects were informed that those completing each follow-up would become eligible for a $50 prize to be awarded by random lottery. At 12 months, 35 subjects (83%) completed the interview. Collateral interviews were completed in 24 (68%) of these cases.

Results

Sample Characteristics

Of the 42 subjects (18 women), 19 were currently married and 30 were employed full or part time. By group means they were, on average, 40 years of age, had 15 years of education, and had been experiencing alcohol-related problems for 7.2 years. On the Michigan Alcoholism Screening Test (Selzer, 1971), they achieved a mean score of 14.6. A history of parental alcohol problems was reported for nine fathers and three mothers. Only 1 subject was a purely episodic drinker; the remainder were classified as steady ($n = 19$) or combination steady and episodic drinkers (Miller & Marlatt, 1984). For 26 (62%), this was the first time they had ever sought help or consultation of any kind with regard to their drinking.

Integrity of Interventions

For purposes of analyses, we combined therapist behavior codes into nine groups and client behavior codes into seven groups, consistent with the general strategy of Patterson and Forgatch (1985). The two therapist styles were compared on behavior

categories by combining the counts of the two raters for each session. Therapists in
the directive style differed ($p < .05$) on four of nine domains, showing more confrontational behaviors and fewer listening, questioning, and restructuring responses
(see Table 1). Two of these differences remained significant after Bonferroni adjustment for Type I error ($.05/9 = .0056$).

Integrity of Group Equivalence

Comparing clients receiving the DCU with those assigned to the waiting-list control
group, we found no differences on the eight variables chosen: age, marital status,
years of education, age at first drink and at first intoxication, total Michigan Alcohol
Screening Test score, projected peak BAC, and total weekly consumption; the largest
obtained value was $F(1, 40) = -1.45$, $p > .05$.

Integrity of Client Self-Reports

For projected peak intoxication, agreement between subjects' and collaterals' reports
was significant at both intake, $r(24) = .59$, $p < .001$, and 12 months, $r(18) = .54$, $p
< .02$. For weekly alcohol consumption (SEC/week), subject and collateral reports
were not significantly correlated at intake, $r(24) = .31$, $p < .08$, but by 12-month
follow-up, convergence was significant, $r(19) = .65$, $p < .001$. This replicated an
unexpected pattern observed in our prior studies (Graber & Miller, 1988; Miller et
al., 1979).

Planned Experimental Contrasts

Effects of the Check-Up Intervention

To test the immediate experimental effect of the DCU, we contrasted treated ($n =
28$) and waiting-list ($n = 14$) groups at Week 7. At this point, 6 weeks had elapsed

Table 1—*Therapist Behaviors During Directive Versus Client-Centered Sessions*

Behavior category	Directive		Client centered		$F(1, 40)^a$	p
	M	SD	M	SD		
Confront	23.5	33.4	3.0	5.0	45.17	.000
Direct	56.3	28.8	40.0	32.1	1.25	.632
Listen	60.1	44.5	103.9	82.2	3.42	.010
Query	27.0	29.5	60.0	50.5	2.93	.023
Restructure	6.5	6.3	10.6	14.5	5.26	.001
Support	17.1	16.9	19.0	15.7	1.15	.752
Teach	354.8	150.8	305.4	145.5	1.07	.874
Understand	22.1	36.5	37.4	32.5	1.26	.611
Other	17.1	19.3	21.0	19.9	1.06	.906

[a]One audiotape was lost, reducing the sample to 41 cases.

since the DCU for treated subjects, whereas the controls had been waiting 6 weeks without intervention. Summary statistics and results of this contrast are reported in Tables 2 and 3. Intake measures were used as covariates, with the pooled means of the DCU groups serving as constant covariate values for each member in the waiting group. One-tailed tests were applied separately for each of three dependent measures. The DCU group reported less weekly consumption, lower peak BAC levels, and fewer drinking days relative to waiting-list controls (effect sizes of .54, .56, and .78, respectively, on the basis of unadjusted means). The between-groups difference for drinking days per week remained significant after Bonferroni adjustment for three one-tailed tests (.05/3 = .0167). With large effect sizes of .54 and .56, the absence of significance after Bonferroni correction on the other two variables was attributable to insufficient sample size and power.

Effects of Therapist Style

The second planned contrast was between the two therapeutic styles, ignoring whether subjects received immediate or delayed DCU. Again, one-tailed tests were used for each measure in this comparison, and individual intake measures were used as covariates. No experimental effects were found on weekly alcohol consumption, peak BAC, or number of days drinking per week between directive and client-centered approaches at any follow-up point—largest obtained $F(1, 39) < 1$, $p > .05$ —and this absence of main effect did not appear to be due to insufficient power (effect sizes of .03, .19, and .16, respectively). Therapist styles did, however, evoke significantly different client behaviors during the feedback session. Clients in the directive style were more likely to argue with, interrupt, and ignore (off task) the therapist. They were also more likely to deny (negative) and less likely to acknowl-

Table 2—*Effects of the Drinker's Check-Up*

Measure	Waiting (n = 14) M	SD	Directive (n = 14) M	SD	Client centered (n = 14) M	SD
Weekly consumption (SEC)						
Intake (before DCU)	35.71	37.21	37.71	32.76	49.00	49.74
6 Weeks after DCU	15.07	13.98	22.21	30.07	15.14	23.10
12-Month follow-up	23.18	18.48	17.00	12.42	12.00	8.90
Weekly peak BAC (mg%)						
Intake (before DCU)	137.4	128.6	157.7	167.9	164.1	183.7
6 Weeks after DCU	68.9	69.4	81.5	89.2	71.4	103.5
12-Month follow-up	74.9	42.1	59.1	50.1	56.2	46.2
Drinking days per week						
Intake (before DCU)	5.79	2.08	6.36	1.45	4.36	2.10
6 Weeks after DCU	4.71	2.95	4.07	2.84	3.36	2.59
12-Month follow-up	6.18	2.14	5.33	2.65	4.10	2.38

Note. Sample means and standard deviations are unadjusted by condition across time. SEC = standard ethanol content; DCU = Drinker's Check-Up; BAC = blood alcohol concentration.

Table 3—*Planned Contrasts: Directive (D; n = 14) and Client-Centered (CC; n = 14) Groups Combined Versus Waiting-List Group at Week 7*

Dependent measure	D + CC		Waiting		F(1, 39)	p
	M	SD	M	SD		
Weekly consumption (SEC)	18.9	26.9	35.5	37.2	3.08	<.09
Peak intoxication (BAC)	77.0	94.9	136.9	128.6	3.20	<.08
Days drinking per week	3.7	2.7	5.8	2.1	6.32	<.01

Note. Means and standard deviations are adjusted. SEC = standard ethanol content; BAC = blood alcohol concentration.

edge problems (positive). These differences are reflected in Table 4. Four clients were totally abstinent at 12-month follow-up, all of whom were in the client-centered condition.

Post Hoc Contrasts

Effects of Therapist Behavior

Because there was evident variability among therapists in the delivery of assigned styles (see the standard deviations in Table 1), we sought to examine the relation between actual therapist behaviors and client outcomes. Our sample was too small to permit multiple regression, so we examined simple correlations between in-session processes and drinking outcomes. A single therapist behavior significantly predicted client drinking 1 year later: The more the therapist *confronted*, the more the client drank, $r(34) = .65$, $p < .001$. In this coding system, therapist "confronting" responses consisted of challenging, disagreeing, head-on disputes, incredulity, emphasizing negative client characteristics, and sarcasm. Larger intercorrelations among therapist and client behaviors during feedback sessions are reported in Table 5. In general, client resistance behaviors were strongly correlated with therapist confrontational responses. Positive, self-motivational client responses, on the other hand, were related to therapist listening and restructuring.

Table 4—*Client Behaviors During Directive Versus Client-Centered Sessions*

Behavior category	Directive		Client centered		F(1, 40)[a]	p
	M	SD	M	SD		
Argue	3.4	10.7	1.0	1.8	35.02	.000
Follow	394.0	203.8	387.3	242.4	1.42	.453
Interrupt	4.1	12.0	1.2	1.9	38.90	.000
Negative	8.3	14.4	7.0	8.3	3.00	.019
Off task	5.8	14.6	3.5	4.3	11.23	.000
Positive	21.3	16.8	43.6	38.4	5.22	.001
Other	143.0	81.4	150.4	102.0	1.57	.332

[a]One audiotape was lost, reducing the sample to 41 cases.

Table 5—*Relationships Among Therapist and
Client Behaviors*

Therapist	Client	r
Teach	Follow	.94
Confront	Argue	.88
Confront	Interrupt	.87
Confront	Off task	.81
Restructure	Positive	.80
Listen	Positive	.77
Listen	Follow	.74
Confront	Negative	.74

Note. In the 6×8 matrix (excluding general talk categories), there were 29 significant correlations ($p < .05$). Given the number of analyses, we have reported only those coefficients greater than or equal to .60. For all of the correlations, the sample size was 41 and the probability level was .0001.

Effects of Client Behavior

Client behavior during the feedback session was likewise a good predictor of long-term outcome. Clients' 12-month alcohol consumption was predictable from any one of four resistance behaviors during the session 1 year earlier: interrupting ($r = .65$, $p < .001$); arguing ($r = .62$, $p < .001$); off-task responses such as inattention, silence, or side-tracking ($r = .58$, $p < .001$); and negative responses such as blaming others, disagreeing, excusing, claiming impunity, minimizing, pessimism, and expressed reluctance or unwillingness to change ($r = .45$, $p < .01$). Neither therapist nor client behaviors during sessions predicted drinking levels 6 weeks after feedback. These effects were apparent only at the 12-month follow-up. Immediate behavior changes (at Week 7) were only modestly related to enduring changes at 12 months ($rs = .20$ for consumption, .29 for peak BAC, and .42 for drinking days per week). Thus, client in-session resistance behavior was more strongly (and inversely) related to long-term outcome than was immediate behavior change.

Effects of Client Beliefs

Peele (1987) has suggested that responsiveness to alternative treatments is related to individual and cultural differences in conceptions of alcoholism. We wondered, in retrospect, whether clients' responsiveness to the two therapeutic styles might be affected by their pretreatment beliefs about alcoholism (Miller & Marlatt, 1984, Item C87). Using our three dependent measures, 2×2 analyses of covariance were conducted by crossing client belief (disease vs. bad habit) and therapeutic style (directive vs. client centered) with intake measures used as covariates. A significant post hoc interaction was found for number of drinking days per week, $F(1, 37) = 6.04$, $p < .02$. Familywise protected simple main effects of adjusted means showed that within the client-centered condition, clients believing alcoholism to be more like a bad habit drank on significantly fewer days per week ($M = 1.33$, $SD = 1.41$) than did clients viewing alcoholism more as a disease ($M = 5.04$, $SD = 2.41$), $F(1, 18) = 13.47$, $p < .05$. Within the directive condition, number of drinking days was not moderated by client beliefs (for bad habit, $M = 4.06$, $SD = 3.11$; for disease, $M = 3.60$, $SD = 2.61$).

Discussion

Consistent with prior findings (Miller et al., 1988), the DCU exerted relatively large effects (.54–.78) on alcohol consumption within 6 weeks after feedback, and this reduction was maintained and was confirmed by collateral reports at 12-month follow-up. After receiving the DCU, waiting-list controls showed a rapid and comparable reduction on consumption variables. This was consistent with our earlier study (Miller et al., 1988) and the findings of other investigations of brief feedback interventions with problem drinkers (Bien et al., 1993).

The between-groups effects of *assigned* therapist style failed to reach statistical significance, but one *actual* therapist behavior (confrontation) proved to be predictive of client drinking 12 months after the single feedback session. Client resistance behavior during the feedback session was likewise a potent predictor of long-term change in drinking.

This raises one potential alternative explanation of the relation between therapist style and outcome. It could be argued that resistant clients both inspire more negative therapist behavior and suffer poorer long-term outcomes. This explanation was rendered less plausible because therapist behaviors related to outcome were strongly determined in this study by the experimental manipulation. Therapist confrontational responses in particular were eight times higher in the directive condition and represented the strongest discriminant variable between assigned conditions. Furthermore, all four of the client resistance responses that were predictive of long-term outcome were shown to be strongly affected by the experimental effect of assigned therapist style. This indicates that both therapist style and client resistance were largely (but not fully) determined by the experimental manipulation. These findings are consistent with prior research associating positive outcomes with an empathic therapist style.

It is noteworthy that although the DCU itself showed an immediate impact on drinking at Week 7, the effects of treatment process events (therapist and client behaviors during the feedback session) were not evident until the 12-month follow-up. This suggests that different elements of treatment may influence short-term gains and the long-term maintenance of such change.

Confrontation and empathy are not, we believe, inherently incompatible. In its etymology, confrontation literally means "to bring face to face," which does not necessarily mean going head to head. To confront is to help another person face the facts. In this sense, confrontation is a *goal* rather than a therapeutic procedure (Miller & Rollnick, 1991). What constitutes the most effective means for accomplishing this goal remains an open question.

It is of interest that the effects of therapist style on long-term drinking outcomes have been relatively large both in this and in prior research (e.g., Miller et al., 1980; Valle, 1981). This is consistent with a broader literature outside of alcoholism associating a directive and controlling therapist style with poor outcomes, although these effects have tended to be weak and inconsistent (Beutler, Crago, & Arizmendi, 1986; Lieberman, Yalom, & Miles, 1973). One reason for this inconsistency may be a "treatment-matching" phenomenon: different types of people respond optimally to directive and client-centered styles (e.g., McLachlan, 1972). Some evidence for this was found in the interaction between client beliefs about alcoholism and responsiveness to therapeutic styles. It is also possible that the availability of a relatively clear outcome measure, such as drinking behavior, reduces research noise and permits better detection of therapist effects. Finally, our data indicate the need to examine actual therapist behaviors, not only the effects of assigned therapy conditions.

In any event, specific and observed therapist behaviors commonly associated with the term *confrontational* were found to predict poorer outcomes for problem drinkers. These findings are consistent with earlier reports that a directive–confrontational style evokes client resistance (Patterson & Forgatch, 1985) and is associated with unfavorable outcomes in treating alcohol problems (Miller et al., 1980; Valle, 1981). Indeed, the level of client resistance evoked during a treatment session appeared to be negatively related to long-term treatment success. It should be noted that the client resistance responses that predicted negative outcomes were relatively infrequent behaviors, constituting fewer than 3% of total client responses during sessions. The relative *absence* of such in-session client resistance was more strongly related to outcome than was the *presence* of client verbal responses ("positive") commonly thought to mark motivation for change (i.e., agreeing with the therapist and expressing concern, determination, or optimism). More generally successful therapeutic styles, then, may be those that evoke positive motivational responses from clients without engendering resistance. If this is so, the occurrence during sessions of client resistance responses could serve as immediate feedback of probable impact and as a cue for altering therapeutic approach.

The generalizability of these findings to more severe clinical populations is an important question. Other studies have reported a similar relation between empathic style and positive outcomes in problem drinkers seeking treatment (e.g., Miller et al. 1980; Valle, 1981). Two recently completed trials of the DCU have demonstrated still larger effect sizes with outpatients (Bien, 1991) and inpatients (Brown & Miller, 1993) being treated for alcohol problems, and we are currently testing the preventive application of this approach with pregnant drinkers. Similar motivational strategies are being applied and tested with a variety of populations and problem areas (Miller & Rollnick, 1991). Defining the limits and mechanisms of brief motivational interventions is likely to require a broad program of ongoing research (Heather, 1986).

References

Appel, C.-P., & Miller, W. R. (1984). *The self-evaluation of drinking*. Unpublished manuscript, University of New Mexico, Albuquerque.

Beutler, L. E., Crago, M., & Arizmendi, T. G. (1986). Therapist variables in psychotherapy process and outcome. In S. L. Garfield & A. E. Bergin (Eds.), *Handbook of psychotherapy and behavior change* (pp. 257–310). New York: Wiley.

Bien, T. H. (1991). *Motivational intervention with alcohol outpatients*. Unpublished doctoral dissertation, University of New Mexico, Albuquerque.

Bien, T. H., Miller, W. R., & Tonigan, J. S. (1993). Brief interventions for alcohol problems: A review. *Addiction, 88*, 305–325.

Brown, J. M., & Miller, W. R. (1993). Impact of motivational interviewing on participation and outcome in residential alcoholism treatment. *Psychology of Addictive Behaviors, 7,* 211–218.

Cervantes, E. A., Miller, W. R., & Tonigan, J. S. (1990, November). *Comparison of timeline follow-back and averaging methods for quantifying alcohol consumption in treatment research.* Paper presented at the annual meeting of the Association for the Advancement of Behavior Therapy, San Francisco.

Chafetz, M. E. (1961). A procedure for establishing therapeutic contact with the alcoholic. *Quarterly Journal of Studies on Alcohol, 22,* 325–328.

Chamberlain, P., Patterson, G., Reid, J., Kavanagh, K., & Forgatch, M. (1984). Observation of client resistance. *Behavior Therapy, 15,* 144–155.

DiCicco, L., Unterberger, H., & Mack, J. E. (1978). Confronting denial: An alcoholism intervention strategy. *Psychiatric Annals, 8,* 596–606.

Edwards, G., Orford, J., Egert, S., Guthrie, S., Hawker, A., Hensman, C., Mitcheson, M., Oppenheimer, E., & Taylor, C. (1977). Alcoholism: A controlled trial of "treatment" and "advice." *Journal of Studies on Alcohol, 38,* 1004–1031.

Ends, E. J., & Page, C. W. (1957). A study of three types of group psychotherapy with hospitalized male inebriates. *Quarterly Journal of Studies on Alcohol, 18,* 263–277.

Graber, R. A., & Miller, W. R. (1988). Abstinence and controlled drinking goals for problem drinkers: A randomized clinical trial. *Psychology of Addictive Behaviors, 2,* 20–33.

Hazelden Foundation. (1985). You don't have to tear 'em down to build 'em up. *Hazelden Professional Update,* p. 2.

Heather, N. (1986). Minimal treatment interventions for problem drinkers. *Current Issues in Clinical Psychology, 4,* 171–186.

Horn, J. L., Wanberg, K. W., & Foster, F. M. (1987). *Guide to the Alcohol Use Inventory.* Minneapolis, MN: National Computer Systems.

Institute of Medicine. (1989). *Prevention and treatment of alcohol problems: Research opportunities.* Washington, DC: National Academy of Sciences.

Lieberman, M. A., Yalom, I. D., & Miles, M. B. (1973). *Encounter groups: First facts.* New York: Basic Books.

Luborsky, L., McLellan, A. T., Woody, G. E., O'Brien, C. P., & Auerbach, A. (1985). Therapist success and its determinants. *Archives of General Psychiatry, 42,* 602–611.

Markham, M. (1990). *The Blood Alcohol Concentration Computational System (BACCuS)* [Computer program]. Albuquerque, NM: University of New Mexico, Department of Psychology.

McLachlan, J. F. C. (1972). Benefit from group therapy as a function of patient–therapist match on conceptual level. *Psychotherapy: Theory, Research and Practice, 9,* 317–323.

Miller, W. R. (1983). Motivational interviewing with problem drinkers. *Behavioural Psychotherapy, 11,* 147–172.

Miller, W. R., & Baca, L. M. (1983). Two-year follow-up of bibliotherapy and therapist-directed controlled drinking training for problem drinkers. *Behavior Therapy, 14,* 441–448.

Miller, W. R., Crawford, V. L., & Taylor, C. A. (1979). Significant others as corroborative sources for problem drinkers. *Addictive Behaviors, 4,* 67–70.

Miller, W. R., Heather, N., & Hall, W. (1991). Calculating standard drink units: International comparisons. *British Journal of Addiction, 86,* 43–47.

Miller, W. R., Leckman, A. L., Delaney, H. D., & Tinkcom, M. (1992). Long-term follow-up of behavioral self-control training. *Journal of Studies on Alcohol, 53,* 249–261.

Miller, W. R., & Marlatt, G. A. (1984). *Manual for the Comprehensive Drinker Profile.* Odessa, FL: Psychological Assessment Resources.

Miller, W. R., & Marlatt, G. A. (1987). *Manual supplement for the Brief Drinker Profile, Follow-up Drinker Profile, and Collateral Interview Form.* Odessa, FL: Psychological Assessment Resources.

Miller, W. R., & Rollnick, S. (1991). *Motivational interviewing: Preparing people to change addictive behavior.* New York: Guilford Press.

Miller, W. R., Sovereign, R. G., & Krege, B. (1988). Motivational interviewing with problem drinkers: II. The Drinker's Check-up as a preventive intervention. *Behavioural Psychotherapy, 16,* 251–268.

Miller, W. R., & Taylor, C. A. (1980). Relative effectiveness of bibliotherapy, individual and group self-control training in the treatment of problem drinkers. *Addictive Behaviors, 5,* 13–24.

Miller, W. R., Taylor, C. A., & West, J. C. (1980). Focused versus broad-spectrum behavior therapy for problem drinkers. *Journal of Consulting and Clinical Psychology, 48,* 590–601.

Milmoe, S., Rosenthal, R., Blane, H. T., Chafetz, M. E., & Wolf, I. (1967). The doctor's voice: Postdictor of successful referral of alcoholic patients. *Journal of Abnormal Psychology, 72,* 78–84.

Moore, R. C., & Murphy, T. C. (1961). Denial of alcoholism as an obstacle to recovery. *Quarterly Journal of Studies on Alcohol, 22,* 597–609.

Patterson, G. R., & Forgatch, M. S. (1985). Therapist behavior as a determinant for client noncompliance: A paradox for the behavior modifier. *Journal of Consulting and Clinical Psychology, 53,* 846–851.

Peele, S. (1987). Why do controlled-drinking outcomes vary by investigator, by country and by era? Cultural conceptions of relapse and remission in alcoholism. *Drug and Alcohol Dependence, 20,* 173–201.

Rogers, C. R. (1959). A theory of therapy, personality, and interpersonal relationships as developed in the client-centered framework. In S. Koch (Ed.), *Psychology: The study of a science: Vol. 3. Formulations of the person and the social context* (p. 184–256). New York: McGraw-Hill.

Selzer, M. L. (1971). The Michigan Alcoholism Screening Test: The quest for a new diagnostic instrument. *American Journal of Psychiatry, 127,* 1653–1658.

Truax, C. B., & Carkhuff, R. R. (1967). *Toward effective counseling and psychotherapy.* Chicago: Aldine.

Valle, S. K. (1981). Interpersonal functioning of alcoholism counselors and treatment outcome. *Journal of Studies on Alcohol, 42,* 783–790.

World Health Organization, Expert Committee on Mental Health. (1952). *Report on the first session of the Alcoholism Subcommittee* (Tech. Rep. No. 48). Geneva, Switzerland: Author.

Chapter 15
INTERPRETATION AND AROUSAL IN THE COUNSELING PROCESS

Douglas H. Olson and Charles D. Claiborn

Within the social influence model of counseling (e.g., Strong & Claiborn, 1982), interpretation is of particular interest. *Interpretation* may be defined broadly as any intervention that offers the client a discrepant point of view and persuades the client to construe events differently and, consequently, to act differently (Levy, 1963). Understanding how interpretation functions, then, is central to understanding the influence process in counseling (Claiborn, 1982).

Conceptualizing interpretations as discrepant messages, Levy (1963) drew on dissonance theory (Festinger, 1957) to describe conditions under which they are accepted, rejected, or resisted by the client. One set of conditions is especially interesting to us because it concerns the role of arousal in influence, a neglected topic in the counseling literature, and because it addresses the practical question of timing or placement of interpretation in the counseling interview. Specifically, Levy hypothesized that interpretations associated with dissonance reduction would be more readily accepted than interpretations associated with dissonance arousal, because dissonance-reducing interpretations would be associated with greater comfort than dissonance-arousing interpretations. Levy made clear that he was referring to dissonance not only as a cognitive state but as a state of emotional and physiological arousal. Thus, by extension interpretations associated with a decrease in emotional or physiological arousal ought to be more readily accepted than interpretations associated with increased arousal. Stimulated by Levy's thinking, we sought to explore interpretation and arousal in the present study.

In Kiesler and Pallak's (1976) review of dissonance research, they noted that "there is evidence, although largely indirect, suggesting a fairly literal interpretation of dissonance as an arousal state" (p. 1015). The more direct evidence is complicated by the fact that arousal can be operationalized in so many different ways. For example, Croyle and Cooper (1983) found nonspecific skin conductance responses to be greater (which indicates higher arousal) under high dissonance conditions than under low ones. In addition, Gerard (1967) found high dissonance participants to show a constriction of pulse amplitude (an arousal response), and McMillen and Geiselman (1974) found high dissonance participants to have less alpha wave activity (a relaxation response).

Arousal that accompanies cognitive dissonance has also been found to facilitate attitude change, which suggests that dissonance functions as a drive to impel its own

Reprinted from *Journal of Counseling Psychology, 37,* 131–137 (1990). Copyright © 1990 by the American Psychological Association. Used with permission of the first author.

This article is based on a dissertation completed by Douglas H. Olson under the supervision of Charles D. Claiborn and submitted to the Department of Educational Psychology at the University of Nebraska—Lincoln.

We gratefully acknowledge the help of David N. Dixon, who served as co-chair of the dissertation committee.

reduction. Attitude change occurred, for example, in one study when participants were given an amphetamine but told it was a placebo (Cooper, Zanna, & Taves, 1978). The drug-stimulated arousal, denied proper attribution by the placebo procedure, functioned as dissonance, with attitude change as the dissonance-reducing consequence. Other studies have produced consistent results (Pittman, 1975; Zanna & Cooper, 1974).

Two studies have explored the relation between arousal and influence in psychotherapy. Hoehn-Saric, Frank, and Gurland (1968) used ether to manipulate arousal in therapy sessions and verified the effectiveness of the manipulation with pulse and observational ratings. In the sessions the therapists pointed out problematic attitudes of their clients and suggested more appropriate alternative attitudes. The results showed client attitude change to be greater in the ether sessions, but it was unclear whether this was due to arousal or the intrusive procedure for administering ether. A second study replicated the findings of the first but controlled for the effects of the ether administration (Hoehn-Saric et al., 1972). The researchers were therefore able to conclude that attitude change was facilitated by arousal.

In this study we wanted a realistic procedure for manipulating arousal in the counseling interview, one that made use of counseling interventions rather than external agents. In addition, we wanted a measure of physiological arousal that was suitable for checking the arousal manipulation. Research on the physiologically arousing effects of counseling interventions seemed relevant to these aims. In one study McCarron and Appel (1971) found that the galvanic skin response (GSR) of clients was greater after the delivery of interpretations and confrontations than after reflections and probes. They noted that the more arousing interventions were both more specific and discrepant than the less arousing interventions. However, in a second study, Weinstein (1978) found that confrontative and nonconfrontative counseling interventions did not produce different client responses on two other physiological measures, heart rate and skin conductance, even though differences were obtained on paralinguistic cues associated with arousal. Though sparse and inconclusive, these findings at least suggested contrasting interventions and an arousal procedure to use in this study.

The specific context for our study was a single counseling interview focusing on participants' problems with procrastination. Arousal, the independent variable, was manipulated through the use of either confrontation or reflection, interventions that had proven in McCarron and Appel's (1971) study, as well as our pilot testing, to be differentially arousing. In the high arousal interview, the counselor used confrontations just before delivering the interpretations, whereas in the low arousal interview, the counselor used reflections. The interpretations, which offered participants a discrepant point of view with regard to their problem, were the same in both conditions. A third group of control participants did not participate in an interview but completed some measures. Dependent measures assessed participants' physiological arousal (GSR), as well as several influence outcomes.

The first hypothesis of the study was that participants in the high arousal condition would show a GSR decrease after interpretations, whereas participants in the low arousal condition would show an increase. This followed simply from previous research that suggested that interpretation might be less arousing than confrontations but more arousing than reflections (McCarron & Appel, 1971). The second hypothesis, drawn from Levy (1963), was that participants in the high arousal condition would show greater attitude change relevant to the interpretations, greater interpretation acceptance, and greater interpretation recognition than participants in the low arousal condition and that their affective response to the interpretations and their perceptions of the counselor would be more positive. The third hypothesis was that participants in both interview conditions would show greater attitude change and interpretation acceptance than participants in the control condition.

Method

Participants

The participants were 60 undergraduates, 50 women and 10 men, recruited through introductory educational psychology classes. Very few participants were ethnic minorities or outside the typical age range for college sophomores. They received course credit for participating in the study. The criteria for inclusion in the study were that participants (a) reported problems with procrastination and (b) scored at or below the median (a score of 35) on a modified Controllability scale from the Procrastination Inventory (Strong, Wambach, Lopez, & Cooper, 1979). The latter criterion meant that participants were disinclined to attribute procrastination to factors under their direct control.

Experimental Manipulation

The independent variable in the study was arousal, manipulated through counselor interventions to comprise two experimental conditions, high arousal (confrontation) and low arousal (reflection). A no-treatment control condition constituted a third level in some analyses.

In the high arousal condition, confrontations were delivered 1 min before each of the two interpretations—that is, at approximately the 15- and 21-min points in the interview. The confrontations described a discrepancy between participants' statements in the interview and their behavior outside the interview: for example, "You've been telling me that you plan to do something about your procrastination. However, your repeated procrastination at school shows that you are resisting change." Although the basic theme was the same for all participants, the particular content was tailored to each participant's disclosure in the interview. To ensure that the content of the confrontations was appropriate and timely, the counselors anticipated the confrontations with listening responses that focused on each aspect of the discrepancy; thus, the confrontations fit reasonably into the sequence of the interview. The confrontations were two sentences long and were presented in a strong, moderately challenging tone of voice and with the counselor's leaning slightly forward.

In the low arousal condition, reflections of feeling or content were used just before the interpretations. These were no more discrepant than the listening responses used throughout the interview: for example, "It sounds like that was really frustrating." The reflections were brief and presented in a calm, tentative tone of voice and with the counselor's reclining slightly in his chair.

High and low arousal were manipulated in a 30-min counseling interview about procrastination, conducted according to a standardized protocol. In the first 15 min of the interview, the counselor used nondiscrepant listening responses to explore the problem. At approximately the 16- and 22-min points of the interview (e.g., 1 min after the confrontations in the high arousal condition), the counselor delivered the interpretations. As in Levy's (1963) definition, the interpretations were designed to present the participants with a view of procrastination discrepant from their own. They were discrepant in emphasizing the participants' direct control over procrastination and in relating procrastination to such concepts as personal choice, responsibility, and effort. In form, they were not simply explanatory interpretations aimed at producing insight but included a guidance component to link understanding to action. The first interpretation was, "You make the personal choice to procrastinate or not. Taking full responsibility for your own procrastination may be the key to actually doing something about it." The second interpretation was, "Change will come to you through hard work and effort. Choosing to take full responsibility for your procrastination may be one answer to your problem." The appropriateness of the interpretations at each point in the interview derived from their representing the counselor's perspective on the topic at hand (procrastination) and from the fact that they expressed a theme (controllability) that was salient in the participants' exploration of the problem. The interpretations were delivered verbatim, in a firm, straightforward tone of voice, and with the counselor's reclining slightly in his chair.

The control condition was used to partial out the effects of testing, including regression effects, as well as the effects of being connected to GSR equipment. Control participants received the same orientation to GSR procedures but did not participate in counseling interviews. They also completed questionnaires at pretest, posttest, and follow-up.

Counselors

The counselors were three White male doctoral students in counseling psychology. All were experienced counselors, who ranged in age from 27 to 35. They were unfamiliar with the hypotheses of the study. For 2 weeks they rehearsed protocols for the experimental conditions, until they were able to follow them reliably. They used cue sheets during interviews to help them adhere to the protocols.

Trained observers conducted a manipulation check during the interviews to ensure that the protocols were followed. The observers were three doctoral students in counseling psychology, unaware of the purpose of the study. During 1 week of training, they familiarized themselves with the protocols. Then one observer watched each interview through a one-way mirror, checking it against the protocol to ensure that listening responses were used throughout, except when specific reflections, confrontations, and interpretations were required. The counselors adequately followed the protocols in all interviews, though the onset of the manipulation sequence varied within a range of 2 min.

Dependent Measures

Physiological Arousal

GSR was the measure of physiological arousal. The instrument used was a Biologic Devices SR10. It was kept in the interview room behind a partition, out of the view of both counselor and participant, and thus quite unobtrusive. The digital readout faced the one-way mirror so that data could be recorded from the next room. GSR sensors were attached to two of the participant's fingers on one hand.

GSR was chosen because of its effectiveness as an indicator of autonomic arousal after counselor responses (e.g., Dittes, 1957; McCarron & Appel, 1971). A procedural check with five pilot participants was conducted with GSR, an electromyograph, and a measure of hand temperature to make sure GSR was the most responsive to the manipulations used in the study. This proved to be the case. GSR levels after the counselor's confrontations were observed to rise sharply for a brief period (5–45 s). After the arousal period GSR levels decreased to baseline readings over 2–3 min. Observation of this pattern helped determine that interpretations in the high arousal condition ought to be presented about 1 min after the confrontations.

Analyses of the GSR data included five time periods: (a) the 3-min baseline period, recorded during the 11th–13th min of the interview; (b) the 1-min period prior to the first interpretation, which corresponded to the first arousal manipulation (referred to as *Arousal 1*); (c) the 1-min period subsequent to the first interpretation (*Interpretation 1*); (d) the 1-min period prior to the second interpretation, which corresponded to the second arousal manipulation (*Arousal 2*); and (e) the 1-min period subsequent to the second interpretation (*Interpretation 2*).

Two doctoral students in counseling psychology, unaware of the purpose of the study, served as GSR recorders. There was one recorder at each interview. The recorders were trained for 2 weeks to record GSR data on log sheets during interviews. They used an earplug device that beeped every 10 s to log GSR data in 10-s intervals throughout the interviews. The recorders were also familiar with interview protocols and marked on the log sheets the exact intervals at which counselors were presenting the arousal manipulations and interpretations. From the recorders' marks for these intervals, it was possible to determine which intervals constituted Arousals 1 and 2 and Interpretations 1 and 2. The scores for each participant during each time period were the averages of the 10-s interval scores for that period.

Attitude Change

Scores on a shortened version of the Controllability scale from the Procrastination Inventory (Strong et al., 1979) were used as both a criterion for inclusion in the study and a measure of attitude change. The scale was shortened from 16 to 7 items because only these items were relevant to the content of the interpretations presented in the interviews. The scale measured the extent to which subjects attributed their procrastination to factors under their direct control. Each item in the scale was accompanied by a 7-point continuum for indicating extent of agreement. Scores on the scale could range from 7 to 49, wherein higher scores indicate more direct control over procrastination. The scale was administered along with other scales of the Procrastination Inventory, but only the 7 Controllability scale items were scored. The internal consistency (alpha coefficient) of the 7-item scale, based on data from 148 pilot participants, was .66, in contrast to .72 for the original, longer scale.

Interpretation Acceptance

A 2-item measure was used to assess the extent to which participants agreed with the content of the interpretations presented in the study. The measure listed the exact content of each interpretation, accompanied by a 7-point scale (1 = *totally agree* to 7 = *totally disagree*), which was repeated for each item. Scores were summed across the two items. A similar measure was used in Croyle and Cooper's (1983) study of arousal and dissonance.

Interpretation Recognition

A recognition measure was used to assess whether participants accurately received and remembered the content of the interpretations. The measure listed six interpretations and asked participants to indicate which had been presented by the counselor. The six interpretations included the two that had been presented in the interview, two interpretations that conveyed opposite content on the controllability dimension, and two interpretations that presented content irrelevant to that dimension. Each correct summary marked was scored +1, and each incorrect summary, −1. Scores could thus range from 1 to 7, after linear transformation to remove negative values.

Affective Response

A measure adapted from Weinstein (1978) assessed participants' affective response to the interpretations during the minute after their delivery. It was completed by the same observers who performed the manipulation check. The observers, watching through the one-way mirror, rated participants' responses following the interpretation on a scale from 1 to 3. A response was rated 1 if the participant verbally denied the content of the interpretation or if the participant's tone of voice became defensive or tense, as evidenced by increased volume, pitch, or pace. A response was rated 2 if there was no discernible change in the content of the participant's statements or voice quality. A response was rated 3 if the participant seemed to understand and accept the content of the interpretation, as evidenced by their asking for more information, expanding on the interpretation, or making specific feeling statements, or if the participant's voice became relaxed, as evidenced by decreased volume, pitch, or pace. During the observers' training, they became familiar with the interview protocols and the rating system. They then simultaneously observed pilot interviews and made independent ratings. Training continued until agreement on ratings among all three observers over three consecutive interviews reached 90% or greater. There was one observer for each interview during the actual study.

Perceptions of Counselors

The Counselor Rating Form—Short version (CRF-S; Corrigan & Schmidt, 1983) was used to determine whether counselors were differentially perceived on dimensions relevant to their influence, specifically, expertness, attractiveness, and trustworthiness. The scales to measure each of these dimensions consist of four adjectives accompanied by 7-point continua for rating the counselor. Each scale thus yields a score from 4 to 28. Scale reliabilities across counselors and settings have been reported as .85–.94 for expertness, .89–.93 for attractiveness, and .82–.93 for trustworthiness (Corrigan & Schmidt, 1983).

Procedure

A pilot study was run to check experimental procedures and provide practice for all personnel involved with the study. Nineteen undergraduates were assigned to either the high or low arousal condition and participated in 30-min interviews wherein the counselors followed the experimental protocols. Mean levels of GSR during the manipulation phases of the interviews showed that participants became more aroused after the confrontations than after the reflections; participants who received reflections tended to maintain baseline levels of arousal. The experimental manipulations, after refinement, seemed satisfactory for testing the hypotheses of the study.

The actual study was conducted in 3 weeks. The 1st week included an orientation and pretest session. Participants attended in small groups. An experimenter described requirements of the study and administered the Procrastination Inventory. Participants who met the criteria for inclusion were scheduled for sessions during the following 2 weeks. Those who did not meet the criteria or chose not to participate were given experimental credit and an opportunity for referral to a counselor. The participants included in the study were randomly assigned to the high arousal ($n = 19$), low arousal ($n = 20$), and control ($n = 21$) conditions.

In the 2nd week the participants in the experimental and control conditions attended individual sessions. A different experimenter familiarized participants with the interview room and GSR procedures. The experimenter emphasized that the GSR equipment would measure physiological changes during the interview and would do nothing to or for the participants. The experimenter had the participants sit down and attached the GSR sensors to one hand. Participants were asked to keep the hand with the sensory stationary on the arm of the chair. The experimenter then asked participants to complete (with the other hand) a brief survey irrelevant to the experiment and relax alone in the room for 3 min. The survey task was intended simply as a distraction from the GSR procedure. After the resting period the sensors were removed from participants in the control condition, and they completed the Procrastination Inventory a second time. After the resting period for experimental participants, the experimenter introduced the counselor, and the interview began. After the interview the experimental participants again completed the Procrastination Inventory, as well as the CRF-S.

In the 3rd week the participants returned for follow-up testing in small groups. All participants completed the Procrastination Inventory and the interpretation acceptance measure. Experimental participants also completed the interpretation recognition measure. All participants were then debriefed about the nature of the study, and those who desired further counseling were given appropriate referrals. The participants generally found the study very interesting and useful; no one reported a negative reaction.

Results

Physiological Arousal

Table 1 presents cell means and standard deviations for GSR data by condition and time. A repeated measures analysis of variance (ANOVA), with condition (high and

Table 1—*Means and Standard Deviations for Galvanic Skin Response Scores by Condition and Time*

	Low arousal		High arousal	
Time	*M*	*SD*	*M*	*SD*
Baseline	7.75	6.24	8.35	5.37
Arousal 1	7.59	6.15	9.15	5.84
Interpretation 1	7.82	6.10	8.55	5.61
Arousal 2	7.64	5.92	9.41	5.71
Interpretation 2	7.89	6.34	9.27	6.13

Note. $n = 20$ for the low arousal condition; $n = 19$ for the high arousal condition. Participants' scores for each time period are averages of the 10-s interval scores for that period. Higher scores indicate higher arousal.

low arousal) as the between-subjects variable and time (five repeated measures) the within-subjects variable, yielded a significant main effect for time, $F(4, 34) = 3.71$, $p < .02$, and a significant Condition × Time interaction, $F(4, 34) = 6.76$, $p < .0005$. The simple main effect for time within the high arousal condition was significant, $F(4, 34) = 9.45$, $p < .0001$, which indicates differences across time in that condition. The simple main effect for time within the low arousal condition was not significant.

Tukey tests were conducted to determine differences between means at the five time periods in the high arousal condition (see Table 1); significance level was set at .05. Arousal at Arousal 1 was significantly higher than at baseline, which indicates that the first confrontation (the arousal manipulation in this condition) was accompanied by increased arousal, as intended. Arousal at Interpretation 1 was significantly lower than at Arousal 1 but not different from baseline; thus the first interpretation was accompanied by decreased arousal. Arousal at Arousal 2 was significantly higher than at Interpretation 1 and baseline but not at Arousal 1; again, as intended, the second confrontation was also accompanied by increased arousal. Arousal at Interpretation 2 did not differ from Arousal 2, however, which indicates that the second interpretation was not accompanied by decreased arousal. In summary, the arousal manipulations created a contrasting context for the delivery of the interpretations. However, the interpretations were only partially associated with reduced arousal in the high arousal condition and were not associated with increased arousal in the low arousal condition.

Effects of Interpretations

Means and standard deviations for measures of attitude (controllability), interpretation acceptance, interpretation recognition, affective response to the interpretations, and perceptions of the counselors are presented in Table 2 by condition and time.

A repeated measures ANOVA on the attitude measure, with condition (high arousal, low arousal, and control) as the between-subjects variable and time (pretest, posttest, and follow-up) as the within-subjects variable, yielded a significant main effect for time, $F(2, 114) = 18.79$, $p < .0001$, but not a significant interaction. Attitudes changed in the direction of greater controllability in all conditions, including

Table 2—*Means and Standard Deviations on the Nonphysiological Measures by Condition*

Measure	Low arousal		High arousal		Control	
	M	SD	M	SD	M	SD
Attitude						
Pretest	29.5	3.9	29.6	5.0	29.8	3.9
Posttest	31.6	4.4	34.3	5.6	32.3	4.8
Follow-up	31.7	5.0	35.2	6.7	31.8	6.4
Acceptance	11.6	2.8	13.0	1.3	11.4	1.7
Recognition	4.7	1.2	4.8	1.2		
Affective response						
Interpretation 1	2.6	0.7	3.0	0.0		
Interpretation 2	2.6	0.8	2.4	1.0		
Expertness	24.2	2.7	22.8	3.5		
Attractiveness	23.9	3.5	22.5	3.2		
Trustworthiness	24.7	1.9	23.2	3.2		

Note. $n = 20$ for the low arousal condition; $n = 19$ for the high arousal condition; $n = 21$ for the control condition. Attitude scores are from the modified Controllability scale of the Procrastination Inventory; possible range is 7–49, wherein higher scores indicate greater controllability. Possible range for the interpretation acceptance measure is 2–14, wherein higher scores indicate greater acceptance. Possible range for the interpretation recognition measure is 1–7, wherein higher scores indicate more accurate recognition. Possible range for the affective response measure is 1–3, wherein higher scores indicate a more positive response. Expertness, attractiveness, and trustworthiness scores are from the Counselor Rating Form—Short version; possible range for each scale is 4–28, wherein higher scores indicate higher levels of these variables.

the control, which suggests regression effects. Though the Condition × Time interaction was not significant, we note that the attitude change effect size in the high arousal condition from pretest to follow-up was well over twice that in the other two conditions (.82 versus .33 and .30 for low arousal and control, respectively, with the largest cell standard deviation, 6.7, as the standard for measurement).

A one-way ANOVA on the interpretation acceptance measure, with condition (high arousal, low arousal, and control) as the independent variable, yielded a significant effect, $F(2, 57) = 3.65$, $p < .05$. Tukey tests, with significance set at .05, indicated that participants in the high arousal condition were significantly more accepting of the interpretation content than those in the control condition, but that participants in the low arousal condition were not (see Table 2).

An independent t test was used to analyze differences between the high and low arousal conditions on the interpretation recognition measure. The participants in the two conditions did not differ in their recognition of the interpretation content. Participants showed moderate recognition scores overall ($M = 4.8$, $SD = 1.2$).

A repeated measures ANOVA on the affective response measure, with condition (high and low arousal) as the between-subjects variable and time (first and second interpretation) as the within-subjects variable, yielded a significant main effect for time, $F(1, 37) = 6.60$, $p < .02$, and a significant Condition × Time interaction, $F(1, 37) = 4.81$, $p < .05$. Follow-up t tests showed a difference between conditions for the first interpretation only, $t(37) = 2.05$, $p < .05$. Participants in the high arousal condition showed greater behavioral evidence of understanding and accepting the first interpretation than participants in the low arousal condition. The participants' scores on this measure also showed that they received both interpretations quite positively (overall $M = 2.7$, $SD = 0.6$).

Finally, a two-way multivariate analysis of variance was performed on the three CRF-S scores, with condition (high and low arousal) and counselor (the three counselors) as the independent variables. There were no significant main effects or interactions. This indicated that the arousal manipulations in the two conditions did not affect perceptions of the counselor along social influence dimensions and that the individual counselors in the study were not perceived differently. CRF-S scores were quite high overall (cell $Ms > 22.5$, $SDs < 3.5$), which suggests that the counselors were positively perceived on the three dimensions in both conditions.

Discussion

This study addresses two problems in the use of interpretation in counseling. The first is the question of timing or placement of interpretation in the interview. As Spiegel and Hill (1989) noted, interpretations cannot be assumed to have the same impact regardless of when they occur. Spiegel and Hill recommended that researchers attend to the timing of interpretations so that guidelines for delivering interpretations may not rest simply on untested clinical lore. In this study we conceptualized timing in terms of the placement of interpretations in the context of arousal. The second problem addressed in this study concerns the diversity of interpretation impact. As every practitioner knows, some interpretations create a sense of discomfort in the client, whereas other interpretations have the opposite effect. Levy (1963) argued that the latter ought to be more facilitative of attitude change than the former, an idea we sought to explore in our study.

Our first hypothesis concerns the arousal context of the interpretations. To begin with, we found that the arousal manipulations functioned as intended: Confrontations produced significant arousal over baseline, and reflections did not. This replicates the finding of McCarron and Appel (1971) that confrontations are more arousing than reflections. However, we were only partially successful in creating the conditions for testing Levy's (1963) hypothesis. In the low arousal condition, interpretations were not effective in increasing arousal, and in the high arousal condition, interpretation did reduce arousal after the first confrontation but not after the second. The fact that interpretations in this study were not very arousing, despite their discrepancy, may have been due to their particular form or content. Perhaps purely insight-oriented interpretations are more arousing, particularly those having "Aha!" or "I never thought of that!" effects. Research to explore form and content variables may help to establish a clearer link between interpretation and arousal.

We hypothesized that interpretations in the two arousal conditions would have different effects, and this was the case on some measures. The more positive affective responses of high arousal participants than low arousal participants to the first interpretation is at least consistent with Levy's (1963) hypothesis that arousal reduction may facilitate interpretation acceptance. Only for the first interpretation did arousal reduction occur in one condition but not the other. No differences in response could be expected for the second interpretation, because in neither condition did that interpretation alter arousal.

Participants in the high arousal condition also reported a greater overall acceptance of the interpretations than control participants, a difference not obtained for the low arousal condition. The attitude change findings followed this same pattern, though nonsignificantly. We cannot fully account for these findings with Levy's (1963) explanation, because the measures in question were given after both interpretations had been delivered and because the second interpretations in the two conditions did not exhibit the arousal pattern prescribed by Levy. However, the differential impact of the interpretations almost certainly derived from differences in the experimental manipulations. The confrontations and reflections given in the interviews differed in verbal content by drawing attention to different aspects of participants' experience. The two interventions also differed in nonverbal presentation. Differing levels of arousal resulting from such manipulations, evidenced by the GSR data, may have accounted for the differential impact of the interpretations. This possibility is consistent, certainly, with findings of Hoehn-Saric and colleagues (Hoehn-Saric et al., 1968, 1972) that have indicated that arousal facilitates interpretation.

Other aspects of the experimental manipulation may account for the obtained differences as well. To begin with, the confrontations may have been more interesting or involving than the reflections and thus prompted participants to be more attentive to the interpretations in the high arousal condition. Though data that bear directly on this possibility were not collected, neither the CRF-S nor the recognition data are consistent with it. The counselors themselves were not perceived differently, as may have been expected if the interventions were differentially involving, nor did participants appear to be differentially attentive to the interpretations, at least to an extent that may have affected recognition.

Alternatively, the confrontations may have been perceived as offering more support for the interpretations than the reflections did and thereby made the interpretations in the high arousal condition more convincing. This possibility is taken from the elaboration likelihood model of persuasion (Petty & Cacioppo, 1986), and in particular, from the notion that strong arguments for a message promote more cognitive processing in favor of the message and consequently more attitude change in the direction of the message. If the confrontations in this study served as stronger arguments for the interpretations, as evidenced by perceptual and cognitive response data (Petty & Cacioppo, 1986), this can account for the superiority of interpretations in the high arousal condition. Measures suitable for exploring this possibility were not used in this study, and so it must await further research.

The results of this study are clearly limited by the methodology. Our interpretations differed from the typical insight-producing interventions usually called by that name, though they were consistent with Levy's (1963) conceptualization of interpretation as a discrepant message. Nevertheless, generalization of these results to the interpretive process as a whole must proceed cautiously pending further research. The use of planned interventions, delivered according to a protocol, allowed for the careful control of content in the interview as well as the manipulation of discrepancy. On the other hand, counseling is not typically conducted in this way, and one may wonder as to the appropriateness of the interventions in particular instances. We believe the interventions were generally appropriate, because of the careful protocol design and counselor training. Moreover, the affective response and CRF-S data indicate that participants responded positively to the interpretation and to the entire interview. The analogue methodology used in this study met all of Strong's (1971) boundary conditions for realistic laboratory research in counseling. However, in addition to the artificiality imposed by the protocols, we must also point out that the participants were not real clients, and the treatment lasted only one session. Furthermore, a host of variables characteristic of the counseling process were tightly controlled here, including the characteristics of the counselors, the nature of the problem, and the form and content of the interventions. These variables do not render the results inapplicable to counseling but rather constrain their applicability. The results obtained under these conditions, and other experimental conditions that extend them, must be confirmed ultimately in actual counseling before their implications can be fully appreciated. Studies like ours, we believe, set the stage for such research by clarifying aspects of the change process and sharpening the focus on the mechanisms that underlie it.

References

Claiborn, C. D. (1982). Interpretation and change in counseling. *Journal of Counseling Psychology, 29,* 439–453.

Cooper, J., Zanna, M. P., & Taves, P. A. (1978). Arousal as a necessary condition for attitude change following induced compliance. *Journal of Personality and Social Psychology, 36,* 1101–1106.

Corrigan, J. D., & Schmidt, L. D. (1983). Development and validation of revisions in the Counselor Rating Form. *Journal of Counseling Psychology, 30,* 64–75.

Croyle, R. T., & Cooper, J. (1983). Dissonance arousal: Physiological evidence. *Journal of Personality and Social Psychology, 45,* 782–791.

Dittes, J. E. (1957). Galvanic skin response as a measure of patient's relation to therapist's permissiveness. *Journal of Abnormal and Social Psychology, 55,* 295–303.

Festinger, L. (1957). *A theory of cognitive dissonance.* Stanford, CA: Stanford University Press.

Gerard, H. B. (1967). Choice difficulty, dissonance, and the decision sequence. *Journal of Personality, 35,* 91–108.

Hoehn-Saric, R., Frank, J. D., & Gurland, B. J. (1968). Focused attitude change in neurotic patients. *Journal of Nervous and Mental Diseases, 147,* 124–133.

Hoehn-Saric, R., Liberman, B., Imber, S. D., Stone, A. R., Pande, S. K., & Frank, J. D. (1972). Arousal and attitude change in neurotic patients. *Archives of General Psychiatry, 26,* 51–56.

Kiesler, C. A., & Pallak, M. S. (1976). Arousal properties of dissonance manipulations. *Psychological Bulletin, 83,* 1014–1025.

Levy, L. H. (1963). *Psychological interpretation.* New York: Holt, Rinehart & Winston.

McCarron, L. T., & Appel, V. H. (1971). Categories of therapist verbalizations and patient–therapist autonomic response. *Journal of Consulting and Clinical Psychology, 37,* 123–134.

McMillen, D. L., & Geiselman, J. H. (1974). Effect of cognitive dissonance on alpha frequency activity: The search for dissonance. *Personality and Social Psychology Bulletin, 1,* 150–151.

Petty, R. E., & Cacioppo, J. T. (1986). *Communication and persuasion: Central and peripheral routes to attitude change.* New York: Springer-Verlag.

Pittman, T. S. (1975). Attribution of arousal as a mediator in dissonance reduction. *Journal of Experimental Social Psychology, 11,* 53–63.

Spiegel, S. B., & Hill, C. E. (1989). Guidelines for research on therapist interpretation: Toward greater methodological rigor and relevance to practice. *Journal of Counseling Psychology, 36,* 121–129.

Strong, S. R. (1971). Experimental laboratory research in counseling. *Journal of Counseling Psychology, 18,* 106–110.

Strong, S. R., & Claiborn, C. D. (1982). *Change through interaction: Social psychological processes of counseling and psychotherapy.* New York: Wiley.

Strong, S. R., Wambach, C. A., Lopez, F. G., & Cooper, R. K. (1979). Motivational and equipping functions of interpretation in counseling. *Journal of Counseling Psychology, 26,* 98–107.

Weinstein, P. A. (1978). The feeling brain: The impact of confrontation on the neural affective systems (Doctoral dissertation, University of Nebraska—Lincoln, 1978). *Dissertation Abstracts International, 39,* 4060B.

Zanna, M. P., & Cooper, J. (1974). Dissonance and the pill: An attribution approach to studying the arousal properties of dissonance. *Journal of Personality and Social Psychology, 29,* 703–709.

Chapter 16
THERAPIST BEHAVIOR AS A DETERMINANT
FOR CLIENT NONCOMPLIANCE:
A Paradox for the Behavior Modifier

G. R. Patterson and M. S. Forgatch

For the present studies, noncompliance was presumed to be a ubiquitous behavior for children and adults alike. It is paradoxical that certain situations (e.g., parent training) designed to help the client may actually stimulate the client to work against the therapist. Analyses of videotaped parent training sessions by Chamberlain, Patterson, Reid, Kavanagh, and Forgatch (1984) showed that the average rate of parent noncompliant behavior was .17 responses per minute during the initial stages of treatment. This increased significantly to more than .30 responses per minute during the midstages of treatment. These findings led to the hypothesis that therapists' efforts to change parent behavior may function as an important determinant for parent noncompliance during treatment. The present studies tested this hypothesis.

Client noncompliance is viewed as the outcome of two sets of variables (Patterson, 1984). The first set, thought to be major determinants for initial levels, involves personal and social factors brought by the parent to treatment. The second set of variables come to play an increasingly important role during middle and late treatment. They consist of measures of therapist efforts to directly intervene (i.e., teach or confront).

The formulation rests on a set of assumptions about the nature of client noncompliance (Patterson, 1984). It assumes bidirectional effects for parent and therapist, each altering the other's behavior. It also assumes that noncompliance should be analyzed at micro- and macrolevels. The microlevel concerns observable events in the therapy sequence; the macrolevel refers to compliance between sessions in carrying out assignments. The model requires that the two measures covary. In a pilot study (Patterson, 1984), observers viewed videotapes of treatment and rated the parents' between-sessions noncompliance. The ratings correlated .64 with the microlevel measure of noncompliance. Although not yet tested, the two measures together are assumed to provide the best predictor for treatment outcome.

The real power of an analytic focus on client–therapist exchanges lies in its

Reprinted from *Journal of Consulting and Clinical Psychology, 53,* 846–851 (1985). Copyright © 1985 by the American Psychological Association. Used with permission of the first author.

A series of studies on therapy process and client noncompliance, of which the two present studies were part, was supported by a grant from the John D. and Catherine T. MacArthur Foundation. Final write-up of this manuscript was supported in part by National Institute of Mental Health Grant 1 R01 MH 38318.

An earlier version of this article was presented at the annual meeting of the American Psychological Association, July 1982, Washington, DC.

We gratefully acknowledge the contribution of J. Reid and P. Chamberlain, who critiqued earlier drafts of this article and assisted development of the concepts presented herein, and to I. August, T. Dishion, P. Gabrielson, K. Gardner, K. Kavanagh, and S. McCarthy for their careful coding of innumerable videotapes.

ability to identify, on a moment-by-moment basis, what one person does that alters the behavior of another (Gottman & Bakeman, 1979). In the present context, this implies studying what the therapist does that has an immediate impact on parent noncompliance. The important restriction is the failure to identify delayed effects. A micromeasure could generate false negative errors if client noncompliance is delayed by minutes, hours, or days.

The present two studies examined the immediate impact of therapist behavior on client noncompliance. The first study analyzed data for six therapist–client pairs, comparing the conditional likelihood of parent noncompliance given therapist efforts to teach or confront with the base-rate likelihood of parent noncompliance. The hypothesis tested for each dyad was that the conditional likelihood of noncompliance would be higher than the base-rate likelihood. The second study tested the hypothesis that therapist efforts to teach and confront are causally related to parent noncompliance. These therapist behaviors were manipulated in a set of single-subject ABAB reversal designs. The hypothesis tested was that increases in therapist "teach" and "confront" behaviors during experimental (B) phases would be accompanied by increases in client noncompliance; when these therapist behaviors were decreased (A phases), reductions in client noncompliance were expected. An analysis of variance (ANOVA) for repeated measures tested the significance of the comparisons.

Study 1

This study tested the hypothesis that therapist efforts to teach and confront would be followed by increased likelihoods for noncompliance. There was a related interest in determining whether therapist efforts to facilitate, reframe, and support would be accompanied by immediate reductions in parent noncompliance.

The analyses were carried out separately for each of six therapist–mother dyads. In each analysis, six therapist behaviors were examined for their potential impact on the mothers' behavior that immediately followed the event.

Method

Sample

Subjects were six families with child management problems: Five families were referred because the target child was socially aggressive, and one was referred because the boy was chronically delinquent. Target children were five boys and one girl; the mean age was 9.9 (range = 4.0 to 13.1 years). The mean socioeconomic status of the families as measured by Hollingshead's (1975) four-factor index of social status was 31.9 (range = 11 to 50). Fifty percent of the families were absent a father.

General Procedure

The sample was composed of treated cases with complete sets of videotapes. Data were combined from all phases of treatment. Although other family members were typically present during treatment sessions, only mother data were analyzed in this study. Cases were randomly assigned to coders by family and by treatment session to prevent bias due to either familiarity with the family or expectation based on sequence.

Client behavior and therapist behavior were scored independently from videotapes using two separate groups of coders. Client behavior was scored first by one set of coders using the Client Noncompliance Code; in doing so, they also earmarked space for therapist behaviors. The second time through, the new group of coders categorized the therapist behaviors using the Therapist Behavior Code. Behavior was coded on time lines to retain the sequence of therapist–client interaction for a treatment session.

A unit consisted of a therapist speech episode followed by a client reaction. In some instances, the therapist might be characterized by two code categories; the client behavior was reflected in only one category. Coded sessions averaged 47 min (range = 20 to 86); average number of sessions was 21 (range = 12 to 35).

Client Noncompliance Code. Developed by Kavanagh, Gabrielson, and Chamberlain (1982), the Client Noncompliance Code (CNC) is a mutually exclusive, exhaustive six-category coding system designed to study client noncompliant behavior in therapy sessions. Five categories describe noncompliant behavior ("interrupt," "negative attitude," "confront," "own agenda," "not tracking"), and one category describes all cooperative behavior. To facilitate the statistical analyses, the data from the five noncompliant categories were combined, constituting the denominator used to calculate the conditional probability values.

Therapist Behavior Code. Developed by Forgatch and Chamberlain (1982), the Therapist Behavior Code (TBC) consists of seven exhaustive and mutually exclusive categories that describe therapist verbal behavior during a treatment session. The categories include: "support," "teach," "question," "confront," "reframe," "talk," and "facilitate."

Treatment

The treatment procedures developed over the past decade (Forgatch, Chamberlain, Patterson, & Gabrielson, 1982; Patterson, 1984; Patterson, Reid, Jones, & Conger, 1975) call for teaching parents a set of consistent methods for altering both the pro- and antisocial behaviors of the problem child. This requires that parents alter their reactions to the target child and his or her siblings. The treatment requires an average of 20 hr of professional time (range = 10 to 30 hr).

Therapists

Therapists were three female master's-level and two (one female, one male) doctorate-level clinicians. Our prior pilot studies with small samples of therapists have not shown a significant effect for sex of therapist in determining level of client noncompliance.

The range of experience for the master's-level clinicians was 2 to 6 years and for the doctorate-level clinicians, 7 to 15 years. All therapists had worked at the center for at least one year. Cases were assigned to therapists on a nonsystematic basis.

Results

Reliabilities

To determine the reliability of the CNC, 13 videotapes were randomly drawn from a total sample of 115 and coded independently by two observers. The mean entry-by-entry percentage of agreement was .74. The comparable analysis of the TBC showed a 75% agreement.

The critical consideration was the reliability of the six conditional probability values serving as dependent variables in analyses. These values were calculated separately for the 13 videotapes viewed by the pairs of observers. The correlation between their scores was .60 ($p < .01$) for the likelihood of client noncompliance given therapist "support"; .77 ($p < .001$) for therapist "teach"; .66 ($p < .01$) for therapist "question"; .47 ($p < .07$) for therapist "confront"; .61 ($p < .05$) for therapist "reframe"; and .49 ($p < .05$) for therapist "facilitate." The mean correlation for the combined conditionals was .78 ($p < .001$).

Impact of Therapist Behavior

To test the hypothesis concerning the covariation in therapist and client reaction sequences, the data were analyzed separately for each therapist–client dyad. Table 1 summarizes the relevant data for each subject. For each subject, the conditional probability value was compared with the base-rate likelihood of noncompliance (non-comply/comply + noncomply). The binomial z was used to determine the level of significance for each comparison.[1]

The main hypothesis was that directive therapist behaviors (i.e., "teach" and "confront") would tend to elicit immediate client noncompliance. Support for the hypothesis would require that for each dyad the conditional likelihood of client noncompliance given therapist "teach" or "confront" could be significantly higher than the base-rate likelihood for client noncompliance. It can be seen (row 1 of Table 1) that for "teach," the comparisons were in the expected direction in four of the six comparisons. More intrusive efforts to reeducate the parent, as in the category "confront" (row 2), were associated with significant increases over the base-rate likelihood in three of the six comparisons.

The data offer consistent support for the main hypothesis. Efforts of experienced staff to teach family management procedures are likely to produce an immediate increase in the noncompliance for mothers of antisocial children.

The secondary analysis examined the possibility that some therapist behaviors

---

[1]Sackett (1977) and Gottman and Bakeman (1979) argued that the assumptions underlying the z statistic are violated when base-rate values are close to .01 and/or the number of behaviors in the denominator falls below N_{25}. Approximately 18% of the therapist behaviors had base rates of .01 or less in the present study. Furthermore, it should be noted that the binomial z is not an exact test, and the values should be thought of as only approximations to a t test.

Table 1—*Likelihood of Subject Noncompliance Given Various Therapist Behaviors*

	Therapist behavior					
Subject	Teach (.223)[a]	Confront (.031)	Facilitate (.243)	Support (.185)	Reframe (.047)	Question (.215)
1 (.032)[b]						
p (X$_1$)	.207	.018	.319	.175	.033	.208
Cond. p	.041	.079	.099	.022	.055	.026
z	2.28*	2.56*	−7.22***	−2.08*	1.74*	−1.40
2 (.143)						
p (X$_1$)	.293	.036	.163	.157	.046	.237
Cond. p	.130	.035	.020	.052	.135	.031
z	−1.46	−2.94**	−7.93***	−5.81***	−.24	−9.43***
3 (.072)						
p (X$_1$)	.205	.009	.228	.243	.021	.233
Cond. p	.092	—	.016	.039	.097	.029
z	2.74**	—	−7.16***	−4.72***	.770	−5.78***
4 (.141)						
p (X$_1$)	.171	.051	.311	.176	.079	.163
Cond. p	.189	.225	.039	.109	.170	.091
z	5.83***	4.68***	−17.76***	−3.80***	2.06*	−5.61***
5 (.218)						
p (X$_1$)	.231	.037	.188	.208	.044	.221
Cond. p	.327	.338	.097	.172	.253	.082
z	7.75***	2.53*	−6.51***	−2.71**	.80	−8.18***
6 (.135)						
p (X$_1$)	.232	.032	.246	.149	.059	.227
Cond. p	.097	.127	.064	.088	.084	.030
z	−4.46***	−.26	−8.44***	−3.79***	−2.29*	−11.22***

Note. p (X$_1$) = base-rate likelihood of the behavior. Cond. p = conditional probability of subject noncompliance to the therapist behavior. z = level of significance of comparison of cond. p with base-rate likelihood of subject noncompliance.
[a]Mean percentage of therapist behavior.
[b]Base-rate likelihood of noncompliance of subject.
*$p < .05$.   **$p < .01$.   ***$p < .001$.

(e.g., "support" and "facilitate") are associated with immediate decreases in the conditional probability of noncompliant client behavior. Both of these therapist behaviors were associated with highly significant decreases in the conditional probability of noncompliance in all six cases. A comparison of base-rate values for noncompliance to the conditional likelihood for "reframe" showed a trend to increase noncompliance in four of the six comparisons; only one significantly decreased noncompliance.

The data provide modest but consistent support for two of the three hypotheses. Therapist efforts to reeducate parents (i.e., "teach" and "confront") were associated with increases in client noncompliance. Therapist "facilitate" and "support" were accompanied by decreased likelihoods of client noncompliance.

Study 2

Finding significant associations between therapist behaviors and subsequent client noncompliance does not, of course, prove that the former causes the latter. Even though the therapist behavior precedes the client behavior in the sequence, some third unknown variable could have produced the effect. Study 2 examined whether the causal status of the behaviors found in Study 1 was associated with an increase in the base rate of the client's immediate noncompliance.

Each of seven therapist–parent dyads participated in a single-subject ABAB design. During the B phases, the therapists increased their "teach" and "confront" behaviors; during the A phases, they refrained as best they could from using these behaviors. The hypothesis was tested by comparing the likelihood of client noncompliance during experimental periods with the likelihood for the baseline period. If therapist "teach" and "confront" serve as significant determinants, then client noncompliance should be higher when these variables are increased and lower when they are reduced. It should also be the case that a repeated measures ANOVA would demonstrate significant differences between the conditions.

Method

Subjects

Subjects were seven families with child management problems. One family from Study 1 took part in Study 2. Four of the families were referred because the target child was socially aggressive; three families were referred for child abuse. Target children were four girls and three boys, with a mean age of 7.8 years (range = 3.8 to 12.8). The mean socioeconomic status (Hollingshead, 1975) of the families was a relatively low 27.4 (range = 20 to 45). Five were father-absent families.

Therapists

Therapists were the same as in Study 1 (except for the male doctorate-level clinician with 15 years' experience).

Measures

Sessions were videotaped and coded using the CNC and TBC in the same fashion as in Study 1.

General Procedure

Cases were selected for this study only if they had been in treatment for a minimum of 5 weeks. Therapists role-played the procedure with another therapist prior to this study. The study used an $A_1B_1A_2B_2$ design. Phases were planned to last 8 to 12 min ($M = 9.9$; range, 6 to 22). During the experimental (B) phases, therapists were to use frequent "confront" and "teach" behaviors. During the A phases, therapists were to refrain from using either "teach" or "confront." Following the last B phase, a nonexperimental (A_3) period ensued, allowing the therapist use of the full spectrum of behaviors to conduct business, sum up, give assignments, and so on.

To decrease the intrusive effect of the manipulation, therapists timed the shift from one phase to another. When appropriate, they would manipulate a readily visible notepad as a sign to the observers that the shift had occurred. During the A phases, they held their notepad in their laps; during the B phases they placed the notepad on the floor beside them.

Results

Reliability

For the CNC and TBC, two of the seven videotapes were coded independently by two observers. The mean entry-by-entry percentage of agreement was .65 (range = .63 to .68) and .75 (range = .72 to .79) for the CNC and TBC, respectively.

Effects of Experimental Manipulation

The data show that the manipulated control of client noncompliance was clearly related to therapist "teach" and "confront" behavior: In both experimental phases, client noncompliance increased when therapist "teach" and "confront" increased. In B_1, as the rate of therapist "teach" and "confront" was increased from 0.06 to 1.02 per minute, the rate of client noncompliant behaviors rose from 0.45 to 0.76 per minute; in B_2, the increased rate of therapist "teach" and "confront" behaviors from 0.11 to 1.66 per minute was matched by an increased rate of client noncompliant behaviors from 0.51 to 0.69 per minute. When therapists reduced their level of "teach" and "confront," client behaviors returned to baseline levels.

While "teach" and "confront" increased in rate from B_1 to B_2, there was a slight drop in client noncompliance, suggesting that variables other than therapist "teach" and "confront" may also function as determinants for client noncompliance.

During the baseline periods, the therapists were not perfectly controlled: They practically doubled their rates of "teach" and/or "confront" during the second, compared with the first, baseline (.06 per minute during A_1 and .11 during A_2).

A statistical comparison of the mean values for maternal noncompliance across the four phases showed significant differences. A repeated measures ANOVA was carried out after transforming the data using natural logs. The F value comparing the four phases was $F(1, 5) = 11.74$, $p < .02$. Baseline to experimental comparison was $F(3, 15) = 3.48$, $p < .05$.

Discussion

Both studies provide strong support for the hypothesis that therapist efforts to teach and confront during parent training produce significant increases in the likelihood that the client's immediate reaction will be noncompliant. Therapist "support" and "facilitate" were also accompanied by reduced likelihoods of noncompliance. The paradox is that even the efforts of well-trained therapists may be met with client noncompliance.[2] If this is the case, it seems that social learning therapists require a dual set of technologies. One set describes parent training skills; the other describes means for coping effectively with client noncompliance.

From the interactional stance taken in this article, it is assumed that client noncompliance alters the behavior of the therapist. Given prolonged noncompliance, the therapist may come to evaluate the family in a negative way. In effect, the client may teach the therapist to remain distant, to refrain from teaching parenting skills, to neglect following up on missed appointments, and eventually to not bring this apparently hopeless case up for staff review. We see weekly staff meetings as a necessary component because they serve as an antidote to such effects produced by client noncompliance, and the staff supports the therapist, providing new bursts of enthusiasm and generating new ideas on how to cope with noncompliance.

The results from these two studies are promising. They suggest that it may be possible to subject hypotheses about client noncompliance to empirical analyses that are both significant and clinically meaningful. The findings also emphasize the necessity for studying the key question: Given that necessary therapist behaviors increase client noncompliance, how does a skilled therapist reduce noncompliance?

References

Chamberlain, P., Patterson, G. R., Reid, J. B., Kavanagh, K., & Forgatch, M. S. (1984). Observation of client resistance. *Behavior Therapy, 15,* 144–155.

Forgatch, M. S., & Chamberlain, P. (1982). *The Therapist Behavior Code.* Unpublished instrument and technical report, Oregon Social Learning Center, Eugene.

Forgatch, M. S., Chamberlain, P., Patterson, G. R., & Gabrielson, P. (1982). *Time out* [Videotape]. Eugene, OR: Castalia.

Gottman, J. M., & Bakeman, R. (1979). The sequential analysis of observation data. In S. Suomi, M. Lamb, & G. Stephenson (Eds.), *Social interaction analysis: Methodological issues* (pp. 185–206). Madison: University of Wisconsin Press.

Hollingshead, A. B. (1975). *Four-factor index of social status.* Unpublished manuscript, Yale University.

Kavanagh, K., Gabrielson, P., & Chamberlain, P. (1982). *Manual for coding client resistance* (Tech. Rep. No. A.2). Eugene, OR: Oregon Social Learning Center.

Patterson, G. R. (1984). *Treatment process: A problem at three levels* (NIMH proposal MH 38730). Eugene, OR: Oregon Social Learning Center.

Patterson, G. R., Reid, J. B., Jones, R. R., & Conger, R. E. (1975). *A social learning approach to family intervention: Families with aggressive children* (Vol. 1). Eugene, OR: Castalia.

Sackett, G. P. (1977). The lag sequential analysis of contingency and cyclicity in behavioral interaction research. In J. Osofsky (Ed.), *Handbook of infant development* (pp. 623–649). New York: Wiley.

---

[2]It would also be of interest to discover what determines when the therapists will teach or confront. Is it client noncompliance itself that leads the therapist to initiate these behaviors? A comparison of the base rate for therapist "teach" with the conditional probability of "teach" given client noncompliance produced large shifts in probability for only two of the five therapists.

Part V

Insight Stage—Interpretation

INTRODUCTION

Psychoanalytic therapists regard interpretations as the "pure gold" of therapy, the central skill used to help clients gain self-knowledge (Hill & O'Brien, 1999). Not surprisingly, then, some of the best and most innovative research in the helping skills area has been on therapist interpretation. In fact, it was difficult to choose among studies because there were so many excellent ones. Although the studies are presented in alphabetical order, we discuss them here in chronological order to draw attention to the significant advances that have been made over time studying the effects of interpretation in therapy.

In 1959, Speisman (see chapter 21) found that moderately deep interpretations led to more exploration and less resistance than deep or superficial interpretations. Because this study has been cited so often in helping skills literature, it is instructive to examine this study closely. Speisman rated interpretive activity in every therapist statement on a 7-point scale and then divided the scale into three levels of interpretation: superficial (levels 1.0–2.4), moderate (levels 2.5–4.4), and deep (levels 4.5–7.0). He examined interpretive activity within all therapist statements rather than just those therapist statements that were identified as interpretations. A comparison of these definitions with those used by Hill and O'Brien (1999) suggests that Speisman's superficial interpretations were restatements, his moderate interpretations were accurate interpretations, and his deep interpretations were inaccurate interpretations. Hence, this scale seems to have at least two dimensions: type and quality of intervention. Reformulating Speisman's results from this perspective would indicate that good interpretations lead to more exploration and less resistance than inaccurate interpretations or restatements.

The 1985 Claiborn and Dowd (see chapter 17) study was chosen to represent several experimental studies that tested interpretation in terms of social psychological principles about therapy as a persuasion process (e.g., Claiborn, Crawford, & Hackman, 1983; Claiborn, Ward, & Strong, 1981; Forsyth & Forsyth, 1982; Hoffman & Teglasi, 1982; Strong, Wambach, Lopez, & Cooper, 1979). In this study, Claiborn and Dowd tested the effects of the attributional content of interpretations (i.e., the cause to which the client attributed their behavior). The depressed clients used in the study had either a behavioral attributional style (i.e., belief that negative emotions were due to behaviors and could be changed) or a characterological attributional style (i.e., belief that negative emotions were due to personalities and could not be changed easily). The clients were given either behavioral interpretations (e.g., "When you choose to skip your brother's wedding, you feel guilty") or characterological interpretations (e.g., "The way you have been describing yourself tells me you are a perfectionistic type of person, which can lead to loneliness"). Although the content of the interpretations (e.g., behavioral vs. characterological) was irrelevant to change in clients' negative emotions, attributional styles, and problem-related attributions, clients who had characterological attributional styles responded more favorably to characterological interpretations than to behavioral interpretations. The authors suggested that hypothesized results for the behavioral group might not have been found because the clients were more at the midpoint instead of being strongly behavioral in their attributions.

Silberschatz, Fretter, and Curtis (1986) conducted an important study on three therapy cases and found that the suitability of therapist interpretations was more predictive of client productivity than was type of interpretation (transference vs. nontransference). In 1988, Crits-Christoph, Cooper, and Luborsky (see chapter 18) followed up on the Silberschatz et al. study by using a larger sample. They examined the effects of the accuracy of therapist interpretations, basing their definition of accuracy on the similarity of the interpretation to judgments of the client's central relationship pattern. The relationship pattern was assessed though the core conflictual relationship theme (CCRT) method, which codes client wishes, responses of the other person, and responses of the self in narratives about relationships told by clients in therapy. Crits-Christoph et al. found that the accuracy of interpretations in terms of client wishes and responses from the other person was significantly related to treatment outcome. Furthermore, this relationship was not influenced by general therapist errors in technique or the quality of the therapeutic alliance.

In 1993, Piper, Joyce, McCallum, and Azim (see chapter 20) examined the effects of transference interpretations (i.e., interpretations that focus on the client's reactions to the therapist) on therapeutic alliance and treatment outcome. They found a minimal correlation between the frequency of occurrence of transference interpretation (which they called *concentration*) and accuracy (which they called *correspondence*). Furthermore, they found that for clients with low interpersonal capacity, concentration was not related to the therapeutic alliance or treatment outcome, but correspondence was negatively related to the therapeutic alliance and follow-up outcome. The authors suggested that therapists should avoid using transference interpretations with clients who have interpersonal deficits because such interpretations might make these clients feel rejected and abandoned. In contrast, clients with high interpersonal capacity may be more likely to benefit from transference interpretations given the results that they had the best outcome at follow-up when they were given infrequent but highly accurate transference interpretations. We emphasize, however, that the Crits-Christoph et al. and Piper et al. studies both examined the correlation between transference interpretations and outcome rather than examining the immediate effects of specific transference interpretations.

Taking a different approach, Elliott et al. (1994, see chapter 19) first identified events in which clients indicated that they had gained insight and then worked backward to determine the antecedents of the insight. Using comprehensive process analysis, they found that the most common therapist interventions leading to client insight were therapist interpretations that were well-grounded in the client material; exemplified the therapist's orientation; and were delivered in a firm, persistent, but interactive style. Elliott et al. showed that it was not just a simple therapist interpretation—client insight sequence that accounted for the gains in client insight. Rather, several stages could be distinguished, which involved the development of the therapeutic alliance and background information about the client, the client expressing puzzlement over their reactions, the therapist giving an interpretation, the client thinking over the interpretation, the client coming to an insight, and then the client exploring and elaborating on the insight.

In summary, therapist interpretation seems to be effective in leading to high levels of client exploration, experiencing, insight and to low levels of resistance. However, characteristics of the interpretation seem to moderate their effects on clients. For example, the depth of the interpretation, the amount of discrepancy between the interpretation and the client's beliefs, and the accuracy of the interpretation for the individual client seem to play a role in the outcome of the interpretation. Furthermore, transference interpretations may by useful for interpersonally-adept clients when used infrequently but may be contraindicated for clients with interpersonal deficits. Finally, it appears that interpretations are highly dependent on the context of therapy and take some time to be incorporated by clients, so examining the stages of the impact of interpretation may be more appropriate than examining a simplistic one-step sequence such as therapist interpretation leading to client insight.

References

Claiborn, C. D., Crawford, J. B., & Hackman, H. W. (1983). Effects of intervention discrepancy in counseling for negative emotions. *Journal of Counseling Psychology, 30,* 164–171.

Claiborn, C. D., Ward, S. R., & Strong, S. R. (1981). Effects of congruence between counselor interpretation and client beliefs. *Journal of Counseling Psychology, 28,* 101–109.

Forsyth, N. L., & Forsyth, D. R. (1982). Internality, controllability, and the effectiveness of attributional interpretations in counseling. *Journal of Counseling Psychology, 29,* 140–150.

Hill, C. E., & O'Brien, K. M. (1999). *Helping skills: Facilitating exploration, insight, and action.* Washington, DC: American Psychological Association.

Hoffman. M. A., & Teglasi, H. (1982). The role of causal attributions in counseling shy subjects. *Journal of Counseling Psychology, 29,* 132–139.

Silberschatz, G., Fretter, P. B., & Curtis, J. T. (1986). How do interpretations influence the process of psychotherapy? *Journal of Consulting and Clinical Psychology, 54,* 646–652.

Speisman, J. C. (1959). Depth of interpretation and verbal resistance in psychotherapy. *Journal of Consulting Psychology, 23,* 93–99.

Strong, S. R., Wambach, C. A., Lopez, F. G., & Cooper, R. K. (1979). Motivational and equipping functions of interpretation in counseling. *Journal of Counseling Psychology, 26,* 98–107.

Chapter 17
ATTRIBUTIONAL INTERPRETATIONS IN COUNSELING:
Content Versus Discrepancy

Charles D. Claiborn and E. Thomas Dowd

One of the most puzzling questions in the study of interpretation in counseling is the role played by interpretation content. Discussing the failure of researchers to demonstrate that the content of interpretation is relevant to its functioning, Claiborn (1982) speculated that perhaps the right content variables had simply not been identified. He suggested that interpretation researchers focus on client problems for which specific content variables have been shown to be important; these problem-relevant variables might enhance the contribution of interpretation content to the change process.

One such problem area is negative emotions. Recent research has revealed that emotional difficulties, particularly those characterized by depressed affect, have identifiable attributional components. Seligman, Abramson, Semmel, and von Baeyer (1979) found that depressed, as compared with nondepressed, individuals attributed bad outcomes to internal (to the person), stable (over time), and global (across situation) causes; this led the authors to postulate a depressive attributional style. Peplau, Russell, and Heim (1979) found that although lonely individuals attributed their loneliness to various causes, they were more likely to be depressed if their attributions were internal and stable. Research of Peterson, Schwartz, and Seligman (1981), however, indicated that characterological attributions, which combine internality with stability and globality, were associated with depressive symptoms, whereas behavioral attributions, also internal but neither stable nor global, were not. Presumably, behavioral causes are more accessible to personal control and modification than characterological causes, and give individuals a greater sense of efficacy in coping with negative emotions.

This research has immediate implications for the study of interpretation content. If some problems are maintained by the attributions clients make about events in their lives—as Abramson, Seligman, and Teasdale (1978) have suggested in the case of depression—then it is likely that interventions designed to alter these attributions would contribute to improvement. Conversely, interventions offering attributions compatible with the problem would be less effective, because they would do little to remove attributional components of the problem. This prediction of differential effectiveness as a function of certain content variables—in this case, the attributional dimensions of interventions—is the sort of content hypothesis Claiborn (1982) recommended to interpretation researchers. Such a hypothesis, drawn from the attri-

Reprinted from *Journal of Counseling Psychology, 32,* 188–196 (1985). Copyright © 1985 by the American Psychological Association. Used with permission of the first author.

An earlier version of this article was presented at the annual meeting of the American Psychological Association, Anaheim, California, August 1983.

The authors wish to thank Laura Boettcher, Tom Guck, Mike Kavan, Doug Olson, and Joe Swoboda for helping with the study.

butional theory of depression (Abramson et al., 1978), was tested in the present study of interpretation for clients with negative emotions: It was hypothesized that interpretations advocating behavioral attributions would produce greater improvement than interpretations advocating characterological attributions.

The content hypothesis has received little support in previous interpretation research (e.g., Hoffman & Teglasi, 1982; Strong, Wambach, Lopez, & Cooper, 1979), although content in these studies was not manipulated on dimensions specifically related to client problems. Because support was weak, however, the present study also examined a contrasting hypothesis cited by Claiborn (1982) that has received stronger support: the discrepancy hypothesis. Several researchers have found that the discrepancy of interpretations from client beliefs is important to their functioning (Claiborn, Crawford, & Hackman, 1983; Claiborn, Ward, & Strong, 1981; Forsyth & Forsyth, 1982). It seems that using interpretation to offer clients a set of concepts or beliefs divergent from their own facilitates change, independent of interpretation content. Although the optimal degree of discrepancy is not entirely clear (see Claiborn et al., 1983), moderate discrepancies have tended to be more effective than very large ones (Claiborn et al., 1981; Forsyth & Forsyth, 1982). Interpretations that do not differ greatly from client beliefs are perhaps more easily understood and assimilated by clients. This aspect of the discrepancy hypothesis was further explored in this study as an alternative to the content hypothesis. Thus, it was hypothesized that interpretations only moderately discrepant from client attributional styles (the client-beliefs variable in this study) would produce greater improvement than highly discrepant interpretations, regardless of interpretation content.

The content and discrepancy hypotheses were tested in a study of brief counseling for negative emotions. The study was conducted according to a $2 \times 2 \times 2$ factorial design, with client attributional style and the attributional content of interpretations as independent variables and repeated measures as the third factor. Clients exhibiting either behavioral or characterological attributional styles were given interpretations that contained either behavioral or characterological attributions. Thus, interpretation discrepancy was determined by the complete crossing of two kinds of client attributional style with two kinds of interpretation content to make two moderately discrepant and two highly discrepant conditions. (A match between client attributional style and interpretation content—as when both are behavioral, for example—was considered moderately discrepant rather than nondiscrepant, because interpretations always differ somewhat from client beliefs, often relabeling and clarifying beliefs with which they essentially agree; see Claiborn et al., 1983.) Repeated measures assessed changes in clients' attributional styles, particular problem-related attributions, and negative emotions.

Method

Clients

Clients were 38 college students, 29 females and 9 males, recruited through introductory educational psychology courses. They received course credit for participating. Criteria for inclusion in the study were that they (a) currently were experiencing problematic negative emotions (feeling depressed, down, blue, or discouraged) such as might result from a recent failure, rejection, or loss; (b) scored between 10 and 32 (mildly to moderately depressed) on the Beck Depression Inventory (BDI; Beck, 1967); and (c) exhibited either a behavioral (internal, unstable, specific) or characterological (internal, stable, global) attributional style for bad outcomes on the Attributional Style Questionnaire (ASQ; Peterson et al., 1982).

Independent Variables

Client Attributional Style

Median splits on the stability and globality subscales of ASQ placed clients into either behavioral or characterological attributional style groups, as defined by Peterson et al. (1981). Clients below the median on both subscales were placed in the behavioral group; clients above the median on both subscales were placed in the characterological group. The clients generally tended toward characterological attributional styles, as might be expected given the relationship between this style and problematic negative emotions; medians on both stability and globality were somewhat above the subscale midpoints of 24. Thus, in the behavioral group, about half of the scores on at least one of these subscales fell between 24 and 31, that is, slightly to the characterological side. As a consequence, attributional styles of the behavioral group were not distinctly behavioral but represented the middle of the behavioral–characterological continuum. However, they were clearly less characterological than the attributional styles of the characterological group.

Interpretation Content

The interpretations attributed the client's negative emotions, or events that had precipitated them, to either behavioral or characterological causes. *Behavioral* and *characterological* were operationalized according to the guidelines of Peterson et al. (1981): Behavioral causes included particular overt actions and cognitions of the client in particular situations. For example, one behavioral interpretation was: "Your feelings are caused by how you react to situations. When you chose to [behavior], you set yourself up to feel [negative emotion]." The behaviors, in this case, might be something like "skip your brother's wedding" or "not tell her what was bothering you," and the negative emotions, "guilty" or "resentful," respectively. Characterological causes were qualities or traits of the client. One of the characterological interpretations was: "The way you have been describing yourself tells me that you are a [stable, global trait] kind of person. This can cause you to feel [negative emotion]." The trait, in this case, might be "perfectionistic," and negative emotion, "disappointed with the ways things turn out"; or the trait might be "introverted," and the negative emotion, "left out" or "lonely." Whereas the emphasis of the behavioral interpretations was on the temporal instability and situational specificity of the client's behavior, characterological interpretations focused on the stability of the client's characteristics over time and their globality across situations. Behavioral and characterological interpretations were used in the study primarily because of the behavioral–characterological distinction in the attributional theory of depression, and less because of an interest in them as treatments. However, they were not unlike interpretations found in cognitive–behavioral and trait–factor (or even psychody-namic) approaches to counseling, respectively.

Counseling was administered in two 30-min interviews, each containing two interpretations in the latter half of the interview and a summary interpretation at the end. The interviews were conducted according to a standardized format to help con-trol for the irrelevant effects of content. The first half of each interview was devoted to problem exploration by means of probes, reflection, and paraphrase. The second half of each interview continued this exploration as influenced by the interpretations, which were spaced 5–7 min apart. Each interpretation was approximately 20 words long and delivered according to the predetermined wording, except that supporting data from the client's life were included to enhance its personal relevance. The summary interpretation integrated the content of the interpretations previously given. The use of a standardized interview format to manipulate interpretation content has been quite successful in previous counseling research (e.g., Claiborn et al., 1983; Strong et al., 1979). The present study closely followed these models.

Manipulation Check

A manipulation check was conducted after the completion of the study to determine whether the interpretations were perceived as intended. Twelve students, recruited from the same undergraduate courses as the clients in the study and exhibiting BDI scores comparable to those of the clients, attended a single interview containing either behavioral or characterological interpretations. The interpretations were ad-ministered in exactly the same way as in the first interview of the actual study, and by two of the three counselors from that study. The students were randomly assigned to interpretation treatments and counselors. After the interview, they completed two instruments: The first, a recall instrument, was a blank page on which the students were instructed to "list as many things as you remember that your counselor said to you about your negative emotions in the interview." Second, a recognition instrument listed five interpretation summaries, each two sentences long, and instructed students to place a check mark beside any summary "very close to the general idea" of what the counselor said to them in the interview. The five summaries included one each of the behavioral and characterological causal frameworks and three other summaries (adapted from interpretations used in similar research) that were neither behavioral nor characterological. Interpretation summaries were used instead of verbatim inter-pretations because interpretations delivered in the interviews were to some extent individually tailored. However, this gave the instrument the added advantage of test-ing whether the theme, as opposed to the wording, of the interpretations could be recognized.

Data from both instruments indicated that the interpretations were perceived as intended. On the recall instrument, two judges, blind to the interpretation treatments to which students had been assigned, were able to place all 12 students' responses into behavioral and characterological categories correctly. Students in the behavioral group, in every case, indicated that particular thoughts or behaviors "trigger" (to quote one student) the negative emotions; students in the characterological group consistently identified traits (e.g., "self-critical," "dependent," "perfectionistic") as the source of their problems. On the recognition instrument, all 12 students checked the interpretation summary appropriate to their treatment. Three of the students also checked a second summary, but not as a function of either treatment or counselor; moreover, it was a different incorrect summary in each case.

Counselors

The counselors in the study were three male doctoral students in counseling psychology. All were experienced counselors, having worked at least 2 years in an agency setting and completed two semesters of practicum. They were also quite verbally articulate. They were unfamiliar with the purpose of the study. Over a 2-week period, they rehearsed the standardized interview format with each set of interpretations until they were able to follow it reliably and deliver the interpretations appropriately. During the interviews, they used nonverbal cues associated with both expertness and attractiveness, including a relaxed, open posture; assured tone of voice; and occasional smiles, head nods, and hand gestures. They highlighted the interpretations with an emphatic tone of voice. They used cue sheets to insure that they conducted the interviews as intended, and they occasionally took notes during the interview in order to better remember and use client data.

Instruments

The Beck Depression Inventory was used to assess the degree of negative affect experienced by the clients. It consists of 21 clusters of four symptoms, with the symptoms in each cluster listed in order of severity. A client's score on each cluster is the number (from 0 to 3) attached to the most severe symptom he or she reports having. Scores thus range from 0 to 63. Reliability and validity of the instrument are reported by Beck (1967).

The Attributional Style Questionnaire was used to assess the general attributional style of clients. Attributional style refers to a characteristic way of forming attributions across events; like a style of communicating, it may be relatively stable, but not unmodifiable. On the ASQ, attributional styles are assessed along dimensions of internality, stability, and globality. Internality refers to the extent to which causes of events reside in or with the person, stability is the extent to which causes remain the same over time, and globality is the extent to which causes apply to events other than the one in question. The instrument presents 12 events, 6 with bad and 6 with good outcomes, and asks the individual to list the major cause of the event and then to rate the internality, stability, and globality of that cause on separate 7-point continua. Ratings are summed across events to yield six subscale scores indicating the internality, stability, and globality of attributions for bad and good outcomes. In this study the whole ASQ was administered, but only the subscales for bad outcomes were scored, because they have been found to be most directly associated with problematic negative emotions (Peterson et al., 1981). Internal consistency reliabilities (alpha coefficients) for these three subscales are .46 (internality), .59 (stability), and .69 (globality); test–retest reliabilities range from $r = .57$ to $r = .69$ (Peterson et al., 1982). With regard to construct validity, Peterson et al. (1982) reported that attributional styles as measured by this instrument have been found to correspond to the attributions that individuals make about significant life events.

An Individualized Attributional Style Questionnaire (ASQ–I), designed by the experimenters, was used to assess clients' attributions regarding their specific problems with negative emotions. The ASQ–I was included in the study to determine whether changes in attributional styles, which concern nonproblem events, would correspond to changes in attributions clients made about their problems. The ASQ–I was like the ASQ in format but contained events specific to each client. Clients were asked to choose three events related to their problems that had a negative outcome. For each event, clients were to supply the same information they had given about events on the ASQ, namely, the major cause of the event and, on separate 7-point continua, ratings of the internality, stability, and globality of each cause. Scores were summed across the three events to yield a single score for each attributional dimension.

A version of the Barrett-Lennard Relationship Inventory (BLRI; Barrett-Lennard, 1964; Mann & Murphy, 1975; Strong et al., 1979) was used to measure perceptions of the counseling relationship. The 36-item version measures empathy, genuineness, unconditionality of regard, and level of regard in separate 8-item subscales and re-sistance in a 4-item subscale. Each item consists of a statement about the relationship, followed by a 7-point continuum for indicating degree of agreement with the state-ment. Internal consistency (alpha coefficients) of the subscales ranges from .53 to .82 (Strong et al., 1979). In this study, the BLRI was used primarily as a check on the differential functioning of the three counselors and secondarily to determine whether differential treatment effects could be attributed to relationship factors. No differences on the BLRI subscales were expected or hypothesized.

Procedure

The study was conducted in 4 weeks. A week prior to the first interview, 83 potential clients completed the BDI, ASQ, and ASQ–I. If they met the criteria for inclusion, they were scheduled for interviews the following 2 weeks; if they did not meet the criteria or choose to participate, they were given experimental credit and the oppor-tunity for referral to a counselor. Clients in each attributional style group were ran-domly assigned to interpretation treatments and counselors. Assignment to treatments constituted the manipulation of discrepancy; clients were assigned to an interpretation treatment that was either moderately or highly discrepant from their own attributional styles. All counselors administered both treatments. Following the second interview, clients completed the BLRI. At a posttest session, a week after the second interview, clients again completed the BDI, ASQ, and ASQ–I. The posttest on the ASQ–I contained the same three events that the clients had chosen on the pretest. All clients were then debriefed thoroughly about the nature of the study, and clients wishing to continue in counseling were allowed to do so.

Data Analysis

To check for counselor differences on the BLRI, subscale scores were analyzed with a one-way multivariate analysis of variance (MANOVA) with the three counselors as levels of the independent variable. The BLRI subscale scores were then reanalyzed with a two-way MANOVA, with client attributional style and interpretation content as independent variables, to determine whether there were any relationship differences as a function of these variables.

To test the hypotheses, scores from the BDI and subscales of the ASQ and ASQ–I were analyzed with separate three-way analyses of variance (ANOVAs), with client attributional style and interpretation content as between-subjects variables and time of testing a within-subjects variable. Separate ANOVAs, rather than a multivariate analysis, were used with ASQ and ASQ–I data, because correlations among the subscales of these instruments at pretest were low ($.07 < rs < .48$; mean $r = .29$); however, to minimize the possibility of Type 1 error, isolated findings at or near the .05 alpha level were not interpreted. Differential changes over time on the dependent measures would provide evidence for the hypotheses in the following way: The content hypothesis would be supported by significant Interpretation Content × Time interactions, with behavioral interpretations producing greater improvement than characterological interpretations. The discrepancy hypothesis would be supported by significant Client Attributional Style × Interpretation Content × Time interactions, with greater improvement occurring in the moderately than in the highly discrepant conditions. Improvement on the BDI was, of course, a reduction in score; improvement on the ASQ and ASQ–I was a reduction in subscale scores, indicating movement away from characterological attributions.

Results

The one-way MANOVA of BLRI data indicated no significant differences among the three counselors in perceived relationship. In terms of the possible scale ranges (8–56), the counselors were perceived to be emphatic ($M = 45.4$), genuine ($M = 48.1$), and both unconditional ($M = 41.1$) and positive ($M = 47.8$) in their regard for their clients. They also aroused little resistance ($M = 8.8$; possible scale range, 4–28). The two-way MANOVA of BLRI data yielded no significant differences in perceived relationship as a function of client attributional style, interpretation content, or the interaction of these. The fact that the counselors were perceived positively and consistently across conditions provided some justification for not considering counselor an independent variable in analyses of the other data, as well as a rationale for not attributing differential treatment effects to relationship factors.

Means and standard deviations for the BDI and ASQ and ASQ–I subscales are presented in Table 1 by independent variable and time of testing. The ANOVA of BDI scores yielded a significant main effect for time, $F(1, 34) = 74.35$, $p < .0001$, indicating that clients in all four conditions exhibited improvement in negative emotions, from pretest ($M = 17.4$) to posttest ($M = 8.4$). The Client Attributional Style × Interpretation Content interaction was significant, $F(1, 34) = 5.38$, $p < .03$, but this effect was not over time so could have been (and apparently was) as affected by pretest differences among the four conditions as by posttest differences. The two interactions relevant to testing the hypotheses of the study were nonsignificant, ($ps > .60$).

Results of ANOVAs on the ASQ and ASQ–I data are reported together by subscale (that is, attributional dimension) to facilitate comparison of changes that occurred on the two instruments. On the internality subscale of the ASQ, there was a significant main effect for time, $F(1, 34) = 6.72$, $p < .02$. Clients' attributional styles for bad

Table 1—*Means and Standard Deviations for the BDI, ASQ, and ASQ–I by Independent Variable and Time of Testing*

Independent variable[a] and time	BDI		ASQ						ASQ–I					
			Internality		Stability		Globality		Internality		Stability		Globality	
	M	SD	M	SD	M	SD	M	SD	M	SD	M	SD	M	SD
B–B[b]														
Pre	17.8	6.3	29.0	5.6	24.0	3.0	26.0	2.6	14.0	3.0	14.1	3.5	13.6	3.4
Post	11.3	7.0	27.6	6.5	25.3	3.6	22.8	5.9	15.4	3.2	14.4	3.5	14.1	4.3
B–C[c]														
Pre	15.4	5.3	27.5	3.2	23.9	3.3	25.0	2.6	11.9	3.7	13.2	2.3	12.1	2.7
Post	8.0	5.1	25.1	4.0	23.5	4.9	21.5	7.5	12.8	2.9	14.5	2.0	13.2	3.7
C–B[d]														
Pre	15.9	4.7	30.0	4.6	31.4	5.8	31.2	4.6	13.2	3.8	14.2	3.4	15.8	3.2
Post	5.7	3.5	26.6	5.8	31.3	5.7	27.3	6.4	16.0	3.2	15.2	1.7	14.9	3.3
C–C[e]														
Pre	20.4	6.0	30.1	5.8	30.7	3.3	31.4	3.7	13.1	5.3	15.5	3.8	14.0	3.5
Post	14.7	5.1	26.5	5.8	26.4	4.0	27.2	6.1	15.2	4.1	15.5	2.6	13.8	2.2

Note. BDI = Beck Depression Inventory; scale range is 0–63. ASQ = Attributional Style Questionnaire; subscale ranges are 6–42. ASQ–I = Individualized Attributional Style Questionnaire; subscale ranges are 3–21. B = behavioral; C = characterological.
[a]In the names of the four conditions, the client attributional style variable is given first and the interpretation content variable second. [b]n = 8. [c]n = 10. [d]n = 9. [e]n = 11.

outcomes became less internal from pretest ($M = 29.1$) to posttest ($M = 26.3$). On the internality subscale of the ASQ–I, there was also a significant main effect for time, $F(1, 34) = 10.44$, $p < .003$, but here the change was in the opposite direction. Clients' problem-related attributions became more internal from pretest ($M = 13.0$) to posttest ($M = 14.8$). On both subscales, the interactions relevant to testing the hypotheses were nonsignificant ($ps > .60$).

On the stability subscale of the ASQ, there was an expected significant main effect for client attributional style, $F(1, 34) = 21.25$, $p < .0001$, produced by the median split on that dimension. Both the Client Attributional Style × Time and Interpretation Content × Time interactions were significant, $F(1, 34) = 4.35$, $p < .05$, and $F(1, 34) = 5.34$, $p < .03$, respectively; the interactions were not the result of pretest differences. Both interactions seemed to be due to change occurring in only one of the four conditions: Clients with characterological attributional styles who received characterological interpretations showed a decrease in the temporal stability of their attributional styles for bad outcomes from pretest ($M = 30.7$) to posttest ($M = 26.4$). Clients with the same attributional style who received behavioral interpretations did not change on this dimension, nor did any of the clients with behavioral attributional styles, regardless of the interpretations they received. The three-way interaction in this subscale was nonsignificant, $F(1, 34) = 1.04$, $p > .30$. There were no significant effects on the stability subscale of the ASQ–I, including the interactions relevant to testing the hypotheses ($ps > .45$).

On the globality subscale of the ASQ, there was an expected significant main effect for client attributional style, $F(1, 34) = 15.24$, $p < .0004$, produced by the median split on that dimension. Otherwise, only the main effect for time was significant, $F(1, 34) = 17.48$, $p < .0002$, indicating that clients in all four conditions became more situationally specific (less global) in their attributional styles from pretest ($M = 28.5$) to posttest ($M = 24.8$). There were no significant effects on the globality subscale of the ASQ–I. On both subscales, the interactions relevant to testing the hypotheses were nonsignificant ($ps > .60$).

Discussion

The content hypothesis, that interpretations containing behavioral attributions would produce greater improvement than those containing characterological attributions, received no support in this study. Clients' negative emotions improved regardless of the content of the interpretations they received. Moreover, interpretation content had no differential effect on the dimensions of clients' attributional styles or of their problem-related attributions, even though interpretation content explicitly varied along the dimensions of stability and globality. That the clients did not perceive the interpretations differentially is unlikely. The interpretations were developed according to the specifications of attribution researchers, expressed in a clear and simple language, and applied directly to events in the clients' lives. Moreover, the manipulation check indicated that their attributional content could be recognized and recalled after a single interview. Thus, it must be concluded that interpretation content is irrelevant to its functioning, at least in the early part of counseling. This finding is consistent with the bulk of previous interpretation research (e.g., Claiborn et al., 1983; Hoffman & Teglasi, 1982; Strong et al., 1979). Unique to this study, however, this finding was obtained in a problem area to which specific content had been linked theoretically, that is, in the attributional model of depression. In light of this, the lack of evidence for the content hypothesis is perhaps even more significant.

The discrepancy hypothesis, that interpretations moderately discrepant from client attributional styles would produce greater improvement than highly discrepant interpretations, fared just slightly better in this study. None of the three-way interactions that would have provided clear support for this hypothesis were significant. The significant two-way interactions on the stability subscale of the ASQ, taken together, indicated that interpretation content had a differential impact for clients with characterological attributional styles, but not for those with behavioral styles. For clients with characterological styles, characterological interpretations produced a decrease in the stability of attributions for bad outcomes, whereas behavioral interpretations did not. This, incidentally, represented further evidence against the content hypothesis, because the characterological interpretations contained more stable attributions than the behavioral interpretations did. But the finding is consistent with the discrepancy hypothesis in that change in a positive direction (less stable attributions for bad outcomes) occurred in the moderately but not the highly discrepant condition for these clients. Beyond this, the discrepancy hypothesis was not supported by the data. Clients' negative emotions improved regardless of whether the interpretations they received were moderately or highly discrepant from their attributional styles; nor were the changes obtained on internality and globality dimensions of their attributions a function of discrepancy.

The mild (and partial) support for the discrepancy hypothesis in this study is somewhat at odds with research that has more clearly shown moderately discrepant interpretations to be superior (Claiborn et al., 1981; Forsyth & Forsyth, 1982). It is more consistent with other research indicating that some discrepancy (that is, the use of any interpretation at all) is better than none (Claiborn et al., 1983; Hoffman & Teglasi, 1982; Strong et al., 1979); the present study, however, did not include a no-interpretation treatment to test this idea directly. Failure to replicate stronger discrepancy effects from earlier studies, particularly the Claiborn et al. (1981) study, which was similar in design, may simply have been due to the use of different content dimensions on which to manipulate discrepancy. An alternative explanation stems from the fact that the attributional styles of the behavioral group were not distinctly behavioral but more toward the middle of the behavioral–characterological continuum. Thus, matched (that is, behavioral) interpretations for this group could have been more discrepant than matched (characterological) interpretations for the characterological group. If so, perhaps they were too discrepant to be useful to the clients in the way the discrepancy hypothesis predicted. That support for the discrepancy hypothesis occurred only in the characterological group is consistent with this explanation.

A number of changes occurred for clients in all conditions as a function of neither content nor discrepancy but of treatment itself. Negative emotions, as measured by the BDI, improved considerably. Degree of improvement was comparable to that obtained in the interpretation treatment groups in highly similar studies of negative emotions conducted in the same setting (Beck & Strong, 1982; Claiborn et al., 1983). Furthermore, it was superior to the improvement of a control group (Beck & Strong, 1982) and a no-interpretation treatment group (Claiborn et al., 1983), both drawn from the same client population and tested over the same period of time as clients in the present study. Thus, it is unlikely that improvement was wholly due either to regression effects, although clients were chosen for having initially high scores on the BDI, or to nonspecific relationship factors, though these were present at high levels. The use of interpretation itself must also have contributed to improvement. Interpretation in this study gave clients an explicit attributional framework for thinking about their experiences with negative emotions. Though clients did not always change their attributions in the direction of the interpretation content, they did change them. The attributional framework they received, then, did not influence clients in a straightforward manner. Rather, it communicated to them that how they construe causes for events in their lives has an impact on their negative emotions. This prompted them to think about and reconstrue these causes, sometimes in a way divergent from the attributional content of the interpretations.

The attributional data indicate how clients in the study came to construe experiences differently and how that may have contributed to the improvement in negative emotions observed on the BDI. On the ASQ, clients' attributional styles for bad outcomes became less internal and less global; both changes are in the direction of styles that Peterson et al. (1981) called "incompatible with depression: a style of attributing ... [bad outcomes] externally or a style of attributing them to one's behavior" (p. 258). Construing negative events as more externally caused and more situationally specific both reduces the likelihood of self-blame and increases one's sense that the events are changeable. Both beliefs would seem important for resolving problems with negative emotions.

Changes on the ASQ did not correspond to changes on the ASQ–I. As clients' attributional styles became less internal, their problem-related attributions, as measured by the ASQ–I, became more internal. It could be that, as a result of treatment, clients were less inclined to attribute bad outcomes to themselves generally but more inclined to assume personal responsibility (make internal attributions) for the kinds of problems for which they had entered counseling. Both changes could constitute improvement. In addition, the fact that the stability and globality of problem-related attributions did not increase with increasing internality indicates, at least, that these attributions did not become more chatacterological but simply more internal.

The fact that ASQ and ASQ–I data showed different change patterns, along with low to moderate correlations between comparable subscales of the two instruments at pretest ($.20 < rs < .45$), indicates either that the ASQ and ASQ–I are not comparably reliable or that they measure different things. The ASQ assesses the kinds of attributions that the individual forms in response to a variety of events, regardless of whether these events are problematic for or even relevant to that individual. The ASQ–I gathers similar data, but about a very restricted range of events, events moreover that have been generated by the individual and considered relevant to his or her problems. Only further research can explore the nature of the attributional style construct and the extent to which it should be predictive of attributions about particular events. Certainly, the present data challenge validity claims that Peterson et al. (1982) have made about the ASQ.

Change patterns on the two attributional measures, considered separately and together, suggest several areas for further research. These findings do not just demonstrate that interpretation content is irrelevant to its function, though they strengthen the case against Claiborn's (1982) content hypothesis. They also suggest that independent of its content, interpretation effects change in quite specific ways. Interpretation changes client beliefs—in this case, attributions—but not always (or not simply) through a straightforward influence process. How else, then, might interpretation function? Besides continued research on discrepancy, research exploring how interpretation prompts clients to think differently, along specific dimensions, and about themselves and events in their lives is needed to answer that question. The attributional changes produced by the interpretations in this study, as well as specific belief changes obtained in other studies (e.g., Claiborn et al., 1983; Hoffman & Teglasi, 1982), may serve as a starting point for that research.

References

Abramson, L. Y., Seligman, M. E. P., & Teasdale, J. D. (1978). Learned helplessness in humans: Critique and reformulation. *Journal of Abnormal Psychology, 87,* 49–74.

Barrett-Lennard, G. T. (1964). *The Relationship Inventory.* Armidale, Australia: University of New England.

Beck, A. T. (1967). *Depression: Clinical, experimental, and theoretical aspects.* New York: Harper & Row.

Beck, J. T., & Strong, S. R. (1982). Stimulating therapeutic change with interpretations: A comparison of positive and negative connotation. *Journal of Counseling Psychology, 29,* 551–559.

Claiborn, C. D. (1982). Interpretation and change in counseling. *Journal of Counseling Psychology, 29,* 439–453.

Claiborn, C. D., Crawford, J. B., & Hackman, H. W. (1983). Effects of intervention discrepancy in counseling for negative emotions. *Journal of Counseling Psychology, 30,* 164–171.

Claiborn, C. D., Ward, S. R., & Strong, S. R. (1981). Effects of congruence between counselor interpretations and client beliefs. *Journal of Counseling Psychology, 28,* 101–109.

Forsyth, N. L., & Forsyth, D. R. (1982). Internality, controllability, and the effectiveness of attributional interpretations in counseling. *Journal of Counseling Psychology, 29,* 140–150.

Hoffman, M. A., & Teglasi, H. (1982). The role of causal attributions in counseling shy subjects. *Journal of Counseling Psychology, 29,* 132–139.

Mann, B., & Murphy, K. C. (1975). Timing of self-disclosure, reciprocity of self-disclosure, and reactions to an initial interview. *Journal of Counseling Psychology, 22,* 304–308.

Peplau, L. A., Russell, D., & Heim, M. (1979). The experience of loneliness. In I. H. Frieze, D. Bar-Tal, & J. S. Carroll (Eds.), *New approaches to social problems* (pp. 53–78). San Francisco: Jossey-Bass.

Peterson, C., Schwartz, S. M., & Seligman, M. E. P. (1981). Self-blame and depressive symptoms. *Journal of Personality and Social Psychology, 41,* 253–259.

Peterson, C., Semmel, A., von Baeyer, C., Abramson, L. Y., Metalsky, G. I., & Seligman, M. E. P. (1982). The Attributional Style Questionnaire. *Cognitive Therapy and Research, 6,* 287–300.

Seligman, M. E. P., Abramson, L. Y., Semmel, A., & von Baeyer, C. (1979). Depressive attributional style. *Journal of Abnormal Psychology, 88,* 242–247.

Strong, S. R., Wambach, C. A., Lopez, F. G., & Cooper, R. K. (1979). Motivational and equipping functions of interpretation in counseling. *Journal of Counseling Psychology, 26,* 98–107.

Chapter 18
THE ACCURACY OF THERAPISTS' INTERPRETATIONS
AND THE OUTCOME OF DYNAMIC PSYCHOTHERAPY

Paul Crits-Christoph, Andrew Cooper, and Lester Luborsky

Within the clinical psychoanalytic literature, interpretation has been described as the "supreme agent in the hierarchy of therapeutic principles" (Bibring, 1954, p. 763). Focal dynamic psychotherapy specifies the task of the psychotherapist as (a) arriving at a succinct formulation of the patient's main maladaptive relationship pattern and (b) centering interpretations around this pattern. For example, in his manual for psychoanalytic psychotherapy, Luborsky (1984) suggested that the therapist focus interpretations around the main maladaptive relationship pattern, which he labeled the *core conflictual relationship theme*. In addition, Luborsky and colleagues developed an objective method of measuring this pattern (Luborsky, 1977; Luborsky et al., 1985; Luborsky, Crits-Christoph, & Mellon, 1986). Similarly, Strupp and Binder's (1984) manual for time-limited dynamic psychotherapy described the concept of the "dynamic focus" (recently renamed "cyclical maladaptive patterns"; Schacht, 1986) that becomes the central aspect of therapy and guides the therapist's interpretations.

Despite clinical emphasis on the importance of interpretation, empirical studies in this area have been scarce. Early studies (Harway, Dittman, Raush, Bordin, & Rigler, 1955; Speisman, 1959) have examined the depth of interpretations, but no studies have been performed relating this construct to psychotherapy outcome. Additionally, the results of several process studies on interpretation have been limited by methodological or conceptual problems. For example, both Garduk and Haggard (1972) and Luborsky, Bachrach, Graff, Pulver, and Christoph (1979) have examined the immediate impact of interpretations on patients' levels of resistance, insight, and other variables. However, the small number of patients in these two investigations restricted the generalizability of the results and prohibited meaningful conclusions about the relation of interpretation to outcome. In one of the few outcome studies on interpretation, Marziali (1984) found significant relations between frequency of interpretations and outcome. In contrast, Piper, Debbane, Bienvenu, De Carufel, and Garant (1986) failed to replicate these results using more sophisticated research methodology.

These studies, however, were conducted before a reliable measure of central relationship patterns was developed. Therefore, they did not question whether interpretations that accurately bear on this central theme are a primary curative factor in psychotherapy. This issue has been examined by Silberschatz, Fretter, and Curtis (1986): In a series of three single-case studies, they demonstrated high correlations between the accuracy of interpretation, as assessed by the compatibility between the

Reprinted from *Journal of Consulting and Clinical Psychology, 56,* 490–495 (1988). Copyright © 1988 by the American Psychological Association. Used with permission of the first author.

This research was supported in part by National Institute of Mental Health (NIMH) Grants RO1-MH40472 and RO1-MH39673 and by NIMH Research Scientist Award MH40710 to Lester Luborsky.

content of the interpretation and the content of the patient's "plan diagnosis" (Rosenberg, Silberschatz, Curtis, Sampson, & Weiss, 1986) and patients' levels of experiencing (Klein, Mathieu, Gendlin, & Kiesler, 1970) immediately following the interpretations.

The aims of this study were (a) to develop a measure of the accuracy of therapist interpretations based on the core conflictual relationship theme method and (b) to predict the outcome of dynamic psychotherapy from the newly developed measure. We also examined whether the accuracy of interpretations would predict outcome only in the context of a positive therapeutic alliance as well as the overlap between the accuracy of interpretation and a more general measure of therapist technical skill, the Errors in Technique subscale of the Vanderbilt Negative Indicators Scale, which has been shown to predict therapy outcome (Sachs, 1983).

Method

Patients

Descriptive characteristics of the patients are presented in Table 1, and patient diagnoses are summarized in Table 2. These diagnoses were obtained from the *Diagnostic and Statistical Manual of Mental Disorders*, second edition (*DSM–II*; American Psychiatric Association, 1968), diagnoses made by a clinical evaluator as part of a semistructured prognostic interview (Auerbach, Luborsky, & Johnson, 1972). Two clinicians worked together using the *DMS–II* diagnoses and case notes to translate them from second edition to third edition (*DSM–III*; American Psychiatric Association, 1980) diagnoses. The majority of patients were diagnosed with

Table 1—*Descriptive Characteristics of Patients*

Variable	Number
Age (years)	
15–24	28
25–34	10
35–44	4
45–49	1
Sex	
Female	30
Male	13
Marital status	
Single	29
Married	8
Divorced/separated/widowed	6
Education	
High school degree	5
Some college	21
College degree	6
Some graduate or professional school	7
Graduate or professional school	4

Table 2—*Patient Diagnoses*

Diagnosis	Number
DSM–III Axis I[a]	
Atypical eating disorder	1
Dysthymic disorder	16
Ego dystonic homosexuality	2
Generalized anxiety disorder	11
Inhibited sexual excitement	2
Obsessive–compulsive disorder	2
No Axis I diagnosis	13
DSM–III Axis II	
Atypical personality disorder	1
Compulsive personality disorder	4
Histrionic personality disorder	4
Narcissistic personality disorder	1
Passive–aggressive personality disorder	4
Schizoid personality disorder	8
Schizotypal personality disorder	3
Mixed personality disorder	1
No Axis II diagnosis	13

Note.   DSM–III = Diagnostic and Statistical Manual of Mental Disorders (3rd ed.). Numbers total more than sample size (43) because several patients had more than one diagnosis.

[a]Axis 1 patients who additionally had an Axis II diagnosis included 8 with dysthymic disorder, 1 with ego dystonic homosexuality, and 4 with generalized anxiety disorder.

dysthymic disorder, generalized anxiety disorder, or a variety of personality disorders.

Therapists

Twenty-eight therapists participated in the research project. Each therapist usually treated 1 or 2 patients. The therapists ranged in age from 27 to 55 years ($M = 35.6$). The therapists had between 1–22 years of prior clinical experience, with an average of 5.4 years. Twelve of the therapists were psychiatrists in private practice. The remaining 16 therapists were supervised psychiatric residents.

Treatment Characteristics

All patients were seen in individual psychodynamic psychotherapy. Approximately two thirds of the patients were treated at the outpatient clinic of the Hospital of the University of Pennsylvania. The remaining patients were seen in private settings. Treatment length varied among the patients, ranging from 21 to 149 weeks, with an average length of 53.5 weeks.

Measures

Identifying Interpretations

Two judges coded therapist statements into interpretations versus all other types of responses. A response was considered an interpretation if it met at least one of the following criteria: (a) the therapist explained possible reasons for a patient's thoughts, feelings, or behavior (e.g., "One of the benefits of using drugs is that it keeps you in the role of the child") and/or (b) the therapist alluded to similarities between the patient's present circumstances and other life experiences (e.g., "What's happening is that you keep getting yourself into these kinds of situations like what happened on Saturday where you put yourself in for a hell of a big rejection experience").

Interrater reliability, based on the judges' ratings for all 43 cases, was assessed for distinguishing interpretations from other statements. Interjudge agreement was 95% and Cohen's (1960) kappa was .56 ($p < .0001$). Only statements that were coded by both judges as interpretations were retained. The number of interpretations obtained per patient ranged from 1 to 16 ($M = 6.1$).

Core Conflictual Relationship Theme (CCRT) Method

This method (Luborsky, 1977) establishes guidelines for clinical judgments about the content of patients' central relationship patterns from psychotherapy session material. The primary data to be scored are the explicit narrative episodes about relationships that patients commonly tell during psychotherapy sessions. Typical narratives are about fathers, mothers, brothers, sisters, friends, bosses, and therapists. These relationship episodes are identified by a separate set of independent judges before the transcripts are given to the CCRT judges. A minimum of 10 relationship episodes is usually used as a basis for scoring the CCRT.

The CCRT judge reads the relationship episode in the transcript and identifies three components: (a) the patient's main wishes, needs, or intentions toward the other person in the narrative; (b) the responses of the other person; and (c) the responses of the self. For the responses, both positive and negative types are identified. Within each component, the types with the highest frequency across all relationship episodes are identified; their combination constitutes the CCRT.

The steps in the CCRT method formalize the usual inference process of clinicians in formulating transference patterns. The clinician/judge first identifies the wishes and responses to the wishes in each of the episodes and, from these, makes a preliminary CCRT formulation (Steps 1 and 2); the same judge then reviews and reformulates (Steps 1' and 2').

Thus, in Step 1 the judge identifies the types of wishes and responses (both from other and of self) in each relationship episode, and in Step 2 the judge formulates a preliminary CCRT based on the frequency of each of the types of each component. In Step 1' the judge reviews, where needed, the types of wishes and responses based on the Step 2 preliminary CCRT, and in Step 2' the judge reformulates, where needed, based on the recount of all wishes and responses in Step 1'.

The CCRT judges work independently of each other. Judges are trained by first reading the CCRT guide (Luborsky, 1986), trying several standard practice cases, and receiving feedback from the research team about their performance after each. Further descriptions of the CCRT method, with case examples, can be found in Luborsky (1984) and Luborsky, Crits-Christoph, and Mellon (1986).

Interjudge agreement on delineating relationship episodes and formulating CCRTs was recently reported (Crits-Christoph et al., 1988). Weighted kappa values were .61 for wish and negative response of self and .70 for negative response from other.

Preliminary applications of the CCRT method have indicated that it is useful as a measure of transference. In a sample of 8 patients (Luborsky et al., 1985), CCRT results were found to correspond to Freud's (1912/1966) observations about transference that could be restated operationally. For example, it was found that one main theme predominates, that the pattern is relatively unique for each person, that the pattern remains relatively stable over time, and that the relationship with the therapist mimics the general transference pattern.

Two or (occasionally) three judges scored each of the 43 patients for the CCRT. For each case, the final CCRT selected for inclusion in the study was a composite of the judges' CCRT formulations. These formulations included three components: wish, negative response from other, and negative response of self. Because judges occasionally used different wordings in describing their CCRT formulations, their specific wordings were coded into a standardized language to permit direct comparisons between formulations (Luborsky, 1986). This task was accomplished by having three judges code the CCRT judges' formulations into standardized wordings provided by standard lists of wishes, responses from other, and responses of self. This coding task was highly reliable (i.e., greater than 95% agreement between judges).

Once formulations were coded into standard wordings, a composite CCRT was derived by selecting the most frequent wishes and responses that were noted by the different CCRT judges. The final CCRT formulation for each patient consisted of up to two wishes, three negative responses from other, and three negative responses of self.

Accuracy of Interpretations

Accuracy of interpretation represents the degree of congruence between the contents of the patient's CCRT and the contents of the therapist's interpretations. A 4-point rating scale was used to assess the degree to which a clinical judge believed that the therapist had addressed a particular CCRT wish, response from other, or response of self in his or her interpretation.

The following CCRT and therapist interpretation, drawn from one of the cases used in this study, is presented to illustrate the nature of the accuracy ratings. The patient's CCRT consisted of one wish (to make contact with others, to be close), one negative response from other (rejects, distant), and three responses of self (lonely, depressed, anxious). The therapist's interpretation follows:

> I'm beginning to get a picture of a lot of involvement that you have with this guy still, even though he's cut things off; you haven't. And you're not able to begin replacing him yet—the emotional investment, emotional tie you've got still to him, and pretty strongly. And that's inhibiting you. Now, what's behind that . . . obviously he was very important to you, more important than any other guy has been. And that

makes it harder to give him up. And the fact that he really is the one who decided—made the choice to break, not you—makes it harder to give him up too. I see some reaction: What's going on?

This was regarded as an accurate interpretation of the wish and the response from other but not of the response of self.

For each case, three judges were presented with composite CCRT formulations and interpretations that were extracted from transcripts. The judges were directed to familiarize themselves with the patient's CCRT formulation and to make ratings of the accuracy of each wish, response from other, and response of self contained therein.

Ratings for the wishes were averaged to form a composite wish dimension for each patient. Similarly, ratings for the responses from other and responses of self were averaged to yield composites on each. For each patient, these accuracy scores were then averaged across all interpretations. Interrater reliability of the accuracy scales was computed using the intraclass correlation coefficient. Based on the sample of 43 cases, the pooled interjudge reliabilities were (a) .84 for accuracy of the patient's wishes, (b) .76 for accuracy of the patient's responses from other, and (c) .83 for accuracy of the patient's responses of self. Because of a sizable correlation ($r =$ .68) between wish and response from other, these two dimensions were combined into a composite accuracy dimension to avoid the multicolinearity of predictors in subsequent multiple regression analyses.

Errors in Technique Subscale

The Errors in Technique subscale of the Vanderbilt Negative Indicators Scale (Strupp et al., 1981) is a set of 10 items that is hypothesized to be inversely related to beneficial treatment outcome. Item descriptions and reliability and validity data on the scale were provided by Sachs (1983). For each case in the present study, two judges rated the first 15 min and the second 15 min of each of two early therapy sessions. The ratings were averaged across the two segments, and the scores of the two sessions were then combined.

Helping Alliance Scale

The helping alliance counting signs method (Luborsky, Crits-Christoph, Alexander, Margolis, & Cohen, 1983) was applied by two judges to the first 30 min of each of the two early sessions for each patient. The score for positive helping alliance signs was selected for use in this analysis because this measure proved to be the most successful predictor of outcome in a comparison of the 10 most improved and 10 least improved cases from the Penn Psychotherapy Project (Luborsky et al., 1983).

Treatment Outcome

Two outcome measures were used: residual gain and rated benefits (each was described in detail by Mintz, Luborsky, & Christoph, 1979). The residual gain score was derived from general adjustment ratings made by the patient and a clinical observer that were obtained pre- and posttherapy and were statistically adjusted for the effects of the patient's initial level of functioning. The rated benefits measure consisted of ratings by the patient and the therapist assessing actual change. Residual gain and rated benefits scores were highly correlated, $r(41) = .76$.

Judges

With the exception of one judge who coded interpretations and one judge who marked off relationship episodes (both trained research assistants), judges were experienced clinicians (clinical psychologists and psychiatrists) trained in each task. All judges were blind to treatment outcome and worked independently. Separate sets of judges scored each measure.

Results

Table 3 provides the means and standard deviations of the accuracy dimensions. As can be seen, the average level of accuracy was low, yet enough variability was present to allow for relations with other variables to emerge.

The relations among the predictors were examined as a preliminary step to the prediction of outcome. None of the correlations attained statistical significance.

Multiple regression analyses were performed using the two accuracy measures (wish plus response from other, response of self), the Errors in Technique subscale, and the Helping Alliance Scale as predictors and the rated benefits and residual gain measures as outcome criteria. Table 4 presents simple correlations between each predictor and the two outcome measures as well as partial correlations (with each variable controlling for the others) and a multiple correlation combining the predictors.

Most striking was the accuracy on the wish plus response from other measure, which was the best predictor of outcome, yielding statistically significant results in all cases (using both outcome measures and simple and partial correlations). The Errors in Technique subscale and the accuracy on the response of self measure were

Table 3—*Means and Standard Deviations for Accuracy Dimensions*

Dimension	M	SD
Response of self	1.69	.41
Wish	1.81	.56
Response from other	1.49	.38
Wish plus response from other	1.65	.43

Note. The accuracy dimensions were rated on a 1–4 scale, with 1 indicating no congruence between the content of the interpretation and the patient's core conflictual relationship theme and 4 indicating high congruence.

Table 4—*Prediction of Outcome From Accuracy, Helping Alliance,*
and Errors in Technique

Measure	Simple correlations (df = 41)		Partial correlations (df = 38)	
	Rated benefits	Residual gain	Rated benefits	Residual gain
Accuracy				
Wish plus response from other	.38*	.44**	.36*	.43**
Response of self	.16	.07	.07	−.02
Helping alliance	.31*	.36*	.26	.35*
Errors in techniques	−.21	−.10	−.16	−.04

Note. All tests were two-tailed. Multiple correlations were as follows: For rated benefits, $R(4, 38) = .49$, $p < .05$; for residual gain, $R(4, 38) = .54$, $p < .01$. When a Bonferroni adjustment was made for the number of simple correlations computed with each outcome measure, only the accuracy on wish plus response from other correlations remained significant at $p < .05$.

*$p < .05$. **$p < .01$.

not significantly related to outcome. The Helping Alliance Scale showed significant simple correlations with both outcome measures, as had been expected from the Luborsky et al. (1983) study that included a sample of 20 patients, which overlapped with our sample of 43 patients. In addition, the Helping Alliance Scale demonstrated a significant partial correlation with residual gain and a nearly significant effect with rated benefits. Thus, the predictive effects of accuracy and the Helping Alliance Scale appeared to be independent.

To test the hypothesis that accuracy interacts with helping alliance (i.e., accurate interpretations have an impact only when the therapeutic alliance is positive), cross-product terms between accuracy on the wish plus response from other measure and helping alliance were entered after main effects in the multiple regressions. These interactions were nonsignificant.

Because one item ("failure to address maladaptive behaviors or distorted apperceptions") of the Errors in Technique subscale overlapped conceptually with the concept of accuracy of interpretation, we examined the correlations of this item with the accuracy scales. For both accuracy scales, the correlations were nonsignificant: For wish plus response from other, $r(41) = -.11$; for response of self, $r(41) = -.19$.

Discussion

In discussing the main results of the study, it is important to note that the interrater reliability of the accuracy scales was reasonably high compared with the level of reliability usually found for psychotherapy process measures (see, for example, Luborsky et al., 1980). The very specific nature of the rating task (the scales were tailored to each patient's CCRT) and the use of experienced clinical research judges probably contributed to the reliability level. By combining the ratings made on all interpretations identified in each of two complete therapy sessions and by averaging the ratings over three judges, a robust measure was constructed.

The major hypothesis of this research received strong support: A statistically significant and moderately strong relation was found between accuracy of interpretations (i.e., on the wish plus response from other dimension) and treatment outcome. These results extend the findings of Silberschatz et al. (1986), who studied the immediate impact of accuracy (i.e., the convergence of the plan diagnosis with interpretations) in the psychotherapies of three patients. Although a relation between accuracy and therapy outcome was also observed in that study, the significance of the finding was limited by the size of the sample. In the current research, larger and more diverse groups of patients and therapists were examined, allowing for the first systematic investigation of the relation between the accuracy of interpretations and treatment outcome.

The results suggest that what the therapist does in dynamic psychotherapy has an impact on outcome. The overall pattern of results also suggests that a specific and not a general technique factor accounts for the finding. The predictive strength of accuracy on wish plus response from other was not accountable by other variables such as errors in technique or the quality of the therapeutic alliance.

It is of interest that accuracy on wish plus response from other rather than accuracy on response of self-predicted treatment outcome. It appears that correctly addressing the patient's stereotypical patterns of needs and wishes, followed by addressing the responses of others, is an effective strategy. However, limiting the focus of interpretations to the patient's usual responses (typical feeling states) in interpersonal situations is not by itself a productive technique. The lack of a significant relation between accuracy on the response of self with outcome is not inconsistent with the research concerning the therapeutic effects of focusing on patient affect. In their review of the few studies on the relation between affect focus and outcome, Orlinsky and Howard (1986) found that focusing on patient affect is only occasionally helpful, although it is probably not harmful.

The lack of a significant interaction between accuracy of interpretations and the quality of the therapeutic alliance was surprising given the clinical lore that a strong alliance is necessary for patients to tolerate and make use of interpretations. Perhaps this relation would emerge with more severely disturbed patients than the sample used here, particularly if there was a higher frequency of poor alliances. In our study, only three therapist–patient dyads showed no signs at all of a positive alliance.

The results for the Errors in Technique subscale are discrepant from the findings of the Sachs (1983) study, which showed a significant inverse relation between errors in technique and outcome. There are a few possible reasons for the nonsignificant finding for errors in technique in the current research. First, the relatively limited reliability of the Errors in Technique subscale in this study may partly explain the results. The limited reliability may have been a function of the generally low level of errors in our sample (4 of 10 items did not occur, and several others occurred infrequently). In addition, items on this scale may be more appropriate for time-limited psychotherapy. Treatment in Sachs's (1983) study was specified as brief therapy (maximum of 6 months) compared with the open-ended therapy used in the current research (average length of about 1 year).

Interpretation of our main findings is subject to the inherent limitations of all correlational research, such as the possible role of a third variable that may have accounted for the relation between accuracy and outcome. In addition, the direction of the relation can be questioned. For example, it is possible that patients who are making good progress in treatment may be more likely to elicit accurate interpretations from their therapists, particularly if they are becoming aware of their own relationship patterns and can articulate these issues during the sessions. However, the fact that the finding was observed very early in treatment (usually by the fifth session) provides some support for the opposite position in which accuracy leads to favorable outcome.

The study also provided new information concerning the validity of the CCRT measure. By basing the assessment of interpretation accuracy on the CCRT method, the significant relation between accuracy on wish plus response from other with treatment outcome indirectly lends the method further validity.

References

American Psychiatric Association. (1968). *Diagnostic and statistical manual of mental disorders* (2nd ed.). Washington, DC: Author.

American Psychiatric Association. (1980). *Diagnostic and statistical manual of mental disorders* (3rd ed.). Washington, DC: Author.

Auerbach, A., Luborsky, L., & Johnson, M. (1972). Clinicians' predictions of outcome of psychotherapy: A trial of a prognostic index. *American Journal of Psychiatry, 128*, 830–835.

Bibring, E. (1954). Psychoanalysis and the dynamic psychotherapies. *Journal of the American Psychoanalytic Association, 2*, 745–770.

Cohen, J. (1960). A coefficient of agreement for nominal scales. *Educational and Psychological Measurement, 20*, 37–46.

Crits-Christoph, P., Luborsky, L., Dahl, L., Popp, C., Mellon, J., & Mark, D. (1988). Clinicians can agree in assessing relationship patterns in psychotherapy: The core conflictual relationship theme method. *Archives of General Psychiatry, 45*, 1001–1004.

Freud, S. (1966). The dynamics of the transference. In J. Strachey (Ed. and Trans.), *The standard edition of the complete psychological works of Sigmund Freud* (Vol. 12, pp. 99–108). London: Hogarth Press. (Original work published 1912)

Garduk, E., & Haggard, E. (1972). Immediate effects on patients of psychoanalytic interpretations. *Psychological Issues, 7*(4, Monograph 28).

Harway, N., Dittman, A., Raush, H., Bordin, E., & Rigler, D. (1955). The measurement of depth of interpretation. *Journal of Consulting Psychology, 19*, 247–253.

Klein, M., Mathieu, P., Gendlin, E., & Kiesler, D. (1970). *The experiencing scale: A research and training manual.* Madison: Wisconsin Psychiatric Institute.

Luborsky, L. (1977). Measuring a pervasive psychic structure in psychotherapy: The core conflictual relationship theme. In N. Freedman & S. Grand (Eds.), *Communicative structures and psychic structures* (pp. 367–395). New York: Plenum Press.

Luborsky, L. (1984). *Principles of psychoanalytic psychotherapy: A manual for supportive–expressive (SE) treatment.* New York: Basic Books.

Luborsky, L. (1986). *The core conflictual relationship theme method: Guide to scoring and rationale.* Unpublished manuscript.

Luborsky, L., Bachrach, H., Graff, H., Pulver, S., & Christoph, P. (1979). Preconditions and consequences of transference interpretations: A clinical quantitative investigation. *Journal of Nervous and Mental Disease, 167*, 391–401.

Luborsky, L., Crits-Christoph, P., Alexander, L., Margolis, M., & Cohen, M. (1983). Two helping alliance methods for predicting outcomes of psychotherapy: A counting signs versus a global rating method. *Journal of Nervous and Mental Disease, 171*, 480–492.

Luborsky, L., Crits-Christoph, P., & Mellon, J. (1986). Advent of objective measures of the transference concept. *Journal of Consulting and Clinical Psychology, 54*, 39–47.

Luborsky, L., Mellon, J., Alexander, K., van Ravenswaay, P., Childress, A., Levine, F., Cohen, K. D., Hole, A. V., & Ming, S. (1985). A verification of Freud's grandest clinical hypothesis: The transference. *Clinical Psychology Review, 5*, 231–246.

Luborsky, L., Mintz, J., Auerbach, A., Christoph, P., Bachrach, H., Todd, T., Johnson, M., & O'Brien, C. P. (1980). Predicting the outcomes of psychotherapy: Findings of Penn Psychotherapy Project. *Archives of General Psychiatry, 37*, 471–481.

Marziali, E. (1984). Prediction of outcome of brief psychotherapy from therapist interpretive interventions. *Archives of General Psychiatry, 41*, 301–304.

Mintz, J., Luborsky, L., & Christoph, P. (1979). Measuring the outcomes of psychotherapy: Findings of the Penn Psychotherapy Project. *Journal of Consulting and Clinical Psychology, 47*, 319–334.

Orlinsky, D., & Howard, K. (1986). Process and outcome in psychotherapy. In S. Garfield & A. Bergin (Eds.), *Handbook of psychotherapy and behavior change* (3rd ed., pp. 311–381). New York: Wiley.

Piper, W., Debbane, E., Bienvenu, J., De Carufel, F., & Garant, J. (1986). Relationships between the object focus of therapist interpretations and outcome in short term individual psychotherapy. *British Journal of Medical Psychology, 59*, 1–11.

Rosenberg, S. E., Silberschatz, G., Curtis, J. T., Sampson, H., & Weiss, J. (1986). A method for establishing reliability of statements from psychodynamic case formulations. *American Journal of Psychiatry, 143*, 1454–1456.

Sachs, J. S. (1983). Negative factors in brief psychotherapy: An empirical assessment. *Journal of Consulting and Clinical Psychology, 51*, 557–564.

Schacht, T. (1986, June). *Modeling recurrent relationship patterns: The Vanderbilt approach.* Paper presented at the meeting of the Society for Psychotherapy Research, Wellesley, MA.

Silberschatz, G., Fretter, P. B., & Curtis, J. T. (1986). How do interpretations influence the process of psychotherapy. *Journal of Consulting and Clinical Psychology, 54*, 646–652.

Speisman, J. (1959). Depth of interpretation and verbal resistance in psychotherapy. *Journal of Consulting Psychology, 23*, 93–99.

Strupp, H. H., & Binder, J. L. (1984). *Psychotherapy in a new key: A guide to time-limited dynamic psychotherapy.* New York: Basic Books.

Strupp, H. H., Moras, K., Sandell, J., Waterhouse, G., O'Malley, S., Keithly, L., & Gomes-Schwartz, B. (1981). *Vanderbilt Negative Indicators Scale: An instrument for identification of deterrents to progress in time-limited dynamic psychotherapy.* Unpublished manuscript, Vanderbilt University.

Chapter 19
COMPREHENSIVE PROCESS ANALYSIS OF INSIGHT EVENTS IN COGNITIVE–BEHAVIORAL AND PSYCHODYNAMIC–INTERPERSONAL PSYCHOTHERAPIES

Robert Elliott, David A. Shapiro, Jenny Firth-Cozens, William B. Stiles, Gillian E. Hardy, Susan P. Llewelyn, and Frank R. Margison

What is insight? A key concept in psychotherapy theories since Freud, insight seems at once both simple and difficult to define. The sense of suddenly seeing a previously missed perceptual pattern, or the *ah-hah* experience of solving a difficult intellectual or personal puzzle, is a familiar one. Although insight is a central concept in the modern institution of psychotherapy and counseling, relatively little is actually known about it. For example, the defining features of insight have not been properly clarified, nor is it clear what factors give rise to therapeutic insight, how insight unfolds, or what its consequences are.

An analysis of standard words, definitions, and usage, as well as client accounts (Elliott, 1984), suggests that insight may have four major elements. The first element is metaphorical vision, or seeing with figurative eyes (e.g., "It made me see I have a tremendous conflict there"). This element also includes the metaphorical illumination that makes the "seeing into" possible ("The light went on"). This visual metaphor is in keeping with the etymology of the word *insight* as "internal seeing" (*Compact Edition of the Oxford English Dictionary*). The second element is connection, including both the perception of patterns or links ("He really put together all the pieces"). These connections may involve reasons, causes, categorizations, or parallels. The third element is suddenness: Clients may describe something "clicking" or may report feeling surprised ("I was sort of amazed. Wow!"). The fourth element is newness, the sense of discovering something not previously known ("It was just something I never thought of"). This element of newness appears to have been slighted in dictionary and scientific definitions. These four features appear to distinguish prototypic instances of insight and may be useful for distinguishing insight from awareness (cf. Elliott & Wexler, 1994).

The existing therapy research literature on insight, briefly summarized below, has addressed four issues: definitions and measurement of insight, frequency of insight, relation of insight to outcome, and factors that contribute to client insight (for another perspective, see Crits-Christoph, Barber, Miller, & Beebe, 1993).

The first research definition of client insight occurred in Snyder's (1945) pioneering therapy process study. The available definitions generally have emphasized

Reprinted from *Journal of Counseling Psychology*, 41, 449–463 (1994). Copyright © 1994 by the American Psychological Association. Used with permission of the first author.

This research was completed while Robert Elliott and William B. Stiles were visiting researchers at the MRC/ESRC Social and Applied Psychology Unit. A copy of the full analysis of the two example events is available from Robert Elliott. We thank Lorraine Jackson and Hans Strupp for their helpful suggestions.

the visual metaphor and connection aspects of insight (e.g., Elliott, James, Reimschuessel, Cislo, & Sack, 1985; Weiss & Sampson, 1986). Suddenness and newness are referred to much less often in definitions, although they are given somewhat more frequently as examples (e.g., Weiss & Sampson, 1986). The frequency with which personal insight occurs in therapy may be one source of information about its importance in the process of change. In reviewing the literature on types of specific therapeutic impact, Elliott and James (1989) found insight to be among the most commonly studied or reported as important by clients, occurring in 12 of the 21 sources reviewed. Hill, Helms, Spiegel, and Tichenor (1988) reported that about 4% of all therapist interventions resulted in some degree of client self-reported insight and that clients typically gave these interventions very high ratings for helpfulness.

In studies in which clients have been given postsession questionnaires to describe the most helpful event in the session, the rate of insight events has varied considerably. Llewelyn (1988) and Llewelyn, Elliott, Shapiro, Firth, and Hardy (1988) reported rates of 12% and 10%, respectively; however, for data presented by Elliott et al. (1985), the rate was 34% (which possibly was due to the nature of the sample or the rating method used). The 10% figure obtained by Llewelyn et al. (1988) is the corpus from which the present insight events were drawn. These rates suggest that client insight is an important therapeutic phenomenon, at least in terms of its incidence.

On the other hand, direct evidence for the effectiveness of client insight (including client posttreatment reports and process–outcome correlations) is somewhat mixed. In a review of 13 studies of clients' posttreatment perceptions of the most helpful aspects of therapy, Elliott and James (1989) found only 4 studies in which insight was among the four most helpful aspects later reported by clients. (By comparison, therapist being warm and understanding was reported in 10 of the 13 studies.)

In the only large-scale ($N = 40$) study of the relationship of insight to treatment outcome, Llewelyn et al. (1988) failed to find significant correlations between client insight and outcome. On the other hand, several case studies with small sample sizes have reported more positive relationships: Luborsky, Bachrach, Graff, Pulver, and Christoph (1979) found that, among 3 clients in long-term psychoanalytic therapy, the most successful client evidenced the highest levels of insight following transference interpretations. Hill et al. (1988), with a sample size of 5, found a substantial correlation between proportion of in-session client-reported insight and outcome. In this study, the level of client-rated insight was the client impact that best predicted client postsession scores on Stiles's (1980) Session Evaluation Questionnaire (SEQ).

In the small amount of literature devoted to the understanding of what brings about client insight, all but one of the available studies have found insight to be related to therapist interpretation (Elliott, 1984; Elliott et al., 1985; Frank & Sweetland, 1962; Garduk & Haggard, 1972; Hill, Helms, Tichenor, et al., 1988; Luborsky et al., 1979; Weiss & Sampson, 1986); only in Elliott's (1985) nonclinical sample was this relationship not found.

The present study built on a series of studies by Elliott and colleagues (Elliott, 1985; Elliott et al., 1985; Elliott & Shapiro, 1988). In particular, it extended and elaborated Elliott (1984), which was an analysis of the contexts and unfolding effects of four insight events involving an early version of the comprehensive process analysis (CPA; Elliott, 1989, 1993) method used in this study. Three of these events took place in initial sessions with dynamically oriented therapists. Some of the main results were as follows: The events occurred in a context in which (a) clients and therapists were pursuing client self-understanding tasks and (b) clients were working well but experiencing some distress and were indirectly requesting therapist help in self-understanding. The significant therapist interventions were interpretations; addressed a core conflict relationship theme; were delivered interactively, with softening and warmth; and were imperfect. The immediate effects of these interventions proceeded through three stages: (a) processing, (b) insight, and (c) unfolding.

In this article, we present an investigation of a collection of significant insight events from the First Sheffield Psychotherapy Project (Shapiro & Firth, 1987), three from psychodynamic–interpersonal therapy and three from cognitive–behavioral therapy. These events were analyzed by means of CPA, a systematic, interpretive qualitative research procedure for analyzing significant events.

This article presents the two main kinds of CPA study, analyses of single events and cross-analyses of collections of similar events (Elliott, 1993). The first kind of CPA study, single-event analysis, has the purpose of developing an exhaustive understanding, or thick description, of the factors involved in particular significant change events. In this investigation, six insight events were analyzed in depth; in our presentation, one analysis each from the psychodynamic–interpersonal and the cognitive–behavioral therapy events has been selected to represent the corpus. The second kind of CPA study, event cross-analysis, has the purpose of discovering factors across events of a particular type, which either generally characterize that kind of event (the common factors) or which distinguish important variations within that kind of event (here, factors that discriminate between insight events in cognitive–behavioral and psychodynamic–interpersonal treatments). An added feature of the cross-analysis presented in this study was an analysis of possible observer biases through a comparison of obtained results with those that we had expected.

Method

Analyses of Individual Events

CPA is based on the assumption that it is impossible to understand a phenomenon in general without first understanding particular instances of that phenomenon. Thus, CPA research begins with intensive analyses of a one or more significant therapy events of a particular type: events whose major perceived effect on the client was to produce personal insight. Specifically, to truly understand each event, we wanted to know (a) what features of the key response engendered the insight, (b) how the event's effects unfolded, both during and after the session, and (c) what features of the context fostered the emergence of the event.

Participants

In the First Sheffield Psychotherapy Project (Shapiro & Firth, 1987), 40 clients with depressive or anxiety disorders received eight sessions each of an interpersonal–

psychodynamic treatment and a cognitive–behavioral treatment in a crossover design.

The insight events were selected on the basis of the following criteria: (a) the event occurred within a successful eight-session phase of therapy, defined by means of the amount of change on the Present State Examination (PSE), a structured diagnostic interview (Wing, Cooper, & Sartorius, 1974); (b) two analysts (Robert Elliott and Susan P. Llewelyn) agreed that the client's description of the most helpful event in the session (obtained with Llewelyn's 1988, Helpful Aspects of Therapy Form; HAT) involved personal insight (defined as realizing something new about self; Elliott et al., 1985); and (c) the therapist, using the tape of the session, was able to identify a specific segment that corresponded to the client's description of the event. The application of these three criteria yielded three exploratory and three prescriptive therapy insight events.

All of the clients and therapists were of Anglo–British ethnicity. Four of the clients were women, and two were men. The two therapists (one man and one woman) were highly experienced in both modes of treatment; each was involved with three of the events presented in this collection.

Measures

In this study, clients were assessed on a variety of standard quantitative measures. These measures played a minor role in the predominantly qualitative analyses, mainly providing an index of the clinical significance of the events.

The HAT Form (Llewelyn et al., 1988) was the key measure used in this study. Administered after each session, the measure asks clients to describe in their own words the most helpful and hindering events in the session. It was used in this study to identify sessions in which insight events occurred and to locate the events within sessions. Client descriptions on the HAT Form also provided information on their experience of the significant event, including event content, therapist actions, and client within-session reactions.

In addition, clients completed Stiles's (1980) SEQ after each session, which uses semantic–differential-style items to rate two dimensions of session evaluative experience, depth–value and smoothness–ease. Finally, the Personal Questionnaire (PQ; Phillips, 1986) provided a weekly, 10-item individualized change measure.

Procedure: Comprehensive Process Analysis

CPA involves a number of different procedures and steps (Elliott, 1989, 1993). In particular, qualitative analysts apply a general sensitizing framework, encompassing a wide range of factors that may be important for the understanding of a significant therapy event. These factors were developed from earlier analyses of the literature (see Elliott, 1991) and over the course of previous CPA studies (e.g., Elliott, 1984, 1989). The framework is divided into three broad domains.

The first domain, context, encompasses the factors and events that lead up to or are exemplified by the event. Four levels of context are analyzed (Elliott, 1991). First, *background* refers to relevant features of the client and the therapist that preceded and were brought to the treatment, including client interpersonal conflict themes (Luborsky & Crits-Christoph, 1990; e.g., fears and criticism), problems (e.g., poor interpersonal problem-solving skills), coping style (e.g., self-observant), history (e.g., rejected by father or husband), and current life situation (e.g., helping professional), as well as therapist personal characteristics (e.g., same gender as client) and treatment principles (operating guidelines that can be seen in the therapist's responses; e.g., link themes across domains). Second, *presession context* covers relevant events that have occurred since treatment began, either in earlier sessions (e.g., therapist interpretation in previous session) or outside of therapy (e.g., recent humiliation by fellow teacher). Third, *session context* involves relevant features of the session in which the event occurred, including client and therapist session tasks (e.g., deal with painful insight from previous session), therapeutic alliance (e.g., strong with periodic stresses), and earlier responses in session (e.g., client reports failure to complete therapeutic homework). Finally, *episode context* refers to important features of the conversational episode that contains the significant event, including client and therapist episode tasks (e.g., explore relationship with mother) and client and therapist responses leading up to the event (e.g., client expresses bitterness).

The second domain is key responses. It consists of four aspects of the most helpful therapist or client responses: action (e.g., therapist interpretation), content (e.g., interpersonal fears), style (e.g., gentle), and quality or skillfulness (e.g., appropriate and evocative use of key word).

The third domain, effects, refers to the sequentially unfolding consequences of an event, including its immediate effects within the episode (e.g., client agrees strongly), its delayed effects within the same session or in later sessions (e.g., talks with coworkers about problem), and the clinical significance of the event, given in terms of quantitative ratings of the effectiveness of the event (e.g., client helpfulness ratings), the session within which the event occurred (e.g., SEQ Depth ratings), or across the client's entire treatment (e.g., improvement on PSE ratings).

This framework directs analysts' attention to the kinds of things that often help to explain significant events, but does not constrain the specific nature of their explanations. For example, analysts are asked to consider the client's therapeutic tasks for the session as partial explanations for an event, but are given the freedom to describe these tasks in any way that they see fit.

We all were CPA analysts in this study, and two (David A. Shapiro and Jenny Firth-Cozens) were the two therapists whose events are presented in this study. All of the analysts were trained, experienced clinicians and psychotherapy researchers of diverse theoretical orientations; three were women, and all were Anglo-British or European-American in ethnicity.

To train the analysts, Robert Elliott presented an overview of the CPA method. Analysts then read an article on CPA (Elliott, 1989), and questions about the method were answered. The researchers then analyzed one psychodynamic–interpersonal and one cognitive–behavioral therapy event. After this, for efficiency, the analysts were divided into two teams of four each in order to carry out studies of the remaining four events (two events for each team; Elliott served on both teams, and teams always included the therapist involved in the event).

After the event had been identified, the entire session in which it occurred was transcribed by a research assistant. The analysts followed the steps for CPA (Elliott, 1989, 1993).

First, each analyst independently explicated the implicit meanings in the key therapist speaking turns and the client's postsession description of the event. Explication is an interpretive process of completing the speakers' acts of reference (e.g., taken-for-granted knowledge and meaning implied through stylistic cues; Elliott, 1993).

Second, the analysts met to develop a consensus explication of these meanings, following Gadamer's (1979) principle of "unforced consensus through open dialogue." Specifically, this meeting involved an equalitarian group atmosphere, a systematic hearing of all versions, a voicing of unique descriptions, and a spirit of compromise (Elliott, 1993).

Third, each analyst independently applied the CPA framework to the available information, filling in relevant descriptions and explanations of the event's key responses, effects, and context. For these analyses, the primary source of information for all of the three analysts was the session tape and transcript. In addition, the therapist reviewed his or her notes from the previous and following sessions, while the other analysts also relied on research data available in the client's file (e.g., posttreatment interview and outcome data). Analysts began with a microanalysis of the key therapist responses in the event and then carried out the effects analysis of the consequences of the event. Finally, they analyzed its context, working from the most immediate context (local cue or immediatly preceding speaking turn) to the most general context (client and therapist personal characteristics).

In considering each possible explanatory element, each analyst tested it against three criteria: (a) the element had to be present in the data, (b) the element could not be redundant with other elements within the same CPA heading, and (c) the element had to be relevant to explaining the event. In general, the analysts' perspective was that of outside observers attempting to encompass and respect all of the available information, including the discrepancies between client, therapist, and the views of multiple observers (cf. Elliott & Shapiro, 1992).

Fourth, the analysts met to develop a consensus version of their separate analyses of the event. In this process, the analysts used the same three criteria and followed the same order as in the original analyses.

Cross-Analysis of Insight Events

After analyzing the individual events, the entire team of judges carried out a cross-analysis of the six events, aimed at identifying common and discriminating factors. Specifically, we wanted to answer two questions: (a) What factors appear to be common to client insight across the psychodynamic–interpersonal and cognitive–behavioral treatments (general factors)? and (b) What factors appear to distinguish insight events in the two treatments (discriminating factors)?

Thematic Analysis

For the cross-analysis, we used the open-coding procedure from grounded theory (Rennie et al., 1988) to classify *themes*, that is, replicable features found in at least two of the six insight events. Thus, each judge independently categorized themes for each of the headings in the CPA framework; the team then met and developed a consensus for the definition of each theme and the events that contained it. For example, five of the six events were judged to come from sessions in which the client had the overall task of expressing feelings.

Because of the small number of events in the collection, only the strongest themes were used for model building, which involved inferring connections between explanatory elements. A general theme had to occur in all or in all but one of the six events, whereas a discriminating theme had to be characteristic of all events of one type and none of the other (e.g., an interpersonal therapy discriminating theme had to occur in all three psychodynamic–interpersonal events and no cognitive–behavioral events).

Expectation Ratings

After the analyses were completed, we used 4-point scales to rate each obtained theme for the extent to which they had expected it to be (a) a general theme, characteristic of both kinds of insight events, or (b) a discriminating theme, characteristic of one but not the other kind of insight event. Expectation ratings were averaged across raters and dichotomized at the scale midpoint (1.5). Expectations were obtained retrospectively so that expectations that emerged during the analyses could be detected. Post hoc ratings of the obtained themes provided a measure of possible expectation biases. The analysis of expectations also enabled us to identify unexpected themes (i.e., discoveries).

Results

Analysis of Psychodynamic–Interpersonal Therapy Insight Event

On the postsession HAT Form, the selected psychodynamic–interpersonal insight event was described by the client (Client 57 in Session 15) as follows:

> I was very upset at the thought of consistently "seducing" people—the therapist called the behavior of seduction a sham and linked it to the "sham" that I experienced as a child.

The client was a 37-year-old male social services worker, seen by an experienced male therapist (Shapiro). He sought treatment because of "manic" behavior at work and depression related to a recent affair of his wife's. The event occurred in the second-to-last session of the treatment, the seventh in the psychodynamic–interpersonal phase of treatment.

When we first identified this event, it confronted us with a circumstance we had not previously seen. Even though the client's description revealed that he saw it as a single unified event, the event actually involved therapist actions that occurred in two different parts in the session. Part 1 ("the therapist called the behavior of seduction a sham") took place about 20 min into the session, whereas Part 2 ("and linked it to the 'sham' that I experienced as a child") occurred some 15 min after the first part. The two key therapist interventions are T22 and T40–T41 in Table 1. For clarity, the results of our analysis are presented as a narrative, in temporal order

Table 1—*Transcript of Psychodynamic–Interpersonal Insight (Client 57, Session 15)*

Speaker/turn	Text
	Part 1 of event
T18	[T's first attempt to link C's seductiveness to dishonesty.] *Hmm* (12.0) It's painful to think of seducing people, as being dishonest. (10.3)
C19	((sigh)) (9.3) ((sigh)) [local cue: C disagrees and reiterates pain.] Well, it's painful I don't know whether it's because I feel it's dishonest, it's, (8.2) it's just painful. (15.8)
T19	[T backs down, offers empathy.] To feel yourself to be a seducer, (1.9) °is painful°. (3.6)
C20	[Side sequence regarding: Reaction to previous session begins here.] 'h I- I- I- I don't know uh (19.1) I'm surprised I'm so upset (T: *Mmm*) about it because I've, it's been around with me and interestingly I've been (1.0) very aware of some of the day-to-day interactions and I've thought, you know (T: *Mhm*) the bell's gone/and I've thought, "Well I'm doing it again."
T20	Well that's almost, and that's wh], and that's been quite a good feeling in a way to have that knowledge. Yeah? (1.2)
C21	Yes.=
T21	In a way, yes.=
C22	[Mutual agreement ends side sequence.] Yeah (0.5)
T22[a]	But- but somehow (1.0) (uh), getting into it here is like a painful thing of, (2.4) is it feeling bad about yourself? Is it a kind of you as a sham, you as a:? (<0.5)
C23	Yeah, I have to admit it,/yes) (T: Yeah) it's-, yeah (1.1) I-, yes. I think it's got to do with:- with that somehow [= Process Step 1: strong agreement]. h Yes. (2.9) I suppose that's a very basic sort of simple concept and [insight marker:] I don't know why I didn't think of it [elaboration:] but I, yes, I feel (2.7) (I) remember reading an interview about somebody creative who- and say famous and he, (1.0) 'h he actually said, you know, "One day I- I, you know, I- I fear I may uh, I may be found out." (and) I'm just- (T: *Hmm*) I'm just, 'h and I really sort of identified with that [= Step 2]/but
	Part 2 of event
C39	(20.1) I certainly sought my *mother's* approval 'cause she made life so bloody unpleasant if you didn't get it, you know. [= relevant event] (15.0)
T39	And- and your memory is very much of *not* getting it, isn't it? Very much (1.6) suffering =
C40	'hh Well the- it, when it was given it sort of came over in such great *do*llops of blancmange in front of other people, you know that you, it was ex*cru*ciatingly (T: *Hmm*) em*bar*rassing c-, and you knew that once these people sort of, disappeared, or what have you, that (2.1) her reactions'd be different [= local cue] (0.5)
T40[a]	So you felt her affection was a sham? (1.0)
C41	*Right* [= strong agreement] (5.0)/Hmm
T41[a]	And tha]t's maybe part of your, your pain at your, your seduction being a sham. (13.0) And there's a lot of anger about being stopped from being a loving person by the way you were mistreated as a child.

Table continues

Table 1—*Continued*

Speaker/turn	Text
C42	(25.0) I'm s-, did you say lovable or loving person? [= side sequence] (0.6)
T42	"Lov*ing*" I said (C: (laughs)) but uh the other is maybe also there. (C: *Hmm*) Uh (20.0)
C43	[Connection form of insight marker:] I- I'm uh think there's bound to be a connection betwee:n (1.9) what we've just been talking about and the fact that I go *so* upset when I said, you know, "That I'm, (1.6) I'm upset about being a sham." (T: *Hmm, Hmm,* [1.6] *Hmm*) (8.0) [elaboration:] But so much of my background as a child was a, was a sham. I mean (12.0) and I, and really got *seduced* into that. I mean I was sent away to schoo:l (1.8) u:m (5.0) a real "cra:p" (1.7) Catholic boarding school (7.0) and yet I was from a working class [place name] background.

Note. Transcription symbols (from Sacks, Schegloff, & Jefferson, 1974) are as follows: h = out-breath; 'h = in-breath; 'hh = long in-breath; : = prolongation of sound; ° = softer than expected; *Mmm* = backchannel utterances; text in parentheses, e.g., (and) = unclear hearing; / = beginning of interruption;] = end of interruption; numbers in parentheses are timings of internal and interresponse pauses; the "=" symbol stands for the absence of an expected pause; T = therapist; C = client.

ᵃKey therapist intervention.

(context, key responses, and effects) and somewhat simplified. (In addition, space limitations preclude presenting explication analyses.)

Context Analysis

In our analysis, we looked at four levels of context.

Background: What general characteristics of client and therapist explain the insight? In our search for the broadest context of this event, we examined the role played by the background characteristics that the client and the therapist brought to the treatment. To do this, we examined the session transcript and the therapist's case notes (for client background information); we also drew on our general knowledge of the treatment model and of the therapist (for therapist background).

Analyzing the client's background helps to explain why the equation of interpersonal seductiveness with "sham" in key response T20 was so important to him. The client had strong conflicting wishes both to be in control and to receive the affection and approval of others (= conflicts). His strategy for meeting these wishes was to act in a manipulatively charming (i.e., seductive) manner (= style). Moreover, he was in a helping profession and worked with acting-out adolescents, which had sensitized him to issues of interpersonal pretense and dishonesty (seductiveness).

The client's open, insightful style and his life situation as a helping professional also suggested that he knew what was expected and useful in therapy. This information helped to explain the strong positive alliance observed, which allowed the client to feel helped in spite of the painfulness of the content.

The therapist's background also helped to make sense of the event. For one thing, his key responses and the therapeutic tasks he pursued in the session and episode can be seen as expressing two psychodynamic–interpersonal therapy treatment principles: (a) that it is useful to link themes across areas of the client's life and (b) that interpersonal themes should be tied together at the end of treatment. Two therapist personal characteristics were also important for the therapist alliance: his similarities to the client (in terms of gender and profession) were a positive influence, whereas his typically high activity level was evident at times during the session when he pushed the client too hard, generating temporary alliance disruptions.

Presession: What recent events led to the insight? In the previous session, the therapist had interpreted the client's interpersonal behavior as seductive. The client was upset by this during the ensuing week.

Session: What features of the present session led to the insight? The client came to this session with the task of exploring his painful reaction to the previous session. In addition, the client and therapist generally shared the session tasks of dealing with interpersonal themes and issues related to termination.

Furthermore, for this session the task aspect of the alliance appearred to be generally strong, evidence by the degree to which the client was working at (rather than avoiding) appropriate therapeutic tasks throughout the session and particularly in the responses before and after the key therapist responses. On the other hand, the bond aspect of the alliance, although also generally good, suffered from periodic disruptions, apparently induced by the therapist pushing too hard, to the point where the client at times felt misunderstood or criticized.

Analysis of the session context also explained how the client and therapist got from the concept that seduction equals sham (T22) to the idea that the client's present pain was related to the pain he experienced as a child when his mother shammed affection for him (T40 and T41). The bridge was a narrative (= relevant event) about turning down a recent unreasonable request from his parents. This narrative raised the issue of the client's desire for his parents' approval, which in turn led to Part 2 of the event, an exploration of his relationship with his mother when he was a child.

Episode: What was the immediate context? Because the significant event has two parts, there are two different episode contexts. The episode context for the first part of the event corresponds to speaking turns C15–C22 (partially presented in Table 1), leading up to the therapist peak at T22. (In Table 1, relevant events and local cues are noted in brackets, as are several other orgainzational features.) The episode was organized by the shared task of searching for the meaning of the painful insight generated by the previous therapy session. The local cue is unusual in that it did not immediately precede the key therapist response. In T18, the therapist first attempted to describe the client's discomfort but used the wrong word (*dishonest* instead of sham). The client rejected this attempt (C19), signaling the need for another try and providing the local cue for the key response (T22). However, the degree of pain expressed by the client (C19) prompted the therapist to provide breathing room in the form of a short, supportive side sequence before returning to the task.

The episode context for the second part of the event occurred within a later episode of the session. Client and therapist were now exploring the client's relationship with his mother. In the local cue (C40), the client offered the therapist the key element for a genetic interpretation by describing his childhood pain at the contrast between his mother's public affection toward him and her private coldness.

Microanalysis of Key Responses

In our process analysis of the key therapist response in Part 1 of the event (T22), we found that at the end of T22 ("is it kind of you as a sham?"), the therapist finally hit upon an acceptable formula (i.e., interpretation) for explaining the client's painful reaction to the seduction theme (= action). This formula linked the painful reaction to shamming, which became the key to a network of meanings and memories (= content). Finally, the therapist's delivery of this response skillfully balanced searching and persistence with gentle collaboration (= style and quality).

The key therapist responses in Part 2 of the event were also judged as skillfully balancing style with content and action. Specifically, the therapist used a gentle, meditative style (with 13-s internal pause), and a small number of evocative words to convey a painful interpretation. These responses clarified the painful meaning the word shamming had for the client.

Effects Analysis

This part of the analysis entailed a close examination of the sequence of events immediately after each part of the event, as well as a tracing of the event's delayed effects and the quantitative data that bore on its effectiveness (Elliott, 1993).

Immediate effects.   As the narrative in Table 1 shows, the key therapist response in Part 1 (T22) led immediately to strong agreement by the client, followed by an insight marker (C23: "I don't know why I didn't think of it"); the client then elaborated on this insight. The insight marker provides evidence that the newness characteristic of insight is present in this event. The episode ended (T23, not in transcript) when the therapist attempted to deflect attention to the therapeutic relationship.

In Part 2 of the event (Table 1), the immediate effects were complex. They began with the client's strong, bitter agreement (C41) between the two parts of the therapist response (T40 and T41). A long, reflective silence follows, ended by a brief "repair sequence" (C42–T42). The episode ends when the therapist deflects attention to the client's relationship with his son (not in transcript). It is interesting that both parts of this event ended by apparently unhelpful therapist responses, producing temporary strains in the therapeutic alliance.

Later effects.   Two weeks after the session in which the insight event occurred, the client was asked to describe any particularly helpful aspects of therapy as part of the posttreatment assessment. The following responses appear to be relevant to this event:

> I was made to look at some very painful feelings that I have had since my childhood . . . My ambivalent feelings about my mother was something I have *looked at* before, and been aware of, but I felt I was made to stay with the pain of some of those feelings—getting in touch with feelings is not an intellectual exercise . . . I was made to look at how and why I try to please people.

Thus, it appears that the delayed effect of this event and the related therapeutic work was primarily an enhanced awareness regarding painful feelings about self and mother, with perhaps a hint of insight ("how and why I try to please people"). Our interpretation is that the immediate client reaction of insight became transformed over time into awareness.

Clinical significance of event. The effects analysis also involved a range of quantitative effectiveness data, much of which supported the clinical significance of this event. The client gave the session high ratings for helpfulness (5 = *very helpful*) and SEQ Depth–Value (6.0), while the therapist gave very high ratings for SEQ Depth–Value (6.75). Using the guidelines suggested in Elliott (1993), we found that a majority of the available indicators of clinical significance were positive.

Analysis of Cognitive–Behavioral Therapy Insight Event

The cognitive–behavioral therapy event selected for detailed presentation was described by the client (Client 40 in Session 4) as follows:

> We went over a situation which happened today, where I had thought I'd let myself down and made a fool of myself, and when the therapist pointed out that it was [a] fairly common situation and quite funny, I suddenly saw another side to it and felt much better.

The client was a 34-year-old female school teacher, referred by her physician for "depression and inability to cope with relationships." She was seen by an experienced female clinical psychologist (Firth-Cozens) for eight sessions of cognitive therapy followed by eight sessions of interpersonal therapy. The event came from Session 4 of the initial, cognitive phase of treatment; in earlier sessions, she had been taught relaxation, instructed to keep a diary, and introduced to some assertion strategies. The transcript of the event is presented in Table 2.

Context Analysis

Background. The client background context helped to explain the significance of the event for the client. During this and other sessions, the client had described a history of rejection by important men in her life, including her father and ex-husband, at the same time revealing a basic interpersonal conflict of desiring respect and approval while fearing humiliation and rejection. The client's typical way of meeting her needs (= style) had been through self-abnegation and joking in order to please others, coupled with vigilance against being betrayed. As a result, she had poor interpersonal problem-solving skills (necessitating assertiveness training) and vacillated between excessively negative and positive views of self (= problems). In the face of this, the client was enmeshed in a continuing conflict with a male fellow teacher (D), with whom she had previously enjoyed a friendly relationship and whose class she had taken over (= situation).

The therapist background was relevant to the event in two ways. To begin with, the therapist's actions were guided by two general cognitive–behavioral treatment principles: (a) that clients should be helped to make external reattributions of negative events, which was the message of the key therapist response, and (b) that clients should be encouraged to assert themselves, which was the intent of the larger task within which the event occurred. In addition, the therapist being of the same gender as the client (= personal characteristic) appeared to facilitate the therapeutic alliance.

Presession. The presession context for this significant event included a number of extratherapy life events, each reported by the client during the session. During

Table 2—*Transcript of Cognitive–Behavioral Insight Event (Client 40, Session 4)*

Speaker/turn	Text
C1	'hh I think it [a useful incident for us to go through] would be, being found out to be wrong in front of D. You, you know (T: *Hmm*) if he sort of of uh, do, just uh as he does little tiny things all the time that that annoy me, t- to death. [Begins narrative.] He, he, one thing he did this week was, and it's nothing, absolutely nothing but it annoyed me, 'h he walked through the hall just as we were finishing off after P.E. when the buzzer had gone, you know, it was playtime and there were just about three mats to put away and you can bet your life you'll get somebody fooling with a mat when D walks through. [complaint about self:] It happens to me every ti:me, you know, that (T: *Hmm*) I look a fool 'h and, and I, I/ don't look a fool but I feel a fool.
T2	But do you, no you don't.] (1.2)
C2	But he's, he's just *got* to do something like just move the piano a little bit further out of the way (T: Yea:h) where it *should* be. That's the thing that hurts. (T: *Hmm*) I should have seen that the piano was too close to the mat stand (T: *Hmm*) but I haven't. (T: *Hmm*) [local cue: tentative reattribution:] But anybody else would just walk through (T: *Hmm*) but D's just got to put it right. (<0.5)
T3ᵃ	I think you're probably quite *right* about D. I mean I think/he is a pain in- yes, *yeah*
C3	He's a bit of a pain ((laughing)) = ((continues laughing))/'hh
T4	That's right (<0.5)
C4	*Ye(h)s.*/There is that.
T5	U:m I think he is] probably very worried about his own position at the/ moment and uh
C5	Yeah, Ye:ss,]/that's it, that's the get-out, isn't it?
T6	and, and probably] uh may be in some ways might be quite jealous of you in, in little ways. Maybe your relationship with the kids is better 'hh or something like this or he, I should think he sees you as a bit of a threat. (C: Yeah) U:m and his only way of controlling that sort of feeling is to keep putting his finger on little things and (C: Yeah, yeah) everybody, *nothing* is ever going to be perfect.

Note. Transcription symbols (from Sacks, Schegloff, & Jefferson, 1974) are as follows: h = out-breath; 'h = in-breath; 'hh = long in-breath; : = prolongation of sound; *Mmm* = backchannel utterances; text in parentheses, e.g., (and) = unclear hearing; / = beginning of interruption;] = end of interruption; numbers in parentheses are timings of internal and inter-response pauses; the "=" symbol stands for the absence of an expected pause; T = therapist; C = client; D = C's coworker.
ᵃKey therapist intervention.

the week prior to the session, she had generally been feeling tense and angry without apparent reason and had experienced a humiliating interaction with an annoying fellow teacher (who was referred to in the event). Also, she had not carried out therapeutic homework having to do with assertion.

Session. In analyzing the overall session context for this significant event, we noted that the therapist entered into the session with the agenda of helping the client to practice assertion (= therapist session task). As the session progressed, the therapist added emergent tasks of teaching the client to make positive reattributions and of supporting the client and bolstering her motivation, which were evident in the key response. For her part, the client attempted to explain her discomfort and anger in problematic life situations and to obtain therapist support with regard to these difficulties (= client session tasks). The significant event was anticipated by earlier reattributional work regarding another coworker; shortly before the episode in which the event took place, the client admitted that she had not completed a therapeutic homework assignment (= relevant events).

    Episode. The episode context in which the significant therapist response occurred was initiated by the therapist at T1 (Table 2) as an attempt to remediate the missing homework. Initially, the therapist attempted to obtain an example of a difficult situation for anxiety management and assertiveness training, while the client attempted to comply with this (= episode tasks). However, supporting the client also emerged as an important therapist task during the episode, as she told her story (in C1 and C2) of being publicly embarrassed by fellow teacher D. The client's tentative reattribution (end of C2) provided the immediate stimulus (= local cue) for the key therapist response, T3.

Microanalysis of Key Response

As the narrative in Table 2 indicates, this event is much simpler than the previous one, centering on a single brief therapist response. The explication and process analysis indicated that the therapist's main action in this response was a reassurance and an interpretation of a third party (the fellow teacher), which was intended to reassure the client that she was justified in her view of D. The reassurance was carried by the therapist's interpreting the client as correct and offering her judgment of D as "a pain" ("in the ass" was understood by both as implied). T3 also reveals the therapist task of reinforcing the client's tentative reattribution given at the end of her previous response (C2, the local cue).

    The content of the therapist's reassurance was the truth of what the client had been saying and suggests an external reattribution of the situation reported by the client: The situation was the fellow teacher's fault because he is a "pain" (i.e., generally overzealous and rude). The style of the therapist's response was friendly and definite ("quite right") and revealed a responsiveness to client feedback, as the therapist became more critical of the other during the course of her response. Finally, the judges were impressed with the therapist's having quickly responded to the opportunity to reinforce the client's tentative reattribution (= quality).

Effects Analysis

    Immediate Effects. The immediate effects of the key therapist response (Table 2) began with the client agreeing with the therapist's appraisal of D, followed by laughter at D's expense (C3). This short conversational sequence that negatively characterized D ended with mutual agreement (T4 and C4). The therapist then went on to elaborate her externalizing reattribution of the problem as D's: It is not just that D is a pain; in particular, he may be jealous or feel threatened by the client, both of which imply positive attributes about the client. The client's actions and manner suggest that she initially felt relieved and supported by the therapist, and then she moved into cognitive elaboration in the form of external attribution and decreased negative views of self.

Later effects.   The delayed postsession effects of the event were revealed in the client's report several sessions later that she had sought out and discussed D's behavior with several other colleagues; these colleagues confirmed her perceptions of D. An additional benefit of this event was that she improved her relationship with her team-teacher, with whom she had been having some conflicts. It is important to note, however, that the client's relationship with D had been an important topic in the intervening sessions; it is thus not clear whether this particular response was solely responsible for the client's later action. Nevertheless, the later action was in keeping with what happened in this event (i.e., discussing D in negative terms with a supportive other and getting confirmation from them). At the very least, the event was part of a larger therapeutic process involving in-session rehearsal and interpersonal support.

Clinical significance of event.   The quantitative effectiveness data show some support for the event's clinical significance. In particular, the client rated the event and the session as very helpful (a 5). The client showed substantial improvement on the change measures over this phase of treatment. On the other hand, client and therapist SEQ ratings were within one standard deviation of their sample means (6.25 for client and 5.00 for therapist), and the client showed a moderate increase in client distress on the PQ during the week after the session (from 55 to 65). Overall, the clinical significance indicators for this event were not nearly as strong as for the psychodynamic–interpersonal event.

Cross-Analysis of Interpersonal and Cognitive Insight Events

One hundred nine themes were identified as applying to two or more of the six events analyzed; an additional 15 quantitative impact variables were also included (e.g., client SEQ Depth).

General Themes for the Insight Events

We found 19 general themes (7 occurred in all events and 12 in all but one event). These themes offer a general picture of the common features of insight events in the two therapies and are presented in Table 3.

Context.   Regardless of the treatment model, the clients' history and current life situation of ongoing interpersonal difficulties (e.g., conflict with a fellow teacher) were relevant to understanding the events. Recent painful life events, related to these general difficulties led the clients to enter the current session with the task of first expressing, then exploring the uncomfortable feelings engendered. The significant event was immediately preceded by the clients describing their reaction to this life event.

Clients and their therapies were also found to share important demographic similarities, which were judged to facilitate the therapeutic alliance in the face of peri-

Table 3—*General Theme Characteristics of Insight Events in Both Psychodynamic–*
Interpersonal and Cognitive–Behavioral Therapies

CPA heading	Theme
	Context
Background	
Client situation	Client is involved in recurrent, ongoing relationship difficulties (e.g., previous failed marriage). (5/6)
	Client experiences interpersonal difficulties at work. (5/6)
Therapist characteristics	Therapist is similar to client (e.g., age and sex). (5/6)
Presession	
Extratherapy events	During previous week, the client has experienced a puzzling or painful life event. (5/6)
Session	
Client task	The client seeks to express feelings. (5/6)
Alliance	The therapeutic alliance is generally strong and positive. (6/6)
	The therapeutic alliance is marked by periodic conflicts; it is fragile or limited in some way. (6/6)
Episode	
Client task	The client attempts to explore painful or puzzling feelings or events. (5/6)
Relevant event	The client describes a painful emotional or puzzling reaction. (5/6)
	Key response
Action or response mode	Therapist interpretation is present in the key response (6/6); interpretation is the major action (predominant over other response modes). (5/6)[a]
Content	The key response refers to a basic interpersonal conflict theme (fear, wish, or both). (5/6)[a]
	The key response refers to a painful or puzzling personal reaction related to a general theme (e.g., reattribution or interpersonal conflict theme). (6/6)[a]
Style	The therapist's manner is firm and persistent. (5/6)[a]
	The therapist's response is interactive (i.e., responsive to client feedback). (6/6)
Quality	The therapist makes skillful use of the treatment model. (5/6)
	The key response is well-grounded in client material. (6/6)
	Effects
Process impact	The client's initial response is implicit or explicit agreement. (6/6)

Note. Numbers in parentheses indicate how many of the six change events contained the theme. CPA = comprehensive process analysis.
[a]Unexpected theme.

odic strains or difficulties (e.g., the bond between client and therapist was strong, but the client was not doing her homework).

Key response. Unexpectedly, cognitive–behavioral as well as psychodynamic–interpersonal events were found to contain therapist interpretations. The content of the two types of insight event was also unexpectedly similar: the therapists' interpretations formulated the clients' painful reaction (a) as a problem to be addressed further (e.g., externally reattributing the problem) and (b) as relevant to a general interpersonal conflict theme (cf. Luborsky & Crits-Christoph, 1990; e.g., fears, humiliation). The interpretations were delivered in a style that was both firm and persistent and yet also allowed for feedback from the clients. Finally, the therapists' interventions were judged as being well-grounded in client material and skillful within the guidelines for the respective treatment model.

Effects. In all of the events, the clients' first response was to agree, either implicitly or explicitly (e.g., "Yeah, I have to admit, yes" and "He's a bit of a pain, yeah").

Psychodynamic–Interpersonal Therapy Event Themes

Thirteen themes and one quantitative variable were present in all three psychodynamic–interpersonal therapy events and in none of the cognitive–behavioral therapy events; these discriminating themes are presented in the middle column of Table 4.

The discriminating themes tell the following story about the psychodynamic–interpersonal insight events. Model-specific treatment principles guided the therapists' behavior, including offering interpretive links involving multiple life domains (e.g., the client's current interpersonal behavior and his childhood relationship with his mother) and guiding the continued exploration and linking of central issues raised in earlier therapy sessions. In this context, the therapists were helping the clients to explore painful or puzzling experiences (e.g., a strong reaction to the previous session).

The key responses were immediately preceded by an initial therapist interpretation (T18: "It's painful to think of seducing people as being dishonest") and the clients' expression of a strong, difficult emotional reaction (C19: "It's just painful"). In this response, the therapists picked a major theme from a previous session (e.g., seductiveness), delivering it in a negotiating manner and making appropriate and evocative use of a key word (e.g., sham). The clients reacted to this response with apparently greater awareness of theme-related unwanted experiences, accompanied by painful emotion. As a result, the clients experienced the session as a whole as rough or difficult.

Cognitive–Behavioral Therapy Event Themes

Six themes and two effectiveness variables discriminated cognitive–behavioral therapy insight events from those in psychodynamic–interpersonal therapy. These themes suggest that the events involved clients with substantial pretreatment clinical distress and low self-esteem. Perhaps responding to this, their therapists emphasized treatment principles having to do with external reattribution of negative life events and

Table 4—*Psychodynamic–Interpersonal and Cognitive–Behavioral*
Insight Event Discriminating Themes

CPA heading	Psychodynamic–Interpersonal	Cognitive–Behavioral
	Context	
Background		
Client symptoms	None	Clients show lower self-esteem and greater distress on pretests on the PSE and the Rosenberg SES.
Treatment principles	It is useful to link themes acorss life domains. It is useful to focus on primary/ early relationships. It is useful to negotiate under-standings with the client.	It is useful to help clients to reattribute (externalize negative events or inter-nalize positive events). It is useful to encourage cli-ents to assert self or to take control.
Presession	A core interpersonal theme was raised in an earlier session.[a]	None
Session		
Therapist task	Therapist is attempting to ex-plore and link themes, issues, and relationships; therapist explains these to client.	None
Episode		
Therapist task	Therapist is attempting to ex-plore painful or puzzling feelings and events.	None
Relevant event	Early in episode, therapist in-terprets or connects relevant event to core theme.	Client and therapist engage in collaborative informa-tion gathering activities.[a]
Local cue	The immediate stimulus for the key therapist response is cli-ent expression of a strong painful or puzzling emotional reaction.	None
	Key therapist response	
Content	Key response builds on a major theme or proposition dis-cussed in a previous session.[a]	Key response is about exter-nal reattribution (shifting blame).[a]
Style	Therapist manner is negotiating.	None
Quality	Therapist makes appropriate and evocative use of a key word.[a]	None
	Effects	
Client experience	Client experiences strong or painful emotion.	Client disowns or reattributes negative events.[a]

Table continues

Table 4—*Continued*

CPA heading	Psychodynamic–Interpersonal	Cognitive–Behavioral
Effectiveness	Client experiences awareness of unwanted, puzzling experience related to them.[a] Session rougher (for the SEQ, *M* = 2.80).	SCL-90: Client shows distress at posttest (*mdn* symptom total was 83 for prescriptive vs. 14 for exploratory). Rosenberg SES: Client shows lower self-esteem at posttest (*mdn* was 21 for prescriptive vs. 44 for exploratory).

Note. CPA = comprehensive process analysis; PSE = Present State Examination; SES = Self-Esteem Scale; SCL-90 = Symptom Checklist–90.
[a]Unexpected theme.

greater self-assertion. The key therapist responses were external reattributions, which shifted blame from the client to others (e.g., the therapist noted that a colleague of the client's was, in fact, "a pain"). These responses occurred in the context of collaborative, information-gathering activities, suggesting the possibility that the insight emerged serendipitously (e.g., while verbally reconstructing a situation in preparation for a behavioral role play).

The clients then followed their therapist's lead in externally reattributing the negative events. The clients in the three cognitive–behavioral insight events also remained more distressed and with lower self-esteem at posttest (however, both sets of clients were roughly equivalent in amount of improvement over treatment).

Analysis of Possible Observer Bias: Expected Versus Obtained Themes

Finally, we supplemented our predominantly qualitative analysis with a statistical comparison of the analysts' retrospective expectations with what they actually found. The relationship between expected and obtained themes was statistically reliable but suggested that no more than about a quarter of the variance in the obtained results could be attributed to the analysts' expectations or biases, $\phi = .44$, $p < .01$; $r = .51$, $p < .01$; $N = 109$. Similarly, for the discriminating themes, the relationship between expected and obtained themes was statistically reliable but small enough to indicate that expectations could not have played a large role in determining the obtained results, $\phi = .39$, $p < .01$; $r = .45$, $p < .01$; $N = 109$.

Several strongly expected general themes (with mean ratings greater than 2.50) were not found, including the expectations that the therapists would generally manifest skill in the events, that the content of the event would generally be raised earlier in the current session rather than in an earlier session, and that the key responses would differentially attempt to foster external reattribution (expected for cognitive–behavioral events) or explain painful reactions (expected for psychodynamic–interpersonal events).

More important, a number of unexpected general themes were found, which are indicated in Tables 3 and 4. These themes include the general themes of a key therapist response that refers to client core conflicts and problematic personal reactions and that is delivered in a firm, persistent style. Similarly, the reattributional content and effect of the cognitive–behavioral insight events was an unexpected finding.

Discussion

A General Model of Insight Events

The two significant events presented in-depth as well as the analysis of themes in the larger collection of six events share a number of common features, suggesting the possibility of a general model of insight events.

The events illustrate the general role of recent painful or puzzling life events that occur in a broader context of chronic situational difficulties. In these events, clients expressed some puzzlement over their reactions. In particular, the two events presented in greater detail involved "problematic reaction points" (Rice & Sapiera, 1984) introduced by the clients as a primary therapeutic task for the episode in which the event occurred. The therapeutic intervention used in all events to address this task was interpretation, well-grounded in client material, exemplifying the treatment model and delivered in a firm, persistent, but interactive style.

All of the events thus involved what Rice and Sapiera (1984) called a *meaning bridge*, linking the client's reaction to its context, so that the reaction comes to make sense. In the first event, the client came to understand a link that united his pain of defining his interpersonal behavior as seductive to his childhood pain of his mother's shamming affection toward him. In the second event, the client linked feeling pain (at being incompetent) to her fellow teacher's being a pain.

Our analyses thus suggest a refinement of Elliott's (1984) three-stage (processing– insight–elaboration) microprocess model of insight, incorporating many of the common themes identified. In particular, the current version of CPA provided a much more detailed analysis of context in this study, complementing the more detailed analysis of immediate effects made possible in the earlier study by the availability of rich recall data. Combining the results of the two studies yielded the following sequential model:

1. *Contextual priming.* Earlier therapy sessions have provided the therapist with relevant thematic information and allowed the development of the therapeutic alliance (cf. Luborsky et al., 1979). The client has recently experienced a painful problematic life event, which is narrated to the therapist.
2. *Novel information.* The client is then presented with new information that is both relevant to the recent painful event and in keeping with more general themes about the client's functioning. This new information generally takes the form of therapist interpretation (cf. Garduk & Haggard, 1972; Hill, Helms, Tichenor, et al., 1988).
3. *Initial distantiated processing.* The client's immediate reaction to this novel

information is to mull it over, typically briefly and in a fairly unemotional manner, while agreeing to its general accuracy (cf. Elliott, 1984).

4. *Insight.* The client's initial pondering is followed by a clear sense of connection or reconnection, which may take any of a number of forms (e.g., interpersonal conflict pattern or causal reattribution). In the events studied so far, this insight is conveyed to the therapist in the form of an observable emotional expression of surprise (e.g., "I don't know why I didn't think of it"), which also indicates the presence of the hallmark experience of newness. (Private, or unmarked, insight events clearly exist, but have not been studied.)

5. *Elaboration.* The insight then stimulates the client to further exploration, which elaborates the emotional or other implications of the insight (e.g., painful awareness or relief). This elaboration indicates that the insight is not merely intellectual (cf. the psychoanalytic debate on intellectual vs. emotional insight; Crits-Christoph et al., 1993).

This model, based on the analyses reported here and in Elliott (1984), suggests that therapist interpretation is necessary for client insight. However, data from Elliott et al. (1985) indicated that clients can generate their own insights, without therapist interpretation, though perhaps stimulated by open questions from the therapist. The issue of when therapist interpretation should be offered to facilitate client insight is an important one and needs further investigation. In addition, the issue of private insight also warrants further study.

Differences Between Insight Events

The two kinds of insight events studied were also very different and in ways that reflect important differences found between the two contrasting treatment approaches. For one thing, the emotional effect of the psychodynamic–interpersonal therapy events involved painful awareness (e.g., bitterness at mother's shammed affection), a feature that is generally lacking in the insight events of cognitive–behavioral therapy.

In addition, the content of the two kinds of insight events contrasted sharply: Cognitive–behavioral events were primarily reattributional in nature (e.g., it was the coworker's fault, not the client's), while psychodynamic–interpersonal events involved connection to a conflict theme from a previous session (e.g., the client's painful reaction to being described as seductive). This study suggests that useful interpretations in psychodynamic treatments may involve cross-session linking of core interpersonal conflict themes, balanced by a tentative, negotiating style (i.e., supportive). On the other hand, the shift in emphasis toward causal reattribution in cognitive therapy (e.g., Antaki & Brewin, 1982) is also supported by our findings. It is thus important not to assume that insight is the same in the two treatments.

Implications of the Analysis of the Psychodynamic–Interpersonal Event

The analysis presented of the psychodynamic–interpersonal insight event has several implications. First, the event illustrates the phenomenon of a significant event that is perceived by the client as a psychological unit yet that contains more than one part. After this event was identified, we found that clients using tape-assisted recall (Elliott & Shapiro, 1988) sometimes identify events consisting of two or even three parts, each separated by 5–15 min of intervening material. This event illustrates three factors that may facilitate multipart significant events: (a) the use of therapist interpretations to link different aspects of client experience that are discussed at different points in a session, (b) the organization of treatment around important, shared key themes or tasks, (c) and the temporary interruption of an important therapeutic task by irrelevant or distracting material. If these factors are important, then multipart events are more likely to occur in treatments in which more linking interpretations are used, in which central themes or tasks are clear and shared, or in which important therapeutic tasks have been left incomplete.

Second, this event, unlike the insight events examined in Elliott (1984), depended in large part on the choice of a single key word. Much of the episode context for the first part of this event was taken up with a search for the right way of expressing the client's painful experience. Here, what appeared to matter was the specific word and its connotative network of associations, that is, a lexically indexed emotion scheme (cf. Greenberg, Rice, & Elliott, 1993). The importance of word choice has been noted by researchers studying clients' experience of being understood or misunderstood (e.g., Elliott, 1985) and their attempts to make sense out of painful events.

Third, this event illustrates how clients actively and selectively process therapeutic material. For example, during the session the client rejected the therapist's attempts to link the client's feelings to the therapeutic relationship (in Part 1) and to the client's relationship with his son (in Part 2). In addition, the event itself also was a selection by the client of what he regarded as most helpful in the session.

Implications of the Analysis of the Cognitive–Behavioral Event

The insight event from cognitive–behavioral therapy also raises interesting issues. For example, the event selected may appear to an outside observer as too small to be a clinically significant event. However, an important but inevitable result of studying client-identified significant events is the discovery that some of these events are seemingly minor occurrences (cf. Elliott, 1989). Here, the client selected a moment in which her therapst agreed with her and shared a bit of humor at another person's expense. The intervention was not out of the ordinary for cognitive–behavioral therapy, but neither was it an example of a key form of intervention in this treatment.

Our analysis sheds light on why the client valued such a seemingly minor event. Because of the client's vulnerabilities, an extratherapy incident with a coworker held great signifiance for the client. The client perceived her self-esteem as a competent teacher to be at stake in the incident she described. Therefore, it mattered deeply to her that her therapist agreed with her that her coworker was inappropriately critical. In addition, the incident exemplified many similar incidents in her relationship with the coworker. The significance of the helpful event was in part borrowed from the importance of a particular type of interpersonal interaction in the client's life—that is, it was a familiar script. The successful external reattribution of blame might be expected to provide a model for this depressed client to use in other similar situations.

Finally, the therapist allowed herself to depart momentarily from her usual professional manner. Such glimpses of the therapist as a person are often cited by clients as helpful (e.g., Hill, Helms, Tichenor, et al., 1988).

Limitations and Implications for Further Research

The work reported here advances previous CPA studies (Elliott, 1984, 1989) in a number of ways, including the provision of more complete analysis of context and the use of a broader range of data on the effects of events. In addition, the analyses show that the method was applicable to events in cognitive–behavioral therapies, as well as to events identified without the use of client recall procedures.

It is important to remember that CPA is an interpretive research method, meaning that its aim is to develop comprehensive constructions or theories of the nature of each event and the factors that contributed to it. Although we attempted to stay as close to the data as possible, constantly grounding our interpretations in the data, we expect that different research teams would have come up with somewhat different analyses of the same events.

From the point of view of traditional research designs in clinical and counseling psychology, CPA has four major flaws: (a) the small sample limits external validity, (b) the observers' expectations may introduce bias, (c) the group consensus processes may distort the results, and (d) the themes obtained may be a result of chance combinations of data that are due to the fishing-expedition nature of the analyses.

Although the problem of obvserver expectancy bias cannot be completely ruled out, the method clearly showed its ability to disconfirm the expected and to turn up the unexpected. A greater concern is the likelihood that some of the obtained themes reflect random processes rather than meaningful variations. The results also depend on the quality of the judges and a positive group process of open dialogue (Elliott, 1993); we assume that the method's validity is a function of the perceptiveness of the analysts and a good group process. All of these problems could be addressed by a replication of the study involving a different set of judges and another sample of significant insight events from the same two therapies. Such a replication could use the same open-ended method, or it could use a set of quantitative rating scales based on the themes found in this study. It would also be useful for researchers to study insight events in an experiential therapy (e.g., Greenberg et al., 1993) in order to evaluate how insight occurs in the absence of therapist interpretive responses.

In spite of the limitations, we believe that the advantages of CPA merit its addition to the canon of useful counseling and psychotherapy research methods. CPA offers a systematic outline for producing "thick descriptions" of appropriate polydimensionality (Stiles, 1993). The central strength of thoroughly discovery-oriented methods such as CPA is that they facilitate the discovery of new clinical phenomena. Among other things, this study uncovered the critical role of therapist key, evocative words in facilitating client insight in psychodynamic–interpersonal therapy. Even a large battery of quantitative process measures might have missed this or other of the patterns that were obtained.

In addition, the CPA analyses described in this study led to the development of the assimilation model (Stiles et al., 1990), which proposes that insight develops out of problematic experiences through a sequence that moves from unwanted thoughts to vague awareness to problem clarification to insight. Further CPA research is underway to evaluate the accuracy of the assimilation model (Manford et al., 1994).

References

Antaki, C., & Brewin, C. (Eds.). (1982). *Attributions and psychological change.* San Diego, CA: Academic Press.

Crits-Christoph, P., Barber, J. P., Miller, N. E., & Beebe, K. (1993). Evaluating insight. In N. E. Miller, L. Luborsky, J. P. Barber, & J. P. Docherty (Eds.), *Psychodynamic treatment research* (pp. 407–422). New York: Basic Books.

Elliott, R. (1984). A discovery-oriented approach to significant events in psychotherapy: Interpersonal process recall and comprehensive process analysis. In L. N. Rice & L. S. Greenberg (Eds.), *Patterns of change* (pp. 249–286). New York: Guilford Press.

Elliott, R. (1985). Helpful and nonhelpful events in brief counseling interviews: An empirical taxonomy. *Journal of Counseling Psychology, 32,* 307–322.

Elliott, R. (1989). Comprehensive process analysis: Understanding the change process in significant therapy events. In M. Packer & R. B. Addison (Eds.), *Entering the circle: Hermeneutic investigation in psychology* (pp. 165–184). Albany: State University of New York Press.

Elliott, R. (1991). Five dimensions of therapy process. *Psychotherapy Research, 1,* 92–103.

Elliott, R. (1993). *Comprehensive process analysis: Mapping the change process in psychotherapy.* Unpublished research manual. (Available from author, Department of Psychology, University of Toledo, Toledo, OH 43606.)

Elliott, R., & James, E. (1989). Varieties of client experience in psychotherapy: An analysis of the literature. *Clinical Psychology Review, 9,* 443–467.

Elliott, R., James, E., Reimschuessel, C., Cislo, D., & Sack, N. (1985). Significant events and the analysis of immediate therapeutic impacts. *Psychotherapy, 22,* 620–630.

Elliott, R., & Shapiro, D. A. (1988). Brief structured recall: A more efficient method for identifying and describing significant therapy events. *British Journal of Medical Psychology, 61,* 141–153.

Elliott, R., & Shapiro, D. A. (1992). Clients and therapists as analysts of significant events. In S. G. Toukmanian & D. L. Rennie (Eds.), *Two perspectives on psychotherapeutic change: Theory-guided and phenomenological research strategies* (pp. 163–186). Newbury Park, CA: Sage.

Elliott, R., & Wexler, M. M. (1994). Measuring the impact of sessions in process–experiential therapy of depression: The Session Impacts Scale. *Journal of Counseling Psychology, 41,* 166–174.

Frank, G. H., & Sweetland, A. A. (1962). A study of the process of psychotherapy: The verbal interaction. *Journal of Consulting Psychology, 26,* 135–138.

Gadamer, H. G. (1979). *Truth and method.* London: Sheed & Ward.

Garduk, E. L., & Haggard, E. A. (1972). Immediate effects on patients of psychoanalytic interpretations. *Psychological Issues, 7* (28).

Greenberg, L. S., Rice, L. N., & Elliott, R. (1993). *Facilitating emotional change: The moment-by-moment process.* New York: Guilford Press.

Hill, C. E., Helms, J. E., Spiegel, S. B., & Tichenor, V. (1988). Development of a system for assessing client reactions to therapist interventions. *Journal of Counseling Psychology, 35,* 27–36.

Hill, C. E., Helms, J. E., Tichenor, V., Spiegel, S. B., O'Grady, K., & Perry, E. S. (1988). Effects of therapist response modes in brief psychotherapy. *Journal of Counseling Psychology, 35,* 222–233.

Llewelyn, S. P. (1988). Psychological therapy as viewed by clients and therapists. *British Journal of Clinical Psychology, 27,* 223–238.

Llewelyn, S. P., Elliott, R., Shapiro, D. A., Firth, J., & Hardy, G. (1988). Client perceptions of significant events in prescriptive and exploratory periods of individual therapy. *British Journal of Clinical Psychology, 27,* 105–114.

Luborsky, L., Bachrach, H., Graff, H., Pulver, S., & Christoph, P. (1979). Preconditions and consequences of transference interpretations: A clinical–quantitative investigation. *Journal of Nervous and Mental Diseases, 169,* 391–401.

Luborsky, L., & Crits-Christoph, P. (1990). *Understanding transference: The CCRT method.* New York: Basic Books.

Manford, M. J., Elliott, R., Wunderlich, D., Earl, C., Kechisen, S., & Woods, C. (1994, February). *From awareness to problem solution: A comprehensive process analysis of a significant event in experiential therapy.* Paper presented at meeting of the North American Society for Psychotherapy Research, Santa Fe, NM.

Phillips, J. P. N. (1986). Shapiro personal questionnaire and generalized personal questionnaire techniques: A repeated measures individualized outcome measurement. In L. S. Greenberg & W. M. Pinsof (Eds.), *The psychotherapeutic process: A research handbook* (pp. 557–590). New York: Guilford Press.

Rennie, D. L., Phillips, J. R., & Quartaro, G. K. (1988). Grounded theory: A promising approach to conceptualization in psychology? *Canadian Psychology, 29,* 139–150.

Rice, L. N., & Sapiera, E. P. (1984). Task analysis and the resolution of problematic reactions. In L. N. Rice & L. S. Greenberg (Eds.), *Patterns of change* (pp. 29–66). New York: Guilford Press.

Sacks, H., Schegloff, E. A., & Jefferson, G. (1974). A simplest systematics for the organization of turn-taking in conversation. *Language, 50,* 696–735.

Shapiro, D. A., & Firth, J. (1987). Prescriptive vs. exploratory psychotherapy: Outcomes of the Sheffield psychotherapy project. *British Journal of Psychiatry, 151,* 790–799.

Snyder, W. U. (1945). An investigation of the nature of nondirective psychotherapy. *Journal of General Psychology, 33,* 193–223.

Stiles, W. B. (1980). Measurement of the impact of psychotherapy sessions. *Journal of Consulting and Clinical Psychology, 48,* 176–185.

Stiles, W. B. (1993). Quality control in qualitative research. *Clinical Psychology Review, 13,* 593–618.

Stiles, W. B., Elliott, R., Llewelyn, S. P., Firth-Cozens, J. A., Margison, F. R., Shapiro, D. A., & Hardy, G. (1990). Assimilation of problematic experiences by clients in psychotherapy. *Psychotherapy, 27,* 411–420.

Weiss, J., & Sampson, H. (with the Mount Zion Psychotherapy Research Group). (1986). *The psychoanalytic process: Theory, clinical observation, and empirical research.* New York: Guilford Press.

Wing, J. K., Cooper, J. E., & Sartorius, N. (1974). *Measurement and classification of psychiatric symptoms.* Cambridge, England: Cambridge University Press.

Chapter 20
CONCENTRATION AND CORRESPONDENCE OF TRANSFERENCE INTERPRETATIONS IN SHORT-TERM PSYCHOTHERAPY

William E. Piper, Anthony S. Joyce, Mary McCallum, and Hassan F. A. Azim

One of the central and distinguishing technical features of psychoanalytically oriented psychotherapy (subsequently referred to as dynamic therapy) is the interpretation of transference. By interpretation, we refer to the actual statements made by the therapist to the patient in an attempt to enhance the patient's understanding of his or her experiences. This is related to, but distinct from, the therapist's internal process of understanding the patient. In general, the intent of interpretation is to produce an alteration in the patient's intrapsychic conflicts to permit improved functioning (Brenner, 1976). Transference interpretations focus on the patient's reactions to the therapist. They may be, but are not necessarily, linked to the patient's reactions to other important people. This article provides a review of research that has examined the relationship between aspects of transference interpretation and outcome in dynamic therapy. In addition, the results of a study of time-limited therapy that was recently completed in our center is presented.

The investigation of the impact of transference interpretation is an important area in the field of psychotherapy process research. A general problem in this field, which was highlighted by Garfield (1990), is a deficiency of replication and cross-validation of findings; this involves both a scarcity of replication attempts and inconsistent results when replications have been attempted. In recent years, however, some lines of convergence regarding the impact of interpretation have emerged in studies conducted in independent settings. Our article highlights that convergence.

During the past 20 years, increasing importance has been attributed to relationship factors (e.g., therapeutic alliance), compared with technique factors (e.g., interpretation), in explaining the results of psychotherapy. Several types of research findings have been cited to support this position. First, well-known reviews of pyschotherapy outcome research of both the box score (Luborsky, Singer, & Luborsky, 1975) and meta-analytic (Smith, Glass, & Miller, 1980) varieties and certain carefully conducted individual studies (Strupp & Hadley, 1979) have reported general success for psychotherapy regardless of the type or, presumably, the technique used. Second, other reviews (Horvath & Symonds, 1991; Luborsky, Crits-Christoph, Mintz, & Auerbach, 1988) have identified significant relationships between the patient—therapist alliance and favorable outcome in many studies. Third, as indicated earlier,

Reprinted from *Journal of Consulting and Clinical Psychology*, *61*, 586–595 (1993). Copyright © 1993 by the American Psychological Association. Used with permission of the first author.

This research was supported by Grant 6609-136746 from the National Health Research and Development Program, Health and Welfare Canada; Grant 55-66043 from the Alberta Mental Health Research Fund; and an equipment grant from the Special Services and Research Committee, University of Alberta Hospitals.

there has been a deficiency of methodologically strong studies, which have been replicated and cross-validated, that have demonstrated that variation in technique makes a difference. In light of the existing evidence, the burden of proof rests with those who believe in the importance of technique. That is a reasonable conclusion and a challenge.

Yet the evidence used to discount the importance of technique is not without its shortcomings. Box score reviews have reported similar benefits for different therapies; however, small sample sizes and corresponding low statistical power in many of the studies, as well as methodological weaknesses, represent compelling alternative explanations for the nonsignificant findings. The findings for meta-analytic reviews have been based on the extensive averaging of several components. For each measure, each patient's outcome score was averaged with other patients' scores to create an effect size. Then, effect sizes were averaged across measures and across studies to test general hypotheses. In the process of averaging, it is likely that variability caused by other factors (e.g., therapist technique) was obscured. For certain individual studies, the investigators reported considerable variability of outcome among the patients. The tendency has been to attribute such variability to patient characteristics (Strupp, 1980). The role of technique, which is often interdependent with patient characteristics, has remained in the background. This may partly be due to the fact that patient characteristics are often easier to measure than technique. Clearly, most of the outcome studies reviewed have not carefully assessed the nature and range of the techniques used.

In studies that have demonstrated significant associations between alliance and outcome, many researchers have relied on patient self-report measures for both types of variables. This raises the possibility that the measures of alliance may, in part, represent early reports of outcome. If so, significant associations should not be surprising. Despite that ambiguity, few would disagree with the notion that a strong alliance is important to the work and outcome of psychotherapy. Similarly, few would argue with the idea that technique and alliance are interdependent and that both should be used in predicting outcome. The position advocated in this article is not that technique has a more important impact on outcome than such factors as patient characteristics and alliance but that technique should not be prematurely rejected as an important variable. What appears to be lacking in the literature is an accumulation of studies with large sample sizes that include careful assessment of technique and outcome, with adequate range where other potentially confounding variables (e.g., therapist experience) have been controlled. Also needed are studies that consider the interaction of technique with such factors as patient characteristics and alliance. Some of the studies reviewed in this article meet these conditions.

What the literature provides is an enumeration of a large number of aspects of interpretations that may have an impact on the outcome of dynamic therapy (Sandler, Dare, & Holder, 1971). They include content (e.g., conflictural components), persons (e.g., therapist), correctness (e.g., correspondence with a central conflict), unconscious material, timing, sequencing, linkage, and dosage. Most of these aspects have been offered by clinicians in the context of providing practical guidelines for effective technique (Hammer, 1968; Menninger, 1958; Paul, 1963). Whereas some aspects such as dosage are quantitative in nature, others such as correctness, timing, and sequencing refer to the quality of interpretations. Few aspects have been carefully investigated in clinical outcome studies. This article focuses on only a limited set of aspects. They include the quantitative aspect of dosage and the qualitative aspect of correctness, or in our research, what we have preferred to label as *concentration* and *correspondence*, respectively. By studying transference interpretations, we have also chosen to focus on the person of the therapist.

Transference Interpretation

Because transference interpretation has been regarded as a hallmark of the technique of dynamic therapy, both the terms *transference* and *interpretation* have received considerable attention in the literature. Unfortunately, they have assumed a variety of meanings over the years. In regard to transference, there has been disagreement about what it encompasses and whether additional concepts such as therapeutic alliance or real relationship are required to account for the patient's reaction to the therapist (Ehrenreich, 1989). Similarly, the literature on interpretation suggests a number of possible definitions. Some seem to reflect stages in the evolution of psychoanalytic theory. Rather than contradicting one another, however, they represent complementary perspectives. For example, from the topographical point of view, an interpretation makes the unconscious conscious. From the dynamic point of view, an interpretation makes reference to the components of intrapsychic conflict. Clinicians are able to use both of these definitions to guide their practice, but researchers encounter considerable problems in attempting to use both. That has been our experience because of the difficulty of distinguishing what was conscious from what was unconscious. To achieve a reliable operational definition while maintaining clinical meaningfulness, we adopted the dynamic point of view. In our research, an interpretation was defined as the therapist's reference to the components of intrapsychic conflict.

Although a variety of definitions of transference and interpretation have been provided, there is consensus that the exploration of the patient's transferential reaction to the therapist is a unique opportunity for insight and psychic change. Because the transference reaction occurs in the present, the extent to which it is inappropriate can be explored in a situation that is immediate and compelling. Recognition of the importance of transference was originally made by Freud (1912/1958) and later elaborated by Strachey (1934), who outlined a process in which transference interpretations are capable of reversing the patient's "neurotic vicious circle." This involves the patient making a distinction between the analyst and early influential figures. The importance of linking the patient's reactions to the therapist and reactions to parental figures was later emphasized by Malan (1976b) in the area of short-term therapy. Gill (1982) has also written extensively about the importance of transference interpretations, but with a different technical emphasis. He advocates that priority be given to exploring the here-and-now transference reaction to the therapist rather than linking the reaction to its original sources. A similar position has been taken by Strupp and Binder (1984) in regard to short-term therapy.

Because transference interpretation has been regarded as a particularly powerful technique, many who have investigated it have assumed that it would be possible to detect a direct relationship between the use of transference and interpretation and the outcome of treatment. In their process-and-outcome model of psychotherapy, Orlinsky and Howard (1986) posited several intervening variables between therapist interventions and treatment outcome, which they referred to as macro-outcome. The variables included other events during the session (therapy process), events after each session (postsession outcome), and events in the patient's life between sessions (micro-outcome). Their model and review of the literature suggested that the detection of a strong direct relationship between transference interpretation and treatment outcome would be difficult.

Review of Research Investigating Dosage of Transference Interpretations

Economic and other practical factors have been influential in sustaining interest in short-term dynamic therapy. Enthusiasm about innovations in technique is also evident in the writings of many of the proponents of short-term therapy during the 1970s (Davanloo, 1978; Malan, 1976a; Mann, 1973; Sifneos, 1976). One innovative feature involves the early and active interpretation of transference. An early attempt to provide research justification for this approach was made by Malan (1976b). In a sample of 22 brief-therapy patients, Malan correlated the proportion of transference interpretations relative to all interpretations with the outcome of the treatment. Although that correlation was nonsignificant, he reported finding a significant correlation between the proportion of transference and parental linking (T/P) interpretations and outcome. T/P interpretations indicate the similarity between the patient's reactions to the therapist and the patient's previous reactions to his or her parents. This was an intriguing finding, but its validity remained in question because of serious methodological problems with the study. Marziali and Sullivan (1980) overcame one of the problems (lack of rater blindness) by rerating Malan's data. They did not report findings concerning the relationship between simple (patient–therapist, nonlinked) transference interpretations and outcome but did report confirming the significant relationship between T/P interpretations and outcome.

Marziali (1984) subsequently attempted to replicate Malan's findings in an independent study of 25 patients in brief (20-session) therapy. The study overcame many of the methodological weaknesses of the earlier study. The data were derived from audio recordings, raters were blind to outcome, and data analyses were controlled for pretherapy patient differences. Four main types of outcome variables were included (patient global outcome rating, therapist global outcome rating, patient symptom index, and independent assessor dynamic outcome ratings). For simple transference interpretations, no significant correlations were found; as for T/P interpretations, a significant correlation was found for one of the four outcome variables, the dynamic change ratings, which Marziali highlighted as replicating Malan's (1976b) findings. However, because raw frequency rather than proportion of T/P linking was used, it is possible that interpretation was confounded with such variables as the activity or the involvement of the therapist.

Another opportunity to test relationships between transference interpretations and outcome in short-term individual therapy came from a comparative outcome study that W. E. Piper and his colleagues conducted in Montreal (Piper, Debbane, Bienvenu, & Garant, 1984). In one of the conditions of the study, 21 patients were treated with an average of 23 sessions of individual therapy. A reliable system for categorizing interpretations, the Therapist Intervention Rating System (TIRS; Piper, Debbane, de Carufel, & Bienvenu, 1987) was applied to audio recordings of the sessions.

According to the TIRS, an interpretation makes reference to one or more dynamic components. A dynamic component is one part of a patient's conflict that exerts an internal force on another aspect of the patient (e.g., wish, anxiety, or defense). The TIRS also assesses the type of object (person) included in the intervention. Proportions of transference and T/P interpretations, as well as interpretations that included reference to other types of persons and linkings, were correlated with many outcome variables from several different sources (Piper, Debbane, Bienvenu, de Carufel, & Garant, 1986). An inverse relationship between simple transference interpretations and improvement in sexual adjustment was found at posttherapy. For T/P interpretations, a direct relationship with overall usefulness as rated by therapist was found at posttherapy, and an inverse relationship with improvement in relationships with friends was found at follow-up. Overall, however, only a few significant correlations were found relative to the total that had been calculated.

The studies reviewed thus far have provided no evidence of a direct relationship between the dosage of simple transference interpretations and favorable outcome, and only weak evidence for such a relationship between T/P interpretations and favorable outcome. Piper et al. (1986) even suggested that inverse relationships may exist for certain outcome variables. To be fair, however, we also note that the sample sizes were small, the dosages of T/P interpretations were low, and variation may have been limited, all of which would have worked against the detection of significant differences. In contrast, the next study (Piper, Azim, Joyce, & MacCullum, 1991), which was conducted in our center, involved a large sample and a considerable range in dosage of transference interpretations.

The database for the dosage study (Piper, Azim, Joyce, & McCallum, 1991) came from a controlled clinical trial of time-limited, short-term individual psychotherapy that involved the random assignment of 125 patients to immediate treatment or delayed treatment (wait-list) conditions (Piper, Azim, McCallum, & Joyce, 1990). Garfield (1990) has argued that it is wise to establish the efficacy of treatment before expending effort in studying process variables. The clinical trial clearly demonstrated the efficacy of the treatment. The dosage study was based on a sample of 64 of the 86 therapy completers that was well balanced on several variables. The TIRS was used to reliably rate over 22,500 interventions from the sessions of the 64 patients. An intervention was defined as a therapist statement that occurred between patient statements or silences of 30 s or longer. Interventions ranged from brief facilitative remarks to complex statements. The average number of interventions, interpretations, and transference interpretations per session were 44, 11, and 5, respectively.

The transference interpretation dosage variable, which we labeled *concentration*, was a proportion defined as the frequency of transference interpretations divided by the total number of interventions. A large set of outcome variables was reduced to three factors (general symptoms and dysfunction, individualized objectives, and social–sexual adjustment) by means of a principal-component analysis. Two additional types of variables were measured, a patient characteristic that we have labeled *quality of object relations* (QOR; Azim, Piper, Segal, Nixon, & Duncan, 1991) and therapeutic alliance. QOR was defined as a person's internal enduring tendency to establish certain types of relationships, ranging from primitive to mature. Therapeutic alliance was defined as the nature of the working relationshp between the patient and therapist. Three alliance factors (patient-rated impression, therapist-rated immediate impression, and therapist-rated reflective impression) were derived from a principal-components analysis of ratings of six items that were made by the patient and therapist after each session or each third of therapy.

Table 1 presents correlations between concentration and alliance and between concentration and outcome measured at posttherapy and a 6-month follow-up. The square of concentration was used in the analyses because curvilinear rather than linear relationships best represented the patterns. The strongest findings involved the high QOR patients. Concentration was significantly (or near significantly) and inversely related to all but two of the therapeutic alliance and outcome factors. None of the correlations for low QOR patients were significant. Because the study was naturalistic rather than experimental in design, more than one causal explanation of the significant correlations is plausible. With regard to alliance, a high concentration of transference interpretations could have weakened the alliance with subsequent negative effects on outcome, a weak alliance could have prompted a high concentration from the therapist, or both could have occurred. Further examination of session material provided evidence that was consistent with both explanations. It was also clear that continuation of a high concentration of transference interpretations either within or across sessions did not serve to strengthen a weak alliance and that both were predictive of poorer outcome. As an additional step, we plotted dose–response relationships for concentration and outcome at posttherapy. An effective response occurred for 50% or more of the patients when the concentration was equal to or less than one interpretation in every 12 interventions. Although the results of the study were open to more than one explanation, we felt that they were sufficiently strong to warrant alerting clinicians to the possibility of negative treatment effects when high concentrations of transference interpretations are used with certain types

Table 1—*Correlations Between Concentration of Transference Interpretations and Therapeutic Alliance Factors, Posttherapy Outcome Factors, and Follow-Up Outcome Factors*

Sample, r, and n	Therapeutic alliance factors			Posttherapy outcome factors			Follow-up outcome factors		
	I	II	III	I	II	III	I	II	III
High QOR									
r	−.38**	−.46***	−.48***	.60****	.61****	.34*	.38*	.19	.11
n	32	32	32	32	32	32	27	28	27
Low QOR									
r	−.20	−.32*	−.09	.21	.02	.03	.03	.01	−.07
n	32	32	32	30	32	31	22	26	26
All									
r	−.28**	−.38***	−.27	.37***	.23*	.17	.19	.05	.02
n	64	64	64	62	64	63	49	54	53

Note. The square of concentration of transference interpretations was used in the correlations. For therapeutic alliance, Factor I = patient-rated impression, Factor II = therapist-rated immediate impression, and Factor III = therapist-rated reflective impression. For outcome, Factor I = general symptoms and dysfunction, Factor II = individualized objectives, and Factor III = social–sexual adjustment. High outcome scores are undesirable. QOR = quality of object relations.

*p < .10. **p < .05. ***p < .01. ****p < .001.

of patients who receive short-term therapy. In the process of presenting and publishing our findings, we learned that we had measured the concentration but not the "correctness" of therapist interpretations. It was possible that these two variables were confounded. Therefore, we conducted a subsequent study that included a measure of correctness. Before presenting the results of that study, we will present a selective review of research that has focused on correctness.

Review of Research Investigating Correctness of Transference Interpretations

Correctness, among other terms, has been used to refer to the degree to which an interpretation "fits" or "is relevant to" a formulation about the patient. Formulations have typically included the components of recurrent conflicts and maladaptive outcomes in the patient's life. Other terms that have been used rather than correctness are *focality, congruence, suitability, compatibility, accuracy,* and *correspondence.* For practical reasons concerning the need to use time efficiently, there has been a good deal of interest among advocates of time-limited therapy in constructing focused formulations to which interpretations can be addressed. French (1958) was among the first to write about the patient's "nuclear conflict" and the need for the therapist to address it by means of interpretation. Similarly, Malan (1976a) emphasized the importance of interpreting the patient's "basic neurotic conflict." Some proponents of brief therapy have suggested interpreting particular conflict areas such as oedipal issues (Sifneos, 1976) or separation issues (Mann, 1973), whereas others have advocated focusing on the interpersonal aspects of conflict regardless of the specific content area (Strupp & Binder, 1984). Perhaps the first attempt to quantitatively measure correctness can be credited to Luborsky, who developed a rating method for assessing the degree to which the therapist responded to the patient's main communication (Auerbach & Luborsky, 1968).

Research investigating the correlates of correctness began with Malan's (1976a) examination of the concept of focality. There have been two meanings associated with this concept that should be distinguished because they have often been confused in the literature. The first meaning concerns focality as a patient characteristic. As such, it is not a representation of correctness of interpretations, because it refers only to the degree to which the patient's problem can be conceptualized in terms of a focal conflict. Malan (1976a) and others, such as Sifneos (1976) believe that focality of conflict is an important patient selection criterion for brief therapy. However, when Malan correlated ratings of focality with outcome in his study of 22 patients, the result was nonsignificant. Similar nonsignificant results for focality as a patient predictor were found in two additional studies (Husby, Dahl, Dahl, Heiberg, Olafsen, & Weisoth, 1985; Piper, de Carufel, & Szkrumelak, 1985). Thus, the evidence to date has indicated that the usefulness of focality as a selection criterion is questionable.

The second meaning concerns focality as a technical variable, which constitutes a representation of correctness. In Malan's terms, it refers to the extent to which the therapist sticks to a single theme or focus for his or her interpretations. Ratings of this variable were significantly correlated with outcome in his study. While Malan's work represents an important beginning in the area of correctness research, the methodology that he used was crude by today's standards. For example, his measure of focality was a global rating applied to a written summary of an entire therapy session. Such ratings are susceptible to other global qualities that characterize "good" and "bad" sessions. In addition, no reliability data were provided for the measure. In contrast, the measures of correctness in the subsequent studies we review were more complex (i.e., comprised several components) and were applied to each of the therapist's interpretations. Considerable efforts were made to establish their reliabilities.

The first of these measures was developed by the Mount Zion Psychotherapy Research Group in San Francisco. The rationale for their measure, as well as the theory associated with the therapy that they provide, is presented in a book by Weiss, Sampson, and the Mount Zion Psychotherapy Research Group (1986). According to the theory, a patient has unconscious pathogenic beliefs that serve to perpetuate symptomatology and maladaptive behavior. The origins of these beliefs are usually attributed to traumatic childhood experiences. It is also assumed that a patient in therapy attempts to test his or her beliefs through interaction with the therapist. Although the patient would like to better understand and disconfirm his beliefs, he or she runs the risk of confirming them. The patient's strategy for disconfirmation is called his or her plan. It is the therapist's task to discover the plan and pass the tests that are presented. To increase the likelihood that this is achieved, the therapist should generate a written plan formulation. The formulation includes four components (patient goals, pathogenic beliefs, tests, and insights). The Mount Zion Group has demonstrated that the components of the plan can be judged reliably (Curtis, Silberschatz, Sampson, Weiss, & Rosenberg, 1988; Rosenberg, Silberschatz, Curtis, Sampson, & Weiss, 1986). According to these investigators, an interpretation is "correct," or to use their terminology, "suitable," if it is compatible with the patient's plan (i.e., if it passes the test). However, from a consideration of some of the examples that they provide (Silberschatz, Curtis, & Nathans, 1989), it is not entirely clear whether an interpretation to be rated as suitable must strictly pass the test or whether, at times, it might only have to sensitively address the conflicts indicated in the plan formulation.

Silberschatz, Fretter, and Curtis (1986) used their measure to study the relationship between suitability of interpretation and immediate patient productivity. The latter was measured by the Experiencing Scale (Klein, Mathieu, Gendlin, & Kiesler, 1970) for 3 patients in brief therapy. Following Malan (1976a), an interpretation was defined as an intervention in which the therapist suggested or implied an emotional content in the patient beyond what the patient had already said. A transference interpretation made reference to the patient's feelings about the therapist or the therapy. For all 3 patients, a significant direct relationship between suitability and experiencing was found. For 2 of the patients, no significant relationship between the use of transference interpretations and experiencing was found, but for the third patient, a significant inverse relationship emerged. The investigators also provided anecdotal data that suggested that suitability was positively related to treatment outcome. They believed that their study supported the importance of suitability but were also clear in acknowledging the need to replicate their findings with a larger sample of patients and therapists.

The second of the measures was developed by investigators from the Department of Psychiatry at the University of Pennsylvania in Philadelphia. They defined accuracy of interpretation as the degree of congruence between the content of the patient's Core Conflictual Relationship Theme (CCRT; Luborsky & Crits-Christoph,

1990) and the content of the therapist's interpretation. The CCRT is a representation of the patient's central relationship patterns. It is derived from narrative episodes provided by the patient concerning his or her relationships. Such narratives are frequently presented in assessment interviews and early therapy sessions. A CCRT specifies three components: the patient's main wishes, needs, or intentions toward other persons; the responses of other persons; and the responses of the self. The process of constructing a CCRT involves several steps. An independent judge reviews some of the patient's narratives and then, through a process of formulation and reformulation, arrives at a specification of the three components. Adequate reliability for the formulations has been demonstrated (Crits-Christoph, Luborsky, Dahl, Popp, Mellon, & Mark, 1988).

Chrits-Christoph, Cooper, and Luborsky (1988) used their measure to study the relationship between accuracy of interpretation and therapy outcome for 43 patients in moderate-length (approximately 1 year) therapy. The ratings for accuracy were based on two early-in-treatment sessions. An interpretation was defined as (a) explaining possible reasons for a patient's thoughts, feelings, or behavior; (b) alluding to similarities between the patient's present circumstances and other life experiences; or (c) both. In this study, transference interpretations were not distinguished from nontransference interpretations. Two composite outcome variables were constructed. One was a residual gain score derived from adjustment ratings provided by the patient and a clinical observer, and the other was a rated-benefits score based on ratings by the patient and the therapist. The two were highly correlated. The investigators found a significant direct relationshp between accuracy (reflecting two combined CCRT components, wish and response from others) and treatment outcome. The relationship held even when therapeutic alliance and errors in technique variables were partialled out. Crits-Christoph et al. concluded that the results were consistent with the principle that correctly addressing the patient's pattern of wishes and responses of others is an effective technique. At the same time, they cautioned against inferring causality from correlational findings.

Edmonton Correspondence of Transference Interpretation Study

The third of the measures was developed in our research center. As indicated earlier, after investigating the relationships between the concentration (proportion) of transference interpretations and both therapeutic alliance and treatment outcome, we sought to investigate correctness. We wanted to know whether the two variables were confounded, but we were also interested in studying the relationship between correctness, either as a single variable or in interaction with concentration, and both therapeutic alliance and treatment outcome. We did not have plan formulations or CCRT formulations for the patients from which we could derive a measure of correctness, but we did have a psychodynamic formulation that had been constructed by each patient's therapist after the first two therapy sessions. The therapist had described a repetitive conflict for the patient that involved similar maladaptive outcomes and similar objects (types of people).

The derivation of an accuracy score involved several steps. From each formulation, which was in the form of a narrative, A. S. Joyce extracted information about five topics: (a) patient wishes and needs, (b) patient anxieties and fears, (c) patient defensive processes, (d) patient maladaptive outcomes, and (e) objects. The reliability of this process of extraction was checked by having an independent judge perform the process with 12 cases. A third judge rated the agreement between the two extractions for each of the five areas. Agreement across the five areas averaged 86% (range, 75%–92%). We defined correctness, which we preferred to call *correspondence*, as the degree of correspondence between the content of the interpretation and the content of the therapist's formulation (Joyce, 1991). An independent judge rated the degree of correspondence using a 3-point rating scale (1 = no, 2 = moderate, and 3 = strong) with half-point ratings permitted. In our study, we were interested in the correspondence of transference interpretations. Because the therapist as object was not included in the therapist's formulation, the degree of correspondence for transference interpretations focused only on the first four areas of the formulation. The object (person) of the therapist could take the role of any relationship pattern explained in the formulation.

The information extracted from one of the therapist's formulations and actual examples of high and low correspondence transference interpretations from the therapy of the patient, a 28-year-old woman, are provided.

Wishes:
1. Wishes to be dependent on others, have others care for her and make decisions for her and thereby show their love for her.
2. Wishes for mother to show her love.

Anxieties:
1. Terrified of involvement as she becomes overwhelmed —consumed by it to the exclusion of any other activity.
2. Afraid she'll be punished by someone for her over-attachment because she has taken that person away from others who need them, i.e., fearful of reprisal from others.

Defensive processes:
1. Has brought her life to a standstill; doing very little dating, work, school, or other activity—little involvement in normal activities.
2. Becomes over-involved with others to the exclusion of other relationships or activities.

Maladaptive outcomes:
1. Feeling depressed, nonproductive and uninvolved.
2. Crying
3. Repeatedly feeling disappointed by significant others.

Objects:
1. Mother
2. Father
3. Boyfriends
4. Bosses
5. Male siblings
6. "Mother substitutes," others.

Interpretation 1. "It makes a great deal of sense. You have been looking for someone all your life to tell you how to do things, and if it's right or wrong. I'm no different. In fact, it's very clear that you wish for someone to do it as you wanted your mother to do things for you, which she did not." This interpretation received the maximal correspondence rating of 3 because of the strong correspondence to the wish in the formulation.

Interpretation 2. "It's very terrifying for you to even hear me say that your father's wishes for you and your mother's wishes for you were contradictory." This interpretation received the minimal correspondence rating of 1 because of the lack of correspondence between the fears identified in the interpretation and the formulation.

Correspondence ratings were made for the same set of transference interpretations that were in the concentration study. The sample included 2,381 transference interpretations from approximately 22,500 interventions that had been made during 8 of the 20 therapy sessions for each of the 64 patients. To investigate rater reliability, a second judge independently rated correspondence for all transference interpretations for 16 randomly selected patients—a quarter of the sample. An intraclass correlation coefficient (ICC; 2, 1) was calculated for each of the 16 patients. The average ICC was .60 (SD = .21; range, .10–.96), which indicated moderate reliability. One factor that worked against a higher ICC was a large number of "no correspondence" ratings, 60% for the first judge and 72% for the second. Even with this basement effect, reliability was reasonable. The average correspondence rating for all transference interpretations was 1.46 (SD = .25; range, 1.0–3.0).

We first examined the relationship between concentration and correspondence. Pearson product–moment correlation coefficients for the two variables were low and nonsignificant for high-QOR patients, $r(30)$ = .10, low-QOR patients, $r(30)$ = .21, and all 64 patients, $r(62)$ = .14, which indicated considerable independence. Thus, concentration was not confounded by correspondence in the previous study. That alleviated our concern that the interpretations given in high concentration had perhaps been of low correspondence. The independence also facilitated the multivariate analyses that are reported below.

Before conducting the multivariate analyses, we conducted a set of univariate correlations between correspondence and alliance and between correspondence and outcome measured at posttherapy and at 6-month follow-up. The results are reported in Table 2. For correspondence findings, the results differed for high- and low-QOR patients. For low-QOR patients, significant inverse relationships with the patient- and therpist-rated reflective alliance factors were found. In addition, a significant inverse relationship with favorable outcome regarding individualized objectives was found at follow-up. For high-QOR patients, no significant relationships with the alliance or posttherapy outcome factors were found. However, a significant direct relationship with favorable outcome regarding general symptoms and dysfunction was found at follow-up.

The inverse relationships between correspondence and both alliance and follow-up outcome for low-QOR patients represented new findings. Again, because of their correlational nature, the findings are open to more than one explanation. Low-QOR patients, who report a history of relatively nongratifying relationships, may be more in need of forming a gratifying relationship with the therapist than exploring their pattern of nongratifying relationships in therapy. Accordingly, high correspondence by emphasizing similarities between past abusive relationships and the current transferential one could weaken the alliance. Alternatively, a weak alliance could elicit high correspondence by the therapist in an effort to encourage work. In regard to follow-up outcome, high-QOR patients, in contrast to low-QOR patients, may continue to recognize and work through transferential projections beyond the therapy sessions because of their ability to incorporate the analytic function of the therapist during therapy. For the low-QOR patients, consideration of the therapist as another

Table 2—*Correlations Between Correspondence of Transference Interpretations and Therapeutic Alliance Factors, Posttherapy Outcome Factors, and Follow-Up Outcome Factors*

Sample, r, and n	Therapeutic alliance factors			Posttherapy outcome factors			Follow-up outcome factors		
	I	II	III	I	II	III	I	II	III
High QOR									
r	.08	−.21	−.13	.16	−.12	.21	−.39**	−.10	.13
n	32	32	32	32	32	32	27	28	27
Low QOR									
r	−.37**	−.04	−.37**	.27	.25	−.03	.23	.49**	.05
n	32	32	32	30	32	31	22	26	26
All									
r	−.10	−.14	−.23*	−.22*	.08	.11	−.10	.18	.11
n	64	64	64	62	64	63	49	54	53

Note. For therapeutic alliance, Factor I = patient-rated impression, Factor II = therapist-rated immediate impression, and Factor III = therapist-rated reflective impression. For outcome, Factor I = general symptoms and dysfunction, Factor II = individualized objectives, and Factor III = social–sexual adjustment. High outcome scores are undesirable. QOR = quality of object relations.

*$p < .10$.   **$p < .05$.

nongratifying object may render them feeling criticized, rejected, or abandoned during and after therpay, which contributes to a poorer outcome. Thus, it is perhaps most beneficial for high-QOR patients to use the therapeutic relationship to appreciate their role in creating unsatisfactory relationships, whereas low-QOR patients can use the therapeutic relationship to appreciate that not all relationships need to be abusive. These explanations are, of course, tentative and in need of future verification.

Next, a series of hierarchical, multiple-regression analyses were conducted. For each analysis, the independent variables were concentration, correspondence, and the interaction (product) of the two single variables, with the dependent variable being one of the alliance, posttherapy outcome, or follow-up outcome factors. The analyses were conducted separately for high-QOR and low-QOR patients. The analyses, which were clearly exploratory in nature, allowed us to determine several things: (a) whether either single variable (concentration or correspondence) was a significant predictor, (b) whether the other single variable significantly improved the prediction, and (c) whether the interaction (product) significantly improved the prediction after the effects of the single variables had been accounted for.

For all of the therapeutic alliance factors and the posttherapy outcome factors, the multiple regression analyses did not provide any new information. Univariate (i.e., single variable) predictions were not significantly enhanced by addition of the second single variable or by addition of the interaction product. That was also true for the follow-up outcome factors in the case of the low-QOR patients. In contrast, new information was obtained for the first follow-up outcome factor (general symptoms and dysfunction) in the case of high-QOR patients. The regression results are presented in Table 3. At Step 1, correspondence accounted for 15% of the variance; at Step 2, concentration accounted for an additional 18%; and at Step 3, the interaction product accounted for an additional 10%, for a total of 43% of the variance, which is substantial.

Methods for examining the interaction of continuous variables in regression analyses as described by Cohen and Cohen (1983) and by Aiken and West (1991) were used to interpret the results. Figure 1 illustrates the pattern. As the level of concentration decreased, correspondence changed from having a negative effect to having a positive effect on outcome. The slope of the regression line for low concentration significantly differed from 0 ($p < .01$), the slope of the regression line for average concentration almost significantly differed from 0 ($p < .06$), but the slope of the regression line for high concentration did not. Thus, the best follow-up outcome was associated with low concentration and high correspondence. For correspondence (or what can generally be regarded as correctness in transference interpretations) to have a favorable effect, a less concentrated use of transference interpretations may be required. Although intriguing, because of the number of variables and regression analyses, the significant results must be interpreted with caution and regarded as tentative until replicated.

Discussion

In the course of reviewing clinical investigations of the relationshp between the use of transference interpretations and outcome in dyanmic therapy, several impressions have emerged. In general, few studies have been conducted, particularly those with large samples, large ranges for the variables, and controls for possible confounding factors. The studies that have been conducted have tended to focus on short-term rather than long-term dynamic therapy. In regard to design, the studies have been correlational rather than experimental, which has increased the number of potential explanations for the findings. In addition, the impact of other variables (e.g., patient characteristics) has been identified as important. Finally, more recent studies are considerably stronger than earlier studies in regard to methodology.

From the more recent studies, two characteristics of transference interpretations

Table 3—*Multiple Regression Results for Follow-Up Outcome Factor I (General Symptomatology and Dysfunction) for Patients With High Quality of Object Relations*

Predictor variable	R	R^2	Overall F ratio	Partial F ratio for the added variable
Correspondence	.39	.15	4.52*	
Concentration	.57	.33	5.86**	6.26*
Interaction product	.66	.43	5.84**	4.22*

Note. The relationship between favorable outcome on Factor I and correspondence was direct, whereas the relationship between favorable outcome on Factor I and concentration was inverse.

*$p < .05$.   **$p < .01$.

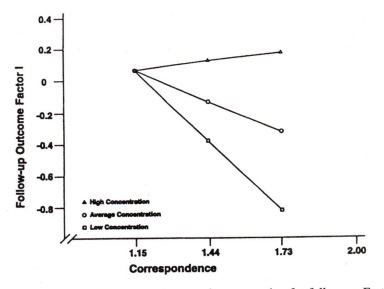

Figure 1. Interaction of correspondence and concentration for follow-up Factor I.

have been highlighted—dosage and correctness. The results of our present study suggest that the two are distinct concepts, each of which is significantly related to certain forms of therapeutic alliance and treatment outcome. The study also indicated that the relationships differed according to whether patients were low or high on QOR. This personality variable, which represents the quality of the patient's lifelong pattern of relationships, has previously been shown to be a better predictor of alliance and outcome than measures of recent interpersonal functioning (Piper, Azim, Joyce, McCallum, Nixon, & Segal, 1991).

The clinical implications of our findings must remain tentative at this stage. The findings suggest that, in the interest of enhancing favorable outcome in brief therapy, therapists might consider providing low concentrations of highly correspondent transference interpretations to high-QOR patients and avoiding highly correspondent transference interpretations to low-QOR patients. However, as we have noted, our studies have focused on only a limited set of variables that characterize therapist interventions. Concentration and correspondence are but two representations of the quantity and quality of interpretations. An interpretation of high correspondence may also be of low quality on other criteria such as timing or sequencing. The context in which interpretations are provided is extremely important, a point that clinicians have made for many years and an area that psychotherapy process researchers have begun to investigate. Future work in this area should provide an even stronger predictive model.

In reference to all of the studies reviewed, there appears to be greater convergence of findings for the variable correctness. The more recent studies have provided data from three independent settings (San Francisco, CA; Philadelphia, PA; and Edmonton, Canada) that indicate a direct relationship between correctness and favorable process or outcome for certain types of patients. These findings are consistent with those previously reported by Malan (1976a). The convergence is more representative of cross-validation than replication because the definitions and measures of correctness have varied. An important difference between our measure and those of others is the use of the therapist rather than a team of independent assessors to generate the patient formulation. Given that it is the therapist who actually makes the interpretations, we believe that our method has an advantage in terms of clinical applicability.

Whether our measure has an advantage in regard to predictive validity remains to be demonstrated. Future research that compares the validity of the different concepts and measures would be useful. Another worthwhile topic for future research concerns the advisability of changing the patient's formulation and the corresponding focus of interpretations as therapy proceeds. Hatcher, Huebner, and Zakin (1986) have provided data that indicate that formulations do change during time-limited therapy. The implication for research concerning correctness is that the criterion for correctness should change as therapy progresses. In more intensive psychotherapy, particularly psychoanalysis, such a strategy would seem to be even more imperative.

Overall, we believe that the findings reviewed indicate that variation in technique may make a difference in brief dynamic therapy. It is likely that variability in technique and its effects have been masked in some previous studies and reviews. Thus, the effects of appropriate technique and inappropriate technique may have cancelled each other out. In addition to the technical characteristics highlighted in this article, there are others (e.g., timing and sequencing) that are of potential theoretical and practical importance that have not been carefully investigated in any large-scale studies. If studied, they too will need to be examined in the context of other potentially interacting variables.

References

Aiken, L. S., & West, S. G. (1991). *Multiple regression: Testing and interpreting interactions.* Newbury Park, CA: Sage Publications.

Auerbach, A., & Luborsky, L. (1968). Accuracy of judgments of psychotherapy and the nature of the "good hour." In J. Shlien, H. F. Hunt, J. P. Matarazzo, & C. Savage (Eds.), *Research in psychotherapy* (Vol. 3, pp. 155–168). Washington, DC: American Psychological Association.

Azim, H. F. A., Piper, W. E., Segal, P. M., Nixon, G. W. H., & Duncan, S. C. (1991). The Quality of Object Relations Scale. *Bulletin of the Menninger Clinic, 55*(3), 323–343.

Brenner, C. (1976). *Psychoanalytic technique and psychic conflict.* New York: International Universities Press.

Cohen, J., & Cohen, P. (1983). *Applied multiple regression: Correlation analysis for the behavioral sciences.* Hillsdale, NJ: Erlbaum.

Crits-Christoph, P., Cooper, A., & Luborsky, L. (1988). The accuracy of therapist's interpretations and the outcome of dynamic psychotherapy. *Journal of Counsulting and Clinical Psychology, 56,* 490–495.

Crits-Christoph, P., Luborsky, L., Dahl, L., Popp, C., Mellon, J., & Mark, D. (1988). Clinicians can agree in assessing relationship patterns in psychotherapy: The core conflictual relationship theme method. *Archives of General Psychiatry, 45,* 1001–1004.

Curtis, J. T., Silberschatz, G., Sampson, H., Weiss, J., & Rosenberg, S. (1988). Developing reliable psychodynamic case formulations: An illustration of the plan diagnosis method. *Psychotherapy, 25,* 256–265.

Davanloo, H. (Ed.). (1978). *Basic principles and techniques in short-term dynamic psycho-therapy*. New York: Spectrum Publications.

Ehrenreich, J. H. (1989). Transference: One concept or many? *Psychoanalytic Review*, *76*, 37–65.

French, T. M. (1958). *The integration of behavior* (Vol. 3). Chicago: University of Chicago Press.

Freud, S. (1958). The dynamics of the transference. In J. Strachey (Ed.), *The standard edition of the complete psychological works of Sigmund Freud* (Vol. 12, pp. 97–108). London: Hogarth Press. (Original work published 1912)

Garfield, S. L. (1990). Issues and methods in psychotherapy process research. *Journal of Consulting and Clinical Psychology*, *58*, 273–280.

Gill, M. M. (1982). *Analysis of transference: Theory and technique* (Vol. 1). Madison, CT: International Universities Press.

Hammer, E. F. (Ed.). (1968). *Use of interpretation in treatment: Technique and art*. New York: Grune & Stratton.

Hatcher, S. L., Huebner, D. A., & Zakin, D. F. (1986). Following the trail of the focus in time-limited psychotherapy. *Psychotherapy*, *23*, 513–520.

Horvath, A., & Symonds, B. D. (1991). Relation between working alliance and outcome in psychotherapy: A meta-analysis. *Journal of Consulting and Clinical Psychology*, *38*, 139–149.

Husby, R., Dahl, A. A., Dahl, C. I., Heiberg, A. N., Olafsen, O. M., & Weisoth, L. (1985). Short-term dynamic psychotherapy: II. Prognostic value of characteristics of patients studied by a 2-year follow-up of 39 neurotic patients. *Psychotherapy and Psychosomatics*, *43*, 8–16.

Joyce, A. S. (1991). *Preconditions and responses to dynamic interpretation in short-term individual psychotherapy*. Unpublished doctoral dissertation, University of Alberta, Edmonton.

Klein, M. H., Mathieu, P. L., Gendlin, E. T., & Kiesler, D. J. (1970). *The Experiencing Scale: A research and training manual*. Madison: Wisconsin Psychiatric Institute.

Luborsky, L., & Crits-Christoph, P. (1990). *Understanding transference: The core conflictual relationship theme method*. New York: Basic Books.

Luborsky, L., Crits-Christoph, P., Mintz, J., & Auerbach, A. (1988). *Who will benefit from psychotherapy?* New York: Basic Books.

Luborsky, L., Singer, B., & Luborsky, L. (1975). Comparative studies of psychotherapy. *Archives of General Psychiatry*, *32*, 995–1008.

Malan, D. H. (1976a). *The frontier of brief psychotherapy*. New York: Plenum Press.

Malan, D. H. (1976b). *Toward the validation of dynamic psychotherapy*. New York: Plenum Press.

Mann, J. (1973). *Time-limited psychotherapy*. Cambridge, MA: Harvard University Press.

Marziali, E. A. (1984). Prediction of outcome of brief psychotherapy from therapist interpretive interventions. *Archives of General Psychiatry*, *41*, 301–304.

Marziali, E. A., & Sullivan, J. M. (1980). Methodological issues in the content analysis of brief psychotherapy. *British Journal of Medical Psychology*, *53*, 19–27.

Menninger, K. (1958). *Theory of psychoanalytic technique*. New York: Basic Books.

Orlinsky, D. E., & Howard, K. I. (1986). Process and outcome in psychotherapy. In S. L. Garfield & A. E. Bergin (Eds.), *Handbook of psychotherapy and behavior change* (3rd ed., pp. 311–381). New York: Wiley.

Paul, L. (Ed.). (1963). The logic of psychoanalytic interpretation. In *Psychoanalytic clinical interpretation* (pp. 249–272). New York: Free Press of Glencoe.

Piper, W. E., Azim, H. F. A., Joyce, A. S., & McCallum, M. (1991). Transference interpretations, therapeutic alliance and outcome in short-term individual psychotherapy. *Archives of General Psychiatry*, *48*, 946–953.

Piper, W. E., Azim, H. F. A., Joyce, A. S., McCallum, M., Nixon, G. W. H., & Segal, P. S. (1991). Quality of object relations vs. interpersonal functioning as predictors of therapeutic alliance and psychotherapy outcome. *Journal of Nervous and Mental Disease, 179*, 432–438.

Piper, W. E., Azim, H. F. A., McCallum, M., & Joyce, A. S. (1990). Patient suitability and outcome in short-term individual psychotherapy. *Journal of Consulting and Clinical Psychology, 58*, 475–481.

Piper, W. E., Debbane, E. G., Bienvenu, J. P., de Carufel, F., & Garant, J. (1986). Relationships between the object focus of therapist interpretations and outcome in short-term individual psychotherapy. *British Journal of Medical Psychology, 59*, 1–11.

Piper, W. E., Debbane, E. G., Bienvenu, J. P., & Garant, J. (1984). A comparative study of four forms of psychotherapy. *Journal of Consulting and Clinical Psychology, 52*, 268–279.

Piper, W. E., Debbane, E. G., de Carufel, F. L., & Bienvenu, J. P. (1987). A system for differentiating therapist interpretations and other interventions. *Bulletin of the Menninger Clinic, 51*, 532–550.

Piper, W. E., de Carufel, F., & Szkrumelak, N. (1985). Patient predictors of process and outcome in short-term individual psychotherapy. *The Journal of Nervous and Mental Disease, 173*(12), 726–733.

Rosenberg, S. E., Silberschatz, G., Curtis, J. T., Sampson, H., & Weiss, J. (1986). A method for establishing reliability of statements from psychodynamic case formulations. *American Journal of Psychiatry, 143*, 1454–1456.

Sandler, J., Dare, C., & Holder, A. (1971). Basic psychoanalytic concepts: X. Interpretations and other interventions. *British Journal of Psychiatry, 118*, 53–59.

Sifneos, P. E. (1976). *Short-term dynamic psychotherapy evaluaton and technique.* New York: Plenum Press.

Silberschatz, G., Curtis, J. T., & Nathans, S. (1989). Using the patient's plan to assess progress in psychotherapy. *Psychotherapy, 26*, 40–46.

Silberschatz, G., Fretter, P. B., & Curtis, J. T. (1986). How do interpretations influence the process of psychotherapy? *Journal of Consulting and Clinical Psychology, 54*, 646–652.

Smith, M. H., Glass, G. V., & Miller, T. I. (1980). *The benefits of psychotherapy.* Baltimore, MD: Johns Hopkins University Press.

Strachey, J. (1934). The nature of the therapeutic action of psycho-analysis. *International Journal of Psycho-Analysis, 15*, 127–159.

Strupp, H. H. (1980). Success and failure in time-limited psychotherapy. *Archives of General Psychiatry, 37*, 947–954.

Strupp, H. H., & Binder, J. L. (1984). Historical background: Overview and critique. In *Psychotherapy in a new key.* New York: Basic Books.

Strupp, H. H., & Hadley, S. W. (1979). Specific versus nonspecific factors in psychotherapy. *Archives of General Psychiatry, 36*, 1125–1136.

Weiss, J., Sampson, H., & The Mount Zion Psychotherapy Research Group. (1986). *The psychoanalytic process: Theory, clinical observation, and empirical research.* New York: Guilford Press.

Chapter 21
DEPTH OF INTERPRETATION AND VERBAL RESISTANCE IN PSYCHOTHERAPY[1]

Joseph C. Speisman

Much of the research on psychotherapy has been oriented toward identifying the factors which contribute to the success or failure of various techniques. This study follows a more recent trend toward utilization of the process of psychotherapy as a source for investigating variables of interpersonal behavior (Bordin, Cutler, Dittmann, Harway, Raush, & Rigler, 1954; Collier, 1953; Raush, Sperber, Rigler, Williams, Harway, Bordin, Dittmann, & Hays, 1956).

The purpose of the study was to observe the effects of varying depths of interpretation on resistance. There are many disagreements in the literature on psychotherapy concerning the proper application of interpretation, but it is unclear whether these are truly theoretical distinctions or problems of definition. The most obvious disagreement is exemplified in Fenichel's (1941) advice to interpret just beyond the preconscious, and Rogers' (1951) suggestions to reflect and clarify only what the patient has already stated. Fenichel and Rogers, however, reach agreement in their opposition to even judicious use of deep interpretations advocated by Berg (1947) and occasionally by others (Klein, 1932; Stekel, 1911).

Auld and Murray (1955) have concluded that research in the area of the effects of therapist interpretations has indicated very little more than, ". . . there is no single type of response by the therapist that works best under all circumstances." While this is undoubtedly true, there remains the problem of specifying the effects of various therapist responses under diverse conditions. The predictions for the present study were derived largely from Fenichel (1941), but they were exploratory in intent. Simply stated, the particular proposition being studied was that deep interpretations lead to the most resistance, moderate interpretations lead to the least resistance, and superficial interpretations fall between the other two levels as to their influence on resistance.

Method and Procedure

Collier (1953) has suggested that interpretive activity in psychotherapy may be scaled on a continuum. Harway et al. (1953) have developed such a scale for depth of interpretation (referred to as D/I), and have provided information on reliability and validity for the instrument (Raush et al., 1956). As the criterion for depth, the scale

Reprinted from *Journal of Consulting Psychology*, *23*, 93–99 (1959). Copyright © 1959 by the American Psychological Association. Used with permission of the author.

[1]Based on a doctoral dissertation submitted to the University of Michigan, 1957. The research was made possible through the support of U.S.P.H.S. Project M-516; Analyses of Therapeutic Interaction, E. S. Bordin, principal investigator. The author wishes to thank the members of the project for their cooperation, and to express particular appreciation to Harold L. Raush for his assistance and guidance.

emphasizes the disparity between the therapist's view of and the patient's awareness of his own emotions and motives. Thus the ratings are independent of the genetic depth of any given interpretation. The seven-point scale ranges from superficial interpretations embodied in restatements of what the patient has just said to deep interpretations characterized as completely beyond the patient's conscious grasp.

For the purposes of this study the scale was divided into three areas which define the three levels of interpretation. Superficial interpretations were either restatements of what the patient had just said or only slightly modified repetitions. These interpretations fall between 1 and 2.4 on the scale (see Table 1). Moderate interpretations presented the material in a different manner or in a new context (between 2.5 and 4.4 on the scale). Deep interpretations were those which were considered to deal with material which was outside the patient's awareness (from 4.5 to 7 on the scale).

Six categories representing verbal aspects of resistance were derived after a search of the literature. The categories were intended to describe the status of communication from patient to therapist. The rationale was that resistance could be measured both positively (i.e., pursuing the therapeutic task) and negatively (i.e., avoiding the therapeutic task in various ways). The therapeutic task in this case was simply that the patient speak as freely and completely as is possible. It was clear that this concept of resistance is limited in that (a) only verbal manifestations of resistance were tapped, and (b) only the superficial or what Glover (1955) has called "obvious" resistances were studied.

The three positive categories were:

> *Exploration category.* Rate the degree to which the patient is actually exploring either new material or material which may have been discussed at some previous time. The patient may be introducing associations, ideas, thoughts, feelings, perceptions, etc., about the new or old material. He is perhaps attempting to verbalize either more extensively or intensively; he is trying to conceptualize, abstract, or concretize some aspect of whatever content is under discussion. Mere mention of an idea or feeling would be rated low; rate higher exploration as the patient investigates further.
>
> *Self-scrutiny category.* Rate the degree to which the patient is examining himself. He may be reacting to his own statements or those of the therapist, but in each case he is investigating reasons for, or expressing reactions to, his own feelings or statements.
>
> *Self-orientation category.* Rate the degree to which the patient is reporting his own feelings, emotional reactions, ideas, etc., in whatever topic is being discussed. This would be contrasted with the patient talking solely about other people's reactions, or about external events without mentioning his own feelings about, or reactions to, these events.

The three negative categories were:

> *Opposition category.* Rate the degree to which the patient's statement contains the qualities of opposition or denial toward the therapist or therapy. The opposition need not have a directly expressed object. You may, for example, rate opposition from a patient statement which expressed doubt or negativism where therapist or therapy as an object is only inferred.
>
> *Superficiality category.* Rate the degree to which the patient is being superficial. Try to evaluate to what extent he is saying only what is surface and obvious. For example, to what extent is he emphasizing details and particulars at the expense of deeper meaning.

Table 1—*Depth of Interpretation Scale*

1	2	3	4	5	6	7
Therapist merely repeats the material of which the patient is fully aware	Restatement of material of which the patient is aware	Implied focusing with regard to material of which the patient is aware	Reformulation of the behavior of the patient during the interview in a way not explicitly recognized previously by patient	Use of preceding patient statement to exemplify a process that has been building up during an interview and of which the patient is seemingly unaware	Therapist speculates as to a possible childhood situation that might relate to current patient feeling	Therapist response deals with inferences about material completely removed from the patient's awareness
			Therapist comments on patient's bodily and facial expressions as manifestations of patient's feelings			

Table 2—*Horst Reliability Indices for Three Judges*
on the Resistance Categories

	Case A $N = 38$	Case B $N = 45$
Exploration	.84	.80
Self-scrutiny	.83	.91
Self-orientation	.78	.84
Superficiality	.85	.78
Opposition	.91	.75
Blocking	.32	.30

Blocking category. Rate the degree to which the patient seems to be substituting an acceptable thought for one he cannot bring himself to express directly. Important cues would be areas which are "glossed over," or instances where the patient abruptly interrupts himself and continues in a different vein. Other cues would be pauses, hesitations, stumbling, stuttering, repetitions, etc.

Reliability and Interrelations of Measures

Interjudge agreement had been obtained on the measures during their development using case material similar to that used in the final procedure, and was also calculated for the case materials under consideration. In every instance interjudge agreement was obtained by means of the Horst reliability index (1949).

The reliability of the D/I measure had received considerable attention, but as a reliability check for this study three judges rated two interviews which were not to be included in the final data. The combined ratings of three judges yielded Horst indices of .77 and .81, and since this index, unlike the usual correlational index, is a direct approximation of the variance accounted for, these reliability figures were deemed sufficient.

Three different judges using the resistance categories independently rated the same two interviews as had been used for the D/I reliability check.

The results from each resistance category are given in Table 2. The reliability for all categories except Blocking was considered acceptable. Interjudge agreement was also checked for the ratings of the final case material and were of the same order as the figures reported in Table 2. The Blocking category reliability figure remained low (e.g., on the order of .20) despite further training, and this category was not included in the final results.

The several resistance categories were then intercorrelated since they had been presumed to measure different aspects of resistance. As can be seen in Table 3, this assumption was unwarranted.

The categories seemingly represent only two independent aspects of resistance: Opposition and either Exploration, Self-scrutiny, Self-observation, or Superficiality.[2]

---

[2]The Superficiality category had been prepared as a negative aspect of resistance, but the scale accompanying this category was reversed, and the judges were rating on some dimension of "meaningfulness"; thus the high positive correlation with Exploration, etc.

Table 3—*Intercorrelations (r) Among Resistance Categories*

	Exploration	Self-scrutiny	Self-orientation	Superficiality	Opposition
Exploration					
Self-scrutiny	.72				
Self-orientation	.58	.61			
Superficiality	.67	.66	.70		
Opposition	.02	.11	.18	.14	

It remains an open question as to whether it was the definitions, the judges, or the conceptualization of resistance which did not permit finer discrimination, but for the purpose of clearer exposition results will be reported fully only for the Exploration and Opposition categories.

Procedure

In order to obtain data from as broad a range of cases as possible and still provide the detailed and extensive information usually required to make judgments about psychotherapy, the data were collected in two ways. One source was all responses in a sequence of five consecutive interviews from a single case (Intensive case). The second source was 21 different cases from which units of 11 successive responses were randomly selected (Extensive cases). All cases were described by their therapists as neurotic problems although no attempt was made to select cases by nosological classification. The schools represented by the therapists included nondirective, modified psychoanalytic, Adlerian, and eclectic. Therapists were psychologists and psychiatrists, and ranged from approximately one to ten years in experience.

Judges were advanced graduate students or faculty members in clinical psychology at the University of Michigan, and all judges had 100 hours or more of supervised experience as psychotherapists. Three judges, none of whom had been involved in the original reliability checks, did all of the ratings on the resistance categories. A total of 12 new judges rated D/I. Each interview was rated by three judges, and ratings were done independently. All ratings were done on transcriptions of interviews taken directly from audiotapes. Typescripts were done by a secretary trained to follow a uniform procedure. In addition to actual conversation all pauses, stutters, slurs, etc. and expressions such as laughter, sighs, gasps, groans, etc. were included. All names, places, and other identifiable materials were coded to ensure confidentiality for the patient. Judges were given general instructions which cautioned them not to read ahead of the responses they were rating, and not to change a rating once they read further in the interview. For each interview, judges were given a rating booklet with blank seven-point scales, and either the D/I definition and scale or the category definitions, each of which was accompanied by an illustrative seven-point scale with only the end points identified.

Judges who rated D/I rated therapist responses in the sequence in which they appeared in the interview. A response was defined as a therapist statement occurring between two patient statements, and judges were requested to rate each response.

Since rating D/I requires of the judges an estimation of the patient's awareness it was necessary to include the patient statements in the material as well as the therapist remarks.

Judges who rated resistance were presented with only the patient statements in their proper sequence. Therapist remarks were deleted in order to avoid the possibility that the ratings might be influenced by judges' theoretical biases as to the relationship between therapist and patient statements (see Harway et al. [1953], for a discussion of this procedure).

The ratings on the intensive case included all of the reponses in the interviews, and no additional context material was provided. In the extensive series the rater was allowed to read that portion of the interview which preceded the 11 responses to be rated.

Results

All analyses were done by a modification of Kendall's tau (1947), which allows for ties in ranks to the extent of both variables being dichotomized, and in the case of complex tables direction of association is more readily obtainable than with the more commonly used chi square procedures.

Table 4 presents the taus and significance levels for comparisons among each of the three levels of interpretations as to their effects on Exploration and Opposition. In addition, the ratings of responses following Deep interpretations were compared with a pool of the ratings of responses following Modedrate and Superficial interpretations (Not Deep in the table). The data presented in Table 4 indicate that both Superficial and Moderate interpretations were followed by more Exploration and less Opposition (i.e., lower resistance) than were Deep interpretations, and that Moderate interpretations were followed by patient statements rated lower on resistance than were Superficial interpretations. These results support the formulation advanced ear-

Table 4—*Relationships Between Levels of Interpretation and Degree of Resistance*

Comparison of Interpretation Levels	Exploration				Opposition	
	Intensive		Extensive		Intensive	Extensive
	N^a	Tau	N^a	Tau	Tau	Tau
Not Deep vs. Deep[b]	137	.18**	228	.14*	−.10	−.22**
Superficial vs. Deep	42	.19	110	.16*	−.14	−.31**
Moderate vs. Deep	102	.24**	128	.22**	−.18*	−.29**
Moderate vs. Superficial	130	.24**	218	.17**	−.19**	.00

[a]Number of comparisons, N, are the same for Exploration and Opposition in each instance.

[b]The table is read as follows: Not Deep interpretations when compared with Deep interpretation are positively associated with Exploration and negatively associated with Opposition, etc.

*Significant beyond .05 level.

**Significant beyond .01 level.

Table 5—*Comparisons of the Effects of Shifts in Level of Interpretation
on Changes in Degree of Resistance*

	Increase or Decrease of Resistance					
	Exploration				Opposition	
	Intensive		Extensive		Intensive	Extensive
Shift in Interpretation	N^a	Tau	N^a	Tau	Tau	Tau
Not Deep to Deep vs. Deep to Not Deep	13	.69*	13	.54	−.69*	−.54
Moderate to Superficial vs. Superficial to Moderate	38	.37*	94	.47**	−.58**	−.23*

ªNumber of comparisons, *N*, are the same for Exploration and Opposition in each instance.

ªNumber of comparisons, *N*, are the same for Exploration and Opposition in each instance.

*Significant beyond .05 level.

**Significant beyond .01 level.

lier that Deep interpretations lead to the most resistance, Moderate interpretations lead to the least resistance, and Superficial interpretations fall between the other two levels as to their influence on resistance.

While all the results were in the predicted direction and 12 of the 16 comparisons were statistically significant, the degree of association indicated by the taus was not high.[3] Presumably other factors, including other aspects of resistance, operate in the expression of opposition and exploration.

As another approach to the problem, shifts from one interpretation level to another were compared with the reverse shifts. That is, shifts from Moderate to Superficial interpretations were compared with shifts from Superficial to Moderate interpretations, etc. as to the influence of each shift on the expression of Exploration and Opposition. This allowed a more direct approach to the interaction between the various depths of interpretations than the earlier analyses, which only compared each of the levels of interpretation as to their general influence within or across cases.

Table 5 presents the taus and significance levels for the comparisons of the effects of shifts in interpretation levels. The data indicated that shifts from Deep to Not Deep (i.e., combination of Moderate and Superficial) interpretations were followed by increased Exploration and decreased Opposition (lowered resistance), while higher resistance followed the reverse shift. Shifts from Moderate to Superficial interpretations were followed by increased resistance, and shifts from Superficial to Moderate interpretations were followed by decreased resistance.

As had the previous results, these data indicated that Deep interpretations were followed by the highest levels of resistance, and Moderate interpretations were followed by lower resistance than Superficial interpretations. For these analyses, however, the relationship between Superficial and Deep interpretations was indeterminate. Individual comparisons of shifts between Deep and Moderate and Superficial interpretations could not be made, since the *N* in these cases became too small. It

---

[3]All comparisons including those with the resistance categories not reported in this section were in the predicted direction, and the number of significant results was comparable to those reported.

should be noted that in contrast to the previous analyses, the amount of variance accounted for is substantial.

Validity

An integral part of this study was the development of the resistance measures, and thus the question of validity, as well as reliability and interrelationships, requires some comment. In the absence of outside criteria, one relevant procedure was a statement of extent of support, weight of evidence, or construct validity. In this sense the two categories of resistance were successful measures. Exploration provided seven significant results in eight comparisons, and Opposition provided five out of eight; both beyond chance expectation. These results must be interpreted with caution because of the circularity involved in this use of construct validity, and because some comparisons involved the same data as others.

Another, perhaps indirect, approach to validity was to demonstrate the invalidity of obvious alternative interpretations of the results. One potential criticism of the Exploration category was that it measured nothing more than the amount of verbiage the patient produced and that this did not necessarily indicate the relative absence of resistance that the category was supposed to represent. Some relationship was to be expected between number of words and Exploration given the general instructions to patients to speak freely, but this should account for only a minimum of the category's usefulness. A Pearson r of .35 was obtained between number of words and Exploration ratings, and this correlation was compared with reliability figures of .88 and .79 for Exploration. As a further check, partial correlations were obtained with Exploration, Self-scrutiny, and Superficiality, in each case holding constant the number of words. Exploration and Self-scrutiny correlated .72, and the resulting partial correlation was .66. Exploration and Superficiality correlated .67, and when number of words was held constant the correlation obtained was .60. Both the comparison of correlation between Exploration and number of words, and the partial correlations were considered to support the idea that Exploration involves more than the mere length of the patient's statement.

Effects of Resistance on Interpretation

It is quite conceivable that the therapist's level of interpretation is influenced by the degree of resistance he encounters. For example, if a therapist is faced with high resistance, he may resort to more extreme, and thus deeper, interpretations in an effort to reduce the level of resistance. Accordingly, the degree of resistance preceding various levels of interpretation were explored. No significant relationships were found, although Opposition appeared to have more of an influence on subsequent interpretation than did Exploration. The relationship between preceding Exploration and following levels of interpretation was indicated by taus of .02 and .06 for intensive and extensive cases respectively, and comparisons between preceding Opposition and subsequent interpretation levels yielded taus of .13 and .10.

Discussion

Within the limits of the study, three general conclusions may be stated: (*a*) Therapist interpretations systematically influence patient responses; (*b*) the resistance level of a patient remark does not significantly influence the depth of the immediately following therapist interpretation; and (*c*) the Moderate level of interpretation is most effective in maintaining minimum levels of that aspect of resistance which varies with interpretative activity, and when Moderate interpretations follow Deep or Superficial interpretations they are more likely to reduce resistance than are the reverse orders.

Very little work has been done which can be compared directly with the present investigation. There have been several studies of the effects of therapist activity on such concepts as insight or progress, but the results appear to be contradictory. Dittmann (1952) found that patient "Progress" was enabled primarily by interpretations which were somewhat beyond the reflective level. Bergman (1951), on the other hand, concludes that "Reflection of Feeling" was the only technique which led to "Insight" or "Continued Exploration." Insofar as the definitions and operations coincide among the various studies, the results obtained in the investigation reported here would support Dittmann's findings and would not support Bergman.

Gillespie (1953) approached the concept of resistance directly, but his results were equivocal. Gillespie found that Hostile Expressions were directed torard the therapist or toward the therapy process following Interpretation. Since his definition of interpretation was closest to the Moderate level used here, Gillespie's results conflict with the results obtained with the Opposition category. These conflicting findings may be due solely to differences in definition and operationalization of the concepts. On the other hand, nondirective therapy, from which Gillespie's work stems, is directly concerned with hostile expressions as indicators of resistance and as indicators of negative findings for the progress of therapy in general, and Gillespie's findings may reflect factors peculiar to nondirective procedures which were masked in the present study. Contrary to his expectations, Gillespie found that indices of resistance other than Hostile Expressions were associated wtih "accurate clarification" and "restatement of content" which would tend to support the results obtained with the Superficial level of interpretation in the current study.

The results of this study lend support to Fenichel (1941) from whom the hypotheses were drawn. Within the framework that this theorist has presented, the findings may be most generally stated as follows: Moderate interpretations encourange free expression by producing a new frame of reference or by making new connections for materials which are close to consciousness. Deep interpretations, if accurate, impinge on materials at their most regressed stage, but do not stimulate expression because there is no direct connection with the conscious ego. Conversely, Superficial interpretations function only with what is already part of the conscious ego, and so do not provide encouragement for further expression.

Summary

Three levels of interpretation, Deep, Moderate, and Superficial, and two aspects of verbal resistance, Opposition and Exploration, were rated in psychotherapy protocols.

The three levels of interpretation were compared as to the degree of resistance which followed each level, and as to the change in degree of resistance when the therapist shifted from one interpretive level to another. Moderate interpretations were more effective than were Superficial or Deep interpretations in maintaining lower levels of resistance and in reducing levels of resistance. Reference was made to the reliability, validity, and interrelations among several categories of resistance. Previous relevant studies and some aspects of theoretical positions were briefly discussed.

References

Auld, F., & Murray, E. J. Content-analysis studies of psychotherapy. *Psychol. Bull.*, 1955, **52,** 377–395.

Berg, C. *Deep analysis.* New York: Norton, 1947.

Bergman, D. V. Counseling method and client responses. *J. Consult. Psychol.*, 1951, **15,** 216–224.

Bordin, E. S., Cutler, R. L., Dittmann, A. T., Harway, N. I., Raush, H. L., & Rigler, D. Measurement problems in process research. *J. Consult. Psychol.,* 1954, **18,** 79–82.

Collier, R. M. A scale for rating the responses of the psychotherapist. *J. Consult. Psychol.,* 1953, **17,** 321–326.

Dittmann, A. T. The interpersonal process in psychotherapy: Development of a research method. *J. Abnorm. Soc. Psychol.,* 1952, **47,** 236–244.

Fenichel, O. *Problems of psychoanalytic technique.* Albany, N. Y.: Psychoanal. Quart., 1941.

Gillespie, J. F. Verbal signs of resistance in client-centered therapy. In W. U. Snyder (Ed.), *Group report of research in psychotherapy.* University Park: Pennsylvania State Univer., 1953.

Glover, E. *The technique of psychoanalysis.* London: Bailliere, Tindall & Cox, 1955.

Harway, N. I., Dittmann, A. T., Raush, H. L., Bordin, E. S., & Rigler, D. The measurement of depth of interpretation. *J. Consult. Psychol.,* 1953, **19,** 247–253.

Horst, P. A generalized expression for the reliability of measure. *Psychometrika,* 1949, **14,** 21–31.

Kendall, M. G. The variance of tau when both rankings contain ties. *Biometrika,* 1947, **34,** 297–298.

Klein, M. *The psychoanalysis of children.* New York: Norton, 1932.

Raush, H. L., Sperber, Z., Rigler, D., Williams, J., Harway, N. I., Bordin, E. S., Dittmann, A. T., & Hays, W. L. A dimensional analysis of depth of interpretation. *J. Consult. Psychol.,* 1956, **20,** 43–48.

Rogers, C. R. *Client-centered therapy.* Cambridge: Houghton Mifflin, 1951.

Stekel, W. *Die Sprache des Traumes* [The speech of dreams]. Wiesbaden, Germany: Bergmann, 1911.

Part VI

Insight Stage—Self-Disclosure

INTRODUCTION

Self-disclosure is one of the most interesting helping skills because it is not as clearly related to one of the three stages as other skills. For example, it can be used in the exploration stage to provide information about the therapist and the therapy process and to encourage the client to talk about thoughts and feelings. It can be used in the insight stage to encourage insight. It can also be used in the action stage to suggest strategies. Furthermore, self-disclosure is interesting because of the controversy that surrounds it theoretically. Psychoanalytic theorists strongly recommend against using self-disclosure because of fears of contaminating the transference, whereas humanistic therapists adamantly encourage using self-disclosure because it can enable a real, genuine relationship between the therapist and client and can model appropriate self-disclosure for the client. Hence, empirical research on therapist self-disclosure is particularly important to help resolve some of the controversy.

Hill, Helms, Tichenor, et al. (1988, see chapter 4) investigated the frequency of occurrence of therapist self-disclosure and the immediate impact of therapist self-disclosure on client and therapist ratings of helpfulness and client level of experiencing. They found that therapist self-disclosure occurred infrequently (1% of all therapist sentences involved self-disclosure). Clients gave the highest helpfulness ratings and had the highest levels of experiencing to therapist self-disclosure, whereas therapists gave the lowest helpfulness ratings to therapist self-disclosure. It is important to note that Hill et al. did not distinguish different types of self-disclosure in their analyses, so it is not clear whether these results apply to all types of therapist self-disclosure.

In 1978, McCarthy and Betz (see chapter 23) compared self-disclosing disclosures (which Hill & O'Brien, 1999, called *self-disclosures*) with self-involving disclosures (which Hill & O'Brien called *immediacy*). In their analogue study, McCarthy and Betz had undergraduates listen to an audiotape of a session in which a therapist used either 10 self-disclosing or 10 self-involving statements interspersed among several exploration skills (open questions, restatements, and reflections of meaning). The therapist was rated as more expert and trustworthy when using self-involving than self-disclosing statements. Furthermore, in written responses to therapist statements, undergraduates asked more questions about the therapist and made more self-referents to the therapist who gave self-disclosing statements rather than self-involving statements. Hence, it appeared that undergraduates focused on the therapists more than on themselves after self-disclosing statements. In contrast, undergraduates made more self-referents and used more present-tense statements with self-involving than self-disclosing statements. Hence, self-involving statements seemed to stimulate observers to speak more about themselves in the immediate moment. These results need to be replicated in the therapy setting.

In a 1997 qualitative study, Knox, Hess, Petersen, and Hill (chapter 23) asked clients in long-term therapy to describe experiences of and reactions to specific helpful therapist disclosures. Clients, who reported that the disclosures had a positive impact on their therapy, thought that their therapists had made the disclosures (which were typically about personal historical information) to normalize their feelings and be reassuring. Finally, clients also indicated that the disclosures led to new insights or perspectives, made therapists seem more real and human, improved the therapeutic relationship, and resulted in clients feeling more "normal" or reassured.

In an innovative experimental approach, Barrett and Berman (in press) asked therapists at a university counseling center to either increase the number of reciprocal self-disclosures (disclosures in response to similar client disclosures) they made during treatment of one client or to refrain from making self-disclosures during treatment of another client. Clients who received more reciprocal therapist self-disclosures reported less symptom distress after four sessions of treatment and liked their therapists more, although they did not increase in the number or intimacy of their own self-disclosures. It should be noted that even in the increased disclosure condition, therapists gave only about five disclosures per session. This study was not included in this collection because it was not published at the time we went to press; however, we encourage readers to seek out this study.

Clearly, these studies show that therapist self-disclosure can have a very positive impact on clients (perhaps only if they are used infrequently though). However, at least two methodological problems have plagued this literature. First, a vast majority of the studies that have been conducted on therapist self-disclosure have used analogue methodologies, in which researchers ask nonclient participants to read transcripts or listen to tapes of scripted sessions (see reviews by Hill & Knox, in press; and Watkins, 1990). These analogue studies have limited applicability to therapy. Although naturalistic research is difficult because therapists disclose infrequently in therapy, we recommend that researchers study naturally occurring therapy rather than simulations of therapy. Simulations cannot recreate the experience that clients have within therapy after a relationship has been established. For example, a research volunteer might react negatively to a therapist disclosure on a videotape simulation, whereas a client might react positively to the same self-disclosure if he or she knows that the therapist means well and there is a good relationship.

Another problem is that there are several very different types of self-disclosure (disclosures of facts or credentials, feelings, insights, immediate personal experiences of the client, and strategies), but most studies fail to indicate the type of disclosure. Furthermore, given that Hill and O'Brien (1999) classified self-disclosure and immediacy as separate skills, they particularly need to be considered separately in future research.

In addition, Barrett and Berman (in press) suggested that it is important to examine whether disclosures are in response to similar client disclosures (i.e., reciprocal) or not. Researchers also need to determine whether the self-disclosures are reassuring or challenging. Hence, future researchers need to carefully delineate the type of self-disclosure and the context (e.g., in response to a client disclosure or not) given that different types of self-disclosure and different contexts could have very different effects on the therapy process.

References

Barrett, M. S., & Berman, J. S. (in press). Is psychotherapy more effective when therapists disclose information about themselves? *Journal of Consulting and Counseling Psychology*.

Hill, C. E., & Knox, S. (in press). The role of therapist self-disclosure in therapy. In J. Norcross (Ed.), *A guide to psychotherapy relationships that work*. Oxford, England: Oxford University Press.

Hill, C. E., & O'Brien, K. M. (1999). *Helping skills: Facilitating exploration, insight, and action*. Washington, DC: Author.

Watkins, C. E., Jr. (1990). The effects of counselor self-disclosure: A research review. *The Counseling Psychologist, 18*, 477–500.

Chapter 22
A QUALITATIVE ANALYSIS OF CLIENT PERCEPTIONS OF THE EFFECTS OF HELPFUL THERAPIST SELF-DISCLOSURE IN LONG-TERM THERAPY

Sarah Knox, Shirley A. Hess, David A. Petersen, and Clara E. Hill

The use of thearpist self-disclosure in psychotherapy is controversial. In the psychodynamic tradition, therapists often severely limit their self-disclosure for fear of diluting transference (Basescu, 1990; Kaslow, Cooper, & Linsenberg, 1979; Mathews, 1988). Those with humanistic, existential, and eclectic orientations, on the other hand, claim to use this intervention more freely, equating realness with a fully open, honest, genuine, and personally involved stance (Simon, 1988) and viewing therapist self-disclosure as a means of demystifying the psychotherapy process (Kaslow et al. 1979).

Although therapist self-disclosure has been studied frequently (cf. Watkins, 1990), this research has most often used volunteer (nonclinent) participants in single, contrived sessions. This existing research (e.g., Fox, Strum, & Walters, 1984; Mahrer, Fellers, Durak, Gervaize, & Brown, 1981; Mathews, 1988; Nilsson, Strassberg, & Bannon, 1979; Robitschek & McCarthy, 1991; Rosie, 1980) thus does not capture actual client internal experience of the dynamics of therapist self-disclosure in genuine therapy settings, nor does it give information about the perceived consequences, if any, of this intervention on clients in long-term psychotherapy.

Hill et al. (1988), in one of the few studies of actual therapy, found that although therapist self-disclosures occurred only 1% of the time, they received the highest client helpfulness ratings. This study is useful in illuminating the potentially profound impact of this rare intervention, but it again does not capture qualitatively the inner perceptions of clients in long-term therapy. Thus, our understanding of how clients internally experience this intervention remains limited. We do not, for instance, know what clients perceive as the effects of therapist self-disclosure on themselves, on the therapy, or on their relationships with their therapists. Such information would illuminate both the process and outcome of therapy. If therapists gained a deeper understanding of how clients experience self-disclosure, they might more effectively use self-disclosure in their work with clients.

We were interested in studying three potential consequences of therapist self-

Reprinted from *Journal of Counseling Psychology*, *44*, 274–283 (1997). Copyright © 1997 by the American Psychological Association. Used with permission of the first author.

The order of the second and third authors was determined alphabetically. This study, based on a master's thesis by Sarah Knox completed under the direction of Clara E. Hill, was supported in part by the Graduate School and the Department of Psychology at the University of Maryland College Park. A version of this article was presented in June 1996 at the 27th Annual Meeting of the Society for Psychotherapy Research in Amelia Island, Florida.

We express our appreciation to Charles Gelso and Mary Ann Hoffman for serving on the thesis committee. We also express our thanks to Paula Alarid, Samantha Erskine, Julie Hudnall, Craig McManus, Rhonda Rose, Susanna Tipermus, Amy Venema, Maggie Weil, and Mike Wood for their assistance with transcription.

disclosure for long term clients, which seemed reasonable on the basis of the literature. First, therapist self-disclosures could influence the "real relationship" in that clients might see their therapists as more human or more as persons. The real relationship, according to Gelso and Carter (1994), is that portion of the total relationship that is essentially nontransferential. The real relationship consists of genuineness, or the ability and willingness to be what one truly is in the relationship, and realistic perceptions, or those uncontaminated by transference distortions and other defenses. Theoretical statements have been proposed regarding the effects of therapist self-disclosure on the balance of power or control in the therapy, an aspect of the real relationship. It has been suggested, for example, that therapists' revelations of negative information would not result in loss of status (Chelune, 1979), that therapists' openness with clients about past and present secrets would lead to a balance of power in the relationship (Lander & Nahon, 1992), and that therapist self-disclosure would encourage an equal and balanced alliance between client and therapist (Kaslow et al., 1979). These theoretical propositions, however, have been the focus of minimal, if any, actual research.

A second potential consequence that has been explored is the effect of therapist self-disclosure on feelings of universality. Clients often feel most distressed at the thought that they suffer alone (Yalom, 1975). Therapist self-disclosure, however, might alleviate this despair, for such an intervention might give clients a sense of shared experience or universality, normalizing their ordeals and reassuring them that they are not alone (Chelune, 1979). Mathews (1988) posited that therapist self-disclosure makes clients feel less alone, less crazy, and more hopeful.

A third potential consequence is modeling. Mann and Murphy (1975) suggested that when therapists display disclosing behavior, the clients learn through imitation to do the same. Kaslow et al. (1979) noted that therapists serve as a model of form or process, in this case the form or process of disclosure in therapy. Clients might also see therapists as models of content—that is, as examples of individuals who demonstrate thoughts, emotions, or behaviors clients seek to adopt. Therapists could thus serve as broad and encompassing models of disclosure within the therapy sessions. On the basis of the content of therapist self-disclosure, then, clients might alter their thoughts, feelings, or behaviors, both within and beyond the session itself. Simon (1988) addressed this possibility and found that modeling of adult behavior as a demonstration of problem-solving skills, coping skills, self-acceptance, or assertiveness was the predominant reason therapists cited for self-disclosure. She based her assumptions not on research with clients, however, but on interviews with experienced clinicians. Although this perspective is useful and valuable, it does not lead to any conclusions that are based on clients' internal experiences in therapy sessions. We were open to other possible consequences that might emerge from clients' responses and considered the three mentioned above merely as a good place to start, but surely not to finish.

Prior to being able to investigate therapist self-disclosure, however, we faced a major definitional problem. Previous studies have used widely discrepant definitions of therapist self-disclosure, which makes it difficult to generalize across studies. Weiner (1983), for example, described therapist self-disclosure as occurring when the therapist gives more than just professional expertise or when the therapist is purposely more open and genuine with the client. This openness could take the form of the therapist's revealing such things as his or her feelings, attitudes, opinions, associations, fantasies, experiences, or history. Others have defined self-disclosure as intrapersonal (therapist reveals information about his or her personal life outside of counseling) and interpersonal (therapist reveals feelings about the client's problems or the counseling relationship; Nilsson et al., 1979). Still another definition describes self-disclosure in terms of intrapersonal past (therapist reveals information about his or her own past history), intrapersonal present (therapist reveals information about his or her present personal experiences), and self-involving statements (therapist expresses feelings about or reactions to statements or behaviors of the client; Cherbosque, 1987). Yet other researchers define this intervention along different lines, subdividing therapist self-disclosure into positive or negative, personal or demographic, similar or dissimilar, past or present, and self-involving (Watkins, 1990) or describing it as consisting of self-involving and self-disclosing self-referent statements, whether positive or negative (Andersen & Anderson, 1985; Robitschek & McCarthy, 1991). Still others have defined self-disclosure as the therapist's revealing factual information about his or her life, revealing feelings he or she has experienced in his or her life, or revealing feelings he or she experiences regarding the client (Mathews, 1989), a system of classification echoed by Wachtel (1993), who discussed disclosure of within-session reactions versus disclosure of other characteristics of the therapist. Finally, Palombo (1987) introduced the concept of spontaneous therapist self-disclosure, which he defined as an intervention that is not intentional or a conscious part of the treatment strategy.

Out of these various definitions, a trend can be discerned: There is generally a distinction between information that therapists reveal about themselves as individuals and information that therapists reveal about their experiences of and with the client in the session as it occurs. In this vein, Hill, Mahalik, and Thompson (1989) studied self-disclosing and self-involving therapist statements but considered both types as forms of therapist self-disclosure. Similarly, Watkins (1990) stated that "although self-involving statements are often contrasted with self-disclosing statements, self-involving statements are still regarded as a form of self disclosure" (pp. 478–479).

Given such definitional complexity, we used a global conceptualization of therapist self-disclosure, following the lead of Hill et al. (1989) and Watkins (1990), and we included in our study both self-involving and self-disclosing therapist statements. Because this was an exploratory study and a first attempt to qualitatively capture actual clients' inner experience of this intervention, we considered it wiser to examine as many data as possible about the broader phenomenon of therapist self-disclosure. For this study, then, we defined therapist self-disclosure for clients as "an interaction in which the therapist reveals personal information about him/herself, and/or reveals reactions and responses to the client as they arise in the session."

A qualitative approach seemed appropriate for this exploratory stage of inquiry because it allows the probing of inner experiences without predetermining the responses. We used the consensual qualitative research (CQR) methodology developed by Hill, Thompson, and Williams (1997) and used by Rhodes, Hill, Thompson, and Elliott (1994) and Hill, Nutt-Williams, Heaton, Thompson, and Rhodes (1996). Accoring to Hill et al. (1997), the key features of this approach are the following: (a) The method relies on words to describe phenomena rather than using numbers; (b) a small number of cases is studied intensively; (c) the context of the whole case is used to understand parts of the experience; (d) the process is inductive, with theory being built from observations of the data rather than a structure or theory being imposed on the data ahead of time; (e) the process involves dividing responses to open-ended questions from questionnaires or interviews into domains (i.e., topic areas), constructing core ideas (i.e., abstracts or brief summaries) for all the material within each domain for each individual case, and developing categories to describe the themes in the core ideas within domains across cases (cross-analyses). In the CQR process, all judgments are made by a primary team of from three to five judges so that a variety of opinions is available about each decision; consensus is used to ensure that the "best" construction is developed that considers all of the data. One or two auditors are used to check the consensus judgments in order to ensure that the primary team does not overlook important data. Finally, the primary team continually goes back to the raw data to check to make sure that their interpretations and conclusions are accurate and based on the data.

Hence, our purpose in this study was to use a qualitative approach to examine the antecedents, events, and consequences of helpful examples of therapist self-disclosure as identified by clients.

Method

Participants

Clients

Thirteen clients (9 women and 4 men, all European American) who were currently in long-term therapy participated in the study. These clients ranged in age from 26 to 50 years ($M = 37.69$, $SD = 6.94$), had been in therapy with their therapists from 5 to 192 months ($M = 60.62$, $SD = 61.41$), and were in long-term individual psychotherapy with no planned termination in sight. The number of times clients had been in therapy prior to the present relationship ranged from 0 to 14 ($M = 2.23$; $SD = 2.61$). Clients identified the following presenting problems (not mutually exclusive): depression ($n = 8$), anxiety ($n = 3$), sexuality issues ($n = 3$), drug–alcohol rehabilitation ($n = 1$), borderline personality disorder ($n = 1$), dealing with sudden disability ($n = 1$), eating disorder ($n = 1$), anger ($n = 1$), relationship issues ($n = 1$), dealing with elderly parents ($n = 1$), and life skills ($n = 1$). Clients were seen in the therapists' private practice.

Therapists

As indicated by clients' perceptions, the 5 female and 8 male therapists were all European American and ranged in age at the time of the study from 36 years to older than 51 years. Clients' assessments of their therapists' orientations (not mutually exclusive) were as follows: behavioral–cognitive-behavioral ($n = 5$), psychoanalytic–psychodynamic ($n = 4$), eclectic ($n = 3$), and humanistic–experiential ($n = 2$). Clients reported the frequency of their therapists' self-disclosures as equally balanced between "often" ($n = 4$), "occasionally" ($n = 4$), and "rarely" ($n = 5$).

Judges and Interviewer

Three European American graduate students (2 women and 1 man aged 34–42 years) in a doctoral program in counseling psychology participated in this project as the primary research team and served as judges (Sarah Knox, Shirley A. Hess, and David A. Petersen). A European American, a 47-year-old female professor who helped to develop the qualitative method (Clara E. Hill), served as the auditor. Sarah Knox, who also served as one of the judges, conducted all of the interviews. In terms of theoretical orientations, Sarah Knox's is humanistic–psychodynamic, Shirley A. Hess and David A. Petersen's are psychodynamic–humanistic, and Clara E. Hill's is humanistic–psychodynamic.

Measures

Demographic Form

This form asked for basic demographic information about the participant: age, gender, and race of both participant and therapist, therapy history, and current therapy information (age when client began current therapy, months in current therapy, number of sessions in current therapy, approximate number of sessions anticipated yet to occur in current therapy, and reason or reasons client sought current therapy). The form also asked the participant to indicate the therapist's theoretical orientation by checking the appropriate label. Finally, the form asked for a first name and phone number for further contact.

First Interview

The first interview began with a "grand tour" question about the early therapeutic relationship; this question was used to encourage the participant to reenter his or her experiences in the therapy. A second question asked the participant to estimate the frequency of the therapist self-disclosure she or he experienced (per session, per every other session, etc.) and how often therapist self-disclosure had any perceived impact. Clients were asked to describe the general nature of the disclosures their therapists gave. From there, the focus moved to a request for a specific example of a helpful therapist self-disclosure (as determined by the client, following the definition of therapist self-disclosure given in the packet and at the start of the interview) and for a description of its immediate effects on the participant, on the therapy, and on the therapy relationship. Although going into the study, we had postulated possible effects of therapist self-disclosure on the real relationship, on universality, and on modeling, the interviewer was careful to probe for whatever emerged and to follow the clients' lead in order to reduce the possible influence of interviewer bias. Thus, all client comments were probed as part of the interview process. The next question asked the participant to discuss a specific unhelpful therapist self-disclosure (as determined by the client, following the definition of therapist self-disclosure given in the packet and at the start of the interview) and likewise asked about its immediate effects on the participant, on the therapy, and on the therapy relationship. The interviewer next asked about the current therapeutic relationship in order to assess changes over the course of therapy. Finally, the interviewer gave the interviewee a chance to make any final comments and established a time for the follow-up interview.

Follow-Up Interview

The follow-up interview gave both researcher and participant a chance to ask further questions, to clarify issues, and to amend previous comments. In addition, the interviewer asked the participant if she or he was willing to receive and then correct or amend the transcripts of the two interviews. Finally, the interview concluded with a short debriefing paragraph that once more informed the participant of the study's focus on clients' perceptions of the effects of therapist self-disclosure.

Procedures

Recruiting Clients

Twenty-one experienced therapists, all PhD psychologists known to or by the counseling psychology faculty at a large mid-Atlantic U.S. university, were contacted by phone and asked to invite their clients to participate. They were informed that the study would examine clients' perceptions of the effects of therapist self-disclosure. The 14 who agreed to participate were asked to give a research packet to no more than 5 of their adult (at least 18 years old) long-term clients. These clients must have already had at least 10 sessions with the therapist, must have had no planned termination in sight, and must have otherwise been appropriate for participation as determined by their therapist. Each therapist received between two and five packets, for a total of 57 packets. Of these 57, therapists reported that they actually distributed 40 packets.

The first contact between the primary researcher (Sarah Knox) and the potential participants occurred through the research packet, which was distributed by the therapists to those clients who met the above criteria. The packet included a letter to the client containing information about the nature of the study and assuring confidentiality, the client consent form, a demographic form, and a list of the questions that would be asked in the first interview. Clients were informed in the letter that the study was examining clients' inner experience of therapist self-disclosure in psychotherapy, and they were provided with the definition of therapist self-disclosure used in this study as well as examples of therapist self-disclosure. They were told that their consent meant that they would be volunteering to participate in two audiotaped phone interviews and their therapist would know of their participation only if they chose to tell him or her. Potential participants were then asked to choose whether to continue their participation. For those who refused, their involvement was at an end. Those who agreed to participate completed and returned the consent form and the demographic form. Materials were returned by 20 clients, who were then scheduled for an interview.

Interviewing

The primary researcher interviewed the 20 clients using the interview protocols, which included a restatement of the definition of therapist self-disclosure. At the end of each interview, the researcher made brief field notes indicating how long the interview took, the participant's mood, and the interviewer's ability to develop rapport with the participant. To determine what needed to be clarified in the second interview, the interviewer reviewed the tape of the first interview prior to the second interview, which occurred approximately 2 weeks later. Initial interviews ranged in length from 25 to 60 min ($M = 43.46$, $SD = 8.14$); follow-up interviews ranged in length from 10 to 40 min ($M = 27.31$, $SD = 9.49$).

Transcripts

The interviews were transcribed verbatim (except for minimal encouragers, silences, and stutters) for each participant by undergraduate research assistants. All identifying information was removed from the transcripts, and each participant was assigned a code number to maintain his or her confidentiality. All clients were given the option to review their transcripts, but only 4 clients chose to do so, and the changes they suggested (only 2 of the 4 suggested any changes) were minimal and were typically of a grammatical nature.

Selection of Cases

Because our recruiting was so successful, we had more cases than we needed. Qualitative research typically includes 8–15 cases, which is usually adequate for reaching some stability of results. Hence, we decided to select 13 cases, balancing as much as possible across client and therapist gender, therapist theoretical orientation, and when the interview was conducted. Initial analyses were done on these 13 cases, and then a 14th case was examined to determine whether it contributed anything new to the categories. The judges determined that no new data were added, so the categories were considered stable. Only the 13 analyzed cases were considered as part of the final sample.

Selection of Data

As we began the analyses, we realized that the data generated from the question on general self-disclosure were too diffuse to be useful because of the wide variations in the responses. In addition, when analyzing clients' experience of unhelpful therapist self-disclosures, we discovered that several clients had no unhelpful examples and so responded with less helpful examples that were not distinguishable from the helpful examples. Hence, we dropped both the general and unhelpful therapist self-disclosures from the analyses.

Bracketing Biases

Prior to coding data, all three judges and the auditor explored their expectations—biases by responding to each interview protocol as they expected participants to respond. Thus, for each interview question the judges and auditor individually wrote responses they felt would be typical of clients who chose to participate in the study. The judges and auditor were then asked to bracket, or set aside, their suppositions and to approach the data with as much objectivity as possible.

Sarah Knox believed that the helpful disclosures would make the clients feel more comfortable in some way, would provoke the clients to think about something from a new perspective, would change the clients' view of themselves, and would also positively affect the therapy relationship. Shirley A. Hess felt that helpful therapist self-disclosures would make clients think more about how they were coming across and would also enable the clients to see the therapists as more real. She felt that clients would consider these disclosures as intended to make the clients become more aware of the effects of their actions and to help the clients understand why they respond as they do. David A. Petersen felt that helpful disclosures would serve to normalize clients' problems, with clients feeling a stronger bond with their therapist as a result of the disclosure. Clara E. Hill (the auditor) expected that therapist self-disclosures of experiences similar to what the clients were going through would have a positive effect because the clients would feel a sense of universality, an increase in the real relationship between therapists and clients, and a desire to model the therapists. Furthermore, she thought clients would be able to use the disclosures, perhaps as models for encouraging "self-talk" when facing challenging situations.

Procedures for Analyzing Data

Consensus

The heart of this type of qualitative research is arriving at consensus about the meaning, significance, and categorization of the data. Consensus is accomplished through team members' discussing their individual conceptualizations and then agreeing on a final interpretation that is satisfactory to all. Initial disagreement is the norm and is then followed by eventual agreement (consensus) on the analysis of the data. Because the three members of the primary team were all graduate students at the same level of training and because they were friends and respectful of each other, power dynamics were not a problem and could be discussed openly.

Determination of Domains

Domains (topic areas) were initially developed out of the first few interview cases, were refined by going through additional cases, and were continually modified to fit the emerging data. The final domains included the following: early relationship between therapist and client, later relationship between therapist and client, antecedent of the self-disclosure, client's perception of therapist's intention for the self-disclosure, the self-disclosure event, and consequences of the self-disclosure.

Assignment to Domains

The three judges independently assigned each block of data (one complete thought consisting of a phrase or several sentences related to the same topic, e.g., "client thinks that therapist is not able to understand her struggle with drugs, so client asks him if he's ever tried street drugs"; "therapist disclosed that he had a family member who died of AIDS"; "client senses universality of her problem") from each case into one or more domains. The judges discussed the assignment of these blocks to domains until they reached consensus.

Core Ideas

Each judge independently read all data within each domain for a specific case and wrote what he or she considered to be the core ideas that expressed the general ideas in more concise and abstract terms (e.g., "clients perceived their early and later relationships with their therapists as a mixture of positive and negative attributes"). Judges discussed the wording of each core idea until they reached consensus. A consensus version for each case was then developed, which consisted of the core ideas and the raw data for each of the domains.

Audit

The auditor examined the consensus version of each case and evaluated the accuracy of both the domain coding and the wording of the core ideas. The judges then discussed the auditor's comments and made those changes agreed upon by consensus judgment. The judges thus again reached consensus for domains and wording of the core ideas in the revised consensus version. The auditor then reviewed these changes and suggested further modifications, which the judges similarly considered for another revised consensus version.

Cross-Analysis

The purpose of cross-analysis was to compare the core ideas within domains across cases. After listing the core ideas of each domain for each case, the judges examined each domain and looked for similarities in core ideas across cases. They then placed these core ideas into coherent themes or categories, seeking to reach a small number of categories within each domain. Although the number of categories varied from domain to domain, the judges and auditor sought to identify those categories that most efficiently and most clearly captured the essence of the domain. For example, several categories were formulated under consequences of helpful therapist self-disclosure: "gave client insight or new perspective to make changes," "allowed client to view therapist as more real and more human," "normalized or universalized client's struggles," and "enabled client to use therapist as model."

After this initial set of categories was developed, the judges returned to the consensus version of each case to determine whether the case contained evidence not previously coded for any of the categories. If such evidence was discerned (as determined by a consensus judgment of the primary team), the consensus version of the case was altered accordingly to reflect this category, and the core idea was added to the appropriate category in the cross-analysis.

The auditor then reviewed the cross-analysis along with the revised consensus version for each case. Suggestions made by the auditor were considered by the primary team and incorporated if agreed upon by consensus judgment. Once again, the auditor suggested additional changes, which the team discussed.

Results

All 13 cases described an example of a helpful therapist self-disclosure. Following the CQR methodology, we considered categories in each domain to be general if they applied to all cases, typical if they applied to at least half but not all cases, and variant if they applied to at least 3 but fewer than half of the cases. In all domains, categories that were applicable to only 1 or 2 cases were dropped from further consideration, because such infrequently occurring categories were considered less typical. Table 1 contains the summary of findings that emerged from the cross-analyses.

Therapeutic Relationship

The early relationship was typically described as having a mixture of positive and negative attributes. For example, 1 client had difficulty trusting her therapist but also saw him as open, patient, and reliable; another client censored what she said yet felt that her therapist's consistency and persistence made her feel comfortable; a 3rd client became disappointed that the therapist did not "fix" everything, yet she also looked forward to her sessions as her "Friday night date."

Like the early relationship, the later relationship was typically described as having a mixture of positive and negative characteristics. For example, 1 client felt the relationship was more comfortable but admitted that the increased closeness occasionally made her feel scared; another said that although she was more comfortable with the process of therapy and felt that her therapist was helpful, caring, and insightful, she occasionally still felt anxious and nervous; a 3rd acknowledged that although she felt more mature in her present relationship and saw this relationship as more real and more equal, she still questioned at time whether her therapist cared for her.

Antecedents

The helpful therapist self-disclosures typically involved the same antecedent: Clients were discussing important personal issues. There was a wide variety in the content of what clients were discussing, but the common factor was that clients reported that they were discussing topics of concern to them. For example, 1 client was questioning whether her therapist would be able to understand her struggles with drugs because she thought he had never tried street drugs, another client was discussing her difficult adolescent experiences, and a 3rd client was discussing her depression.

Table 1—*Summary of General, Typical, and Variant Categories of Helpful Therapist Self-Disclosures*

Domain	Category	Frequency
Relationship	Mixture of positive and negative attributes	Typical
Antecedent	Client discusses important personal issues	Typical
Intent	Normalize or reassure	Typical
	Help client make constructive change to deal with an issue	Variant
	Client unsure about intention	Variant
Event	Therapist disclosed personal nonimmediate information	General
	(a) Family	Variant
	(b) Leisure	Variant
	(c) Similar experience	Variant
Consequences	Positive	Typical
	(a) Gave client insight or perspective to make changes	Typical
	(b) Therapist seen as more real or relationship seen as improved or equalized	Typical
	(c) Normalized or reassured	Typical
	(d) Client used therapist as model	Variant
	Negative feelings or reactions; negative influence on therapy or therapy relationship	Variant
	Neutral	Variant

Note. $N = 13$. General = category applied to all cases; typical = category applied to at least half of the cases; variant = category applied to fewer than half of the cases. Categories represented by only one or two cases were dropped.

Intent

Clients typically believed that their therapists disclosed to normalize their experiences or to reassure them. For instance, 1 client felt that her therapist disclosed to show her understanding, as a mother, of what the client was feeling about her daughter. Another client believed that her therapist disclosed to ease the client's feelings about upcoming medical tests. Two variant categories also emerged. First, some clients were unsure of their therapists' intentions. One client, for instance, had thought about it quite a bit but remained unsure about why her therapist self-disclosed; another client was uncertain of his therapist's intention. Second, a few clients felt that their therapists disclosed to help clients make constructive changes to deal with issues. For example, 1 client stated that she thought her therapist's disclosure was intended to reduce her self-imposed pressure to resolve difficulties perfectly and immediately; another client felt the disclosure was given to encourage her to confront her issues.

Event

In all 13 helpful therapist self-disclosure examples, therapists disclosed personal nonimmediate information. These disclosures were often from the past, and none were immediate to the therapy relationship, despite instructions to clients that encompassed both self-disclosing and self-involving therapist statements. Variant subcategories within this larger category of personal nonimmediate information were (a) disclosures about family (e.g., 1 therapist discussed spending time at the shore during his childhood, another disclosed having a young son), (b) disclosures about leisure activities (e.g., 1 disclosed about having tried street drugs, another about his hobby of fly-fishing), and (c) disclosures of similar difficult experiences (e.g., 1 disclosed her difficulty arranging transportation because of a disability, another how her coming out as a lesbian affected her relationships with her family).

Consequences

One broad typical category emerged for the consequences of the helpful therapist self-disclosures: They resulted in positive consequences. Within this larger category of positive consequences, four more specific subcategories also emerged. First, clients typically gained insight or a new perspective to make changes (e.g., 1 client began to see solutions to her problems; another client was able to recall good times in her childhood and see her parents as sick instead of evil; a 3rd client was able to use the perspective gained through the therapist self-disclosure to communicate with her partner about the struggles she faced in relationships with her family). Second, clients typically were able to see their therapists as more real, human, or imperfect, which was associated with an improved or equalized therapeutic relationship (e.g., 1 client viewed her therapist as more human and the relationship as more balanced; a 2nd client sensed her therapist as a kindred spirit; a 3rd client stated that the disclosure made his therapist seem more real and more human and showed that his therapist had flaws like all others and did not have all the answers). Third, the disclosures typically normalized or reassured clients, making them feel better (e.g., 1 client sensed the universality of her problem and felt less anxious about her situation; another client felt less alone and less crazy; and a 3rd was able to be more accepting of his own feelings). Fourth, a few clients used therapists as models to make positive changes in themselves or to increase client self-disclosure (e.g., 1 client stated that the disclosure facilitated her own openness and honesty in the therapy, allowing her to feel less protective, whereas another client used her image of how her therapist would respond to situations to guide her as she interacted with others).

The helpful therapist self-disclosures also occasionally evoked negative effects in the form of negative feelings, reactions, or negative influences on the therapy or therapy relationship. Thus, even within disclosures that clients perceived on the whole as helpful, negative effects were also experienced. One client, for instance, was wary about therapy boundaries and questioned what she was supposed to know as a result of the disclosure, and another client feared the closeness engendered by the disclosure and wanted to push it away.

Finally, a few clients also reported neutral consequences of the therapist self-disclosure. One client stated that the disclosure did not change her views about herself or the therapy process; another said that the disclosure may have been a helpful example of people learning to cope with problems but that it did not add much to his ability to cope with his problems.

Narrative Account of a Helpful Therapist Self-Disclosure

The examples of helpful therapist self-disclosure followed a typical pattern (involving all categories for which we found general or typical results). At the time of the disclosure, clients were discussing important personal issues. They surmised that the therapists disclosed in order to normalize their feelings or to reassure them. The disclosure itself concerned nonimmediate personal information about the therapist. The revelation of the therapist self-disclosure led to positive consequences in the clients in the form of insight, realness or equalization of the relationship, and normalization or reassurance.

Illustrative Example of a Helpful Therapist Self-Disclosure

An example of a helpful disclosure is from a 33-year-old female client who had been seeing her male therapist for 11 years at the time of the interview. She had struggled with drug addiction and chronic depression and was later diagnosed with borderline personality disorder. She described her therapist's theoretical orientation as a combination of behavioral–cognitive-behavioral and humanistic–experiential and indicated that he often disclosed. In their early relationship, this client had difficulty trusting her therapist and thus encountered difficulty in opening up to him. She expressed confusion about what the relationship should be and often tested her therapist to see if he would be trustworthy. At times, she needed him to be responsive, and he was not. She did, however, view him as patient, open, and reliable and stated that she felt comfortable with him right away. At the time of the disclosure, she thought that he would not be able to understand her struggle with drugs, so she asked him if he had ever tried street drugs. She believed he thought that he had no other recourse and needed to stop the argument, so he disclosed to her that he had tried street drugs. This disclosure shocked the client ("It stopped the argument cold"), made her rethink her assumptions and stereotypes, enabled her to recognize the benefits of healthy disagreement, and allowed her to use the therapy relationship as a learning ground for other relationships in her life. She thus became more assertive in expressing her needs and opinions rationally. This disclosure also changed her perspective of her therapist, making him more human and more similar to her, thereby increasing her respect for him, making her feel closer to him, and balancing the relationship. She said, "It snapped me right out of that self-righteous thing, you know, that 'How would you know?' . . . like I was different than him. At that moment it made him a lot more human than I was feeling at the time . . . and changed the whole perspective immediately . . . it made him sort of a kindred spirit in a way."

Discussion

In looking globally at these experiences of specific helpful therapist self-disclosures in long-term therapy, we found that clients perceived self-disclosures to be important events in their therapies. Clients were indeed affected by these revelations, an affirmation of the potency of therapist self-disclosure that is consistent with earlier research (e.g., Hill et al., 1988).

To set the context for these results more completely, we note that the early and later relationships for all cases were described as a mixture of positive and negative attributes. These clients characterized their relationships neither as purely "good" nor as purely "bad" but instead reflected perhaps a more realistic view of their connections to their therapists. Perhaps the presence of at least some positive features in the early relationship allowed the clients the safety and comfort necessary to continue in therapy. Were the negative characteristics not offset by positive elements, these clients may not have remained in therapy and thus may not have been eligible for participation in this study. The negative traits did not seem to drive them from therapy in the beginning, nor did they apparently impede the progress or work of therapy at its later stages. Perhaps the good attributes were indeed strong enough, and thus the relationship itself strong enough, to survive the inevitable difficulties of therapy. These participants, then, represent those who have weathered the potentially tumultuous seasons of the therapy relationship.

These clients typically perceived that immediately preceding the disclosure, they were discussing important personal issues such as relationship difficulties, personal struggles with physical disabilities or substance abuse, or upsetting events with family members. After such antecedents, these clients perceived their therapists as having a clear intention for the disclosure: They saw their therapists as seeking to normalize or reassure them through the disclosure. This reassurance sometimes took the form of letting the client know that things often do work out, of demonstrating the therapist's understanding of the client's struggle, or of letting the client know that his or her feelings were neither unusual nor unexpected. The perception of such positive intentions may have contributed to the clients' experience of these disclosures as helpful.

All of the helpful therapist self-disclosures cited by these clients were of personal nonimmediate information, whether about family, leisure activities, or similar experiences between clients and therapists. Although this information was personal, it was largely historical rather than immediate. Despite instructions that permitted clients to describe either self-disclosing or self-involving therapist statements, these clients cited only the former. These qualitative findings thus differ from the suggestions of other literature that the most helpful self-referent responses are immediate and reassuring (i.e., depict present-tense, direct communications to the client of the therapists' feelings or cognitions regarding the client or the therapy and reveal the therapists' support for, reinforcement for, or legitimization of the clients' perspective, way of thinking, feeling, or behaving; e.g., Hoffman & Spencer, 1977; Hoffman-Graff, 1977; McCarthy & Betz, 1978). This self-involving type of therapist statement was never cited by these clients as an example of a helpful therapist self-disclosure, much less a most helpful therapist self-disclosure. Perhaps clients were better able to recall the distinct historical disclosures, whereas any immediate disclosures that may have occurred were more rapidly forgotten or subsumed under the client's general impression of the therapeutic relationship. Perhaps these clients found the historical disclosures more interesting in providing them with a fuller view of the therapist, whereas the self-involving therapist statements remained less memorable or less helpful because they lacked such revelation. Perhaps also the immediate disclosures were percieved as too intimate or threatening and therefore were not viewed as helpful, whereas the more historical or autobiographical statements enabled these clients to learn more about their therapists and thus feel a greater sense of safety and comfort. Several potential explanations for these clients' citing only self-disclosing therapist statements as examples of helpful therapist self-disclosure are surely possible, but the fact that none of these clients referred to a self-involving therapist statement as an example of a helpful therapist self-disclosure is intriguing, especially because the definition with which they were provided encompassed both types of statement.

In terms of consequences these clients perceived as arising from the disclosures, the helpful self-disclosures resulted in both positive and negative consequences, although there were more positive than negative consequences. One positive consequence was the client's perception of the therapist as more human and more real and of the relationship as more balanced. Thus, therapist self-disclosure did seem to affect the real relationship between these therapists and clients. It is interesting that this increased realness did not, however, appear to result in any loss of status for the therapist, a possibility raised by Andersen and Anderson (1985). Although the clients did not explicitly state that no loss of status occurred, neither did they describe a diminishment of the therapist's status. In addition, the disclosures appeared to equalize the power in the relationship, as suggested by Chelune (1979), Kaslow et al. (1979), Lander and Nahon (1992), and Robitschek and McCarthy (1991). The revelations of the therapist self-disclosures evidently contributed to a more balanced distribution of power in the therapeutic relationship, perhaps again because the clients were able to see their therapists as human and real. These clients seemed to appreciate the realness of their therapists and did not experience this realness as a threat to the therapists' stature. In fact, they described such realness as enhancing the connection between therapists and clients, thus fostering the therapeutic work.

An unexpected positive consequence was that these therapist self-disclosures resulted in client insights or new perspectives. The clients were apparently able to learn, to understand something new about themselves or their experiences, and to view things from a new point of view. They were encouraged to rethink old assumptions about themselves or about others, were able to see solutions to their problems, acquired a better sense of a developmental process with which they were struggling, and were able to translate these into interpersonal or intrapersonal changes.

In addition, positive effects appeared to emerge in the helpful instances of therapist self-disclosure through these clients' feeling reassured, feeling that their struggles were normalized, or acquiring a sense of universality. As suggested by Chelune (1979), Mathews (1988), Robitschek and McCarthy (1991), and Yalom (1975), this sense of not being alone in their struggles confirmed the clients' essential connection with others and thus made them feel better.

Another apparent positive consequence was that these clients used therapists as models to make changes in themselves. As suggested in the literature (Egan, 1990; Kaslow et al., 1979; Simon, 1988; Watkins, 1990), such modeling may help clients with the basic act of disclosure in that clients are encouraged by the therapists' disclosing to increase their own disclosure in their session. Some clients in this study cited just such a consequence, for they seemed to use their therapists' disclosure to spur them on to disclose more themselves. Modeling may also occur when clients use their therapists' disclosed traits, characteristics, or modes of behaving as a guide for themselves outside of therapy. This, too, appeared to occur here, for clients remarked that they internalized attributes demonstrated by their therapists in their own interactions and considered such internalization a positive change in themselves. These clients seemed to use the helpful disclosures, then, as a guide for their own thoughts, feelings, and behaviors, both inside and outside of therapy. In their therapists, they perceived traits they sought in themselves, and then they altered their own interactions by incorporating the therapist as a model.

Some negative consequences also occurred, though these were clearly, and expectedly, not the primary consequences of these interventions. A few clients reported negative effects either in terms of feelings and reactions or in terms of the influence on therapy or the therapy relationship. Apparently, even helpful therapist self-disclosures have the potential for some negative impact.

Limitations

The small sample size brings into question the potential representativeness of these participants. All clients and therapists were European Americans and from one geographical region and thus may not represent the experiences of individuals from other cultures and locations. In addition, all were seen in private practice and may represent only those people who are able to afford long-term psychotherapy.

Furthermore, bias is always a concern in qualitative research. We tried to address this potential limitation by using three individuals on the primary team as well as an auditor. Each of us bracketed our expectations and then tried to set them aside. In addition, we tried to stay very close to the data, typically using the clients' own words in developing the core ideas. At the data analysis stage, Clara E. Hill's function was solely as an auditor, which provided her with even greater objectivity in scrutinizing the work of the primary team.

Another limitation was that the definition of therapist self-disclosure used here was broad and encompassing. In the future, researchers should consider using a more limited definition, perhaps one that distinguishes between self-involving and self-disclosing self-referent statements. In addition, no distinctions were made between the degree of intimacy or risk level of the therapists' self-disclosures. Disclosures of having tried street drugs may have a different effect than revelations of enjoying fly-fishing.

Client characteristics, as well, may have created limitations for this project. As explicated by Nisbett and Wilson (1977), people have varying abilities to recall their internal experiences. Some encounter great difficulty in describing their mental processes when a situation is ambiguous (when the client is unaware of the stimuli that trigger such responses). This may have affected clients' perceptions and responses, especially because we did not know how distal or proximal the cited disclosures were.

Furthermore, clients who agreed to participate may have differed from those who did not, which suggests the possibility of self-selection. We also interviewed only clients who were still in therapy and thus do not have the perspective of those who had already terminated. Clients who have terminated may have left for a variety of reasons, one of which could have been the nature of their experiences with therapist self-disclosure. In addition, therapists might have asked only certain types of clients (e.g., the most compliant or successful) to participate.

The therapists who participated were also a sample of convenience and thus were perhaps not truly representative. Their affiliation with the counseling psychology faculty at a large, mid-Atlantic university, as well, may have influenced their desire to participate. In addition, we investigated only the clients' views of the experience of therapist self-disclosure, which might differ from the therapists' perspectives. Given these limitations, one should exercise caution when attempting to generalize from these results.

Implications

This study enabled an examination of the client's experiences of helpful therapist self-disclosure. We learned more about these clients' actual feelings about therapists and therapy through an "inside view" provided by this qualitative design, a view often inaccessible or even hidden from the therapist in the sessions themselves. By learning about the effects of therapist self-disclosure on these clients, therapists may be able to make more appropriate decisions regarding this intervention with their own clients. Self-disclosing therapist statements seem useful in long-term therapy because they evoke positive consequences within clients. For example, clients often acquired insight or a change in perspective, were able to see their therapist as more human and more real, and felt reassured as a result of therapist self-disclosure. Such consequences are certainly worthy of attention when therapists consider making self-disclosures.

Although there were not enough data for us to investigate this fact more fully, different types of clients seemed to react differently to therapist self-disclosure. Some of these clients were voracious in their desire for therapist self-disclosure, wishing their therapists had disclosed more often or even arranging to meet with another client of the same therapist to share information about the therapist. These clients seemed to want to merge in some way with their therapists. Other clients, however, were less desirous of disclosures, worrying at times that the disclosures blurred the boundaries of the relationship or distinctly stating that self-disclosures were inappropriate because they removed the focus from the client and were unprofessional in their revelations about the therapist. This contrast between those clients who sought therapist self-disclosure and those who preferred more distance from their therapists is worthy of further investigation because it may provide information about how client factors influence whether therapist self-disclosure is seen as an appropriate intervention and, if so, what types of self-disclosure are considered appropriate.

In addition, our understanding of how therapist self-disclosure is experienced by clients may be enhanced by further research into the differential effects of various types of disclosure (i.e., self-involving vs. self-disclosing). As an exploratory investigation, this study qualitatively examined clients' internal experiences of therapist self-disclosure as broadly defined. Similarly designed research into how clients perceive and experience the different types of therapist self-disclosure, however, could prove informative.

Future research into the therapists' perspective regarding therapist self-disclosure would also be instructive in determining whether their perceptions are similar to clients'. We chose not to interview these clients' therapists in this initial study, but comparing therapists' perspectives would be important in future studies.

Finally, given the results suggesting that therapist self-disclosure affects the real relationship between therapist and client, the clients' sense of universality, the clients' ability to use the therapist as a model, and the clients' acquisition of insight, it would be useful to develop ways to assess these effects more concretely and quantitatively. For example, a self-report measure of the effects of therapist self-disclosure could be developed that could be administered after therapy sessions. Furthermore, investigation into whether other therapeutic interventions (e.g., interpretation, reflection of feeling) yield these same effects would also be informative.

References

Andersen, B., & Anderson, W. (1985). Client perceptions of counselors using positive and negative self-involving statements. *Journal of Counseling Psychology, 32*, 462–465.

Basescu, S. (1990). Tools of the trade: The use of self in psychotherapy. *Group, 14*, 157–165.

Chelune, G. J. (1979). *Self-disclosure: Origins, patterns, and implications of openness in interpersonal relationships*. San Francisco: Jossey-Bass.

Cherbosque, J. (1987). Differential effects of counselor self-disclosure statements on perception of the counselor and willingness to disclose: A cross-cultural study. *Psychotherapy, 24*, 434–437.

Egan, G. (1990). *The skilled helper: A systematic approach to effective helping*. Pacific Grove, CA: Brooks/Cole.

Fox, S. G., Strum, C. A., & Walters, H. A. (1984). Perceptions of therapist disclosure of previous experience as a client. *Journal of Clinical Psychology, 40*, 496–498.

Gelso, C. J., & Carter, J. A. (1994). Components of the psychotherapy relationship: Their interaction and unfolding during treatment. *Journal of Counseling Psychology, 41*, 296–306.

Hill, C. E., Helms, J. E., Tichenor, V., Spiegel, S. B., O'Grady, K. E., & Perry, E. S. (1988). Effects of therapist response modes in brief psychotherapy. *Journal of Counseling Psychology, 35*, 222–233.

Hill, C. E., Mahalik, J. R., & Thompson, B. J. (1989). Therapist self-disclosure. *Psychotherapy: Theory, Research, and Practice, 26*, 290–295.

Hill, C. E., Nutt-Williams, E., Heaton, K. J., Thompson, B. J., & Rhodes, R. H. (1996). Therapist restrospective recall of impasses in long-term psychology: A qualitative analysis. *Journal of Counseling Psychology, 43*, 207–217.

Hill, C. E., Thompson, B. J., & Williams, E. N. (1997). A guide to conducting consensual qualitative research. *The Counseling Psychologist, 25*, 517–572.

Hoffman, M. A., & Spencer, G. P. (1977). Effect of interviewer self-disclosure and interviewer–subject sex pairing on perceived and actual subject behavior. *Journal of Counseling Psychology, 24*, 383–390.

Hoffman-Graff, M. A. (1977). Interviewer use of positive and negative self-disclosure and interviewer–subject sex pairing. *Journal of Counseling Psychology, 24*, 184–190.

Kaslow, F., Cooper, B., & Linsenberg, M. (1979). Family therapist authenticity as a key factor in outcome. *International Journal of Family Therapy, 1*, 194–199.

Lander, N. R., & Nahon, D. (1992). Betrayed within the therapeutic relationship: An integrity therapy perspective. *Psychotherapy Patient, 8,* 113–125.

Mahrer, A. R., Fellers, G. L., Durak, G. M., Gervaize, P. A., & Brown, S. D. (1981). When does the counsellor self-disclose and what are the in-counseling consequences? *Canadian Counsellor, 15,* 175–179.

Mann, B., & Murphy, K. C. (1975). Timing of self-disclosure, reciprocity of self-disclosure, and reactions to an initial interview. *Journal of Counseling Psychology, 22,* 304–308.

Mathews, B. (1988). The role of therapist self-disclosure in psychotherapy: A survey of therapists. *American Journal of Psychotherapy, 42,* 521–531.

Mathews, B. (1989). The use of therapist self-disclosure and its potential impact on the therapeutic process. *Journal of Human Behavior and Learning, 6,* 25–29.

McCarthy, P. R., & Betz, N. E. (1978). Differential effects of self-disclosing versus self-involving counselor statements. *Journal of Counseling Psychology, 25,* 251–256.

Nilsson, D. E. Strassberg, D. S., & Bannon, J. (1979). Perceptions of counselor self-disclosure: An analogue study. *Journal of Counseling Psychology, 26,* 399–404.

Nisbett, R. E., & Wilson, T. D. (1977). Telling more than we can know. *Psychological Review, 84,* 231–259.

Palombo, J. (1987). Spontaneous self disclosures in psychotherapy. *Clinical Social Work Journal, 15,* 107–120.

Rhodes, R. H., Hill, C. E., Thompson, B. J., & Elliott, R. (1994). Client retrospective recall of resolved and unresolved misunderstanding events. *Journal of Counseling Psychology, 41,* 473–483.

Robitschek, C. G., & McCarthy, P. R. (1991). Prevalence of counselor self-reference in the therapeutic dyad. *Journal of Counseling and Development, 69,* 218–221.

Rosie, J. S. (1980). The therapist's self-disclosure in individual psychotherapy: Research and psychoanalytic theory. *Canadian Journal of Psychiatry, 25,* 469–472.

Simon, J. C. (1988). Criteria for therapist self-disclosure. *American Journal of Psychotherapy, 42,* 404–415.

Wachtel, P. L. (1993). *Therapeutic communication: Principles and effective practice.* New York: Guilford Press.

Watkins, C. E., Jr. (1990). The effects of counselor self-disclosure: A research review. *The Counseling Psychologist, 18,* 477–500.

Weiner, M. F. (1983). *Therapist disclosure: The use of self in psychotherapy* (2nd ed.). Baltimore: University Park Press.

Yalom, I. D. (1975). *Therapy and practice of group psychotherapy* (2nd ed.). New York: Basic Books.

Chapter 23
DIFFERENTIAL EFFECTS OF SELF-DISCLOSING VERSUS SELF-INVOLVING COUNSELOR STATEMENTS

Patricia R. McCarthy and Nancy E. Betz

In a recent article in this journal, Goodstein and Russell (1977) stress the need for greater attention to definitional issues in research on self-disclosure. This need is particularly evident in the body of research concerning the effects of counselor use of self-disclosure on the process and outcome of counseling. Studies of self-disclosure have frequently utilized definitions that are too vague to permit replication of the study or to communicate clearly how the response is to be accomplished. For example, Jourard and Jaffee (1970) considered self-disclosure to be the way one person willingly makes himself known to others, and Luft (1969) said that self-disclosure concerns what is going on between persons in the present.

Not only are such definitions vague, but in many cases there is a lack of agreement among investigators as to the kinds of responses that should be labeled as self-disclosing. For example, Cozby (1973) indicated that self-disclosure is any information about oneself that a person verbally communicates to another, while Shapiro, Krauss, and Truax (1969) indicated that self-disclosure may be accomplished through nonverbal, as well as verbal, behaviors.

Most importantly, however, definitions of self-disclosure have failed to distinguish self-disclosing responses from another potentially important type of counselor response, that is, a self-involving response. Although both self-disclosing and self-involving responses may be classified as self-referent responses, differences between them suggest that they may have very different effects on clients. According to Danish, D'Augelli, and Brock (1976), a self-disclosing response is "a statement of factual information on the part of the helper about himself or herself" (p. 261). In contrast, a self-involving response is "a statement of the helper's personal response to statements made by the helpee" (p. 261). Thus, self-disclosing responses are statements referring to the past history or personal experiences of the counselor, while self-involving responses are direct present expressions of the counselor's feelings about or reactions to the statements or behaviors of the client.

Failure to distinguish self-disclosing and self-involving responses is demonstrated in definitions of self-disclosure provided by Culbert (1968), Dies (1973), and Johnson and Noonan (1972); in their definitions, self-disclosure is a response in which an individual gives information about himself, his concerns, and his conflicts, or is one in which he talks about his here-and-now reactions and feelings to persons or situations. According to Danish et al. (1976), the first part of the definition would refer to self-disclosing responses, but the second part would refer to self-involving responses.

Reprinted from *Journal of Counseling Psychology, 25,* 251–256 (1978). Copyright © 1978 by the American Psychological Association. Used with permission of the first author.

The authors gratefully acknowledge the advice of Dr. Steven J. Danish of Pennsylvania State University.

Differences in the definitions of these two types of counselor responses suggest the possibility that they have rather different effects on the client. The use of self-disclosing versus self-involving responses may lead, first, to differences in the way the client perceives the counselor. Further, the differences in focus of self-disclosing versus self-involving counselor statements may be expected to influence the nature and focus of subsequent client resopnses. Self-disclosure, since it is oriented toward past experiences of the counselor, may elicit client responses that continue to emphasize the counselor's past experience. Thus, these responses may often be phrased in the past tense and refer primarily to the counselor's rather than the client's experience. Self-involving responses, on the other hand, are present centered and refer to the counselor's affective responses to the client. Such responses may demand from the client a present-centered response focused on himself or herself and responsive to the affect verbalized by the counselor. Thus, self-involving responses would appear to enhance the process of client self-exploration in the present to a greater extent than would self-disclosing responses.

The major purpose of this study was to investigate the differential effects of counselor use of self-disclosing versus self-involving responses. It was hypothesized that the two types of counselor responses would lead to differences in client perceptions of the counselor and to qualitative differences in client response to counselor statements.

The design of the study involved the presentation of counseling interview stimulus material containing either counselor self-disclosure or counselor self-involving responses. Subjects rated the counselors on the dimensions of expertness, attractiveness, and trustworthiness and provided a *client response* to each self-disclosing or self-involving statement made by the counselor.

Method

Construction of Audiotaped Stimulus Materials

Tape recordings of two simulated counseling sessions involving a male counselor and a female client were developed. On one tape, the counselor made 10 self-disclosing statements but no self-involving statements. On the other tape, the counselor made 10 self-involving statements but no self-disclosing statements.

The counselor, played by an experienced counseling psychologist, and the client, played by a graduate student in a counseling-related field, role played the two interviews using prepared scripts.[1] The scripts, adapted from counselor–client interchanges utilized in the *Helping Skills Verbal Response Rating Tape* (Danish, D'Augelli, & Brock, Note 1), were identical except for the insertion of self-disclosing versus self-involving counselor statements. Both scripts involved discussions of the client's dissatisfaction with herself, her lack of friends, and her problems relating to her parents. This discussion was divided into 10 segments; the first segment was 2 minutes in length to provide initial interview content, and the 9 subsequent segments were each 1 minute in length. With the exception of the last response in each segment

---

[1]Scripts are avaliable upon request from the second author.

(made by the counselor), all counselor responses were either open-ended questions, reflections of content, or reflections of feeling.

The last response in each segment was either a self-disclosing or a self-involving counselor statement made by the counselor. Self-disclosing and self-involving counselor statements were written to be positive rather than negative in nature. That is, a positive self-disclosing statement was one expressing similarity, rather than dissimilarity, of personal experiences, and a positive self-involving statement was an expression of positive, rather than negative, feelings about or reactions to the client. On one tape, all segments ended with a positive self-disclosing statement, and on the other tape, all segments with a positive self-involving statement.

Subjects

Subjects were 107 female undergraduates enrolled in an introductory psychology course at Ohio State University. Subjects were randomly assigned to one of the two experimental conditions, with 54 subjects assigned to the self-disclosure condition and 53 assigned to the self-involving condition.

Dependent Measures

Perceptions of the Counselor

The Counselor Rating Form (CRF; Barak & LaCrosse, 1975) was used to assess subjects' perceptions of the expertness, attractiveness, and trustworthiness of the self-disclosing or the self-involving counselor. The CRF consists of 36 7-point bipolar items, 12 on each of the three dimensions. Scores on each dimension may range from 12 to 84. Studies using the CRF have demonstrated reliable differences in perceived expertness, attractiveness, and trustworthiness as a function of appropriate experimental manipulations (Barak & Dell, 1977; Barak & LaCrosse, 1975; LaCrosse & Barak, 1976).

Client Responses

Client responses were obtained by asking subjects to write a response to the last counselor statement (either self-disclosing or self-involving) in each segment of the interview. These responses were analyzed in terms of eight relevant dimensions: (a) total number of words; (b) number of questions about the counselor, for example, "So what did you do after you flunked math in high school?"; (c) proportion of counselor referents to total number of words; (d) proportion of self (i.e., client) referents to total number of words; (e) proportion of affective words to total words; (f) proportion of past tense verbs to total number of verbs; (g) proportion of present tense verbs to total number of verbs; and (h) proportion of future tense verbs to total number of verbs.[2]

---

[2]Definitions of client response dimensions and specific instructions for rating each dimension are available upon request from the second author.

Content analyses of the written client responses were done by three raters care-fully trained to identify the presence or absence of each response category and with-out knowledge of the condition (i.e., self-disclosing versus self-involving) under which the client response was obtained.

Procedure

The experiment was conducted in a laboratory with a central tape system and 20 individual carrels equipped with headphones. Subjects, tested in groups of 20, were told that they would hear a tape of several segments of an initial counseling session. Instructions for writing client responses and for completing the CRF were given. For each subject group, either the tape using counselor self-disclosing responses or that using counselor self-involving responses was played. After hearing each of the 10 segments of the tape, subjects were given 1 minute to respond in writing to the counselor in the way they thought the client would respond. After the completion of the entire taped interview, subjects were given the CRF and asked to rate the coun-selor as they believed the client on the tape would rate him.

Analysis

Means and standard deviations of scores on the three dimensions of perceptions of the counselor and on the eight client response dimensions were obtained for the counselor self-disclosure and counselor self-involving conditions. Statistical com-parisons of the two conditions were made using t tests for independent groups. Although the nature of self-disclosing versus self-involving responses suggested di-rectional hypotheses on some of the client response dimensions, two-tailed tests were used in all comparisons to control for the increased probability of Type I error inherent when several separate comparisons are made.

Results

Perceptions of the Counselor

Means and standard deviations of subjects' ratings of the expertness, attractiveness, and trustworthiness of the self-disclosing and the self-involving counselor are pre-sented in Table 1; for each dimension the results of t tests for the significance of the difference between the two counselors are also shown.

Table 1 shows that in the condition where counselor self-involving responses were utilized, the counselor was rated as significantly more expert ($p = .03$) and significantly more trustworthy ($p = .004$) than he was in the condition where coun-selor self-disclosing responses were utilized. In addition, ratings of counselor attrac-tiveness were somewhat higher in the self-involving condition than in the self-disclosing condition.

Table 1—*Means, Standard Deviations, and t-test Comparisons of Perceived Expertness, Attractiveness, and Trustworthiness of Self-disclosing Versus Self-involving Counselor*

Dimension	Self-disclosing[a]		Self-involving[b]		t^c	p
	M	*SD*	*M*	*SD*		
Expertness	63.1	14.6	68.5	11.1	−2.17	.03
Attractiveness	63.6	9.6	67.0	9.3	−1.88	.06
Trustworthiness	63.6	14.0	70.9	11.5	−2.95	.004

Note. Scores on each dimension may range from a minimum of 12 to a maximum of 84.

[a]$n = 54$. [b]$n = 53$. [c]$df = 105$.

Client Responses

Scores on each of the eight client responses dimensions were calculated by adding the number of times a given response occurred over all 10 responses provided by each subject. Thus, the *total number of words* score represents the total words utilized in 10 responses to either a self-disclosing or self-involving counselor, while *number of questions about counselor* refers to the frequency of this response over 10 client responses. Scores on use of counselor or self-referents, affective words, and verb tenses are expressed in proportions to control for intersubject differences in number of words or number of verbs used in responses.

Means and standard deviations of the eight dimensions of client responses are presented in Table 2; again, results of *t*-test comparisons of the self-disclosing versus the self-involving counselor are indicated.

Results indicated significant differences on four of the eight dimensions of client response to a self-disclosing versus self-involving counselor. As shown in the table, responses to the self-disclosing counselor contained significantly more questions about the counselor ($p = .001$) and a significantly larger proportion of counselor referents relative to the total number of words used ($p = .005$) than did responses to the self-involving counselor. On the other hand, responses to the self-involving counselor contained significantly more self (i.e., client) referents relative to total number of words ($p = .001$) and were significantly more likely to be phrased in the present tense ($p = .04$) than were responses to the self-disclosing counselor. No significant differences were found in the total number of words used, the proportion of affective words to total words, or in proportionate use of past and future tense verbs.

Discussion

Generally, the results of this study suggest that counselor self-disclosing versus self-involving responses have differential effects on client perceptions of the counselor and on the nature of the client responses they elicit. The counselor who used self-involving statements was rated as significantly more expert and significantly more trustworthy than was the counselor who used self-disclosing responses. In addition,

Table 2—*Means, Standard Deviations, and t-Test Comparisons of Eight Dimensions of Client Responses to Self-Disclosing Versus Self-Involving Counselor Statements*

Dimension	Self-disclosing[a]		Self-involving[b]		t^c	p
	M	SD	M	SD		
Total number of words	212.0	74.8	203.0	58.7	.69	.49
Number of questions about counselor	2.8	3.5	.1	.5	5.43	.001
Proportion of counselor referents	.03	.03	.02	.01	2.88	.005
Proportion of self-referents	.12	.04	.15	.02	-3.93	.001
Proportion of affective words to total words	.02	.01	.02	.01	-.62	.53
Proportionate use of verb tenses						
Past	.06	.07	.04	.04	1.50	.14
Present	.78	.14	.83	.13	-2.08	.04
Future	.16	.12	.13	.12	1.62	.11

Note. Scores on each dimension represent the sum over the 10 responses made by each subject.
[a]n = 54. [b]n = 53. [c]df = 105.

counselor self-disclosing responses elicited from the client significantly more questions about the counselor and significantly more counselor referents, while counselor self-involving responses elicited significantly more self-referents. Finally, while most verb usage in client responses was in the present tense, counselor self-involving responses elicited a significantly larger proportion of present tense verbs relative to total number of verbs used than did counselor self-disclosing responses. Self-disclosing and self-involving responses did not differ significantly in the total number of words elicited in client responses or in the tendency of these responses to contain affective words and past or future tense verbs.

The results of this study have important implications both for the practice of counseling and for continued research on counselor self-referent responses, in particular, self-disclosure. For the practice of counseling, these results suggest that counselor use of self-involving responses enhances his or her expertness and trustworthiness to a greater extent than does counselor use of self-disclosing responses. Since a self-involving response requires the counselor to express his or her immediate feelings about or reactions to the client, it involves a greater degree of personal risk than does a self-disclosing response, which is often focused in the past and does not refer directly to the client. Willingness to risk oneself may be viewed as a quality of experts and, in necessitating that the counselor trust the client with his or her personal feelings, may enhance the trust the client has in the counselor.

Further, these results suggest that counselor self-involving responses may be more likely to enhance the process of client self-exploration in the present and to maintain the focus of the counseling relationship on the client rather than on the counselor. Because the counselor is revealing his or her feelings toward the client, the client and his or her behavior remain the focus of conversation; client responses tend to be present tense "I" statements rather than questions about or references to the counselor. Counselor self-disclosure statements, on the other hand, may detract from the process of client self-exploration when their effect is to shift the focus of counseling to the counselor and his or her past experiences and problems. Counselors using self-disclosure need to be aware of this potential effect of their statements.

The findings of significant differences in the effects of two previously undifferentiated types of counselor self-referent responses suggest the need for more specific definition and careful differentiation of response types in further research on the use of self-disclosure and other self-referent responses and behaviors. From both the definitional problems pointed out in the introductory section and the results of this study, it is clear that studies of the effects of self-disclosure and related responses on the process and outcome of counseling will not be maximally useful, either theoretically or practically, until there is greater specificity in and agreement on the kinds of responses that do and do not constitute self-disclosure.

A possible limitation of this study derives from its analogue nature. Subjects listened to an interview and were asked to both rate the counselor on several dimensions and to generate responses that they thought the client in that situation would make. Generalization of these findings to real counseling situations will necessitate studies of the perceptions and responses of clients whose counselors are utilizing some combination of self-disclosing and self-involving responses. Further, only female subjects were utilized in this study; additional research is needed to determine the effects of self-disclosing and self-involving counselor statements on male subjects or clients. Finally, the simulated interview portrayed a male counselor and a female client; thus, studies employing systematic variation in the sex of counselor, client, and subjects are necessary to establish the generalizability of these findings.

In conclusion, it is hoped that the results of this study will stimulate further research on the effects of specific counselor behaviors on counseling process and outcome. Attention to definitional issues should enhance the utility of research findings both for other investigators and for practicing counselors.

Reference Note

1. Danish, S. J., D'Augelli, A. R., & Brock, G. W. *Helping Skills Verbal Response Rating Tape*. Unpublished transcript, Pennsylvania State University, 1976.

References

Barak, A., & Dell, D. M. Differential perceptions of counselor behavior: Replication and extension. *Journal of Counseling Psychology*, 1977, *24*, 288–292.

Barak, A., & LaCrosse, M. B. Multidimensional perception of counselor behavior. *Journal of Counseling Psychology*, 1975, *22*, 471–476.

Cozby, P. C. Self-disclosure: A literature review. *Psychological Bulletin*, 1973, *79*, 73–91.

Culbert, S. A. Trainer self-disclosure and member growth in two T-groups. *Journal of Applied Behavioral Science*, 1968, *4*, 47–73.

Danish, S. J., D'Augelli, A. R., & Brock, G. W. An evaluation of helping skills training: Effects on helpers' verbal responses. *Journal of Counseling Psychology*, 1976, *23*, 259–266.

Dies, R. R. Group therapist self-disclosure: An evaluation by clients. *Journal of Counseling Psychology*, 1973, *20*, 344–348.

Goodstein, L. D., & Russell, S. W. Self-disclosure: A comparative study of reports by self and others. *Journal of Counseling Psychology*, 1977, *24*, 365–369.

Johnson, D. W., & Noonan, M. P. Effects of acceptance and reciprocation of self-disclosures on the development of trust. *Journal of Counseling Psychology*, 1972, *19*, 411–416.

Jourard, S. M., & Jaffee, P. E. Influence of an interviewer's disclosure on the self-disclosing behavior of interviewees. *Journal of Counseling Psychology*, 1970, *17*, 252–257.

LaCrosse, M. B., & Barak, A. Differential perception of counselor behavior. *Journal of Counseling Psychology*, 1976, *23*, 170–172.

Luft, J. *Of human interaction*. Palo Alto, CA: National Press, 1969.

Shapiro, J. G., Krauss, H. H., & Truax, C. B. Therapeutic conditions and disclosure beyond the therapeutic encounter. *Journal of Counseling Psychology*, 1969, *16*, 290–294.

Part VII

Action Stage

INTRODUCTION

An exciting new area of research is focused on determining the effects of the stages of the Hill and O'Brien (1999) helping skills model, in this case the action stage. Humanistic and psychodynamic theorists claim that a separate action stage is not necessary because clients will naturally move on to action on their own after their actualizing potential is released through exploration or after insight into their underlying dynamics is gained. Empirical investigation is important in helping determine whether the action stage does indeed add significantly to the model.

In 2000, Wonnell and Hill (see chapter 27) studied the question of the effects of the action stage in dream interpretation. The three-stage model of dream interpretation investigated (Hill, 1996) is similar to the Hill and O'Brien (1999) helping skills model. They found that volunteer clients who received the full model (exploration, insight, action) gained more from dream interpretation sessions in terms of problem solving and wrote better action plans than did volunteer clients who received the truncated model (exploration, insight). Therapists indicated that it was easiest to do the action stage with clients who were psychologically minded, who were involved in the session, and who presented a recent dream; when therapists felt comfortable with an action orientation; and when there had been thorough exploration and insight before beginning the action stage. Further work is needed on the steps of the action stage as proposed by Hill and O'Brien (Hill, 1996; Hill & O'Brien, 1999) and on how clients carry out action between sessions.

In 1994, Mahrer, Gagnon, Fairweather, Boulet, and Herring (see chapter 25) investigated how therapists gain client commitment and resolve to carry out recommended postsession behaviors. They found that in giving recommendations, therapists used a combination of about five methods per session to get clients to the point where they said they would carry out recommendations. To encourage clients to say that they were going to reduce maladaptive behaviors, therapists were concrete and specific about what changes were needed, provided rationales for why change was important or desirable, provided encouragement and pressure to make the changes, and assigned homework. To encourage clients to say that they would increase new ways of behaving, therapists encouraged clients to initiate discussion of the desired new behaviors, highlighted client readiness and control, were concrete and specific about what changes were needed, clarified the behavior and context involved in the change, and rehearsed the new behaviors in the session.

The 1999 Scheel, Seaman, Roach, Mullin, and Mahoney study (see chapter 26) was selected to represent the growing body of work (Conoley, Padula, Payton, & Daniels, 1994; Worthington, 1986; Wright & Strong, 1982) on therapist recommendations for things clients could do or think between sessions (which Hill & O'Brien, 1999, called *directives*). Scheel et al. found that therapists gave at least one recommendation in 89% of sessions, with an average of about two per session. Validation of internal experiences, social interactions, reframing meanings, decision making, request for action, and elicitation of strength were all typical types of recommendations given by therapists. Clients were most likely to implement the therapist's recommendation if they perceived it as not being too difficult, if it fit with their perceptions of the problem formulation and theory of change, and if they perceived the therapist as having influence (being expert, attractive, and trustworthy), although the type of recommendation did not matter. So, the manner in which therapists present homework assignments seems to be important.

We need to know more, however, about client's reactions to different therapist interventions to encourage clients to make changes. We also need to investigate how clients think about and implement suggestions between sessions, and we need more research on process advisement or therapist suggestions for what clients can do within sessions.

In 1997, Hanson, Claiborn, and Kerr (see chapter 24) investigated the effects of different styles of test interpretation within the context of career counseling. According to the Hill and O'Brien definitions, test interpretation is a form of information giving because it provides data and facts to clients, and so this study belongs in the action stage. In the delivered style, the therapist labeled and described the constructs relevant to the highest and lowest scores on two tests (the Personality Research Form and the Vocational Preference Inventory), gave two behavioral examples of each construct, and then summarized the results for the client and asked for questions. In the interactive style, the therapist asked the client to note particularly high or low scores on the same two tests, described the construct relevant to that score for the client, asked the client to give two behavioral examples of each construct, and asked the client to summarize the results. Clients rated the sessions deeper and therapists as more influential (i.e., expert, attractive, and trustworthy) in the interactive than in the delivered condition. These results emphasize the importance of involving clients in the information-giving process.

Unfortunately, other than studies such as the Hanson et al. study on test interpretation, not much research has been conducted on information giving by therapists in therapy. This lack of research is distressing, especially given that information giving is one of the most frequently used skills in therapy (see Hill, Helms, Tichenor, et al., 1988, see chapter 4). The paucity of research may reflect the eschewal by psychodynamic theories of information giving, but because even psychodynamic therapists give a lot of information, it needs further investigation. It is important to note, however, that there are many types of information (about the helping process; giving facts, data, and opinions; giving feedback about the client), and these need to be distinguished in future research.

References

Conoley, C. W., Padula, M. A., Payton, D. S., & Daniels, J. A. (1994). Predictors of client implementation of counselor recommendations: Match with problem, difficulty level, and building client strengths. *Journal of Counseling Psychology, 41,* 3–7.

Hill, C. E. (1996). *Working with dreams in psychotherapy.* New York: Guilford Press.

Hill, C. E., & O'Brien, K. M. (1999). *Helping skills: Facilitating exploration, insight, and action.* Washington, DC: American Psychological Association.

Worthington, E. L., Jr. (1986). Client compliance with homework directives during counseling. *Journal of Counseling Psychology, 33,* 124–130.

Wright, R. M., & Strong, S. R. (1982). Stimulating therapeutic change with directives: An exploratory study. *Journal of Counseling, 29,* 199–202.

Chapter 24
DIFFERENTIAL EFFECTS OF TWO TEST-INTERPRETATION STYLES IN COUNSELING: A Field Study

William E. Hanson, Charles D. Claiborn, and Barbara Kerr

Counselors have traditionally used tests for assessment and diagnosis, as well as to facilitate client change (Campbell, 1990; Duckworth, 1990; Tinsley & Bradley, 1986). When used to facilitate change, test results constitute interventions in and of themselves and are believed to lead to such outcomes as greater awareness, knowledge, and self-understanding. The therapeutic utility of test interpretations, however, should be an empirical consideration rather than a clinical assumption. Therefore, the question remains, Do psychological tests and their interpretation actually contribute to changes in client self-perceptions, cognitions, and subsequent behavior?

Although a considerable amount of research has examined the effects of receiving ambiguous, or even false, test feedback (referred to as the *Barnum effect*; see, e.g., Furnham & Schofield, 1987), less attention has been given to accurate test-interpretation processes and outcomes. Goodyear (1990) provided one of the first critical reviews of the literature in this area. He concluded that "clients who receive test interpretations—regardless of format or of the particular outcome criteria employed—do experience greater gains than do those in control conditions" (p. 242). Unfortunately, the outcomes examined in this research have been quite varied, and thus the specific sorts of gains produced by test interpretations have not been conclusively documented.

More recently, Finn and Tonsager (1992) have produced additional support for Goodyear's conclusion about test-interpretation gains and have provided more specific information about these gains. For example, they found that when they compared attention-control participants with clients who received Minnesota Multiphasic Personality Inventory—2 interpretations, the latter group exhibited increased self-esteem and optimism about overcoming their problems, as well as decreased symptomatology, when measured after a brief interval. In addition to learning more about such outcomes, we would find it helpful to understand the processes underlying test interpretations as thearpeutic interventions. One aim of our research was therefore to explore how clients cognitively consider the information they receive in test interpretations.

Goodyear (1990) noted that most studies of test interpretation have used recall of test results as the outcome criterion without relating recall either to understanding or to use of the results. Another common criterion is the difference between clients'

Reprinted from *Journal of Counseling Psychology*, 44, 400–405 (1997). Copyright © 1997 by the American Psychological Association. Used with permission of the first author.

An earlier version of this article was presented at the 103rd Annual Convention of the American Psychological Association, New York, NY, August 1995. We gratefully acknowledge the help of Julie Beasley, Jennifer Boyce, Laurie Burke, Michael Gottfried, Michelle Kirton, Holly Mull, Richard Sheehy, and Sonja Van Laar in conducting the study.

pre- and postinterpretation self-estimates on the characteristics measured by the test (e.g., Lister & Ohlsen, 1965). This criterion is consistent with a social influence perspective of counseling, particularly the idea that test interpretations constitute influential messages that change relevant client beliefs (Claiborn & Hanson, 1999). Still, pre–post changes in client self-estimates say little about how the client processes test data and how this results in change.

Our study was based more explicitly than earlier research on a social influence perspective (Claiborn & Hanson, 1999). In this perspective, the counselor not only influences the client to take a test, by providing a rationale for its usefulness, but also influences the client's beliefs about the test, for example, its validity for a particular use. Additionally, the test interpretation itself comprises a whole set of influence messages, which are intended to change the influence outcomes, that is, the clients' views of themselves. Many of the counselor, message, and client variables found to be important in influence processes in counseling generally (see Heppner & Claiborn, 1989) may be expected to be important in test interpretation as well. Thus, our study focused not only on the impact of the test interpretation as message but also on the perceptions of the counselor as influence agent, the evaluation of the session as influence situation, and the active processing of the client as influence recipient.

With respect to client processing, recent social psychological findings, especially those stimulated by the Elaboration Likelihood Model (ELM; Petty & Cacioppo, 1986), suggest that a recipient's involvement in the influence exchange has strong implications for influence outcomes. When recipients process messages thoughtfully, the resulting attitude change has been found to be more durable, more resistant to counterinfluence, and more likely to be reflected in the recipient's behavior. All of these are relevant outcomes for counseling. Within the context of test interpretation, however, research findings on the variable of involvement are inconclusive. Early studies indicated that passively received interpretations were largely ineffective in promoting client change (Berdie, 1954; Folds & Gazda, 1966; Froehlich & Moser, 1954). A few other studies found only a modest relationship between client involvement and changes in self-understanding (Dressel & Matteson, 1950; Lister & Ohlsen, 1965). Rogers (1954) and Finn and Tonsager (1992), on the other hand, obtained relatively positive changes for clients who participated actively in the interpretation of their test data. In addition, clients have been found to rate their test interpretations as significantly more attractive (an influence variable) when they are involved in making sense of the results (Rubinstein, 1978). In spite of some promising findings, there have been few systematic comparisons of test-interpretation styles that vary in the degree of client involvement and no studies at all that have examined how client involvement in the interpretation affects their processing of test data. Thus, these questions became aims of our research, as well.

Another contribution of the ELM and related social psychological research is the focus on the cognitive processing of influence. According to Petty and Cacioppo (1986), the degree to which influence messages are thoughtfully processed, or elaborated, is positively associated with influence outcomes. In addition, favorability of the thoughts toward the message is itself a measure of attitude change; more favorable thoughts are associated with attitude change in the direction of the influence. Clearly, both elaboration and favorability are as relevant to the study of influence in counseling as they are to influence generally (Heppner & Claiborn, 1989; McNeill

& Stoltenberg, 1989); for this reason, we chose these concepts to guide the exploration of process in this study.

In this study, then, we used a social influence perspecive, including the ELM
concepts of elaboration and favorability, to examine how clients process and respond
to the test interpretations they receive in counseling. Specifically, in the second session of career counseling, clients received interpretations of their results on the Personality Research Form (PRF; Jackson, 1987) and the Vocational Preference Inventory (VPI; Holland, 1985b). The interpretations were either delivered to the client,
with little client involvement in the process, or conducted interactivley, with considerable client involvement. Clients completed thought-listing measures immediately
after the interpretation of each test. Clients evaluated the session and the counselor
after the session on dimensions relevant to the influence situation and the influence
agent, respectively. We hypothesized that the interactive style of test interpretation
would produce greater elaboration and favorability of thoughts than would the delivered style, because greater client interaction with the counselor would be associated with greater client cognitive activity regarding the tests. We also hypothesized
that clients would view interactive test interpretation as having more impact than
delivered interpretation, in that it would be associated with greater influence. We
measured impact in this study in terms of session depth. Similarly, we hypothesized
that clients would consider counselors using interactive interpretation to be more
influential on dimensions of expertness, trustworthiness, and attractiveness than they
would counselors using delivered interpretation.

Method

Participants

Clients were 26 traditionally aged undergraduate honors students who were receiving
career counseling at a Southwestern university. They included 20 women and 6 men
(21 Anglo Americans, 3 Latinos, and 2 Asian Americans). Clients were not compen-
sated for their participation but received counseling free of charge.

Counselors were 15 graduate students in counseling and counseling psychology.
All were Anglo American, and 13 were women. All had completed at least one
supervised practicum prior to their participation in the study.

Judges for the thought-listing measure were three graduate students in counseling
or counseling psychology and one graduate student in business, all of whom were
otherwise unconnected with the study. The judges included two women and two men
(three Anglo Americans and one African American).

Dependent Measures

Thought Listing

The thought-listing technique is intended to assess a person's cognitions in response
to a message (Cacioppo & Petty, 1981). In this study, immediately after the interpretation of each test, clients listed on a designated sheet of paper all the thoughts

they were having at that moment, and they put the sheet in an envelope to return to the experimenter after the session. They were assured that the counselor would not have access to the thought-listing data.

Thought listing yielded two scores: (a) an elaboration score, which was based on the number of thoughts listed and were relevant to the interpretation the client had just received, and (b) a favorability score, which was based on the number of relevant thoughts favorable to the interpretation the client had received. Thoughts were considered relevant and were thus included in the elaboration score if they concerned the test itself, the interpretation content, the interpretation process, or the counselor. Thoughts were considered favorable if they expressed a positive attitude toward the test, acceptance of interpretation content, or positive reactions to the interpretation process or the counselor. We summed elaboration and favorability scores across the two administrations of the thought-listing measure. Prior to scoring, two pairs of judges rated the thought-listing data in terms of elaboration and favorability. We obtained kappa coefficients (Cohen, 1960) of .85 and .63 for these ratings, respectively.

Session Evaluation Questionnaire (SEQ)

The SEQ is a 24-item semantic differential measure of clients' reactions to counseling sessions. The items, consisting of bipolar adjective pairs separated by 7-point scales, are divided into two sections: session evaluation and postsession mood. Session evaluation subscales include Depth and Smoothness; postsession mood subscales include Arousal and Positivity. Though the entire instrument was administered, the Depth subscale was of primary relevance to this study because it concerns the perceived value or impact of a session. Subscale scores are reported on a 7-point scale; higher scores indicate a greater degree of the dimension. The SEQ dimensions, most notably depth and smoothness, have been used frequently in process research and have demonstrated adequate internal consistency, stability, and validity (Stiles, 1980; Stiles & Snow, 1984). The dimensions have also been associated with important therapeutic outcomes (Stiles, Shapiro, & Firth-Cozens, 1990), including premature termination and engagement in counseling (Tryon, 1990).

Counselor Rating Form (CRF)

Barak and LaCrosse (1975) developed the CRF to assess clients' perceptions of three counselor attributes that are relevant to the counselor's ability to influence: expertness, trustworthiness, and attractiveness. The CRF consists of 36 seven-point bipolar items in a semantic differential format, with 12 items relevant to each attribute. Reliabilities for the three attribute subscales range from .75 to .92 (LaCrosse & Barak, 1976), but the subscales are also highly intercorrelated. Therefore, the CRF total score was used in this study; it could range from 36 to 252. The CRF has been widely used to differentiate counselor behaviors relevant to influence and to predict influence outcomes (Heppner & Claiborn, 1989).

Procedure

The clients signed up to participate in a three-session counseling program jointly sponsored by the Honors College and a counselor training center at the university. They were informed that the counseling program would include data collection for several research projects, one of which was this study, and consent to participate in the research was obtained. It was possible for clients to participate in the counseling program without participating in the research, though no one chose this option. It was also possible for the clients to continue in counseling beyond three sessions, and some clients chose to do so. We randomly assigned clients to conditions and counselors, within the limitations imposed by scheduling. As a consequence, there were 11 and 15 clients in the delivered and interactive conditions, respectively. Counselors conducted both conditions, except for the few counselors who received only one client.

Counselors were thoroughly trained in the use of the tests to be interpreted in the study, as well as in the delivered and interactive test-interpretation protocols. Training occurred in three 4-hour sessions during the 3 weeks prior to the study. Three supervisors, two licensed counseling psychologists, and an advanced student in counseling psychology conducted the training. Counselors learned the protocols by observing supervisors' demonstrations and rehearsing in observed role-playing, for which supervisors gave feedback. Two of the supervisors, using the written protocols as checklists, closely monitored the final role-playings of each counselor. The supervisors required that role-playings be reattempted, as necessary, until each element of the protocols was followed accurately. In discussions with the counselors, the supervisors also ensured that the counselors had an accurate understanding of the constructs measured by each test.

During the study, all counseling sessions were observed by at least one of the supervisors and audiotaped. Observation and inspection of the tapes by the supervisors, who again used the written protocols as checklists, indicated that the protocols were closely followed in the 26 cases included in the study. In one additional case, in which an urgent situation arose, the supervisor interrupted the session briefly and asked the counselor to diverge from the protocol. Supervisors also met weekly with the counselors as a group to develop test interpretations for upcoming sessions and to discuss completed sessions.

The first session of counseling that the clients received was devoted to gathering information about the client and setting goals. Between the first and second sessions, clients completed the PRF–Form E (Jackson, 1987) and the VPI (Holland, 1985b). We chose these tests for our study primarily because of their demonstrated value in career and life planning (e.g., Kerr & Erb, 1991). Both tests are widely used and highly respected but differ considerably in focus: The PRF, based on Murray's (1938) need theory, is a general measure of normal personality; the VPI, based on Holland's (1985a) theory of careers, is a measure of interests. Reliability and validity of both tests are generally sound and amply documented (Holland, 1985c; Jackson, 1984).

The tests were interpreted in the second session of counseling. Prior to this session, an experimenter explained the thought-listing procedure to the client and gave the client an envelope with two thought-listing sheets, one to be completed following the interpretation of each test. The counselor began the second session by asking the client if he or she had any questions or comments about the first session or about taking the tests. The counselor explored only markedly negative reactions. Then the counselor explained what each test measured and provided general reliability and validity information about each test. Finally, the counselor interpreted each test according to either the delivered or interactive protocol. The order in which the two tests were interpreted was counterbalanced within the conditions.

We developed the protocols for the two styles of test interpretation (delivered and interactive). They were identical except for the interventions themselves, which constituted about half of the session, or 20–25 min. The protocol for the delivered style of interpretation had the following elements: First, in the overview of the session, the counselor indicated that the test results would be interpreted for the client. Second, taking the tests one at a time, the counselor labeled and described the constructs relevant to the client's notable scores. These descriptions were consistent with the interpretive manuals of the tests (Holland, 1985c; Jackson, 1984). Notable scores were generally the two or three highest and the two or three lowest, if those scores departed significantly from the average range of the scale, as indicated in the interpretative manuals. No other scores were interpreted. After describing the construct, the counselor gave one or two behavioral examples of the construct at that score level. Specifically, the counselor said, "You scored [very high, high, low, very low] on this scale, which suggests that you [behavioral descriptor appropriate to the scale and the client]." The terms *very high* and *very low* were used when scores were more than a standard deviation from the mean. The behavioral descriptors were informed, whenever possible, by information disclosed by the client in the first session. For example, behavioral descriptors for the Autonomy scale of the PRF might have been "need to be free to come and go as you please, and to work on your own, toward your own goals." At the end of the session, the counselor summarized the test interpretations and asked for questions or comments, in response to which the counselor restated or clarified the interpretations but offered no new material.

The protocol for the interactive style of interpretation had the following elements: First, in the overview of the session, the counselor indicated that the client would be involved in interpreting the test results. Second, taking the tests one at a time, the counselor asked the client to note particularly high or low scores. If the client noted scores that did not meet the criteria for notable scores in the delivered protocol, the counselor revised the client's selection to fit those criteria; thus, scores meeting the same criteria were interpreted regardless of the protocol. Then, exactly as in the delivered protocol, the counselor briefly described the construct relevant to that score, using descriptions consistent with the interpretive manuals of the tests. After describing the construct, the counselor asked the client to give one or two behavioral examples of the construct. If the examples were appropriate, as they generally were, the counselor affirmed them; otherwise, the counselor modified them, as necessary, to fit the manual descriptions. At the end of the session, the counselor asked the client to summarize his or her own test interpretations and then asked the client, "What are some conclusions about yourself that you can draw from these tests?" The counselor responded briefly to the client's answer.

In both protocols, immediately after each test had been interpreted, the counselor said, "It's time to thought list," whereupon the client took the appropriate thought-listing sheet and used up to the next 3 min to complete it. While the client listed his or her thoughts, the couneslor wrote session notes. After thought listing, the client placed the sheet in the envelope, and the session continued. After the session, the client gave the envelope to the experimenter, who then administered the SEQ and CRF to the client. Finally, the client was scheduled for the third session. Debriefing, including arrangements for continued counseling, was handled by the experimenter after the third session.

Results

Means and standard deviations for the dependent variables are presented in Table 1 by interpretation style, and intercorrelations among the variables are presented in Table 2. Because of the large number of dependent variables, we conducted three analyses for the three conceptually distinct sets of variables: those from the thought-listing measure, the SEQ, and the CRF. We performed two multivariate analyses of variance (MANOVAs), with interpretation style as the independent variable, on the elaboration and favorability scores from the thought-listing measure and on the four subscale scores from the SEQ. We performed a univariate analysis of variance (ANOVA), with interpretation style as the independent variable, on the CRF total score.

The MANOVA on thought-listing data indicated that clients in the two conditions did not differ on elaboration or favorability, $F(2, 23) = 2.59$, $p < .10$. According to the η^2 statistic, the independent variable accounted for 18% of the variance in elaboration and favorability scores taken together and for 14% of the variance in favorability scores alone.

The MANOVA on SEQ subscale scores yielded a significant effect, $F(4, 21) = 3.68$, $p < .05$, suggesting that clients in the interactive condition considered the session more valuable on the SEQ variables taken together than did clients in the

Table 1—*Means and Standard Deviations on the Thought-Listing, Session, and Counselor Measures by Interpretation Style*

Measure	Interpretation style			
	Delivered (n = 11)		Interactive (n = 15)	
	M	SD	M	SD
Thought listing				
Elaboration	8.63	3.56	9.73	3.22
Favorability	4.91	2.39	7.33	3.52
SEQ				
Depth	3.66	0.49	4.35	0.40
Smoothness	4.47	0.41	4.43	0.46
Arousal	2.17	0.75	2.59	1.04
Positivity	3.82	0.73	4.16	0.66
CRF	217.91	18.92	236.53	12.00

Note. Thought-listing scores are frequencies. Session Evaluation Questionnaire (SEQ) subscale ranges are 1–7. Counselor Rating Form (CRF) total score range is 36–252. Higher scores indicate a greater degree of each dimension.

Table 2—*Intercorrelations Among the Thought-Listing, Session, and Counselor Measures*

Measure	1	2	3	4	5	6	7
1. Elaboration	—						
2. Favorability	.79**	—					
3. Depth	−.02	.11	—				
4. Smoothness	−.34	−.24	.00	—			
5. Arousal	−.09	.11	.33	.08	—		
6. Positivity	−.30	−.16	.50**	.34	.44*	—	
7. CRF	−.00	.01	.77**	.14	.22	.49*	—

Note. Elaboration and favorability are thought-listing scores. Depth, Smoothness, Arousal, and Positivity are subscales of the Session Evaluation Questionnaire. CRF is the total score of the Counselor Rating Form. Higher scores indicate a greater degree of each dimension.

*p < .05, two-tailed.   **p < .01, two-tailed.

delivered condition. Follow-up univariate analyses, with alpha adjusted to .01 to control for inflation, yielded a significant difference on depth but not on the other three variables. Clients in the interactive condition found the session to have greater depth than did clients in the delivered condition, $F(1, 24) = 15.71$, $p < .001$. According to the η^2 statistic, the independent variable accounted for 40% of the variance in SEQ scores taken together and also in the depth scores alone.

The ANOVA on the CRF total score was significant, $F(1, 24) = 9.44$, $p < .01$. Clients in the interactive condition perceived the counselor as more influential on the expertness, trustworthiness, and attractiveness dimensions taken together than did clients in the delivered condition. According to the η^2 statistic, the independent variable accounted for 28% of the variance in CRF total scores.

Discussion

This study sought to determine the effects of two styles of test interpretation, delivered and interactive, on clients' (a) cognitive processing of the test results, (b) evaluations of the test-interpretation session, and (c) perceptions of the counselor. The results were consistent across these three sets of dependent variables, though the cognitive-processing effects were not significant. Delivered and interactive interpretations differentially affected clients' session evaluations and perceptions of counselors. Sessions in which interactive interpretations occurred were evaluated as having more impact, especially as measured by scores on the Depth subscale of the SEQ. However, clients in the two conditions did not consider the conditions to be differentially relaxed and comfortable, as evidenced by scores on the Smoothness subscale of the SEQ. In addition, clients did not consider the two conditions to be differentially arousing and positive in their effects on client mood.

Counselors who interpreted clients' test results interactively were perceived as more influential on the combined dimensions of expertness, trustworthiness, and attractiveness. This finding is consistent with Rubinstein (1978), who reported that participants viewed interactive interpretations more favorably and rated counselors in the interactive condition as more attractive than counselors in noninteractive conditions. Somewhat ironically, though not unreasonably, it seems that counselors who attempt to involve clients in the interpretive process—acknowledging the clients' expertise in collaborating with them—are perceived as more influential than counselors who do most of the interpreting themselves.

These findings are generally consistent with the results of other studies in which client involvement was either directly manipulated (Dressel & Matteson, 1950; Rogers, 1954) or at least encouraged (Finn & Tonsager, 1992; Lister & Ohlsen, 1965). The ELM (Petty & Cacioppo, 1986) offers a possible explanation for these results. According to the ELM, change is strongly affected by the recipient's ability and motivation to process the influence message—in this case, the test interpretation. Perhaps interactive interpretations are more understandable and personally relevant to clients, and clients are correspondingly more able and motivated to process the interpretations, when the clients themselves play an active part in generating and supporting the interpretations. If this is the case, it is all the likelier that clients will engage in the central route processing so crucial to enduring change (McNeill & Stoltenberg, 1989; Petty & Cacioppo, 1986). Unfortunately, the thought-listing data from this study were not entirely supportive of this explanation, because elaboration and favorability scores did not differ between the two groups. The fact, however, that the independent variable accounted for 14% of favorability scores at least points to the need for further investigation of cognitive-processing effects in test interpretation and the adequacy of the ELM to account for them. A design with more statistical power is recommended.

A related issue arises from the fact that test-interpretation style in this study was manipulated directly in terms of counselor behavior. Counselors either acted to involve clients verbally in the interpretive process or they did not. Clients in the interactive condition certainly complied with the counselor's requests throughout the interview, and clients in the delivered condition had few requests with which to comply. Still, there was no actual measure of client involvement, either actual or percieved, in the study. So it is impossible to say with confidence that clients in the interactive condition were, or saw themselves as being, more verbally involved than clients in the delivered condition; thus, it is difficult to link clients' cognitive processing (a type of involvement) with their behavioral participation in the session. Future research in the area may benefit from including such involvement measures.

Given that this study was conducted in the context of ongoing career counseling, external validity was enhanced at the occasional expense of internal validity. As a consequence, other explanations can account for the results. Perhaps most important, it was virtually impossible for the counselors to be unaware of the experimental manipulation, and so despite their strict adherence to the protocols, as verified by training and supervisor monitoring, counselors may have preferred one interpretation style over the other. Because the counselors generally conducted both types of sessions, there is a real possibility of counselor bias. No data were collected to determine counselor preferences, though counselors reported being comfortable with both styles. The comparability of the counselors' work in the two conditions is further suggested by the lack of differences on the Smoothness, Arousal, and Positivity subscales of the SEQ. Further research in the area should use other measures of nonspecific effects to rule out unintended differential effects of treatment.

External validity was also limited because all of the participants were Honors College undergraduate students, whose processing abilities and motivation probably differ from those found in more general populations. Whether or not these differences exist and affect the generalizability of the results is also a topic for further research.

The failure to find cognitive-processing differences in this study may have some methodological explanations. First, the thought-listing data were difficult to rate for favorability. Even after considerable training, two different sets of judges (different still from the elaboration judges) failed to exceed a rather modest interrater reliability. The particular difficulty seemed to be that the judges were not fully aware of the interpretations the clients had received; these had to be inferred from the thoughts themselves. A solution for future research might be to have clients rate the elaboration and favorability of their own thoughts, following the session; social psychological researchers have used this approach with some success (Petty & Cacioppo, 1986). Alternatively, judges could observe or listen to audiotapes of sessions to learn what the interpretations were before doing the ratings.

In addition to addressing these concerns, future research might examine how clients' cognitive processing of test results relates to McGuire's (1985) influence outcomes. A logical step might be to assess clients' memory for and acceptance of test interpretations in the short- and the long-term. Also, it might be worthwhile to manipulate the valence of test interpretations—that is, whether they suggest positive or negative attributes to the client. Research on the Barnum effect suggests that this content dimension affects the acceptance of bogus interpretations, though this finding has not been confirmed with accurate interpretations (Goodyear, 1990).

Although Dressel and Matteson (1950) called early on for increased attention to variables that might affect the acceptance and use of test results, little work has been done on this topic (Goodyear, 1990). Because ours was one of the first studies to examine client cognitive processing of test interpretations, additional reseasrch is needed to clarify and confirm the findings reported here. Nevertheless, along with other recent research (e.g., Finn & Tonsager, 1992), our study shows that test interpretations, as interventions, affect the counseling process in clinically meaningful and measurable ways. If interactive interpretations prove to be superior to delivered interpretations, as suggested by this study, such evidence would enhance our understanding of this important intervention and point to ways of making it more efficient and valuable to clients.

References

Barak, A., & LaCrosse, M. (1975). Multidimensional perception of counselor behavior. *Journal of Counseling Psychology, 22*, 471–476.

Berdie, R. F. (1954). Changes in self-rating as a method of evaluating counseling. *Journal of Counseling Psychology, 1*, 49–54.

Cacioppo, J. T., & Petty, R. E. (1981). Social psychological procedures for cognitive response assessment: The thought-listing technique. In T. V. Merluzzi, C. R. Glass, & M. Genest (Eds.), *Cognitive assessment* (pp. 309–342). New York: Guilford Press.

Campbell, V. L. (1990). A model for using tests in counseling. In C. E. Watkins & V. L. Campbell (Eds.), *Testing in counseling practice* (pp. 1–7). Hillsdale, NJ: Erlbaum.

Claiborn, C. D., & Hanson, W. E. (1999). Test interpretation: A social influence perspective.

In J. W. Lichtenberg & R. K. Goodyear (Eds.), *Scientist–practitioner perspectives on test interpretation* (pp. 151–166). Needham Heights, MA: Allyn & Bacon.

Cohen, J. (1960). A coefficient of agreement for nominal scales. *Educational and Psychological Measurement, 20,* 37–46.

Dressel, P. L., & Matteson, R. W. (1950). The effect of client participation in test interpretation. *Educational and Psychological Measurement, 10,* 693–706.

Duckworth, J. (1990). The counseling approach to the use of testing. *The Counseling Psychologist, 18,* 198–204.

Finn, S. E., & Tonsager, M. E. (1992). Therapeutic effects of providing MMPI–2 test feedback to college students awaiting therapy. *Psychological Assessment, 4,* 278–287.

Folds, J. H., & Gazda, G. M. (1966). A comparison of the effectiveness and efficiency of three methods of test interpretation. *Journal of Counseling Psychology, 13,* 318–324.

Froehlich, C. P., & Moser, W. E. (1954). Do counselees remember test scores? *Journal of Counseling Psychology, 1,* 149–152.

Furnham, A., & Schofield, S. (1987). Accepting personality test feedback: A review of the Barnum effect. *Current Psychological Research and Reviews, 6,* 162–178.

Goodyear, R. K. (1990). Research on the effects of test interpretation: A review. *The Counseling Psychologist, 18,* 240–257.

Heppner, P. P., & Claiborn, C. D. (1989). Social influence research in counseling: A review and critique [Monograph]. *Journal of Counseling Psychology, 36,* 365–387.

Holland, J. L. (1985a). *Making vocational choices: A theory of personality types and work environments.* Englewood Cliffs, NJ: Prentice-Hall.

Holland, J. L. (1985b). *Vocational Preference Inventory (VPI)—1985 edition.* Odessa, FL: Psychological Assessment Resources.

Holland, J. L. (1985c). *Vocational Preference Inventory (VPI)—1985 edition professional manual.* Odessa, FL: Psychological Assessment Resources.

Jackson, D. N. (1984). *Personality Research Form manual* (3rd ed.). Port Huron, MI: Sigma Assessment Systems.

Jackson, D. N. (1987). *Personality Research Form—Form E.* Port Huron, MI: Sigma Assessment Systems.

Kerr, B. A. & Erb, C. E. (1991). Career counseling with academically talented students: Effects of a value-based intervention. *Journal of Counseling Psychology, 38,* 309–314.

LaCrosse, M., & Barak, A. (1976). Differential perception of counselor behavior. *Journal of Counseling Psychology, 23,* 170–172.

Lister, J. L., & Ohlsen, M. M. (1965). The improvement of self-understanding through test interpretation. *Personnel and Guidance Journal, 43,* 804–810.

McGuire, W. J. (1985). Attitudes and attitude change. In G. Lindzey & E. Aronson (Eds.), *Handbook of social psychology* (3rd. ed., Vol. 2, pp. 233–346). New York: Random House.

McNeill, B. W., & Stoltenberg, C. D. (1989). Reconceptualizing social influence in counseling: The elaboration likelihood model. *Journal of Counseling Psychology, 36,* 24–33.

Murray, H. A. (1938). *Explorations in personality.* Cambridge, MA: Harvard University Press.

Petty, R. E. & Cacioppo, J. T. (1986). The elaboration likelihood model of persuasion. *Advances in Experimental Social Psychology, 19,* 123–205.

Rogers, L. B. (1954). A comparison of two kinds of test interpretation interview. *Journal of Counseling Psychology, 1,* 224–231.

Rubinstein, N. R. (1978). Integrative interpretation of Vocational Interest Inventory results. *Journal of Counseling Psychology, 25,* 306–309.

Stiles, W. B. (1980). Measurement of the impact of psychotherapy sessions. *Journal of Consulting and Clinical Psychology, 48,* 176–185.

Stiles, W. B., Shapiro, D. A., & Firth-Cozens, J. A. (1990). Correlations of session evaluations with treatment outcome. *British Journal of Clinical Psychology, 29,* 13–21.

Stiles, W. B., & Snow, J. S. (1984). Counseling session impact as viewed by novice counselors and their clients. *Journal of Counseling Psychology*, *31*, 3–12.

Tinsley, H. E. A., & Bradley, R. W. (1986). Test interpretation. *Journal of Counseling and Development*, *64*, 462–466.

Tryon, G. S. (1990). Session depth and smoothness in relation to the concept of engagement in counseling. *Journal of Counseling Psychology*, *37*, 248–253.

Chapter 25
CLIENT COMMITMENT AND RESOLVE TO CARRY OUT POSTSESSION BEHAVIORS

Alvin R. Mahrer, Robin Gagnon, David R. Fairweather,
Donald B. Boulet, and Colin B. Herring

In some sessions, there is a point where the therapist recommends or requests that the client carry out a postsession behavior. For example, a postsession behavior might be to have the client either keep a daily log of times when he or she feels anxious or deliberately not smoke the whole day following the session. The therapist merely recommends or tells the client to carry out the postsession behavior and obtains the client's simple acknowledgment or agreement to carry it out (Brady, 1972; Harcum, 1989; Papajohn, 1982; Prochaska & DiClemente, 1982). "Generally, clients are expected to carry out requested behavior both within and outside of sessions" (Nelson & Borkovec, 1989, p. 155; cf. Lopez & Wambach, 1982; Wright & Strong, 1982). In behavior therapies, this is generally referred to as a homework assignment (Boutin, 1978; Flanders & McNamara, 1985; Goldfried & Davison, 1976; Kanfer & Grimm, 1980; Montgomery & Montgomery, 1975).

The focus of this study is a related but different kind of event. Instead of the therapist's simply assigning or requesting that the client carry out the homework, the therapist uses methods designed to obtain the client's manifest commitment and resolve, intention, readiness, and determination to undertake the postsession behavior. The clinical and research literatures highlight the relative absence of studies of effective methods for achieving this level of client commitment and resolve and of the kinds of postsession behaviors that warrant such methods, but the literature does suggest that such methods may be appropriate when the postsession behavior seems to be a significantly new departure or when an ordinary simple assignment or request is thought to be insufficient for the client to carry it out (Bandura & Adams, 1977; Brady, 1972; Cormier & Cormier, 1979; Goldfried, 1982; Goldfried & Davison, 1976; Haley, 1984; Kanfer & Grimm, 1980; Linehan, 1993; Mahrer, 1989; Mahrer, Dessaulles, Nadler, Gervaize, & Sterner, 1987; Mahrer & Nadler, 1986; Mahrer, Nadler, Gervaize, Sterner, & Talitman, 1988; Mahrer, White, Howard, Gagnon, & MacPhee, 1992; Mahrer, White, Soulière, MacPhee, & Boulet, 1991; Montgomery & Montgomery, 1975; Omer, 1985; Prochaska & DiClemente, 1982; Tosi & Henderson, 1983).

It seems useful to study this target to provide some guidelines for practitioners. In some sessions, practitioners may face the questions of what kinds of postsession behaviors may call for the client's manifest commitment and resolve and what methods should be used to obtain this commitment and resolve. Accordingly, the purpose is to answer two questions: (a) What therapist methods are used to obtain manifest commitment and resolve to carry out postsession behaviors? and (b) for what cate-

Reprinted from *Journal of Counseling Psychology, 41,* 407–414 (1994). Copyright © 1994 by the American Psychological Association. Used with permission of the first author.

gories of postsession behaviors do therapists obtain clients' manifest commitment and resolve?

The focus of this study is the client's manifest expression of commitment and resolve to carry out the postsession behavior, rather than whether the client actually carried out the postsession behavior. There have been many studies on client compliance or adherence to in-session recommendations, and this topic has been reviewed by Meichenbaum and Turk (1987). For example, researchers have examined relationships between the carrying out of the postsession behavior and successful outcome (e.g., Kothandapani, 1971; Levy, 1977; Levy & Clark, 1980; Patterson, 1984; Patterson & Forgatch, 1985; Prochaska, 1979; Wurtele, Galanos, & Roberts, 1980). Researchers have also examined relationships between the subsequent carrying out of the postsession behaviors and antecedent in-session factors such as the match between the recommended postsession behavior and the presenting problem, the difficulty level of the homework assignment, the client's strengths, the clarity of the recommended postsession behavior, and the client's attitude toward the assigned postsession behavior (Conoley, Padula, Payton, & Daniels, 1994; Prochaska, DiClemente, & Norcross, 1992; Worthington, 1986).

Accordingly, the focus is not on whether clients carried out the postsession behavior, nor on in-session factors related to the carrying out of the postsession behavior, nor on the therapist's assigning, recommending, or merely telling the client to carry out the postsession behavior. Rather, the focus is on therapist methods that are used, and the kinds of postsession behaviors for which they are used, to obtain the client's manifest commitment and resolve to carry out the postsession behaviors. In this study, the valued event is the in-session occurrence of the client's manifest commitment and resolve, not whether the client actually carried out the postsession behavior.

The general research strategy was to examine verbatim sessions from varying approaches and to identify instances in which clients manifested a substantive level of commitment, resolve, intention, readiness, and willingness to carry out postsession behaviors. Judges were then to identify the methods used to obtain this target event and the kinds of postsession behaviors for which these methods were used.

Method

Judges

The 10 judges were members of a continuing psychotherapy research team. The team included three professional clinicians, and the balance consisted of advanced doctoral students in clinical and counseling psychology. Six of the judges were male; four were female, and their mean age was 34.62 years. Because of the continuing nature of the research team, judges ranged from 25 hr to approximately 500 hr of experience, with a mean of 210 hr ($SD = 48.83$), in using the procedures and methods similar to those used in the present study. Judges were trained by means of didactic presentation and participant practice.

Procedure

Selection of Transcripts

The 10 judges were given a formal definition of client commitment and resolve to carry out postsession behaviors, of which the salient features are as follows: There is an explicit, manifest indication of commitment, resolve, intention, readiness, willingness, and determination to carry out the postsession behavior. The indication is to be clearly explicit and manifest rather than implicit and is to include either direct statements of commitment and resolve rather than such minimal indicators as saying *uh-huh*, *yes*, or *OK* or an implicit understanding that the client is to carry out the postsession behavior.

An exhaustive search of published transcripts yielded 241 transcripts of complete, unedited sessions with individual adult clients, exclusive of intake, demonstration, or termination sessions. Because the transcripts were published and available, we did not deem seeking client consent an issue. On the basis of indicated orientation, the transcripts included the following: cognitive–behavioral (14%); behavioral (18%); psychodynamic (28%), humanistic, Gestalt, and client centered (12%); integrative–eclectic (17%); and other (11%). From the 241 transcripts, two judges independently determined the presence of the target event. Criterion consisted of agreement by both judges. On this basis, 31 transcripts were identified that represented 31 different therapists.

The 31 transcripts, identified by the two judges, were turned over to a separate group of 10 judges who were asked to independently identify the presence of the target events in the transcripts. Of the 31 transcripts, only 22 attained criterion of 70% agreement among the 10 judges as containing at least one target event, and the 22 transcripts contained a total of 28 instances of client commitment and resolve to carry out the postsession behaviors. Accordingly, the 22 transcripts and 28 target events served as the data for this study. As indicated in the published transcripts, the theoretical orientations of the 22 transcripts were cognitive–behavioral (32%); behavioral (14%); psychodynamic (14%); humanastic, Gestalt, and client centered (32%); and integrative–eclectic (10%).

Ten transcripts were of male therapists and male clients, and the balance of 12 transcripts included male therapists and female clients. Demographic data on clients and therapists accompanied the transcripts with insufficient frequency for meaningful reporting. Of the 22 transcripts, client presenting problems included depression (7), obesity (1), test anxiety (1), self-destructive behavior (1), alcoholism (1), anxiety (3), delinquency (2), obsessive–compulsive problems (1), pain (1), procrastination (1), psychotic ideation (1), social anxiety (1), relationship difficulties (1), and phobias (2). The total is greater than the number of sessions because of the presentation of multiple problems by some clients.

Identification of the Target Events

The purpose of the first step was to identify the target events. Instructions enabled each judge individually to examine the entire transcript and to identify client statements containing commitment and resolve to carry out the postsession behavior.

Judges were to identify all the statements indicating commitment and resolve to carry out the given postsession behavior, whether the commitment and resolve were indicated in a single client statement or in a set of client statements. If a transcript included several postsession behaviors, judges were to identify client statements containing each of the postsession behaviors. Criterion was a 70% level of interjudge agreement on the specific client statements containing the target event. Examples of statements indicating commitment and resolve to carry out the postsession behavior are listed in Appendix A.

By means of this procedure, judges identified 28 target events in which clients indicated commitment and resolve to carry out the postsession behavior. Although the criterion level of interjudge agreement was 70%, the obtained mean level of interjudge agreement was 81.66%.

Identification of Therapist Methods of Obtaining Client Commitment and Resolve to Carry out the Postsession Behavior

Once the target event was identified, the purpose of the second step was to determine the therapist methods judged as useful in obtaining client commitment and resolve to carry out the postsession behavior. The instructions emphasized that judges were to examine the antecedent therapist and client statements, judges were free to examine any number of antecedent statements, including the opening statements of the session, and judges were free to examine sequences and patterns of therapist and client interlocking interactions to identify client conditions or participation in the use of the methods. Given the idiosyncratic nature of the task and the purpose of discovering the specific methods and procedures used by therapists, the procedure relied on careful clinical analysis to generate categories of therapist methods rather than on using category systems with predetermined classes of therapist methods.

Judges were to submit their individual descriptions in writing. The instructions emphasized that the descriptions were (a) to exclude technical jargon and vocabulary that represented any given therapeutic approach, (b) to be in the midrange between relatively loose generalizations and the actual words said by therapist and client, and (c) to be aimed toward providing practitioner-useful working principles and methods for obtaining the target event under various client conditions or states.

For each of the target events, two independent researchers content-analyzed the individual written clinical analyses of each of the 10 judges to generate a single composite of the therapist methods used to obtain client commitment and resolve to carry out the postsession behavior. Each of the two researchers arrived at the composite description by mapping all the elements contained in the judges' clincial analyses and then synthesizing the elements into a single composite (cf. Hycner, 1985). For each of the composites, differences between the provisional composites of the two researchers were discussed until a single composite was arrived at with regard to the therapist methods of attaining client commitment and resolve for each of the target events.

By proceeding sequentially through each of the 28 target events, the therapist methods of each subsequent target event were compared with the methods identified in the previous target events. For each target event, the two researchers put the therapist methods into the provisional category system of therapist methods that were based on the previous composites. Differences between the two researchers were again discussed to add to or confirm the provisionally generated category system of therapist methods. For each of the 28 target events, the provisionally generated category system of therapist methods was given to the 10 judges so that they could determine the goodness-of-fit of the therapist methods from the given target event and the provisionally generated category system. A criterion level of 70% interjudge agreement was used to finalize the sequentially generated category system. By following this procedure sequentially over the 28 target events, a category system was generated of the therapist methods judged to be those used to obtain client commitment and resolve to carry out the postsession behaviors.

Identification of the Categories of Postsession Behavior

After the identification of the therapist methods, the purpose of the next step was to determine the categories of postsession behavior. To maximize practitioner usefulness, we focused on examining the category of postsession behavior in relation to the context of the entire session. Accordingly, each judge was instructed to examine the entire transcript to identify the category of postsession behavior rather than to focus predominantly on the restricted content of the postsession behavior itself. The instructions directed the judges to go beyond the specific content of the postsession behavior—for example, as vocational, sexual, or interpersonal—and to identify the category on the basis of the context of the entire session.

Judges were to submit their individual descriptions in writing. As given in the second step, two independent researchers independently content analyzed the 10 judges' written clinical analyses to arrive at a single composite for categorizing each of the target events. Differences between the composites of the two researchers were discussed so as to arrive at a single composite category system of postsession behaviors.

By proceeding sequentially through each of the 28 target events, we compared each subsequent composite description with the provisionally generated category system on the basis of the antecedent composite descriptions. For example, the two researchers arrived at a single composite description of the second target event and determined a provisional overall category system. The 10 judges were then given the composite descriptions of the first two target events to confirm, disconfirm, refine, or modify the provisional overall category system determined by the two researchers, using a 70% level of interjudge agreement among the 10 judges. By following this procedure progressively for each of the 28 target events, an overall category system was generated, on the basis of the composite descriptions of the 28 target events. To verify use of the genrated category system, we gave the judges the transcripts, including the identified 28 postsession behaviors, and we instructed them to assign the postsession behaviors to the appropriate category of the system. Criterion was 70% interjudge agreement among the 10 judges.

We examined each transcript before proceeding on to the next. The transcripts were examined in random order. For each transcript, the first step was to identify client statements indicating commitment and resolve to carry out the postsession behavior; the second step was to identify the categorized therapist methods used to attain client commitment and resolve, and the third step was to identify the category of the postsession behavior in the context of the session.

Results

Therapist Methods

Using the written clinical analyses of the 10 judges, two researchers determined the composite description of each method and the sequentially generated set of therapist methods. The 10 judges then verified or modified the composite set of therapist methods. The criterion level of interjudge agreement was 70% among the 10 judges. Obtained mean level of interjudge agreement was 83.48%. The following is the set of 16 therapist methods in the verbatim words of the judges, as determined in the composite descriptions by the two researchers and meeting the criterion level of interjudge agreement of the 10 judges:

1. *Seeing client as new person.* The counselor regards the client as a qualitatively new person, or invites the client to be a new person, in considering and in carrying out the postsession behavior. It is as if the new person could, should, and will be committed to carrying out the postsession behavior.

2. *Client initiation.* The client is predominantly the one who comes up with the explicit postsession behavior, or with a more general behavior that may be refined into one that is more specific and explicit. The counselor neither blocks nor reduces the client's initiative in achieving commitment for carrying out the postsession behavior.

3. *Client readiness and control.* The counselor highlights the client's right, readiness, and willingness to carry out or to decline to carry out the postsession behavior. The counselor inquires into the client's readiness, hesitation, or uncertainty about the postsession behavior.

4. *Contingent conditions.* The counselor makes provision of other, sought-after parts of the treatment program explicitly contingent on the client's agreement to carry out the postsession behavior.

5. *Concrete specificity.* The counselor is quite specific in defining the concrete and specific postsession behavior, the situational context, the other persons who might be involved, and when and how to carry out the postsession behavior.

6. *Behavior–context clarification.* The counselor works to clarify the behavior, the situational context, or both. Typically, the counselor starts with a behavior or situational context that is somewhat loose or vague, and the process involves increasing clarification.

7. *Negotiation and custom fitting.* The counselor negotiates with the client in regard to the number, nature, content, and difficulty of the postsession behaviors.

8. *Justifying rationales.* The counselor provides justifying reasons, arguments, and rationales for how and why the postsession behaviors are important and desirable. Typically, this includes drawing linkages between carrying out the postsession behaviors and the counseling aims, purposes, and goals.

9. *Reluctance-countering rationales.* If the client is reluctant, hesitant, resistant, or negative, the counselor uses additional justifying reasons, arguments, and rationales for undertaking the postsession behaviors.

10. *Encouragement–pressure.* The counselor pushes, presses, and encourages the client to carry out the postsession behaviors.

11. *Acknowledgment of failure.* The counselor openly acknowledges failure in obtaining client commitment to carrying out the postsession behavior.

12. *Assignment of homework.* The client is simply requested, told, or instructed to carry out the postsession behavior as homework.

13. *Clarification and reassignment of homework.* If the client is unclear or not adequately agreeable, the counselor clarifies the assigned postsession behavior, increases commitment, and reassigns the postsession homework.

14. *In-session tryout, rehearsal, and refinement–elaboration.* The counselor has the client try out the postsession behavior in the session and enables the client to see how it feels and to repeat, refine, and elaborate the postsession behavior.

15. *Counselor accompaniment.* The counselor joins with the client in trying out and in carrying out the prospective postsession behavior in the session.

16. *Contractual agreement–commitment.* The counselor and client arrive at a contractual agreement that the postsession behavior will be carried out.

Over the 28 instances of client commitment and resolve, the mean number of therapist methods was 5.07 ($SD = 2.39$). In none of the 28 target events was just one therapist method used, whereas 10 of the 16 therapist methods were used in 3 instances of client commitment and resolve.

Frequency distributions of the 16 therapist methods are presented in Table 1. As indicated in Table 1, the most commonly used methods were Method 5 (concrete specificity, 64.21%), Method 2 (client initiation, 50.00%), Method 3 (client readiness and control, 46.43%), Method 10 (encouragement–pressure, 42.86%), and Method 16 (contractual agreement–commitment, 42.86%). The remaining 11 methods were used with lower frequencies, as is shown in Table 1.

Postsession Behaviors

Data consisted of the postsession behaviors as identified within the context of the entire transcript. A sample of the 28 postsession behaviors appears in Appendix B.

Results indicated that the 10 judges organized the 28 postsession behaviors into a twofold category system. The first category was identified as postsession behaviors to facilitate problem reduction. In the verbatim words of the composite, the postsession behaviors were to be instrumental in facilitating the reduction or resolution of the problematic concern, condition, or state identified in the session. The second category was identified as postsession behaviors to facilitate the occurrence of new ways of being and behaving, deeper personality processes, or qualities that were identified in the session and were valued and welcomed by the client. Judges were then given the transcripts and asked to assign each of the 28 postsession behaviors to the appropriate one of the two categories. Criterion level of interjudge agreement was 70%. The obtained level of interjudge agreement was 91.42%. All 28 postsession behaviors met criterion agreement.

Table 1—*Frequency Distribution of Therapist Methods
in Two Categories of Postsession Behaviors*

| | All data (n = 28) | | Category of postsession behavior | | | |
| | | | Facilitation of problem reduction (n = 14) | | Facilitation of new ways of being– behaving (n = 14) | |
Method	n	%	n	%	n	%
1. Seeing client as new person	7	25.00	0	0.00	7	50.00
2. Client initiation	14	50.00	1	7.14	13	92.86
3. Client readiness and control	13	46.43	2	14.29	11	78.57
4. Contingent conditions	2	7.14	1	7.14	1	7.14
5. Concrete specificity	18	64.29	10	71.43	8	57.14
6. Behavior–context clarification	9	32.14	1	7.14	8	57.14
7. Negotiation and custom fitting	2	7.14	1	7.14	1	7.14
8. Justifying rationales	9	32.14	8	57.14	1	7.14
9. Reluctance-countering rationales	4	14.29	4	28.57	0	0.00
10. Encouragement–pressure	12	42.86	7	50.00	5	35.70
11. Acknowledgment of failure	1	3.57	0	0.00	1	7.14
12. Assignment of homework	8	28.57	8	57.14	0	0.00
13. Clarification and reassignment of homework	2	7.14	2	14.29	0	0.00
14. In-session tryout, rehearsal, and refinement–elaboration	11	39.29	3	21.43	8	57.14
15. Counselor accompaniment	6	21.43	0	0.00	6	42.85
16. Contractual agreement–commit-ment	12	42.86	6	42.85	6	42.85

Therapist Methods and Categories of Postsession Behaviors

As indicated in Table 1, of the 28 postsession behaviors, 14 were judged as instrumental in facilitating problem reduction, and 14 were judged as facilitating the occurrence of new ways of being and behaving. These results enable a comparison of the two distributions to determine whether there was a difference in the distribution of methods used to promote commitment and resolve to carry out postsession behaviors that were instrumental in facilitating problem reduction, as compared with the distribution of methods of promoting commitment and resolve to carry out postsession behaviors for facilitating the occurrence of new ways of being and behaving. Table 1 shows the frequency distribution for each of the 16 methods under the two categories of postsession behaviors. For example, the frequency of Method 1 was 0 under problem reduction and 7 under facilitation of new way of being and behaving.

There was a significant difference between the two distributions, $\chi^2(15, N = 16)$ = 41.8, $p \leq .01$. However, frequencies for the individual 16 therapist methods were too low to determine which therapist methods occurred with significantly higher frequency under one of the two categories of postsession behaviors. Nevertheless, with regard to the facilitation of problem reduction, Table 1 indicates that four therapist methods were used with frequencies of 50% or more: Method 5 (concrete specificity), Method 8 (justifying rationales), Method 10 (encouragement–pressure), and Method 12 (assignment of homework). With regard to the facilitation of new ways of being and behaving, the five methods used with frequencies of 50% or more were Method 2 (client initiation), Method 3 (client readiness and control), Method 5 (concrete specificity), Method 6 (behavior–context clarification), and Method 14 (in-session tryout, rehearsal, and refinement–elaboration). Only one higher frequency therapist method was used more than 50% in both categories of postsession behavior, namely, Method 5 (concrete specificity).

Discussion

For therapists who are inclined to achieve client commitment and resolve to carry out postsession behaviors, the main findings identified 16 methods used by therapists in attaining client commitment and resolve. Of these 16 methods, only 1 consisted of the common method in which the client is simply requested, told, or instructed to carry out a postsession behavior as a homework assignment (cf. Brady, 1972; Harcum, 1989; Papajohn, 1982; Prochaska & DiClemente, 1982). Methods used with relatively higher frequency include Method 2, in which the client initiates defining of the postsession behavior; Method 3, which highlights the client's readiness and willingness to undertake the postsession behavior; Method 5, in which the therapist is concretely specific in defining the postsession behavior and situational context; Method 10, in which the therapist encourages, presses, and urges the client to carry out the postsession behavior; and Method 16, in which therapist and client arrive at a contractual understanding and agreement that the client will carry out the postsession behavior. In addition to these 16 methods, the findings warrant a suggestion that therapists use a set of methods, perhaps a mean of approximately 5 methods, to attain client commitment and resolve.

Because the judges were looking for what therapists seemed to do that promoted client commitment and resolve, some of the commonly shared judges' observations are reported. Although we did not examine these carefully, so many judges mentioned them so often that perhaps they may be the focus of further study. One of the observations is that therapists seemed to use methods over and over until commitment and resolve were obtained. A second was a high level of mutual cooperativeness, sometimes culminating in a small flurry of several postsession behaviors. Perhaps commitment and resolve occurs when therapists use a package of approximately 5 of the 16 methods in these two ways.

The results also indicated a twofold category system of postsession behaviors. In one, the postsession behaviors were to be instrumental in facilitating the reduction or resolution of the problematic concern, condition, or state identified in the session. For example, if the patient's problem was excessive smoking, the postsession behavior of giving up smoking for a day was understood as facilitating the reduction of the excessive smoking. In the other category, the postsession behaviors were to facilitate the occurrence of new ways of being and behaving, deeper personality processes, or qualities that were identified in the session and valued and welcomed by the client. For example, if the session identified a deeper personality process or quality such as being theatrical or performing, the postsession behavior of trying out for a local play was understood as facilitating the occurrence of the deeper personality process or quality.

Postsession behaviors were equally divided between the two categories. In addition, what may have stronger implications for practitioners is that a significant difference was obtained between the distributions of methods used to facilitate problem reduction and those used to facilitate the occurrence of new ways of being and behaving. Each of the two categories generally seems to be associated with its own set of methods. Although the frequencies for each of the methods were too low to see which methods go with which category, some useful indications may be provided by the higher frequency methods.

As indicated in Table 1, two higher frequency methods occurred in both categories: Method 5, in which the therapist is concretely specific in defining the postsession behavior and situational context, and Method 16, in which therapist and client arrive at a contractual understanding and agreement that the client will carry out the postsession behavior. The provisional suggestion is that, to obtain commitment and resolve to carry out postsession behaviors for facilitating problem reduction, in addition to Methods 5 and 16, practitioners may use a set of methods including Method 8, in which the therapist provides a justifying rationale for the postsession behavior; Method 10, in which the therapist encourages, presses, and urges the client to carry out the postsession behavior; and Method 12, in which the client is requested or instructed to carry out the postsession behavior as a homework assignment. It is intersting that Method 12, which is commonly accepted as perhaps the method of choice, is only one of a number of high-frequency methods in the package, and it occurs only with regard to facilitating problem reduction, not with regard to facilitating new ways of being and behaving.

For practitioners inclined toward obtaining commitment and resolve to carry out postsession behaviors for facilitating new ways of being and behaving, in addition to Methods 5 and 16, the high-frequency methods include Method 1, in which the therapist regards the client as a qualitatively new person; Method 2, in which the client initiates defining of the postsession behavior; Method 3, which highlights the client's readiness and willingness to undertake the postsession behavior; Method 6, in which the behavior and situational context are increasingly clarified; Method 14, in which the postsession behavior is rehearsed and modified; and Method 15, in which the therapist joins with the client in rehearsing and trying out the postsession behavior in the session.

It appears that the methods associated with each of the two categories differ. However, these are provisional indications that are based on the higher frequency methods for each category. What is called for, especially for practitioner usefulness, is sufficient data to determine which methods are associated with obtaining commitment and resolve to carry out which kinds of postsession behaviors. This is a call both for more data, to have sufficient confidence in the methods that are used, and for further ways of usefully organizing postsession behaviors. The present study yielded a category of postsession behaviors aimed at problem reduction and a second category aimed at facilitating new ways of being and behaving. This twofold category system bears some similarity to clinical suggestions of organizing postsession behaviors along dimensions of, for example, the degree of departure from the client's ordinary behavioral repertoire or the likelihood that simple homework assignment would be effective in obtaining the client's commitment and resolve to carry out the behavior (cf. Bandura & Adams, 1977; Brady, 1972; Cormier & Cormier, 1979; Goldfried & Davison, 1976; Haley, 1984; Kanfer & Grimm, 1980; Linehan, 1993; Mahrer, 1989; Montgomery & Montgomery, 1975; Omer, 1985; Prochaska & Di-Clemente, 1982; Tosi & Henderson, 1983).

With so few target events, it was difficult to have methodological confidence in identifying the methods and in identifying which methods occurred together. Our way of arriving at the methods relied on careful clinical analyses from a relatively large number of judges and on content analyses of the written descriptions provided by the judges. It seems important to improve the rigor of this way of arriving at an identification of therapist methods. The related problem of how to determine the overlap among the categories seems to call both for larger numbers of target events to determine which methods go with which other methods and for an improved procedure for arriving at the overall number of therapist methods that were identified. The present design and procedure yielded 16 methods. We expect that both a larger data pool and an improved content analytic procedure may well yield a somewhat different set of therapist methods for promoting commitment and resolve for carrying out postsession behaviors.

In summary, the results may be taken as yielding the following provisional practitioner-related propositions:

1. Therapists seemed to draw from and to use a rather large number of methods to promote client commitment and resolve to carry out postsession behaviors. We arrived at 16 methods and a mean of 5.07 methods used in each instance of promoting commitment and resolve.
2. Therapists seemed to use somewhat different sets of methods to promote commitment and resolve to carry out postsession behaviors for facilitating reduction in problem behaviors, as compared with postsession behaviors for facilitating the occurrence of new ways of being and behaving.

References

Bandura, A., & Adams, N. E. (1977). Analysis of self-efficacy theory of behavioral change. *Cognitive Therapy and Research, 1*, 287–310.

Boutin, G. E. (1978). Treatment of test anxiety by rational stage directed hypnotherapy: A case study. *American Journal of Clinical Hypnosis, 21*, 42–57.

Brady, J. P. (1972). Systematic desensitization. In W. S. Agras (Ed.), *Behavior modification: Principles and clinical applications* (pp. 127–153). Boston: Little, Brown.

Conoley, C. W., Padula, M. A., Payton, D. S., & Daniels, J. A. (1994). Predictors of client implementation of counselor recommendations: Match with problem, difficulty level, and building on client strengths. *Journal of Counseling Psychology, 41*, 3–7.

Cormier, W. H., & Cormier, L. S. (1979). *Interviewing strategies for helpers.* Monterey, CA: Brooks/Cole.

Flanders, P. A., & McNamara, J. R. (1985). Enhancing acne medication compliance: A comparison of strategies. *Behaviour Research and Therapy, 23*, 225–227.

Goldfried, M. R. (1982). Resistance and clinical behavior therapy. In P. L. Wachtel (Ed.), *Resistance: Psychodynamic and behavioral approaches* (pp. 95–113). New York: Plenum.

Goldfried, M. R., & Davison, G. C. (1976). *Clinical behavior therapy.* New York: Holt, Rinehart & Winston.

Haley, J. (1984). *Ordeal therapy: Unusual ways to change behavior.* San Francisco: Jossey-Bass.

Harcum, E. R. (1989). Commitment to collaboration as a prerequisite for existential commonality in psychotherapy. *Psychotherapy, 26,* 200–209.

Hycner, R. H. (1985). Some guidelines for the phenomenological analysis of interview data. *Human Studies, 8,* 279–303.

Kanfer, F. H., & Grimm, L. G. (1980). Managing clinical change: A process model of therapy. *Behavior Modification, 4,* 419–444.

Kothandapani, V. (1971). Validation of feeling, belief, and intention to act as three components of attitude and their contribution to prediction of contraceptive behavior. *Journal of Personality and Social Psychology, 19,* 321–333.

Levy, R. L. (1977). Relationship of an overt commitment to task compliance in behavior therapy. *Journal of Behavior Therapy and Experimental Psychiatry, 8,* 25–29.

Levy, R. L., & Clark, H. (1980). The use of an overt commitment to enhance compliance: A cautionary note. *Journal of Behavior Therapy and Experimental Psychiatry, 11,* 105–107.

Linehan, M. M. (1993). *Cognitive–behavioral treatment of borderline personality disorder.* New York: Guilford Press.

Lopez, F. G., & Wambach, C. A. (1982). Effects of paradoxical and self-control directives in counseling. *Journal of Counseling Psychology, 29,* 115–124.

Mahrer, A. R. (1989). *How to do experiential psychotherapy: A manual for practitioners.* Ottawa, Ontario, Canada: University of Ottawa Press.

Mahrer, A. R., Dessaulles, A., Nadler, W. P., Gervaize, P. A., & Sterner, I. (1987). Good and very good moments in psychotherapy: Content, distribution, and facilitation. *Psychotherapy, 24,* 7–14.

Mahrer, A. R., & Nadler, W. P. (1986). Good moments in psychotherapy: A preliminary review, a list, and some promising research avenues. *Journal of Consulting and Clinical Psychology, 54,* 10–15.

Mahrer, A. R., Nadler, W. P., Gervaize, P. A., Sterner, I., & Talitman, E. A. (1988). Good moments in rational–emotive therapy: Some unique features of this approach. *Journal of Rational–Emotive and Cognitive–Behavior Therapy, 6,* 146–161.

Mahrer, A. R., White, M. V., Howard, M. T., Gagnon, R., & MacPhee, D. (1992). How to bring about some very good moments in psychotherapy sessions. *Psychotherapy Research, 2,* 252–265.

Mahrer, A. R., White, M. V., Soulière, M. D., MacPhee, D. C., & Boulet, D. B. (1991). Intensive process analysis of significant in-session client change events and antecedent therapist methods. *Journal of Integrative and Eclectic Psychotherapy, 10,* 38–55.

Meichenbaum, D., & Turk, D. C. (1987). *Facilitating treatment adherence.* New York: Plenum.

Montgomery, A. G., & Montgomery, D. J. (1975). Contractual psychotherapy: Guidelines and strategies for change. *Psychotherapy: Theory, Research, and Practice, 12,* 348–352.

Nelson, R. A., & Borkovec, T. D. (1989). Relationship of client participation to psychotherapy. *Journal of Behavior Therapy and Experimental Psychiatry, 20,* 155–162.

Omer, H. (1985). Fulfillment of therapeutic tasks as a precondition for acceptance in therapy. *American Journal of Psychotherapy, 39,* 175–186.

Papajohn, J. C. (1982). *Intensive behavior therapy.* New York: Pergamon Press.

Patterson, G. R. (1984). Treatment process: A problem at three levels. (National Institute of Mental Health Proposal MH 38730). Eugene, OR: Oregon Social Learning Center.

Patterson, G. R., & Forgatch, M. S. (1985). Therapist behavior as a determinant for client noncompliance: A paradox for the behavior modifier. *Journal of Consulting and Clinical Psychology, 53,* 846–851.

Prochaska, J. O. (1979). *Systems of psychotherapy: A transtheoretical analysis*. Homewood, IL: Dorsey Press.

Prochaska, J. O., & DiClemente, C. C. (1982). Transtheoretical therapy: Toward a more integrative model of change. *Psychotherapy: Theory, Research, and Practice, 19*, 276–288.

Prochaska, J. O., DiClemente, C. C., & Norcross, J. C. (1992). In search of how people change: Applications to addictive behaviors. *American Psychologist, 47*, 1102–1114.

Tosi, D. J., & Henderson, G. W. (1983). Rational stage-directed therapy: A cognitive experiential system using hypnosis, imagery, cognitive restructuring, and developmental staging. *Journal of Rational Emotive Therapy, 1*, 15–19.

Worthington, E. L., Jr. (1986). Client compliance with homework directives during counseling. *Journal of Counseling Psychology, 33*, 124–130.

Wright, R. M., & Strong, S. R. (1982). Stimulating therapeutic change with directives: An exploratory study. *Journal of Counseling Psychology, 29*, 199–202.

Wurtele, S. K., Galanos, A. N., & Roberts, M. C. (1980). Increasing return compliance in a tuberculosis detection drive. *Journal of Behavioral Medicine, 3*, 311–318.

Appendix A

Example Statements of Commitment and Resolve to Carry Out a
Postsession Behavior

1. All right, yes, I will do it.
2. Yes, I'm going to do that.
3. I know what I can do; here's what I can do: I'll send her a dozen roses.
4. Yes, OK, sure; I'll try it.
5. I'll do that, I can do that; I know just how.
6. I'm going to; I'll try it with Joe, together.
7. It's a little bit, you know, different for me, but I'll do it by Wednesday.
8. I think I can do it; yeah, I will take one every three hours.
9. Yes, I agree; I'll call her and do it.
10. I know I will be able to, sure.
11. Yes, and maybe I can go even further too.

Appendix B

Examples of Postsession Behaviors Identified in the Transcript

1. Giving up smoking cigarettes for one full day.
2. Telephoning a particular person to whom the client is attracted.
3. Posting a calorie chart on the refrigerator.
4. Identifying and challenging specific irrational thoughts when they occur.
5. Using significantly smaller sized dishware at mealtime.
6. Bringing the client's father to her apartment and telling him how much she loves him.
7. Deliberately making oneself even more anxious when studying for the important examination.
8. Talking to his aunt about some things he wants to learn about his early childhood.
9. Visualizing violent accidents happening to specific people she dislikes.
10. Telling her husband that she no longer wants to play tennis with him and his tennis buddies.

Chapter 26
CLIENT IMPLEMENTATION OF THERAPIST RECOMMENDATIONS PREDICTED BY CLIENT PERCEPTION OF FIT, DIFFICULTY OF IMPLEMENTATION, AND THERAPIST INFLUENCE

Michael J. Scheel, Scott Seaman, Kenneth Roach, Thomas Mullin, and Karen Blackwell Mahoney

Ultimately, the success of therapy hinges on the possibility that clients will generalize changes beyond the context of therapy. To move the change process along, therapists may offer suggestions through recommendations that call for out-of-session actions. Recommendations, whether delivered from the therapist's expert stance or collaboratively constructed with the client, can be thought of as attempts to generalize treatment beyond the therapy session. Client perspective, as framed through the concept of treatment acceptability, was used in this investigation to highlight the subjective experience of the client at junctures in the therapeutic process when a recommendation is offered. The overall purpose of this study was to provide increased insight about the occurrence of the recommendation–acceptability event in therapy and to assess the relative strengths of elements of acceptability that contribute to the prediction of client implementation of a recommendation.

Therapist Recommendations

Therapist recommendations can take many forms and are sometimes referred to as homework, directives, prescriptions, or suggestions. Therapist recommendations can be defined as out-of-session activities suggested during therapy to be performed by the client. One example from rational–emotive therapy is Ellis's well-known recommendation to clients to perform shame-attacking exercises (Ellis & Dryden, 1987). A client may be instructed to go to a public place and announce in town crier fashion that "It's 2 o'clock and all's well" as a means of demonstrating to himself or herself that an embarrassing experience is not catastrophic. In rational–emotive therapy, as with other therapies that include homework assignments, influences on the implementation of recommendations by clients are unclear.

Recommendations seem to follow routinely from in-session process in several forms of psychotherapy. For instance, homework assignments are emphasized in brief therapies in an effort to extend treatment (de Shazer et al., 1986; Fisch, Weakland, & Segal, 1982). Practicing skills learned in therapy and keeping thought logs are common recommendations in cognitive–behavioral orientations. Sometimes therapists may simply recommend that clients experiment with new thoughts or feelings

Reprinted from *Journal of Counseling Psychology, 46,* 308–316 (1999). Copyright © 1999 by the American Psychological Association. Used with permission of the first author.

between sessions. Homework is thought to occur most typically within cognitive–behavioral and systemic-based therapies (Hay & Kinnier, 1998).

Contributions of Implementation to Therapy

Therapist presentations of recommendations that clients find acceptable and implement may be important contributors to positive psychological outcomes. Recommended actions may suggest divergence from past problematic patterns and may provide impetus for further change by clients. On the other hand, recommendations may not be helpful when clients perceive them as inappropriate for their presenting complaints and, therefore, do not implement them. Therapists may perceive psychological resistance if implementation does not occur. In mandated brief therapy formats, resistance is a negative factor. In addition, clients might feel misunderstood, discouraged, or overwhelmed by therapist requests when they are unsuccessful in implementing recommendations.

Given that failure to implement a recommendation might contribute to negative outcomes and that creating momentum for change away from client feelings of "stuckness" and stagnation is desirable, understanding of factors that maximize the possibility of implementation seems tremendously important. Several researchers have examined methods used by therapists to gain client commitment or compliance to in-session directives (Mahrer, Gagnon, Fairweather, Boulet, & Herring, 1994; Prochaska, DiClemente, & Norcross, 1992; Worthington, 1986; Wright & Strong, 1982). The focus of these studies has been on therapist behaviors that influence client commitment to the recommended action; client perceptions and beliefs concerning post-session assignments have not been examined.

Treatment Acceptability

Treatment acceptability provides a useful lens to identify client constructions of meaning in relation to a therapist recommendation. Acceptability has previously been defined as "judgments by clients of whether treatment procedures are appropriate, fair, and reasonable for the problem or client" (Kazdin, 1981, p. 493). It has also been linked to implementation behavior (Conoley, Conoley, Ivey, & Scheel, 1991; Kazdin, 1980; Reimers, Wacker, & Koeppl, 1987; Witt & Elliott, 1985). Yet, a client may perceive a treatment as appropriate, fair, and reasonable and still not implement it. An intent of this investigation was to broaden the definition of treatment acceptability by linking it to its behavioral counterpart, implementation. Hence, acceptability was defined as client perception that the therapist's request for action outside the session fits with the client's understanding of his or her problem, the client's ability to implement the recommendation, and the client's theory of how change can occur for him or her.

The Conoley et al. (1991) model of acceptability was selected for use in the present investigation. In this model, factors that contribute to overall acceptability are thought to be (a) the client's perception of fit between the problem and the intervention; (b) the client's belief about the intervention's level of difficulty, effectiveness, and humaneness; and (c) the client–therapist relationship. Implementation is seen as a product of acceptability and the client's ability to carry out the intervention. Intervention maintenance is seen as occurring through (a) client implementation of the original intervention, (b) tolerable disruption, and (c) creation of sufficient change. The Conoley et al. (1991) model is appealing for an adult psychotherapy setting as a result of its therapeutic relationship component. Further attraction of this model results from the link between the recommendation and implementation as well as a focus on the subjective experience of the client.

In 1994, Conoley, Padula, Payton, and Daniels assessed the strength of three variables in the prediction of implementation while acknowledging that their study was only a partial test of the 1991 model. Match between the recommendation and the client's presenting problem, the level of difficulty of the recommendation, and the incorporation of client strengths in the recommendation were assessed by judges who viewed archival counseling tapes. Each variable contributed significantly to the prediction of implementation.

The present investigation extended the Conoley et al. (1994) study by directly assessing client perceptions. A means to access client perceptions instead of reliance on rater judgment seems crucial, because the essence of the Conoley et al. (1991) model is the unique meaning of clients in relation to recommendations. Several questionnaires exist that assess client reports of acceptability of classroom behavioral interventions in schools using a consultant–consultee relationship (e.g., the Semantic Differential [Kazdin, 1980]; the Intervention Rating Profile—15 [IRP-15; Witt, Martens, & Elliott, 1984]; and the Behavior Intervention Rating Scale [BIRS; Von Brock, 1985]). The construct of treatment acceptability is purportedly measured through the BIRS, and the factors of the BIRS (acceptability, effectiveness, and time) possess some similarity to the conceptual framework of the Conoley model. Hence, even though the BIRS was not adequate as a representation of the Conoley et al. (1991) model, it could be used as a comparison measure.

The complete Conoley et al. (1991) model has never been considered. The fit of the recommendation for the client was originally specified in the 1991 model to include the client's problem formulation. Subsumed within problem formulation are clients' viewpoints about how change can occur for them and their beliefs about the origin, cause, and attributions related to the problem. In the 1994 study, raters judged a less detailed variable that was described as the match between the recommendation and the presenting problem.

Clients' perceptions of difficulties related to implementation of the recommendation can take many forms. In the Conoley et al. (1991) model, difficulties were represented as client perceptions of anxiety elicited, lack of understanding of what is required, disruptiveness, complexity, extensive time requirements, and whether the task is within the scope of the ability and resources of the client. In the 1994 study, independent judges rated only the time required, anxiety elicited, and client resources available.

The therapist–client relationship as perceived by the client was referred to in this investigation as the client's impression of therapist influence. Strong (1968) originally defined therapist influence as expertness, attractiveness, and trustworthiness. If clients do not perceive their therapist as expert in the role and about their situation, do not sense some attraction to and identification with their therapist, and do not trust and feel safe with their therapist, there seems little likelihood of implementation of any therapist recommendations. Hence, it seems of vital importance to include therapist influence in the prediction of implementation. In the 1994 study, therapist influence was assessed through rater judgments via the Counselor Rating Form—Short (CRF-S; Corrigan & Schmidt, 1983). Only cases in the top quarter of the Likert categories of the CRF-S were included. The predictive strength of therapist influence over its full range was not assessed. Therefore, a further extension of this research to more fully depict the 1991 acceptability model should involve the inclusion of therapist influence in the predictive equation of implementation as well as broader depictions of the categories of fit and difficulties.

Purposes and Research Questions

Initially, this investigation was devised with the particular interest of assessing therapist recommendations and client perceptions of acceptability in their natural setting. It was not known whether recommendations occurred in sufficient frequency to conduct a study of implementation. Before the goals of the study could be realized, we had to assess how often recommendations actually occurred. An additional intent of this research became the description of the types of recommendations that occurred. If recommendations occurred in sufficient numbers, then a predictive model of implementation could be constructed. The relative contributions of fit, difficulties, and therapist influence, the three major components of Conoley's 1991 model, had never been completely tested, because the contribution of therapist influence had not previously been combined with the other variables in a predictive equation of implementation. In addition, client perceptions had never been directly measured. To assess client perceptions of fit, difficulties, and therapist influence, we had to construct a scale and gather validation evidence.

In summary, the research questions were as follows: (a) What is the frequency of therapist recommendations? (b) What types of recommendations occur? (c) Do certain types of recommendations occur more often, and are certain types associated more with implementation than other types? and (d) What are the relative strengths of client perceptions of fit, difficulties of implementation, and therapist influence in the prediction of implementation?

Method

Participants

Clients ($N = 102$) from a university counseling center agreed to participate in a study of "the occurrence of therapist recommendations and client perceptions of those recommendations." Seventy women and 32 men composed the client sample. Clients eligible for services at the counseling center are undergraduate and graduate students as well as university faculty and staff. The participants were primarily Caucasian (88%), with the remainder being Asian American (6%), Hispanic (3%), African American (2%), and American Indian (1%). The mean age of the sample was 23.73 years ($SD = 4.24$). This counseling center uses a brief therapy format with a 12-session limit. Clients presenting with problems of a more chronic nature are referred to outside agencies.

A large number of therapists were needed to minimize the nested effect that might be due to individual therapists. Twenty-seven of 36 therapists agreed to participate in the study (8 senior staff psychologists, 8 predoctoral psychology interns, and 11 advanced practicum students). Fifteen women and 13 men composed this group. Therapists were asked to check off as many theoretical approaches as seemed to apply or with which they identified from a list of 20 approaches. The mean number of orientations checked was 5.32 (SD = 2.11). All 20 approaches were checked at least once; the top 5 were cognitive–behavioral (n = 19), person centered (n = 17), feminist (n = 12), psychodynamic (n = 11), and systems (n = 9). Seven therapists indicated one primary approach while using a secondary group of theories. The primary approaches were person centered (n = 2), systems (n = 2), interpersonal, feminist, and constructivist. The mean number of years of experience was 7.50 (SD = 6.74). Most practicum therapists had only 1 year of experience, whereas 1 senior staff psychologist had worked in the field for 22 years. Regarding ethnicity, 1 therapist identified as African American and 1 as Hispanic; all others identified as Caucasian. The age of therapists was not reported.

Instruments

Construction and Validation of the Recommendation Rating Scale

The first stage of this study consisted of the item construction and instrument development of the Recommendation Rating Scale (RRS). The purpose of the RRS is to apply the fit–difficulties–influence model of acceptability in adult psychotherapy. The RRS was developed as a self-report measure of client beliefs concerning a designated recommendation.

The theoretical basis for the RRS was derived from the Conoley et al. (1991) model of acceptability and implementation and the Conoley et al. (1994) investigation of recommendation match with problem, difficulties, and client strengths as predictors of implementation. After examination of the 1991 model and the 1994 study, we designed a conceptual framework from which items for an acceptability scale could be written. Three broad conceptual areas were apparent—fit, difficulties, and therapist influence—under which all elements of the model could be categorized. Fit was defined as "the client's perceived match between the recommendation and the client's beliefs about his or her problem formulation and theory of change." The difficulties category was defined as "the client's perception of disruption, lack of ability, time required, expense, complexity, lack of understanding, and anxiety elicited due to the recommendation." Therapist influence was based on Strong's (1968) social influence model and was defined as "the client's perception of his or her therapist as expert, attractive, and trustworthy." Considerations of clients' perception of comfort, identification, and satisfaction with their therapist and in the relationship were also included as elements of therapist influence.

Some modifications of the 1991 model were made on the basis of the results of Conoley et al. (1994), a review of the literature on treatment acceptability, and item analysis. "Client strengths" was not mentioned specifically in the 1991 model but was used in the 1994 investigation. The match between the recommendation and client strengths was designated as an element of fit as a result of its conceptual relation to the client's theory of change. A second modification involved the "effectiveness" of a recommendation. Client perception of effectiveness was considered an element of fit, even though Conoley et al. (1991) included it in the difficulties category. This amendment was made on the basis of results of the pilot study in which items about effectiveness correlated more with the Fit scale than with the Difficulties scale. Furthermore, effectiveness conceptually seemed to be, by definition, related to the client's theory of change rather than difficulties of the recommendations. Clients' perception of their "lack of understanding" of what is required was included as a difficulty because it was mentioned in previous literature about acceptability as a prerequisite to implementation (Reimers et al., 1987).

Item Construction and Pilot Study

Items were written for the RRS in a 6-point anchored, Likert-type format (1 = *strongly disagree*, 6 = *strongly agree*). A blank space is provided at the beginning of the questionnaire to insert the recommendation for which the client would respond. After item construction, a pilot study was conducted with 50 college students who were asked to assume the role of client. Each participant was given a problem scenario and a corresponding recommendation and asked to imagine that the presenter of the research was his or her therapist. Responses to 34 items in the original RRS yielded interitem correlation and internal consistency reliability estimates for each of the three subscales. Two items were dropped because their item correlation was higher with another scale than with their own scale. Thirty-two items were retained after this initial analysis, with 9 under fit, 12 under difficulties, and 11 under therapist influence. To be included, an item had to correlate the most with the subscale for which it had been written. Interitem correlations ranged from .43 to .80 for the Fit scale, .45 to .77 for the Difficulties scale, and .49 to .80 for the Therapist Influence scale. Internal consistency alphas for Fit, Difficulties, and Therapist Influence, respectively, were .86, .85, and .92, with a full-scale alpha of .92. Moderate correlation was found among the three subscales (Fit and Difficulties: $r = .26$, $p < .05$; Fit and Therapist Influence, $r = .59$, $p < .01$; and Difficulties and Therapist Influence: $r = .49$, $p < .01$).

Further Validation and Refinement

Further evidence of the validity of the RRS was collected through the present investigation as well as additional refinement of the item pools for the three categories of the RRS. Results from principal-components analysis, item-to-scale correlation, ratings of content from expert judges, and reliability estimates were considered in decisions about the final composition of the Fit, Difficulties, and Therapist Influence scales.

Scores from the 91 participants who completed the RRS were submitted to a principal-components analysis using an oblique rotation (given that the three subscales moderately correlated in the pilot investigation and given the common underlying construct of client perceptions). Although the 3.3 respondents per item for this investigation reflects a small sample size for a principal-components analysis, support exists for the stability of the resulting factor structure. Arrindell and van der Ende (1985) investigated the stability of factors as a function of the ratio of number of participants to number of variables for principal-components analysis. These researchers found support for the stability of factors even with a ratio of 1.3 respondents per item.

An initial analysis resulted in six factors with eigenvalues greater than 1.00 (7.49, 3.63, 2.21, 1.51, 1.37, and 1.22), accounting for 65% of the variance. After examination of the scree plot, a three-factor solution was selected (Gorsuch, 1983). The three-factor solution accounted for 49.35% of the variance, whereas a two-factor solution explained 41% and a four-factor solution accounted for 55%.

Five items were problematic. Two from the Fit scale had factor loadings that were higher for the Difficulties factor (Item 19 ["The recommendation goes against my beliefs about how positive change can occur in my situation"] and Item 29 ["The recommendation conflicts with my beliefs"]). Two items from the Difficulties scale had a factor loading of less than .40 (Item 22 ["The recommendation requires me to do something that I have been successful at before"] and Item 13 ["The recommendation would cost me much in money to do"]). One item from the Therapist Influence scale (Item 3 ["I feel safe talking with my counselor"]) had a factor loading of only .43 with its scale. Table 1 displays the factor loadings and items of the final RRS.

Item-to-scale correlation for the three scales was also tabulated. The results of this analysis are exhibited in Table 1. Corrections were made to correlate item scores with their own scale after eliminating that item from the scale to prevent inflated results. As can be detected in Table 1, each item in the final scale correlated most highly with its own scale. All items had correlations above .44 with their own scale. The most overlap among the scales was detected between the Fit and Therapist Influence items; the Difficulties scale items were most independent.

Internal consistency estimates were also calculated. Alphas were .82 for Fit, .81 for Difficulties, and .86 for Therapist Influence; the full-scale alpha was .87.

Six PhD counseling psychologists judged the content of the items for each of the three scales. Definitions of the three scales were provided for the judging procedure. The experts were instructued to categorize each item as belonging to the Fit, Difficulties, or Therapist Influence scale. Items 19 and 29 were the only items in the Fit category with less than 100% agreement (33% and 50% agreement, respectively). In the Difficulties section, only two of the six experts categorized Item 22 as a Difficulty item. At least five of the six raters agreed on all other Difficulties items. There was 100% agreement on all Therapist Influence scale items.

In the final scale, Items 3, 13, 19, 22, and 29 were dropped when at least two of the three criteria (low factor loadings, low item-to-scale correlation, and lack of agreement among experts) were present. The final RRS contained 27 items after the deletions. The variance accounted for in the principal-components analysis was maintained at 48%, and reliability remained relatively constant despite the lower number of items. The final scale contained 7 Fit items, 10 Difficulties items, and 10 Therapist Influence items. Moderate correlations existed between the Therapist Influence scale and the other two scales (Fit and Therapist Influence: $r = .49$, $p < .01$; Fit and Difficulties: $r = .12$; Therapist Influence and Difficulties: $r = .26$, $p < .05$).

Table 1—*Recommendation Rating Scale (RRS) Items, Factor Loadings Obtained With the Pattern Matrix of the Oblique Solution, and Item Correlations With Fit, Difficulties, and Therapist Influence Subscales*

RRS item	Factor			Correlations		
	1	2	3	Fit	Difficulties	Therapist influence
Therapist Influence subscale						
7. I have tremendous confidence in my counselor	.79	−.07	.16	.47**	.18	.75**
15. I find my counselor to be a likeable person	.63	−.02	.32	.51**	.15	.69**
17. I am very satisfied with my counselor so far in our work together	.87	−.11	−.07	.42**	.14	.79**
18. I find it difficult to identify with my counselor	.66	.06	.04	.35***	.24*	.59***
20. I'm open and expressive with my counselor	.67	.10	−.03	.27***	.21*	.59***
23. I view my counselor as an expert in helping me	.71	−.03	.18	.27***	.21*	.59***
24. In counseling situations I am reluctant to be open with a counselor	.62	.06	−.13	.18	.20	.46***
26. When I talk to my counselor I feel uncomfortable	.72	.11	−.19	.15	.25*	.57***
28. It seems like my counselor is on my side	.54	−.08	.30	.48***	.10	.53***
31. I'm comfortable discussing any subject with my counselor	.44	−.01	.21	.34**	.12	.46***
Difficulties subscale						
2. The recommendation would be difficult for me to accomplish	−.15	.61	−.12	−.11	.41**	−.04
5. The recommendation creates anxiety for me	.10	.55	−.16	.01	.51**	.12
6. I understand what is required to accomplish the recommendation	−.02	.70	.27	.23*	.53***	.28
8. Following this recommendation would interrupt my daily routines	.09	.48	−.21	−.02	.45***	.07
9. If I try this recommendation I think I will be able to complete it	−.09	.81	.22	.21*	.65***	.20
10. The recommendation would require a lot of time for me to accomplish	.14	.49	−.23	−.05	.42***	.13
16. The recommendation creates discomfort for me	.21	.55	−.13	.09	.55***	.24*
25. I am capable of accomplishing the recommendation	−.07	.74	.33	.26*	.56***	.27***
27. The recommendation seems complex to me	−.10	.63	.12	.16	.52***	.30**
32. I understand what it would take to do this recommendation	−.05	.72	.29	.28**	.57***	.26*

Fit subscale

1. The recommendation fits with at least one of the reasons for which I have come to counseling	.18	−.13	.66	.57**	.08	.43**
4. The recommendation matches my beliefs about what has caused my current situation	.14	−.05	.59	.54**	.04	.37**
11. This recommendation utilizes my personal strengths	−.04	.03	.61	.47**	.05	.23*
12. If I complete this recommendation I believe it will be a stimulus for change in my life	−.02	−.03	.78	.68**	.05	.32**
14. This recommendation would be helpful in creating positive change in my situation	.17	.05	.59	.55**	.13	.39**
21. I understand the connection between the counselor's recommendation and my most important reason for coming to counseling	.02	.23	.61	.53**	.24*	.33**
34. If I implement this recommendation it may supply enough changes to make important differences in my life	.19	−.05	.68	.70**	.06	.42**

Note. Items 3, 13, 19, 22, 29, 30, and 33 were eliminated as a result of insufficient evidence of validity.
*p < .05. **p < .01.

Behavior Intervention Rating Scale

To adapt the BIRS to an adult psychotherapy situation, we performed a modification in the wording of the items. For instance, "The child's behavior problem was severe enough to warrant use of this consultation model" was altered to read "The situation is severe enough to warrant use of this recommendation." The BIRS is a 24-item questionnaire with each item rated on a 6-point Likert-type scale. Witt et al. (1984) expanded the BIRS from the IRP-15. Three factors were determined through a factor analysis of the BIRS: (a) acceptability, (b) effectiveness, and (c) time. Alpha coefficients were .97 for the full scale and .97, .92, and .87 for acceptability, effectiveness, and time, respectively (Elliott, 1988).

Implementation Measure

Clients rated their level of implementation immediately before the second therapy session ("The recommendation was fully implemented"; 1 = *strongly disagree*, 6 = *strongly agree*). A primary recommendation designated by the therapist in the previous session had been written in the space provided at the top of the rating sheet by one of the researchers.

Procedure

Therapists agreed to allow the recruitment of their clients each quarter of the academic year. Therapists and clients were both informed that the study involved "an investigation of the counselor recommendations that might occur during a therapy session." In addition, therapists were encouraged to conduct their sessions in their typical manner. Therapists screened 7 clients that they judged to be inappropriate candidates over the 2 years of recruitment as a result of the possible disruption of the therapy process for these clients.

Eligible clients in Sessions 2 through 8 of therapy were selected randomly from participating therapist caseloads and recruited by graduate-level counseling students while waiting for their counseling appointments over 1-week periods during each quarter of 2 school years. The mean number of sessions at recruitment was 4.32 (*SD* = 1.69). Particular care was taken in recruitment to avoid any messages that might be interpreted as coercive by the clients. The graduate students were also instructed beforehand to not attempt to recruit clients who seemed particularly anxious in the waiting room. In addition, clients were also informed that their therapist would not know whether they had been asked to participate, leaving clients free to choose without feeling their decision might in some way affect the therapeutic relationship. Therapists were informed of their client's participation after the client had consented. Clients were also offered $5 to stay after their session and complete questionnaires about any recommendation that might have occurred in the session that day. Sixty-eight percent of clients who were recruited agreed to participate.

Recommendations were defined for the therapist "as anything the therapist suggests a client do or think about between sessions." Immediately after a therapy session, the client moved to a separate room while the therapist stayed in the therapy room and wrote down her or his recollection of all recommendations that had occurred, designating one recommendation as primary. The researcher then wrote the primary recommendation in the space provided at the top of the questionnaire. The client subsequently rated the primary recommendation using the RRS and BIRS. The questionnaires were administered in alternating order.

After the first session, the researcher noted when the next therapy session was scheduled. The next session was required to occur between 1 and 3 weeks later. The data from any client whose next session was not within this window of time were not included in the analyses. Some attrition occurred when the therapist reported that no recommendation was given or when the client did not return in at least 3 weeks. Seventy-five clients who had received a recommendation returned for their next session within 3 weeks. Returning clients were asked to rate their level of implementation of the primary recommendation from the previous session while in the waiting room before sessions. Again, care was taken to not pressure clients in some way as they waited for their next session.

A content analysis of all recommendations that therapists recorded after the first session was conducted. One researcher who was a PhD counseling psychologist initially examined the 182 recommendations (both primary and secondary) that occurred and established 11 categories with accompanying descriptions. The categories were not meant to depict any one theoretical orientation but were intended to reflect the commonality of therapy practice. Five raters who were graduate students in counseling independently judged 20 recommendations and compared categorizations. The 11 categories were reduced to 8 after reviews for completeness and clarity. The 8 categories were social interactions, stress management, promotion of self-esteem, validation of internal experience, reframing meaning, referral, decision making, and request for action.

Each recommendation received an agreement rating. For instance, if four of the five raters judged a recommendation to be in the same category, the agreement rating was 80%. The five raters judged a second set of 20 recommendations and revised category descriptions twice more before achieving an overall mean agreement of 84%. The final mean agreement among the five judges after rating all of the recommendations was 79%.

Results

Occurrence and Type of Recommendations

Therapists reported giving at least 1 recommendation in 91 of the 102 sessions, and they reported a total of 182 recommendations. The mean number of recommendations given in a session was 1.85 ($SD = 1.36$), with a median of 1.00. The therapist reported more than 3 recommendations in 13 different sessions. As stated previously, the therapist designated 1 recommendation as primary immediately after the therapy session.

Table 2 displays the final eight categories, their descriptions, an example of one recommendation that occurred in each category, and the percentage of the total number of primary recommendations in each category as well as the percentage of total recommendations in each category. A one-way analysis of variance revealed no significant differences in implementation among the eight types of recommendations,

Table 2—*Category, Description of Category, Examples, and Percentage Occurrence of Types of Recommendations*

Category	Description	Example	Primary %	Total %
Social interactions	Encourage the practice of clear, assertive, or new behaviors in interactions with others	"Communicate more with spouse with less mind reading"	15	16
Stress management	Stress-reduction activities are specifically designated as the goal	"Try to detach emotionally from complainants at work to relieve stress"	4	2
Promotion of self-esteem	Promotion of self-acceptance, positive thoughts, affirmations, or self-nurturance	"Trust in your judgments and acceptance of self in rebuilding self-confidence"	13	13
Validation of internal experience	Promotion of awareness of feelings and thoughts; a focus on internal experiences, perhaps through feeling logs, journaling, messages to pay attention to internal experiences	"List cognitions in difficult situations, describe the situation, and describe feelings associated with the thoughts"	20	20
Reframing meaning	Suggestions of different understandings or shifts in perspective. This may involve discovery through outside readings, use of visualization, or metaphors	"Notice your wall around yourself and decide if it is serving a purpose"	16	15
Referral	Referral for evaluation by another professional, testing, a different form of therapy (e.g., group modality; medical) or training (e.g., assertiveness group)	"Make an appointment for a medical evaluation"	4	6
Decision making	Focus on an active problem-solving approach of appraisal, goal-setting, and decision making	"Consider option of leaving current relationship"	16	14
Request for action	Request to pursue goal-oriented behavior after a decision is made	"Call and set up volunteer work and internship to complete bachelor's degree"	10	14

$F(7, 67) = 1.50$, $p = .18$. No category was predominant, with validation of internal experience, social interactions, reframing meanings, decision making, request for action, and elicitation of strength all occurring from 13% to 20% of the time. Less frequent were referrals and stress management recommendations.

Consideration of Therapist Effects

Therapist effect can positively bias estimates of treatment, increasing the probability of Type I error (Burlingame, Kircher, & Taylor, 1994). Our interest in this study was in estimating the relative strengths of components of client acceptability. To assess the effect of these variables, any influence due to therapist effect must first be tested. Twenty-seven therapists participated. Therapists in this investigation had from 1 to 5 clients who also participated, thus representing possible nested effects due to therapist. Before proceeding with the analysis of interst, we tested differences among therapists. Twenty-six dummy vectors were created representing the 27 therapists. These vectors were entered as a block in a regression analysis. According to Kirk (1982), if therapist effects are negligible, it is not necessary to treat therapist as a factor in the design. Therapist effects are considered negligible if they are nonsignificant when tested with a liberal alpha value of .25 (Burlingame et al., 1994; Kirk, 1982; Winer, 1962, 1971). This preliminary analysis was nonsignificant, $F(1, 26) = 1.08$, $p = .39$. Thus, a significant effect due to therapist was not revealed, and consequently therapist effects were not considered in the remainder of the analyses.

Correlation and Simultaneous Regression Analysis

Next, a correlation matrix was constructed for the Fit, Difficulties, and Therapist Influence scales; the rating of implementation that served as the dependent variable for the planned regression analysis; and the total scale scores of the RRS and BIRS (see Table 3). Comparisions using a Pearson product–moment correlation of .57 ($p < .01$) were made between the BIRS and the RRS.

Table 3—*Mean, Sample Size, Standard Deviation, and Intercorrelation of Variables Entered Into Regression Equation and Implementation Ratings*

Scale	n	M	SD	1	2	3	4	5	6
1. Fit	91	35.66	4.12	—					
2. Difficulties	91	47.98	6.80	.12	—				
3. Therapist Influence	91	52.26	5.71	.49**	.26*	—			
4. Client Imp.	75	4.67	1.03	.30**	.34**	.41**	—		
5. BIRS (total)	91	114.47	12.01	.58**	.29**	.46**	.44**	—	
6. RRS (total)	91	135.90	12.07	.64**	.73**	.79**	.49**	.57**	—

Note. Fit = client's perception of fit assessed with the RRS; Difficulties = client's perception of the difficulties of implementation of the recommendation assessed with the RRS; Therapist Influence = client's perception of therapist influence assessed with the RRS; Client Imp. = client report of implementation; BIRS = Behavior Intervention Rating Scale; RRS = Recommendation Rating Scale.

*$p < .05$. **$p < .01$.

A simultaneous regression analysis was performed in which client ratings of implementation were the dependent variables and the Fit, Difficulties, and Therapist Influence scales were the predictor variables; this analysis yielded an overall statistically significant model and significant unique contributions from Difficulties and Therapist Influence (see Table 4). Simultaneous entry was performed because no justification for the order of entry of the predictor variables could be discerned.

Discussion

Our investigation of therapist recommendations illuminated this aspect of the therapy process that previously was vaguely understood. Our results shed light on the rate of recommendation occurrence, the types of recommendations that can occur, the amount of client-rated implementation, and the predictors of implementation. We discovered a high frequency of recommendations (about 9 of every 10 sessions), with most sessions containing multiple recommendations. These recommendations were determined to take eight different forms, validation of internal experience, reframed meanings, social interactions, and decision-making recommendations being the most predominant types. Less popular but still prevalent were referrals, requests for action, stress management, and promotion of self-esteem. Clients tended on the whole to report a high level of implementation immediately before the subsequent therapy session. Client perceptions of therapist influence and of the difficulties of implementation were both found to be significant predictors of client-reported implementation. Client perceptions concerning the fit of recommendations overlapped too much with therapist influence to be a unique contributor to the prediction of implementation.

Some specific examples of recommendations in our study serve to illustrate the predictive value of our variables of interest. One client was provided the assignment to "identify ways to validate and substantiate (the client's) world view." This recommendation was classified as a validation of internal experience. Immediately after the therapy session, the client rated, via the RRS, both the fit of the recommendation with the problem and therapist influence as high. This client also indicated that the recommendation would be difficult to implement. This last rating proved to be predictive in that, the following week, the client reported a low level of implementation. Our impression of this particular example was that most people would view the act of substantiating and validating their worldview as difficult. Furthermore, the failure to accomplish such a task might be discouraging to the client and possibly "invalidating." Perhaps the recommendation was too vague to be considered as anything

Table 4—*Simultaneous Multiple Regression to Predict Client Rating of Implementation*

Variable	B	$SE\ B$	β	$t(71)$	p
Fit	.032	.029	.13	1.12	.266
Difficulties	.045	.017	.26	2.44	.017
Therapist influence	.053	.022	.29	2.37	.021

Note. $N = 75$. $R_{total} = .495$. $R^2_{total} = .245$. $F(3, 71) = 7.69$, $p < .001$.

other than difficult. Consequently, we wonder from this example whether more specificity in delivery of a recommendation might facilitate implementation.

A second example of low implementation occurred with a recommendation to "try to detach emotionally from complainants at work to relieve stress." This recommendation was categorized as a stress management type. The client rated difficulty as only moderate but rated therapist influence and fit as low. Our initial reaction was that most people would find it hard to emotionally distance themselves in a work situation and also gain relief from stress, yet the client in question did not view this as a particularly difficult thing to do. Instead, lack of implementation was more related to the lack of influence of the therapist and to the lack of fit of the recommendation with the client's problem formulation. We believe this example serves to highlight the individualistic and unique nature of perceptions of recommendations that occur during therapy.

Examples of recommendations that were reported by clients as fully implemented also are informative. The client in each of the following perceived the recommendation as a good fit, not difficult, and involving high therapist influence: "Take as much time as you need to make a decision, and if you make a decision, make sure that you are OK with it"; "Take less responsibility for your husband's problems"; "Spend more time alone and focus on career issues during that time"; "List cognitions in difficult situations and associated feelings"; "Write out positives of relationship. Write out negatives of relationship"; "Write down what it means to be integrated and also what it means to you to not be integrated"; "Reflect on how your I-J scores on the MBTI shed light on events of your life"; and "Change to a nurse practitioner for meds." We found a pattern difficult to discern from these recommendations that might help in providing additional understanding of implementation. These recommendations represented several types, including decision making, promotion of self-esteem, validation of internal experience, reframed meanings, and referral. The importance of assessment based on the subjective reality of each client rather than the universal nature of a type of recommendation is emphasized to us through the collection of these as well as the many other recommendations of this study. The result in our investigation concerning the lack of differences in implementation across types of recommendations further supports the premise that recommendations must be uniquely assessed for appropriateness with each client.

We gained a description of the types of recommendations that occurred. These types were derived from the data in our study rather than from a theoretical formulation. Our content analysis provided a construal of meaning about the types that therapists reported. A difficulty of the content analysis was that raters discovered recommendations that seemed to fit more than one category. Judgments had to be made about the primacy of categories based on criteria that were established for this purpose. For instance, "Nurture and protect [oneself] however possible by going to football games, being with friends, and getting more sleep" was categorized as promotion of self-esteem. Social interactions were also suggested through the recommendation, but the main purpose of the recommendation was judged to be the promotion of well-being and self-esteem. Social interaction seems, in this case, to be a means by which clients nurture themselves. Hence, this recommendation was a promotion of self-esteem as a result of the decision rule to consider the main purpose of the recommendation above all else.

Limitations

Limitations on the generalizability of our results are due to sampling from Sessions 2 through 8 of therapy and collecting data at a university counseling center using a time-limited format. For instance, our results probably do not translate to long-term therapy with clients who demonstrate severe and chronic psychological disorders.

Nonetheless, our results are supportive of the premise that recommendations are common in many forms of psychotherapy rather than based on any one type of theoretical orientation. Of course, therapists may have been influenced in some way by the research conditions to deviate from normal practice to attend more to recommendations. Therapists were encouraged to conduct therapy in their usual manner. Even so, it is impossible to know the influence of our research on the frequency of recommendations given. However, if recommendations are in reality given only half as often as we discovered, we would still consider the event of a therapist recommendation to be common practice.

Another limitation was due to the nature of the data that were collected. Both acceptability and implementation were derived from client self-report measures. Consequently, results that confirm the association between the two measures may at least partially be due to response bias. We were dependent on client reports of implementation, because it was impossible to directly assess implementation.

A final limitation of this investigation was the artificial factor of the therapist writing down a primary recommendation after the conclusion of the session. We believed this was necessary to conduct the research. During the therapy session, more elaboration about the recommendation may have occurred. Discussion of the recommendation during the session probably contributed to client meanings concerning fit, difficulties, and therapist influence.

Implications for Future Research

The complete model depicting the Conoley et al. (1991) conceptualization of acceptability and implementation was realized and examined in its relationship with implementation. Even with the advancements accomplished through this investigation, results left room for further work. Client perceptions about the primary recommendation accounted only moderately for implementation. Results indicate that acceptability, as conceptualized in this investigation, is related to client-reported implementation, but other factors are probably involved as well. Perhaps the Conoley et al. (1991) conceptualization of acceptability and implementation can be expanded to account for more or other factors separate from acceptability.

Methods of delivering recommendations that maximize the possibility of implementation also should be examined. The amount of collaboration between client and therapist in designing a recommendation and the rationales provided by therapists explaining why clients should follow through with recommendations are two processes that might influence implementation. Mahrer et al. (1994) have suggested tactics similar to these that therapists might use to gain more commitment from clients. In future research, results from their research could possibly be combined with the focus of this investigation.

The contributions of fit, difficulties, and therapist influence to the prediction of implementation were assessed. Other conceptualizations may have meaning and may predict implementation as well. Certainly, factors other than fit, difficulties, and relationship contribute to client implementation. Depression comes to mind as a mediating influence on perceptions. A depressed client may demonstrate some impairment to initiate a new action. If depression is alleviated, clients may perceive higher levels of fit and fewer difficulties, and they may even view their therapist as more influential. Investigation of other client personality characteristics that serve as mediators of client perceptions concerning therapist suggestions for action may also aid in the prediction of implementation.

References

Arrindell, W. A., & van der Ende, J. (1985). An empirical test of the utility of the observations-to-variables ratio in factor and components analysis. *Applied Psychological Measurement, 9*, 165–178.

Burlingame, G. M., Kircher, J. C., & Taylor, S. (1994). Methodological considerations in group psychotherapy research: Past, present, and future practices. In A. Fuhriman & G. M. Burlingame (Eds.), *Handbook of group psychotherapy: An empirical and clinical synthesis* (pp. 41–80). New York: Wiley.

Conoley, C. W., Conoley, J. C., Ivey, D. C., & Scheel, M. J. (1991). Enhancing consultation by matching the consultee's perspectives. *Journal of Counseling and Development, 69*, 546–549.

Conoley, C. W., Padula, M. A., Payton, D. S., & Daniels, J. A. (1994). Predictors of client implementation of counselor recommendations: Match with problem, difficulty level, and building client strengths. *Journal of Counseling Psychology, 41*, 3–7.

Corrigan, J. D., & Schmidt, L. D. (1983). Development and validation of revisions in the Counselor Rating Form. *Journal of Counseling Psychology, 30*, 64–75.

de Shazer, S., Berg, I., Lipchik, E., Nunnally, E., Molnar, A., Gingerich, W., & Weiner-Davis, M. (1986). Brief therapy: Focused solution development. *Family Process, 25*, 207–222.

Elliott, S. N. (1988). The acceptability of behavioral treatments. In J. C. Witt, S. N. Elliott, & F. M. Gresham (Eds.), *Handbook of behavior therapy in education.* New York: Plenum Press.

Ellis, A., & Dryden, W. (1987). *The practice of rational–emotive therapy.* New York: Springer.

Fisch, R., Weakland, J. H., & Segal, L. (1982). *The tactics of change: Doing therapy briefly.* San Francisco: Jossey-Bass.

Gorsuch, R. L. (1983). *Factor analysis* (2nd ed.). Hillsdale, NJ: Erlbaum.

Hay, C. E., & Kinnier, R. T. (1998). Homework in counseling. *Journal of Mental Health Counseling, 20*, 122–132.

Kazdin, A. E. (1980). Acceptability of alternative treatments for deviant child behavior. *Journal of Applied Behavior Analysis, 13*, 259–273.

Kazdin, A. E. (1981). Acceptability of child treatment techniques: The influence of treatment efficacy and adverse side effects. *Behavior Therapy, 12*, 493–506.

Kirk, R. (1982). *Experimental design: Procedures for the behavioral sciences* (2nd ed.). Monterey, CA: Brooks/Cole.

Mahrer, A. R., Gagnon, R., Fairweather, D. R., Boulet, D. B., & Herring, C. B. (1994). Client commitment and resolve to carry out postsession behaviors. *Journal of Counseling Psychology, 41*, 407–414.

Prochaska, J. O., DiClemente, C. C., & Norcross, J. C. (1992). In search of how people change: Applications to addictive behaviors. *American Psychologist, 47*, 1102–1114.

Reimers, T. M., Wacker, D. P., & Koeppl, G. (1987). Acceptability of behavioral treatments: A review of the literature. *School Psychology Review, 16,* 212–227.

Strong, S. R. (1968). Counseling: An interpersonal influence process. *Journal of Counseling Psychology, 15,* 215–224.

Von Brock, M. B. (1985). *The influence of effectiveness information on teachers' ratings of acceptability.* Unpublished master's thesis, Louisiana State University, Baton Rouge.

Winer, B. J. (1962). *Statistical principles in experimental design.* New York: McGraw-Hill.

Winer, B. J. (1971). *Statistical principles in experimental design* (2nd ed.). New York: McGraw-Hill.

Witt, J. C., & Elliott, S. N. (1985). Acceptability of classroom management strategies. In T. R. Kratochwill (Ed.), *Advances in school psychology* (Vol. 4, pp. 251–288). Hillsdale, NJ: Erlbaum.

Witt, J. C., Martens, B. K., & Elliott, S. N. (1984). Factors affecting teachers' judgments of the acceptability of behavioral interventions: Time involvement, behavior problem severity, type of intervention. *Behavior Therapy, 15,* 204–209.

Worthington, E. L., Jr. (1986). Client compliance with homework directives during counseling. *Journal of Counseling Psychology, 33,* 124–130.

Wright, R. M., & Strong, S. R. (1982). Stimulating therapeutic change with directives during counseling. *Journal of Counseling Psychology, 29,* 199–202.

Chapter 27
EFFECTS OF INCLUDING THE ACTION STAGE IN DREAM INTERPRETATION

Teresa L. Wonnell and Clara E. Hill

The Hill (1996) model of dream interpretation involves three stages: exploration, insight, and action. In the exploration stage of the model, the therapist asks the dreamer to describe and associate to each of the images and feelings in the dream. Thorough exploration is considered necessary to set the foundation for later stages. In the insight stage, the therapist works with the dreamer to construct an understanding of the meaning of the dream on one or more possible levels such as recent waking life or past memories. In the action stage, ideas for behavioral changes or changes in the dream are explored, and actual changes in waking life are encouraged. A focus on action is considered necessary to consolidate the insignt gained and to help the client make changes.

In testing the Hill model of dream interpretation, taking the model apart is a way to determine empirically the effects of the different stages (e.g., Kazdin, 1994). A reasonable starting point in this deconstruction process is to test the effects of the action stage because although almost all models of dream interpretation include steps that encourage exploration and insight, not all models include an action component. For instance, models based on experiential and psychoanalytic theories are grounded on the assumption that the reexperiencing of the dream or the insight gained during the interpretation process is the ultimate goal of working with dreams (e.g., Craig & Walsh, 1993; Freud, 1900/1965; Perls, 1969; Schwartz, 1990). In contrast, other dream interpretation models include an action step in which dreamers are encouraged, during sessions, to explore taking action of some kind outside of the session on the basis of what they learn about themselves during the interpretation process (Cartwright & Lamberg, 1992; Gendlin, 1986; Hill, 1996; Johnson, 1986; Mahrer, 1989). The proponents of action-oriented models believe that although insight into the dream is important, it does not typically lead spontaneously to behavior change. Rather, they suggest that it is often necessary for therapists and clients to consider explicitly what the client can do differently in waking life and develop plans for how he or she could go about making changes.

This debate about the effects of focusing on insight versus action is also present in the broader counseling and psychotherapy literature. Psychoanalytic theories (e.g.,

Reprinted from *Journal of Counseling Psychology*, 47, 372–379 (2000). Copyright © 2000 by the American Psychological Association. Used with permission of the first author.

This study was completed as a master's thesis for Teresa L. Wonnell at the University of Maryland, College Park, under the direction of Clara E. Hill. This study was presented in June 1998 at the annual meeting of the Society for Psychotherapy Research, Snowbird, Utah, and in August 1998 at the 106th Annual Convention of the American Psychological Association, San Francisco.

We thank Deanna Koestel, Suzanne Gill, Sharon Quarles, Jonathan Slocum, Russell Washington, Bina Sheladia, Misty Kolchakian, and Julie Quimby for assisting with the study and Aaron Rochlen, Misty Kolchakian, and Jason Zack for reading earlier versions of the article. We also thank Janet Helms and Mary Ann Hoffman for their guidance and helpful comments in the various phases of this project.

Greenson, 1967) promote insight with the expectation that change will occur as a consequence of the insight. In contrast, behavioral theories (e.g., Goldfried & Davison, 1994) stress the need for concerted attention to action at the expense of insight. Recent developments in theory, however, have involved the integration of various theories because all approaches to psychotherapy seem to offer valuable and occasionally even unique contributions to research and practice (Gold, 1993; Prochaska & Norcross, 1994). Working with dreams provides practical opportunities for testing questions about the effects of insight and action given that both can be offered in a single session.

Our primary purpose in the present study was to test the effect of including an action stage on clients' perceived progress toward problem solution and clients' ideas for taking postsession action. Several empirical studies have demonstrated that clients do gain insight from the dream interpretation process using this model (Cogar & Hill, 1992; Diemer, Lobell, Vivino, & Hill, 1996; Heaton, Hill, Petersen, Rochlen, & Zack, 1998; Hill, Diemer, & Heaton, 1997; Hill, Diemer, Hess, Hillyer, & Seeman, 1993; Hill et al., 2000; Rochlen, Ligiero, Hill, & Heaton, 1999; Zack & Hill, 1998), but no studies of this or any other model have investigated the effects of including an action stage on client progress in terms of action.

In this study, volunteer clients were randomly assigned to one of two conditions: dream interpretation sessions conducted using the full three-stage Hill model (exploration/insight/action condition) and dream interpretation sessions conducted without the action stage (exploration/insight condition). We hypothesized that volunteer clients who participated in sessions including the action stage would generate significantly clearer, more detailed plans for taking action, would report having a better sense of problem definition and solution, and would report higher levels of other action-related gains than would volunteer clients who participated in sessions without the action stage. Because clients in both conditions were able to explore their dreams and gain some insight into them, we also hypothesized that the level of insight attained and satisfaction with the quality of sessions would not differ.

In the present study, *client action* is defined as relatively short-term "micro-outcomes," or small, intentional changes or actions that a client might report between sessions or after a single session (Orlinsky & Howard, 1986), as well as referring to relatively large-scale or long-term intentional changes one might expect after multiple sessions of therapy. Furthermore, client action is defined as including thoughts and emotions as well as physical behaviors. For example, self-talk would be considered an action as long as it is intentional on the client's part.

We were also interested in exploring therapists' experiences in facilitating the action stage. In the past, therapists have reported anecdotally that the action stage is the most difficult part of doing a dream interpretation using the Hill model and that it is often the stage with which they feel least competent. As evidence supporting these anecdotal reports, therapists in previous studies have rated their adherence to the Hill model lower for the action stage than for the exploration and insight stages (Heaton et al., 1998; Hill et al., 1997). Therapists in those studies also rated themselves higher on humanistic orientations than on cognitive–behavioral orientations and thus may have been less comfortable facilitating action than would therapists who are more cognitive–behaviorally oriented. Hence, we were interested in learning about what factors, from the therapist perspective, contribute to the ease or difficulty of doing the action stage in hopes that any knowledge gained could be used to modify the model and improve the training of therapists. Because this area had not been explored before, we did not form specific hypotheses but instead examined therapists' descriptions of their experiences in facilitating the action stage for those sessions in which the action stage was included. Nonetheless, because of our experience in working with dreams and supervising therapists in dream studies, we did have some expectations of what factors therapists might mention. Specifically, we expected therapists to mention client characteristics and characteristics of dreams.

In this study, we had therapists participate in both conditions (dream interpretation with the action stage or without the action stage) to control for confounding therapist variables. We recognized, however, that therapist belief in one condition over the other could influence results (e.g., Robinson, Berman, & Neimeyer, 1990), so we assessed difference in therapist belief across conditions to determine if it was a confounding variable. In addition, because we did not want length of session to be a confounding variable between conditions, we required therapists to keep sessions in both conditions about the same length.

Method

Participants

Volunteer Clients

Forty-three undergraduate psychology students (32 women, 11 men: 29 European Americans, 7 Asian Americans, 5 African Americans, and 2 Hispanic Americans), ranging in age from 17 to 24 years ($M = 18.67$, $SD = 1.36$), volunteered to serve as clients. Volunteer clients were unaware of the hypotheses of the study and received course credit for participating.

Therapists

Twenty-two therapists (15 women, 7 men: 17 European Americans, 4 Asian Americans, and 1 Asian), including Teresa L. Wonnell, participated in the study. Therapists were doctoral students or interns from counseling and clinical programs at a large mid-Atlantic U.S. university. All had completed at least one practicum course. Their ages ranged from 24 to 40 years ($M = 29.55$, $SD = 4.57$), and the amount of therapy experience ranged from 1 to 6 years ($M = 2.89$, $SD = 1.72$). The average number of dream interpretation sessions done previously (including practice sessions) ranged from 2 to 30 ($M = 6.14$, $SD = 6.85$), and 15 of the therapists had participated in previous studies using the Hill dream interpretation model. Using 5-point scales ($5 = high$) to rate their theoretical orientation, therapists rated themselves as 3.95 ($SD = 0.79$) on humanistic–experiential, 3.50 ($SD = 1.22$) on psychodynamic, and 2.95 ($SD = 0.90$) on cognitive–behavioral orientations. Pairwise t tests with a Bonferonni correction of .017 (.05/3) indicated that therapists rated themselves higher on humanistic–experiental than on cognitive–behavioral orientation ($t = 3.69$, $p < .001$). Because of the involvement of Teresa L. Wonnell, we planned to check for a therapist effect by comparing the means of all session outcome variables for her versus all other therapists.

Judges

Four undergraduate raters (3 women, 1 man: 1 European American, 2 African Americans, 1 Asian American; age $M = 24.83$ years, $SD = 5.63$) and Teresa L. Wonnell rated clients' action plans on the basis of the dream, from written records. Two undergraduate judges (2 women: 1 European American and 1 Asian American; age $M = 30.21$ years, $SD = 3.35$) rated whether or not the action stage was present from session audiotapes. Judges were unaware of the experimental condition when making ratings. Two graduate student judges (2 European American women, age $M = 24$ years, $SD = 1.41$) and Teresa L. Wonnell placed into categories therapists' written statements about the ease or difficulty of doing the action stage.

Measures

Therapist Belief in Condition

Therapists were asked in writing how much they believed in the helpfulness of both conditions used in the study, on a scale of 1 (*low*) to 5 (*high*). A difference index was calculated for each therapist by subtracting belief ratings for the exploration/insight condition from belief ratings for the exploration/insight/action condition. This item was developed for the study, and, hence, no validity or reliability data are available.

Recency of the Dream

Volunteer clients filled out a questionnaire that asked "How long ago did you have the dream that you worked on in the dream interpretation session?" They responded using the following options: "Within the last seven days," "More than seven days ago but within the past month," "More than one month ago but less than a year ago," and "More than one year ago."

The Depth Scale from the Session Evaluation Questionnaire (SEQ) Form 4 (Stiles & Snow, 1984) is a widely used self-report measure of session quality. It consists of five bipolar adjective pairs: *valuable–worthless*, *full–empty*, *special–ordinary*, *weak–powerful*, and *shallow–deep*. The items are related on 7-point Likert-type scales (7 = *high*), in which higher scores reflect higher ratings of session depth. The reported score of this measure is the mean of the five individual item scores. Stiles and Snow (1984) reported high internal consistency ($\alpha = .91$ for therapists and .87 for volunteer clients) with a sample of graduate students and volunteer student clients. In a second study, Stiles et al. (1994) reported that the Depth Scale was moderately to strongly correlated ($r = .44$ to .72) with several subscales of the Session Impacts Scale (the Understanding, Problem Solving, and Relationship subscales; Stiles et al., 1994), providing evidence of concurrent validity of this measure because both are measures of session impact. In the present study, the internal consistency estimate (Cronbach's alpha) for clients was .86.

The Session Impacts Scale—Problem Solving (SIS-PS; Stiles et al., 1994) is a self-report measure designed to measure the extent to which understanding gained by the client from a therapy session has been applied to problem solving. It was used in this study as a measure of problem-solving impacts: ideas clients gained about problem definition and possible problem-solving actions. Part of a larger, 17-item measure (SIS), the Problem-Solving scale consists of two items scored in a 5-point Likert-type scale (5 = *high*), and it probes for a client's sense of problem definition and ideas for coping with a problem. Stiles et al. (1994) reported an internal consistency alpha estimate of .82. Exploratory factor analysis confirmed the distinctness of the scale. As evidence of construct validity, Stiles et al. (1990) found that clients rated cognitive–behavioral sessions as significantly higher than psychodynamic–interpersonal sessions on this measure. In the present study, the internal consistency (Cronbach's alpha) was .84.

The Gains From Dream Interpretation (GDI; Heaton et al., 1998) is a measure of the specific gains that clients report from dream interpretation sessions. It was developed from client responses to a set of open-ended questions about what they felt they gained from single dream-interpretation sessions using the Hill model. The measure consists of 14 items rated on 9-point Likert-type scales (9 = *high*). A factor analysis performed by Heaton et al. (1998) using data from 115 undergraduate volunteer clients who participated in single dream-interpretation sessions indicated three scales: Exploration–Insight (7 items, α = .83), Action (5 items, α = .82), and Experiential (2 items, α = .79). In other studies, Cronbach's alpha for the Experiential scale has been low, so this scale was not used in the present study. The GDI correlates positively and significantly ($p \leq .05$) with more general session-outcome measures such as the SEQ–Depth, the Mastery–Insight Scale, and the SIS-U (Zack & Hill, 1998). In the present study, internal consistency estimates (Cronbach's alphas) were .84 (Exploration–Insight) and .75 (Action).

Client Action Plan

Clients were asked to write a response to the following question: "Based on this dream interpretation session, what changes would you like to make in your current life; and, how would you go about making those changes?" The quality of intended action was assessed by trained judges using a 9-point Likert-type scale (1 = *no action*, 9 = *high action*). Quality of action was assessed in terms of the relationship of the written plan to the dream (does the plan seem to be connected to the dream?), the number of action ideas expressed, whether the plan was clear and detailed, and whether it would be possible to carry out the plan. The interrater reliability estimate (Cronbach's alpha) among three judges in the Hill, Nakayama, and Wonnell (1998) study was .95. Ratings on this measure correlated moderately and significantly (r = .41) with judges' ratings of insight in volunteer client-written dream interpretations (Hill et al., 1998). In the present study, the interrater reliability estimate (Cronbach's alpha) among five judges was .96.

An example of an action plan that received a low rating (3) was in response to the following dream: A volunteer client dreamed that after much anticipation she visited her boyfriend in another locale. When she arrived and he barely noticed her, she felt devastated. Her action plan was as follows: "I would like to become more independent and more secure with my relationship. I am not sure exactly how to go about this, but as time goes on, I am sure it will become evident." This action plan was given a low rating because although it did identify changes that the volunteer client wanted to make, it did not include any plan about how to make changes.

An example of an action plan given a rating of 5 was in response to a dream of a male volunteer client of being on a high bridge with some friends. Everybody was planning on jumping into the river. His friends told him to go first, but as he jumped over the side railing, he tripped and fell twisting through the air out of control. He interpreted the tripping and falling as "different hurdles and obstacles causing confusion and disarray." His action plan was to "learn to face oncoming distractions, by standing up for my need to study . . . organize myself, and follow my needs." This action plan was given a moderate rating because it did list some changes the volunteer client would like to make and mentioned ideas about how to make changes, but the ideas were rather vague.

An example of an action plan with a high rating (8) was for a volunteer client who dreamed she was in a classroom with fellow workers and young children. Colors were bright, and everybody seemed to be enjoying themselves. Her interpretation (which was rather long) included the following: "I feel comfortable sticking with the familiar . . . I want to leave my current job, but I don't want to risk the loss of the relationships I've made . . . so I need to ease into the next step of growth by leaving my job but not abruptly." Her action plan was as follows:

> I would like to let the people I work with know that I enjoy working with them, but at the same time I would like to move on and get a job that is more fulfilling for me . . . I could have some sort of closure when I decide to leave my present job: small going away party or go out for dinner.

This plan was detailed and plausible, expressed more than one idea for action, and seemed connected to the dream and to the interpretation.

Action-Stage Ease–Difficulty Measure

After sessions in which they conducted an action stage, therapists rated on a 9-point scale how easy it was to conduct the stage in that session, in which 1 = *very easy* and 9 = *very difficult*. An open-ended question was then asked: "To what factors do you attribute the ease or difficulty of doing the action stage in this session? (e.g., client factors, the dream, your familiarity or lack of familiarity with the model, or any other factor)."

On the basis of written responses to the above open-ended question, we developed seven categories, arranged in four larger categories: client factors (with subcategories of involvement, psychological mindedness, and miscellaneous factors), dream factors (with subcategories of dream recency and other), therapist factors, and exploration/insight. A team of three judges then assigned each statement that a therapist made in response to the above question to one of the seven categories. The interjudge agreement, estimated by averaging kappas across each pair of judges, was .88.

Adherence Check

Therapists rated their adherence to the stages of the Hill model and their overall competence on 9-point Likert scales ($9 = high$). Evidence of validity for this method of measuring adherence includes significant correlations found by Heaton et al. (1998) between observer-rated adherence and therapist-rated adherence (.68, .52, and .40 for the exploration, insight, and action stages, respectively). For sessions in which the action stage was done, it was decided a priori that therapists had to rate themselves at least 4 out of 9 on each of the four scales. For sessions in which the action stage was not done, therapists had to rate their adherence to the action stage as less than 4 but their adherence to the other two stages as at least 4.

Manipulation Check

Two judges who were unaware of which condition was used listened to the last 20 min of all tapes and independently rated the extent to which the action stage was present. Judges focused on therapist statements and rated, using a 9-point Likert-type scale ranging from 1 (*not at all*) to 9 (*quite a bit*), the extent to which therapists did each of the following: (a) encouraged volunteer client to change the dream, (b) encouraged volunteer client to think of ways to continue to work with the dream, (c) encouraged volunteer client to identify specific changes to make in his or her life, and (d) helped volunteer client develop specific behavioral strategies to make changes come about. Judges also timed the length of the action stage (e.g., from the time any statement was made, that indicated the action stage had begun, to the end of the session). For a session to be categorized as including the action stage, we decided a priori that it needed to last at least 8 min and receive a rating of 5 on at least one of the four action scales (therapists doing the action stage were required to engage in only one of the possible types of action).

Procedures

Therapist Training

Therapists were trained in both conditions. All therapists recruited for this study participated in an 8-hr training workshop on using the Hill model of dream interpretation. Prior to the workshop, participants were expected to read or reread Hill (1996). The first hour of the workshop consisted of a didactic presentation of the model, focusing on how to do the two different conditions. Participants then practiced a dream interpretation as a group for 2 hr using the three-stage model. During the second 3 hr, participants split up into dyads and practiced conducting one of the two experimental conditions with each other, switching roles so that every participant got a chance to be in the therapist's role. In the final 2 hr of training (occurring at a different time), therapists practiced the other experimental condition with a volunteer client while being observed by a supervisor who afterward provided feedback using a checklist of behaviors for each of the stages.

Client Recruitment

Volunteer clients were recruited from the introductory psychology research pool at a large, mid-Atlantic university. Sign-up sheets were posted on a bulletin board designated for the recruitment of such students. The sign-up sheets advertised a study on "Dream Interpretation." By mentioning dreams in the title, we hoped to recruit volunteer clients who were at least somewhat interested in working with their dreams. The sign-up sheet also informed students that to participate they had to bring a written dream that they were willing to discuss to the session and had to be willing to be audiotaped. Forty-nine volunteer clients were randomly assigned to condition and to therapist.

Presession Check

The 49 volunteer clients first read and signed a consent form and completed a demographic form. A researcher, either an undergraduate assistant or Teresa L. Wonnell, checked to make sure that volunteer clients brought a typed copy of a dream. Volunteer clients who did not bring a copy of their dream were asked to write one at the time. The researcher also checked the length of dreams, and if they seemed very long, clients were asked to choose a portion on which they were most interested in focusing because dreams that are long are difficult to work with in a single session. Finally, the researcher introduced the volunteer client to the therapist.

Dream Interpretation Sessions

The therapist guided the volunteer client through a dream interpretation, using the Hill cognitive–experiential method. Half of the sessions were conducted using the entire three-stage model (exploration/insight/action condition) whereas the other half were conducted without the action stage (exploration/insight condition). Most therapists (21 out of 22) conducted an equal number of sessions in each condition. The type of condition that a particular therapist conducted first was randomly determined. After the first session, therapists conducted sessions in an alternating fashion. In advance of the first session, therapists were told which condition to do first.

Sessions lasted 50 to 100 min. Therapists were instructed to aim for a session length of 75 to 80 min, regardless of condition, in an attempt to make the times equivalent across conditions. When doing the exploration/insight/action condition, therapists were encouraged to spend about 45 min in the exploration stage, 15 to 25 min in the insight stage, and at least 10 min in the action stage. When doing the exploration/insight condition, therapists were encouraged to spend about 50 to 55 min in the exploration stage and about 20 to 30 min in the insight stage.

Postsession Testing

Therapists completed the therapist adherence measure and the action-stage ease–difficulty measure. Volunteer clients completed the SIS–PS, the SEQ—Depth scale, and the GDI; wrote an action plan for the dream that they had worked on in the session; and reported the recency of the dream. These measures were completed in random order.

Action Rating

Raters were given a definition of action and practiced rating using data from a previous study until an interrater reliability (alpha) of .90 was reached. Each volunteer client's dream was read aloud, then the action plan was read aloud, and finally each rater independently gave the action plan a rating. To ensure that condition was unknown when ratings were made, dreams and action plans were identified only by code number and were randomly ordered. Teresa L. Wonnell did not do ratings for sessions in which she was a therapist.

Categorization of Factors to Which Therapists Attributed the Ease or Difficulty of Doing the Action Stage

To categorize therapsts' responses, two of the three judges first read over therapists' open-ended responses and by consensus divided them into segments such that each segment contained a single idea. Next, the three judges independently assigned each segment to one of seven categories. Then, judges compared answers, and any discrepancies were assigned to one category by consensus.

Results

For the purpose of significance testing, an alpha level of .05 was used. Means and standard deviations of variables are shown in Table 1, and correlations between variables are shown in Table 2.

Preliminary Analyses

Therapist Effects

Comparisons, using t tests, of the means of session outcome variables for Teresa L. Wonnell versus all other therapists revealed no significant differences. Furthermore, no other effects were found among therapists.

Therapist Belief in Condition

A difference index was calculated for each therapist by subtracting belief ratings for the exploration/insight condition from belief ratings for the exploration/insight/action condition. The mean belief difference index was 0.95 ($SD = 0.87$). Values of the index ranged from 0 to 3, indicating that therapists ranged from reporting no differences in their belief of the efficacy of the conditions to reporting that they believed the exploration/insight/action condition was more helpful than the exploration/insight

Table 1—*Means and Standard Deviations of Experimental Variables by Condition*

Measure	Insight (n = 23)		Action (n = 20)	
	M	*SD*	*M*	*SD*
Client-rated outcome variables				
Depth[a]	6.09	.98	6.17	.91
Gains: Exploration–Insight[b]	7.88	1.06	7.99	1.00
Gains: Action[b]	6.10	1.24	6.98	1.45
Problem Solving[c]	3.04	1.30	3.95	1.06
Judge-rated outcome variables				
Action plan[b]	3.15	1.75	4.90	1.85
Therapist-rated variables				
Adherence: exploration stage[b]	7.30	1.18	7.65	1.14
Adherence: insight stage[b]	7.04	1.26	7.30	1.08
Adherence: action stage[b]			7.30	1.13
Competence[b]	6.96	1.26	7.00	1.12
Ease–difficulty of action stage[b]			4.12	2.32
Session variables				
Session length (min)	66.50	10.62	73.55	13.34
Action stage length (min)			12.74	2.78

Note. High scores indicate high levels on all variables; for therapist-rated ease–difficulty, high scores indicate difficult sessions. Depth = Depth scale of the Session Evaluation Questionnaire; Gains = Gains from Dream Interpretation; Problem Solving = Problem Solving subscale of the Session Impacts Scale.

[a]Rated on a 9-point scale.   [b]Rated on a 7-point scale.   [c]Rated on a 5-point scale.

condition (note that no one reported the exploration/insight condition as being more helpful). This index was not significantly correlated with any outcome variable (see Table 2), therefore we concluded that therapists' differing beliefs did not affect session outcome.

Adherence and Manipulation Checks

Means and standard deviations of therapist-rated adherence and competence are shown in Table 1. A multivariate analysis of variance (MANOVA) with condition as the independent variable and therapists' adherence ratings of the exploration and insight stages and competence ratings as dependent variables was not significant, $F(3, 38) = 0.52$, $p > .05$. Hence, no differences between conditions were found for ratings of adherence to the first two stages or for ratings of competence. Furthermore, scores for therapist-rated adherence were within 1 *SD* of adherence scores reported for dream interpretation sessions by Heaton et al. (1998) and by Hill et al. (1997). Hence, these sessions appeared to be comparable with those of previous studies in terms of therapist-reported adherence to the stages and therapist-reported competence.

In all, 49 sessions were conducted. Two sessions were dropped because therapists' self-ratings of adherence and competence were below the a priori-determined

Table 2—*Correlations Among Variables*

Measure	1	2	3	4	5	6	7	8	9	10	11
Client-rated outcome variables											
1. Depth	—										
2. Gains: Exploration–Insight	.56**	—									
3. Gains: Action	.47**	.62**	—								
4. Problem Solving	.23	.36*	.79**	—							
Judge-rated outcome variables											
5. Action plan	.13	.26	.49**	.54**	—						
Therapist variables											
6. Belief index	.09	-.14	.08	.12	.07	—					
7. Experience: overall	.33*	.25	.13	.05	-.04	.10	—				
8. Experience: dreams	-.11	-.03	.14	.16	-.02	-.18	-.25	—			
9. Ease–difficulty of action stage (n = 20)	-.77**	-.75**	-.74**	-.79**	-.54*	-.30	-.11	.18	—		
Session variables											
10. Session length	.21	.14	.17	.10	.25	-.27	.01	-.11	.00	—	
11. Action stage length (n = 20)	-.03	.06	-.05	.23	.05	-.01	.43	-.24	-.07	.03	—
Other											
12. Recency of dream[a]	-.16	-.43**	-.29	-.12	-.07	.03	-.13	-.21	.51*	-.07	-.16

Note. $N = 43$ unless otherwise noted. All correlations are Pearson correlation coefficients unless otherwise noted. Depth = Depth scale of the Session Evaluation Questionnaire; Gains = gains from dream interpretation; Problem Solving = Problem Solving subscale of the Session Impacts Scale.

[a]Spearman correlation coefficients.

*p < .05. **p < .01.

cutoffs. Two undergraduate judges who were unaware of condition listened to tapes of the remaining 47 sessions and judged which condition the therapist was conducting. Three more sessions were dropped because either the action stage was not at lest 8 min or the judges indicated that the therapist was conducting a condition other than the assigned one. A final session was dropped because the volunteer client's scores on all the outcome measures were 2 standard deviations or more below the mean and, therefore, this case was considered an outlier. Hence, although 49 volunteer clients completed sessions, analyses were conducted on 43 sessions (23 in the exploration/insight condition and 20 in the exploration/insight/action condition).

Differences Between Conditions

Using chi-square analyses, we found no differences between the exploration/insight condition and the exploration/insight/action condition for client age, gender, or race. Furthermore, t tests showed that mean session length and the recency of dreams did not differ between conditions.

Comparison of Outcome Variables With Dream Interpretation Norms

Sessions were perceived by volunteer clients as comparable with previous dream interpretation studies on client-reported depth (Hill et al., 1997; Hill, Diemer, Hess, Hillyer, & Seeman, 1993), exploration–insight gains, and action gains (Heaton et al., 1998; Zack & Hill, 1998).

Effect of Condition on Client-Perceived Session Quality

Client-perceived session quality, as assessed by the Depth Scale, was not significantly different between the two conditions, $t(41) = -0.28$, $p > .05$. Hence, as hypothesized, no differences were found for volunteer client-reported session depth.

Effect of Condition on Client Insight

No differences were found for GDI–Exploration–Insight, $t(41) = -0.37$, $p > .05$. Hence, as hypothesized, no differences were found between conditions on volunteer client-reported insight.

Effect of Condition on Client Action

As can be seen in Table 2, the three measures used to assess action immediately postsession (GDI–Action, SIS–Problem-Solving, and judge-rated client action plans) were all positively correlated (rs ranged from .49 to .79). Hence, they were analyzed in one MANOVA with condition as the independent variable. The MANOVA was significant, $F(3, 39) = 3.66$, $p < .05$. Follow-up univariate tests with an adjusted alpha of .017 (.05/3) revealed that volunteer clients in the exploration/insight/action condition scored higher than did volunteer clients in the exploration/insight condition on the SIS–Problem-Solving scale, $F(1, 41) = 6.17$, $p = .017$, and on judge-related action plans, $F(1, 41) = 10.15$, $p < .017$. No difference was found on the GDI – Action, $F(1, 41) = 4.65$, $p > .017$. Hence, volunteer clients in the exploration/insight/ action condition gained more in terms of action than did volunteer clients in the exploration/insight condition.

Ease or Difficulty of Working With Clients in the Action Stage

Therapists reported a mean ease–difficulty rating of 4.12 ($SD = 2.32$). Table 2 shows that therapists' action-stage ease–difficulty ratings were significantly correlated with the recency of the dream, therapists' ratings of adherence to the action stage, client-reported depth, exploration/insight gains, action gains, problem-solving, and judge-rated action plans. Hence, therapists reported that it was easier to do the action stage with more recent dreams and reported higher adherence when the action stage was easier. Also, when therapists reported that the action stage was easier, volunteer clients reported more depth, more insight, and more action gains and problem-solving impacts, and had higher quality action plans.

Therapists listed an average of 1.95 ($SD = 1.00$) factors per session. Table 3 shows four factors to which therapists attributed the ease or difficulty of doing the action stage. First, client factors were mentioned in 70% of the sessions, with client involvement and psychological mindedness being the most frequently mentioned

Table 3—*Percentage of Sessions in Which Factors Were Mentioned by Therapists as Influencing the Ease or Difficulty of Doing the Action Stage (N = 20)*

Factor	Example[a]
Client factors (70%)	
a. Client was involved, motivated, open vs. passive, unmotivated, resistant (55%)	"Client was very motivated to make . . . concrete changes"
b. Client was psychologically minded, insightful vs. not psychologically minded (25%)	"Client was very psychologically minded"
c. Miscellaneous or unspecified client factors (20%)	"[Client] is already taking action"
Dream factors (55%)	
a. Dream was recent vs. old (15%)	"The dream was several years old" [Difficult session]
b. Miscellaneous or unspecified dream factor (40%)	"Dream was a good metaphor"
Therapist factors (35%)	"I feel comfortable with the action stage"
Exploration and insight (25%)	"The insights seemed to lead to obvious actions"

Note. Therapists typically listed more than one factor per session, and, therefore, the percentages do not add up to 100%.

[a]Unless otherwise noted, examples are from sessions that therapists rated as easy.

factors. Second, some aspect of the dream was mentioned in 55% of the sessions. Specifically, the recency of the dream was mentioned in 15% of the sessions, such that older dreams were more difficult to work with. Third, therapist factors such as experience, confidence, and comfort with facilitating the action stage were mentioned in 35% of the sessions. Fourth, attainment (or lack thereof) of the goals of the exploration and insight stages was listed in 25% of sessions. Hence, therapists reported that it was easiest to do the action stage when they were confident of their skills and were working with volunteer clients who were motivated, who were psychologically minded, who presented recent dreams, and who had been able to explore their dream thoroughly and gain insight prior to the action stage.

Discussion

Volunteer clients who went through the action stage scored higher on a measure of problem solving and wrote clearer, more specific action plans that contained more ideas for actions than did volunteer clients who did not go through the action stage. Thus, the action stage seemed to have an impact on volunteer clients immediately after a dream-interpretation session. It seemed to help volunteer clients identify and define things they wanted to change and to help them generate ideas about what specific actions to take. Including the action stage did not, however, seem to affect volunteer clients' insight into their dreams over and above what was gained in the insight stage. Conversely, not including the action stage did not compromise the achievement of insight, which is one of the major goals of the Hill model of dream interpretation.

Therapists reported that facilitating the action stage (i.e., helping clients explore behavioral changes or changes in the dream and encouraging waking life changes) was easier when volunteer clients were interested, motivated, and involved. This finding is consistent with the literature about client involvement, which has been found to be a good predictor of therapy outcome (Gomes-Schwartz, 1978) and a good predictor of positive session evaluations by both therapist and client (Eugster & Wampold, 1996).

The type of dream that the volunteer client brought into the session also influenced whether the therapist rated the action stage as easy or difficult. Of the many aspects of dreams that were mentioned, the only one that was mentioned consistently was the recency of the dream. The finding that older dreams were harder to work with could stem from several things. Older dreams may have seemed less relevant to volunteer clients' current waking life, and they may have been less motivated to explore making any changes based on the dream. Also, the older dreams may have been less vividly remembered, with fewer details, making them more difficult to link to action.

In addition, therapist factors were mentioned as influencing the ease or difficulty of facilitating the action stage. Some therapists reported feeling comfortable or confident doing the action stage. However, results showed that the ease ratings for the action stage were not related to overall experience as a therapist or to the amount of experience in doing dream interpretations using the Hill model. Although we are not sure of the explanation for this finding, perhaps characteristics of particular sessions, such as client or dream factors, are more important than are therapist experience or training.

A final factor related to the ease or difficulty of conducting the action stage was previous events of the session. Therapists said that thorough exploration or the achievement of plausible insights made conducting the action stage easier. This finding underscores the importance of not rushing through the first two stages of the dream interpretation model or trying to force action too quickly. Thorough exploration of dream images and understanding the dream as a whole seem necessary for developing action ideas.

Limitations

An a priori power analysis indicated that a sample size of 100 would have been needed to detect medium effect sizes with a power of .70, and, therefore, any small or medium effects in the present study, in which the sample size was 43, would have been difficult to detect. In addition, volunteer clients only participated in single sessions of dream interpretation and were relatively nondistressed volunteers rather than clients seeking counseling, so generalizations to a client population must be made cautiously. Particularly relevant to this study, volunteer clients who are relatively nondistressed may not be as motivated to consider changes in their lives as clients who seek counseling would be, although research is needed to test this hypothesis. Another limitation is that therapists reported being more humanistically than behaviorally oriented. Therapists with more of a behavioral orientation may have conducted the action stage differently. A final limitation is that we do not know whether volunteer clients who went through the action stage left the session with any more intention to take action and whether they actually carried out their action plans more often than volunteer clients who did not go through the action stage.

Implications

The primary implication of this study is that the action stage can be a helpful component of the Hill dream-interpretation model. Hence, therapists should consider including the action stage in sessions to help volunteer clients identify changes they want to make and to help them develop plans for carrying out changes, especially when clients are involved and motivated and present a recent dream. The results of this study also suggest that awareness of certain factors (e.g., client involvement, the recency of the dream) can help therapists anticipate whether to spend much time in the action stage.

A broader implication is that focusing on action as well as insight produced effects that were not realized by focusing on insight alone. Furthermore, focusing on action as well as insight did not compromise the amount of insight gained. Although any generalizations to psychotherapy that do not involve working with dreams or volunteer clients must be made cautiously, the results of this study provide evidence that integrating insight and action within one session is feasible and potentially beneficial.

More needs to be known about the relative usefulness of the specific tasks that therapists use in the action stage and whether some tasks lead to better outcome with some clients or dreams than others. Presently, therapists often start the action stage by asking clients how they would change their dream, as a creative way to begin exploring ideas for change. Should therapists always start the action stage in this manner? If not, what factors should therapists consider when deciding whether to use this or other tasks in the action stage? Also, as mentioned above, we need to know whether immediate session outcome is related to postsession behavior, and to what extent clients actually carry out their action plans.

Given the encouraging results of this study, it seems worthwhile to replicate it under conditions that better approximate therapy. Clients who desire counseling (and value their dreams) should be recruited and should go through several sessions of dream interpretation. Also, an accurate method for assessing client actions and change outside of dream sessions needs to be developed so that action can be linked to therapeutic outcome.

References

Cartwright, R. D., & Lamberg, L. (1992). *Crisis dreaming: Using your dreams to solve your problems*. New York: HarperCollins.

Cogar, M. M., & Hill, C. E. (1992). Examining the effects of brief individual dream interpretation. *Dreaming, 2*, 239–248.

Craig, E., & Walsh, S. J. (1993). The clinical use of dreams. In G. Delaney (Ed.), *New directions in dream interpretation* (pp. 103–154). Albany, NY: SUNY Press.

Diemer, R., Lobell, L., Vivino, B., & Hill, C. E. (1996). A comparison of dream interpretation, event interpretation, and unstructured sessions in brief psychotherapy. *Journal of Counseling Psychology, 43*, 99–112.

Eugster, S. L., & Wampold, B. E. (1996). Systematic effects of participant role on evaluation of the psychotherapy session. *Journal of Consulting and Clinical Psychology, 64*, 1020–1028.

Freud, S. (1965). *The interpretation of dreams*. New York: Avon Books. (Original work published 1900)

Gendlin, E. T. (1986). *Let your body interpret your dreams*. Wilmette, IL: Chiron.

Gold, J. R. (1993). The sociohistorical context of psychotherapy integration. In G. Stricker & J. R. Gold (Eds.), *Comprehensive handbook of psychotherapy integration* (pp. 3–8). New York: Plenum Press.

Goldfried, M. R., & Davison, G. C. (1994). *Clinical behavior therapy*. New York: Wiley.

Gomes-Schwartz, B. (1978). Effective ingredients in psychotherapy: Prediction of outcome from process variables. *Journal of Consulting and Clinical Psychology, 46*, 1023–1035.

Greenson, R. R. (1967). *The technique and practice of psychoanalysis* (Vol. 1). Madison, CT: International Universities Press.

Heaton, K. J., Hill, C. E., Petersen, D., Rochlen, A. B., & Zack, J. (1998). A comparison of therapist-facilitated and self-guided dream interpretation sessions. *Journal of Counseling Psychology, 45*, 115–122.

Hill, C. E. (1996). *Working with dreams in psychotherapy*. New York: Guilford Press.

Hill, C. E., Diemer, R. A., & Heaton, K. J. (1997). Dream interpretation: Who volunteers, who benefits, and what volunteer clients view as most and least helpful. *Journal of Counseling Psychology, 44*, 53–62.

Hill, C. E., Diemer, R. A., Hess, S., Hillyer, A., & Seeman, R. (1993). Are the effects of dream interpretation on session quality, insight, and emotions due to the dream itself, to projection, or to the interpretation process? *Dreaming, 3*, 269–279.

Hill, C. E., Nakayama, E. Y., & Wonnell, T. L. (1998). The effects of description, direct association, or combined description/association in exploring dream images. *Dreaming*, *8*, 1–13.

Hill, C. E., Zack, J. S., Wonnell, T. L., Hoffman, M. A., Rochlen, A. B., Goldberg, J. L., Nakayama, E. Y., Heaton, K. J., Kelley, F. A., Eiche, K., Tomlinson, M. J., & Hess, S. (2000). Structured brief therapy with a focus on dreams or loss for clients with troubling dreams and recent loss. *Journal of Counseling Psychology*, *47*, 90–101.

Johnson, R. (1986). *Inner work*. San Francisco: Harper & Row.

Kazdin, A. E. (1994). Methodology, design, and evaluation in psychotherapy research. In A. E. Bergin & S. L. Garfield (Eds.), *Handbook of psychotherapy and behavior change: An empirical analysis* (4th ed., pp. 19–71). New York: Wiley.

Mahrer, A. R. (1989). *Dream work in psychotherapy and self-change*. New York: Norton.

Orlinsky, D. E., & Howard, K. I. (1986). Process and outcome of psychotherapy. In S. L. Garfield & A. E. Bergin (Eds.), *Handbook of psychotherapy and behavior change: An empirical analysis* (3rd ed., pp. 311–384). New York: Wiley.

Perls, F. (1969). *Gestalt therapy verbatim*. New York: Bantam.

Prochaska, J. O., & Norcross, J. C. (1994). *Systems of psychotherapy: A transtheoretical analysis* (3rd ed.). Pacific Grove, CA: Brooks/Cole.

Robinson, L. A., Berman, J. S., & Neimeyer, R. A. (1990). Psychotherapy for the treatment of depression: A comprehensive review of controlled outcome research. *Psychological Bulletin*, *108*, 30–49.

Rochlen, A. B., Ligiero, D. P., Hill, C. E., & Heaton, K. J. (1999). The effects of training for dream recall/attitudes, dream interpretation skills, and counseling education on dream recall, attitudes, and dream interpretation outcome. *Journal of Counseling Psychology*, *46*, 27–34.

Schwartz, W. (1990). A psychoanalytic approach to dreamwork. In S. Krippner (Ed.), *Dreamtime and dreamwork: Decoding the language of the night* (pp. 49–58). Los Angeles: Tarcher.

Stiles, W. B., Elliott, R., Llewelyn, S. P., Firth-Cozens, J. A., Margison, F. R., Shapiro, D. A., & Hardy, G. (1990). Assimilation of problematic experiences by clients in psychotherapy. *Psychotherapy*, *27*, 411–420.

Stiles, W. B., Reynolds, S., Hardy, G. E., Rees, A., Barkham, M., & Shapiro, D. A. (1994). Evaluation and description of psychotherapy sessions by clients using the Session Evaluation Questionnaire and the Session Impacts Scale. *Journal of Counseling Psychology*, *41*, 175–185.

Stiles, J., & Snow, J. S. (1984). Dimensions of psychotherapy session impact across sessions and across clients. *British Journal of Clinical Psychology*, *23*, 59–63.

Zack, J., & Hill, C. E. (1998). Predicting outcome of dream interpretation sessions by dream valence, dream arousal, attitudes towards dreams, and waking life stress. *Dreaming*, *8*, 169–185.

ABOUT THE EDITOR

Clara Hill, PhD, is a professor in the Department of Psychology at the University of Maryland, College Park. She received her PhD in 1974 from Southern Illinois University in Carbondale and has been at the University of Maryland since then. Her major areas of research are the process and outcome of counseling and psychotherapy, training students in how to conduct counseling and psychotherapy, dream interpretation, supervision, and qualitative research. She is past president of the North American Society for Psychotherapy Research and of the International Society for Psychotherapy Research. She served as an associate editor and then editor of the *Journal of Counseling Psychology* from 1991 to 1999. She is the author of three books: *Therapist Techniques and Client Outcomes: Eight Cases of Brief Psychotherapy* (1989), *Working With Dreams in Psychotherapy* (1996), and *Helping Skills: Facilitating Exploration, Insight, and Action* (1999, with Karen O'Brien).